Henry Hallam
The Middle Ages, Vol. I

The World's Great Books

Committee of Selection

Édition de Grand Luxe

View of the State of Europe During the Middle Ages

By
Henry Hallam

With a Critical and Biographical Introduction
by George Lincoln Burr

Illustrated
Volume I

New York
D. Appleton and Company
1899

HALLAM'S "MIDDLE AGES"

IN 1818 the press of John Murray, in London, gave to the world, in two quarto volumes, Henry Hallam's "View of the State of Europe during the Middle Ages." This was its author's earliest book; but its author was no unknown man.

Born in 1777, of that old Lincolnshire family which in the fifteenth century gave to the see of Salisbury the prelate who stood so manfully for reform at Pisa and at Constance, Henry Hallam was already in ripe manhood, and the eyes of the leaders of thought had long been upon him. His father, Dr. John Hallam, Canon of Windsor and Dean of Bristol, a man distinguished both by learning and by character, and possessed of ample fortune, had given his only son the best education England could offer. To his mother he owed a strain of west-country blood and a rare refinement and delicacy of soul; and it must have meant much to the beginnings of young Hallam's career that her brother, Dr. Roberts, a clerical verse writer of some repute and a lover of society, was Provost of Eton at the boy's advent there in 1790. The lad showed at school the same precocity which at home had made him a devourer of books at four and a sonnet writer at ten. He led his fellows in the class-room, and his Latin verse won a place in the Musæ Etonenses. At Oxford, to which he passed in 1794, his talent was not less marked. Here, a student at Christ Church, he gave especial thought to history. In 1799, taking his degree, he entered on his studies for the bar. These completed, he was for a few years a practising advocate in the Oxford circuit. But not his singular love of jurisprudence, nor that judicial insight and temper which seemed to insure him a lofty place upon the bench, had power to wean him from historical studies. Already in 1801 he had become a member of the Society of Antiquaries. His appointment to a commissionership of stamps, an office of large salary and light duties, soon gave him a home in London and the leisure needed for the scholar's life. He turned forever from the active practice of the law, though never to lose the tastes and habits of mind it had bred in him.

Hallam's friendship with Francis Horner brought him into early connection with that brilliant band of young scholars who, in 1802, had launched the "Edinburgh Review," and his first contribution (a review of a now forgotten history of France) not only dispelled the doubts Horner had uttered to Jeffrey as to how Hallam could write, but strikingly foreshadowed the direction to be taken by his studies. "Man, so studious to record his crimes and his miseries, casts a careless eye," wrote the young critic, "upon the laws which protect, the arts which adorn, and the commerce which enriches him. It was not indeed till lately that the great and leading uses of historical knowledge seem to have been well understood, or that philosophy, with Montesquieu as her high priest, taught us to consider the progress of the species as of more importance than the pedigree of kings, and commissioned those painful though sometimes refractory drudges, the antiquarians, to labour as her pioneers in the collection of facts, which her more favoured sons must afterwards combine and generalize." Such a pen the Edinburgh Reviewers did not leave idle, nor could they long hide its identity; and with them he was pilloried by the indignant Byron as

> "Classic Hallam, much renowned for Greek"

—the charge being that Hallam had scored Payne Knight for Greek verses which were really Pindar's. That Hallam wrote the review is clear, not only from its style, but from his published correspondence with Horner; but De Morgan long ago pointed out that Hallam was wholly right, since the only line actually borrowed from Pindar is so garbled as to be precisely what Hallam called it—"nonsense."

In January, 1807, Hallam took a wife—Julia, daughter of Sir Abraham Elton, a Somersetshire magnate. In 1812 his father

died, leaving him a landed competence, which still more completely lifted him above sordid cares. He had now entered upon
the researches which fruited in his " Middle Ages," and its first
chapter, with much of the second, was already penned; but he
did not let these exacting studies cost him his touch with the
literary world. George Ticknor tells us how, in 1815, when he
first visited London, he was taken by Gifford " to a handsome
room over Murray's bookstore, which he has fitted up as a sort
of literary lounge, where authors resort to read newspapers and
talk literary gossip." There Ticknor found, with others, " Lord
Byron's ' Classic Hallam, much renowned for Greek,' now as
famous for being one of his lordship's friends." Thus, doubtless, arose the acquaintance which made Mr. Murray, early in
1818, the publisher of Hallam's book.

The middle ages were no new theme for a British historian.
Twice before, within a half century, they had furnished material
for a masterpiece. In 1769 Robertson had published, as an introduction to his " History of Charles the Fifth," that eloquent
" View of the State of Society in Europe," which is still perhaps
the best-known survey of the mediæval centuries; and from 1776
to 1788 Gibbon had held a fascinated world in suspense by the
successive volumes of his " Decline and Fall." Hallam was, of
course, profoundly familiar with both; in his attitude, his matter, his method, his style, their influence is plain, and the debt
is frankly confessed. Nor was he, more than they, a child of
that romantic reaction which in his day rewrote so much of
mediæval history. Yet his book and its aim were his own. Robertson had sketched in glowing chapters the progress of civilization and liberty; Gibbon had mournfully " described the triumph
of barbarism and religion." Hallam held no brief for either faith
or doubt, progress or regress. A decade before Ranke's work
began he had grasped the thought that history needs only to
teach " wie es eigentlich gewesen ist," and it was in the spirit of
the judge on the bench that he would review its evidence. Yet,
even more than its predecessors, his book is a " philosophic history "—its narrative but a thread for criticism and inference.

The reception of Hallam's work, both by the public and by
scholars, was cordial, even flattering. Mr. Murray had bought

outright the first three editions for a handsome sum (£1,400), and he had no reason to regret his bargain. The book was speedily translated into French, and both at home and over Channel its author at once took rank among the foremost historians of his time.

But success did not divert him from his ardour as a student. Vast as was the scope of his " Middle Ages," he never had meant it for more than a vestibule to a vaster structure. " It had been my first intention," he tells us, " to have prosecuted that undertaking to a general continuation "—to write, that is, the modern history of Europe—" and when experience taught me to abandon a scheme projected early in life with very inadequate views of its magnitude, I still determined to carry forward the constitutional history of my own country." In 1827, less than a decade after the issue of his " Middle Ages," he gave to the world his " Constitutional History of England."

Turning then to another topic scarcely less " congenial to his studies and habits of mind," and grasping again far back, he brought to completion, in 1837-'39, after another decade of arduous labour, his " Introduction to the Literature of Europe in the Fifteenth, Sixteenth, and Seventeenth Centuries "—a continuation of the ninth chapter of his " Middle Ages," as the " Constitutional History " had been a continuation of the eighth.

But his first book had not meanwhile been forgotten. Its successive editions showed enrichment in text and notes; and, the " Literature of Europe " once off his hands, he set about a more thorough revision of the " Middle Ages," producing in 1848 a volume of supplemental notes, which aimed to bring his work nearer the level of later research, and in the tenth edition of the book (1853)—the last prepared under the author's eye—these supplemental notes were incorporated with the text.

The qualities which to his contemporaries marked Hallam's greatness as a historian nobody has better stated than his friend and rival Macaulay: " He has great industry and great acuteness. His knowledge is extensive, various, and profound. His mind is equally distinguished by the amplitude of its grasp and by the delicacy of its tact. His speculations have none of that

vagueness which is the common fault of political philosophy. . . .
The language, even where most faulty, is weighty and massive,
and indicates strong sense in every line. It often rises to an
eloquence, not florid or impassioned, but high, grave, and sober,
such as would become a state paper or a judgment delivered by
a great magistrate, a Somers or a D'Aguesseau. In this respect
the character of Mr. Hallam's mind corresponds strikingly with
that of his style. His work is eminently judicial. Its whole
spirit is that of the bench, not that of the bar. He sums up with
a calm, steady impartiality, turning neither to the right nor to
the left, glossing over nothing, exaggerating nothing, while the
advocates on both sides are alternately biting their lips to hear
their conflicting misstatements and sophisms exposed."

But there were defects also to which his own time was not
blind: his want of the sympathetic imagination; the Latinity, the
frequent stiffness, the occasional harshness of his style; his dog-
matic and oracular temper; the almost pedantic obtrusion of his
learning; his impatience of enthusiasm, in himself or in others—
he declares it "little else than superstition put in motion"; in
fine, that "extreme austerity" which forced even from Macaulay
the admission that Hallam, though a judge, is "a hanging judge."
To the modern student still other blemishes begin to appear.
Not even the philosophic historian may longer take his research
so largely at second hand. Hallam usually, indeed, verified his
references, and is not often caught in such a misquotation as that
famous one from St. Eligius, which he admits borrowing through
Robertson from a faulty translation of Mosheim. He dipped
freely and fruitfully into the sources for himself. Yet it is safe
to say that all his work would have been the better could he but
for a single chapter have been willing to become one of those
"painful drudges" who "labour in the collection of facts," and
so have mastered the criticism of sources as well as of conclusions. His very dogmatism savours of the dilettante: with all
his learning he is the educated gentleman, not the trained
scholar.

But it was the Germans who were to teach us thorough-
ness; and Hallam, alas! knew next to nothing of the Germans.
Of their tongue he late in life gained a smattering. So much

one may not doubt, since Sir George Lewis knew the governess who taught him, though with Sir George one may well believe the smattering slight. Their history, though it was that of the mediæval empire, interested him so little that even in his latest edition he gave it less than fifty pages—a seventh as much as to France—and in this chapter, the weakest in his book, he cites no German work save two or three of the last century, and these only in translation. A footnote in his latest edition does, indeed, mention Ranke; but it is only Ranke's "History of the Reformation," which Mrs. Austin's translation had made familiar to English readers. Of the still more pertinent untranslated works of that master, or of those studies of his pupils which have revolutionized our knowledge of the mediæval empire and of the earlier middle ages, and which, in the words of Lord Acton, laid "the foundation for what has been for so long incomparably the first school of history in the world," Hallam knows naught. Even that great work by which, for a decade before Hallam laid down his pen, Georg Waitz was pouring new light upon the early institutions of all the Germanic races, seems as little to have caught his eye as the earlier books of Eichhorn or of Hüllmann. When he speaks of bringing his volumes "nearer to the boundaries of the historic domain, as it has been enlarged within our own age," it is of Sismondi, of Michelet, of Guizot, that he thinks. Nor, familiar though he is with Muratori and the great French collections, does he appear to know aught of the "Monumenta Germaniæ" or of the "Regesta" of Böhmer.

To the present generation, now giving such thought to Byzantine studies, his treatment of the Greek Empire may seem not less stepfatherly; and many are his other lapses from what we should count proportion. But it would be rash to suppose that Hallam himself did not know and intend these inequalities. His book was written for British readers, and he knew well what they then cared to learn and he to teach. It needed no apology if his Europe stopped at the Rhine, if he gave to the period of the Hundred Years' War the larger half of his long chapter on France, or if he halted his story for a three-page discussion of a point in the Treaty of Brétigny. However broad his tolerance or impartial his judgments, he was himself, everywhere and frankly, a Briton, an Anglican, and a Whig.

That the historian of mediæval institutions who wrote before Waitz and Brunner, Stubbs and Lea and Maitland, Fustel de Coulanges and Luchaire, is now out of date, goes without saying. But Hallam's " Middle Ages " belongs to the history of thought. Without it none can understand what the mediæval centuries meant to men of English speech in the first half of the nineteenth century.

Besides his three books and an occasional review, the historian published little. But these labours of the closet were by no means all his activity. In 1824 he had become the permanent Vice-President of the Society of Antiquaries, and, though refusing its presidency, the busiest promoter of its enterprises. He was one of the founders of the Statistical Society, and became its treasurer. He was an energetic trustee of the British Museum. Nor was he indifferent to contemporary politics. He took a hearty interest in the abolition of the slave-trade, and in all movements for social or constitutional progress. Yet he steadfastly declined to enter political life, even after his retirement from the stamp office made possible his acceptance of a seat in Parliament. Sir Henry Holland tells us that he even refused a baronetcy pressed upon him by Peel; and probably no man whose name was known so well was so little known by face and figure to the British public.

But that face and figure were no strangers in the best literary and political circles of England. One meets him everywhere in the memoirs of the time—now hobnobbing with Tom Moore, now breakfasting at Rogers's or dining at Wordsworth's, now joining Mackintosh at his " King of Clubs," or taking a hand with Davy and Faraday, Scott and Croker, in the founding of the Athenæum (whose great library is much his debtor), now revelling in high debate with Whewell or Milman or Macaulay at that still more famous club which once had heard Johnson storm and Burke descant. At Holland House and at Bowood no guest was more frequent or more welcome. In his own home, too, that " dark house in the long unlovely street " of which Tennyson sings in " In Memoriam," he ministered a generous hospitality to scholars of every land. There Gladstone remembered first meeting Sydney Smith. There Irving and Ticknor and Prescott and Everett crossed wits with Campbell or Rogers, Macaulay or Lord Mahon.

"All that he was," says the French historian Mignet, who had met Hallam more than once, "his person itself bespoke. Large and of fine figure, the refined purity of his life, the sustained dignity of his character, the keen insight of a robust mind, the untroubled equity of a superior judgment, his affability, gracious and firm at once, his quiet modesty, his unvarying uprightness, depicted themselves in his noble face." Yet it was not precisely in this rôle of the stately scholar that " the judicious Hallam " was best known among his friends. " The stranger would find him," writes Harriet Martineau, who knew him long and well, " the most rapid talker in company, quick in his movements, genial in his feelings, earnest in narrative, rather full of dissent from what everybody said, innocently surprised when he found himself agreeing with anybody, and pretty sure to blurt out something awkward before the day was done." " Never," wrote Lord Carlisle in his journal after a breakfast with him, " were such torrents of good talk as burst and sputtered over from Macaulay and Hallam."

His passion for setting others right was a special temptation to the wit of his close friend Sydney Smith. Fanny Kemble relates how, " a party having been made to go and see the boa constrictor soon after its first arrival at the Zoölogical Gardens, Sydney Smith, who was to have been there, failed to come, and, questioned at dinner why he had not done so, said, ' Because I was detained by the Bore Contradictor—Hallam.' " Still more amusing is the great wit's picture of Hallam kept awake by a cold: " And poor Hallam was tossing and tumbling in his bed when the watchman came by and called, ' Twelve o'clock, and a starlight night!' Here was an opportunity for controversy when it seemed most out of the question! Up jumped Hallam with ' I question that, I question that! Starlight! I see a star, I admit, but I doubt whether that constitutes starlight.' Hours more of tossing and tumbling, and then comes the watchman again, ' Past two o'clock, and a cloudy morning!' ' I question,

I question that!' says Hallam. And he rushes to the window
and throws up the sash, influenza notwithstanding. 'Watchman,
do you mean to call this a cloudy morning? I see a star. And
I question its being past two o'clock; I question it, I question it!'"

Yet this love of contradiction meant no lack of kindliness.
"He is such a man," wrote Ticknor in 1838, "as I should have
desired to find him; a little sensitive and nervous, perhaps, but
dignified, quiet, and wishing to please." "Mr. Hallam is, I suppose," adds Ticknor, "about sixty, gray-headed, hesitates a little
in his speech, is lame, and has a shy manner, which makes him
blush, frequently, when he expresses as decided an opinion as
his temperament constantly leads him to entertain. Except his
lameness, he has a fine, dignified person, and talked pleasantly,
with that air of kindness which is always so welcome to a
stranger."

His lameness, the result of a fall at the Lakes of Killarney,
crippled him during all the later years of his life. It was but
the least of many blows dealt him by fortune. All the world
knows the brilliant promise and the untimely death of that son
Arthur to whose memory the sweetest of English poets has
chanted the noblest of all elegies. Henry Hallam was his son's
companion on that sad last journey, and was with him at the
end. And when "those whose eyes must long be dim with
tears," as the stricken father wrote to Tennyson, had "brought
him to rest among his kindred and in his own country," he was
not long to rest alone. Only four years later, in 1837, his sister
Ellen passed as suddenly from life to death. In 1846, with like
suddenness, died their mother, the historian's beloved wife; and
in 1850 a younger son, Henry, scarcely less brilliant and admired
than Arthur, fell like him at the very opening of manhood. Of
the historian's eleven children few grew to maturity, and only
one daughter survived him. These griefs, so bitter to a man
whose domestic affections were singularly warm, were borne
with a touching gentleness and dignity. His powers were
unbroken almost to the last. Motley, who met him first in
the summer before his death, and had a half-hour's talk with
him, found him, though paralyzed in leg, arm, and tongue,

bright of mind and light of spirit, with "nothing senile in his aspect."

On January 21, 1859, but a few months before his old friend Macaulay, he sank to rest, more than an octogenarian. He sleeps beside his sons—

> "by the pleasant shore,
> And in the hearing of the wave.
>
> "There twice a day the Severn fills;
> The salt sea-water passes by,
> And hushes half the babbling Wye,
> And makes a silence in the hills"—

his fitting monument the austerely simple tablet inscribed by Tennyson to "Henry Hallam the historian."

GEORGE LINCOLN BURR.

FAMOUS AND UNIQUE MANUSCRIPT AND
BOOK ILLUSTRATIONS.

A series of fac-similes, showing the development of manuscript and
book illustrating during four thousand years.

MY LADY'S TABLE.

Miniature from a fifteenth-century manuscript in the Library of the
Arsenal at Paris, showing costumes of the period.

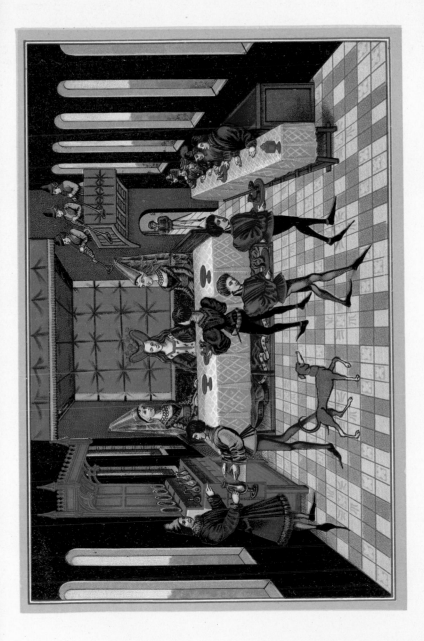

THE AUTHOR'S PREFACE
TO THE FIRST EDITION

———◆◆◆———

IT is the object of the present work to exhibit, in a series of historical dissertations, a comprehensive survey of the chief circumstances that can interest a philosophical inquirer during the period usually denominated the middle ages. Such an undertaking must necessarily fall under the class of historical abridgments: yet there will perhaps be found enough to distinguish it from such as have already appeared. Many considerable portions of time, especially before the twelfth century, may justly be deemed so barren of events worthy of remembrance that a single sentence or paragraph is often sufficient to give the character of entire generations and of long dynasties of obscure kings.

> "Non ragioniam di lor, ma guarda e passa."

And even in the more pleasing and instructive parts of this middle period it has been my object to avoid the dry composition of annals, and aiming, with what spirit and freedom I could, at a just outline rather than a miniature, to suppress all events that did not appear essentially concatenated with others, or illustrative of important conclusions. But as the modes of government and constitutional laws which prevailed in various countries of Europe, and especially in England, seemed to have been less fully dwelt upon in former works of this description than military or civil transactions, while they were deserving of far more attention, I have taken pains to give a true representation of them, and in every instance to point out the sources from which the reader may derive more complete and original information.

Nothing can be further from my wishes than that the following pages should be judged according to the critical laws of historical composition. Tried in such a balance they would be eminently defective. The limited extent of this work, compared with the subjects it embraces, as well as its partaking more of the character of political dissertation than of narrative, must necessarily preclude that circumstantial delineation of events and of characters upon which the beauty as well as usefulness of a regular history so mainly depends. Nor can I venture to assert that it will be found altogether perspicuous to those who are destitute of any previous acquaintance with the period to which it relates; though I have only presupposed, strictly speaking, a knowledge of the common facts of English history, and have endeavoured to avoid, in treating of other countries, those allusive references which imply more information in the reader than the author designs to communicate. But the arrangement which I have adopted has sometimes rendered it necessary to anticipate both names and facts which are to find a more definite place in a subsequent part of the work.

This arrangement is probably different from that of any former historical retrospect. Every chapter of the following volumes completes its particular subject, and may be considered in some degree as independent of the rest. The order consequently in which they are read will not be very material, though, of course, I should rather prefer that in which they are at present disposed. A solicitude to avoid continual transitions, and to give free scope to the natural association of connected facts, has dictated this arrangement, to which I confess myself partial. And I have found its inconveniences so trifling in composition that I can not believe they will occasion much trouble to the reader.

The first chapter comprises the history of France from the invasion of Clovis to the expedition, exclusively, of Charles VIII against Naples. It is not possible to fix accurate limits to the middle ages; but though the ten centuries from the fifth to the fifteenth seem, in a general point of view, to constitute that period, a less arbitrary division was necessary to render the commencement and conclusion of a historical narrative satisfactory. The continuous chain of transactions on the stage of human society is ill divided by mere lines of chronological demarcation. But as the subversion of the Western Empire is manifestly the natural termination of ancient history, so the establishment of the Franks in Gaul appears the most convenient epoch for the commencement of a new period. Less difficulty occurred in finding the other limit. The invasion of Naples by Charles VIII was the event that first engaged the principal states of Europe in relations of alliance or hostility which may be deduced to the present day, and is the point at which every man who traces backward its political history will be obliged to pause. It furnishes a determinate epoch in the annals of Italy and France, and nearly coincides with events which naturally terminate the history of the middle ages in other countries.

The feudal system is treated in the second chapter, which I have subjoined to the history of France, with which it has a near connection. Inquiries into the antiquities of that jurisprudence occupied more attention in the last age than the present, and their dryness may prove repulsive to many readers. But there is no royal road to the knowledge of law; nor can any man render an obscure and intricate disquisition either perspicuous or entertaining. That the feudal system is an important branch of historical knowledge will not be disputed when we consider not only its influence upon our own constitution, but that one of the parties which at present divide a neighbouring kingdom professes to appeal to the original principles of its monarchy, as they subsisted before the subversion of that polity.

The four succeeding chapters contain a sketch, more or less rapid and general, of the histories of Italy, of Spain, of Germany, and of the Greek and Saracenic Empires. In the seventh I have endeavoured to develop the progress of ecclesiastical power—a subject eminently distinguishing the middle ages, and of which a concise and impartial delineation has long been desirable.

The English constitution furnishes materials for the eighth chapter. I can not hope to have done sufficient justice to this theme, which has cost me considerable labour; but it is worthy of remark that since the treatise of Nathaniel Bacon, itself open to much exception, there has been no historical development of our constitution, founded upon extensive researches, or calculated to give a just notion of its character. For those parts of

B

Henry's history which profess to trace the progress of government are still more jejune than the rest of his volumes; and the work of Professor Millar, of Glasgow, however pleasing from its liberal spirit, displays a fault too common among the philosophers of his country—that of theorizing upon an imperfect induction, and very often upon a total misapprehension of particular facts.

The ninth and last chapter relates to the general state of society in Europe during the middle ages, and comprehends the history of commerce, of manners, and of literature. None, however, of these are treated in detail, and the whole chapter is chiefly designed as supplemental to the rest, in order to vary the relations under which events may be viewed, and to give a more adequate sense of the spirit and character of the middle ages.

In the execution of a plan far more comprehensive than what with a due consideration either of my abilities or opportunities I ought to have undertaken, it would be strangely presumptuous to hope that I can have rendered myself invulnerable to criticism. Even if flagrant errors should not be frequently detected, yet I am aware that a desire of conciseness has prevented the sense of some passages from appearing sufficiently distinct; and though I can not hold myself generally responsible for omissions in a work which could only be brought within a reasonable compass by the severe retrenchment of superfluous matter, it is highly probable that defective information, forgetfulness, or too great a regard for brevity, have caused me to pass over many things which would have materially illustrated the various subjects of these inquiries.

I dare not, therefore, appeal with confidence to the tribunal of those superior judges who, having bestowed a more undivided attention on the particular objects that have interested them, may justly deem such general sketches imperfect and superficial; but my labours will not have proved fruitless if they shall conduce to stimulate the reflection, to guide the researches, to correct the prejudices, or to animate the liberal and virtuous sentiments of inquisitive youth:

> " Mî satis ampla
> Merces, et mihi grande decus, sim ignotus in ævum
> Tum licet, externo penitusque inglorius orbi."

April, 1818.

THE AUTHOR'S PREFACE

TO THE SUPPLEMENTAL NOTES[1] PUBLISHED IN 1848

————————

THIRTY years have elapsed since the publication of the work to which the following notes relate, and almost forty since the first chapter and part of the second were written. The occupations of that time rendered it impossible for me to bestow such undivided attention as so laborious and difficult an undertaking demanded; and at the outset I had very little intention of prosecuting my researches, even to that degree of exactness which a growing interest in the ascertainment of precise truth, and a sense of its difficulty, led me afterward in some parts to seek, though nowhere equal to what with a fuller command of time I should have desired to attain. A measure of public approbation accorded to me far beyond my hopes has not blinded my discernment to the deficiencies of my own performance; and as successive editions have been called for, I have continually felt that there was more to correct or to elucidate than the insertion of a few foot-notes would supply, while I was always reluctant to make such alterations as would leave to the purchasers of former editions a right to complain. From an author whose science is continually progressive, such as chemistry or geology, this is unavoidably expected; but I thought the case not quite the same with a mediæval historian.

In the meantime, however, the long period of the middle ages had been investigated by many of my distinguished contemporaries with signal success, and I have been anxious to bring my own volumes nearer to the boundaries of the historic domain as

[1] In this edition the Supplemental Notes have been incorporated with the original work, partly at the foot of the pages, partly at the end of the second volume.—EDITOR.

xvii

it has been enlarged within our own age. My object has been, accordingly, to reconsider those portions of the work which relate to subjects discussed by eminent writers since its publication, to illustrate and enlarge some passages which had been imperfectly or obscurely treated, and to acknowledge with freedom my own errors. It appeared most convenient to adopt a form of publication by which the possessors of any edition may have the advantage of these Supplemental Notes, which will not much affect the value of their copy.

The first two chapters, on the history of France and on the feudal system, have been found to require a good deal of improvement. As a history, indeed, of the briefest kind, the first pages are insufficient for those who have little previous knowledge, and this I have, of course, not been able well to cure. The second chapter embraces subjects which have peculiarly drawn the attention of continental writers for the last thirty years. The whole history of France—civil, constitutional, and social—has been more philosophically examined, and yet with a more copious erudition, by which philosophy must always be guided, than in any former age. Two writers of high name have given the world a regular history of that country—one for modern as well as mediæval times, the other for these alone. The great historian of the Italian republics, my guide and companion in that portion of the "History of the Middle Ages," published in 1821 the first volumes of his "History of the French"; it is well known that this labour of twenty years was very nearly terminated when he was removed from the world. The two histories of Sismondi will, in all likelihood, never to be superseded; if in the latter we sometimes miss, and yet we do not always miss, the glowing and vivid pencil, guided by the ardour of youth and the distinct remembrance of scenery, we find no inferiority in justness of thought, in copiousness of narration, and especially in love of virtue and indignation at wrong. It seems, indeed, as if the progress of years had heightened the stern sentiments of republicanism with which he set out, and to which the whole course of his later work must have afforded no gratification, except that of scorn and severity. Measuring not only their actions but characters by a rigid standard, he sometimes demands from the men of past times more than human frailty and ignorance could have given; and his history would leave but a painful impression from the gloominess of the picture were not this constantly relieved by the peculiar softness and easy grace of his style. It can not be said that Sismondi is very diligent in probing obscurities or in weighing evidence; his general views, with which most of his chapters begin, are luminous and valuable to the ordinary reader, but sometimes sketched too loosely for the critical investigator of history.

Less full than Sismondi in the general details, but seizing particular events or epochs with greater minuteness and accuracy—not emulating his full and flowing periods, but in a style concise, rapid, and emphatic, sparkling with new and brilliant analogies—picturesque in description, spirited in sentiment, a poet in all but his fidelity to truth—M. Michelet has placed his own " History of France " by the side of that of Sismondi. His quotations are more numerous, for Sismondi commonly gives only references, and when interwoven with the text, as they often are, though not quite according to the strict laws of composition, not only bear with them the proof which an historical assertion may fail to command, but exhibit a more vivid picture.

In praising M. Michelet we are not to forget his defects. His pencil, always spirited, does not always fill the canvas. The consecutive history of France will not be so well learned from his pages as from those of Sismondi; and we should protest against his peculiar bitterness toward England were it not ridiculous in itself by its frequency and exaggeration.

I turn with more respect to a great name in historical literature, and which is only less great in that sense than it might have been, because it belongs also to the groundwork of all future history—the whole series of events which have been developed on the scene of Europe for twenty years now past. No envy of faction, no caprice of fortune, can tear from M. Guizot the trophy which time has bestowed—that he for nearly eight years, past and irrevocable, held in his firm grasp a power so fleeting before, and fell only with the monarchy which he had sustained, in the convulsive throes of his country.

"Cras vel atrâ
Nube polum Pater occupato,
Vel sole puro : non tamen irritum,
Quodcunque retro est, efficiet."

It has remained for my distinguished friend to manifest that high attribute of a great man's mind—a constant and unsubdued spirit in adversity, and to turn once more to those tranquil pursuits of earlier days which bestow a more unmingled enjoyment and a more unenvied glory than the favour of kings or the applause of senates.

The " Essais sur l'Histoire de France," by M. Guizot, appeared in 1820; the " Collection de Mémoires relatives à l'Histoire de France " (a translation generally from the Latin, under his superintendence and with notes by him), if I mistake not, in 1825; the lectures on the civilization of Europe, and on that of France, are of different dates, some of the latter in 1829. These form, by the confession of all, a sort of epoch in mediæval history by their philosophical acuteness, the judicious choice of their subjects, and the general solidity and truth of the views which they present.

I am almost unwilling to mention several other eminent names, lest it should seem invidious to omit any. It will sufficiently appear by these notes to whom I have been most indebted. Yet the writings of Thierry, Fauriel, Raynouard, and not less valuable, though in time almost the latest, Lehuerou, ought not to be passed in silence. I shall not attempt to characterize these eminent men; but the gratitude of every inquirer into the mediæval history of France is especially due to the Ministry of Public Instruction under the late government for the numerous volumes of " Documens Inédits," illustrating that history, which have appeared under its superintendence and at the public expense, within the last twelve years. It is difficult not to feel, at the present juncture, the greatest apprehension that this valuable publication will at least be suspended.

Several chapters which follow the second in my volumes have furnished no great store of additions, but that which relates to the English constitution has appeared to require more illustration. Many subjects of no trifling importance in the history of our ancient institutions had drawn the attention of men very conversant with its best sources; and it was naturally my desire to impart in some measure the substance of their researches to my readers. In not many instances have I seen ground for materially altering my own views; and I have not, of course, hesitated to differ from those whom I often quote with much respect. The publications of the Record Commission—the celebrated " Report of the Lords' Committee on the Dignity of a Peer "— the work of my learned and gifted friend, Sir Francis Palgrave, " On the Rise and Progress of the English Commonwealth," replete with omnifarious reading and fearless spirit, though not always commanding the assent of more sceptical tempers—the approved and valuable contributions to constitutional learning by Allen, Kemble, Spence, Starkie, Nicolas, Wright, and many others —are full of important facts and enlightened theories. Yet I fear that I shall be found to have overlooked much, especially in that periodical literature which is too apt to escape our observation or our memory; and can only hope that these notes, imperfect as they must be, will serve to extend the knowledge of my readers and guide them to the sources of historic truth. They claim only to be supplemental, and can be of no service to those who do not already possess the " History of the Middle Ages."

June, 1848.

CONTENTS

ILLUSTRATIONS

VIEW OF THE STATE OF EUROPE DURING THE MIDDLE AGES

———••——

CHAPTER I

HISTORY OF FRANCE, FROM ITS CONQUEST BY CLOVIS TO THE INVASION OF NAPLES BY CHARLES VIII

Fall of the Roman Empire—Invasion of Clovis—First race of French kings—Accession of Pepin—State of Italy—Charlemagne—His reign and character—Louis the Debonair—His successors—Calamitous state of the empire in the ninth and tenth centuries—Accession of Hugh Capet—His first successors—Louis VII—Philip Augustus—Conquest of Normandy—War in Languedoc—Louis IX—His character —Digression upon the crusades—Philip III—Philip IV—Aggrandizement of French monarchy under his reign—Reigns of his children—Question of Salic law—Claim of Edward III—War of Edward III in France—Causes of his success—Civil disturbances of France—Peace of Bretigni—Its interpretation considered—Charles V— Renewal of the war—Charles VI—His minority and insanity—Civil dissensions of the parties of Orleans and Burgundy—Assassination of both these princes—Intrigues of their parties with England under Henry IV—Henry V invades France —Treaty of Troyes—State of France in the first years of Charles VII—Progress and subsequent decline of the English arms—Their expulsion from France—Change in the political constitution—Louis XI—His character—Leagues formed against him—Charles, Duke of Burgundy—His prosperity and fall—Louis obtains possession of Burgundy—His death—Charles VIII—Acquisition of Brittany.

BEFORE the conclusion of the fifth century the mighty fabric of empire which valour and policy had founded upon the seven hills of Rome was finally overthrown in all the west of Europe by the barbarous nations from the north, whose martial energy and whose numbers were irresistible. A race of men, formerly unknown or despised, had not only dismembered that proud sovereignty, but permanently settled themselves in its fairest provinces, and imposed their yoke upon the ancient possessors. The Vandals were masters of Africa; the Suevi held part of Spain; the Visigoths possessed the remainder, with a large portion of Gaul; the Burgundians occupied the provinces watered by the Rhône and Saône; the Ostrogoths almost all Italy. The northwest of Gaul, between the Seine and the

Loire, some writers have filled with an Armorican republic;[1] while the remainder was still nominally subject to the Roman Empire, and governed by a certain Syagrius, rather with an independent than a deputed authority.

At this time Clovis, King of the Salian Franks, a tribe of Germans long connected with Rome, and originally settled upon the right bank of the Rhine,[2] but who had latterly penetrated as far as Tournay and Cambray,[3] invaded Gaul, and defeated Syagrius at Soissons. The result of this victory was the subjugation of those provinces which had previously been considered as Roman. But as their allegiance had not been very strict, so their loss was not very severely felt, since the Emperors of Constantinople were not too proud to confer upon Clovis the titles of consul and patrician, which he was too prudent to refuse.[4]

Some years after this Clovis defeated the Allemanni, or Swabians, in a great battle at Zulpich, near Cologne. In consequence of a vow, as it is said, made during this engagement,[5] and at the instigation of his wife Clotilda, a princess of Burgundy, he became a convert to Christianity. It would be a fruitless inquiry whether he was sincere in this change; but it is certain, at least, that no policy could have been more successful. The Arian sect, which had been early introduced among the barbarous nations,

[1] It is impossible not to speak sceptically as to this republic, or rather confederation of independent cities under the rule of their respective bishops, which Dubos has with great ingenuity raised upon a passage of Zosimus, but in defiance of the silence of Gregory, whose see of Tours bordered upon their supposed territory. Yet his hypothesis is not to be absolutely rejected, because it is by no means deficient in internal probability, and the early part of Gregory's history is brief and negligent. Dubos, " Hist. Critique de l'Etablissement des Français dans les Gaules," tome i, p. 253. Gibbon, c. 38, after following Dubos in his text, whispers as usual his suspicions in a note. [Note I.]

[2] [Note II.]

[3] The system of Père Daniel, who denies any permanent settlement of the Franks on the left bank of the Rhine before Clovis, seems incapable of being supported. It is difficult to resist the presumption that arises from the discovery of the tomb and skeleton of Childeric, father of Clovis, at Tournay, in 1653. See Montfaucon, " Monumens de la Monarchie Française," tome i, p. 10.

[4] The theory of Dubos, who considers Clovis as a sort of lieutenant of the emperors, and as governing the Roman part of his subjects by no other title, has justly seemed extravagant to later critical inquirers into the history of France. But it may nevertheless be true that the connection between him and the empire, and the emblems of Roman magistracy

which he bore, reconciled the conquered to their new masters. This is judiciously stated by the Duke de Nivernois, " Mém. de l'Acad. des Inscrip.," tome xx, p. 174. [Note III.] In the sixth century, however, the Greeks appear to have been nearly ignorant of Clovis's countrymen. Nothing can be made out of a passage in Procopius, where he seems to mention the Armoricans under the name Ἀρβόρυχοι ; and Agathias gives a strangely romantic account of the Franks, whom he extols for their conformity to Roman laws, πολιτείᾳ ὡς τὰ πολλὰ χρῶνται Ῥωμαϊκῇ, καὶ νόμοις τοῖς αὐτοῖς, καὶ τὰ ἄλλα ὁμοίως ἀμφί τε τὰ συμβόλαια καὶ γάμους καὶ τὴν τοῦ θείου θεράπειαν νομίζουσι . . . . ἐμοί γε δοκοῦσι σφόδρα εἶναι κόσμιοί τε καὶ ἀστειότατοι, οὐδέν τε ἔχειν τὸ διάλλαττον. ἢ μόνον τὸ βαρβάρικον τῆς στολῆς, καὶ τὸ τῆς φωνῆς ἰδιαζον. He goes on to commend their mutual union, and observes particularly that, in partitions of the kingdom, which had frequently been made, they had never taken up arms against each other, nor polluted the land with civil bloodshed. One would almost believe him ironical. The history of Agathias comes down to A. D. 559. At this time many of the savage murders and other crimes which fill the pages of Gregory of Tours, a writer somewhat more likely to know the truth than a Byzantine rhetorician, had taken place.

[5] Gregory of Tours makes a very rhetorical story of this famous vow, which, though we can not disprove, it may be permitted to suspect.—L. ii, c. 30.

was predominant, though apparently without intolerance,[6] in the Burgundian and Visigoth courts; but the clergy of Gaul were strenuously attached to the Catholic side, and, even before his conversion, had favoured the arms of Clovis. They now became his most zealous supporters, and were rewarded by him with artful gratitude, and by his descendants with lavish munificence. Upon the pretence of religion, he attacked Alaric, King of the Visigoths, and, by one great victory near Poitiers overthrowing their empire in Gaul, reduced them to the maritime province of Septimania, a narrow strip of coast between the Rhône and the Pyrenees. The last exploits of Clovis were the reduction of certain independent chiefs of his own tribe and family, who were settled in the neighbourhood of the Rhine.[7] All these he put to death by force or treachery; for he was cast in the true mould of conquerors, and may justly be ranked among the first of his class, both for the splendour and the guiltiness of his ambition.[8]

[6] " Hist. de Languedoc, par Vich et Vaissette," tome i, p. 238; Gibbon, c. 37. A specious objection might be drawn from the history of the Gothic monarchies in Italy, as well as Gaul and Spain, to the great principles of religious toleration. These Arian sovereigns treated their Catholic subjects, it may be said, with tenderness, leaving them in possession of every civil privilege, and were rewarded for it by their defection or sedition. But in answer to this it may be observed: 1. That the system of persecution adopted by the Vandals in Africa succeeded no better, the Catholics of that province having risen against them upon the landing of Belisarius. 2. That we do not know what insults and discouragements the Catholics of Gaul and Italy may have endured, especially from the Arian bishops, in that age of bigotry; although the administrations of Alaric and Theodoric were liberal and tolerant. 3. That the distinction of Arian and Catholic was intimately connected with that of Goth and Roman, of conqueror and conquered; so that it is difficult to separate the effects of national from those of sectarian animosity.

The tolerance of the Visigoth sovereigns must not be praised without making an exception for Euric, predecessor of Alaric. He was a prince of some eminent qualities, but so zealous in his religion as to bear hardly on his Catholic subjects. Sidonius Apollinaris loudly complains that no bishoprics were permitted to be filled, that the churches went to ruin, and that Arianism made a great progress. (Fauriel, " Hist. de la Gaule Méridionale," vol. i, p. 578.) Under Alaric himself, however, as well as under the earlier kings of the Visigothic dynasty, a more liberal spirit prevailed. Salvian, about the middle of the fifth century, extols the Visigothic government, in comparison with that of the empire, whose vices and despotism had met with a deserved termination. Eu-

cherius speaks of the Burgundians in the same manner. (Id. ibid., and vol. ii, p. 28.) Yet it must have been in itself mortifying to live in subjection to barbarians and heretics; not to mention the hospitality, as it was called, which the natives were obliged to exercise toward the invaders, by ceding two thirds of their lands. What, then, must the Western Empire have been, when such a condition was comparatively enviable! But it is more than probable that the Gaulish bishops subject to the Visigoths hailed the invasion of the Franks with sanguine hope, and were undoubtedly great gainers by the exchange.

[7] Modern historians, in enumerating these reguli, call one of them King of Mans. But it is difficult to understand how a chieftain, independent of Clovis, could have been settled in that part of France. In fact, Gregory of Tours, our only authority, does not say that this prince, Regnomeris, was King of Mans, but that he was put to death in that city: apud Cenomannis civitatem jussu Chlodovechi interfectus est.

The late French writers, as far as I have observed, continue to place a kingdom at Mans. It is certain, nevertheless, that Gregory of Tours, and they have no other evidence, does not assert this; and his expressions rather lead to the contrary; since, if Regnomeris were King of Mans, why should we not have been informed of it? It is, indeed, impossible to determine such a point negatively from our scanty materials; but if a Frank kingdom had been formed at Mans before the battle of Soissons, this must considerably alter the received notions of the history of Gaul in the fifth century; and it seems difficult to understand how it could have sprung up afterward during the reign of Clovis.

[8] The reader will be gratified by an admirable memoir, by the Duke de Nivernois, on the policy of Clovis, in the twentieth volume of the Academy of Inscriptions.

Clovis left four sons; one illegitimate, or at least born before his conversion; and three by his queen Clotilda. These four made, it is said, an equal partition of his dominions, which comprehended not only France, but the western and central parts of Germany, besides Bavaria, and perhaps Swabia, which were governed by their own dependent, but hereditary, chiefs. Thierry, the eldest, had what was called Austrasia, the eastern or German division, and fixed his capital at Metz; Clodomir, at Orleans; Childebert, at Paris; and Clotaire, at Soissons.[9] During their reigns the monarchy was aggrandized by the conquest of Burgundy. Clotaire, the youngest brother, ultimately reunited all the kingdoms; but upon his death they were again divided among his four sons, and brought together a second time by another Clotaire, the grandson to the first. It is a weary and unprofitable task to follow these changes in detail, through scenes of tumult and bloodshed, in which the eye meets with no sunshine, nor can rest upon any interesting spot. It would be difficult, as Gibbon has justly observed, to find anywhere more vice or less virtue. The names of two queens are distinguished even in that age for the magnitude of their crimes: Fredegonde, the wife of Chilperic, of whose atrocities none have doubted; and Brunehaut, Queen of Austrasia, who has met with advocates in modern times, less, perhaps, from any fair presumptions of

[9] Quatuor filii regnum accipiunt, et inter se æquâ lance dividunt.—Greg. Tur., l. iii, c. 1. It would rather perplex a geographer to make an equal division of Clovis's empire into portions, of which Paris, Orleans, Metz, and Soissons should be the respective capitals. I apprehend, in fact, that Gregory's expression is not very precise. The kingdom of Soissons seems to have been the least of the four, and that of Austrasia the greatest. But the partitions made by these princes were exceedingly complex ; insulated fragments of territory, and even undivided shares of cities, being allotted to the worse-provided brothers, by way of compensation, out of the larger kingdoms. It would be very difficult to ascertain the limits of these minor monarchies. But the French Empire was always considered as one, whatever might be the number of its inheritors; and from accidental circumstances it was so frequently reunited as fully to keep up this notion.

M. Fauriel endeavours to show the equality of this partition (" Hist. de la Gaule Méridionale," vol. ii, p. 92). But he is obliged to suppose that Germany beyond the Rhine, part of which owned the dominion of Clovis, was counted as nothing, not being inhabited by Franks. It was something, nevertheless, in the scale of power; since from this fertile source the Austrasian kings continually recruited their armies. Aquitaine—that is, the provinces south of the Loire—was divided into three, or rather perhaps two portions. For though Thierry and Childebert had considerable territories, it seems not certain that Clodomir took any share, and improbable that Clotaire had one. Thierry, therefore, King of Austrasia, may be reckoned the best provided of the brethren. It will be obvious from the map that the four capitals, Metz, Soissons, Paris, and Orleans, are situated at no great distance from each other, relatively to the whole of France. They were, therefore, in the centre of force; and the brothers might have lent assistance to each other in case of a national revolt.

The cause of this complexity in the partition of France among the sons of Clovis has been conjectured by Dubos, with whom Sismondi (vol. i, p. 242) agrees, to have been their desire of owning as subjects an equal number of Franks. This is supported by a passage in Agathias, quoted by the former, " Hist. de l'Établissement, vol. ii, p. 413. Others have fancied that Aquitaine was reckoned too delicious a morsel to be enjoyed by only one brother. In the second great partition, that of 567 (for that of 561 did not last long), when Sigebert, Gontran, and Chilperic took the kingdoms of Austrasia, Burgundy, and what was afterward called Neustria, the southern provinces were again equally divided. Thus Marseilles fell to the King of Paris, or Neustria, while Aix and Avignon were in the lot of Burgundy.

her innocence than from compassion for the cruel death which she underwent.[10]

But after Dagobert, son of Clotaire II, the Kings of France dwindled into personal insignificance, and are generally treated by later historians as insensati, or idiots.[11] The whole power of the kingdom devolved upon the mayors of the palace, originally officers of the household, through whom petitions or representations were laid before the king.[12] The weakness of sovereigns rendered this office important, and still greater weakness suffered it to become elective; men of energetic talents and ambition united it with military command; and the history of France for half a century presents no names more conspicuous than those of Ebroin and Grimoald, mayors of Neustria and Austrasia, the western and eastern divisions of the French monarchy.[13] These, however, met with violent ends; but a more successful usurper of the royal authority was Pepin Heristal, first mayor, and afterward duke, of Austrasia; who united with almost an avowed sovereignty over that division a paramount command over the French or Neustrian provinces, where nominal kings of the Merovingian family were still permitted to exist.[14] This authority he transmitted to a more renowned hero, his son, Charles Martel, who, after some less important exploits, was called upon to encounter

[10] Every history will give a sufficient epitome of the Merovingian dynasty. The facts of these times are of little other importance than as they impress on the mind a thorough notion of the extreme wickedness of almost every person concerned in them, and consequently of the state to which society was reduced. But there is no advantage in crowding the memory with barbarian wars and assassinations. [Note IV.]

For the question about Brunehaut's character, who has had partisans almost as enthusiastic as those of Mary of Scotland, the reader may consult Pasquier, "Recherches de la France," l. viii, or Velly, "Hist. de France," tome i, on one side, and a dissertation by Gaillard, in the "Memoirs of the Academy of Inscriptions," tome xxx, on the other. The last is unfavourable to Brunehaut, and perfectly satisfactory to my judgment.

Brunehaut was no unimportant personage in this history. She had become hateful to the Austrasian aristocracy by her Gothic blood, and still more by her Roman principles of government. There was evidently a combination to throw off the yoke of civilized tyranny. It was a great conflict, which ended in the virtual dethronement of the house of Clovis. Much, therefore, may have been exaggerated by Fredegarius, a Burgundian by birth, in relating the crimes of Brunehaut. But, unhappily, the antecedent presumption, in the history of that age, is always on the worse side. She was unquestionably endowed with a masculine energy of mind, and very superior to such a mere imp of audacious wickedness as Fredegonde. Brunehaut left a great and almost fabulous name; public causeways, towers, castles, in different parts of France, are popularly ascribed to her. It has even been suspected by some that she suggested the appellation of Brunechild in the "Nibelungen Lied." That there is no resemblance in the story, or in the character, courage excepted, of the two heroines, can not be thought an objection.

[11] An ingenious attempt is made by the Abbé Vertot, "Mém. de l'Académie," tome vi, to rescue these monarchs from this long-established imputation. But the leading fact is irresistible, that all the royal authority was lost during their reigns. However, the best apology seems to be that, after the victories of Pepin Heristal, the Merovingian kings were, in effect, conquered, and their inefficiency was a matter of necessary submission to a master.

[12] [Note V.]

[13] The original kingdoms of Soissons, Paris, and Orleans were consolidated into that denominated Neustria, to which Burgundy was generally appendant, though distinctly governed by a mayor of its own election. But Aquitaine, the exact bounds of which I do not know, was, from the time of Dagobert I, separated from the rest of the monarchy, under a ducal dynasty, sprung from Aribert, brother of that monarch. [Note VI.]

[14] [Note VII.]

a new and terrible enemy. The Saracens, after subjugating Spain, had penetrated into the very heart of France. Charles Martel gained a complete victory over them between Tours and Poitiers,[15] in which three hundred thousand Mohammedans are hyperbolically asserted to have fallen. The reward of this victory was the province of Septimania, which the Saracens had conquered from the Visigoths.[16]

Such powerful subjects were not likely to remain long contented without the crown; but the circumstances under which it was transferred from the race of Clovis are connected with one of the most important revolutions in the history of Europe. The mayor Pepin, inheriting his father Charles Martel's talents and ambition, made, in the name and with the consent of the nation, a solemn reference to the Pope Zacharias as to the deposition of Childeric III, under whose nominal authority he himself was reigning. The decision was favourable; that he who possessed the power should also bear the title of king. The unfortunate Merovingian was dismissed into a convent, and the Franks, with one consent, raised Pepin to the throne, the founder of a more illustrious dynasty.[17] In order to judge of the importance of this revolution to the see of Rome, as well as to France, we must turn our eyes upon the affairs of Italy.

The dominion of the Ostrogoths was annihilated by the arms of Belisarius and Narses in the sixth century, and that nation appears no more in history. But not long afterward the Lombards, a people for some time settled in Pannonia, not only subdued that northern part of Italy which has retained their name, but, extending themselves southward, formed the powerful duchies of Spoleto and Benevento. The residence of their kings was in Pavia; but the hereditary vassals, who held those two duchies,

[15] Tours is above seventy miles distant from Poitiers; but I do not find that any French antiquary has been able to ascertain the place of this great battle with more precision ; which is remarkable, since, after so immense a slaughter, we should expect the testimony of " grandia effossis ossa sepulcris." It is now, however, believed that the slaughter at the battle near Poitiers was by no means immense, and even that the Saracens retired without a decisive action. (Sismondi, ii, 132; Michelet, ii, 13.) There can be no doubt that the battle was fought much nearer to Poitiers than to Tours.

The victory of Charles Martel has immortalized his name, and may justly be reckoned among those few battles of which a contrary event would have essentially varied the drama of the world in all its subsequent scenes; with Marathon, Arbela, the Metaurus, Châlons, and Leipsic. Yet do we not judge a little too much by the event, and follow, as usual, in the wake of fortune? Has not more frequent experience condemned those who set the fate of empires upon a single cast, and risk a general battle with invaders, whose greater peril is in delay? Was not this the fatal error by which Roderic had lost his kingdom? Was it possible that the Saracens could have retained any permanent possession of France, except by means of a victory? And did not the contest upon the broad champaign of Poitou afford them a considerable prospect of success, which a more cautious policy would have withheld?

[16] This conquest was completed by Pepin in 759. The inhabitants preserved their liberties by treaty; and Vaissette deduces from this solemn assurance the privileges of Languedoc.—" Hist. de Lang.," tome i, p. 412.

[17] [Note VIII.]

might be deemed almost independent sovereigns.[18] The rest of
Italy was governed by exarchs, deputed by the Greek emperors,
and fixed at Ravenna. In Rome itself neither the people nor the
bishops, who had already conceived in part their schemes of ambition, were much inclined to endure the superiority of Constantinople; yet their disaffection was counterbalanced by the
inveterate hatred, as well as jealousy, with which they regarded
the Lombards. But an impolitic and intemperate persecution,
carried on by two or three Greek emperors against a favourite
superstition, the worship of images, excited commotions throughout Italy, of which the Lombards took advantage, and easily
wrested the exarchate of Ravenna from the Eastern Empire. It
was far from the design of the popes to see their nearest enemies
so much aggrandized; and any effectual assistance from the Emperor Constantine Copronymus would have kept Rome still faithful. But having no hope from his arms, and provoked by his
obstinate intolerance, the pontiffs had recourse to France; [19] and
the service they had rendered to Pepin led to reciprocal obligations of the greatest magnitude. At the request of Stephen II
the new King of France descended from the Alps, drove the Lombards from their recent conquests, and conferred them upon the
Pope. This memorable donation nearly comprised the modern
provinces of Romagna and the March of Ancona.[20]

The state of Italy, which had undergone no change for nearly
two centuries, was now rapidly verging to a great revolution.
Under the shadow of a mighty name the Greek Empire had concealed the extent of its decline. That charm was now broken:
and the Lombard kingdom, which had hitherto appeared the only
competitor in the lists, proved to have lost its own energy in
awaiting the occasion for its display. France was far more than
a match for the power of Italy, even if she had not been guided
by the towering ambition and restless activity of the son of Pepin.
It was almost the first exploit of Charlemagne, after the death
of his brother Carloman had reunited the Frankish Empire under
his dominion,[21] to subjugate the kingdom of Lombardy. Neither
Pavia nor Verona, its most considerable cities, interposed any
material delay to his arms: and the chief resistance he encoun-

---

[18] The history, character, and policy of
the Lombards are well treated by Gibbon, c. 45. See, too, the fourth and fifth
books of Giannone, and some papers by
Gaillard in the "Memoirs of the Academy
of Inscriptions," tome xxxii, xxxv, xlv.

[19] There had been some previous overtures to Charles Martel as well as to
Pepin himself; the habitual sagacity of
the court of Rome perceiving the growth
of a new western monarchy, which would
be, in faith and arms, their surest ally.
(Muratori, "Ann. d'Ital.," A. D. 741.)

[20] Giannone, l. v, c. 2.
[21] Carloman, younger brother of
Charles, took the Austrasian or German
provinces of the empire. The custom of
partition was so fully established that
those wise and ambitious princes, Charles
Martel, Pepin, and Charlemagne himself,
did not venture to thwart the public
opinion by introducing primogeniture.
Carloman would not long have stood
against his brother; who, after his death,
usurped the inheritance of his two infant
children.

tered was from the Dukes of Friuli and Benevento, the latter of whom could never be brought into thorough subjection to the conqueror. Italy, however, be the cause what it might, seems to have tempted Charlemagne far less than the dark forests of Germany. For neither the southern provinces, nor Sicily, could have withstood his power if it had been steadily directed against them. Even Spain hardly drew so much of his attention as the splendour of the prize might naturally have excited. He gained, however, a very important accession to his empire by conquering from the Saracens the territory contained between the Pyrenees and the Ebro. This was formed into the Spanish March, governed by the Count of Barcelona, part of which at least must be considered as appertaining to France till the twelfth century.[22]

But the most tedious and difficult achievement of Charlemagne was the reduction of the Saxons. The wars with this nation, who occupied nearly the modern circles of Westphalia and Lower Saxony, lasted for thirty years. Whenever the conqueror withdrew his armies, or even his person, the Saxons broke into fresh rebellion, which his unparalleled rapidity of movement seldom failed to crush without delay. From such perseverance on either side destruction of the weaker could alone result. A large colony of Saxons were finally transplanted into Flanders and Brabant, countries hitherto ill peopled, in which their descendants preserved the same unconquerable spirit of resistance to oppression. Many fled to the kingdoms of Scandinavia, and, mingling with the Northmen, who were just preparing to run their memorable career, revenged upon the children and subjects of Charlemagne the devastation of Saxony. The remnant embraced Christianity, their aversion to which had been the chief cause of their rebellions, and acknowledged the sovereignty of Charlemagne—a submission which even Witikind, the second Arminius of Germany, after such irresistible conviction of her destiny, did not disdain to make. But they retained, in the main, their own laws; they were governed by a duke of their own nation, if not of their own election, and for many ages they were distinguished by their original character among the nations of Germany.[23]

The successes of Charlemagne on the eastern frontier of his empire against the Slavonians of Bohemia and Huns or Avars of Pannonia, though obtained with less cost, were hardly less eminent. In all his wars the newly conquered nations, or those

---

[22] The Counts of Barcelona always acknowledged the feudal superiority of the Kings of France till some time after their own title had been merged in that of Kings of Aragon. In 1180 legal instruments executed in Catalonia ceased to be dated by the year of the King of France; and as there certainly remained no other mark of dependence, the separation of the principality may be referred to that year. But the rights of the French crown over it were finally ceded by Louis IX in 1258. De Marca, " Marca Hispanica," p. 514; "Art de vérifier les Dates," tome ii, p. 291.

[23] [Note IX.]

BAPTISM OF WITIKIND.

Photogravure from a painting by Paul Thumann.

whom fear had made dependent allies, were employed to subjugate their neighbours, and the incessant waste of fatigue and the sword was supplied by a fresh population that swelled the expanding circle of dominion. I do not know that the limits of the new Western Empire are very exactly defined by contemporary writers, nor would it be easy to appreciate the degree of subjection in which the Slavonian tribes were held. As an organized mass of provinces, regularly governed by imperial officers, it seems to have been nearly bounded, in Germany, by the Elbe, the Saale, the Bohemian mountains, and a line drawn from thence crossing the Danube above Vienna, and prolonged to the Gulf of Istria. Part of Dalmatia was comprised in the duchy of Friuli. In Italy the empire extended not much beyond the modern frontier of Naples, if we exclude, as was the fact, the duchy of Benevento from anything more than a titular subjection. The Spanish boundary, as has been said already, was the Ebro.[24]

A seal was put to the glory of Charlemagne when Leo III, in the name of the Roman people, placed upon his head the imperial crown. His father, Pepin, had borne the title of patrician, and he had himself exercised, with that title, a regular sovereignty over Rome.[25] Money was coined in his name, and an oath of fidelity was taken by the clergy and people. But the appellation of emperor seemed to place his authority over all his subjects on a new footing. It was full of high and indefinite pretension, tending to overshadow the free election of the Franks by a fictitious descent from Augustus. A fresh oath of fidelity to him as emperor was demanded from his subjects. His own discretion, however, prevented him from affecting those more despotic prerogatives which the imperial name might still be supposed to convey.[26]

[24] I follow in this the map of Koch, in his "Tableau des Révolutions de l'Europe," tome i. That of Vaugondy, Paris, 1752, includes the dependent Slavonic tribes, and carries the limit of the empire to the Oder and frontiers of Poland. The authors of "L'Art de vérifier les Dates" extend it to the Raab. It would require a long examination to give a precise statement.

[25] The Patricians of the lower empire were governors sent from Constantinople to the provinces. Rome had long been accustomed to their name and power. The subjection of the Romans, both clergy and laity, to Charlemagne, as well before as after he bore the imperial name, seems to be established. See "Dissertation Historique, par le Blanc," subjoined to his "Traité de Monnoyes de France," p. 18; and St. Marc, "Abrégé Chronologique de l'Histoire de l'Italie," tome i. The first of these writers does not allow that Pepin exercised any authority at Rome. A good deal of obscurity rests over its internal government for near fifty years; but there is some reason to believe that the nominal sovereignty of the Greek emperors was not entirely abrogated. Muratori, "Annali d'Italia," ad. ann. 772; St. Marc, tome i, pp. 356, 372. A mosaic, still extant in the Lateran palace, represents our Saviour giving the keys to St. Peter with one hand, and with the other a standard to a crowned prince, bearing the inscription Constantine V. But Constantine V did not begin to reign till 780; and if this piece of workmanship was made under Leo III, as the authors of "L'Art de vérifier les Dates" imagine, it could not be earlier than 795. Tome i, p. 262; Muratori ad ann. 798. However this may be, there can be no question that a considerable share of jurisdiction and authority was practically exercised by the popes during this period. Vid. Murat. ad ann. 789.

[26] [Note X.]

In analyzing the characters of heroes it is hardly possible to separate altogether the share of fortune from their own. The epoch made by Charlemagne in the history of the world, the illustrious families which prided themselves in him as their progenitor, the very legends of romance, which are full of his fabulous exploits, have cast a lustre around his head, and testify the greatness that has embodied itself in his name. None, indeed, of Charlemagne's wars can be compared with the Saracenic victory of Charles Martel; but that was a contest for freedom, his for conquest and fame is more partial to successful aggression than to patriotic resistance. As a scholar, his acquisitions were probably little superior to those of his unrespected son; and in several points of view the glory of Charlemagne might be extenuated by an analytical dissection.[27] But rejecting a mode of judging equally uncandid and fallacious, we shall find that he possessed in everything that grandeur of conception which distinguishes extraordinary minds. Like Alexander, he seemed born for universal innovation: in a life restlessly active, we see him reforming the coinage and establishing the legal divisions of money; gathering about him the learned of every country; founding schools and collecting libraries; interfering, but with the tone of a king, in religious controversies; aiming, though prematurely, at the formation of a naval force; attempting, for the sake of commerce, the magnificent enterprise of uniting the Rhine and Danube;[28] and meditating to mould the discordant codes of Roman and barbarian laws into a uniform system.

The great qualities of Charlemagne were, indeed, alloyed by the vices of a barbarian and a conqueror. Nine wives, whom he divorced with very little ceremony, attest the license of his private life, which his temperance and frugality can hardly be said to redeem. Unsparing of blood, though not constitutionally cruel, and wholly indifferent to the means which his ambition prescribed, he beheaded in one day four thousand Saxons—an act of atrocious butchery, after which his persecuting edicts, pronouncing the pain of death against those who refused baptism, or even who ate flesh during Lent, seem scarcely worthy of notice. This union of barbarous ferocity with elevated views of national improvement might suggest the parallel of Peter the Great. But the degrading habits and brute violence of the Muscovite place him at an immense distance from the restorer of the empire.

[27] Eginhard attests his ready eloquence, his perfect mastery of Latin, his knowledge of Greek so far as to read it, his acquisitions in logic, grammar, rhetoric, and astronomy. But the anonymous author of the life of Louis the Debonair attributes most of these accomplishments to that unfortunate prince.

[28] See an essay upon this project in the "Memoirs of the Academy of Inscriptions," tome xviii. The rivers which were designed to form the links of this junction were the Altmuhl, the Regnitz, and the Main; but their want of depth, and the sponginess of the soil, appear to present insuperable impediments to its completion.

A strong sympathy for intellectual excellence was the leading characteristic of Charlemagne, and this undoubtedly biassed
him in the chief political error of his conduct—that of encouraging the power and pretensions of the hierarchy. But, perhaps,
his greatest eulogy is written in the disgraces of succeeding times
and the miseries of Europe. He stands alone, like a beacon upon
a waste, or a rock in the broad ocean. His sceptre was the bow
of Ulysses, which could not be drawn by any weaker hand. In
the dark ages of European history the reign of Charlemagne
affords a solitary resting place between two long periods of turbulence and ignominy, deriving the advantages of contrast both
from that of the preceding dynasty and of a posterity for whom
he had formed an empire which they were unworthy and unequal
to maintain.[29]

Pepin, the eldest son of Charlemagne, died before him, leaving a natural son, named Bernard.[30] Even if he had been legitimate, the right of representation was not at all established during these ages; indeed, the general prejudice seems to have
inclined against it. Bernard, therefore, kept only the kingdom
of Italy, which had been transferred to his father; while Louis,
the younger son of Charlemagne, inherited the empire.[31] But,
in a short time, Bernard, having attempted a rebellion against
his uncle, was sentenced to lose his eyes, which occasioned his
death—a cruelty more agreeable to the prevailing tone of manners than to the character of Louis, who bitterly reproached himself for the severity he had been persuaded to use.

Under this prince, called by the Italians the Pious, and by
the French the Debonair, or Good-natured,[32] the mighty struc-

[29] The " Life of Charlemagne," by
Gaillard, without being made perhaps so
interesting as it ought to have been, presents an adequate view both of his actions and character. Schmidt, " Hist. des
Allemands," tome ii, appears to me a
superior writer.

An exception to the general suffrage
of historians in favour of Charlemagne is
made by Sismondi. He seems to consider him as having produced no permanent effect, the empire, within half a
century, having been dismembered, and
relapsing into the merest weakness :
" Tellement la grandeur acquise par les
armes est trompeuse, quand elle ne se
donne pour appui aucune institution
bienfaisante; et tellement le règne d'un
grand roi demeure stérile, quand il ne
fonde pas la liberté de ses concitoyens "
(vol. iii, p. 97). But certainly some of
Charlemagne's institutions were likely to
prove beneficial if they could have been
maintained, such as the Scabini and the
Missi Dominici. And when Sismondi
hints that Charlemagne ought to have
given a charte constitutionnelle, it is difficult not to smile at such a proof of his
inclination to judge past times by a

standard borrowed from the theories of
his own. M. Guizot asks whether the
nation was left in the same state in which
the emperor found it. Nothing fell with
him, he remarks, but the central government, which could only have been
preserved by a series of men like himself. (" Essais sur l'Hist. de France,"
pp. 276–294; " Hist. de la Civilisation en
France," leçon ii, p. 39.) Some, indeed,
of his institutions can not be said to have
long survived him; but this again must
be chiefly attributed to the weakness of
his successors. No one man of more than
common ability arose in the Carlovingian
dynasty after himself, a fact very disadvantageous to the permanence of his policy, and perhaps rather surprising ;
though it is a theory of Sismondi that
royal families naturally dwindle into imbecility, especially in a semi-barbarous
condition of society.

[30] A contemporary author, Thegan, ap.
Muratori, A. D. 810, asserts that Bernard
was born of a concubine. I do not know
why modern historians represent it otherwise.

[31] [Note XI.]

[32] These names, as a French writer ob-

ture of his father's power began rapidly to decay. I do not know that Louis deserves so much contempt as he has undergone; but historians have in general more indulgence for splendid crimes than for the weaknesses of virtue. There was no defect in Louis's understanding or courage; he was accomplished in martial exercises, and in all the learning which an education, excellent for that age, could supply. No one was ever more anxious to reform the abuses of administration; and whoever compares his capitularies with those of Charlemagne will perceive that, as a legislator, he was even superior to his father. The fault lay entirely in his heart; and this fault was nothing but a temper too soft and a conscience too strict.[33] It is not wonderful that the empire should have been speedily dissolved; a succession of such men as Charles Martel, Pepin, and Charlemagne could alone have preserved its integrity, but the misfortunes of Louis and his people were immediately owing to the following errors of his conduct.

Soon after his accession Louis thought fit to associate his eldest son, Lothaire, to the empire, and to confer the provinces of Bavaria and Aquitaine, as subordinate kingdoms, upon the two younger, Louis and Pepin. The step was, in appearance, conformable to his father's policy, who had acted toward himself in a similar manner. But such measures are not subject to general rules, and exact a careful regard to characters and circumstances. The principle, however, which regulated this division was learned from Charlemagne, and could alone, if strictly pursued, have given unity and permanence to the empire. The elder brother was to preserve his superiority over the others, so that they should neither make peace nor war, nor even give answer to ambassadors, without his consent. Upon the death of either no further partition was to be made; but whichever of his children might become the popular choice was to inherit the whole kingdom, under the same superiority of the head of the family.[34] This compact was from the beginning disliked by the younger brothers, and an event, upon which Louis does not seem to have calculated, soon disgusted his colleague Lothaire. Judith of Bavaria, the emperor's second wife, an ambitious woman, bore him a son, by name Charles, whom both parents were naturally anxious to place on an equal footing with his brothers. But

---

serves, meant the same thing. Pius had, even in good Latin, the sense of mitis, meek, forbearing, or what the French call débonnaire. " Synonymes de Rouband," tome i, p. 257. Our English word debonair is hardly used in the same sense, if indeed it can be called an English word; but I have not altered Louis's appellation, by which he is so well known.

[33] Schmidt, " Hist. des Allemands," tome ii, has done more justice than other historians to Louis's character. Vaissette attests the goodness of his government in Aquitaine, which he held as a subordinate kingdom during his father's life. It extended from the Loire to the Ebro, so that the trust was not contemptible.— " Hist. de Languedoc," tome i, p. 476.
[34] " Baluzii Capitularia," tome i, p. 575.

this could only be done at the expense of Lothaire, who was ill disposed to see his empire still further dismembered for this child of a second bed. Louis passed his life in a struggle with three undutiful sons, who abused his paternal kindness by constant rebellions.

These were rendered more formidable by the concurrence of a different class of enemies, whom it had been another error of the emperor to provoke. Charlemagne had assumed a thorough control and supremacy over the clergy; and his son was perhaps still more vigilant in chastising their irregularities and reforming their rules of discipline. But to this, which they had been compelled to bear at the hands of the first, it was not equally easy for the second to obtain their submission. Louis therefore drew on himself the inveterate enmity of men who united with the turbulence of martial nobles a skill in managing those engines of offence which were peculiar to their order, and to which the implicit devotion of his character laid him very open. Yet, after many vicissitudes of fortune, and many days of ignominy, his wishes were eventually accomplished. Charles, his youngest son, surnamed the Bald, obtained, upon his death, most of France, while Germany fell to the share of Louis, and the rest of the imperial dominions, with the title, to the eldest, Lothaire. This partition was the result of a sanguinary, though short, contest; and it gave a fatal blow to the empire of the Franks. For the Treaty of Verdun, in 843, abrogated the sovereignty that had been attached to the eldest brother and to the imperial name in former partitions: each held his respective kingdom as an independent right.[35] This is the epoch of a final separation between the French and German members of the empire. Its millenary was celebrated by some of the latter nation in 1843.[36]

The subsequent partitions made among the children of these brothers are of too rapid succession to be here related. In about

[35] " Baluzii Capitularia," tome ii, p. 42; Velly, tome ii, p. 75. The expressions of this treaty are perhaps equivocal; but the subsequent conduct of the brothers and their families justifies the construction of Velly, which I have followed.

[36] The partition, which the Treaty of Verdun confirmed, had been made by commissioners specially appointed in the preceding year. " Le nombre total des commissaires fut porté à trois cents; ils se distribuérent toute la surface de l'empire, qu'ils s'engagèrent à parcourir avant le mois d' août de l'année suivante; cet immense travail etoit en effet alors nécessaire pour se procurer les connoissances qu'on obtient aujourd'hui en un instant, par l'inspection d'une carte géographique: malheureusement on écrivoit à cette époque aussi peu qu'on lisoit. Le rapport des commissaires ne fut point mis par écrit, ou point déposé dans les archives. S'il nous avoit été conservé, ce seroit le plus curieux de tous les monumens sur l'état de l'Europe au moyen âge." (Sismondi, " Hist. des Franç.," iii, 76.) For this he quotes Nithard, a contemporary historian.

In the division made on this occasion the kingdom of France, which fell to Charles the Bald, had for its eastern boundary the Meuse, the Saône, and the Rhône; which, nevertheless, can only be understood of the Upper Meuse, since Brabant was certainly not comprised in it. Lothaire, the elder brother, besides Italy, had a kingdom called Lorraine, from his name (Lotharingia), extending from the mouth of the Rhine to Provence, bounded by that river on one frontier, by France on the other. Louis took all beyond the Rhine, and was usually styled The Germanic.

forty years the empire was nearly reunited under Charles the Fat, son of Louis of Germany, but his short and inglorious reign ended in his deposition. From this time the possession of Italy was contested among her native princes; Germany fell at first to an illegitimate descendant of Charlemagne, and in a short time was entirely lost by his family; two kingdoms, afterward united, were formed by usurpers out of what was then called Burgundy, and comprised the provinces between the Rhône and the Alps, with Franche Comté, and a great part of Switzerland.[37] In France the Carlovingian kings continued for another century; but their line was interrupted two or three times by the election or usurpation of a powerful family, the Counts of Paris and Orleans, who ended, like the old mayors of the palace, in dispersing the phantoms of royalty they had professed to serve.[38] Hugh Capet, the representative of this house upon the death of Louis V, placed himself upon the throne, thus founding the third and most permanent race of French sovereigns. Before this happened the descendants of Charlemagne had sunk into insignificance, and retained little more of France than the city of Laon. The rest of the kingdom had been seized by the powerful nobles, who, with the nominal fidelity of the feudal system, maintained its practical independence and rebellious spirit.[39]

These were times of great misery to the people, and the worst, perhaps, that Europe has ever known. Even under Charlemagne we have abundant proofs of the calamities which the people suffered. The light which shone around him was that of a consuming fire. The free proprietors, who had once considered themselves as only called upon to resist foreign invasion, were harassed by endless expeditions, and dragged away to the Baltic Sea or the banks of the Drave. Many of them, as we learn from his capitularies, became ecclesiastics to avoid military conscription.[40] But far worse must have been their state under the lax

---

[37] These kingdoms were denominated Provence and Transjurane Burgundy. The latter was very small, comprising only part of Switzerland; but its second sovereign, Rodolph II, acquired by treaty almost the whole of the former; and the two united were called the kingdom of Arles. This lasted from 933 to 1032, when Rodolph III bequeathed his dominions to the Emperor Conrad II.—"Art de vérifier les Dates," tome ii, p. 427-432.

[38] The family of Capet is generally admitted to possess the most ancient pedigree of any sovereign line in Europe. Its succession through males is unequivocally deduced from Robert the Brave, made governor of Anjou in 864, and father of Eudes, King of France, and of Robert, who was chosen by a party in 922, though, as Charles the Simple was still acknowledged in some provinces, it is uncertain whether he ought to be counted in the royal list. It is, moreover, highly probable that Robert the Brave was descended, equally through males, from St. Arnoul, who died in 640, and consequently nearly allied to the Carlovingian family, who derive their pedigree from the same head. See "Preuves de la Généalogie de Hughes Capet," in "L'Art de vérifier les Dates," tome i, p. 566.

[39] [Note XII.]
At the close of the ninth century there were twenty-nine hereditary fiefs of the crown. At the accession of Hugh Capet, in 987, they had increased to fifty-five. (Guizot, "Civilis en France," Leçon 24.) Thierry maintains that those between the Loire and the Pyrenees were strictly independent and bound by no feudal tie. ("Lettres sur l'Hist. de France," lettre ix.)

[40] "Capitularia," A. D. 805. Whoever

government of succeeding times, when the dukes and counts, no longer checked by the vigorous administration of Charlemagne, were at liberty to play the tyrants in their several territories, of which they now became almost the sovereigns. The poorer landholders accordingly were forced to bow their necks to the yoke, and, either by compulsion or through hope of being better protected, submitted their independent patrimonies to the feudal tenure.

But evils still more terrible than these political abuses were the lot of those nations who had been subject to Charlemagne. They, indeed, may appear to us little better than ferocious barbarians; but they were exposed to the assaults of tribes, in comparison of whom they must be deemed humane and polished. Each frontier of the empire had to dread the attack of an enemy. The coasts of Italy were continually alarmed by the Saracens of Africa, who possessed themselves of Sicily and Sardinia, and became masters of the Mediterranean Sea.[41] Though the Greek dominions in the south of Italy were chiefly exposed to them, they twice insulted and ravaged the territory of Rome; nor was there any security even in the neighbourhood of the maritime Alps, where, early in the tenth century, they settled a piratical colony.[42]

Much more formidable were the foes by whom Germany was assailed. The Slavonians, a widely extended people, whose language is still spoken upon half the surface of Europe, had occupied the countries of Bohemia, Poland, and Pannonia,[43] on the eastern confines of the empire, and from the time of Charlemagne acknowledged its superiority. But at the end of the ninth century a Tartarian tribe, the Hungarians, overspreading that country which since has borne their name, and moving forward like a vast wave, brought a dreadful reverse upon Germany.

possessed three mansi of allodial property was called upon for personal service, or at least to furnish a substitute. Nigellus, author of a poetical life of Louis I, seems to implicate Charlemagne himself in some of the oppressions of his reign. It was the first care of the former to redress those who had been injured in his father's time.—" Recueil des Historiens," tome vi. N. B.—I quote by this title the great collection of French historians, charters, and other documents illustrative of the middle ages, more commonly known by the name of its first editor, the " Benedictine Bouquet." But as several learned men of that order were successively concerned in this work, not one half of which has yet been published, it seemed better to follow its own title-page.

[41] These African Saracens belonged to the Aglabites, a dynasty that reigned at Tunis for the whole of the ninth century, after throwing off the yoke of the Abbas-

site Khalifs. They were overthrown themselves in the next age by the Fatimites. Sicily was first invaded in 827: but the city of Syracuse was only reduced in 878.

[42] Muratori, " Annali d'Italia," ad. ann. 906, et alibi. These Saracens of Frassineto, supposed to be between Nice and Monaco, were extirpated by a Count of Provence in 972. But they had established themselves more inland than Frassineto. Creeping up the line of the Alps, they took possession of St. Maurice, in the Valais, from which the feeble kings of Transjurane Burgundy could not dislodge them.

[43] I am sensible of the awkward effect of introducing this name from a more ancient geography, but it saves a circumlocution still more awkward. Austria would convey an imperfect idea, and the Austrian dominions could not be named without a tremendous anachronism.

Their numbers were great, their ferocity untamed. They fought with light cavalry and light armour, trusting to their showers of arrows, against which the swords and lances of the European armies could not avail. The memory of Attila was renewed in the devastations of these savages, who, if they were not his compatriots, resembled them both in their countenances and customs. All Italy, all Germany, and the south of France felt this scourge; [44] till Henry the Fowler and Otho the Great drove them back by successive victories within their own limits, where, in a short time, they learned peaceful arts, adopted the religion and followed the policy of Christendom.

If any enemies could be more destructive than these Hungarians, they were the pirates of the north, known commonly by the name of Normans. The love of a predatory life seems to have attracted adventurers of different nations to the Scandinavian seas, from whence they infested, not only by maritime piracy, but continual invasions, the northern coasts both of France and Germany. The causes of their sudden appearance are inexplicable, or at least could only be sought in the ancient traditions of Scandinavia. For, undoubtedly, the coasts of France and England were as little protected from depredations under the Merovingian kings, and those of the Heptarchy, as in subsequent times. Yet only one instance of an attack from this side is recorded, and that before the middle of the sixth century, [45] till the age of Charlemagne. In 787 the Danes, as we call those northern plunderers, began to infest England, which lay most immediately open to their incursions. Soon afterward they ravaged the coasts of France. Charlemagne repulsed them by means of his fleets; yet they pillaged a few places during his reign. It is said that, perceiving one day from a port in the Mediterranean some Norman vessels which had penetrated into that sea, he shed tears in anticipation of the miseries which awaited his empire. [46] In Louis's reign their depredations upon the coast were more incessant, [47] but they did not penetrate into

[44] In 924 they overran Languedoc. Raymond-Pons, Count of Toulouse, cut their army to pieces; but they had previously committed such ravages that the bishops of that province, writing soon afterward to Pope John X, assert that scarcely any eminent ecclesiastics, out of a great number, were left alive.— "Hist. de Languedoc," tome ii, p. 60. They penetrated into Guienne, as late as 951.—Flodoardi Chronicon, in "Recueil des Historiens," tome viii. In Italy they inspired such terror that a mass was composed expressly deprecating this calamity: Ab Ungarorum nos defendas jaculis! In 937 they ravaged the country as far as Benevento and Capua.—Muratori, "Ann. d'Italia."

[45] "Greg. Turon.," l. iii, c. 3.

[46] In the ninth century the Norman pirates not only ravaged the Balearic Isles and nearer coasts of the Mediterranean, but even Greece.—De Marca, "Marca Hispanica," p. 327.

[47] Nigellus, the poetical biographer of Louis, gives the following description of the Normans:
"Nort quoque Francisco dicuntur nomine manni.
Veloces, agiles, armigerique nimis:
Ipse quidem populus latè pernotus habetur,
Lintre dapes quærit, incolitatque mare.
Pulcher adest facie, vultuque statuque decorus."—L. iv.
He goes on to tell us that they worshipped Neptune. Was it a similarity of name or of attributes that deceived him?

the inland country till that of Charles the Bald. The wars between that prince and his family, which exhausted France of her noblest blood, the insubordination of the provincial governors, even the instigation of some of Charles's enemies, laid all open to their inroads. They adopted a uniform plan of warfare both in France and England; sailing up navigable rivers in their vessels of small burden, and fortifying the islands which they occasionally found, they made these intrenchments at once an asylum for their women and children, a repository for their plunder, and a place of retreat from superior force. After pillaging a town, they retired to these strongholds or to their ships; and it was not till 872 that they ventured to keep possession of Angers, which, however, they were compelled to evacuate. Sixteen years afterward they laid siege to Paris, and committed the most ruinous devastations on the neighbouring country. As these Normans were unchecked by religious awe, the rich monasteries, which had stood harmless amid the havoc of Christian war, were overwhelmed in the storm. Perhaps they may have endured some irrecoverable losses of ancient learning; but their complaints are of monuments disfigured, bones of saints and kings dispersed, treasures carried away. St. Denis redeemed its abbot from captivity with six hundred and eighty-five pounds of gold. All the chief abbeys were stripped about the same time, either by the enemy or for contributions to the public necessity. So impoverished was the kingdom that, in 860, Charles the Bald had great difficulty in collecting three thousand pounds of silver to subsidize a body of Normans against their countrymen. The Kings of France, too feeble to prevent or repel these invaders, had recourse to the palliative of buying peace at their hands or rather precarious armistices, to which reviving thirst of plunder soon put an end. At length Charles the Simple, in 918, ceded a great province, which they had already partly occupied, partly rendered desolate, and which has derived from them the name of Normandy. Ignominious as this appears, it proved no impolitic step. Rollo, the Norman chief, with all his subjects, became Christians and Frenchmen; and the kingdom was at once relieved from a terrible enemy, and strengthened by a race of hardy colonists.[48]

The accession of Hugh Capet had not the immediate effect of restoring the royal authority over France. His own very extensive fief was now, indeed, united to the crown; but a few great vassals occupied the remainder of the kingdom. Six of these obtained, at a subsequent time, the exclusive appellation of peers

[48] An exceedingly good sketch of these Norman incursions, and of the political situation of France during that period, may be found in two memoirs by M. Bonamy, " Mém. de l'Acad. des Inscript.," tomes xv and xvii. These I have chiefly followed in the text. [Note XIII.]

2

of France—the Count of Flanders, whose fief stretched from the Scheldt to the Somme; the Count of Champagne; the Duke of Normandy, to whom Brittany did homage; the Duke of Burgundy, on whom the Count of Nivernois seems to have depended; the Duke of Aquitaine, whose territory, though less than the ancient kingdom of that name, comprehended Poitou, Limousin, and most of Guienne, with the feudal superiority over the Angoumois, and some other central districts; and, lastly, the Count of Toulouse, who possessed Languedoc, with the small countries of Quercy and Rouergue, and the superiority over Auvergne.[49] Besides these six, the Duke of Gascony, not long afterward united with Aquitaine, the Counts of Anjou, Ponthieu, and Vermandois, the Viscount of Bourges, the lords of Bourbon and Coucy, with one or two other vassals, held immediately of the last Carlovingian kings.[50] This was the aristocracy, of which Hugh Capet usurped the direction; for the suffrage of no general assembly gave a sanction to his title. On the death of Louis V he took advantage of the absence of Charles, Duke of Lorraine, who, as the deceased king's uncle, was nearest heir, and procured his own consecration at Rheims. At first he was by no means acknowledged in the kingdom; but his contest with Charles proving successful, the chief vassals ultimately gave at least a tacit consent to the usurpation, and permitted the royal name to descend undisputed upon his posterity.[51] But this was almost the sole attribute of sovereignty which the first kings of the third dynasty enjoyed. For a long period before and after the accession of that family France has, properly speaking, no national history. The character or fortune of those who were called its kings was little more important to the majority of the nation than those of foreign princes. Undoubtedly the degree of influence which they exercised with respect to the vassals of the crown varied according to their power and their proximity. Over Gui-

[49] Auvergne changed its feudal superior twice. It had been subject to the Duke of Aquitaine till about the middle of the tenth century. The Counts of Toulouse then got possession of it; but early in the twelfth century the Counts of Auvergne again did homage to Guienne. It is very difficult to follow the history of these fiefs.

[50] The immediacy of vassals in times so ancient is open to much controversy. I have followed the authority of those industrious Benedictines, the editors of " L'Art de vérifier les Dates."

[51] The south of France not only took no part in Hugh's elevation, but long refused to pay him any obedience, or rather to acknowledge his title, for obedience was wholly out of the question. The style of charters ran, instead of the king's name, Deo regnante, rege expec-

tante, or absente rege terreno. He forced Guienne to submit about 990. But in Limousin they continued to acknowledge the sons of Charles of Lorraine till 1009. —Vaissette, " Hist. de Lang.," tome ii, pp. 120, 150. Before this Toulouse had refused to recognise Eudes and Raoul, two Kings of France who were not of the Carlovingian family, and even hesitated about Louis IV and Lothaire, who had an hereditary right.—Idem.
These proofs of Hugh Capet's usurpation seem not to be materially invalidated by a dissertation in the fiftieth volume of the " Academy of Inscriptions," p. 553. It is not, of course, to be denied that the northern parts of France acquiesced in his assumption of the royal title, if they did not give an express consent to it.

enne and Toulouse the first four Capets had very little authority; nor do they seem to have ever received assistance from them in either civil or national wars.[52] With provinces nearer to their own domains, such as Normandy and Flanders, they were frequently engaged in alliance or hostility; but each seemed rather to proceed from the policy of independent states than from the relation of a sovereign toward his subjects.[53]

It should be remembered that, when the fiefs of Paris and Orleans are said to have been reunited by Hugh Capet to the crown little more is understood than the feudal superiority over the vassals of these provinces. As the kingdom of Charlemagne's posterity was split into a number of great fiefs, so each of these contained many barons, possessing exclusive immunities within their own territories, waging war at their pleasure, administering justice to their military tenants and other subjects, and free from all control beyond the conditions of the feudal compact.[54] At the accession of Louis VI in 1108 the cities of Paris, Orleans, and Bourges, with the immediately adjacent districts, formed the most considerable portion of the royal domain. A number of petty barons, with their fortified castles, intercepted the communication between these, and waged war against the king almost under the walls of his capital. It cost Louis a great deal of trouble to reduce the lords of Montlhéry and other places within a few miles of Paris. Under this prince, however, who had more activity than his predecessors, the royal authority consid-

---

[52] I have not found any authority for supposing that the provinces south of the Loire contributed their assistance to the king in war, unless the following passage of Gulielmus Pictaviensis be considered as matter of fact, and not rather as a rhetorical flourish. He tells us that a vast army was collected by Henry I against the Duke of Normandy: Burgundium, Arverniam, atque Vasconiam properare videres horribiles ferro; immo vires tanti regni quantum in climata quatuor mundi patent cunctas.—" Recueil des Historiens," tome xi, p. 83. But we have the roll of the army which Louis VI led against the Emperor Henry V, A. D. 1120, in a national war: and it was entirely composed of troops from Champagne, the Isle of France, the Orleannois, and other provinces north of the Loire.— Velly, tome iii, p. 62. Yet this was a sort of convocation of the ban; Rex ut eum tota Francia sequatur, invitat. Even so late as the reign of Philip Augustus, in a list of the knights bannerets of France, though those of Brittany, Flanders, Champagne, and Burgundy, besides the royal domains, are enumerated, no mention is made of the provinces beyond the Loire.—Du Chesne, " Script. Rerum Gallicarum," tome v, p. 262.

[53] [Note XIV.]

[54] In a subsequent chapter I shall illustrate at much greater length the circumstances of the French monarchy with respect to its feudal vassals. It would be inconvenient to anticipate the subject at present, which is rather of a legal than narrative character.

Sismondi has given a relative scale of the great fiefs, according to the number of modern departments which they contained. At the accession of Louis VI the crown possessed about five departments; the Count of Flanders held four; the Count of Vermandois, two; the Count of Boulogne, one; the Count of Champagne, six; the Duke of Burgundy, three; of Normandy, five; of Brittany, five; the Count of Anjou, three. Thirty-three departments south of the Loire he considers as hardly connected with the crown; and twenty-one were at that time dependent on the empire. (Vol. v, p. 7.) It is to be understood, of course, that these divisions are not rigorously exact; and also that, in every instance, owners of fiefs with civil and criminal jurisdiction had the full possession of their own territories, subject more or less to their immediate lord, whether it were the king or another. The real domain of Louis VI was almost confined to the five towns— Paris, Orleans, Estampes, Melun, and Compiègne (Id., p. 86); and to estates, probably large, in their neighbourhood.

erably revived. From his reign we may date the systematic rivalry of the French and English monarchies. Hostilities had several times occurred between Philip I and the two Williams; but the wars that began under Louis VI lasted, with no long interruption, for three centuries and a half, and form, indeed, the most leading feature of French history during the middle ages.[55] Of all the royal vassals, the Dukes of Normandy were the proudest and most powerful. Though they had submitted to do homage, they could not forget that they came in originally by force, and that in real strength they were fully equal to their sovereign. Nor had the conquest of England any tendency to diminish their pretensions.[56]

Louis VII ascended the throne with better prospects than his father. He had married Eleanor, heiress of the great duchy of Guienne. But this union, which promised an immense accession of strength to the crown, was rendered unhappy by the levities of that princess. Repudiated by Louis, who felt rather as a husband than a king, Eleanor immediately married Henry II of England, who, already inheriting Normandy from his mother and Anjou from his father, became possessed of more than one half of France, and an overmatch for Louis, even if the great vassals of the crown had been always ready to maintain its supremacy. One might venture, perhaps, to conjecture that the sceptre of France would eventually have passed from the Capets to the Plantagenets, if the vexatious quarrel with Becket at one time, and the successive rebellions fomented by Louis at a later period, had not embarrassed the great talents and ambitious spirit of Henry.

But the scene quite changed when Philip Augustus, son of Louis VII, came upon the stage. No prince comparable to him in systematic ambition and military enterprise had reigned in France since Charlemagne. From his reign the French monarchy dates the recovery of its lustre. He wrested from the Count of Flanders the Vermandois (that part of Picardy which borders on the Isle of France and Champagne [57]), and subsequently the county of Artois. But the most important conquests of Philip were obtained against the Kings of England. Even Richard I, with all his prowess, lost ground in struggling against an adversary not less active and more politic than himself. But when

[55] Velly, tome iii, p. 40.

[56] The Norman historians maintain that their dukes did not owe any service to the King of France, but only simple homage, or, as it was called, per paragium. —"Recueil des Historiens," tome xi, pref., p. 161. They certainly acted upon this principle; and the manner in which they first came into the country is not very consistent with dependence.

[57] The original Counts of Vermandois were descended from Bernard, King of Italy, grandson of Charlemagne : but their fief passed by the donation of Isabel, the last countess, to her husband, the Earl of Flanders, after her death in 1183. The principal towns of the Vermandois are St. Quentin and Péronne.— "Art de vérifier les Dates," tome ii, p. 700.

John not only took possession of his brother's dominions, but confirmed his usurpation by the murder, as was very probably surmised, of the heir, Philip, artfully taking advantage of the general indignation, summoned him as his vassal to the court of his peers. John demanded a safe-conduct. Willingly, said Philip; let him come unmolested. And return? inquired the English envoy. If the judgment of his peers permit him, replied the king. By all the saints of France, he exclaimed, when further pressed, he shall not return unless acquitted. The Bishop of Ely still remonstrated that the Duke of Normandy could not come without the King of England; nor would the barons of that country permit their sovereign to run the risk of death or imprisonment. What of that, my lord bishop? cried Philip. It is well known that my vassal the Duke of Normandy acquired England by force. But if a subject obtains any accession of dignity, shall his paramount lord therefore lose his rights? [58]

It may be doubted whether, in thus citing John before his court, the King of France did not stretch his feudal sovereignty beyond its acknowledged limits. Arthur was certainly no immediate vassal of the crown for Brittany; and, though he had done homage to Philip for Anjou and Maine, yet a subsequent treaty had abrogated his investiture, and confirmed his uncle in the possession of those provinces.[59] But the vigour of Philip, and the meanness of his adversary, cast a shade over all that might be novel or irregular in these proceedings. John, not appearing at his summons, was declared guilty of felony, and his fiefs confiscated. The execution of this sentence was not intrusted to a dilatory army. Philip poured his troops into Normandy, and took town after town, while the King of England, infatuated by his own wickedness and cowardice, made hardly an attempt at defence. In two years Normandy, Maine, and Anjou were irrecoverably lost. Poitou and Guienne resisted longer; but the conquest of the first was completed by Louis VIII, successor of Philip, and the subjection of the second seemed drawing near, when the arms of Louis were diverted to different but scarcely less advantageous objects.

The country of Languedoc, subject to the Counts of Toulouse, had been unconnected, beyond any other part of France, with the kings of the house of Capet. Louis VII, having married his sister to the reigning count, and travelled himself through the country, began to exercise some degree of authority, chiefly in confirming the rights of ecclesiastical bodies, who were vain, perhaps, of this additional sanction to the privileges which they

[58] Mat. Paris, p. 238, edit. 1684.
[59] The illegality of Philip's proceedings is well argued by Mably, "Observations sur l'Histoire de France," l. iii, c. 6.

already possessed.[60] But the remoteness of their situation, with a difference in language and legal usages, still kept the people of this province apart from those of the north of France. About the middle of the twelfth century certain religious opinions, which it is not easy nor, for our present purpose, material to define, but, upon every supposition, exceedingly adverse to those of the Church,[61] began to spread over Languedoc. Those who imbibed them have borne the name of Albigeois, though they were in no degree peculiar to the district of Albi. In despite of much preaching and some persecution, these errors made a continual progress, till Innocent III, in 1198, despatched commissaries, the seed of the Inquisition, with ample powers both to investigate and to chastise. Raymond VI, Count of Toulouse, whether inclined toward the innovators, as was then the theme of reproach, or, as is more probable, disgusted with the insolent interference of the Pope and his missionaries, provoked them to pronounce a sentence of excommunication against him. Though this was taken off, he was still suspected; and upon the assassination of one of the inquisitors, in which Raymond had no concern, Innocent published a crusade against both the count and his subjects, calling upon the King of France and the nobility of that kingdom to take up the cross, with all the indulgences usually held out as allurements to religious warfare. Though Philip would not interfere, a prodigious number of knights undertook this enterprise, led partly by ecclesiastics, and partly by some of the first barons in France. It was prosecuted with every atrocious barbarity which superstition, the mother of crimes, could inspire. Languedoc, a country, for that age, flourishing and civilized, was laid waste by these desolators; her cities burned; her inhabitants swept away by fire and the sword. And this was to punish a fanaticism ten thousand times more innocent than their own, and errors which, according to the worst imputations, left the laws of humanity and the peace of social life unimpaired.[62]

---

[60] According to the Benedictine historians Vich and Vaissette, there is no trace of any act of sovereignty exercised by the Kings of France in Languedoc from 955, when Lothaire confirmed a charter of his predecessor Raoul in favour of the Bishop of Puy, till the reign of Louis VII. ("Hist. de Languedoc," tome iii, p. 88.) They have published, however, an instrument of Louis VI in favour of the same church, confirming those of former princes. (Appendix, p. 473.) Neither the Counts of Toulouse, nor any lord of the province, were present in a very numerous national assembly at the coronation of Philip I. (Id., p. 200.) I do not recollect to have ever met with the name of the Count of Toulouse as a subscribing witness to the charters of the first Capetian kings in the "Recueil des Historiens," where many are published, though that of the Duke of Guienne sometimes occurs.

[61] For the real tenets of the Languedocian sectaries I refer to the last chapter of the present work, where the subject will be taken up again.

[62] The Albigensian war commenced with the storming of Béziers, and a massacre wherein fifteen thousand persons, or, according to some narrations, sixty thousand, were put to the sword. Not a living soul escaped, as witnesses assure us. It was here that a Cistercian monk, who led on the crusaders, answered the inquiry, how the Catholics were to be distinguished from heretics: Kill them all! God will know his own. Besides Vaissette, see Sismondi, "Littérature du Midi," tome i, p. 201.

The crusaders were commanded by Simon de Montfort, a man, like Cromwell, whose intrepidity, hypocrisy, and ambition marked him for the hero of a holy war. The energy of such a mind, at the head of an army of enthusiastic warriors, may well account for successes which then appeared miraculous. But Montfort was cut off before he could realize his ultimate object, an independent principality; and Raymond was able to bequeath the inheritance of his ancestors to his son. Rome, however, was not yet appeased; upon some new pretence she raised up a still more formidable enemy against the younger Raymond. Louis VIII suffered himself to be diverted from the conquests of Guienne to take the cross against the supposed patron of heresy. After a short and successful war, Louis, dying prematurely, left the crown of France to a son only twelve years old. But the Count of Toulouse was still pursued, till, hopeless of safety in so unequal a struggle, he concluded a treaty upon very hard terms. By this he ceded the greater part of Languedoc; and, giving his daughter in marriage to Alphonso, brother of Louis IX, confirmed to them, and to the king in failure of their descendants, the reversion of the rest, in exclusion of any other children whom he might have. Thus fell the ancient house of Toulouse, through one of those strange combinations of fortune which thwart the natural course of human prosperity, and disappoint the plans of wise policy and beneficent government.[63]

The rapid progress of royal power under Philip Augustus and his son had scarcely given the great vassals time to reflect upon the change which it produced in their situation. The crown, with which some might singly have measured their forces, was now an equipoise to their united weight. And such a union was hard to be accomplished among men not always very sagacious in policy, and divided by separate interests and animosities. They were not, however, insensible to the crisis of their feudal liberties; and the minority of Louis IX, guided only by his mother, the regent, Blanche of Castile, seemed to offer a favourable oppor-

[63] The best account of this crusade against the Albigeois is to be found in the third volume of Vaissette's "History of Languedoc"; the Benedictine spirit of mildness and veracity tolerably counterbalancing the prejudices of orthodoxy. Velly, "Hist. de France," tome iii, has abridged this work.

M. Fauriel edited for the "Collection des Documens Inédits," in 1837, a metrical history of the Albigensian crusade, by a contemporary calling himself William of Tudela, which seems to be an imaginary name. It contains 9,578 verses. The author begins as a vehement enemy of the heretics and favourer of the crusade; but becomes, before his poem is half completed, equally adverse to Montfort, Fol-

quet, and the other chiefs of the persecution, though never adopting heretical opinions.

Sismondi says—bitterly, but not untruly—of Simon de Montfort: "Habile guerrier, austère dans ses mœurs, fanatique dans sa religion, inflexible, cruel, et perfide, il réunissait toutes les qualités qui pouvaient plaire à un moine." (Vol. vi, p. 297.) The Albigensian sectaries had insulted the clergy and hissed St. Bernard; which, of course, exasperated that irritable body and aggravated their revenge. (Michelet, iii, 306.) But the atrocities of that war have hardly been equalled, and Sismondi was not the man to conceal them.

tunity for recovering their former situation. Some of the most considerable barons, the Counts of Brittany, Champagne, and La Marche, had, during the time of Louis VIII, shown an unwilling-ness to push the Count of Toulouse too far, if they did not even keep up a secret understanding with him. They now broke out into open rebellion; but the address of Blanche detached some from the league, and her firmness subdued the rest. For the first fifteen years of Louis's reign the struggle was frequently renewed, till repeated humiliations convinced the refractory that the throne was no longer to be shaken. A prince so feeble as Henry III was unable to afford them that aid from England which, if his grandfather or son had then reigned, might probably have length-ened these civil wars.

But Louis IX had methods of preserving his ascendency very different from military prowess. That excellent prince was per-haps the most eminent pattern of unswerving probity and Chris-tian strictness of conscience that ever held the sceptre in any country. There is a peculiar beauty in the reign of St. Louis, be-cause it shows the inestimable benefit which a virtuous king may confer on his people, without possessing any distinguished genius. For nearly half a century that he governed France there is not the smallest want of moderation or disinterestedness in his actions, and yet he raised the influence of the monarchy to a much higher point than the most ambitious of his predecessors. To the sur-prise of his own and later times, he restored a great part of his conquests to Henry III, whom he might naturally hoped to have expelled from France. It would indeed have been a tedious work to conquer Guienne, which was full of strong places; and the subjugation of such a province might have alarmed the other vassals of his crown. But it is the privilege only of virtuous minds to perceive that wisdom resides in moderate counsels: no sagacity ever taught a selfish and ambitious sovereign to forego the sweetness of immediate power. An ordinary king, in the cir-cumstances of the French monarchy, would have fomented, or, at least, have rejoiced in, the dissensions which broke out among the principal vassals; Louis constantly employed himself to recon-cile them. In this, too, his benevolence had all the effects of far-sighted policy. It had been the practice of his last three prede-cessors to interpose their mediation in behalf of the less powerful classes, the clergy, the inferior nobility, and the inhabitants of chartered towns. Thus the supremacy of the crown became a familiar idea; but the perfect integrity of St. Louis wore away all distrust, and accustomed even the most jealous feudatories to look upon him as their judge and legislator. And as the royal authority was hitherto shown only in its most amiable preroga-tives, the dispensation of favour and the redress of wrong, few

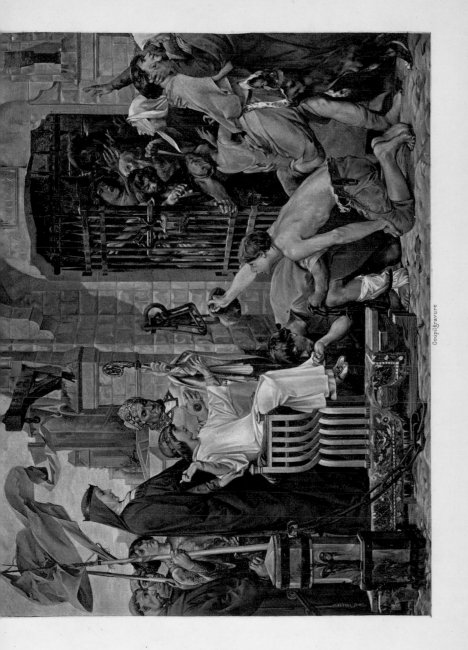

were watchful enough to remark the transition of the French
constitution from a feudal league to an absolute monarchy.
It was perhaps fortunate for the display of St. Louis's virtues
that the throne had already been strengthened by the less innocent exertions of Philip Augustus and Louis VIII. A century
earlier his mild and scrupulous character, unsustained by great
actual power, might not have inspired sufficient awe. But the
crown was now grown so formidable, and Louis was so eminent
for his firmness and bravery—qualities without which every other
virtue would have been ineffectual—that no one thought it safe
to run wantonly into rebellion, while his disinterested administration gave no one a pretext for it. Hence the latter part of his
reign was altogether tranquil, and employed in watching over the
public peace and the security of travellers; administering justice
personally or by the best counsellors; and compiling that code
of feudal customs called the " Establishments of St. Louis," which
is the first monument of legislation after the accession of the
house of Capet. Not satisfied with the justice of his own conduct, Louis aimed at that act of virtue which is rarely practised
by private men, and had perhaps no example among kings—
restitution. Commissaries were appointed to inquire what possessions had been unjustly annexed to the royal domain during
the last two reigns. These were restored to the proprietors, or,
where length of time had made it difficult to ascertain the claimant, their value was distributed among the poor.[64]

It has been hinted already that all this excellence of heart
in Louis IX was not attended with that strength of understanding, which is necessary, we must allow, to complete the usefulness of a sovereign. During his minority Blanche of Castile, his
mother, had filled the office of regent with great courage and
firmness. But after he grew up to manhood, her influence seems
to have passed the limit which gratitude and piety would have
assigned to it; and, as her temper was not very meek or popular,
exposed the king to some degree of contempt. He submitted
even to be restrained from the society of his wife Margaret, daughter of Raymond, Count of Provence, a princess of great virtue
and conjugal affection. Joinville relates a curious story, characteristic of Blanche's arbitrary conduct, and sufficiently derogatory to Louis.[65]

But the principal weakness of this king, which almost effaced
all the good effects of his virtues, was superstition. It would
be idle to sneer at those habits of abstemiousness and mortifica-

---

[64] Velly, tome v, p. 150. This historian
has very properly dwelt for almost a volume on St. Louis's internal administration; it is one of the most valuable parts
of his work. Joinville is a real witness,
on whom, when we listen, it is impossible

not to rely.—" Collection des Mémoires
relatifs à l'Histoire de France," tome ii,
pp. 140–156.
[65] " Collection des Mémoires," tome ii,
p. 241.

tion which were part of the religion of his age, and, at the worst, were only injurious to his own comfort. But he had other prejudices, which, though they may be forgiven, must never be defended. No man was ever more impressed than St. Louis with a belief in the duty of exterminating all enemies to his own faith. With these he thought no layman ought to risk himself in the perilous ways of reasoning, but to make answer with his sword as stoutly as a strong arm and a fiery zeal could carry that argument.[66] Though, fortunately for his fame, the persecution against the Albigeois, which had been the disgrace of his father's short reign, was at an end before he reached manhood, he suffered a hypocritical monk to establish a tribunal at Paris for the suppression of heresy, where many innocent persons suffered death.

But no events in Louis's life were more memorable than his two crusades, which lead us to look back on the nature and circumstances of that most singular phenomenon in European history. Though the crusades involved all the western nations of Europe, without belonging particularly to any one, yet, as France was more distinguished than the rest in most of those enterprises, I shall introduce the subject as a sort of digression from the main course of French history.

Even before the violation of Palestine by the Saracen arms it had been a prevailing custom among the Christians of Europe to visit those scenes rendered interesting by religion, partly through delight in the effects of local association, partly in obedience to the prejudices or commands of superstition. These pilgrimages became more frequent in later times, in spite, perhaps in consequence, of the danger and hardships which attended them. For a while the Mohammedan possessors of Jerusalem permitted, or even encouraged, a devotion which they found lucrative; but this was interrupted whenever the ferocious insolence with which they regarded all infidels got the better of their rapacity. During the eleventh century, when, from increasing superstition and some particular fancies, the pilgrims were more numerous than ever, a change took place in the government of Palestine, which was overrun by the Turkish hordes from the north. These barbarians treated the visitors of Jerusalem with still greater contumely, mingling with their Mohammedan bigotry a consciousness of strength

[66] Aussi vous dis-je, me dist le roy, que nul, si n'est grant clerc, et theologien parfait, ne doit disputer aux Juifs: mais doit l'homme lay, quant il oit mesdire de la foy Chrétienne, defendre la chose, non pas seulement des paroles, mais à bonne espée tranchant, et en frapper les médisans et mescreans a travers le corps tant qu'elle y pourra entrer.—Joinville, in "Collection des Mémoires," tome i, p. 23.

This passage, which shows a tolerable degree of bigotry, did not require to be strained further still by Mosheim, vol. iii, p. 273 (edit. 1803). I may observe, by the way, that this writer, who sees nothing in Louis IX except his intolerance, ought not to have charged him with issuing an edict in favour of the Inquisition in 1229, when he had not assumed the government.

and courage, and a scorn of the Christians, whom they knew
only by the debased natives of Greece and Syria, or by these humble and defenceless palmers.   When such insults became known
throughout Europe, they excited a keen sensation of resentment
among nations equally courageous and devout, which, though
wanting as yet any definite means of satisfying itself, was ripe
for whatever favourable conjuncture might arise.

   Twenty years before the first crusade Gregory VII had projected the scheme of embodying Europe in arms against Asia
—a scheme worthy of his daring mind, and which, perhaps, was
never forgotten by Urban II, who in everything loved to imitate
his great predecessor.[67]   This design of Gregory was founded
upon the supplication of the Greek Emperor Michael, which was
renewed by Alexus Comnenus to Urban with increased impor-
tunity.   The Turks had now taken Nice, and threatened, from the
opposite shore, the very walls of Constantinople.   Every one
knows whose hand held the torch to that inflammable mass of
enthusiasm that pervaded Europe; the hermit of Picardy, who,
roused by witnessed wrongs and imagined visions, journeyed from
land to land, the apostle of a holy war.   The preaching of Peter
was powerfully seconded by Urban.   In the councils of Piacenza
and of Clermont the deliverance of Jerusalem was eloquently
recommended and exultingly undertaken.   " It is the will of
God! " was the tumultuous cry that broke from the heart and
lips of the assembly at Clermont; and these words afford at once
the most obvious and most certain explanation of the leading
principle of the crusades.   Later writers, incapable of sympa-
thizing with the blind fervour of zeal, or anxious to find a pretext
for its effect somewhat more congenial to the spirit of our times,
have sought political reasons for that which resulted only from
predominant affections.   No suggestion of these will, I believe,
be found in contemporary historians.   To rescue the Greek Empire from its imminent peril, and thus to secure Christendom
from enemies who professed toward it eternal hostility, might
have been a legitimate and magnanimous ground of interference;
but it operated scarcely, or not at all, upon those who took the
cross.   It argues, indeed, strange ignorance of the eleventh century to ascribe such refinements of later times even to the princes
of that age.   The Turks were no doubt repelled from the neighbourhood of Constantinople by the crusaders; but this was a collateral effect of their enterprise.   Nor had they any disposition to
serve the interest of the Greeks, whom they soon came to hate,

----

[67] Gregory addressed, in 1074, a sort of
encyclic letter to all who would defend
the Christian faith, enforcing upon them
the duty of taking up arms against the
Saracens, who had almost come up to the
walls of Constantinople.   No mention of
Palestine is made in this letter.   Labbé,
" Concilia," tome x, p. 44.   St. Marc,
" Abrégé Chron. de l'Hist. de l'Italie,"
tome iii, p. 614.

and not entirely without provocation, with almost as much animosity as the Moslems themselves.

Every means was used to excite an epidemical frenzy: the remission of penance, the dispensation from those practices of self-denial which superstition imposed or suspended at pleasure, the absolution of all sins, and the assurance of eternal felicity. None doubted that such as perished in the war received immediately the reward of martyrdom.[68] False miracles and fanatical prophecies, which were never so frequent, wrought up the enthusiasm to a still higher pitch. And these devotional feelings, which are usually thwarted and balanced by other passions, fell in with every motive that could influence the men of that time; with curiosity, restlessness, the love of license, thirst for war, emulation, ambition. Of the princes who assumed the cross, some probably from the beginning speculated upon forming independent establishments in the East. In later periods the temporal benefits of undertaking a crusade undoubtedly blended themselves with less selfish considerations. Men resorted to Palestine, as in modern times they have done to the colonies, in order to redeem their fame or repair their fortune. Thus Gui de Lusignan, after flying from France for murder, was ultimately raised to the throne of Jerusalem. To the more vulgar class were held out inducements which, though absorbed in the overruling fanaticism of the first crusade, might be exceedingly efficacious when it began rather to flag. During the time that a crusader bore the cross he was free from suit for his debts, and the interest of them was entirely abolished; he was exempted, in some instances at least, from taxes, and placed under the protection of the Church, so that he could not be impleaded in any civil court, except on criminal charges or disputes relating to land.[69]

None of the sovereigns of Europe took a part in the first crusade; but many of their chief vassals, great part of the inferior nobility, and a countless multitude of the common people. The priests left their parishes and the monks their cells; and though the peasantry were then in general bound to the soil, we find no check given to their emigration for this cause. Numbers of women and children swelled the crowd; it appeared a sort of sacrilege to repel any one from a work which was considered as the manifest design of Providence. But if it were lawful to interpret the will of Providence by events, few undertakings have been more branded by its disapprobation than the crusades. So many

[68] Nam qui pro Christi nomine decertantes, in acie fidelium et Christianâ militiâ dicuntur, occumbere, non solum infamiæ, verum et peccaminum et delictorum omnimodam credimus abolitionem promereri.—Will. Tyr., l. x, c. 20.
[69] Otho of Frisengen, c. 35, has inserted a bull of Eugenius III in 1146, containing some of these privileges. Others are granted by Philip Augustus in 1214. "Ordonnances des Roi de France," tome i. See also Du Cange, voc. "Crucis Privilegia."

crimes and so much misery have seldom been accumulated in so short a space as in the three years of the first expedition. We should be warranted by contemporary writers in stating the loss of the Christians alone during this period at nearly a million, but at the least computation it must have exceeded half that number.[70] To engage in the crusade and to perish in it were almost synonymous. Few of those myriads who were mustered in the plains of Nice returned to gladden their friends in Europe with the story of their triumph at Jerusalem. Besieging alternately and besieged in Antioch, they drained to the lees the cup of misery: three hundred thousand sat down before that place; next year there remained but a sixth part to pursue the enterprise. But their losses were least in the field of battle; the intrinsic superiority of European prowess was constantly displayed; the angel of Asia, to apply the bold language of our poet, high and unmatchable, where her rival was not, became a fear; and the Christian lances bore all before them in their shock from Nice to Antioch, Edessa, and Jerusalem. It was here, where their triumph was consummated, that it was stained with the most atrocious massacre; not limited to the hour of resistance, but renewed deliberately even after that famous penitential procession to the holy sepulchre, which might have calmed their ferocious dispositions if, through the misguided enthusiasm of the enterprise, it had not been rather calculated to excite them.[71]

The conquests obtained at such a price by the first crusade were chiefly comprised in the maritime parts of Syria. Except the state of Edessa beyond the Euphrates,[72] which, in its best days, extended over great part of Mesopotamia, the Latin possessions never reached more than a few leagues from the sea. Within the barrier of Mount Libanus their arms might be feared, but their power was never established; and the Prophet was still invoked in the mosques of Aleppo and Damascus. The principality of Antioch to the north, the kingdom of Jerusalem, with its feudal dependencies of Tripoli and Tiberias to the south, were assigned, the one to Boemond, a brother of Robert Guiscard, Count of Apulia, the other to Godfrey of Boulogne,[73] whose ex-

[70] William of Tyre says that at the review before Nice there were found 600,000 of both sexes, exclusive of 100,000 cavalry armed in mail. (L. ii, c. 23.) But Fulk of Chartres reckons the same number, besides women, children, and priests. An immense slaughter had previously been made in Hungary of the rabble under Gaultier Sans-Avoir.

[71] The work of Mailly, entitled " L'Esprit des Croisades," is deserving of considerable praise for its diligence and impartiality. It carries the history, however, no further than the first expedition. Gibbon's two chapters on the crusades, though not without inaccuracies, are a brilliant portion of his great work. The original writers are chiefly collected in two folio volumes, entitled " Gesta Dei per Francos," Hanover, 1611.

[72] Edessa was a little Christian principality, surrounded by and tributary to the Turks. The inhabitants invited Baldwin, on his progress in the first crusade, and he made no great scruple of supplanting the reigning prince, who indeed is represented as a tyrant and usurper. (" Esprit des Croisades," tome iv, p. 62; De Guignes, " Hist. des Hun," tome ii, pp. 135–162.)

[73] Godfrey never took the title of King of Jerusalem, not choosing, he said, to

traordinary merit had justly raised him to a degree of influence
with the chief crusaders that has been sometimes confounded
with a legitimate authority.[74] In the course of a few years Tyre,
Ascalon, and the other cities upon the sea-coast were subjected
by the successors of Godfrey on the throne of Jerusalem. But
as their enemies had been stunned, not killed, by the western
storm, the Latins were constantly molested by the Mohammedans
of Egypt and Syria. They were exposed as the outposts of Christendom, with no respite and few resources. A second crusade,
in which the Emperor Conrad II and Louis VII of France were
engaged, each with seventy thousand cavalry, made scarce any
diversion, and that vast army wasted away in the passage of
Natolia.[75]

The decline of the Christian establishments in the East is
ascribed by William of Tyre to the extreme viciousness of their
manners, to the adoption of European arms by the Orientals,
and to the union of the Mohammedan principalities under a single
chief.[76] Without denying the operation of these causes, and
especially the last, it is easy to perceive one more radical than
all the three, the inadequacy of their means of self-defence. The
kingdom of Jerusalem was guarded only, exclusive of European
volunteers, by the feudal service of eight hundred and sixty-six
knights, attended each by four archers on horseback, by a militia
of five thousand and seventy-five burghers, and by a conscription,
in great exigencies, of the remaining population.[77] William of
Tyre mentions an army of thirteen hundred horse and fifteen

wear a crown of gold in that city where
his Saviour had been crowned with
thorns. Baldwin, Godfrey's brother, who
succeeded him within two years, entitles
himself Rex Hierusalem, Latinorum pri-
mus.—Will. Tyr., l. ii, c. 12.
[74] The heroes of the crusade are just
like those of romance. Godfrey is not
only the wisest but the strongest man in
the army. Perhaps Tasso has lost some
part of this physical superiority for the
sake of contrasting him with the imaginary Rinaldo. He cleaves a Turk in
twain, from the shoulder to the haunch.
A noble Arab, after the taking of Jerusalem, requests him to try his sword upon
a camel, when Godfrey, with ease, cuts
off the head. The Arab, suspecting there
might be something peculiar in the blade,
desires him to do the same with his
sword; and the hero obliges him by de-
molishing a second camel.—Will. Tyr., l.
ix, c. 22.
[75] Vertot puts the destruction in the
second crusade at two hundred thousand
men (" Hist. de Malthe," p. 129); and
from William of Tyre's language there
seems no reason to consider this an exaggeration. (L. xvi, c. 19.)
[76] L. xxi, c. 7. John of Vitry also
mentions the change of weapons by the

Saracens, in imitation of the Latins, using
the lances and coat of mail instead of
bows and arrows, c. 92. But, according
to a more ancient writer, part of Soli-
man's (the Kilidge Arslan of De Guignes)
army in the first crusade was in armour,
loricis et galeis et clypeis aureis valde
armati. (Albertus Aquensis, l. ii, c. 27.)
I may add to this a testimony of another
kind, not less decisive. In the Abbey
of St. Denis there were ten pictures, in
stained glass, representing sieges and
battles in the first crusade. These were
made by order of Suger, the minister of
Louis VI, and consequently in the early
part of the twelfth century. In many of
them the Turks are painted in coats of
mail, sometimes even in a plated cuirass.
In others they are quite unarmed, and
in flowing robes. (Montfaucon, " Monumens de la Monarchie Française," tome
i, pl. 50.)
[77] Gibbon, c. 29, note 125. Jerusalem
itself was very thinly inhabited. For all
the heathens, says William of Tyre, had
perished in the massacre when the city
was taken; or, if any escaped, they were
not allowed to return; no heathen being
thought fit to dwell in the holy city.
Baldwin invited some Arabian Christians
to settle in it.

thousand foot as the greatest which had ever been collected, and predicts the utmost success from it if wisely conducted.[78] This was a little before the irruption of Saladin. In the last fatal battle Lusignan seems to have had a somewhat larger force.[79] Nothing can more strikingly evince the ascendency of Europe than the resistance of these Frankish acquisitions in Syria during nearly two hundred years. Several of their victories over the Moslems were obtained against such disparity of numbers that they may be compared with whatever is most illustrious in history or romance.[80] These perhaps were less due to the descendants of the first crusaders, settled in the Holy Land,[81] than to those volunteers from Europe whom martial ardour and religious zeal impelled to the service. It was the penance commonly imposed upon men of rank for the most heinous crimes to serve a number of years under the banner of the cross. Thus a perpetual supply of warriors was poured in from Europe; and in this sense the crusades may be said to have lasted without intermission during the whole period of the Latin settlements. Of these defenders, the most renowned were the military orders of the Knights of the Temple and of the Hospital of St. John;[82] instituted, the one in 1124, the other in 1118, for the sole purpose of protecting the Holy Land. The Teutonic order, established in 1190, when the kingdom of Jerusalem was falling, soon diverted its schemes of holy warfare to a very different quarter of the world. Large estates, as well in Palestine as throughout Europe, enriched the two former institutions; but the pride, rapaciousness, and misconduct of both, especially of the Templars, seem to have balanced the advantages derived from their valour.[83] At length the famous Saladin, usurping the throne of a feeble dynasty which had reigned in Egypt, broke in upon the Christians of Jerusalem; the king and the kingdom fell into his hands; nothing remained but a few strong towns upon the sea-coast.

These misfortunes roused once more the princes of Europe, and the third crusade was undertaken by three of her sovereigns,

[78] L. xxii, c. 27.

[79] A primo introitu Latinorum in terram sanctam, says John de Vitry, nostri tot milites in uno prœlio congregare nequiverunt. Erant enim mille ducenti milites loricati ; peditum autem cum armis, arcubus et balistis circiter viginti millia, infaustæ expeditioni interfuisse dicuntur. (" Gesta dei per Francos," p. 1118.)

[80] A brief summary of these victories is given by John of Vitry, c. 93.

[81] Many of these were of a mongrel extraction, descended from a Frank parent on one side and Syrian on the other. These were called Poulains, Pullani, and were looked upon as a mean, degenerate race. (Du Cange; Gloss. v. Pullani, and

" Observations sur Joinville," in " Collection des Mémoires relatifs à l'Histoire de France," tome ii, p. 190.)

[82] The St. John of Jerusalem was neither the Evangelist nor yet the Baptist, but a certain Cypriot, surnamed the Charitable, who had been patriarch of Alexandria.

[83] See a curious instance of the misconduct and insolence of the Templars, in William of Tyre, l. xx, c. 32. The Templars possessed nine thousand manors, and the Knights of St. John nineteen thousand, in Europe. The latter were almost as much reproached as the Templars for their pride and avarice. (L. xviii, c. 6.)

the greatest in personal estimation as well as dignity—by the
Emperor Frederick Barbarossa, Philip Augustus of France, and
our own Richard Cœur de Lion. But this, like the preceding
enterprise, failed of permanent effect; and those feats of romantic
prowess which made the name of Richard so famous both in
Europe and Asia [84] proved only the total inefficacy of all exertions in an attempt so impracticable; Palestine was never the
scene of another crusade. One great armament was diverted to
the siege of Constantinople, and another wasted in fruitless attempts upon Egypt. The Emperor Frederick II afterward procured the restoration of Jerusalem by the Saracens; but the Christian princes of Syria were unable to defend it, and their possessions were gradually reduced to the maritime towns. Acre, the
last of these, was finally taken by storm in 1291; and its ruin
closes the history of the Latin dominion in Syria, which Europe
had already ceased to protect.

The last two crusades were undertaken by St. Louis. In the
first he was attended by twenty-eight hundred knights and fifty
thousand ordinary troops.[85] He landed at Damietta, in Egypt,
for that country was now deemed the key of the Holy Land,
and easily made himself master of the city. But advancing up
the country, he found natural impediments as well as enemies in
his way; the Turks assailed him with Greek fire, an instrument
of warfare almost as surprising and terrible as gunpowder; he
lost his brother, the Count of Artois, with many knights, at Mas-
soura, near Cairo, and began too late a retreat toward Damietta.
Such calamities now fell upon this devoted army as have scarcely
ever been surpassed: hunger and want of every kind, aggravated
by an unsparing pestilence. At length the king was made prisoner, and very few of the army escaped the Turkish scimetar in
battle or in captivity. Four hundred thousand livres were paid
as a ransom for Louis. He returned to France, and passed near
twenty years in the exercise of those virtues which are his best
title to canonization. But the fatal illusions of superstition were
still always at his heart; nor did it fail to be painfully observed
by his subjects that he still kept the cross upon his garment. His
last expedition was originally designed for Jerusalem. But he
had received some intimation that the King of Tunis was desirous
of embracing Christianity. That these intentions might be carried into effect, he sailed out of his way to the coast of Africa,

---

[84] When a Turk's horse started at a
bush, he would chide him, Joinville says,
with, " Cuides-tu qu'y soit le roi Richard? " Women kept their children quiet
with the threat of bringing Richard to
them.
[85] The Arabian writers give him 9,500
knights and 130,000 common soldiers.

But I greatly prefer the authority of
Joinville, who has twice mentioned the
number of knights in the text. On Gibbon's authority, I put the main body at
50,000; but, if Joinville has stated this,
I have missed the passage. Their vassals
amounted to 1800.

and laid siege to that city. A fever here put an end to his life, sacrificed to that ruling passion which never would have forsaken him. But he had survived the spirit of the crusades; the disastrous expedition to Egypt had cured his subjects, though not himself, of their folly;[86] his son, after making terms with Tunis, returned to France; the Christians were suffered to lose what they still retained in the Holy Land; and though many princes in subsequent ages talked loudly of renewing the war, the promise, if it were ever sincere, was never accomplished.

Louis IX had increased the royal domain by the annexation of several counties and other less important fiefs; but soon after the accession of Philip III (surnamed the Bold) it received a far more considerable augmentation. Alfonso, the late king's brother, had been invested with the county of Poitou, ceded by Henry III, together with part of Auvergne and of Saintonge and held also, as has been said before, the remains of the great fief of Toulouse, in right of his wife Jane, heiress of Raymond VII. Upon his death, and that of his countess, which happened about the same time, the king entered into possession of all these territories. This acquisition brought the sovereigns of France into contact with new neighbours, the Kings of Aragon and the powers of Italy. The first great and lasting foreign war which they carried on was that of Philip III and Philip IV against the former kingdom, excited by the insurrection of Sicily. Though effecting no change in the boundaries of their dominions, this war may be deemed a sort of epoch in the history of France and Spain, as well as in that of Italy, to which it more peculiarly belongs.

There still remained five great and ancient fiefs of the French crown—Champagne, Guienne, Flanders, Burgundy, and Brittany. But Philip IV, usually called the Fair, married the heiress of the first, a little before his father's death; and although he governed that county in her name without pretending to reunite it to the royal domain, it was, at least in a political sense, no longer a part of the feudal body. With some of his other vassals Philip used more violent methods. A parallel might be drawn between

---

[86] The refusal of Joinville to accompany the king in this second crusade is very memorable, and gives us an insight into the bad effects of both expeditions. Le Roy de France et le Roy de Navarre me pressoient fort de me croiser, et entreprendre le chemin du pelerinage de la croix. Mais je leur respondi, que tendis que j'avoie esté oultre-mer au service de Dieu, que les gens et officers du Roy de France avoient trop grevé et foullé mes subjets, tant qu'ils en estoient apovris; tellement que jamès il ne seroit que eulx et moy ne nous en sortissons. Et veoie clerement, si je me mectoie au pelerinage de la croix, que ce seroit la totale destruction de mesdiz povres subjets. Depuis ouy-je dire a plusieurs, que ceux qui luy conseillerent l'enterprinse de la croix firent un trez grant mal, et pecherent mortellement. Car tandis qu'il fust au royaume de France, tout son royaume vivoit en paix, et regnoit justice. Et incontinent qu'il en fust ors, tout commença à décliner et à empirer. (Tome ii, p. 158.)

In the Fabliaux of Le Grand d'Aussy we have a neat poem by Rutubœuf, a writer of St. Louis's age, in a dialogue between a crusader and a non-crusader, wherein, though he gives the last word to the former, it is plain that he designed the opposite scale to preponderate. (Tome ii, p. 163.)

3

this prince and Philip Augustus. But while in ambition, violence of temper, and unprincipled rapacity, as well as in the success of their attempts to establish an absolute authority, they may be considered as nearly equal, we may remark this difference, that Philip the Fair, who was destitute of military talents, gained those ends by dissimulation which his predecessor had reached by force.

The duchy of Guienne, though somewhat abridged of its original extent, was still by far the most considerable of the French fiefs, even independently of its connection with England.[87] Philip, by dint of perfidy, and by the egregious incapacity of Edmund, brother of Edward I, contrived to obtain and to keep for several years the possession of this great province. A quarrel among some French and English sailors having provoked retaliation, till a sort of piratical war commenced between the two countries, Edward, as Duke of Guienne, was summoned into the king's court to answer for the trespass of his subjects. Upon this he despatched his brother to settle terms of reconciliation, with fuller powers than should have been intrusted to so credulous a negotiator. Philip so outwitted this prince, through a fictitious treaty, as to procure from him the surrender of all the fortresses in Guienne. He then threw off the mask, and, after again summoning Edward to appear, pronounced the confiscation of his fief.[88] This business is the greatest blemish in the political character of Edward. But his eagerness about the acquisition of Scotland rendered him less sensible to the danger of a possession in many respects more valuable; and the spirit of resistance among the English nobility, which his arbitrary measures had provoked, broke out very opportunely for Philip to thwart every effort for the recovery of Guienne by arms. But after repeated suspensions of hostilities a treaty was finally concluded, by which Philip restored the province, on the agreement of a marriage between his daughter Isabel and the heir of England.

To this restitution he was chiefly induced by the ill success that attended his arms in Flanders, another of the great fiefs which this ambitious monarch had endeavoured to confiscate. We have not, perhaps, as clear evidence of the original injustice of his proceedings toward the Count of Flanders as in the case of Gui-

---

[87] Philip was highly offended that instruments made in Guienne should be dated by the year of Edward's reign, and not of his own. This almost sole badge of sovereignty had been preserved by the Kings of France during all the feudal ages. A struggle took place about it, which is recorded in a curious letter from John de Greilli to Edward. The French court at last consented to let dates be thus expressed: Actum fuit, regnante P. rege Franciæ, E. rege Angliæ tenente ducatum Aquitaniæ. Several precedents were shown by the English where the

Counts of Toulouse had used the form, Regnante A. Comite Tolosæ. (Rymer, tome ii, p. 1083.) As this is the first time that I quote Rymer, it may be proper to observe that my references are to the London edition, the paging of which is preserved on the margin of that printed at the Hague.

[88] In the view I have taken of this transaction I have been guided by several instruments in Rymer, which leave no doubt on my mind. Velly, of course, represents the matter more favourably for Philip.

enne; but he certainly twice detained his person, once after drawing him on some pretext to his court, and again in violation of
the faith pledged by his generals. The Flemings made, however,
so vigorous a resistance that Philip was unable to reduce that
small country; and in one famous battle at Courtray they discomfited a powerful army with that utter loss and ignominy to which
the undisciplined impetuosity of the French nobles was pre-emi-
nently exposed.[89]

Two other acquisitions of Philip the Fair deserve notice: that
of the counties of Angoulême and La Marche, upon a sentence
of forfeiture (and, as it seems, a very harsh one) passed against
the reigning count; and that of the city of Lyons and its adjacent
territory, which had not even feudally been subject to the crown
of France for more than three hundred years. Lyons was the
dowry of Matilda, daughter of Louis IV, on her marriage with
Conrad, King of Burgundy, and was bequeathed with the rest
of that kingdom by Rodolph, in 1032, to the empire. Frederick
Barbarossa conferred upon the Archbishop of Lyons all regalian
rights over the city, with the title of imperial vicar. France
seems to have had no concern with it, till St. Louis was called in
as a mediator in disputes between the chapter and the city, during
a vacancy of the see, and took the exercise of jurisdiction upon
himself for the time. Philip III, having been chosen arbitrator
in similar circumstances, insisted, before he would restore the
jurisdiction, upon an oath of fealty from the new archbishop.
This oath, which could be demanded, it seems, by no right but
that of force, continued to be taken till, in 1310, an archbishop
resisting what he had thought a usurpation, the city was besieged by Philip IV, and, the inhabitants not being unwilling
to submit, was finally united to the French crown.[90]

Philip the Fair left three sons, who successively reigned in
France: Louis, surnamed Hutin, Philip the Long, and Charles
the Fair; with a daughter, Isabel, married to Edward II of England.[91] Louis, the eldest, survived his father little more than a
year, leaving one daughter, and his queen pregnant. The circumstances that ensued require to be accurately stated. Louis
had possessed, in right of his mother, the kingdom of Navarre,
with the counties of Champagne and Brie. Upon his death,
Philip, his next brother, assumed the regency both of France
and Navarre; and not long afterward entered into a treaty with
Eudes, Duke of Burgundy, uncle of the Princess Jane, Louis's
daughter, by which her eventual rights to the succession were

[89] The Flemings took at Courtray 4,000
pair of gilt spurs, which were only worn
by knights. These Velly, happily enough,
compares to Hannibal's three bushels of
gold rings at Cannæ.

[90] Velly, tome vii, p. 404. For a more
precise account of the political dependence of Lyons and its district, see "L'Art
de vérifier les Dates," tome ii, p. 469.
[91] [Note XV.]

to be regulated. It was agreed that, in case the queen should be delivered of a daughter, these two princesses, or the survivor of them, should take the grandmother's inheritance, Navarre and Champagne, on releasing all claim to the throne of France. But this was not to take place till their age of consent, when, if they should refuse to make such renunciation, their claim was to remain, and right to be done to them therein; but, in return, the release made by Philip of Navarre and Champagne was to be null. In the meantime he was to hold the government of France, Navarre, and Champagne, receiving homage of vassals in all these countries as governor; saving the right of a male heir to the late king, in the event of whose birth the treaty was not to take effect.[92]

This convention was made on the 17th of July, 1316; and on the 15th of November the queen brought into the world a son, John I (as some called him), who died in four days.[93] The conditional treaty was now become absolute—in spirit, at least, if any cavil might be raised about the expression; and Philip was, by his own agreement, precluded from taking any other title than that of regent or governor until the Princess Jane should attain the age to concur in or disclaim the provisional contract of her uncle. Instead of this, however, he procured himself to be consecrated at Rheims; though, on account of the avowed opposition of the Duke of Burgundy, and even of his own brother Charles, it was thought prudent to shut the gates during the ceremony, and to dispose guards throughout the town. Upon his return to Paris, an assembly composed of prelates, barons, and burgesses of that city was convened, who acknowledged him as their lawful sovereign, and, if we may believe a historian, expressly declared that a woman was incapable of succeeding to the crown of France.[94] The Duke of Burgundy, however, made a show of supporting his niece's interests, till, tempted by the prospect of a marriage with the daughter of Philip, he shamefully betrayed her cause, and gave up in her name, for an inconsiderable pension, not only her disputed claim to the whole monarchy, but her unquestionable right to Navarre and Champagne.[95] I have been rather minute in stating these details, because the transaction is misrepresented by every historian, not excepting those

[92] " Hist. de Charles le Mauvais," par Sécousse, vol. ii, p. 2.

[93] Ancient writers, Sismondi tells us (ix, 344), do not call this infant anything but the child who was to be king; the maxim of later times, " Le roi ne meurt pas," was unknown. I suspect, nevertheless, that the strict hereditary succession was better recognised before this time than Sismondi here admits; compare what he says afterward of a period very little later, vol. xi, 6.

[94] Tunc etiam declaratum fuit, quod in regno Franciæ mulier non succedit. Continuation of Gul. Nangis, in " Spicilegio d'Achery," tome iii. This monk, without talents, and probably without private information, is the sole contemporary historian of this important period. He describes the assembly which confirmed Philip's possession of the crown—quamplures proceres et regni nobiles ac magnates unâ cum plerisque prælatis et burgensibus Parisiensis civitatis.

[95] " Hist. de Charles le Mauvais," tome ii, p. 6. Jane and her husband, the Count of Evreux, recovered Navarre, after the death of Charles the Fair.

who have written since the publication of the documents which
illustrate it.[96]

In this contest, every way memorable, but especially on account of that which sprang out of it, the exclusion of females from
the throne of France was first publicly discussed. The French
writers almost unanimously concur in asserting that such an exclusion was built upon a fundamental maxim of their government. No written law, nor even, as far as I know, the direct
testimony of any ancient writer, has been brought forward to
confirm this position. For as to the text of the Salic law, which
was frequently quoted, and has indeed given a name to this exclusion of females, it can only by a doubtful and refined analogy
be considered as bearing any relation to the succession of the
crown. It is certain, nevertheless, that from the time of Clovis
no woman had ever reigned in France; and, although not an instance of a sole heiress had occurred before, yet some of the
Merovingian kings left daughters, who might, if not rendered
incapable by their sex, have shared with their brothers in partitions then commonly made.[97] But, on the other hand, these times
were gone quite out of memory, and France had much in the
analogy of her existing usages to reconcile her to a female reign.
The crown resembled a great fief, and the great fiefs might universally descend to women. Even at the consecration of Philip
himself, Maud, Countess of Artois, held the crown over his head
among the other peers.[98] And it was scarcely beyond the recollection of persons living that Blanche had been legitimate regent
of France during the minority of St. Louis.

For these reasons, and much more from the provisional treaty
concluded between Philip and the Duke of Burgundy, it may be
fairly inferred that the Salic law, as it was called, was not so fixed
a principle at that time as has been contended. But however
this may be, it received at the accession of Philip the Long a sanc-

---

[96] Velly, who gives several proofs of
disingenuousness in this part of history,
mutilates the treaty of the 17th of July,
1316, in order to conceal Philip the Long's
breach of faith toward his niece.

[97] The Treaty of Andely, in 587, will
be found to afford a very strong presumption that females were at that time excluded from reigning in France. (Greg.
Turon., l. ix.)

[98] The continuator of Nangis says indeed of this, de quo aliqui indignati
fuerunt. But these were probably the
partisans of her nephew Robert, who
had been excluded by a judicial sentence
of Philip IV, on the ground that the
right of representation did not take place
in Artois; a decision considered by many
as unjust. Robert subsequently renewed
his appeal to the court of Philip of Valois; but, unhappily for himself, yielded

to the temptation of forging documents
in support of a claim which seems to
have been at least plausible without such
aid. This unwise dishonesty, which is
not without parallel in more private
causes, not only ruined his pretensions
to the county of Artois, but produced a
sentence of forfeiture, and even of capital punishment, against himself. See a
pretty good account of Robert's process
in Velly, tome viii, p. 262.

Sismondi (x, 44) does not seem to be
convinced that Robert of Artois was
guilty of forgery; but perhaps he is led
away by his animosity against kings,
especially those of the house of Valois.
M. Michelet informs us (v, 30) that the
deeds produced by the demoiselle Divi-
on, on which Robert founded his claims,
are in the " Trésor des Chartes," and
palpable forgeries.

tion which subsequent events more thoroughly confirmed. Philip himself leaving only three daughters, his brother Charles mounted the throne; and upon his death the rule was so unquestionably established that his only daughter was excluded by the Count of Valois, grandson of Philip the Bold. This prince first took the regency, the queen dowager being pregnant, and, upon her giving birth to a daughter, was crowned king. No competitor or opponent appeared in France; but one more formidable than any whom France could have produced was awaiting the occasion to prosecute his imagined right with all the resources of valour and genius, and to carry desolation over that great kingdom with as little scruple as if he was preferring a suit before a civil tribunal.

From the moment of Charles IV's death Edward III of England buoyed himself up with a notion of his title to the crown of France, in right of his mother Isabel, sister to the last three kings. We can have no hesitation in condemning the injustice of this pretension. Whether the Salic law were or were not valid, no advantage could be gained by Edward. Even if he could forget the express or tacit decision of all France, there stood in his way Jane, the daughter of Louis X, three of Philip the Long, and one of Charles the Fair. Aware of this, Edward set up a distinction that, although females were excluded from succession, the same rule did not apply to their male issue; and thus, though his mother Isabel could not herself become Queen of France, she might transmit a title to him. But this was contrary to the commonest rules of inheritance; and if it could have been regarded at all, Jane had a son, afterward the famous King of Navarre, who stood one degree nearer to the crown than Edward.

It is asserted in some French authorities that Edward preferred a claim to the regency immediately after the decease of Charles the Fair, and that the States-General, or at least the peers of France, adjudged that dignity to Philip de Valois. Whether this be true or not, it is clear that he entertained projects of recovering his right as early, though his youth and the embarrassed circumstances of his government threw insuperable obstacles in the way of their execution.[99] He did liege homage,

[99] Letter of Edward III addressed to certain nobles and towns in the south of France, dated March 28, 1328, four days before the birth of Charles IV's posthumous daughter, intimates this resolution. (Rymer, vol. iv, p. 344 et seq.) But an instrument, dated at Northampton on the 16th of May, is decisive. This is a procuration to the Bishops of Worcester and Litchfield, to demand and take possession of the kingdom of France, " in our name, which kingdom has devolved and appertains to us as to the right heir "

(p. 354). To this mission Archbishop Stratford refers, in his vindication of himself from Edward's accusation of treason in 1340; and informs us that the two bishops actually proceeded to France, though without mentioning any further particulars. Novit enim qui nihil ignorat, quod cum quæstio de regno Franciæ post mortem regis Caroli, fratris serenissimæ matris vestræ, in parliamento tunc apud Northampton celebrato, tractata discussaque fuisset ; quodque idem regnum Franciæ ad vos hæreditario jure extite-

therefore, to Philip for Guienne, and for several years, while the affairs of Scotland engrossed his attention, gave no sign of meditating a more magnificent enterprise. As he advanced in manhood, and felt the consciousness of his strength, his early designs grew mature, and produced a series of the most important and interesting revolutions in the fortunes of France. These will form the subject of the ensuing pages.

No war had broken out in Europe, since the fall of the Roman Empire, so memorable as that of Edward III and his successors against France, whether we consider its duration, its object, or the magnitude and variety of its events. It was a struggle of one hundred and twenty years, interrupted but once by a regular pacification, where the most ancient and extensive dominion in the civilized world was the prize, twice lost and twice recovered, in the conflict, while individual courage was wrought up to that high pitch which it can seldom display since the regularity of modern tactics has chastised its enthusiasm and levelled its distinctions. There can be no occasion to dwell upon the events of this war, which are familiar to almost every reader: it is rather my aim to develop and arrange those circumstances which, when rightly understood, give the clew to its various changes of fortune.

France was, even in the fourteenth century, a kingdom of such extent and compactness of figure, such population and resources, and filled with so spirited a nobility, that the very idea of subjugating it by a foreign force must have seemed the most extravagant dream of ambition.[100] Yet, in the course of about

rat legitimè devolutum; et super hoc fuit ordinatum, quod duo episcopi, Wigorniensis tunc, nunc autem Wintoniensis, ac Coventriensis et Lichfeldensis in Franciam dirigerent gressus suos, nomineque vestro regnum Franciæ vindicarent et prædicti Philippi de Valesio coronationem pro viribus impedirent; qui juxta ordinationem prædictam legationem iis injunctam tunc assumentes, gressus suos versus Franciam direxerunt; quæ quidem legatio maximam guerræ præsentis materiam ministravit. (Wilkins, " Concilia," tome i, p. 664.)

There is no evidence in Rymer's " Fœdera " to corroborate Edward's supposed claim to the regency of France upon the death of Charles IV; and it is certainly suspicious that no appointment of ambassadors or procurators for this purpose should appear in so complete a collection of documents. The French historians generally assert this, upon the authority of the continuator of William of Nangis, a nearly contemporary, but not always well-informed, writer. It is curious to compare the four chief English historians. Rapin affirms both the claim to the regency on Charles IV's death, and that to the kingdom after the birth of his daughter. Carte, the most exact historian we have, mentions the latter, and

is silent as to the former. Hume passes over both, and intimates that Edward did not take any steps in support of his pretensions in 1328. Henry gives the supposed trial of Edward's claim to the regency before the States-General at great length, and makes no allusion to the other, so indisputably authenticated in Rymer. It is, I think, most probable that the two bishops never made the formal demand of the throne as they were directed by their instructions. Stratford's expressions seem to imply that they did not.

Sismondi does not mention the claim of Edward to the regency after the death of Charles IV, though he supposes his pretensions to have been taken into consideration by the lords and doctors of law, whom he asserts, following the continuator of William of Nangis, to have consulted together, before Philip of Valois took the title of regent. (Vol. x, p. 10.) Michelet, more studious of effect than minute in details, makes no allusion to the subject.

[100] The Pope (Benedict XII) wrote a strong letter to Edward (March, 1340), dissuading him from taking the title and arms of France, and pointing out the impossibility of his ever succeeding. I have no doubt that this was the com-

twenty years of war, this mighty nation was reduced to the lowest state of exhaustion, and dismembered of considerable provinces by an ignominious peace. What was the combination of political causes which brought about so strange a revolution, and, though not realizing Edward's hopes to their extent, redeemed them from the imputation of rashness in the judgment of his own and succeeding ages?

The first advantage which Edward III possessed in this contest was derived from the splendour of his personal character and from the still more eminent virtues of his son. Besides prudence and military skill, these great princes were endowed with qualities peculiarly fitted for the times in which they lived. Chivalry was then in its zenith; and in all the virtues which adorned the knightly character, in courtesy, munificence, gallantry, in all delicate and magnanimous feelings, none were so conspicuous as Edward III and the Black Prince. As later princes have boasted of being the best gentlemen, they might claim to be the prowest knights in Europe—a character not quite dissimilar, yet of more high pretension. Their court was, as it were, the sun of that system which embraced the valour and nobility of the Christian world; and the respect which was felt for their excellences, while it drew many to their side, mitigated in all the rancour and ferociousness of hostility. This war was like a great tournament, where the combatants fought indeed à outrance, but with all the courtesy and fair play of such an entertainment, and almost as much for the honour of their ladies. In the school of the Edwards were formed men not inferior in any nobleness of disposition to their masters—Manni and the Captal de Buch, Knollys and Calverley, Chandos and Lancaster. On the French side, especially after Du Guesclin came on the stage, these had rivals almost equally deserving of renown. If we could forget, what never should be forgotten, the wretchedness and devastation that fell upon a great kingdom, too dear a price for the display of any heroism, we might count these English wars in France among the brightest periods in history.

Philip of Valois and John, his son, showed but poorly in comparison with their illustrious enemies. Yet they both had considerable virtues; they were brave,[101] just, liberal, and the

mon opinion. But the Avignon popes were very subservient to France. Clement VI, as well as his predecessor, Benedict XII, threatened Edward with spiritual arms. (Rymer, tome v, pp. 88 and 465.) It required Edward's spirit and steadiness to despise these menaces. But the time when they were terrible to princes was rather passed by; and the Holy See never ventured to provoke the king, who treated the Church, through-out his reign, with admirable firmness and temper.

[101] The bravery of Philip is not questioned. But a French historian, in order, I suppose, to enhance this quality, has presumed to violate truth in an extraordinary manner. The challenge sent by Edward, offering to decide his claim to the kingdom by single combat, is well known. Certainly it conveys no imputation on the King of France to have de-

latter, in particular, of unshaken fidelity to his word. But neither was beloved by his subjects; the misgovernment and extortion of their predecessors during half a century had alienated the public mind, and rendered their own taxes and debasement of the coin intolerable. Philip was made by misfortune, John by nature, suspicious and austere; and although their most violent acts seem never to have wanted absolute justice, yet they were so ill conducted and of so arbitrary a complexion that they greatly impaired the reputation, as well as interests, of these monarchs. In the execution of Clisson under Philip, in that of the Connétable d'Eu under John, and still more in that of Harcourt, even in the imprisonment of the King of Navarre, though every one of these might have been guilty of treasons, there were circumstances enough to exasperate the disaffected, and to strengthen the party of so politic a competitor as Edward.

Next to the personal qualities of the King of England, his resources in this war must be taken into the account. It was after long hesitation that he assumed the title and arms of France, from which, unless upon the best terms, he could not recede without loss of honour.[102] In the meantime he strengthened himself by alliances with the emperor, with the cities of Flanders, and with most of the princes in the Netherlands and on the Rhine. Yet I do not know that he profited much by these conventions, since he met with no success till the scene of the war was changed from the Flemish frontier to Normandy and Poitou. The troops of Hainault alone were constantly distinguished in his service.[103]

clined this unfair proposal. But Velly has represented him as accepting it, on condition that Edward would stake the crown of England against that of France; an interpolation which may be truly called audacious, since not a word of this is in Philip's letter, preserved in Rymer, which the historian had before his eyes, and actually quotes upon the occasion. (" Hist. de France," tome viii, p. 382.)

[102] The first instrument in which Edward disallows the title of Philip is his convention with the Emperor Louis of Bavaria, wherein he calls him nunc pro rege Francorum se gerentem. The date of this is August 26, 1337, yet on the 28th of the same month another instrument gives him the title of king; and the same occurs in subsequent instances. At length we have an instrument of procuration to the Duke of Brabant. October 7, 1337, empowering him to take possession of the crown of France in the name of Edward; attendentes inclitum regnum Franciæ ad nos fore jure successionis legitimè devolutum. Another of the same date appoints the said duke his vigar-general and lieutenant of France. The king assumed in this commission the title Rex Franciæ et Angliæ ; in other instruments he calls himself Rex Angliæ et Franciæ. It was necessary to obviate the jealousy of the English, who did not, in that age, admit the precedence of France. Accordingly, Edward had two great seals on which the two kingdoms were named in a different order. But, in the royal arms, those of France were always in the first quarter, as they continued to be until the accession of the house of Brunswick.

Probably Edward III would not have entered into the war merely on account of his claim to the crown. He had disputes with Philip about Guienne; and that prince had, rather unjustifiably, abetted Robert Bruce in Scotland. I am not inclined to lay any material stress upon the instigation of Robert of Artois.

[103] Michelet dwells on the advantage which Edward gained by the commerce of England with Flanders: " Le secret des batailles de Crécy, de Poitiers, est aux comptoirs des marchands de Londres, de Bordeaux, et de Bourges " (vol. v, p. 6). France had no internal trade; the roads were dangerous on account of robbers, and heavy tolls were to be paid; fiscal officers had replaced the feudal lords. The value of money was perpetually varying far more than in England. (Id., p. 12.) Certainly the comparative prosperity of the latter country supplied Edward with the sinews of war.

But his intrinsic strength was at home. England had been growing in riches since the wise government of his grandfather, Edward I, and through the market opened for her wool with the manufacturing towns of Flanders. She was tranquil within; and her northern enemy, the Scotch, had been defeated and quelled. The Parliament, after some slight precautions against a very probable effect of Edward's conquest of France, the reduction of their own island into a province, entered as warmly as improvidently into his quarrel. The people made it their own, and grew so intoxicated with the victories of this war that for some centuries the injustice and folly of the enterprise do not seem to have struck the gravest of our countrymen.

There is, indeed, ample room for national exultation at the names of Crécy, Poitiers, and Agincourt. So great was the disparity of numbers upon those famous days that we can not, with the French historians, attribute the discomfiture of their hosts merely to mistaken tactics and too impetuous valour. They yielded rather to that intrepid steadiness in danger which had already become the characteristic of our English soldiers, and which during five centuries has insured their superiority whenever ignorance or infatuation has not led them into the field. But these victories, and the qualities that secured them, must chiefly be ascribed to the freedom of our constitution and to the superior condition of the people. Not the nobility of England, not the feudal tenants, won the battles of Crécy and Poitiers, for these were fully matched in the ranks of France; but the yeomen who drew the bow with strong and steady arms, accustomed to use it in their native fields, and rendered fearless by personal competence and civil freedom. It is well known that each of the three great victories was due to our archers, who were chiefly of the middle class, and attached, according to the system of that age, to the knights and squires who fought in heavy armour with the lance. Even at the battle of Poitiers, of which our country seems to have the least right to boast, since the greater part of the Black Prince's small army was composed of Gascons, the merit of the English bowmen is strongly attested by Froissart.[104]

France could not afford to maintain a well-appointed infantry.

" Une tactique nouvelle," M. Michelet afterward very well observes (p. 81), " sortait de l'état nouveau de la société; ce n'était pas un œuvre de génie, ni de réflexion. Edouard III n'était ni un Gustave Adolphe ni un Frédéric II. Il avait employé les fantassins faute de cavaliers. . . . La bataille de Crécy reveilla un secret dont personne ne se doutait, l'impuissance militaire de ce monde féodal, qui s'était cru le seul monde militaire." Courtray might have given some suspicion of this; but Cour-tray was much less of a "bataille rangée" than Crécy.

[104] Au vray dire, les archres d'Angle-terre faisoient à leurs gens grant avan-tage. Car ils tiroyent tant espessement, que les François ne sçavoyent dequel costé entendre, qu'ils ne fussent con-suyvis de trayt; et s'avançoyent tous-jours ces Anglois, et petit à petit enque-royent terre. (Part I, c. 162.)

It is by an odd oversight that Sismondi has said (x, 295), " Les Anglais étaient accoutumés à se servir sans cesse de l'ar-balète." The cross-bow was looked upon as a weapon unworthy of a brave man;

Yet the glorious termination to which Edward was enabled, at least for a time, to bring the contest, was rather the work of fortune than of valour and prudence. Until the battle of Poitiers he had made no progress toward the conquest of France. That country was too vast and his army too small for such a revolution. The victory of Crécy gave him nothing but Calais; a post of considerable importance in war and peace, but rather adapted to annoy than to subjugate the kingdom. But at Poitiers he obtained the greatest of prizes, by taking prisoner the King of France. Not only the love of freedom tempted that prince to ransom himself by the utmost sacrifices, but his captivity left France defenceless, and seemed to annihilate the monarchy itself. The government was already odious; a spirit was awakened in the people which might seem hardly to belong to the fourteenth century, and the convulsions of our own time are sometimes strongly paralleled by those which succeeded the battle of Poitiers. Already the States-General had established a fundamental principle that no resolution could be passed as the opinion of the whole unless each of the three orders concurred in its adoption.[105] The right of levying and of regulating the collection of taxes was recognised. But that assembly, which met at Paris immediately after the battle, went far greater lengths in the reform and control of government. From the time of Philip the Fair the abuses natural to arbitrary power had harassed the people. There now seemed an opportunity of redress; and however seditious, or even treasonable, may have been the motives of those who guided this assembly of the States, especially the famous Marcel, it is clear that many of their reformations tended to liberty and the public good.[106] But the tumultuous scenes which passed in the capital, sometimes heightened into civil war, necessarily distracted men from the common defence against Edward. These tumults were excited and the distraction increased by Charles, King of Navarre, surnamed the Bad, to whom the French writers have, not perhaps unjustly, attributed a character of unmixed and inveterate malignity. He was grandson of Louis Hutin, by his daughter Jane, and, if Edward's pretence of claiming through females could be admitted, was a nearer heir to the crown; the consciousness of which seems to have suggested itself

a prejudice which afterward prevailed with respect to firearms. A romancer praises the Emperor Conrad:
" Par un effort de lance et d'écu,
Conquérant tous ses ennemis,
Y à arbalestreis ni fu mis ";
quoted by Boucher in his translation of " Il Consolato del Mare," p. 518. Even the long-bow might incur this censure; or any weapon in which the combatants fought eminus. But if we look at the plate armour of the fifteenth century, it may seem that a knight had not much to boast of the danger to which he exposed himself, especially when encountering infantry.
[105] " Ordonnances des Rois de France," tome ii.
[106] I must refer the reader onward to the next chapter for more information on this subject. This separation is inconvenient, but it arose indispensably out of my arrangement and prevented greater inconveniences.

to his depraved mind as an excuse for his treacheries, though he could entertain very little prospect of asserting the claim against either contending party. John had bestowed his daughter in marriage on the King of Navarre; but he very soon gave a proof of his character by procuring the assassination of the king's favourite, Charles de la Cerda. An irreconcilable enmity was the natural result of this crime. Charles became aware that he had offended beyond the possibility of forgiveness, and that no letters of pardon nor pretended reconciliation could secure him from the king's resentment. Thus, impelled by guilt into deeper guilt, he entered into alliances with Edward, and fomented the seditious spirit of Paris. Eloquent and insinuating, he was the favourite of the people, whose grievances he affected to pity, and with whose leaders he intrigued. As his paternal inheritance, he possessed the county of Evreux in Normandy. The proximity of this to Paris created a formidable diversion in favour of Edward III, and connected the English garrisons of the north with those of Poitou and Guienne.

There is no affliction which did not fall upon France during this miserable period. A foreign enemy was in the heart of the kingdom, the king a prisoner, the capital in sedition, a treacherous prince of the blood in arms against the sovereign authority. Famine, the sure and terrible companion of war, for several years desolated the country. In 1348 a pestilence, the most extensive and unsparing of which we have any memorial, visited France, as well as the rest of Europe, and consummated the work of hunger and the sword.[107] The companies of adventure, mercenary troops in the service of John or Edward, finding no immediate occupation after the truce of 1357, scattered themselves over the country in search of pillage. No force existed sufficiently powerful to check these robbers in their career. Undismayed by superstition, they compelled the Pope to redeem himself in

[107] A full account of the ravages made by this memorable plague may be found in Matteo Villani, the second of that family who wrote the history of Florence. His brother and predecessor, John Villani, was himself a victim to it. The disease began in the Levant about 1346; from whence Italian traders brought it to Sicily, Pisa, and Genoa. In 1348 it passed the Alps and spread over France and Spain; in the next year it reached Britain, and in 1350 laid waste Germany and other northern states, lasting generally about five months in each country. At Florence more than three out of five died. (Muratori, " Script. Rerum Italicarum," tome xiv, p. 12.) The stories of Boccaccio's Decamerone, as is well known, are supposed to be related by a society of Florentine ladies and gentlemen retired to the country during this pestilence.

Another pestilence, only less destructive than the former, wasted both France and England in 1361. Sismondi bitterly remarks (x, 342) that between four and five millions who died of the former plague in France merely diminished the number of the oppressed, producing no perceptible effect. But this is exaggerated. The plague caused a truce of several months. The war was, in fact, carried on with less vigour for some years. It is, however, by no means unlikely that the number of deaths has been overrated. Nothing can be more loose than the statistical evidence of mediæval writers. Thus 30,000 are said to have died at Narbonne. (Michelet, v, 94.) But had Narbonne so many to lose? At least, would not the depopulation have been out of all proportion to other cities?

Avignon by the payment of forty thousand crowns.[108] France was the passive victim of their license, even after the pacification concluded with England, till some were diverted into Italy and others led by Du Guesclin to the war of Castile. Impatient of this wretchedness, and stung by the insolence and luxury of their lords, the peasantry of several districts broke out into a dreadful insurrection. This was called the Jacquerie, from the cant phrase Jacques Bonhomme, applied to men of that class, and was marked by all the circumstances of horror incident to the rising of an exasperated and unenlightened populace.[109]

Subdued by these misfortunes, though Edward had made but slight progress toward the conquest of the country, the regent of France, afterward Charles V, submitted to the Peace of Bretigni. By this treaty, not to mention less important articles, all Guienne, Gascony, Poitou, Saintonge, the Limousin, and the Angoumois, as well as Calais and the county of Ponthieu, were ceded in full sovereignty to Edward; a price abundantly compensating his renunciation of the title of France, which was the sole concession stipulated in return. Every care seems to have been taken to make the cession of these provinces complete. The first six articles of the treaty expressly surrender them to the King of England. By the seventh John and his son engaged to convey within a year from the ensuing Michaelmas all their rights

[108] Froissart, p. 187. This troop of banditti was commanded by Arnaud de Cervole, surnamed l'Archiprêtre, from a benefice which, although a layman, he possessed, according to the irregularity of those ages. See a memoir on the life of Arnaud de Cervole, in the twenty-fifth volume of the "Academy of Inscriptions."

[109] The second continuator of Nangis, a monk of no great abilities, but entitled to notice as our most contemporary historian, charges the nobility with spending the money raised upon the people by oppressive taxes, in playing at dice, "et alios indecentes jocos." (D'Achery, "Spicilegium," tome iii, p. 114; folio edition.) All the miseries that followed the battle of Poitiers he ascribes to bad government and neglect of the commonweal: but especially to the pride and luxury of the nobles. I am aware that this writer is biassed in favour of the King of Navarre; but he was an eye-witness of the people's misery, and perhaps a less exceptional authority than Froissart, whose love of pageantry and habits of feasting in the castles of the great seem to have produced some insensibility toward the sufferings of the lower classes. It is a painful circumstance, which Froissart and the continuator of Nangis attest, that the citizens of Calais, more interesting than the common heroes of history, were unrewarded, and begged their bread in misery throughout France. Vil-

laret contradicts this, on the authority of an ordinance which he has seen in their favour. But that was not a time when ordinances were very sure of execution. (Vill., tome ix, p. 470.) I must add that the celebrated story of the six citizens of Calais, which has of late been called in question, receives strong confirmation from John Villani, who died very soon afterward. (L. xii, c. 96.) Froissart, of course, wrought up the circumstances after this manner. In all the colouring of his history he is as great a master as Livy, and as little observant of particular truth. M. de Bréquigny, almost the latest of those excellent antiquaries whose memoirs so much illustrate the French Academy of Inscriptions, has discussed the history of Calais, and particularly this remarkable portion of it. ("Mém. de l'Académie des Inscriptions," tome i.)

Petrarch has drawn a lamentable picture of the state of France in 1360, when he paid a visit to Paris. "I could not believe," he says, "that this was the same kingdom which I had once seen so rich and flourishing. Nothing presented itself to my eyes but a fearful solitude, an extreme poverty, lands uncultivated, houses in ruins. Even the neighbourhood of Paris manifested everywhere marks of destruction and conflagration. The streets are deserted: the roads overgrown with weeds: the whole is a vast solitude." ("Mém. de Pétrarque," tome iii, p. 541.)

over them, and especially those of sovereignty and feudal appeal. The same words are repeated still more emphatically in the eleventh and some other articles. The twelfth stipulates the exchange of mutual renunciations: by John, of all right over the ceded countries; by Edward, of his claim to the throne of France. At Calais the Treaty of Bretigni was renewed by John, who, as a prisoner, had been no party to the former compact, with the omission only of the twelfth article, respecting the exchange of renunciations. But that it was not intended to waive them by this omission is abundantly manifest by instruments of both the kings, in which reference is made to their future interchanges at Bruges, on the feast of St. Andrew, 1361. And, until that time should arrive, Edward promises to lay aside the title and arms of France (an engagement which he strictly kept [110]), and John to act in no respect as king or suzerain over the ceded provinces. Finally, on November 15, 1361, two commissioners are appointed by Edward to receive the renunciations of the King of France at Bruges on the ensuing feast of St. Andrew,[111] and to do whatever might be mutually required by virtue of the treaty. These, however, seem to have been withheld, and the twelfth article of the Treaty of Bretigni was never expressly completed. By mutual instruments, executed at Calais, October 24th, it had been declared that the sovereignty of the ceded provinces, as well as Edward's right to the crown of France, should remain as before, although suspended as to its exercise, until the exchange of renunciations, notwithstanding any words of present conveyance or release in the Treaties of Bretigni and Calais. And another pair of letters-patent, dated October 26th, contains the form of renunciations, which, it is mutually declared, should have effect by virtue of the present letters, in case one party should be ready to exchange such renunciations at the time and place appointed, and the other should make default therein. These instruments executed at Calais are so prolix, and so studiously enveloped, as it seems, in the obscurity of technical language, that it is difficult to extract their precise intention. It appears, nevertheless, that whichever party was prepared to perform what was required of him at Bruges on November 30, 1361, the other then and there making default, would acquire not only what our lawyers might call an equitable title, but an actual vested right, by virtue of the provision in the letters-patent of October 26, 1360. The appointment above mentioned of Edward's commissioners on November 15, 1361, seems to throw upon the French the burden of proving that John sent his envoys with equally full powers to the place

[110] Edward gives John the title of King of France in an instrument bearing date at Calais, October 22, 1360. (Rymer, tome vi, p. 217.) The treaty was signed October 24. (Id., p. 219.)
[111] Rym., tome vi, p. 339.

of meeting, and that the non-interchange of renunciations was owing to the English Government. But though a historian, sixty years later (Juvenal des Ursins), asserts that the French commissioners attended at Bruges, and that those of Edward made default, this is certainly rendered improbable by the actual appointment of commissioners made by the King of England on the 15th of November, by the silence of Charles V after the recommencement of hostilities, who would have rejoiced in so good a ground of excuse, and by the language of some English instruments, complaining that the French renunciations were withheld.[112]   It is suggested by the French authors that Edward was unwilling to execute a formal renunciation of his claim to the crown.   But we can hardly suppose that, in order to evade this condition, which he had voluntarily imposed upon himself by the Treaties of Bretigni and Calais, he would have left his title to the provinces ceded by those conventions imperfect.   He certainly deemed it indefeasible, and acted, without any complaint from the French court, as the perfect master of those countries. He created his son Prince of Aquitaine, with the fullest powers over that new principality, holding it in fief of the crown of England by the yearly rent of an ounce of gold.[113]   And the court of that great prince was kept for several years at Bordeaux.

I have gone something more than usual into detail as to

[112] It appears that, among other alleged infractions of the treaty, the King of France had received appeals from Armagnac, Albret, and other nobles of Aquitaine not long after the peace. For, in February, 1362, a French envoy, the Count de Tancarville, being in England, the privy council presented to Edward their bill of remonstrances against this conduct of France; et semble au conseil le roy d'Angleterre que consideré la fourme de la ditte paix, que tant estoit honourable et proffitable au royaume de France et à toute chrétienté, que la reception desdittes appellacions n'a mie esté bien faite, ne passée si ordenément, ne à si bon affection et amour, comme il droit avoir esté fait de raison parmi l'effet et l'intention de la paix et alliances affermées et entr'eux semble estre moult prejudiciables et contraires à l'onneur et à l'estat du roy et de son fils le prince et de toute la maison d'Angleterre, et pourra estre evidente matière de rebellion des subgiez, et aussi donner tres-grant occasion d'enfraindre la paix, si bon remede sur ce n'y soit mis plus hastivement.   Upon the whole, they conclude that if the King of France would repair this trespass, and send his renunciation of sovereignty, the king should send his of the title of France. (Martenne, " Thes. Anec.," tome i, p. 1487.)

Four princes of the blood, or, as they are termed, Seigneurs des Fleurdelys, were detained as hostages for the due ex-

ecution of the Treaty of Bretigni, which, from whatever pretence, was delayed for a considerable time.   Anxious to obtain their liberty, they signed a treaty at London in November, 1362, by which, among other provisions, it was stipulated that the King of France should send fresh letters, under his seal, conveying and releasing the territories ceded by the peace, without the clause contained in the former letters, retaining the ressort: Et que en ycelles lettres soit expressement compris transport de la souveraineté et du ressort, etc.   Et le roi d'Angleterre et ses enfans ferront semblablement autiels renonciations, sur ce q'il doit faire de sa partie. (Rymer, tome vi, p. 396.)   This Treaty of London was never ratified by the French Government; but I use it as a proof that Edward imputed the want of mutual renunciations to France, and was himself ready to perform his part of the treaty.

[113] Rym., tome vi, pp. 385-389.   One clause is remarkable: Edward reserves to himself the right of erecting the province of Aquitaine into a kingdom.   So high were the notions of this great monarch in an age when the privilege of creating new kingdoms was deemed to belong only to the Pope and the emperor. Etiam si per nos hujusmodi provinciæ ad regalis honoris titulum et fastigium imposterum sublimentur; quam erectionem faciendam per nos ex tunc specialiter reservamus.

these circumstances, because a very specious account is given
by some French historians and antiquaries which tends to throw
the blame of the rupture in 1368 upon Edward III.[114] Unfounded
as was his pretension to the crown of France, and actuated as
we must consider him by the most ruinous ambition, his character was unblemished by ill faith. There is no apparent cause
to impute the ravages made in France by soldiers formerly in
the English service to his instigation, nor any proof of a connection with the King of Navarre subsequently to the Peace of
Bretigni. But a good lesson may be drawn by conquerors from
the change of fortune that befell Edward III. A long warfare
and unexampled success had procured for him some of the richest provinces of France. Within a short time he was entirely
stripped of them, less through any particular misconduct than
in consequence of the intrinsic difficulty of preserving such acquisitions. The French were already knit together as one people; and
even those whose feudal duties sometimes led them into the field
against their sovereign could not endure the feeling of dismemberment from the monarchy. When the Peace of Bretigni was to be
carried into effect, the nobility of the south remonstrated against
the loss of the king's sovereignty, and showed, it is said, in their
charters granted by Charlemagne, a promise never to transfer
the right of protecting them to another. The citizens of Rochelle
implored the king not to desert them, and protested their readiness to pay half their estates in taxes rather than fall under the
power of England. John with heaviness of heart persuaded these
faithful people to comply with that destiny which he had not been
able to surmount. At length they sullenly submitted: we will
obey, they said, the English with our lips, but our hearts shall
never forget their allegiance.[115] Such unwilling subjects might
perhaps have been won by a prudent government; but the temper
of the Prince of Wales, which was rather stern and arbitrary,
did not conciliate their hearts to his cause.[116] After the expedi-

[114] Besides Villaret and other historians, the reader who feels any curiosity
on this subject may consult three memoirs in the fifteenth volume of the
" Academy of Inscriptions," by MM. Sécousse, Salier, and Bonamy. These distinguished antiquaries unite, but the third
with much less confidence and passion
than the other two, in charging the omission upon Edward. The observations in
the text will serve, I hope, to repel their
arguments, which, I may be permitted
to observe, no English writer has hitherto undertaken to answer. This is not said
in order to assume any praise to myself; in fact, I have been guided, in a
great degree, by one of the adverse counsel, M. Bonamy, whose statement of facts
is very fair, and makes me suspect a little
that he saw the weakness of his own cause.

The authority of Christine de Pisan,
a contemporary panegyrist of the French
king, is not, perhaps, very material in
such a question; but she seems wholly
ignorant of this supposed omission on
Edward's side, and puts the justice of
Charles V's war on a very different basis;
namely, that treaties not conducive to
the public interest ought not to be kept.
" Collection des Mémoires," tome v, p.
137.) A principle more often acted upon
than avowed!
[115] Froissart, part i, c. 214.
[116] See an anecdote of his difference
with the Seigneur d'Albret, one of the
principal barons in Gascony, to which
Froissart, who was then at Bordeaux, ascribes the alienation of the southern nobility. chap. 244. Edward III, soon after
the Peace of Bretigni, revoked all his

tion into Castile, a most injudicious and fatal enterprise, he attempted to impose a heavy tax upon Guienne. This was extended to the lands of the nobility, who claimed an immunity from all impositions. Many of the chief lords in Guienne and Gascony carried their complaints to the throne of Charles V, who had succeeded his father in 1364, appealing to him as the prince's sovereign and judge. After a year's delay the king ventured to summon the Black Prince to answer these charges before the peers of France, and the war immediately recommenced between the two countries.[117]

Though it is impossible to reconcile the conduct of Charles upon this occasion to the stern principles of rectitude which ought always to be obeyed, yet the exceeding injustice of Edward in the former war, and the miseries which he inflicted upon an unoffending people in the prosecution of his claim, will go far toward extenuating this breach of the Treaty of Bretigni. It is observed, indeed, with some truth by Rapin, that we judge of Charles's prudence by the event; and that, if he had been unfortunate in the war, he would have brought on himself the reproaches of all mankind, and even of those writers who are now most ready to extol him. But his measures had been so sagaciously taken that, except through that perverseness of fortune, against which, especially in war, there is no security, he could hardly fail of success. The elder Edward was declining through age, and the younger through disease; the ceded provinces were eager to return to their native king and their garrisons, as we may infer by their easy reduction, feeble and ill-supplied. France, on the other hand, had recovered breath after her losses; the sons of those who had fallen or fled at Poitiers were in the field; a king, not personally warlike, but eminently wise and popular, occupied the throne of the rash and intemperate John. She was restored by the policy of Charles V and the valour of Du Guesclin. This hero, a Breton gentleman without fortune or exterior graces, was the greatest ornament of France during that age. Though inferior, as it seems, to Lord Chandos in military skill, as well as in the polished virtues of chivalry, his unwearied activity, his talent of inspiring confidence, his good fortune, the generosity and frankness of his character, have preserved a fresh recollection of his name, which has hardly been the case with our countryman.

In a few campaigns the English were deprived of almost all their conquests, and even, in a great degree, of their original possessions in Guienne. They were still formidable enemies, not

grants in Guienne. (Rymer, tome vi, p. 391.)
[117] On November 20, 1368, some time before the summons of the Prince of Wales, a treaty was concluded between Charles and Henry, King of Castile, wherein the latter expressly stipulates that whatever parts of Guienne or England he might conquer he would give up to the King of France. (Rymer, tome vi, p. 598.)

4

only from their courage and alacrity in the war, but on account
of the keys of France which they held in their hands: Bordeaux,
Bayonne, and Calais, by inheritance or conquest; Brest and Cher-
bourg, in mortgage from their allies, the Duke of Brittany and
King of Navarre. But the successor of Edward III was Richard
II; a reign of feebleness and sedition gave no opportunity for
prosecuting schemes of ambition. The war, protracted with few
distinguished events for several years, was at length suspended
by repeated armistices, not, indeed, very strictly observed, and
which the animosity of the English would not permit to settle
in any regular treaty. Nothing less than the terms obtained at
Bretigni, emphatically called the Great Peace, would satisfy a
frank and courageous people, who deemed themselves cheated
by the manner of its infraction. The war was therefore always
popular in England, and the credit which an ambitious prince,
Thomas, Duke of Gloucester, obtained in that country, was
chiefly owing to the determined opposition which he showed to
all French connections. But the politics of Richard II were of
a different cast, and Henry IV was equally anxious to avoid hostilities with France; so that, before the unhappy condition of
that kingdom tempted his son to revive the claims of Edward in
still more favourable circumstances, there had been thirty years
of respite, and even some intervals of friendly intercourse between
the two nations. Both, indeed, were weakened by internal discord, but France more fatally than England. But for the calamities of Charles VI's reign, she would probably have expelled her
enemies from the kingdom. The strength of that fertile and populous country was recruited with surprising rapidity. Sir Hugh
Calverley, a famous captain in the wars of Edward III, while
serving in Flanders, laughed at the herald, who assured him that
the King of France's army, then entering the country, amounted
to twenty-six thousand lances; asserting that he had often seen
their largest musters, but never so much as a fourth part of the
number.[118] The relapse of this great kingdom under Charles VI
was more painful and perilous than her first crisis, but she recovered from each through her intrinsic and inextinguishable
resources.

Charles V, surnamed the Wise, after a reign which, if we
overlook a little obliquity in the rupture of the Peace of Bretigni,
may be deemed one of the most honourable in French history,
dying prematurely, left the crown to his son, a boy of thirteen,
under the care of three ambitious uncles, the Dukes of Anjou,
Berry, and Burgundy. Charles had retrieved the glory, restored
the tranquility, revived the spirit of his country; the severe trials
which exercised his regency after the battle of Poitiers had dis-

[118] Froissart, part ii, c. 142.

ciplined his mind; he became a sagacious statesman, an encourager of literature, a beneficent lawgiver. He erred, doubtless, though upon plausible grounds, in accumulating a vast treasure, which the Duke of Anjou seized before he was cold in the grave. But all the fruits of his wisdom were lost in the succeeding reign. In a government essentially popular the youth or imbecility of the sovereign creates no material derangement. In a monarchy, where all the springs of the system depend upon one central force, these accidents, which are sure in the course of a few generations to recur, can scarcely fail to dislocate the whole machine. During the forty years that Charles VI bore the name of king, rather than reigned in France, that country was reduced to a state far more deplorable than during the captivity of John.

A great change had occurred in the political condition of France during the fourteenth century. As the feudal militia became unserviceable, the expenses of war were increased through the necessity of taking troops into constant pay; and while more luxurious refinements of living heightened the temptations to profuseness, the means of enjoying them were lessened by improvident alienations of the domain. Hence taxes, hitherto almost unknown, were levied incessantly, and with all those circumstances of oppression which are natural to the fiscal proceedings of an arbitrary government. These, as has been said before, gave rise to the unpopularity of the first two Valois, and were nearly leading to a complete revolution in the convulsions that succeeded the battle of Poitiers. The confidence reposed in Charles V's wisdom and economy kept everything at rest during his reign, though the taxes were still very heavy. But the seizure of his vast accumulations by the Duke of Anjou, and the ill faith with which the new government imposed subsidies, after promising their abolition, provoked the people of Paris, and sometimes of other places, to repeated seditions. The States-General not only compelled the government to revoke these impositions and restore the nation, at least according to the language of edicts, to all their liberties, but, with less wisdom, refused to make any grant of money. Indeed, a remarkable spirit of democratical freedom was then rising in those classes on whom the crown and nobility had so long trampled. An example was held out by the Flemings, who, always tenacious of their privileges, because conscious of their ability to maintain them, were engaged in a furious conflict with Louis, Count of Flanders.[119] The court of France took part in this war ; and, after obtaining a decisive victory over the citizens

[119] The Flemish rebellion, which originated in an attempt, suggested by bad advisers to the count, to impose a tax upon the people of Ghent without their consent, is related in a very interesting manner by Froissart, part ii, c. 37, etc., who equals Herodotus in simplicity, liveliness, and power over the heart. I would advise the historical student to acquaint himself with these transactions and with the corresponding tumults at Paris. They are among the eternal lessons of

of Ghent, Charles VI returned to chastise those of Paris.[120] Unable to resist the royal army, the city was treated as the spoil of conquest; its immunities abridged; its most active leaders put to death; a fine of uncommon severity imposed; and the taxes renewed by arbitrary prerogative. But the people preserved their indignation for a favourable moment, and were unfortunately led by it, when rendered subservient to the ambition of others, into a series of crimes, and a long alienation from the interests of their country.

It is difficult to name a limit beyond which taxes will not be borne without impatience, when they appear to be called for by necessity, and faithfully applied; nor is it impracticable for a skilful minister to deceive the people in both these respects. But the sting of taxation is wastefulness. What high-spirited man could see without indignation the earnings of his labour, yielded ungrudgingly to the public defence, become the spoil of parasites and speculators? It is this that mortifies the liberal hand of public spirit; and those statesmen who deem the security of government to depend not on laws and armies, but on the moral sympathies and prejudices of the people, will vigilantly guard against even the suspicion of prodigality. In the present stage of society it is impossible to conceive that degree of misapplication which existed in the French treasury under Charles VI, because the real exigencies of the state could never again be so inconsiderable. Scarcely any military force was kept up, and the produce of the grievous impositions then levied was chiefly lavished upon the royal household [121] or plundered by the officers of government. This naturally resulted from the peculiar and afflicting circumstances of this reign. The Duke of Anjou pretended to be entitled by the late king's appointment, if not by the constitution of France, to exercise the government as regent during the minor-

history; for the unjust encroachments of courts, the intemperate passions of the multitude, the ambition of demagogues, the cruelty of victorious factions, will never cease to have their parallels and their analogies; while the military achievements of distant times afford in general no instruction, and can hardly occupy too little of our time in historical studies. The prefaces to the fifth and sixth volumes of the " Ordonnances des Rois de France " contain more accurate information as to the Parisian disturbances than can be found in Froissart.
[120] If Charles VI had been defeated by the Flemings, the insurrection of the Parisians, Froissart says, would have spread over France; toute gentillesse et noblesse eût été morte et perdue en France; nor would the Jacquerie have ever been si grande et si horrible (c. 120). To the example of the Gantois he ascribes the tumults which broke out about the same time in England as well as in France (c. 84). The Flemish insurrection would probably have had more important consequences if it had been cordially supported by the English Government. But the danger of encouraging that democratical spirit which so strongly leavened the commons of England might justly be deemed by Richard II's council much more than a counterbalance to the advantage of distressing France. When too late some attempts were made, and the Flemish towns acknowledged Richard as King of France in 1384. (Rymer, tome vii, p. 448.)
[121] The expenses of the royal household, which under Charles V were 94,000 livres, amounted in 1412 to 450,000. (Villaret, tome iii, p. 243.) Yet the king was so ill supplied that his plate had been pawned. When Montagu, minister of the finances, was arrested in 1409, all this plate was found concealed in his house.

ity;[122] but this period, which would naturally be very short, a law of Charles V having fixed the age of majority at thirteen, was still more abridged by consent; and after the young monarch's coronation, he was considered as reigning with full personal authority. Anjou, Berry, and Burgundy, together with the king's maternal uncle, the Duke of Bourbon, divided the actual exercise of government.

The first of these soon undertook an expedition into Italy, to possess himself of the crown of Naples, in which he perished. Berry was a profuse and voluptuous man, of no great talents; though his rank, and the middle position which he held between struggling parties, made him rather conspicuous throughout the revolutions of that age. The most respectable of the king's uncles, the Duke of Bourbon, being further removed from the royal stem, and of an unassuming character, took a less active part than his three coadjutors. Burgundy, an ambitious and able prince, maintained the ascendency until Charles, weary of a restraint which had been protracted by his uncle till he was in his twenty-first year, took the reins into his own hands. The Dukes of Burgundy and Berry retired from court, and the administration was committed to a different set of men, at the head of whom appeared the constable De Clisson, a soldier of great fame in the English wars. The people rejoiced in the fall of the princes by whose exactions they had been plundered; but the new ministers soon rendered themselves odious by similar conduct. The fortune of Clisson, after a few years' favour, amounted to one million seven hundred thousand livres, equal in weight of silver, to say nothing of the depreciation of money, to ten times that sum at present.[123]

---

[122] It has always been an unsettled point whether the presumptive heir is entitled to the regency of France; and, if he be so to the regency, whether this includes the custody of the minor's person. The particular case of the Duke of Anjou is subject to a considerable apparent difficulty. Two instruments of Charles V, bearing the same date of October, 1374, as published by Dupuy ("Traité de Majorité des Rois," p. 161), are plainly irreconcilable with each other; the former giving the exclusive regency to the Duke of Anjou, reserving the custody of the minor's person to other guardians; the latter conferring not only this custody, but the government of the kingdom, on the queen, and on the Dukes of Burgundy and Bourbon, without mentioning the Duke of Anjou's name. Daniel calls these testaments of Charles V, whereas they are in the form of letters-patent; and supposes that the king had suppressed both, as neither party seems to have availed itself of their authority in the discussions that took place after the king's death. ("Hist. de France,"

tome iii, p. 662, edit. 1720.) Villaret, as is too much his custom, slides over the difficulty without notice. But M. de Bréquigni (" Mém. de l'Acad. des Inscript.," tome I, p. 533) observes that the second of these instruments, as published by M. Sécousse, in the "Ordonnances des Rois," tome vi, p. 406, differs most essentially from that in Dupuy, and contains no mention whatever of the government. It is, therefore, easily reconcilable with the first, that confers the regency on the Duke of Anjou. As Dupuy took it from the same source as Sécousse—namely, the "Trésor des Chartes"—a strong suspicion of wilful interpolation falls upon him, or upon the editor of his posthumous work, printed in 1655. This date will readily suggest a motive for such an interpolation to those who recollect the circumstances of France at that time and for some years before, Anne of Austria having maintained herself in possession of a testamentary regency against the presumptive heir.

[123] Froissart, part iv, c. 46.

Charles VI had reigned five years from his assumption of power when he was seized with a derangement of intellect, which continued, through a series of recoveries and relapses, to his death. He passed thirty years in a pitiable state of suffering, neglected by his family, particularly by the most infamous of women, Isabel of Bavaria, his queen, to a degree which is hardly credible.[124] The ministers were immediately disgraced; the princes reassumed their stations. For several years the Duke of Burgundy conducted the government. But this was in opposition to a formidable rival, Louis, Duke of Orleans, the king's brother. It was impossible that a prince so near to the throne, favoured by the queen, perhaps with criminal fondness, and by the people on account of his external graces, should not acquire a share of power. He succeeded at length in obtaining the whole management of affairs, wherein the outrageous dissoluteness of his conduct, and still more the excessive taxes imposed, rendered him altogether odious. The Parisians compared his administration with that of the Duke of Burgundy, and from that time ranged themselves on the side of the latter and his family, throughout the long distractions to which the ambition of these princes gave birth.

The death of the Duke of Burgundy, in 1404, after several fluctuations of success between him and the Duke of Orleans, by no means left his party without a head. Equally brave and ambitious, but far more audacious and unprincipled, his son John, surnamed Sanspeur, sustained the same contest. A reconciliation had been, however, brought about with the Duke of Orleans; they had sworn reciprocal friendship, and participated, as was the custom, in order to render these obligations more solemn, in the same communion. In the midst of this outward harmony the Duke of Orleans was assassinated in the streets of Paris. After a slight attempt at concealment, Burgundy avowed and boasted of the crime, to which he had been instigated, it is said, by somewhat more than political jealousy.[125] From this fatal moment the dissensions of the royal family began to assume the complexion of civil war. The queen, the sons of the Duke of Orleans, with the Dukes of Berry and Bourbon, united against the assassin. But he possessed in addition to his own appanage of Burgundy, the county of Flanders as his maternal inheritance;

[124] Sismondi inclines to speak more favourably of this queen than most have done, " Dans les temps postérieurs on s'est plu à faire un monstre de Isabeau de Bavière." He discredits the suspicion of a criminal intercourse with the Duke of Orleans, and represents her as merely an indolent woman fond of good cheer. Yet he owns that the king was so neglected as to suffer from an excessive want of cleanliness, sometimes even from hun-ger (xii, 218, 225). Was this no imputation on his wife? See, too, Michelet, vi, 42.

[125] Orleans is said to have boasted of the Duchess of Burgundy's favours. (Vill., tome xii, p. 474.) Amelgard, who wrote about eighty years after the time, says, Vim etiam inferre attentare præsumpsit. (" Notices des Manuscrits du Roi," tome i, p. 411.)

and the people of Paris, who hated the Duke of Orleans, readily forgave, or rather exulted, in his murder.[126]

It is easy to estimate the weakness of the government, from the terms upon which the Duke of Burgundy was permitted to obtain pardon at Chartres, a year after the perpetration of the crime. As soon as he entered the royal presence every one rose, except the king, queen, and dauphin. The duke, approaching the throne, fell on his knees; when a lord, who acted as a sort of counsel for him, addressed the king: " Sire, the Duke of Burgundy, your cousin and servant, is come before you, being informed that he has incurred your displeasure, on account of what he caused to be done to the Duke of Orleans, your brother, for your good and that of your kingdom, as he is ready to prove when it shall please you to hear it, and therefore requests you, with all humility, to dismiss your resentment toward him, and to receive him into your favour." [127]

This insolent apology was all the atonement that could be extorted for the assassination of the first prince of the blood. It is not wonderful that the Duke of Burgundy soon obtained the management of affairs, and drove his adversaries from the capital. The princes, headed by the father-in-law of the young Duke of Orleans, the Count of Armagnac, from whom their party was now denominated, raised their standard against him; and the north of France was rent to pieces by a protracted civil war, in which neither party scrupled any extremity of pillage or massacre. Several times peace was made; but each faction, conscious of their own insincerity, suspected that of their adversaries. The king, of whose name both availed themselves, was only in some doubtful intervals of reason capable of rendering legitimate the acts of either. The dauphin, aware of the tyranny which the two

[126] Michelet represents this young prince as regretted and beloved; but his language is full of those strange contrasts and inconsistencies which, for the sake of effect, this most brilliant writer sometimes employs. " Il avait, dans ses emportemens de jeunesse, terriblement vexé le peuple; il fut maudit du peuple, pleuré du peuple. Vivant, il coûta bien de larmes; mais combien plus, mort! Si vous eussiez demandé à la France si ce jeune homme était bien digne de tante d'amour, elle eût repondu, Je l'aimais. Ce n'est pas seulement pour le bien qu'on aime; qui aime, aime tout, les défauts aussi. Celui-ci plut comme il était, mêlé de bien et de mal. (" Hist. de France," vi, 6.) What is the meaning of this love for one who, he has just told us, was cursed by the people? And if Paris was the representative of France, how did the people show their affection for the Duke of Orleans, when they were openly and vehemently the partisans of his murderer? On the first return of the Duke of Burgundy to Paris after the assassination, the citizens shouted Noel, the usual cry on the entrance of the king, to the great displeasure of the queen and other princes. " Et pour vrai, comme dit dessus, il estoit très fort aymé du commun peuple de Paris, et avoient grand espérance qu'iceluy duc eust très grand affection au royaume, et à la chose publicque, et avoient souvenance des grans tailles qui avoient esté mises sus depuis la mort du Duc Philippe de Bourgogne père d'iceluy, jusques à l'heure présente, lesquelles ils entendoient que feust par le moyen dudit Duc d'Orleans. Et pource estoit grandement encouru en l'indignation d'iceluy peuple, et leur sembloit que Dieu de sa grâce les avoit très-grandement   pour récommandez, quand il avoit souffert qu'ils fussent hors de sa subjection et governement, et qu'ils en estoient delivrez." (Monstrelet, 34.) Compare this with what M. Michelet has written.

[127] Monstrelet, part i, f. 112.

parties alternately exercised, was forced, even at the expense of perpetuating a civil war, to balance one against the other, and permit neither to be wholly subdued. He gave peace to the Armagnacs at Auxerre, in despite of the Duke of Burgundy; and, having afterward united with them against this prince, and carried a successful war into Flanders, he disappointed their revenge by concluding with him a treaty at Arras.

This dauphin and his next brother died within sixteen months of each other, by which the rank devolved upon Charles, youngest son of the king. The Count of Armagnac, now Constable of France, retained possession of the government. But his severity, and the weight of taxes, revived the Burgundian party in Paris, which a rigid proscription had endeavoured to destroy. He brought on his head the implacable hatred of the queen, whom he had not only shut out from public affairs, but disgraced by the detection of her gallantries. Notwithstanding her ancient enmity to the Duke of Burgundy, she made overtures to him, and, being delivered by his troops from confinement, declared herself openly on his side. A few obscure persons stole the city keys, and admitted the Burgundians into Paris. The tumult which arose showed in a moment the disposition of the inhabitants; but this was more horribly displayed a few days afterward, when the populace, rushing to the prisons, massacred the Constable d'Armagnac and his partisans. Between three and four thousand persons were murdered on this day, which has no parallel but what our own age has witnessed, in the massacre perpetrated by the same ferocious populace of Paris, under circumstances nearly similar. Not long afterward an agreement took place between the Duke of Burgundy, who had now the king's person as well as the capital in his hands, and the dauphin, whose party was enfeebled by the loss of almost all its leaders. This reconciliation, which mutual interest should have rendered permanent, had lasted a very short time, when the Duke of Burgundy was assassinated at an interview with Charles, in his presence, and by the hands of his friends, though not, perhaps, with his previous knowledge.[128] From whomsoever the crime proceeded, it was

[128] There are three suppositions conceivable to explain this important passage in history, the assassination of John Sanspeur. 1. It was pretended by the dauphin's friends at the time, and has been maintained more lately (St. Foix, "Essais sur Paris," tome iii, p. 209, edit. 1767), that he had premeditated the murder of Charles, and that his own was an act of self-defence. This is, I think, quite improbable: the dauphin had a great army near the spot, while the duke was only attended by five hundred men. Villaret, indeed, and St. Foix, in order to throw suspicion upon the Duke of Burgundy's

motives, assert that Henry V accused him of having made proposals to him which he could not accept without offending God; and conjecture that this might mean the assassination of the dauphin. But the expressions of Henry do not relate to any private proposals of the duke, but to demands made by him and the queen, as proxies for Charles VI in conference for peace, which he says he could not accept without offending God and contravening his own letters-patent. (Rymer, tome ix, p. 790.) It is not, however, very clear what this means. 2. The next hypothesis is, that it was the de-

a deed of infatuation, and plunged France afresh into a sea of perils, from which the union of these factions had just afforded a hope of extricating her.

It has been mentioned already that the English war had almost ceased during the reigns of Richard II and Henry IV. The former of these was attached by inclination, and latterly by marriage, to the court of France; and, though the French Government showed at first some disposition to revenge his dethronement, yet the new king's success, as well as domestic quarrels, deterred it from any serious renewal of the war. A long commercial connection had subsisted between England and Flanders, which the Dukes of Burgundy, when they became sovereigns of the latter country upon the death of Count Louis in 1384, were studious to preserve by separate truces.[129] They acted upon the same pacific policy when their interest predominated in the councils of France. Henry had even a negotiation pending for the marriage of his eldest son with a princess of Burgundy,[130] when an unexpected proposal from the opposite side set more tempting views before his eyes. The Armagnacs, pressed hard by the Duke of Burgundy, offered, in consideration of only four thousand troops, the pay of which they would themselves defray, to assist him in the recovery of Guienne and Poitou. Four princes of the blood—Berry, Bourbon, Orleans, and Alençon—disgraced their names by signing this treaty.[131] Henry broke off his alliance with Burgundy and sent a force into France, which found on its arrival that the princes had made a separate treaty, without the least concern for their English allies. After his death Henry V engaged for some time in a series of negotiations with the French court, where the Orleans party now prevailed, and with the Duke of Burgundy. He even secretly treated at the same time for a marriage with Catherine of France (which seems to have been his favourite, as it was ultimately his successful project), and with a daughter of the duke—a duplicity not creditable to his memory.[132] But Henry's ambition, which aimed at the highest quarry, was not long fettered by negotiation; and, indeed, his proposals of marrying Catherine were coupled with such exorbitant demands as France, notwithstanding all her weakness, could not admit,

liberate act of Charles. But his youth, his feebleness of spirit, and especially the consternation into which, by all testimonies, he was thrown by the event, are rather adverse to this explanation. 3. It remains only to conclude that Tanegui de Chastel, and other favourites of the dauphin, long attached to the Orleans faction, who justly regarded the duke as an infamous assassin, and might question his sincerity or their own safety if he should regain the ascendant, took advantage of this opportunity to commit an act of retaliation, less criminal, but not less ruinous in its consequences, than that which had provoked it. Charles, however, by his subsequent conduct, recognised their deed, and naturally exposed himself to the resentment of the young Duke of Burgundy.

[129] Rymer, tome viii, p. 511; Villaret, tome xii, p. 174.
[130] Rymer, tome viii, p. 721.
[131] Rymer, tome viii, pp. 726, 737, 738.
[132] Rymer, tome ix, p. 136.

though she would have ceded Guienne and given a vast dowry with the princess.[133] He invaded Normandy, took Harfleur, and won the great battle of Agincourt on his march to Calais.[134]

The flower of French chivalry was mowed down in this fatal day, but especially the chiefs of the Orleans party and the princes of the royal blood met with death or captivity. Burgundy had still suffered nothing; but a clandestine negotiation had secured the duke's neutrality, though he seems not to have entered into a regular alliance till a year after the battle of Agincourt, when, by a secret treaty at Calais, he acknowledged the right of Henry to the crown of France, and his own obligation to do him homage, though its performance was to be suspended till Henry should become master of a considerable part of the kingdom.[135] In a second invasion the English achieved the conquest of Normandy; and this, in all subsequent negotiations for peace during the life of Henry, he would never consent to relinquish. After several conferences, which his demands rendered abortive, the French court at length consented to add Normandy to the cessions made in the peace at Bretigni;[136] and the treaty, though labouring under some difficulties, seems to have been nearly completed when the Duke of Burgundy, for reasons unexplained, suddenly came to a reconciliation with the dauphin. This event, which must have been intended adversely to Henry, would probably have broken off all parley on the subject of peace if it had not been speedily followed by one still more surprising, the assassination of the Duke of Burgundy at Montereau.

An act of treachery so apparently unprovoked inflamed the minds of that powerful party which had looked up to the duke as their leader and patron. The city of Paris especially abjured at once its respect for the supposed author of the murder, though the legitimate heir of the crown. A solemn oath was taken by all ranks to revenge the crime; the nobility, the clergy, the Parliament, vying with the populace in their invectives against Charles, whom they now styled only pretended (soi-disant) dauphin. Philip, son of the assassinated duke, who, with all the popularity and much of the ability of his father, did not inherit

[133] The terms required by Henry's ambassadors in 1415 were the crown of France; or, at least, reserving Henry's rights to that, Normandy, Touraine, Maine, Guienne, with the homage of Brittany and Flanders. The French offered Guienne and Saintonge, and a dowry of 800,000 gold crowns for Catherine. The English demanded 2,000,000. (Rymer, tome ix, p. 218.)

[134] The English army at Agincourt was probably of not more that 15,000 men; the French were at the least 50,000, and, by some computations, much more numerous. They lost 10,000 killed, of whom 9,000 were knights or gentlemen. Almost as many were made prisoners. The English, according to Monstrelet, lost 1,600 men; but their own historians reduce this to a very small number. It is curious that the Duke of Berry, who advised the French to avoid an action, had been in the battle of Poitiers fifty-nine years before. (Vill., tome xiii, p. 355.)

[135] Compare Rymer, tome ix, pp. 34, 138, 304, 394. The last reference is to the Treaty of Calais.

[136] Rymer, tome ix, pp. 628, 763. Nothing can be more insolent than the tone of Henry's instructions to his commissioners, p. 628.

all his depravity, was instigated by a pardonable excess of filial resentment to ally himself with the King of England. These passions of the people and the Duke of Burgundy, concurring with the imbecility of Charles VI and the rancour of Isabel toward her son, led to the treaty of Troyes. This compact, signed by the queen and duke, as proxies of the king, who had fallen into a state of unconscious idiocy, stipulated that Henry V, upon his marriage with Catherine, should become immediately regent of France, and, after the death of Charles, succeed to the kingdom, in exclusion not only of the dauphin, but of all the royal family.[137] It is unnecessary to remark that these flagitious provisions were absolutely invalid. But they had at the time the strong sanction of force; and Henry might plausibly flatter himself with a hope of establishing his own usurpation as firmly in France as his father's had been in England. What not even the comprehensive policy of Edward III, the energy of the Black Prince, the valour of their Knollyses and Chandoses, nor his own victories could attain, now seemed, by a strange vicissitude of fortune, to court his ambition. During two years that Henry lived after the Treaty of Troyes he governed the north of France with unlimited authority in the name of Charles VI. The latter survived his son-in-law but a few weeks; and the infant Henry VI was immediately proclaimed King of France and England, under the regency of his uncle, the Duke of Bedford.

Notwithstanding the disadvantage of a minority, the English cause was less weakened by the death of Henry than might have been expected. The Duke of Bedford partook of the same character, and resembled his brother in faults as well as virtues; in his haughtiness and arbitrary temper as in his energy and address. At the accession of Charles VII the usurper was acknowledged by all the northern provinces of France, except a few fortresses, by most of Guienne, and the dominions of Burgundy. The Duke of Brittany soon afterward acceded to the Treaty of Troyes, but changed his party again several times within a few years. The central provinces, with Languedoc, Poitou, and Dauphiné, were faithful to the king. For some years the war continued without any decisive result; but the balance was clearly swayed in favour of England. For this it is not difficult to assign several causes. The animosity of the Parisians and the Duke of Burgundy against the Armagnac party still continued, min-

[137] As if through shame on account of what was to follow, the first articles contain petty stipulations about the dower of Catherine. The sixth gives the kingdom of France after Charles's decease to Henry and his heirs. The seventh concedes the immediate regency. Henry kept Normandy by right of conquest, not in virtue of any stipulation in the treaty, which he was too proud to admit. The Treaty of Troyes was confirmed by the States-General, or rather by a partial convention which assumed the name, in December, 1420. (Rymer, tome x, p. 30.) The Parliament of England did the same. (Id., p. 110.) It is printed at full length by Villaret, tome xv, p. 84.

gled in the former with dread of the king's return, whom they
judged themselves to have inexpiably offended. The war had
brought forward some accomplished commanders in the English
army, surpassing, not indeed in valour and enterprise, but in military skill, any whom France could oppose to them. Of these, the
most distinguished, besides the Duke of Bedford himself, were
Warwick, Salisbury, and Talbot. Their troops, too, were still
very superior to the French. But this, we must in candour allow,
proceeded in a great degree from the mode in which they were
raised. The war was so popular in England that it was easy
to pick the best and stoutest recruits,[138] and their high pay
allured men of respectable condition to the service. We find
in Rymer a contract of the Earl of Salisbury to supply a body of
troops, receiving a shilling a day for every man at arms, and six-
pence for each archer.[139] This is, perhaps, equal to fifteen times
the sum at our present value of money. They were bound, indeed,
to furnish their own equipments and horses. But France was
totally exhausted by her civil and foreign war, and incompetent
to defray the expenses even of the small force which defended the
wreck of the monarchy. Charles VII lived in the utmost poverty
at Bourges.[140] The nobility had scarcely recovered from the fatal
slaughter of Agincourt and the infantry, composed of peasants
or burgesses, which had made their army so numerous upon that
day, whether from inability to compel their services or experience of their inefficacy, were never called into the field. It became almost entirely a war of partisans. Every town in Picardy,
Champagne, Maine, or wherever the contest might be carried
on, was a fortress; and in the attack or defence of these garrisons
the valour of both nations was called into constant exercise.
This mode of warfare was undoubtedly the best in the actual
state of France, as it gradually improved her troops and flushed
them with petty successes. But what principally led to its adoption was the license and insubordination of the royalists, who,
receiving no pay, owned no control, and thought that, provided
they acted against the English and Burgundians, they were free
to choose their own points of attack. Nothing can more evidently
show the weakness of France than the high terms by which
Charles VII was content to purchase the assistance of some Scot-
tish auxiliaries. The Earl of Buchan was made constable; the
Earl of Douglas had the duchy of Touraine, with a new title,
lieutenant general of the kingdom. At a subsequent time Charles

---

[138] Monstrelet, part i, f. 303.
[139] Rymer, tome x, p. 392. This contract was for 600 men-at-arms, including
six bannerets and thirty-four bachelors;
and for 1,700 archers; bien et suffisam-
ment montez, armez, et arraiez comme
a leurs estats appartient. The pay was,

for the earl, 6s. 8d. a day; for a banneret, 4s.; for a bachelor, 2s.; for every
other man-at-arms, 1s.; and for each archer, 6d. Artillerymen were paid higher
than men-at-arms.
[140] Villaret, tome xiv, p. 302.

offered the province of Saintonge to James I for an aid of six thousand men. These Scots fought bravely for France, though unsuccessfully, at Crevant and Verneuil; but it must be owned they set a sufficient value upon their service. Under all these disadvantages it would be unjust to charge the French nation with any inferiority of courage, even in the most unfortunate periods of this war. Though frequently panic-struck in the field of battle, they stood sieges of their walled towns with matchless spirit and endurance. Perhaps some analogy may be found between the character of the French commonalty during the English invasion and the Spaniards of the late peninsular war. But to the exertions of those brave nobles who restored the monarchy of Charles VII Spain has afforded no adequate parallel.

It was, however, in the temper of Charles VII that his enemies found their chief advantage. This prince is one of the few whose character has been improved by prosperity. During the calamitous morning of his reign he shrank from fronting the storm, and strove to forget himself in pleasure. Though brave, he was never seen in war; though intelligent, he was governed by flatterers. Those who had committed the assassination at Montereau under his eyes were his first favourites; as if he had determined to avoid the only measure through which he could hope for better success, a reconciliation with the Duke of Burgundy. The Count de Richemont, brother of the Duke of Brittany, who became afterward one of the chief pillars of his throne, consented to renounce the English alliance and accept the rank of constable on condition that these favourites should quit the court. Two others, who successively gained a similar influence over Charles, Richemont publicly caused to be assassinated, assuring the king that it was for his own and the public good. Such was the debasement of morals and government which twenty years of civil war had produced! Another favourite, La Tremouille, took the dangerous office, and, as might be expected, employed his influence against Richemont, who for some years lived on his own domains, rather as an armed neutral than a friend, though he never lost his attachment to the royal cause.

It can not, therefore, surprise us that with all these advantages the regent Duke of Bedford had almost completed the capture of the fortresses north of the Loire when he invested Orleans in 1428. If this city had fallen, the central provinces, which were less furnished with defensible places, would have lain open to the enemy, and it is said that Charles VII in despair was about to retire into Dauphiné. At this time his affairs were restored by one of the most marvellous revolutions in history. A country girl overthrew the power of England. We can not pretend to explain the surprising story of the Maid of Orleans; for, however easy it may be to suppose that a heated and enthusiastic imagination produced her own visions, it is a much greater problem to account for the credit they obtained and for the success that attended her. Nor will this be solved by the hypothesis of a concerted stratagem; which, if we do not judge altogether from events, must appear liable to so many chances of failure that it could not have suggested itself to any rational person. However, it is certain that the appearance of Joan of Arc turned the tide of war, which from that moment flowed without interruption in Charles's favour. A superstitious awe enfeebled the sinews of the English. They hung back in their own country, or deserted from the army, through fear of the incantations by which alone they conceived so extraordinary a person to succeed.[141] As men always make sure of Providence for an ally, whatever untoward fortune appeared to result from preternatural causes was at once ascribed to infernal enemies; and such bigotry may be pleaded as an excuse, though a very miserable one, for the detestable murder of this heroine.[142]

The spirit which Joan of Arc had roused did not subside. France recovered confidence in her own strength, which had been chilled by a long course of adverse fortune. The king, too, shook off his indolence,[143] and permitted Richemont to exclude his un-

[141] Rymer, tome x, pp. 458–472. This, however, is conjecture; for the cause of their desertion is not mentioned in these proclamations, though Rymer has printed it in their title. But the Duke of Bedford speaks of the turn of success as astonishing, and due only to the superstitious fear which the English had conceived of a female magician. (Rymer, tome x, p. 408.)

[142] M. de l'Averdy, to whom we owe the copious account of the proceedings against Joan of Arc, as well as those which Charles VII instituted in order to rescind the former, contained in the third volume of " Notices des Manuscrits du Roi," has justly made this remark, which is founded on the eagerness shown by the University of Paris in the prosecution, and on its being conducted before an inquisitor ; a circumstance exceedingly remarkable in the ecclesiastical history of France. But another material observation arises out of this. The maid was pursued with peculiar bitterness by her countrymen of the English, or rather Burgundian, faction; a proof that in 1430 their animosity against Charles VII was still ardent. [Note XVI.]

[143] It is a current piece of history that Agnes Sorel, mistress of Charles VII, had the merit of dissuading him from giving up the kingdom as lost at the time when Orleans was besieged in 1428. Mezeray, Daniel, Villaret, and, I believe, every other modern historian, have mentioned this circumstance; and some of them, among whom is Hume, with the addition that Agnes threatened to leave

the court of Charles for that of Henry, affirming that she was born to be the mistress of a great king. The latter part of this tale is evidently a fabrication, Henry VI being at the time a child of seven years old. But I have, to say the least, great doubts of the main story. It is not mentioned by contemporary writers. On the contrary, what they say of Agnes leads me to think the dates incompatible. Agnes died (in childbed, as some say) in 1450, twenty-two years after the siege of Orleans. Monstrelet says that she had been about five years in the service of the queen; and the king taking pleasure in her liveliness and wit, common fame had spread abroad that she lived in concubinage with him. She certainly had a child, and was willing that it should be thought the king's; but he always denied it, et le pouvoit bien avoir emprunté ailleurs. (Part iii, f. 25.) Olivier de la Marche, another contemporary, who lived in the court of Burgundy, says, about the year 1444, le roy avoit nouvellement eslevé une pauvre demoiselle, gentifemme, nommée Agnes Sorel, et mis en tel triumphe et tel pouvoir, que son estat estoit à comparer aux grandes princesses de royaume, et certes c'estoit une des plus belles femmes que je vey oncques, et fit en sa qualité beaucoup au royaume de France. Elle avançoit devers le roy jeunes gens d'armes et gentils compaignons, et dont le roy depuis fut bien servy. (La Marche, " Mém. Hist.," tome viii, p. 145.) Du Clercq, whose memoirs were first published in the same collection, says that Agnes

worthy favourites from the court. This led to a very important consequence. The Duke of Burgundy, whose alliance with England had been only the fruit of indignation at his father's murder, fell naturally, as that passion wore out, into sentiments more congenial to his birth and interests. A prince of the house of Capet could not willingly see the inheritance of his ancestors transferred to a stranger. And he had met with provocation both from the regent and the Duke of Gloucester, who, in contempt of all policy and justice, had endeavoured, by an invalid marriage with Jacqueline, Countess of Hainault and Holland, to obtain provinces which Burgundy designed for himself. Yet the union of his sister with Bedford, the obligations by which he was bound, and, most of all, the favour shown by Charles VII to the assassins of his father, kept him for many years on the English side, although rendering it less and less assistance. But at length he concluded a treaty at Arras, the terms of which he dictated rather as a conqueror than a subject negotiating with his sovereign. Charles, however, refused nothing for such an end; and, in a very short time, the Burgundians were ranged with the French against their old allies of England.

It was now time for the latter to abandon those magnificent projects of conquering France which temporary circumstances

mourut par poison moult jeune. (Ib., tome viii, p. 410.) And the continuator of Monstrelet, probably John Chartier, speaks of the youth and beauty of Agnes, which exceeded that of any other woman in France, and of the favour shown her by the king, which so much excited the displeasure of the dauphin, on his mother's account, and he was suspected of having caused her to be poisoned (fol. 68). The same writer affirms of Charles VII that he was, before the Peace of Arras, de moult belle vie et devote; but afterward enlaidit sa vie tenir malles femmes en son hostel, etc. (fol. 86).

It is for the reader to judge how far these passages render it improbable that Agnes Sorel was the mistress of Charles VII at the siege of Orleans in 1428, and, consequently, whether she is entitled to the praise which she has received, of being instrumental in the deliverance of France. The tradition, however, is as ancient as Francis I, who made in her honour a quatrain which is well known. This probably may have brought the story more into vogue, and led Mezeray, who was not very critical, to insert it in his history, from which it has passed to his followers. Its origin was apparently the popular character of Agnes. She was the Nell Gwyn of France; and justly beloved, not only for her charity and courtesy, but for bringing forward men of merit, and turning her influence, a virtue very rare in her class, toward the public interest. From thence it was natural to bestow upon her, in after-

times, a merit not ill suited to her character, but which an accurate observation of dates seems to render impossible. But whatever honour I am compelled to detract from Agnes Sorel, I am willing to transfer undiminished to a more unblemished female, the injured Queen of Charles VII, Mary of Anjou, who has hitherto only shared with the usurper of her rights the credit of awakening Charles from his lethargy. Though I do not know on what foundation even this rests, it is not unlikely to be true, and, in deference to the sex, let it pass undisputed.

Sismondi (vol. xiii, p. 204), where he first mentions Agnes Sorel, says that many of the circumstances told of her influence over Charles VII are fabulous. " Cependant il faut bien qu'Agnès ait mérité, en quelque manière, la reconnoissance qui s'est attachée à son nom." This is a loose and inconclusive way of reasoning in history; many popular traditions have no basis at all. And in p. 345 he slights the story told in Brantôme to the honour of Agnes, as well he might, since it is ridiculously untrue that she threatened Charles to go to the court of Henry VI, knowing herself to be born to be the mistress of a great king. Sismondi afterward (pp. 497 and 604) quotes, as I have done, Chartier and Jacques du Clercq; but without adverting to the incongruity of their dates with the current story. M. Michelet does not seem to attach much credit to it, though he adopts the earlier date for the king's attachment to Agnes.

alone had seemed to render feasible. But as it is a natural effect of good fortune in the game of war to render a people insensible to its gradual change, the English could not persuade themselves that their affairs were irretrievably declining. Hence they rejected the offer of Normandy and Guienne, subject to the feudal superiority of France, which was made to them at the congress of Arras; [144] and some years afterward, when Paris, with the adjacent provinces, had been lost, the English ambassadors, though empowered by their private instructions to relax, stood upon demands quite disproportionate to the actual position of affairs.[145] As foreign enemies they were odious even in that part of France which had acknowledged Henry; [146] and when the Duke of Burgundy deserted their side, Paris and every other city were impatient to throw off the yoke. A feeble monarchy and a selfish council completed their ruin: the necessary subsidies were raised with difficulty, and, when raised, misapplied. It is a proof of the exhaustion of France that Charles was unable for several years to reduce Normandy or Guienne, which were so ill provided for defence.[147] At last he came with collected strength to the contest, and, breaking an armistice upon slight pretences, within two years overwhelmed the English garrisons in each of these provinces. All the inheritance of Henry II and Eleanor, all the conquests of Edward III and Henry V except Calais and a small adjacent district, were irrecoverably torn from the crown of England. A barren title, that idle trophy of disappointed ambition, was preserved with strange obstinacy to our own age.

In these second English wars we find little left of that generous feeling which had in general distinguished the contemporaries of Edward III. The very virtues which a state of hostility promotes are not proof against its long continuance, and sink at last into brutal fierceness. Revenge and fear excited the two factions of Orleans and Burgundy to all atrocious actions. The troops serving under partisans on detached expeditions, according to the system of the war, lived at free quarters on the people. The histories of the time are full of their outrages, from which, as is the common case, the unprotected peasantry most suf-

[144] Villaret says, Les plénipotentiaires de Charles offrirent la cession de la Normandie et de la Guienne en toute propriété sous la clause de l'hommage à la couronne (tome xv, p. 174). But he does not quote his authority, and I do not like to rely on a historian not eminent for accuracy in fact or precision in language. If his expression is correct, the French must have given up the feudal appeal or ressort which had been the great point in dispute between Edward III and Charles V, preserving only a homage per paragium, as it was called, which implied no actual supremacy. Monstrelet says only, que per certaines conditions luy seroient accordées les seigneuries de Guienne et Normandie.

[145] See the instructions given to the English negotiators in 1439, at length, in Rymer, tome x, p. 724.

[146] Villaret, tome xiv, p. 448.

[147] Amelgard, from whose unpublished memoirs of Charles VII and Louis XI some valuable extracts are made in the " Notices des Manuscrits," tome i, p. 403, attributes the delay in recovering Normandy solely to the king's slothfulness and sensuality. In fact, the people of that province rose upon the English and almost emancipated themselves with little aid from Charles.

fered.[148]   Even those laws of war which the courteous sympathies of chivalry had enjoined were disregarded by a merciless fury. Garrisons surrendering after a brave defence were put to death. Instances of this are very frequent.   Henry V excepts Alain Blanchard, a citizen who had distinguished himself during the siege, from the capitulation of Rouen, and orders him to execution.   At the taking of a town of Champagne, John of Luxemburg, the Burgundian general, stipulates that every fourth and sixth man should be at his discretion, which he exercises by causing them all to be hanged.[149]   Four hundred English from Pontoise, stormed by Charles VII in 1441, are paraded in chains and naked through the streets of Paris, and thrown afterward into the Seine.   This infamous action can not but be ascribed to the king.[150]

At the expulsion of the English, France emerged from the chaos with an altered character and new features of government. The royal authority and supreme jurisdiction of the Parliament were universally recognised.   Yet there was a tendency toward insubordination left among the great nobility, arising in part from the remains of old feudal privileges, but still more from that lax administration which, in the convulsive struggles of the war, had been suffered to prevail.   In the south were some considerable vassals, the houses of Foix, Albret, and Armagnac, who, on account of their distance from the seat of empire, had always maintained a very independent conduct.   The Dukes of Brittany and Burgundy were of a more formidable character, and might rather be ranked among foreign powers than privileged subjects. The princes, too, of the royal blood, who, during the late reign, had learned to partake or contend for the management, were ill inclined toward Charles VII, himself jealous, from old recollec-

[148] Monstrelet, passim. A long metrical complaint of the people of France, curious as a specimen of versification, as well as a testimony to the misfortunes of the time, may be found in this historian, part i, fol. 321.   Notwithstanding the Treaty of Arras, the French and Burgundians made continual incursions upon each other's frontiers, especially about Laon and in the Vermandois.   So that the people had no help, says Monstrelet, si non de crier miserablement à Dieu leur createur vengeance ; et que pis estoit, quand ils obtenoient aucun saufconduit d'aucuns capitaines, peu en estoit entretenu, mesmement tout d'un parti. (Part ii, fol. 139.)   These pillagers were called Écorcheurs, because they stripped the people of their shirts. And this name superseded that of Armagnacs, by which one side had hitherto been known.   Even Xaintrailles and La Hire, two of the bravest champions of France, were disgraced by these habits of outrage. (Ibid., fols. 144, 150, 175; Oliv. de la Marche, in

" Collect. des Mémoires," tome viii, p. 25; tome v, p. 323.)

Pour la plupart, says Villaret, se faire guerrier, ou voleur de grands chemins, signifioit la même chose.

[149] Monstrelet, part ii, f. 79. This John of Luxemburg, Count de Ligny, was a distinguished captain on the Burgundian side, and for a long time would not acquiesce in the Treaty of Arras. He disgraced himself by giving up to the Duke of Bedford his prisoner Joan of Arc for 10,000 francs. The famous Count of St. Pol was his nephew, and inherited his great possessions in the county of Vermandois.   Monstrelet relates a singular proof of the good education which his uncle gave him. Some prisoners having been made in an engagement, si fut le jeune Comte de St. Pol mis en voye de guerre; car le Comte de Ligny son oncle luy en feit occire aucuns, le quel y prenoit grand plaisir. (Part ii, fol. 95.)

[150] Villaret, tome xv, p. 327.

tions, of their ascendency. They saw that the constitution was verging rapidly toward an absolute monarchy, from the direction of which they would studiously be excluded. This apprehension gave rise to several attempts at rebellion during the reign of Charles VII, and to the war, commonly entitled, for the Public Weal (du bien public), under Louis XI. Among the pretences alleged by the revolters in each of these, the injuries of the people were not forgotten; [151] but from the people they received small support. Weary of civil dissension, and anxious for a strong government to secure them from depredation, the French had no inducement to intrust even their real grievances to a few malcontent princes, whose regard for the common good they had much reason to distrust. Every circumstance favoured Charles VII and his son in the attainment of arbitrary power. The country was pillaged by military ruffians. Some of these had been led by the dauphin to a war in Germany, but the remainder still infested the high roads and villages. Charles established his companies of ordonnance, the basis of the French regular army, in order to protect the country from such depredators. They consisted of about nine thousand soldiers, all cavalry, of whom fifteen hundred were heavy armed; a force not very considerable, but the first, except mere body-guards, which had been raised in any part of Europe as a national standing army.[152] These troops were paid out of the produce of a permanent tax, called the taille; an innovation still more important than the former. But the present benefit cheating the people, now prone to submissive habits, little or no opposition was made, except in Guienne, the inhabitants of which had speedy reason to regret the mild government of England, and vainly endeavoured to return to its protection.[153]

[151] The confederacy formed at Nevers in 1441 by the Dukes of Orleans and Bourbon, with many other princes, made a variety of demands, all relating to the grievances which different classes of the state, or individuals among themselves, suffered under the administration of Charles. These may be found at length in Monstrelet, part ii, fol. 193, and are a curious document of the change which was then working in the French constitution. In his answer the king claims the right, in urgent cases, of levying taxes without waiting for the consent of the States-General.
[152] Olivier de la Marche speaks very much in favour of the companies of ordonnance as having repressed the plunderers and restored internal police. ("Collect. des Mémoires," tome viii, p. 148.) Amelgard pronounces a vehement philippic against them, but it is probable that his observation of the abuses they had fallen into was confined to the reign of Louis XI. ("Notices des Manuscrits," ubi supra.)
[153] The insurrection of Guienne in 1452,

which for a few months restored that province to the English crown, is accounted for in the curious memoirs of Amelgard, above mentioned. It proceeded solely from the arbitrary taxes imposed by Charles VII in order to defray the expenses of his regular army. The people of Bordeaux complained of exactions not only contrary to their ancient privileges, but to the positive conditions of their capitulation. But the king was deaf to such remonstrances. The province of Guienne, he says, then perceived that it was meant to subject it to the same servitude as the rest of France, where the leeches of the state boldly maintain as a fundamental maxim that the king has a right to tax all his subjects how and when he pleases; which is to advance that in France no man has anything that he can call his own, and that the king can take all at his pleasure; the proper condition of slaves, whose peculium enjoyed by their master's permission belongs to him, like their persons, and may be taken away whenever he chooses. Thus situated, the people of

It was not long before the new despotism exhibited itself
in its harshest character. Louis XI, son of Charles VII, who
during his father's reign had been connected with the discontented
princes, came to the throne greatly endowed with those virtues
and vices which conspire to the success of a king. Laborious
vigilance in business, contempt of pomp, affability to inferiors,
were his excellences; qualities especially praiseworthy in an age
characterized by idleness, love of pageantry, and insolence. To
these virtues he added a perfect knowledge of all persons eminent
for talents or influence in the countries with which he was connected and a well-judged bounty, that thought no expense wasted
to draw them into his service or interest. In the fifteenth century this political art had hardly been known, except perhaps in
Italy; the princes of Europe had contended with each other by
arms, sometimes by treachery, but never with such complicated
subtlety of intrigue. Of that insidious cunning, which has since
been brought to perfection, Louis XI may be deemed not absolutely the inventor, but the most eminent improver; and its success has led, perhaps, to too high an estimate of his abilities.
Like most bad men, he sometimes fell into his own snare, and
was betrayed by his confidential ministers, because his confidence
was generally reposed in the wicked. And his dissimulation
was so notorious, his tyranny so oppressive, that he was naturally
surrounded by enemies, and had occasion for all his craft to elude
those rebellions and confederacies which might perhaps not have
been raised against a more upright sovereign.[154] At one time the
monarchy was on the point of sinking before a combination which
would have ended in dismembering France. This was the league
denominated of the Public Weal, in which all the princes and
great vassals of the French crown were concerned: the Dukes
of Brittany, Burgundy, Alençon, Bourbon, the Count of Dunois,
so renowned for his valour in the English wars, the families of
Foix and Armagnac; and at the head of all, Charles, Duke of
Berry, the king's brother and presumptive heir. So unanimous
a combination was not formed without a strong provocation from

Guienne, especially those of Bordeaux,
alarmed themselves, and, excited by some
of the nobility, secretly sought about for
means to regain their ancient freedom;
and having still many connections with
persons of rank in England, they negotiated with them, etc. ("Notices des
Manuscrits," p. 433.) The same cause is
assigned to this revolution by Du Clercq,
also a contemporary writer, living in the
dominions of Burgundy. ("Collection
des Mémoires," tome ix, p. 400.) Villaret
has not known, or not chosen to know,
anything of the matter.
    [154] Sismondi (vol. xiv, p. 312) and
Michelet (vol. ix, p. 347) agree in thinking Louis XI no worse than other kings
of his age; in fact, the former seems rarely to make a distinction between one
king and another. Louis was just and
even attentive toward the lower people,
and spared the blood of his soldiers.
But he had imbibed a notion that treachery and cruelty could not be carried too
far against his enemies, and especially
against his rebellious subjects. Louis
composed for his son's use, or caused to
be composed, a political treatise entitled
"Le Rosier des Guerres," which has
never been published. It is written in a
spirit of public morality very unlike his
practice. (Sismondi, vol. xiv, p. 616.)
Thus two royal anti-Machiavels have
satirized themselves.

the king, or at least without weighty grounds for distrusting his intentions; but the more remote cause of this confederacy, as of those which had been raised against Charles VII, was the critical position of the feudal aristocracy from the increasing power of the crown. This war of the Public Weal was, in fact, a struggle to preserve their independence; and from the weak character of the Duke of Berry, whom they would, if successful, have placed upon the throne, it is possible that France might have been in a manner partitioned among them in the event of their success, or, at least, that Burgundy and Brittany would have thrown off the sovereignty that galled them.[155]

The strength of the confederates in this war much exceeded that of the king, but it was not judiciously employed; and after an indecisive battle at Montlhéry they failed in the great object of reducing Paris, which would have obliged Louis to fly from his dominions. It was his policy to promise everything, in trust that fortune would afford some opening to repair his losses and give scope to his superior prudence. Accordingly, by the Treaty of Conflans, he not only surrendered afresh the towns upon the Somme, which he had lately redeemed from the Duke of Burgundy, but invested his brother with the duchy of Normandy as his appanage.

The term appanage denotes the provision made for the younger children of a King of France. This always consisted of lands and feudal superiorities held of the crown by the tenure of peerage. It is evident that this usage, as it produced a new class of powerful feudatories, was hostile to the interests and policy of the sovereign, and retarded the subjugation of the ancient aristocracy. But a usage coeval with the monarchy was not to be abrogated, and the scarcity of money rendered it impossible to provide for the younger branches of the royal family by any other means. It was restrained, however, as far as circumstances would permit. Philip IV declared that the county of Poitiers, bestowed by him on his son, should revert to the crown on the extinction of male heirs. But this, though an important precedent, was not, as has often been asserted, a general law. Charles V limited the appanages of his own sons to twelve thousand livres of annual value in land. By means of their appanages, and through the operation of the Salic law, which made their inheritance of the crown a less remote contingency, the princes of the blood royal in France were at all times (for the remark is applicable long after Louis XI) a distinct and formidable

[155] Sismondi has a just observation on the League of the Public Weal. " Le nom seul du Bien Public, qui fut donné à cette ligue, était un hommage au progrès des lumières; c'était la profession d'un principe qui n'avait point encore été proclamé; c'est que le bien public doit être le but du gouvernement; mais les princes qui s'associaient pour l'obtenir étaient encore bien peu en état de connaître sa nature " (xiv, 161).

class of men, whose influence was always disadvantageous to the reigning monarch, and, in general, to the people.

No appanage had ever been granted to France so enormous as the duchy of Normandy. One third of the whole national revenue, it is declared, was derived from that rich province. Louis could not, therefore, sit down under such terms as, with his usual insincerity, he had accepted at Conflans. In a very short time he attacked Normandy, and easily compelled his brother to take refuge in Brittany; nor were his enemies ever able to procure the restitution of Charles's appanage. During the rest of his reign Louis had powerful coalitions to withstand; but his prudence and compliance with circumstances, joined to some mixture of good fortune, brought him safely through his perils. The Duke of Brittany, a prince of moderate talents, was unable to make any formidable impression, though generally leagued with the enemies of the king. The less powerful vassals were successfully crushed by Louis with decisive vigour; the duchy of Alençon was confiscated; the Count of Armagnac was assassinated; the Duke of Nemours and the Constable of St. Pol, a politician as treacherous as Louis, who had long betrayed both him and the Duke of Burgundy, suffered upon the scaffold. The king's brother Charles, after disquieting him for many years, died suddenly in Guienne, which had finally been granted as his appanage, with strong suspicions of having been poisoned by the king's contrivance.[156] Edward IV of England was too dissipated and too indolent to be fond of war; and, though he once entered France with an army more considerable than could have been expected after such civil bloodshed as England had witnessed, he was induced, by the stipulation of a large pension, to give up the enterprise.[157] So terrible was still in France the apprehension of an English war that Louis prided himself upon no part of his policy so much as the warding this blow. Edward showed a desire to visit Paris; but the king gave him no invitation, lest, he said, his brother should find some handsome women there, who might tempt him to return in a different manner. Hastings, Howard, and others of Edward's ministers were secured by bribes in the interest of Louis, which the first of these did not scruple to receive at the same time from the Duke of Burgundy.[158]

---

[156] Sismondi, however, and Michelet do not believe that the Duke of Guienne was poisoned by his brother; he had been ill for several months.

[157] The army of Edward consisted of 1,500 men at arms and 14,000 archers, the whole very well appointed. (Comines, tome xi, p. 238.) There seems to have been a great expectation of what the English would do, and great fears entertained by Louis, who grudged no expense to get rid of them.

[158] Comines, l. vi, c. 2. Hastings had the mean cunning to refuse to give his receipt for the pension he took from Louis XI. "This present," he said to the king's agent, "comes from your master's good pleasure, and not at my request; and if you mean I should receive it, you may put it here into my sleeve, but you shall have no discharge from me; for I will not have it said that the Great Chamberlain of England is a pensioner of the King of France, nor

This was the most powerful enemy whom the craft of Louis had to counteract. In the last days of the feudal system, when the house of Capet had almost achieved the subjugation of those proud vassals among whom it had been originally numbered, a new antagonist sprang up to dispute the field against the crown. John, King of France, granted the duchy of Burgundy, by way of appanage, to his third son, Philip. By his marriage with Margaret, heiress of Louis, Count of Flanders, Philip acquired that province, Artois, the county of Burgundy (or Franche-comté), and the Nivernois. Philip the Good, his grandson, who carried the prosperity of this family to its height, possessed himself, by various titles, of the several other provinces which composed the Netherlands. These were fiefs of the empire, but latterly not much dependent upon it, and alienated by their owners without its consent. At the Peace of Arras the districts of Macon and Auxerre were absolutely ceded to Philip, and great part of Picardy conditionally made over to him, redeemable on the payment of four hundred thousand crowns.[159] These extensive though not compact dominions were abundant in population and wealth, fertile in corn, wine, and salt, and full of commercial activity. Thirty years of peace which followed the Treaty of Arras, with a mild and free government, raised the subjects of Burgundy to a degree of prosperity quite unparalleled in these times of disorder, and this was displayed in general sumptuousness of dress and feasting. The court of Philip and of his son Charles was distinguished for its pomp and riches, for pageants and tournaments, the trappings of chivalry, perhaps without its spirit; for the military character of Burgundy had been impaired by long tranquility.[160]

During the lives of Philip and Charles VII each understood the other's rank, and their amity was little interrupted. But their

have my name appear in the books of the Chambres des Comptes." (Ibid.)

[159] The Duke of Burgundy was personally excused from all homage and service to Charles VII; but, if either died, it was to be paid by the heir, or to the heir. Accordingly, on Charles's death Philip did homage to Louis. This exemption can hardly, therefore, have been inserted to gratify the pride of Philip, as historians suppose. Is it not probable that, during his resentment against Charles, he might have made some vow never to do him homage, which this reservation in the treaty was intended to preserve?

It is remarkable that Villaret says the Duke of Burgundy was positively excused by the twenty-fifth article of the Peace of Arras from doing homage to Charles, or his successors Kings of France (tome xvi, p. 404). For this assertion, too, he seems to quote the "Trésor des Chartes," where, probably,

the original treaty is preserved. Nevertheless, it appears otherwise, as published by Monstrelet at full length, who could have no motive to falsify it; and Philip's conduct in doing homage to Louis is hardly compatible with Villaret's assertion. Daniel copies Monstrelet without any observation. In the same treaty Philip is entitled duke by the grace of God, which was reckoned a mark of independence, and not usually permitted to a vassal.

[160] P. de Comines, l. i, c. 2 and 3; l. v, c. 9. Du Clercq, in "Collection des Mémoires," tome ix, p. 389. In the investiture granted by John to the first Philip of Burgundy a reservation is made that the royal taxes shall be levied throughout that appanage. But during the long hostility between the kingdom and duchy this could not have been enforced, and by the Treaty of Arras Charles surrendered all right to tax the duke's dominions. (Monstrelet, fol. 114.)

successors, the most opposite of human kind in character, had one common quality—ambition—to render their antipathy more powerful. Louis was eminently timid and suspicious in policy; Charles intrepid beyond all men, and blindly presumptuous: Louis stooped to any humiliation to reach his aim; Charles was too haughty to seek the fairest means of strengthening his party. An alliance of his daughter with the Duke of Guienne, brother of Louis, was what the malcontent French princes most desired and the king most dreaded; but Charles, either averse to any French connection, or willing to keep his daughter's suitors in dependence, would never directly accede to that or any other proposition for her marriage. On Philip's death, in 1467, he inherited a great treasure, which he soon wasted in the prosecution of his schemes. These were so numerous and vast that he had not time to live, says Comines, to complete them, nor would one half of Europe have contented him. It was his intention to assume the title of king; and the Emperor Frederick III was at one time actually on his road to confer this dignity, when some suspicion caused him to retire, and the project was never renewed.[161] It is evident that, if Charles's capacity had borne any proportion to his pride and courage, or if a prince less politic than Louis XI had been his contemporary in France, the province of Burgundy must have been lost to the monarchy. For several years these great rivals were engaged, sometimes in open hostility, sometimes in endeavours to overreach each other; but Charles, though not much more scrupulous, was far less an adept in these mysteries of politics than the king.

Notwithstanding the power of Burgundy, there were some disadvantages in its situation. It presented (I speak of all Charles's dominions under the common name Burgundy) a very exposed frontier on the side of Germany and Switzerland, as well as France; and Louis exerted a considerable influence over the adjacent princes of the empire as well as the United Cantons. The people of Liège, a very populous city, had for a long time been continually rebelling against their bishops, who were the allies of Burgundy; Louis was, of course, not backward to foment their insurrections, which sometimes gave the dukes a good deal

[161] Garnier, tome xviii, p. 62. It is observable that Comines says not a word of this; for which Garnier seems to quote Belcarius, a writer of the sixteenth age. But even Philip, when Morvilliers, Louis's chancellor, uses menaces toward him, interrupted the orator with these words, Je veux que chacun seache que, si j'eusse voulu, je fusse roi. (Villaret, tome xvii, p. 44.)
Charles had a vague notion of history, and confounded the province or duchy of Burgundy, which had always appertained to the French crown, with Franche-comté and other countries which had belonged to the kingdom of Burgundy. Hence he talked at Dijon, in 1473, to the estates of the former, about the kingdom of Burgundy, " que ceux de France ont longtems usurpé et d'icelui fait duché; que tous les sujets doivent bien avoir à regret, et dit qu'il avait en soi des choses qu'il n'appartenait de savoir à nul qu'à dui." Michelet (ix, 162) is the first who has published this.

of trouble. The Flemings, and especially the people of Ghent, had been during a century noted for their republican spirit and contumacious defiance of their sovereign. Liberty never wore a more unamiable countenance than among these burghers, who abused the strength she gave them by cruelty and insolence. Ghent, when Froissart wrote, about the year 1400, was one of the strongest cities in Europe, and would have required, he says, an army of two hundred thousand men to besiege it on every side, so as to shut up all access by the Lys and Scheldt. It contained eighty thousand men of age to bear arms; [162] a calculation which, although, as I presume, much exaggerated, is evidence of great actual populousness. Such a city was absolutely impregnable at a time when artillery was very imperfect both in its construction and management. Hence, though the citizens of Ghent were generally beaten in the field with great slaughter, they obtained tolerable terms from their masters, who knew the danger of forcing them to a desperate defence.

No taxes were raised in Flanders, or, indeed, throughout the dominions of Burgundy, without consent of the three estates. In the time of Philip not a great deal of money was levied upon the people; but Charles obtained every year a pretty large subsidy, which he expended in the hire of Italian and English mercenaries.[163] An almost uninterrupted success had attended his enterprises for a length of time, and rendered his disposition still more overweening. His first failure was before Neuss, a little town near Cologne, the possession of which would have made him nearly master of the whole course of the Rhine, for he had already obtained the landgraviate of Alsace. Though compelled to raise the siege, he succeeded in occupying next year the duchy of Lorraine. But his overthrow was reserved for an enemy whom he despised, and whom none could have thought equal to the contest. The Swiss had given him some slight provocation, for which they were ready to atone; but Charles was unused to for-

[162] Froissart, part ii, c. 67.
[163] Comines, l. iv, c. 13. It was very reluctantly that the Flemings granted any money. Philip once begged for a tax on salt, promising never to ask anything more; but the people of Ghent, and, in imitation of them, the whole county, refused it. (Du Clercq, p. 389.) Upon his pretence of taking the cross, they granted him a subsidy, though less than he had requested, on condition that it should not be levied if the crusade did not take place, which put an end to the attempt. The states knew well that the duke would employ any money they gave him in keeping up a body of gens-d'armes, like his neighbour, the King of France; and though the want of such a force exposed their country to pillage, they were too good patriots to place the means of en-

slaving it in the hands of their sovereign. Grand doute faisoient les sujets, et pour plusieurs raisons, de se mettre en cette sujetion où ils voyoient le royaume de France, à cause de ses gens-d'armes. A la vérité, leur grand doute n'estoit pas sans cause; car quand il se trouva cinq cens hommes d'armes, la volonté luy vint d'en avoir plus, et de plus hardiment entreprendre contre tous ses voisins. (Comines, l. iii, c. 4, 9.)

Du Clercq, a contemporary writer of very good authority, mentioning the story of a certain widow who had re-married the day after her husband's death, says that she was in some degree excusable, because it was the practice of the duke and his officers to force rich widows into marrying their soldiers or other servants (tome ix, p. 418).

bear; and perhaps Switzerland came within his projects of conquest. At Granson, in the Pays de Vaud, he was entirely routed,
with more disgrace than slaughter.[164] But having reassembled
his troops, and met the confederate army of Swiss and Germans
at Morat, near Friburg, he was again defeated with vast loss.
On this day the power of Burgundy was dissipated: deserted by
his allies, betrayed by his mercenaries, he set his life upon another cast at Nancy, desperately giving battle to the Duke of
Lorraine with a small dispirited army, and perished in the engagement.

Now was the moment when Louis, who had held back while
his enemy was breaking his force against the rocks of Switzerland, came to gather a harvest which his labour had not reaped.
Charles left an only daughter, undoubted heiress of Flanders and
Artois, as well as of his dominions out of France, but whose right
of succession to the duchy of Burgundy was more questionable.
Originally the great fiefs of the crown descended to females, and
this was the case with respect to the two first mentioned. But
John had granted Burgundy to his son Philip by way of appanage, and it was contended that the appanages reverted to the
crown in default of male heirs. In the form of Philip's investiture,
the duchy was granted to him and his lawful heirs, without designation of sex. The construction, therefore, must be left to the
established course of law. This, however, was by no means acknowledged by Mary, Charles's daughter, who maintained both
that no general law restricted appanages to male heirs, and that
Burgundy had always been considered as a feminine fief, John
himself having possessed it, not by reversion as king (for descendants of the first dukes were then living), but by inheritance
derived through females.[165] Such was this question of succession
between Louis XI and Mary of Burgundy, upon the merits of
whose pretensions I will not pretend altogether to decide, but
shall only observe that, if Charles had conceived his daughter
to be excluded from this part of his inheritance, he would probably, at Conflans or Peronne, where he treated upon the vantage

[164] A famous diamond, belonging to
Charles of Burgundy, was taken in the
plunder of his tent by the Swiss at Granson. After several changes of owners,
most of whom were ignorant of its value,
it became the first jewel in the French
crown. (Garnier, tome xviii, p. 361.)

[165] It is advanced with too much confidence by several French historians, either
that the ordinances of Philip IV and
Charles V constituted a general law
against the descent of appanages to female heirs, or that this was a fundamental law of the monarchy. (Du Clos, " Hist.
de Louis XI," tome ii, p. 252; Garnier,
" Hist. de France," tome xviii, p. 258.)
The latter position is refuted by frequent

instances of female succession; thus Artois had passed, by a daughter of Louis
le Male, into the house of Burgundy. As
to the above-mentioned ordinances, the
first applies only to the county of Poitiers; the second does not contain a
syllable that relates to succession. (" Ordonnances des Rois," tome vi, p. 54.)
The doctrine of excluding female heirs
was more consonant to the pretended
Salic law, and the recent principles as
to inalienability of domain than to the
analogy of feudal rules and precedents.
M. Gaillard, in his " Observations sur
l'Histoire de Velly, Villaret, et Garnier,"
has a judicious note on this subject (tome
iii, p. 304).

ground, have attempted at least to obtain a renunciation of Louis's claim.

There was one obvious mode of preventing all further contest and of aggrandizing the French monarchy far more than by the reunion of Burgundy. This was the marriage of Mary with the dauphin, which was ardently wished for in France. Whatever obstacles might occur to this connection, it was natural to expect on the opposite side—from Mary's repugnance to an infant husband, or from the jealousy which her subjects were likely to entertain of being incorporated with a country worse governed than their own. The arts of Louis would have been well employed in smoothing these impediments.[166] But he chose to seize upon as many towns as, in those critical circumstances, lay exposed to him, and stripped the young duchess of Artois and Franche-comté. Expectations of the marriage he sometimes held out, but, as it seems, without sincerity. Indeed, he contrived irreconcilably to alienate Mary by a shameful perfidy, betraying the ministers whom she had intrusted upon a secret mission to the people of Ghent, who put them to the torture, and afterward to death, in the presence and amid the tears and supplications of their mistress. Thus the French alliance becoming odious in France, this princess married Maximilian of Austria, son of the Emperor Frederick—a connection which Louis strove to prevent, though it was impossible then to foresee that it was ordained to retard the growth of France and to bias the fate of Europe during three hundred years. This war lasted till after the death of Mary, who left one son, Philip, and one daughter, Margaret. By a treaty of peace concluded at Arras, in 1482, it was agreed that this daughter should become the dauphin's wife, with Franche-comté and Artois, which Louis held already, for her dowry, to be restored in case the marriage should not take effect. The homage of Flanders was reserved to the crown.

Meanwhile Louis was lingering in disease and torments of mind, the retribution of fraud and tyranny. Two years before his death he was struck with an apoplexy, from which he never wholly recovered. As he felt his disorder increasing, he shut himself up in a palace near Tours, to hide from the world the knowledge of his decline.[167] His solitude was like that of Tiberius

---

[166] Robertson, as well as some other moderns, have maintained, on the authority of Comines, that Louis XI ought in policy to have married the young princess to the Count of Angoulême, father of Francis I, a connection which she would not have disliked. But certainly nothing could have been more adverse to the interests of the French monarchy than such a marriage, which would have put a new house of Burgundy at the head of those princes whose confederacies had so often endangered the crown. Comines is one of the most judicious of historians; but his sincerity may be rather doubtful in the opinion above mentioned, for he wrote in the reign of Charles VIII, when the Count of Angoulême was engaged in the same faction as himself.

[167] For Louis's illness and death see Comines, l. vi, c. 7-12, and Garnier, tome xix, p. 112, etc. Plessis, his last resi-

at Capreæ, full of terror and suspicion, and deep consciousness of universal hatred. All ranks, he well knew, had their several injuries to remember: the clergy, whose liberties he had sacrificed to the see of Rome, by revoking the Pragmatic Sanction of Charles VII; the princes, whose blood he had poured upon the scaffold; the Parliament, whose course of justice he had turned aside; the commons, who groaned under his extortion, and were plundered by his soldiery.[168] The palace, fenced with portcullises and spikes of iron, was guarded by archers and cross-bow men, who shot at any that approached by night. Few entered this den; but to them he showed himself in magnificent apparel, contrary to his former custom, hoping thus to disguise the change of his meagre body. He distrusted his friends and kindred, his daughter and his son, the last of whom he had not suffered even to read or write lest he should too soon become his rival. No man ever so much feared death, to avert which he stooped to every meanness and sought every remedy. His physician had sworn that if he were dismissed the king would not survive a week; and Louis, enfeebled by sickness and terror, bore the rudest usage from this man, and endeavoured to secure his services by vast rewards. Always credulous in relics, though seldom restrained by superstition from any crime,[169] he eagerly bought up treasures of this sort, and even procured a Calabrian hermit, of noted sanctity, to journey as far as Tours in order to restore his health. Philip de Comines, who attended him during his infirmity, draws a parallel between the torments he then endured and those he had formerly inflicted on others. Indeed, the whole of his life was vexation of spirit. " I have known him," says Comines, " and been his servant in the flower of his age, and in the time of his greatest prosperity; but never did I see him without uneasiness and care. Of all amusements, he loved only the chase, and hawking in its season. And in this he had almost as much uneasiness as pleasure: for he rode hard and got up early, and sometimes went a great way, and regarded no weather; so that he used to return very weary, and almost ever

---

dence, about an English mile from Tours, is now a dilapidated farmhouse, and can never have been a very large building. The vestiges of royalty about it are few, but the principal apartments have been destroyed, either in the course of ages or at the revolution.

[168] See a remarkable chapter in Philip de Comines, l. iv, c. 19, wherein he tells us that Charles VII had never raised more than 1,800,000 francs a year in taxes; but Louis XI, at the time of his death, raised 4,700,000, exclusive of some military impositions ; et surement c'estoit compassion de voir et scavoir la pauvreté du peuple. In this chapter he declares his opinion that no king can justly levy money on his subjects without their consent, and repels all common arguments to the contrary.

[169] An exception to this was when he swore by the cross of St. Lo, after which he feared to violate his oath. The constable of St. Pol, whom Louis invited with many assurances to court, bethought himself of requiring this oath before he trusted his promises, which the king refused, and St. Pol prudently stayed away. (Garn., tome xviii, p. 72.) Some report that he had a similar respect for a leaden image of the Virgin, which he wore in his hat, as alluded to by Pope:
" A perjured prince a leaden saint revere."

in wrath with some one. I think that from his childhood he
never had any respite of labour and trouble to his death. And
I am certain that if all the happy days of his life, in which he
had more enjoyment than uneasiness, were numbered, they would
be found very few; and at least that they would be twenty of
sorrow for every one of pleasure.[170]

Charles VIII was about thirteen years old when he succeeded
his father Louis. Though the law of France fixed the majority
of her kings at that age, yet it seems not to have been strictly
regarded on this occasion, and at least Charles was a minor by
nature, if not by law. A contest arose, therefore, for the regency,
which Louis had intrusted to his daughter Anne, wife of the lord
De Beaujeu, one of the Bourbon family. The Duke of Orleans,
afterward Louis XII, claimed it as presumptive heir of the
crown, and was seconded by most of the princes. Anne, however, maintained her ground, and ruled France for several
years in her brother's name with singular spirit and address,
in spite of the rebellions which the Orleans party raised up
against her. These were supported by the Duke of Brittany,
the last of the great vassals of the crown, whose daughter, as
he had no male issue, was the object of as many suitors as Mary
of Burgundy.

The duchy of Brittany was peculiarly circumstanced. The
inhabitants, whether sprung from the ancient republicans of
Armorica, or, as some have thought, from an emigration of
Britons during the Saxon invasion, had not originally belonged
to the body of the French monarchy. They were governed by
their own princes and laws, though tributary, perhaps, as the
weaker to the stronger, to the Merovingian kings.[171] In the ninth
century the Dukes of Brittany did homage to Charles the Bald,
the right of which was transferred afterward to the Dukes of
Normandy. This formality, at that time no token of real subjection, led to consequences beyond the views of either party.
For when the feudal chains that had hung so loosely upon the
shoulders of the great vassals began to be straightened by the
dexterity of the court, Brittany found itself drawn among the
rest to the same centre. The old privileges of independence

[170] Comines, l. vi, c. 13.
[171] Gregory of Tours says that the Bretons were subject to France from the death of Clovis, and that their chiefs were styled counts, not kings (l. iv, c. 4). Charlemagne subdued the whole of Brittany. Yet it seems clear from Nigellus, author of a metrical life of Louis the Debonair, that they were again almost independent. There was even a march of the Britannic frontier, which separated it from France. In the ensuing reign of Charles the Bald, Hincmar tells us, regnum undique a Paganis, et falsis Christianis, scilicet Britonibus circumscriptum est. ("Epist.," c. 8. See, too, "Capitularia Car. Calvi," A. D. 877, tit. 23.) At this time a certain Nomenoe had assumed the crown of Brittany, and some others in succession bore the name of king. They seem, however, to have been feudally subject to France. Charles the Simple ceded to the Normans whatever right he possessed over Brittany; and the dukes of that country (the name of king was now dropped) always did homage to Normandy. See Daru, "Hist. de Bretagne."

were treated as usurpation; the dukes were menaced with confiscation of their fief, their right of coining money disputed, their
jurisdiction impaired by appeals to the Parliament of Paris. However, they stood boldly upon their right, and always refused to
pay liege homage, which implied an obligation of service to the
lord, in contradistinction to simple homage, which was a mere
symbol of feudal dependence.[172]

About the time that Edward III made pretension to the crown
of France a controversy somewhat resembling it arose in the
duchy of Brittany, between the families of Blois and Montfort.
This led to a long and obstinate war, connected all along, as a
sort of underplot, with the great drama of France and England.
At last Montfort, Edward's ally, by the defeat and death of his
antagonist, obtained the duchy, of which Charles V soon after
gave him the investiture. This prince and his family were generally inclined to English connections, but the Bretons would
seldom permit them to be effectual. Two cardinal feelings guided
the conduct of this brave and faithful people; the one, an attachment to the French nation and monarchy in opposition to
foreign enemies; the other, a zeal for their own privileges and
the family of Montfort, in opposition to the encroachments of
the crown. In Francis II, the present duke, the male line of that
family was about to be extinguished. His daughter Anne was
naturally the object of many suitors, among whom were particularly distinguished the Duke of Orleans, who seems to have been
preferred by herself; the Lord of Albret, a member of the Gascon
family of Foix, favoured by the Breton nobility, as most likely
to preserve the peace and liberties of their country, but whose
age rendered him not very acceptable to a youthful princess;
and Maximilian, King of the Romans. Brittany was rent by factions and overrun by the armies of the regent of France, who
did not lose this opportunity of interfering with its domestic
troubles and of persecuting her private enemy, the Duke of Orleans. Anne of Brittany, upon her father's death, finding no other
means of escaping the addresses of Albret, was married by proxy
to Maximilian. This, however, aggravated the evils of the country, since France was resolved at all events to break off so dangerous a connection. And as Maximilian himself was unable,
or took not sufficient pains, to relieve his betrothed wife from
her embarrassments, she was ultimately compelled to accept the
hand of Charles VIII.[173] He had long been engaged by the
Treaty of Arras to marry the daughter of Maximilian, and that

[172] Villaret, tome xii, p. 82; tome xv, p.
199.
[173] This is one of the coolest violations
of ecclesiastical law in comparatively
modern times. Both contracts, especially
that of Anne, were obligatory, so far at
least that they could not be dissolved
without papal dispensation. This was
obtained, but it bears date eight days
after the ceremony between Charles and
Anne. (Sismondi, xv, 106.)

princess was educated at the French court. But this engagement
had not prevented several years of hostilities, and continual intrigues with the towns of Flanders against Maximilian. The
double injury which the latter sustained in the marriage of Charles
with the heiress of Brittany seemed likely to excite a protracted
contest; but the King of France, who had other objects in view,
and perhaps was conscious that he had not acted a fair part,
soon came to an accommodation, by which he restored Artois
and Franche-comté. Both these provinces had revolted to Maximilian, so that Charles must have continued the war at some
disadvantage.[174]

France was now consolidated into a great kingdom: the feudal
system was at an end. The vigour of Philip Augustus, the paternal wisdom of St. Louis, the policy of Philip the Fair, had laid
the foundations of a powerful monarchy, which neither the arms
of England, nor seditions of Paris, nor rebellions of the princes,
were able to shake. Besides the original fiefs of the French
crown, it had acquired two countries beyond the Rhône, which
properly depended only upon the empire, Dauphiné, under Philip
of Valois, by the bequest of Humbert, the last of its princes; and
Provence, under Louis XI, by that of Charles of Anjou.[175] Thus
having conquered herself, if I may use the phrase, and no longer
apprehensive of any foreign enemy, France was prepared, under
a monarch flushed with sanguine ambition, to carry her arms into

[174] Sismondi, xv, 135.

[175] The country now called Dauphiné
formed part of the kingdom of Arles or
Provence, bequeathed by Rodolph III to
the Emperor Conrad II. But the dominion of the empire over these new acquisitions being little more than nominal, a
few of the chief nobility converted their
respective fiefs into independent principalities. One of these was the lord or
Dauphin of Vienne, whose family became
ultimately masters of the whole province.
Humbert, the last of these, made John,
son of Philip of Valois, his heir, on condition that Dauphiné should be constantly preserved as a separate possession, not
incorporated with the kingdom of France.
This request was confirmed by the Emperor Charles IV, whose supremacy over
the province was thus recognised by the
Kings of France, though it soon came to
be altogether disregarded. Sismondi (xiv,
3) dates the reunion of Dauphiné to the
crown from 1457, before which time it
was governed by the dauphin for the
time being as a foreign sovereignty.

Provence, like Dauphiné, was changed
from a feudal dependency to a sovereignty, in the weakness and dissolution
of the kingdom of Arles, about the early
part of the eleventh century. By the
marriage of Douce, heiress of the first line
of sovereign counts, with Raymond Be-

renger, Count of Barcelona, in 1112, it
passed into that distinguished family.
In 1167 it was occupied or usurped by
Alfonso II, King of Aragon, a relation,
but not heir, of the house of Berenger.
Alfonso bequeathed Provence to his
second son, of the same name, from whom
it descended to Raymond Berenger IV.
This count dying without male issue in
1245, his youngest daughter Beatrice
took possession by virtue of her father's
testament. But this succession being disputed by other claimants, and especially
by Louis IX, who had married her eldest
sister, she compromised differences by
marrying Charles of Anjou, the king's
brother. The family of Anjou reigned in
Provence, as well as in Naples, till the
death of Joan in 1382, who, having no
children, adopted Louis, Duke of Anjou,
brother of Charles V, as her successor.
This second Angevine line ended in 1481
by the death of Charles III; though
Regnier, Duke of Lorraine, who was descended through a female, had a claim
which it does not seem easy to repel by
argument. It was very easy, however,
for Louis XI, to whom Charles III had
bequeathed his rights, to repel it by
force, and accordingly he took possession
of Provence, which was permanently
united to the crown by letters-patent of
Charles VIII in 1486.*

* " Art de vérifier les Dates," tome ii, p. 445; Garnier, tome xix, pp. 57, 474.

other countries, and to contest the prize of glory and power upon the ample theatre of Europe.[176]

[176] The principal authority, exclusive of original writers, on which I have relied for this chapter, is the "History of France," by Velly, Villaret, and Garnier; a work which, notwithstanding several defects, has absolutely superseded those of Mezeray and Daniel. The part of the Abbé Velly comes down to the middle of the eighth volume (12mo edition), and of the reign of Philip de Valois. His continuator, Villaret, was interrupted by death in the seventeenth volume, and in the reign of Louis XI. In my references to this history, which for common facts I have not thought it necessary to make, I have merely named the author of the particular volume which I quote. This has made the above explanation convenient, as the reader might imagine that I refer to three distinct works. Of these three historians, Garnier, the last, is the most judicious, and, I believe, the most accurate. His prolixity, though a material defect, and one which has occasioned the work itself to become an immeasurable undertaking, which could never be completed on the same scale, is chiefly occasioned by too great a regard to details, and is more tolerable than a similar fault in Villaret, proceeding from a love of idle declamation and sentiment. Villaret, however, is not without merits. He embraces, perhaps more fully than his predecessor Velly, those collateral branches of history which an enlightened reader requires almost in preference to civil transactions, the laws, manners, literature, and in general the whole domestic records of a nation. These subjects are not always well treated ; but the book itself, to which there is a remarkably full index, forms, upon the whole, a great repository of useful knowledge. Villaret had the advantage of official access to the French archives, by which he has no doubt enriched his history; but his references are indistinct, and his composition breathes an air of rapidity and want of exactness. Velly's characteristics are not very dissimilar. The style of both is exceedingly bad, as has been severely noticed, along with their other defects, by Gaillard, in "Observations sur l'Histoire de Velly, Villaret, et Garnier" (4 vols., 12mo, Paris, 1806).

[This history is now but slightly esteemed in France, especially the volumes written by the Abbé Velly. The writers were too much imbued with the spirit of the old monarchy (though no adulators of kings, and rather liberal according to the standard of their own age) for those who have taken the sovereignty of the people for their creed. Nor are they critical and exact enough for the present state of historical knowledge. Sismondi and Michelet, especially the former, are doubtless superior; but the reader will not find in the latter as regular a narration of facts as in Velly and Villaret. Sismondi has as many prejudices on one side as they have on the opposite. (1848.)]

CHAPTER II

THE FEUDAL SYSTEM, ESPECIALLY IN FRANCE

State of ancient Germany—Effects of the conquest of Gaul by the Franks—Tenures of land—Distinction of laws—Constitution of the ancient Frank monarchy—Gradual establishment of feudal tenures—Principles of a feudal relation—Ceremonies of homage and investiture—Military service—Feudal incidents of relief, aid, wardship, etc.—Different species of fiefs—Feudal law-books—Analysis of the feudal system— Its local extent—View of the different orders of society during the feudal ages— Nobility—Their ranks and privileges—Clergy—Freemen—Serfs or villains—Comparative state of France and Germany—Privileges enjoyed by the French vassals— Right of coining money, and of private war—Immunity from taxation—Historical view of the royal revenue in France—Methods adopted to augment it by depreciation of the coin, etc.—Legislative power—Its state under the Merovingian kings and Charlemagne—His councils—Suspension of any general legislative authority during the prevalence of feudal principles—The king's council—Means adopted to supply the want of a national assembly—Gradual progress of the king's legislative power—Philip IV assembles the States-General—Their powers limited to taxation —States under the sons of Philip IV—States of 1355 and 1356—They nearly effect an entire revolution—The crown recovers its vigour—States of 1380, under Charles VI—Subsequent assemblies under Charles VI and Charles VII—The crown becomes more and more absolute—Louis XI—States of Tours in 1484—Historical view of the earliest stage under the first race of kings and Charlemagne—Territorial jurisdiction—Feudal courts of justice—Trial by combat— Code of St. Louis—The territorial jurisdictions give way—Progress of the judicial power of the crown—Parliament of Paris—Peers of France—Increased authority of the Parliament—Registration of edicts—Causes of the decline of the feudal system—Acquisitions of domain by the crown—Charters of incorporation granted to towns—Their previous condition—First charters in the twelfth century—Privileges contained in them—Military service of feudal tenants commuted for money—Hired troops—Change in the military system of Europe—General view of the advantages and disadvantages attending the feudal system.

GERMANY, in the age of Tacitus, was divided among a number of independent tribes, differing greatly in population and importance. Their country, overspread with forests and morasses, afforded no large proportion of arable land. Nor did they ever occupy the same land two years in succession, if what Cæsar tells us may be believed, that fresh allotments were annually made by the magistrates.[1] But this could not have been an absolute abandonment of land once cultivated, which Horace ascribes to the migratory Scythians. The Germans had fixed though not contiguous dwellings; and the inhabitants of the Gau or township must have continued to till

---

[1] Magistratus ac principes in annos singulos gentibus cognationibusque hominum, qui una coierunt, quantum iis, et quo loco visum est, attribuunt agri, at- que anno post alio transire cogunt. Cæsar, l. vi. Tacitus confirms this: Arva per annos mutant. (" De Mor. Germ.," c. 26.)

the same fields, though it might be with varying rights of separate property.[2] They had kings elected out of particular families; and other chiefs, both for war and administration of justice, whom merit alone recommended to the public choice. But the power of each was greatly limited; and the decision of all leading questions, though subject to the previous deliberation of the chieftains, sprang from the free voice of a popular assembly.[3] The principal men, however, of a German tribe fully partook of that estimation which is always the reward of valour and commonly of birth. They were surrounded by a cluster of youths, the most gallant and ambitious of the nation, their pride at home, their protection in the field; whose ambition was flattered, or gratitude conciliated, by such presents as a leader of barbarians could confer. These were the institutions of the people who overthrew the empire of Rome, congenial to the spirit of infant societies, and such as travellers have found among nations in the same stage of manners throughout the world. And although, in the lapse of four centuries between the ages of Tacitus and Clovis, some change was wrought by long intercourse with the Romans, yet the foundations of their political system were unshaken. If the Salic laws were in the main drawn up before the occupation of Gaul by the Franks, as seems the better opinion, it is manifest that lands were held by them in determinate several possession; and in other respects it is impossible that the manners described by Tacitus should not have undergone some alteration.[4]

When these tribes from Germany and the neighbouring countries poured down upon the empire, and began to form permanent settlements, they made a partition of the lands in the conquered provinces between themselves and the original possessors. The Burgundians and Visigoths took two thirds of their respective conquests, leaving the remainder to the Roman proprietor. Each Burgundian was quartered, under the gentle name of guest, upon one of the former tenants, whose reluctant hospitality confined him to the smaller portion of his estate.[5] The Vandals in

---

[2] Cæsar has not written, probably, with accurate knowledge when he says: Vita omnis in venationibus et studiis rei militaris consistit. . . . Agriculturæ non student, nec quisquam agri modum certum aut fines proprios habet. (" De Bello Gallico," I. vi.) These expressions may be taken so as not to contradict Tacitus. But Luden, who had examined the ancient history of his country with the most persevering diligence, observes that Cæsar knew nothing of the Germans, except what he had collected concerning the Suevi or the Marcomanni. (" Geschichte der Deutschen Volker," i, 481.)

[3] De minoribus rebus principes consultant, de majoribus omnes; ita tamen, ut ea quoque, quorum penes plebem arbitrium est, apud principes pertractentur.

(" Tac. de Mor. Germ.," c. xi.) Acidalius and Grotius contend for prætractentur: which would be neater, but the same sense appears to be conveyed by the common reading.

[4] [Note I.]

[5] " Leg. Burgund.," c. 54, 55. Sir F. Palgrave has produced a passage from the Theodosian code, vii, 8, 5, which illustrates this use of the word hospes. It was given to the military quartered upon the inhabitants anywhere in the empire, and thus transferred by analogy to the barbarian occupants. It was needless, I should think, for him to prove that these acquisitions, " better considered as allodial laws," did not contain the germ of feudality. " There is no Gothic feudality unless the parties be connected by

Africa, a more furious race of plunderers, seized all the best lands.[6] The Lombards of Italy took a third part of the produce. We can not discover any mention of a similar arrangement in the laws or history of the Franks. It is, however, clear that they occupied, by public allotment or individual pillage, a great portion of the lands of France.[7]

The estates possessed by the Franks as their property were termed allodial; a word which is sometimes restricted to such as had descended by inheritance.[8] These were subject to no burden except that of public defence. They passed to all the children equally, or, in their failure, to the nearest kindred.[9] But of these allodial possessions there was a particular species, denominated Salic, from which females were expressly excluded. What these lands were, and what was the cause of the exclusion, has been much disputed. No solution seems more probable than that the ancient lawgivers of the Salian Franks prohibited females from inheriting the lands assigned to the nation upon its conquest of Gaul, both in compliance with their ancient usages and in order to secure the military service of every proprietor. But lands subsequently acquired by purchase or other means, though equally bound to the public defence, were relieved from the severity of this rule, and presumed not to belong to the class of Salic.[10]

the mutual bond of vassalage and seigniory." (" Eng. Commonw.," i, 500.)
[6] " Procopius de Bello Vandal.," l. i, c. 5.
[7] [Note II.]
[8] Allodial lands are commonly opposed to beneficiary or feudal; the former being strictly proprietary, while the latter depended upon a superior. In this sense the word is of continual recurrence in ancient histories, laws, and instruments. It sometimes, however, bears the sense of inheritance, and this seems to be its meaning in the famous sixty-second chapter of the Salic law; de Alodis. Alodium interdum opponitur comparato, says Du Cange, in formulis veteribus. Hence, in the charters of the eleventh century, hereditary fiefs are frequently termed alodia. (" Recueil des Historiens de France," tome xi, préface. Vaissette, " Hist. de Languedoc," tome ii, p. 109.) Alodium has by many been derived from All and odh, property. (Du Cange, et alii.) But M. Guizot, with some positiveness, brings it from loos, lot; thus confining the word to lands acquired by lot on the conquest. But in the first place this assumes a regular partition to have been made by the Franks, which he, in another place, as has been seen, does not acknowledge ; and, secondly, Alodium, or, in its earlier form, Alodis, is used for all hereditary lands. (See Grimm, " Deutsche Rechts Alterthümer," p. 492.) In the Orkneys, where feudal tenures were not introduced, the allodial proprietor is called an udaller, thus lend-

ing probability to the former derivation of alod; since it is only an inversion of the words all and odh; but it seems also to corroborate the notion of Luden, as it had been of Leibnitz, that the word adel or ethel, applied to designate the nobler class of Germans, had originally the same sense; it distinguished absolute or allodial property from that which, though belonging to freemen, was subject to some conditions of dependency. (" Gesch. des Deutschen Volkes," vol. i, p. 719.)
The word sors, which seems to have misled several writers, when applied to land means only an integral patrimony, as it means capital opposed to interest when applied to money. It is common in the civil law, and is no more than the Greek κλῆρος ; but it had been peculiarly applied to the lands assigned by the Romans to the soldiery after a conquest, which some suppose, I know not on what evidence, to have been by lot. (Du Cange, voc. Sors.) And hence this term was most probably adopted by the barbarians, or rather those who rendered their laws into Latin. If the Teutonic word loos was sometimes used for a mansus or manor, as M. Guizot informs us, it seems most probable that this was a literal translation of sors, bearing with it the secondary sense.
[9] " Leg. Salicæ," c. 62.
[10] By the German customs, women, though treated with much respect and delicacy, were not endowed at their marriage. Dotem non uxor marito, sed maritus uxori confert. (Tacitus, c. 18.)

Hence, in the Ripuary law, the code of a tribe of Franks settled upon the banks of the Rhine, and differing rather in words than in substance from the Salic law, which it serves to illustrate, it is said that a woman can not inherit her grandfather's estate (hæreditas aviatica), distinguishing such family property from what the father might have acquired.[11] And Marculfus uses expressions to the same effect. There existed, however, a right of setting aside the law, and admitting females to succession by testament. It is rather probable, from some passages in the Burgundian code, that even the lands of partition (sortes Burgundionum) were not restricted to male heirs.[12] And the Visigoths admitted women on equal terms to the whole inheritance.[13]

A controversy has been maintained in France as to the condition of the Romans, or rather the provincial inhabitants of Gaul, after the invasion of Clovis. But neither those who have considered the Franks as barbarian conquerors, enslaving the former possessors, nor the Abbé Dubos, in whose theory they appear as allies and friendly inmates, are warranted by historical

A similar principle might debar them of inheritance in fixed possessions. Certain it is that the exclusion of females was not infrequent among the Teutonic nations. We find it in the laws of the Thuringians and of the Saxons ; both ancient codes, though not free from interpolation. (Leibnitz, " Scriptores Rerum Brunswicensium," tome i, pp. 81 and 83.) But this usage was repugnant to the principles of Roman law, which the Franks found prevailing in their new country, and to the natural feeling which leads a man to prefer his own descendants to collateral heirs. One of the precedents in Marculfus (l. ii, form. 12) calls the exclusion of females, diuturna et impia consuetudo. In another a father addresses his daughter : Omnibus non habetur incognitum, quod, sicut lex Salica continet, de rebus meis, quod mihi ex alode parentum meorum obvenit, apud germanos tuos filios meos minime in hæreditate succedere poteras. (Formulæ Marculfo adjectæ, 49.) These precedents are supposed to have been compiled about the latter end of the seventh century.

The opinion expressed in the text, that the terra Salica, which females could not inherit, was the land acquired by the barbarians on their first conquest, is confirmed by Sismondi (i, 196) and by Guizot (" Essais sur l'Hist. de France," p. 94). M. Guerard, however, the learned editor of the chartulary of Chartres (" Documens Inédits," 1840, p. 22), is persuaded that Salic land was that of the domain, from sala, the hall or principal residence, as opposed to the portion of the estate which was occupied by tenants, beneficiary or servile. This, he says, .he has proved in another work, which I have not seen. Till I have done so, much doubt remains to me as to this explanation. Montesquieu had already started

the same theory, which Guizot justly, as it seems, calls " incomplète et hypothétique." Besides other objections, it seems not to explain the manifest identity between the terra Salica and the hæreditas aviatica of the Ripuarian law, or the alodis parentum of Marculfus. I ought, however, to mention a remark of Grimm, that throughout the Frank domination German countries made use of the words terra Salica. In them it could not mean lands of partition or assignment, but mere alodia. And he thinks that it may, in most cases, be interpreted of the terra dominicalis. (" Deutsche Rechts Alterthümer," p. 493.)

M. Fauriel maintains (" Hist. de la Gaule Méridion.," ii, 18) that the Salic lands were beneficiary, as opposed to the allodial. But the " hæreditas aviatica " is repugnant to this. Marculfus distinctly opposes alodia to comparata, and limits the exclusion of daughters to the former. According to one of the most recent inquirers, " terra Salica " was all the land held by a Salian Frank. (Lehuerou, i, 86.) But the same objections apply to this solution; in addition to which it may be said that the whole Salic law relates to that people, while " terra Salica " is plainly descriptive of a peculiar character of lands.

[11] C. 56.

[12] I had in former editions asserted the contrary of this, on the authority of " Leg. Burgund.," c. 78, which seemed to limit the succession of estates, called sortes, to male heirs. But the expressions are too obscure to warrant this inference; and M. Guizot (" Essais sur l'Hist. de France," vol. i, p. 95) refers to the fourteenth chapter of the same code for the opposite proposition. But this, too, is not absolutely clear, as a general rule.

[13] [Note III.]

facts, though more approximation to the truth may be found in the latter hypothesis. On the one hand, we find the Romans not only possessed of property, and governed by their own laws, but admitted to the royal favour and the highest offices; [14] while the bishops and clergy, who were generally of that nation,[15] grew up continually in popular estimation, in riches, and in temporal sway. Yet it is undeniable that a marked line was drawn at the outset between the conquerors and the conquered. Though one class of Romans retained estates of their own, yet there was another, called tributary, who seem to have cultivated those of the Franks, and were scarcely raised above the condition of predial servitude. But no distinction can be more unequivocal than that which was established between the two nations, in the weregild, or composition for homicide. Capital punishment for murder was contrary to the spirit of the Franks, who, like most barbarous nations, would have thought the loss of one citizen ill repaired by that of another. The weregild was paid to the relations of the slain, according to a legal rate. This was fixed by the Salic law at six hundred solidi for an Antrustion of the king; at three hundred for a Roman conviva regis (meaning a man of sufficient rank to be admitted to the royal table); [16] at two hundred for a

[14] Daniel conjectures that Clotaire I was the first who admitted Romans into the army, which had previously been composed of Franks. From this time we find many in high military command. (" Hist. de la Milice Françoise," tome i, p. 11.) It seems by a passage in Gregory of Tours, quoted by Dubos (tome iii, p. 547), that some Romans affected the barbarian character by letting their hair grow. If this were generally permitted, it would be a stronger evidence of approximation between the two races than any that Dubos has adduced. Montesquieu certainly takes it for granted that a Roman might change his law, and thus become to all material intents a Frank. (" Esprit des Loix," l. xxviii, c. 4.) But the passage on which he relies is read differently in the manuscripts. [Note IV.]

[15] The barbarians by degrees got hold of bishoprics. In a list of thirty-four bishops or priests present at a council in 506, says M. Fauriel (iii, 459), the names are all Roman or Greek. This was at Agde, in the dominion of the Visigoths. In 511 a council at Orleans exhibits one German name. But at the fifth Council of Paris, in 577, where forty-five bishops attended, the Romans are indeed much the more numerous, but mingled with barbaric names, six of whom M. Thierry mentions. (" Récits des Temps Mérovingiens," vol. ii, p. 183.) In 585, at Macon, out of sixty-three names but six are German. Fauriel asserts that, in a diploma of Clovis II dated 653, there are but five Roman names out of forty-five witnesses; and hence he in-

fers that by this time the Franks had seized on the Church as their spoil, filling it with barbarian prelates. But on reference to " Rec. des Hist." (iv, 636), I find but four of the witnesses to this instrument qualified as episcopus: and of these two have Roman names. The majority may have been laymen for any evidence which the diploma presents. In one, however, of Clovis III, dated 693 (id., p. 672), I find, among twelve bishops, only three names which appear Roman. We can not always judge by the modernization of a proper name. St. Leger sounds well enough; but in his life we find a " Beatus Leodegarius ex progenie celsa Francorum ac nobilissima exortus." Greek names are exceedingly common among the bishops, but these can not mislead an attentive reader.

This inroad of Franks into the Church probably accelerated the utter prostration of intellectual power, at least in its literary manifestation, which throws so dark a shade over the seventh century. And it still more unquestionably tended to the secular, the irregular, the warlike character of the higher clergy in France and Germany for many following centuries. Some of these bishops, according to Gregory of Tours, were profligate barbarians.

[16] This phrase was borrowed from the Romans. The Theodosian code speaks of those qui divinis epulis adhibentur, et adorandi principes facultatem antiquitus meruerunt. (Garnier, " Origine du Gouvernement Français," in Leber's " Collection des Meilleures Dissertations relatives à l'Histoire de France," 1838, vol. v,

common Frank; at one hundred for a Roman possessor of lands; and at forty-five for a tributary, or cultivator of another's property. In Burgundy, where religion and length of settlement had introduced different ideas, murder was punished with death. But other personal injuries were compensated, as among the Franks, by a fine, graduated according to the rank and nation of the aggrieved party.[17]

The barbarous conquerors of Gaul and Italy were guided by notions very different from those of Rome, who had imposed her own laws upon all the subjects of her empire. Adhering in general to their ancient customs, without desire of improvement, they left the former habitations in unmolested enjoyment of their civil institutions. The Frank was judged by the Salic or the Ripuary code; the Gaul followed that of Theodosius.[18] This grand distinction of Roman and barbarian, according to the law which each followed, was common to the Frank, Burgundian, and Lombard kingdoms. But the Ostrogoths, whose settlement in the empire and advance in civility of manners were earlier, inclined to desert their old usages, and adopt the Roman jurisprudence.[19] The laws of the Visigoths, too, were compiled by bishops upon a Roman foundation, and designed as a uniform code, by which both nations should be governed.[20] The name of Gaul or Roman was not entirely lost in that of Frenchman, nor had the separation of their laws ceased, even in the provinces north of the Loire, till after the time of Charlemagne.[21] Ultimately, however, the feudal customs of succession, which depended upon principles quite remote from those of the civil law, and the rights of territorial justice which the barons came to

p. 187.) This memoir by Garnier, which obtained a prize from the Academy of Inscriptions in 1761, is a learned disquisition on the relation between the Frank monarchy and the usages of the Roman Empire, inclining considerably to the school of Dubos. I only read it in 1851: it puts some things in a just light; yet the impression which it leaves is that of one-sidedness. The author does not account for the continued distinction between the Franks and Romans, testified by the language of history and of law. Garnier never once alludes to the most striking circumstance, the inequality of composition for homicide.

To return to the words conviva regis, it seems not probable that they should be limited to those who actually had feasted at the royal table; they naturally include the senatorial families, one of whom would receive that honour if he should present himself at court.

[17] "Leges Salicæ," c. 43; "Leges Burgundionum," tit. 2. Murder and robbery were made capital by Childebert, King of Paris; but Francus was to be sent for trial in the royal court, debilior persona in loco pendatur. (Baluz, tome i, p. 17.)

I am inclined to think that the word Francus does not absolutely refer to the nation of the party, but rather to his rank, as opposed to debilior persona; and, consequently, that it had already acquired the sense of freeman or freeborn (ingenuus), which is perhaps its strict meaning. Du Cange, voc. Francus, quotes the passage in this sense. [Note IV.]

[18] Inter Romanos negotia causarum Romanis Legibus præcipimus terminari. Edict. Clotair. 1. circ. 560. ("Baluz. Capitul.," tome i, p. 7.)

[19] Giannone, l. iii, c. 2.

[20] "Hist. de Languedoc," tome i, p. 242. Heineccius, "Hist. Juris German.," c. i, s. 15.

[21] Suger, in his "Life of Louis VI," uses the expression, lex Salica ("Recueil des Historiens," tome xii, p. 24); and I have some recollection of having met with the like words in other writings of as modern a date. But I am not convinced that the original Salic code was meant by this phrase, which may have been applied to the local feudal customs. The capitularies of Charlemagne are frequently termed lex Salica. Many of these are copied from the Theodosian code.

possess, contributed to extirpate the Roman jurisprudence in that part of France. But in the south, from whatever cause, it survived the revolutions of the middle ages, and thus arose a leading division of that kingdom into pays coutumiers and pays du droit écrit; the former regulated by a vast variety of ancient usages, the latter by the civil law.[22]

The kingdom of Clovis was divided into a number of districts, each under the government of a count, a name familiar to Roman subjects, by which they rendered the Graf of the Germans.[23] The authority of this officer extended over all the inhabitants, as well Franks as natives. It was his duty to administer justice, to preserve tranquility, to collect the royal revenues, and to lead, when required, the free proprietors into the field.[24] The title of a duke implied a higher dignity, and commonly gave authority over several counties.[25] These offices were originally conferred

[22] This division is very ancient, being found in the edict of Pistes, under Charles the Bald, in 864; where we read, in illis regionibus, quæ legem Romanam sequuntur. ("Recueil des Historiens," tome vii, p. 664.) Montesquieu thinks that the Roman law fell into disuse in the north of France on account of the superior advantages, particularly in point of composition for offences, annexed to the Salic law; while that of the Visigoths being more equal, the Romans under their government had no inducement to quit their own code. ("Esprit des Loix," l. xxvii, c. 4.) But it does not appear that the Visigoths had any peculiar code of laws till after their expulsion from the kingdom of Toulouse. They then retained only a small strip of territory in France, about Narbonne and Montpellier. However, the distinction of men according to their laws was preserved for many centuries, both in France and Italy. A judicial proceeding of the year 918, published by the historians of Languedoc (tome ii, appendix, p. 56), proves that the Roman, Gothic, and Salic codes were then kept perfectly separate, and that there were distinct judges for the three nations. The Gothic law is referred to as an existing authority in a charter of 1070. (Idem, tome iii, p. 274; De Marca, " Marca Hispanica," p. 1159.) Women in Italy upon marriage usually changed their law and adopted that of their husbands, returning to their own in widowhood; but to this there are exceptions. Charters are found as late as the twelfth century with the expression, qui professus sum lege Longobardicâ [aut] lege Salicâ [aut] lege Alemannorum vivere. But soon afterward the distinctions were entirely lost, partly through the prevalence of the Roman law, and partly through the multitude of local statutes in the Italian cities. (Muratori, " Antiquitates Italiæ Dissertat." 22; Du Cange, v. Lex. Heineccius, " Historia Juris Germanici," c. ii, s. 51. [Note V.]

[23] The word graf was not always equiv-

alent to comes; it took in some countries, as in England, the form gerefa, and stood for the vicecomes or sheriff, the count or alderman's deputy. Some have derived it from grau, on the hypothesis that the elders presided in the German assemblies.

[24] " Marculfi Formulæ," l. i, p. 32.

[25] Houard, the learned translator of Littleton (" Anciens Loix des François," tome i, p. 6), supposes these titles to have been applied indifferently. But the contrary is easily proved, and especially by a line of Fortunatus, quoted by Du Cange and others:

" Qui modo dat Comitis, det tibi jura Ducis."

The cause of M. Houard's error may perhaps be worth noticing. In the above-cited form of Marculfus, a precedent (in law language) is given for the appointment of a duke, count, or patrician. The material part being the same, it was only necessary to fill up the blanks, as we should call it, by inserting the proper designation of office. It is expressed, therefore, actionem comitatus, ducatus, aut patriciatus, in pago illo, quam antecessor tuus ille usque nunc visus est egisse, tibi agendum regendumque commissimus. Montesquieu has fallen into a similar mistake (l. xxx, c. 16), forgetting for a moment, like Houard, that these instruments in Marculfus were not records of real transactions, but general forms for future occasion.

The office of patrician is rather more obscure. It seems to have nearly corresponded with what was afterward called mayor of the palace, and to have implied the command of all the royal forces. Such at least were Celsus and his successor Mummolus under Gontran. This is probable, too, from analogy. The patrician was the highest officer in the Roman Empire from the time of Constantine, and we know how much the Franks themselves, and still more their Gaulish subjects, affected to imitate the style of the imperial court.

during pleasure; but the claim of a son to succeed his father would often be found too plausible or too formidable to be rejected, and it is highly probable that, even under the Merovingian kings, these provincial governors had laid the foundations of that independence which was destined to change the countenance of Europe.[26] The Lombard dukes, those especially of Spoleto and Benevento, acquired very early an hereditary right of governing their provinces, and that kingdom became a sort of federal aristocracy.[27]

The throne of France was always filled by the royal house of Meroveus. However complete we may imagine the elective rights of the Franks, it is clear that a fundamental law restrained them to this family. Such, indeed, had been the monarchy of their ancestors the Germans; such long continued to be those of Spain, of England, and perhaps of all European nations. The reigning family was immutable; but at every vacancy the heir awaited the confirmation of a popular election, whether that were a substantial privilege or a mere ceremony. Exceptions, however, to the lineal succession are rare in the history of any country, unless where an infant heir was thought unfit to rule a nation of freemen. But, in fact, it is vain to expect a system of constitutional laws rigidly observed in ages of anarchy and ignorance. Those antiquaries who have maintained the most opposite theories upon such points are seldom in want of particular instances to support their respective conclusions.[28]

This office was, as far as I recollect, confined to the kingdom of Burgundy; but the Franks of this kingdom may have borrowed it from the Burgundians, as the latter did from the empire. Marculfus gives a form for the grant of the office of patrician, which seems to have differed only in local extent of authority from that of a duke or a count, which was the least of the three, as the same formula expressing their functions is sufficient for all.

[26] That the offices of count and duke were originally but temporary may be inferred from several passages in Gregory of Tours; as l. v, c. 37; l. viii, c. 18. But it seems by the laws of the Alemanni, c. 35, that the hereditary succession of their dukes was tolerably established at the beginning of the seventh century, when their code was promulgated. The Bavarians chose their own dukes out of one family, as is declared in their laws (tit. ii, c. 1, and c. 20). (Lindebrog, "Codex Legum Antiquarum.") This the Emperor Henry II confirms: Nonne scitis (he says), Bajuarios ab initio ducem eligendi liberam habere potestatem? (Ditmar, apud Schmidt, "Hist. des Allemands," tome ii, p. 404.) Indeed, the consent of these German provincial nations, if I may use the expression, seems to have been always required, as in an independent monarchy. Ditmar, a chroni-

cler of the tenth century, says that Eckard was made Duke of Thoringia totius populi consensu. (Pfeffel, "Abrégé Chronologique," tome i, p. 184.) With respect to France, properly so called, or the kingdoms of Neustria and Burgundy, it may be less easy to prove the existence of hereditary offices under the Merovingians. But the feebleness of their government makes it probable that so natural a system of disorganization had not failed to ensue. The Helvetian counts appear to have been nearly independent as early as this period. (Planta's "Hist. of the Helvetic Confederacy," chap. i.)

[27] Giannone, l. iv. [Note VI.]

[28] Hottoman (" Franco-Gallia," c. vi) and Boulainvilliers ("État de la France ") seem to consider the crown as absolutely elective. The Abbé Vertot (" Mémoires de l'Acad. des Inscriptions," tome iv) maintains a limited right of election within the reigning family. M. de Foncemagne (tome i and tome viii of the same collection) asserts a strict hereditary descent. Neither perhaps sufficiently distinguishes acts of violence from those of right, nor observes the changes in the French constitution between Clovis and Childeric III.

It would now be admitted by the majority of French antiquaries that the nearest heir would not have a strict right to the throne; but if he were of full

Clovis was a leader of barbarians, who respected his valour and the rank which they had given him, but were incapable of servile feelings, and jealous of their common as well as individual rights. In order to appreciate the power which he possessed, it has been customary with French writers to bring forward the well-known story of the vase of Soissons. When the plunder taken in Clovis's invasion of Gaul was set out in this place for distribution, he begged for himself a precious vessel belonging to the Church of Rheims. The army having expressed their willingness to consent, " You shall have nothing here," exclaimed a soldier, striking it with his battle-axe, " but what falls to your share by lot." Clovis took the vessel without marking any resentment, but found an opportunity next year of revenging himself by the death of the soldier. The whole behaviour of Clovis appears to be that of a barbarian chief, not daring to withdraw anything from the rapacity or to chastise the rudeness of his followers.

But if such was the liberty of the Franks when they first became conquerors of Gaul, we have good reason to believe that they did not long preserve it. A people not very numerous spread over the spacious provinces of Gaul, wherever lands were assigned to or seized by them. It became a burden to attend those general assemblies of the nation which were annually convened in the month of March, to deliberate upon public business, as well as to exhibit a muster of military strength. After some time it appears that these meetings drew together only the bishops and those invested with civil offices.[29] The ancient inhabitants of Gaul, having little notion of political liberty, were unlikely to resist the most tyrannical conduct. Many of them became officers of state and advisers of the sovereign, whose ingenuity might teach maxims of despotism unknown in the forests of Germany. We shall scarcely wrong the bishops by suspecting

age and in lineal descent, his expectation would be such as to constitute a moral claim never to be defeated or contested, provided no impediment, such as his minority or weakness of mind, stood in the way. After the middle of the seventh century the mayors of the palace selected whom they would. As it is still clearer from history that the Carlovingian kings did not assume the crown without an election, we may more probably suppose this to have been the ancient constitution. The passages in Gregory of Tours which look like a mere hereditary succession such as Quatuor filii regnum accipiunt et inter se æquâ lance dividunt, do not exclude a popular election, which he would consider a mere formality, and which in that case must have been little more.

I must admit, however, that M. Guizot, whose authority is deservedly so high, gives more weight to lineal inheritance than many others have done; and consequently treats the phrases of historians seeming to imply a choice by the people as merely recognitions of a legal right. " The principle of hereditary right," he says, " must have been deeply implanted when Pepin was forced to obtain the Pope's sanction before he ventured to depose the Merovingian prince, obscure and despised as he was." (" Essais sur l'Hist. de France," p. 298.) But surely this is not to the point. Childeric III was a reigning king; and, besides this, the question is by no means as to the right of the Merovingian family to the throne, which no one disputes, but as to that of the nearest heir. The case was the same with the second dynasty. The Franks bound themselves to the family of Pepin, not to any one heir within it.

[29] Dubos, tome iii, p. 327; Mably, " Observ. sur l'Histoire de France," l. i, c. 3.

them of more pliable courtliness than was natural to the long-haired warriors of Clovis.[30] Yet it is probable that some of the Franks were themselves instrumental in this change of their government. The court of the Merovingian kings was crowded with followers, who have been plausibly derived from those of the German chiefs described by Tacitus; men forming a distinct and elevated class in the state, and known by the titles of Fideles, Leudes, and Antrustiones. They took an oath of fidelity to the king, upon their admission into that rank, and were commonly remunerated with gifts of land. Under different appellations we find, as some antiquaries think, this class of courtiers in the early records of Lombardy and England. The general name of vassals (from Gwas, a Celtic word for a servant) is applied to them in every country.[31] By the assistance of these faithful supporters, it has been thought that the regal authority of Clovis's successors was insured.[32] However this may be, the annals of his more immediate descendants exhibit a course of oppression, not merely displayed, as will often happen among uncivilized people, though free, in acts of private injustice, but in such general tyranny as is incompatible with the existence of any real checks upon the sovereign.[33]

But before the middle of the seventh century the kings of this line had fallen into that contemptible state which has been described in the last chapter. The mayors of the palace, who from mere officers of the court had now become masters of the kingdom, were elected by the Franks, not indeed the whole body of that nation, but the provincial governors and considerable proprietors of land.[34] Some inequality there probably existed

[30] Gregory of Tours throughout his history talks of the royal power in the tone of Louis XIV's court. If we were obliged to believe all we read, even the vase of Soissons would bear witness to the obedience of the Franks.

[31] The Gasindi of Italy and the Anglo-Saxon royal Thane appear to correspond, more or less, to the Antrustions of France. The word Thane, however, as will be seen in another chapter, was used in a very extensive sense, and comprehended all free proprietors of land. That of Leudes seems to imply only subjection, and is frequently applied to the whole body of a nation, as well as, in a stricter sense, to the king's personal vassals. This name they did not acquire, originally, by possessing benefices; but rather, by being vassals or servants, became the object of beneficiary donations. In one of Marculfus's precedents (l. i, f. 18) we have the form by which an Antrustion was created. See Du Cange, under these several words, and Muratori's thirteenth dissertation on Italian antiquities. The Gardingi sometimes mentioned in the laws of the Visigoths do not appear to be of the same description.

[32] Boantus . . . vallatus in domo sua, ab hominibus regis interfectus est. (Greg. Tur., l, viii, c. 11.) A few spirited retainers were sufficient to execute the mandates of arbitrary power among a barbarous disunited people.

[33] This is more fully discussed in Note VII.

[34] The revolution which ruined Brunehaut was brought about by the defection of her chief nobles, especially Warnachar, Mayor of Austrasia. Upon Clotaire II's victory over her, he was compelled to reward these adherents at the expense of the monarchy. Warnachar was made Mayor of Burgundy, with an oath from the king never to dispossess him. (Fredegarius, c. 42.) In 626 the nobility of Burgundy declined to elect a mayor, which seems to have been considered as their right. From this time nothing was done without the consent of the aristocracy. Unless we ascribe all to the different ways of thinking in Gregory and Fredegarius, the one a Roman bishop, the other a Frank or Burgundian, the government was altogether changed.

It might even be surmised that the crown was considered as more elective

from the beginning in the partition of estates, and this had been greatly increased by the common changes of property, by the rapine of those savage times, and by royal munificence. Thus arose that landed aristocracy which became the most striking feature in the political system of Europe during many centuries, and is, in fact, its great distinction, both from the despotism of Asia and the equality of republican governments.

There has been some dispute about the origin of nobility in France, which might perhaps be settled, or at least better understood, by fixing our conception of the term. In our modern acceptation it is usually taken to imply certain distinctive privileges in the political order, inherent in the blood of the possessor, and consequently not transferable like those which property confers. Limited to this sense, nobility, I conceive, was unknown to the conquerors of Gaul till long after the downfall of the Roman Empire. They felt, no doubt, the common prejudice of mankind in favour of those whose ancestry is conspicuous, when compared with persons of obscure birth. This is the primary meaning of nobility, and perfectly distinguishable from the possession of exclusive civil rights. Those who are acquainted with the constitution of the Roman Republic will recollect an instance of the difference between these two species of hereditary distinction in the patricii and the nobiles. Though I do not think that the tribes of German origin paid so much regard to genealogy as some Scandinavian and Celtic nations (else the beginnings of the greatest houses would not have been so enveloped in doubt as we find them), there are abundant traces of the respect in which families of known antiquity were held among them.[35]

But the essential distinction of ranks in France, perhaps also in Spain and Lombardy, was founded upon the possession of land or upon civil employment. The aristocracy of wealth preceded that of birth, which, indeed, is still chiefly dependent upon the other for its importance. A Frank of large estate was styled

than before. The author of " Gesta Regum Francorum," an old chronicler who lived in those times, changes his form of expressing a king's accession from that of Clotaire II. Of the earlier kings he says only, regnum recepit. But of Clotaire, Franci quoque prædictum Clotairium regem parvulum supra se in regnum statuerunt. Again, of the accession of Dagobert I: Austrasii Franci superiores, congregati in unum, Dagobertum supra se in regnum statuunt. In another place, Decedente præfato rege Clodoveo, Franci Clotairium seniorem puerum ex tribus sibi regem statuerunt. Several other instances might be quoted.

[35] The antiquity of French nobility is maintained temperately by Schmidt, " Hist. des Allemands," tome i, p. 361, and with acrimony by Montesquieu,

" Esprit des Loix," 1. xxx, c. 25. Neither of them proves any more than I have admitted. The expression of Ludovicus Pius to his freedman, Rex fecit te liberum, non nobilem; quod impossibile est post libertatem, is very intelligible, without imagining a privileged class. Of the practical regard paid to birth, indeed, there are many proofs. It seems to have been a recommendation in the choice of bishops. (" Marculfi Formulæ," 1. i, c. 4, cum notis Bignonii, in Baluzii " Capitularibus.") It was probably much considered in conferring dignities. Fredegarius says of Protadius, mayor of the palace to Brunehaut, Quoscunque genere nobiles reperiebat, totos humiliare conabatur, ut nullus reperiretur, qui gradum, quem arripuerat, potuisset assumere. [Note VIII.]

a noble; if he wasted or was despoiled of his wealth, his descendants fell into the mass of the people, and the new possessor became noble in his stead. Families were noble by descent, because they were rich by the same means. Wealth gave them power, and power gave them pre-eminence. But no distinction was made by the Salic or Lombard codes in the composition for homicide, the great test of political station, except in favour of the king's vassals. It seems, however, by some of the barbaric codes—those, namely, of the Burgundians, Visigoths, Saxons, and the English colony of the latter nation [36]—that the free men were ranged by them into two or three classes, and a difference made in the price at which their lives were valued: so that there certainly existed the elements of aristocratic privileges, if we can not in strictness admit their completion at so early a period. The Antrustions of the Kings of the Franks were also noble, and a composition was paid for their murder treble of that for an ordinary citizen; but this was a personal, not an hereditary, distinction. A link was wanting to connect their eminent privileges with their posterity, and this link was to be supplied by hereditary benefices.

Besides the lands distributed among the nation, others were reserved to the crown, partly for the support of its dignity, and partly for the exercise of its munificence. These are called fiscal lands; they were dispersed over different parts of the kingdom, and formed the most regular source of revenue.[37] But the greater portion of them were granted out to favoured subjects, under the name of benefices, the nature of which is one of the most important points in the policy of these ages. Benefices were, it is probable, most frequently bestowed upon the professed courtiers, the Antrustiones or Leudes, and upon the provincial governors. It by no means appears that any conditions of military service were expressly annexed to these grants: but it may justly be presumed that such favours were not conferred without an expectation of some return; and we read both in law and history that beneficiary tenants were more closely connected with the crown than mere allodial proprietors. Whoever possessed a benefice was expected to serve his sovereign in the field. But of allodial proprietors only the owner of three mansi was called upon for personal service. Where there were three possessors of single mansi, one went to the army, and the others contributed to his equipment.[38] Such, at least, were the regulations of Charle-

[36] " Leg. Burgund.," tit. 26; " Leg. Visigoth," l. ii, tome 2, c. 4 (in Lindebrog.); Du Cange, voc. Adalingus, nobilis; Wilkins, " Leg. Ang. Sax.," passim.
[37] The demesne lands of the crown are continually mentioned in the early writers; the kings, in journeying to different parts of their dominions, took up their abode in them. Charlemagne is very full in his directions as to their management. (" Capitularia," A. D. 797, et alibi.)
[38] " Capitul. Car. Mag.," ann. 807 and 812. I can not define the precise area of

magne, whom I can not believe, with Mably, to have relaxed the obligations of military attendance. After the Peace of Coblentz, in 860, Charles the Bald restored all allodial property belonging to his subjects, who had taken part against him, but not his own beneficiary grants, which they were considered as having forfeited.

Most of those who have written upon the feudal system lay it down that benefices were originally precarious and revoked at pleasure by the sovereign; that they were afterward granted for life; and at a subsequent period became hereditary. No satisfactory proof, however, appears to have been brought of the first stage in this progress.[39] At least, I am not convinced that beneficiary grants were ever considered as resumable at pleasure, unless where some delinquency could be imputed to the vassal. It is possible, though I am not aware of any documents which prove it, that benefices may in some instances have been granted for a term of years, since even fiefs in much later times were occasionally of no greater extent. Their ordinary duration, however, was at least the life of the possessor, after which they reverted to the fisc.[40] Nor can I agree with those who deny the existence of hereditary benefices under the first race of French kings. The codes of the Burgundians and of the Visigoths, which advert to them, are, by analogy, witnesses to the contrary.[41] The precedents given in the forms of Marculfus (about 660) for the grant of a benefice, contain very full terms, extending it to the heirs of the beneficiary.[42] And Mably has plausibly inferred the perpetuity of benefices, at least in some instances, from the language of the treaty at Andely in 587, and of an edict of Clotaire II some years later.[43] We can hardly doubt at least

a mansus. It consisted, according to Du Cange, of twelve jugera; but what he meant by a juger I know not. The ancient Roman juger was about five eighths of an acre; the Parisian arpent was a fourth more than one. This would make a difference as two to one.

[39] [Note IX.]

[40] The following passage from Gregory of Tours seems to prove that, although sons were occasionally permitted to succeed their fathers, an indulgence which easily grew up into a right, the crown had, in his time, an unquestionable reversion after the death of its original beneficiary : Hoc tempore et Wandelinus, nutritor Childeberti regis obiit; sed in locum ejus nullus est subrogatus, eo quod regina mater curam velit propriam habere de filio. Quæcunque de fisco meruit, fisci juribus sunt relata. Obiit his diebus Bodegesilus dux plenus dierum; sed nihil de facultate ejus filiis minutum est (l. viii, c. 22). Gregory's work, however, does not go farther than 595.

[41] "Leges Burgundiorum," tit. i ; "Leges Visigoth.," l. v, tit. 2.

[42] "Marculf. Form.," xii and xiv, l. i. This precedent was in use down to the eleventh century; its expressions recur in almost every charter. The earliest instance I have seen of an actual grant to a private person is of Charlemagne to one John, in 795. ("Baluzii Capitularia," tome ii, p. 1400.)

[43] Quicquid antefati reges ecclesiis aut fidelibus suis contulerunt, aut adhuc conferre cum justitiâ Deo propitiante voluerint, stabiliter conservetur; et quicquid unicuique fidelium in utriusque regno per legem et justitiam redhibetur, nullum ei prejudicium ponatur, sed liceat res debitas possidere atque recipere. Et si aliquid unicuique per interregna sine culpâ sublatum est, audientiâ habitâ restauretur. Et de eo quod per munificentias præcedentium regum unusquisque usque ad transitum gloriosæ memoriæ domini Chlothacharii regis possedit, cum securitate possideat; et quod exinde fidelibus personis ablatum est, de præsenti recipiat. (Fœdus Andeliacum, in "Gregor. Turon.," l. ix, c. 20.)

that children would put in a very strong claim to what their father had enjoyed; and the weakness of the crown in the seventh century must have rendered it difficult to reclaim its property.

A natural consequence of hereditary benefices was that those who possessed them carved out portions to be held of themselves by a similar tenure. Abundant proofs of this custom, best known by the name of subinfeudation, occur even in the capitularies of Pepin and Charlemagne. At a later period it became universal; and what had begun perhaps through ambition or pride was at last dictated by necessity. In that dissolution of all law which ensued after the death of Charlemagne, the powerful leaders, constantly engaged in domestic warfare, placed their chief dependency upon men whom they attached by gratitude and bound by strong conditions. The oath of fidelity which they had taken, the homage which they had paid to the sovereign, they exacted from their own vassals. To render military service became the essential obligation which the tenant of a benefice undertook; and out of those ancient grants, now become for the most part hereditary, there grew up in the tenth century, both in name and reality, the system of feudal tenures.[44]

This revolution was accompanied by another still more important. The provincial governors, the dukes and counts, to whom we may add the marquises or margraves intrusted with the custody of the frontiers, had taken the lead in all public measures after the decline of the Merovingian kings. Charlemagne, duly jealous of their ascendency, checked it by suffering the duchies to expire without renewal, by granting very few counties hereditarily, by removing the administration of justice from the hands of the counts into those of his own itinerant judges, and, if we are not deceived in his policy, by elevating the ecclesiastical order as a counterpoise to that of the nobility. Even in his time the faults of the counts are the constant theme of the capitularies; their dissipation and neglect of duty, their oppression of the poorer proprietors, and their artful attempts to appropriate the crown lands situated within their territory.[45] If Charlemagne was unable to redress those evils, how much must they have increased under his posterity! That great prince seldom gave more than one county to the same person; and as they were generally of moderate size, coextensive with episcopal dioceses, there was less danger, if this policy had been followed, of their becoming independent.[46] But Louis the Debonair, and, in a still greater

---

Quæcunque ecclesiæ vel clericis vel quibuslibet personis a gloriosæ memoriæ præfatis principibus munificentiæ largitate collatæ sunt, omni firmitate perdurent. Edict. Chlotachar I. et potius II in " Recueil des Historiens," tome iv, p. 116.

[44] [Note X.]
[45] " Capitularia Car. Mag. et Lud. Pii.," passim; Schmidt, " Hist. des Allemands," tome ii, p. 158; Gaillard, " Vie de Charlem.," tome iii, p. 118.
[46] Vaissette, " Hist. de Languedoc," tome i, pp. 587, 700, and note 87.

degree, Charles the Bald, allowed several counties to be enjoyed by the same person. The possessors constantly aimed at acquiring private estates within the limits of their charge, and thus both rendered themselves formidable, and assumed a kind of patrimonial right to their dignities. By a capitulary of Charles the Bald, A. D. 877, the succession of a son to the father's county appears to be recognised as a known usage.[47] In the next century there followed an entire prostration of the royal authority, and the counts usurped their governments as little sovereignties, with the domains and all regalian rights, subject only to the feudal superiority of the king.[48] They now added the name of the county to their own, and their wives took the appellation of countess.[49] In Italy the independence of the dukes was still more complete; and although Otho the Great and his descendants kept a stricter rein over those of Germany, yet we find the great fiefs of their empire, throughout the tenth century, granted almost invariably to the male and even female heirs of the last possessor.

Meanwhile, the allodial proprietors, who had hitherto formed the strength of the state, fell into a much worse condition. They were exposed to the rapacity of the counts, who, whether as magistrates and governors, or as overbearing lords, had it always in their power to harass them. Every district was exposed to continual hostilities; sometimes from a foreign enemy, more often from the owners of castles and fastnesses, which, in the tenth century, under pretence of resisting the Normans and Hungarians, served the purposes of private war. Against such a system of rapine the military compact of lord and vassal was the only effectual shield; its essence was the reciprocity of service and protection. But an insulated allodialist had no support; his fortunes were strangely changed since he claimed, at least in right, a share in the legislation of his country, and could compare with pride his patrimonial fields with the temporary benefices of the crown. Without law to redress his injuries, without the royal power to support his right, he had no course left but to compromise with oppression, and subject himself, in return for protection, to a feudal lord. During the tenth and eleventh centuries it appears that allodial lands in France had chiefly become feudal: that is, they had been surrendered by their proprietors, and received back again upon the feudal conditions; or more frequently, perhaps, the owner had been compelled to

[47] " Baluzii Capitularia," tome ii, pp. 263, 269. This is a questionable point, and most French antiquaries consider this famous capitulary as the foundation of an hereditary right in counties. I am inclined to think that there was at least a practice of succession which is implied and guaranteed by this provision. [Note VI.]
[48] It appears, by the record of a process in 918, that the Counts of Toulouse had already so far usurped the rights of their sovereign as to claim an estate on the ground of its being a royal benefice. (" Hist. de Languedoc," tome ii, appen., p. 56.)
[49] Vaissette, " Hist. de Languedoc," tome i. p. 588, and infrà; tome ii, pp. 38, 109, and appendix, p. 56.

acknowledge himself the man or vassal of a suzerain, and thus to confess an original grant which had never existed.[50] Changes of the same nature, though not perhaps so extensive or so distinctly to be traced, took place in Italy and Germany. Yet it would be inaccurate to assert that the prevalence of the feudal system has been unlimited; in a great part of France allodial tenures always subsisted, and many estates in the empire were of the same description.[51]

There are, however, vestiges of a very universal custom distinguishable from the feudal tenure of land, though so analogous to it that it seems to have nearly escaped the notice of antiquaries. From this silence of other writers, and the great obscurity of the subject, I am almost afraid to notice what several passages in ancient laws and instruments concur to prove, that, besides the relation established between lord and vassal by beneficiary grants, there was another species more personal and more closely resembling that of patron and client in the Roman Republic. This was usually called commendation; and appears to have been founded on two very general principles, both of which the distracted state of society inculcated. The weak needed the protection of the powerful, and the government needed some security for public order. Even before the invasion of the Franks, Salvian, a writer of the fifth century, mentions the custom of obtaining the protection of the great by money, and blames their rapacity, though he allows the natural reasonableness of the practice.[52] The disadvantageous condition of the less powerful freemen, which ended in the servitude of one part, and in the feudal vassalage of another, led such as fortunately still preserved their allodial property to insure its defence by a stipulated payment of money. Such payments, called Salvamenta, may be traced in extant charters, chiefly, indeed, of monasteries.[53] In

[50] " Hist. de Languedoc," tome ii, p. 109. It must be confessed that there do not occur so many specific instances of this conversion of allodial tenure into feudal as might be expected, in order to warrant the supposition in the text. Several records, however, are quoted by Robertson, " Hist. Charles V," note 8; and others may be found in diplomatic collections. A precedent for surrendering allodial property to the king, and receiving it back as his benefice, appears even in Marculfus, l. i, form 13. The county of Cominges, between the Pyrenees, Toulouse, and Bigorre, was allodial till 1244, when it was put under the feudal protection of the Count of Toulouse. It devolved by escheat to the crown in 1443. (Villaret, tome xv, p. 346.)

In many early charters the king confirms the possession even of allodial property for greater security in lawless times; and, on the other hand, in those of the tenth and eleventh centuries, the word allodium is continually used for a feud, or hereditary benefice, which renders this subject still more obscure.

[51] The maxim, Nulle terre sans seigneur, was so far from being universally received in France that in almost all southern provinces, or pays du droit écrit, lands were presumed to be allodial, unless the contrary was shown, or, as it was called, franc-aleux sans titre. The parliaments, however, seem latterly to have inclined against this presumption, and have thrown the burden of proof on the party claiming allodiality. For this see Denisart, " Dictionnaire des Décisions," art. Franc-aleu. [Note XI.]

In Germany, according to Du Cange, voc. Baro, there was a distinction between Barones and Semper-Barones; the latter holding their lands allodially.

[52] Du Cange, v. Salvamentum.

[53] Ibid.

the case of private persons it may be presumed that this voluntary contract was frequently changed by the stronger party into a perfect feudal dependence. From this, however, as I imagine, it probably differed, in being capable of dissolution at the inferior's pleasure, without incurring a forfeiture, as well as in having no relation to land. Homage, however, seems to have been incident to commendation, as well as to vassalage. Military service was sometimes the condition of this engagement. It was the law of France, so late, at least, as the commencement of the third race of kings, that no man could take a part in private wars, except in defence of his own lord. This we learn from a historian about the end of the tenth century, who relates that one Erminfrid, having been released from his homage to Count Burchard, on ceding the fief he had held of him to a monastery, renewed the ceremony on a war breaking out between Burchard and another nobleman, wherein he was desirous to give assistance; since, the author observes, it is not, nor has been, the practice in France for any man to be concerned in war except in the presence or by the command of his lord.[54] Indeed, there is reason to infer, from the capitularies of Charles the Bald, that every man was bound to attach himself to some lord, though it was the privilege of a freeman to choose his own superior.[55] And this is strongly supported by the analogy of our Anglo-Saxon laws, where it is frequently repeated that no man should continue without a lord. There are, too, as it seems to me, a great number of passages in Doomsday-book which confirm this distinction between personal commendation and the beneficiary tenure of land. Perhaps I may be thought to dwell too prolixly on this obscure custom; but as it tends to illustrate those mutual relations of lord and vassal which supplied the place of regular government in the polity of Europe, and has seldom or never been explicitly noticed, its introduction seemed not improper.

[54] "Recueil des Historiens," tome x, p. 355.

[55] Unusquisque liber homo post mortem domini sui, licentiam habeat se commendandi inter hæc tria regna ad quemcunque voluerit. Similiter et ille qui nondum alicui commendatus est. (" Baluzii Capitularia," tome i, p. 443, A. D. 806.) Volumus etiam ut unusquisque liber homo in nostro regno seniorem qualem voluerit in nobis et in nostris fidelibus recipiat. (" Capit. Car. Calvi," A. D. 877.) Et volumus ut cujuscunque nostrum homo, in cujuscunque regno sit, cum seniore suo in hostem, vel aliis suis utilitatibus pergat. (Ibid. See, too, Baluze, tome i, pp. 536, 537.)

By the Establishments of St. Louis, c. 87, every stranger coming to settle within a barony was to acknowledge the baron as lord within a year and a day, or pay a fine. In some places he even became the serf or villein of the lord, (" Ordonnances des Rois," p. 187.) Upon this jealousy of unknown settlers, which pervades the policy of the middle ages, was founded the droit d'aubaine, or right to their movables after their decease. See preface to " Ordonnances des Rois," tome i, p. 15.

The article Commendatio in Du Cange's " Glossary " furnishes some hints upon this subject, which, however, that author does not seem to have fully apprehended. Carpentier, in his " Supplement to the Glossary," under the word Vassaticum, gives the clearest notice of it that I have anywhere found. Since writing the above pages I have found the subject touched by M. de Montlosier, " Hist. de la Monarchie Française," tome i, p. 854. [Note XI.]

It has been sometimes said that feuds were first rendered hereditary in Germany by Conrad II, surnamed the Salic. This opinion is perhaps erroneous. But there is a famous edict of that emperor at Milan, in the year 1037, which, though immediately relating only to Lombardy, marks the full maturity of the system and the last stage of its progress.[56] I have remarked already the custom of subinfeudation, or grants of lands by vassals to be held of themselves, which had grown up with the growth of these tenures. There had occurred, however, some disagreement, for want of settled usage, between these inferior vassals and their immediate lords, which this edict was expressly designed to remove. Four regulations of great importance are established therein: that no man should be deprived of his fief, whether held of the emperor or a mesne lord, but by the laws of the empire and the judgment of his peers;[57] that from such judgment an immediate vassal might appeal to his sovereign; that fiefs should be inherited by sons and their children, or, in their failure, by brothers, provided they were feuda paterna, such as had descended from the father;[58] and that the lord should not alienate the fief of his vassal without his consent.[59]

Such was the progress of these feudal tenures, which determined the political character of every European monarchy where they prevailed, as well as formed the foundations of its jurisprudence. It is certainly inaccurate to refer this system, as is frequently done, to the destruction of the Roman Empire by the northern nations, though in the beneficiary grants of those conquerors we trace its beginning. Four or five centuries, however, elapsed before the allodial tenures, which had become incomparably the more general, gave way, and before the reciprocal contract of the feud attained its maturity. It is now time to describe the legal qualities and effects of this relation, so far only as may be requisite to understand its influence upon the political system.

[56] Spelman tells us, in his " Treatise of Feuds," chap. ii, that Conradus Salicus, a French emperor, but of German descent [what can this mean?], went to Rome about 915 to fetch his crown from Pope John X when, according to him, the succession of a son to his father's fief was first conceded. An almost unparalleled blunder in so learned a writer! Conrad the Salic was elected at Worms in 1024, crowned at Rome by John XIX in 1027, and made this edict at Milan in 1037.

[57] Nisi secundùm constitutionem antecessorum nostrorum, et judicium parium suorum; the very expressions of Magna Charta.

[58] " Gerardus noteth," says Sir H. Spelman, " that this law settled not the feud upon the eldest son, or any other son of the feudatory particularly; but left it in the lord's election to please himself with which he would." But the phrase of the edict runs, filios ejus beneficium tenere: which, when nothing more is said, can only mean a partition among the sons.

[59] The last provision may seem strange at so advanced a period of the system; yet, according to Giannone, feuds were still revocable by the lord in some parts of Lombardy. (" Istoria di Napoli," l. xiii, c. 3.) It seems, however, no more than had been already enacted by the first clause of this edict. Another interpretation is possible; namely, that the lord should not alienate his own seigniory without his vassal's consent, which was agreeable to the feudal tenures. This, indeed, would be putting rather a forced construction on the words ne domino feudum militis alienare liceat.

7

The essential principle of a fief was a mutual contract of support and fidelity. Whatever obligations it laid upon the vassal of service to his lord, corresponding duties of protection were imposed by it on the lord toward his vassal.[60] If these were transgressed on either side, the one forfeited his land, the other his seigniory or rights over it. Nor were motives of interest left alone to operate in securing the feudal connection. The associations founded upon ancient custom and friendly attachment, the impulses of gratitude and honour, the dread of infamy, the sanctions of religion, were all employed to strengthen these ties, and to render them equally powerful with the relations of Nature, and far more so than those of political society. It is a question agitated among feudal lawyers whether a vassal is bound to follow the standard of his lord against his own kindred.[61] It was one more important whether he must do so against the king. In the works of those who wrote when the feudal system was declining, or who were anxious to maintain the royal authority, this is commonly decided in the negative. Littleton gives a form of homage, with a reservation of the allegiance due to the sovereign;[62] and the same prevailed in Normandy and some other countries.[63] A law of Frederick Barbarossa enjoins that in every oath of fealty to an inferior lord the vassal's duty to the emperor should be expressly reserved. But it was not so during the height of the feudal system in France. The vassals of Henry II and Richard I never hesitated to adhere to them against the sovereign, nor do they appear to have incurred any blame on that account. Even so late as the age of St. Louis, it is laid down in his " Establishments " that, if justice is refused by the king to one of his vassals, he might summon his own tenants, under penalty of forfeiting their fiefs, to assist him in obtaining redress by arms.[64] The Count of Brittany, Pierre de Dreux, had prac-

[60] Crag., " Jus Feudale," l. ii, tit. 11; Beaumanoir, " Coûtumes de Beauvoisis," c. lxi, p. 311; " Ass. de Jérus.," c. 217; " Lib. Feud.," l. ii, tit. 26, 47.
Upon the mutual obligation of the lord toward his vassal seems to be founded the law of warranty, which compelled him to make indemnification where the tenant was evicted of his land. This obligation, however unreasonable it may appear to us, extended, according to the feudal lawyers, to cases of mere donation. (Crag., l. ii, tit. 4; Butler's " Notes on Co. Litt.," p. 365.)
[61] Crag., l. ii, tit. 4.
[62] Sect. lxxxv.
[63] Houard, " Anc. Loix des François," p. 114. See, too, an instance of this reservation in " Recueil des Historiens," tome xi, p. 447.
[64] Si le sire dit à son homme lige, Venez vous en avec moi, je veux guerroyer mon seigneur, qui me denie le jugement de so cour, le vassal doit re-
pondre, J'irai scavoir s'il est ainsi que vous me dites. Alors il doit aller trouver le supérieur, et luy dire, sire, le gentilhomme de qui je tiens mon fief se plaint que vous lui refusez justice; je viens pour en scavoir la vérité; car je suis semoncé de marcher en guerre contre vous. Si la reponse est que volontiers il fera droit en sa cour, l'homme n'est point obligé de déferer à la requisition du sire; mais il doit, ou le suivre, ou le resoudre à perdre son fief, si le chef seigneur persiste dans son refus. (" Établissemens de St. Louis," c. 49.) I have copied this from Velly, tome vi, p. 213, who has modernized the orthography, which is almost unintelligible in the " Ordonnances des Rois." One manuscript gives the reading Roi instead of Seigneur. And the law certainly applies to the king exclusively; for, in case of denial of justice by a mesne lord, there was an appeal to the king's court, but from his injury there could be no appeal but to the sword.

tically asserted this feudal right during the minority of St. Louis. In a public instrument he announced to the world that, having met with repeated injuries from the regent and denial of justice, he had let the king know that he no longer considered himself as his vassal, but renounced his homage and defied him.[65]

The ceremonies used in conferring a fief were principally three —homage, fealty, and investiture. 1. The first was designed as a significant expression of the submission and devotedness of the vassal toward his lord. In performing homage, his head was uncovered, his belt ungirt, his sword and spurs removed; he placed his hands, kneeling, between those of the lord, and promised to become his man from thenceforward; to serve him with life and limb and worldly honour, faithfully and loyally, in consideration of the lands which he held under him. None but the lord in person could accept homage, which was commonly concluded by a kiss.[66] 2. An oath of fealty was indispensable in every fief; but the ceremony was less peculiar than that of homage, and it might be received by proxy. It was taken by ecclesiastics, but not by minors; and in language differed little from the form of homage.[67] 3. Investiture, or the actual conveyance of feudal lands, was of two kinds: proper and improper. The first was an actual putting in possession upon the ground, either by the lord or his deputy; which is called, in our law, livery of seisin. The second was symbolical, and consisted in the delivery of a turf, a stone, a wand, a branch, or whatever else might have been made usual by the caprice of local custom. Du Cange enumerates not less than ninety-eight varieties of investitures.[68]

Upon investiture, the duties of the vassal commenced. These it is impossible to define or enumerate; because the services of military tenure, which is chiefly to be considered, were in their nature uncertain, and distinguished as such from those incident to feuds of an inferior description. It was a breach of faith to divulge the lord's counsel, to conceal from him the machinations of others, to injure his person or fortune, or to violate the sanctity

[65] Du Cange, Observations sur Joinville, in "Collection des Mémoires," tome i, p. 196. It was always necessary for a vassal to renounce his homage before he made war on his lord if he would avoid the shame and penalty of feudal treason. After a reconciliation the homage was renewed. And in this no distinction was made between the king and another superior. Thus Henry II did homage to the King of France in 1188, having renounced his former obligation to him at the commencement of the preceding war. ("Mat. Paris," p. 126.)
[66] Du Cange, "Hominium," and Carpentier's "Supplement," id., voc. Littleton, s. 85; "Assises de Jérusalem," c.

204; Crag., l. i, tit. 11; "Recueil des Historiens," tome ii, préface, p. 174. Homagium per paragium was unaccompanied by any feudal obligation, and distinguished from homagium ligeum, which carried with it an obligation of fidelity. The Dukes of Normandy rendered only homage per paragium to the Kings of France, and received the like from the Dukes of Brittany. In liege homage it was usual to make reservations of allegiance to the king, or any other lord whom the homager had previously acknowledged.
[67] Littl., s. 91; Du Cange, voc. Fidelitas.
[68] Du Cange, voc. Investitura.

of his roof and the honour of his family.[69] In battle he was bound to lend his horse to his lord when dismounted, to adhere to his side while fighting, and to go into captivity as a hostage for him when taken. His attendance was due to the lord's courts, sometimes to witness, and sometimes to bear a part in the administration of justice.[70]

The measure, however, of military service was generally settled by some usage. Forty days was the usual term during which the tenant of a knight's fee was bound to be in the field at his own expense.[71] This was extended by St. Louis to sixty days, except when the charter of infeudation expressed a shorter period. But the length of service diminished with the quantity of land. For half a knight's fee but twenty days were due; for an eighth part, but five; and when this was commuted for an escuage or pecuniary assessment, the same proportion was observed.[72] Men turned of sixty, public magistrates, and, of course, women, were free from personal service, but obliged to send their substitutes. A failure in this primary duty incurred perhaps strictly a forfeiture of the fief. But it was usual for the lord to inflict an amerce-

[69] " Assises de Jérusalem," c. 265. Home ne doit à la feme de son seigneur, ne à sa fille requerre vilainie de son cors, ne à sa sœur tant com elle est demoiselle en son hostel. I mention this part of feudal duty on account of the light it throws on the statute of treasons, 25 E. III. One of the treasons therein specified is, si omne violast la compaigne le roy, ou leigné file le roy nient marié ou la compaigne leigné fitz et heire le roy. Those who, like Sir E. Coke and the modern lawyers in general, explain this provision by the political danger of confusing the royal blood, do not apprehend its spirit. It would be absurd, upon such grounds, to render the violation of the king's eldest daughter treasonable, so long only as she remains unmarried, when, as is obvious, the danger of a spurious issue inheriting could not arise. I consider this provision, therefore, as entirely founded upon the feudal principles, which make it a breach of faith (that is, in the primary sense of the word, a treason) to sully the honour of the lord in that of the near relations who were immediately protected by residence in his house. If it is asked why this should be restricted by the statute to the person of the eldest daughter, I can only answer that this, which is not more reasonable according to the common political interpretation, is analogous to many feudal customs in our own and other countries, which attribute a sort of superiority in dignity to the eldest daughter.

It may be objected that in the reign of Edward III there was little left of the feudal principle in any part of Europe, and least of all in England. But the statute of treasons is a declaration of the ancient law, and comprehends, undoubtedly, what the judges who drew it could find in records now perished, or in legal traditions of remote antiquity. Similar causes of forfeiture are enumerated in the " Libri Feudorum," 1. i, tit. 5, and l. ii, tit. 24. In the " Establishments of St. Louis," c. 51, 52, it is said that a lord seducing his vassal's daughter intrusted to his custody lost his seigniory; a vassal guilty of the same crime toward the family of his suzerain forfeited his land. A proof of the tendency which the feudal law had to purify public morals, and to create that sense of indignation and resentment with which we now regard such breaches of honour.

[70] " Assises de Jérusalem," c. 222. A vassal, at least in many places, was bound to reside upon his fief, or not to quit it without the lord's consent. (Du Cange, voc. Reseantia, Remanentia, " Recueil des Historiens," tome xi, préface, p. 172.)

[71] In the kingdom of Jerusalem feudal service extended to a year. (" Assises de Jérusalem," c. 230.) It is obvious that this was founded on the peculiar circumstances of that state. Service of castle guard, which was common in the north of England, was performed without limitation of time. (Littelton's " Henry II," vol. ii, p. 184.)

[72] Du Cange, voc. Feudum militis ; Membrum Loricæ. Stuart's " View of Society," p. 382. This division by knight's fees is perfectly familiar in the feudal law of England. But I must confess my inability to adduce decisive evidence of it in that of France, with the usual exception of Normandy. According to the natural principle of fiefs, it might seem that the same personal service would be required from the tenant,

ment, known in England by the name of escuage.[73] Thus, in Philip III's expedition against the Count de Foix in 1274, barons were assessed for their default of attendance at a hundred sous a day for the expenses which they had saved, and fifty sous as a fine to the king; bannerets, at twenty sous for expenses, and ten as a fine; knights and squires in the same proportion. But barons and bannerets were bound to pay an additional assessment for every knight and squire of their vassals whom they ought to have brought with them into the field.[74] The regulations as to the place of service were less uniform than those which regarded time. In some places the vassal was not bound to go beyond the lord's territory,[75] or only so far as that he might return the same day. Other customs compelled him to follow his chief upon all his expeditions.[76] These inconvenient and varying usages betrayed the origin of the feudal obligations, not founded upon any national policy, but springing from the chaos of anarchy and intestine war, which they were well calculated to perpetuate. For the public defence their machinery was totally unserviceable, until such changes were wrought as destroyed the character of the fabric.

Independently of the obligations of fealty and service, which the nature of the contract created, other advantages were derived from it by the lord, which have been called feudal incidents; these were: 1. Relief. 2. Fines upon alienation. 3. Escheats. 4. Aids; to which may be added, though not generally established, 5. Wardship; and 6. Marriage.

1. Some writers have accounted for reliefs in the following manner: Benefices, whether depending upon the crown or its vassals, were not originally granted by way of absolute inherit-

---

whatever were the extent of his land. William the Conqueror, it is said, distributed this kingdom into about 60,000 parcels of nearly equal value, from each of which the service of a soldier was due. He may possibly have been the inventor of this politic arrangement. Some rule must, however, have been observed in all countries in fixing the amercement for absence, which could only be equitable if it bore a just proportion to the value of the fief. And the principle of the knight's fee was so convenient and reasonable that it is likely to have been adopted in imitation of England by other feudal countries. In the roll of Philip III's expedition, as will appear by a note immediately below, there are, I think, several presumptive evidences of it; and though this is rather a late authority to establish a feudal principle, yet I have ventured to assume it in the text.

The knight's fee was fixed in England at the annual value of twenty pounds. Every estate supposed to be of this value, and entered as such in the rolls of the exchequer, was bound to contribute the

service of a soldier, or to pay an escuage to the amount assessed upon knights' fee.

[73] Littleton, l. ii, c. 3; Wright's " Tenures," p. 121.

[74] Du Chesne, " Script. Rerum Gallicarum," tome v, p. 553; Daniel, " Histoire de la Milice Françoise," p. 72. The following extracts from the muster-roll of this expedition will illustrate the varieties of feudal obligations: Johannes d'Ormoy debet servitium per quatuor dies. Johannes Malet debet servitium per viginti dies, pro quo servitio misit Richardum Tichet. Guido de Laval debet servitium duorum militum et dimidii. Dominus Sabrandus dictus Chabot dicit quod non debet servitium domino regi, nisi in comitatu Pictaviensi, et ad sumptus regis, tamen venit ad preces regis cum tribus militibus et duodecim scutiferis. Guido de Lusigniaco Dom. de Pierac dicit, quod non debet aliquid regi præter homagium.

[75] This was the custom of Beauvoisis. (Beaumanoir, c. 2.)

[76] Du Cange, et Carpentier, voc. Hostis.

ance, but renewed from time to time upon the death of the possessor, till long custom grew up into right. Hence a sum of money, something between a price and a gratuity, would naturally be offered by the heir on receiving a fresh investiture of the fief; and length of time might as legitimately turn this present into a due of the lord, as it rendered the inheritance of the tenant indefeasible. This is a very specious account of the matter. But those who consider the antiquity to which hereditary benefices may be traced, and the unreserved expressions of those instruments by which they were created, as well as the undoubted fact that a large proportion of fiefs had been absolute allodial inheritances, never really granted by the superior, will perhaps be led rather to look for the origin of reliefs in that rapacity with which the powerful are ever ready to oppress the feeble. When a feudal tenant died, the lord, taking advantage of his own strength and the confusion of the family, would seize the estate into his hands, either by the right of force or under some litigious pretext. Against this violence the heir could in general have no resource but a compromise; and we know how readily acts of successful injustice change their name and move demurely, like the wolf in the fable, under the clothing of law. Reliefs and other feudal incidents are said to have been established in France [77] about the latter part of the tenth century, and they certainly appear in the famous edict of Conrad the Salic, in 1037, which recognises the usage of presenting horses and arms to the lord upon a change of tenancy.[78] But this also subsisted under the name of heriot, in England, as early as the reign of Canute.

A relief was a sum of money (unless where charter or custom introduced a different tribute) due from every one of full age, taking a fief by descent. This was in some countries arbitrary, or ad misericordiam, and the exactions practised under this pretence both upon superior and inferior vassals ranked among the greatest abuses of the feudal policy. Henry I of England promises in his charter that they shall in future be just and reasonable; but the rate does not appear to have been finally settled till it was laid down in Magna Charta at about a fourth of the annual value of the fief. We find also fixed reliefs among the old customs of Normandy and Beauvoisis. By a law of St. Louis, in 1245,[79] the lord was entitled to enter upon the lands, if the heir could not pay the relief, and possess them for a year. This right existed unconditionally in England under the name of primer seisin, but was confined to the king.[80]

[77] " Ordonnances des Rois de France," tome i, preface, p. 10.
[78] Servato usu valvassorum majorum in tradendis armis equisque suis senioribus. This, among other reasons, leads me to doubt the received opinion that Italian fiefs were not hereditary before the promulgation of this edict.
[79] " Ordonnances des Rois," p. 55.
[80] Du Cange, v. Placitum, Relevium,

2. Closely connected with reliefs were the fines paid to the lord upon the alienation of his vassal's feud, and, indeed, we frequently find them called by the same name. The spirit of feudal tenure established so intimate a connection between the two parties that it could be dissolved by neither without requiring the other's consent. If the lord transferred his seigniory, the tenant was to testify his concurrence; and this ceremony was long kept up in England under the name of attornment. The assent of the lord to his vassal's alienation was still more essential, and more difficult to be attained. He had received his fief, it was supposed, for reasons peculiar to himself or to his family; at least his heart and arm were bound to his superior, and his service was not to be exchanged for that of a stranger, who might be unable or unwilling to render it. A law of Lothaire II in Italy forbids the alienation of fiefs without the lord's consent.[81] This prohibition is repeated in one of Frederick I, and a similar enactment was made by Roger, King of Sicily.[82] By the law of France the lord was entitled, upon every alienation made by his tenant, either to redeem the fief by paying the purchase money or to claim a certain part of the value, by way of fine, upon the change of tenancy.[83] In England even the practice of subinfeudation, which was more conformable to the law of fiefs and the military genius of the system, but injurious to the suzerains, who lost thereby their escheats and other advantages of seigniory, was checked by Magna Charta,[84] and forbidden by the statute

Sporla. By many customs a relief was due on every change of the lord, as well as of the vassal, but this was not the case in England. Beaumont speaks of reliefs as due only on collateral succession. ("Coûtumes de Beauvoisis," c. 27.) And this, according to Du Cange, was the general rule in the customary law of France. In Anjou and Maine they were not even due upon succession between brothers. ("Ordonnances des Rois," tome i, p. 58.) And M. de Pastoret, in his valuable preface to the sixteenth volume of that collection, says it was a rule that the king had nothing upon lineal succession of a fief, whether in the ascending or descending line, but la bouche et les mains—i. e., homage and fealty (p. 20).

[81] "Lib. Feudorum," l. ii, tit. 9 and 52. This was principally levelled at the practice of alienating feudal property in favour of the Church, which was called pro animâ judicare. (Radevicus in " Gestis Frederick I," l. iv, c. 7; "Lib. Feud.," l. i, tit. 7, 16; l. ii, tit. 10.)

[82] Giannone, l. ii, c. 5.

[83] Du Cange, v. Reaccapitum, Placitum, Rachatum. Pastoret, préface au seizième tome des " Ordonnances," p. 20; Houard, " Dict. du Droit Normand," art. Fief Argou; " Inst. du Droit François," l. ii, c. 2. In Beaumanoir's age and district, at least, subinfeudation without the lord's

license incurred a forfeiture of the land; and his reason extends, of course, more strongly to alienation. ("Coûtumes de Beauvoisis," c. 2; Velly, tome vi, p. 187.) But, by the general law of feuds, the former was strictly regular, while the tenant forfeited his land by the latter. Craig mentions this distinction as one for which he is perplexed to account. ("Jus Feudale," l. iii, tit. 3, p. 632.) It is, however, perfectly intelligible upon the original principles of feudal tenure.

[84] Dalrymple seems to suppose that the thirty-second chapter of Magna Charta relates to alienation and not to subinfeudation. ("Essay on Feudal Property," edit. 1758, p. 83. See Sir E. Coke, 2 Inst., pp. 65, 501; and Wright on "Tenures," contrà.) Mr. Hargrave observes that " the history of our law with respect to the powers of alienation before the statute of Quia Emptores terrarum is very much involved in obscurity." ("Notes on Co. Lit.," 43, a.) In Glanville's time apparently a man could only alienate (to hold of himself) rationabilem partem de terrâ suâ (l. vii, c. 1). But this may have been in favour of the kindred as much as of the lord. (Dalrymple's " Essay," ubi suprà.) It is probable that Coke is mistaken in supposing that " at the common law the tenant might have made a feoffment of the whole tenancy to be holden of the lord."

18 Edward I, called Quia Emptores, which at the same time gave the liberty of alienating lands, to be holden of the grantor's immediate lord. The tenants of the crown were not included in this act; but that of 1 Edward III, c. 12, enabled them to alienate, upon the payment of a composition into chancery, which was fixed at one third of the annual value of the lands.[85]

These restraints, placed for the lord's advantage upon the transfer of feudal property, are not to be confounded with those designed for the protection of heirs and preservation of families. Such were the jus protimeseos in the books of the fiefs,[86] and retrait lignager of the French law, which gave to the relations of the vendor a pre-emption upon the sale of any fief, and a right of subsequent redemption. Such was the positive prohibition of alienating a fief held by descent from the father (feudum paternum), without the consent of the kindred on that line.[87] Such, too, were the still more rigorous fetters imposed by the English statute of entails, which precluded all lawful alienation, till, after two centuries, it was overthrown by the fictitious process of a common recovery. Though these partake in some measure of the feudal spirit, and would form an important head in the legal history of that system, it will be sufficient to allude to them in a sketch which is confined to the development of its political influence.

A custom very similar in effect to subinfeudation was the tenure by frérage, which prevailed in many parts of France. Primogeniture, in that extreme which our common law has established, was unknown, I believe, in every country upon the continent. The customs of France found means to preserve the dignity of families and the indivisibility of a feudal homage without exposing the younger sons of a gentleman to absolute beggary or dependence. Baronies, indeed, were not divided; but the eldest son was bound to make a provision in money, by way of appanage, for the other children, in proportion to his circumstances and their birth.[88] As to inferior fiefs, in many places an equal partition was made; in others, the eldest took the chief portion, generally two thirds, and received the homage of his brothers for the remaining part, which they divided. To the lord of whom the fief was held, himself did homage for the whole.[89] In the early times of the feudal policy, when military service was the great object of the relation between lord and

<hr>

[85] 2 Inst., p. 66; Blackstone's "Commentaries," vol. ii, c. 5.
[86] "Lib. Feud.," l. v, tome xiii. There were analogies to this jus προτιμήσεως in the Roman law, and, still more closely, in the constitutions of the latter Byzantine emperors.
[87] Alienatio feudi paterni non valet etiam domini voluntate, nisi agnatis con-

sentientibus. ("Lib. Feud." apud Wright on "Tenures," pp. 108, 156.)
[88] Du Cange, v. Apanamentum, Baro. Baronie ne depart mie entre frères se leur pere ne leur à fait partie; mes li ainsnez doit faire avenant bienfet au puisné, et si doit les filles marier. ("Etablissem. de St. Louis," c. 24.)
[89] This was also the law of Flanders

vassal, this, like all other subinfeudation, was rather advantageous to the former, for when the homage of a fief was divided, the service was diminished in proportion. Suppose, for example, the obligation of military attendance for an entire manor to have been forty days; if that came to be equally split among two, each would owe but a service of twenty. But if, instead of being homagers to the same suzerain, one tenant held immediately of the other, as every feudatory might summon the aid of his own vassals, the superior lord would, in fact, obtain the service of both. Whatever opposition, therefore, was made to the rights of subinfeudation or frérage would indicate a decay in the military character, the living principle of feudal tenure. Accordingly, in the reign of Philip Augustus, when the fabric was beginning to shake, we find a confederate agreement of some principal nobles sanctioned by the king, to abrogate the mesne tenure of younger brothers, and establish an immediate dependence of each upon the superior lord.[90] This, however, was not universally adopted, and the original frérage subsisted to the last in some of the customs of France.[91]

3. As fiefs descended but to the posterity of the first taker, or at the utmost to his kindred, they necessarily became sometimes vacant for want of heirs, especially where, as in England, there was no power of devising them by will. In this case it was obvious that they ought to revert to the lord, from whose property they had been derived. These reversions became more frequent through the forfeitures occasioned by the vassal's delinquency, either toward his superior lord or the state. Various cases are laid down in the "Assises de Jérusalem," where the vassal forfeits his land for a year, for his life, or forever.[92] But under rapacious kings, such as the Norman line in England, absolute forfeitures came to prevail, and a new doctrine was introduced, the corruption of blood, by which the heir was effectually excluded from deducing his title at any distant time through an attainted ancestor.

4. Reliefs, fines upon alienation, and escheats seem to be natural reservations in the lord's bounty to his vassal. He had rights of another class which principally arose out of fealty and intimate attachment. Such were the aids which he was entitled to call for in certain prescribed circumstances. These depended a great deal upon local custom, and were often extorted unreason-

and Hainault. (Martenne, "Thesaurus Anecdotor," tome i, p. 1092.) The customs as to succession were exceedingly various, as indeed they continued to be until the late generalization of French law. ("Recueil des Histor.," tome ii, préface, p. 108; "Hist. de Languedoc," tome ii, pp. 111, 511.) In the former work it is said that primogeniture was introduced by the Normans from Scandinavia.
[90] "Ordonnances des Rois," tome i, p. 29.
[91] Du Cange, "Dissert. III. sur Joinville"; Beauman., c. 47.
[92] C. 200, 201.

ably. Du Cange mentions several as having existed in France; such as an aid for the lord's expedition to the Holy Land, for marrying his sister or eldest son, and for paying a relief to his suzerain on taking possession of his land.[93] Of these, the last appears to have been the most usual in England. But this and other aids occasionally exacted by the lords were felt as a severe grievance; and by Magna Charta three only are retained: to make the lord's eldest son a knight, to marry his eldest daughter, and to redeem his person from prison. They were restricted to nearly the same description by a law of William I of Sicily and by the customs of France.[94] These feudal aids are deserving of our attention, as the beginnings of taxation, of which for a long time they in a great measure answered the purpose, till the craving necessities and covetous policy of kings substituted for them more durable and onerous burdens.

I might here, perhaps, close the enumeration of feudal incidents, but that the two remaining, wardship and marriage, though only partial customs, were those of our own country, and tend to illustrate the rapacious character of a feudal aristocracy.

5. In England and in Normandy, which either led the way to, or adopted, all these English institutions, the lord had the wardship of his tenant during minority.[95] By virtue of this right he had both the care of his person and received to his own use the profits of the estate. There is something in this custom very conformable to the feudal spirit, since none was so fit as the lord to train up his vassal to arms, and none could put in so good a claim to enjoy the fief, while the military service for which it had been granted was suspended. This privilege of guardianship seems to have been enjoyed by the lord in some parts of Germany;[96] but in the law of France the custody of the land was intrusted to the next heir, and that of the person, as in socage tenures among us, to the nearest kindred of that blood which could not inherit.[97] By a gross abuse of this custom in England, the right of guardianship in chivalry, or temporary possession

[93] Du Cange, voc. Auxilium.
[94] Giannone, l. xii, c. 5; Velly, tome vi, p. 200; "Ordonnances des Rois," tome i, p. 138; tome xvi, préface.
[95] "Recueil des Historiens," tome xi, préface, p. 162; Argou, "Inst. au Droit François," l. i, c. 6; Houard, "Anciennes Loix des François," tome i, p. 147.
[96] Schilter, "Institutiones Juris Feudalis,".p. 85.
[97] Du Cange, v. Custodia; "Assises de Jérusalem," c. 178; "Etablissemens de St. Louis," c. 17; Beaumanoir, c. 15; Argou, l. i, c. 6. The second of these uses nearly the same expression as Sir John Fortescue in accounting for the exclusion of the next heir from guardianship of the person; that mauvaise convoitise li fairoit faire la garde du loup.

I know not any mistake more usual in English writers who have treated of the feudal law than that of supposing that guardianship in chivalry was a universal custom. A charter of 1198, in Rymer, tome i, p. 105, seems indeed to imply that the incidents of garde noble and of marriage existed in the isle of Oleron. But Eleanor, by a later instrument, grants that the inhabitants of that island should have the wardship and marriage of their heirs without any interposition, and expressly abrogates all the evil customs that her husband had introduced (p. 112). From hence I should infer that Henry II had endeavoured to impose these feudal burdens (which perhaps were then new even in England) upon his continental dominions. Radulphus de Diceto tells us

of the lands, was assigned over to strangers. This was one of the most vexatious parts of our feudal tenures, and was never, perhaps, more sorely felt than in their last stage under the Tudor and Stuart families.

6. Another right given to the lord by the Norman and English laws was that of marriage, or of tendering a husband to his female wards while under age, whom they could not reject without forfeiting the value of the marriage; that is, as much as any one would give to the guardian for such an alliance. This was afterward extended to male wards, and became a very lucrative source of extortion to the crown, as well as to mesne lords. This custom seems to have had the same extent as that of wardships. It is found in the ancient books of Germany, but not of France.[98] The kings, however, and even inferior lords, of that country, required their consent to be solicited for the marriage of their vassals' daughters. Several proofs of this occur in the history as well as in the laws of France; and the same prerogative existed in Germany, Sicily, and England.[99] A still more remarkable law prevailed in the kingdom of Jerusalem. The lord might summon any female vassal to accept one of three whom he should propose as her husband. No other condition seems to have been imposed on him in selecting these suitors than that they should be of equal rank with herself. Neither the maiden's coyness nor the widow's affliction, neither aversion to the proffered candidates nor love to one more favoured, seem to have passed as legitimate excuses. One, only one plea, could come from the lady's mouth who was resolute to hold her land in single blessedness. It was, that she was past sixty years of age; and after this unwelcome confession it is justly argued by the author of the law-book which I quote, that the lord could not decently press her into matrimony.[100] However outrageous

of a claim made by him to the wardship of Châteauroux in Berry, which could not legally have been subject to that custom. ("Twysden. X Scriptores," p. 599.) And he set up pretensions to the custody of the duchy of Brittany after the death of his son Geoffrey. This might perhaps be justified by the law of Normandy, on which Brittany depended. But Philip Augustus made a similar claim. In fact, these political assertions of right, prompted by ambition and supported by force, are bad precedents to establish rules of jurisprudence. Both Philip and Henry were abundantly disposed to realize so convenient a prerogative as that of guardianship in chivalry over the fiefs of their vassals. (Littleton's "Henry II.," vol. iii, p. 441.)

[98] Schilter, ubi suprà. Du Cange, voc. Disparagare, seems to admit this feudal right in France; but the passages he quotes do not support it. See also the word Maritagium. [M. Guizot has, how-

ever, observed ("Hist. de la Civilisation en France," Leçon 39) that the feudal incidents of guardianship in chivalry by marriage were more frequent than I seem to suppose. The customary law was so variable that it is dangerous to rely on particular instances, or to found a general negative on their absence. 1848.]

[99] "Ordonnances des Rois," tome i, p. 155; "Assises de Jérus.," c. 180, and Thaumassière's note; Du Cange, ubi suprà; Glanvil., l. vii, c. 12; Giannone, l. xi, c. 5; Wright on "Tenures," p. 94. St. Louis in return declared that he would not marry his own daughter without the consent of his barons. (Joinville, tome ii, p. 140.) Henry I of England had promised the same. The guardian of a female minor was obliged to give security to her lord not to marry her without his consent. ("Établissemens de St. Louis," c. 63.)

[100] "Ass. de Jérus.," c. 224. I must observe that Lauriere says this usage pre-

such a usage may appear to our ideas, it is to be recollected that the peculiar circumstances of that little state rendered it indispensable to possess in every fief a proper vassal to fulfil the duties of war.

These feudal servitudes distinguish the maturity of the system. No trace of them appears in the capitularies of Charlemagne and his family, nor in the instruments by which benefices were granted. I believe that they did not make part of the regular feudal law before the eleventh, or, perhaps, the twelfth century, though doubtless partial usages of this kind had grown up antecedently to either of those periods. If I am not mistaken, no allusion occurs to the lucrative rights of seigniory in the " Assises de Jérusalem," which are a monument of French usages in the eleventh century. Indeed, that very general commutation of allodial property into tenure which took place between the middle of the ninth and eleventh centuries would hardly have been effected if fiefs had then been liable to such burdens and so much extortion. In half-barbarous ages the strong are constantly encroaching upon the weak; a truth which, if it needed illustration, might find it in the progress of the feudal system.

We have thus far confined our inquiry to fiefs holden on terms of military service; since those are the most ancient and regular, as well as the most consonant to the spirit of the system. They alone were called proper feuds, and all were presumed to be of this description until the contrary was proved by the charter of investiture. A proper feud was bestowed without price, without fixed stipulation, upon a vassal capable of serving personally in the field. But gradually, with the help of a little legal ingenuity, improper fiefs of the most various kinds were introduced, retaining little of the characteristics, and less of the spirit, which distinguished the original tenures. Women, if indeed that were an innovation, were admitted to inherit them;[101] they were granted for a price, and without reference to military service. The language of the feudal law was applied by a kind of metaphor to almost every transfer of property. Hence pensions of money and allowances of provisions, however remote from right notions of a fief, were sometimes granted under that name; and even where land was the subject of the donation, its conditions were often lucrative, often honorary, and sometimes ludicrous.[102]

vailed en plusieurs lieux, though he quotes no authority. (" Ordonnances des Rois," p. 155.)

[101] Women did not inherit fiefs in the German Empire. Whether they were ever excluded from succession in France I know not; the genius of a military tenure, and the old Teutonic customs, preserved in the Salic law, seem adverse to their possession of feudal lands; yet the practice, at least from the eleventh century downward, does not support the theory.

[102] Crag., " Jus Feudale," l. i, tit. 10; Du Cange, voc. Feudum de Camerâ, etc. In the treaty between Henry I of England and Robert, Count of Flanders, A. D. 1101, the king stipulates to pay annually 400 marks of silver, in feodo, for the military service of his ally. (Rymer, " Fœdera," tome i, p. 2.)

There is one extensive species of feudal tenure which may be distinctly noticed. The pride of wealth in the middle ages was principally exhibited in a multitude of dependents. The court of Charlemagne was crowded with officers of every rank, some of the most eminent of whom exercised functions about the royal person which would have been thought fit only for slaves in the palace of Augustus or Antonine. The freeborn Franks saw nothing menial in the titles of cup-bearer, steward, marshal, and master of the horse, which are still borne by the noblest families in many parts of Europe, and, till lately, by sovereign princes in the empire.[103] From the court of the king this favourite piece of magnificence descended to those of the prelates and barons, who surrounded themselves with household officers called ministerials, a name equally applied to those of a servile and of a liberal description.[104] The latter of these were rewarded with grants of lands, which they held under a feudal tenure by the condition of performing some domestic service to the lord. What was called in our law grand sergeanty affords an instance of this species of fief.[105] It is, however, an instance of the noblest kind; but Muratori has given abundance of proofs that the commonest mechanical arts were carried on in the houses of the great by persons receiving lands upon those conditions.[106]

These imperfect feuds, however, belong more properly to the history of law, and are chiefly noticed in the present sketch because they attest the partiality manifested during the middle ages to the name and form of a feudal tenure. In the regular military fief we see the real principle of the system, which might originally have been defined an alliance of free landholders arranged in degrees of subordination, according to their respective capacities of affording mutual support.

The peculiar and varied attributes of feudal tenures naturally gave rise to a new jurisprudence, regulating territorial rights in those parts of Europe which had adopted the system. For a

[103] The Count of Anjou, under Louis VI, claimed the office of Great Seneschal of France; that is, to carry dishes to the king's table on state days. (Sismondi, v, 135.) Thus the feudal notions of grand sergeanty prepared the way for the restoration of royal supremacy, as the military tenures had impaired it. The wound and the remedy came from the same lance. If the feudal system was incompatible with despotism, and even, while in its full vigour, with legitimate authority, it kept alive the sense of a supreme chief, of a superiority of rank, of a certain subjection to an hereditary sovereign, not yet testified by unlimited obedience, but by homage and loyalty.
[104] Schmidt, "Hist. des Allemands,"

tome iii, p. 92; Du Cange, v. Familia, Ministeriales.
[105] "This tenure," says Littleton, "is where a man holds his lands or tenements of our sovereign lord the king by such services as he ought to do in his proper person to the king, as to carry the banner of the king, or his lance, or to lead his array, or to be his marshal, or to carry his sword before him at his coronation, or to be his sewer at his coronation, or his carver, or his butler, or to be one of his chamberlains at the receipt of his exchequer, or to do other like services." (Sect. 153.)
[106] "Antiq. Ital. Dissert.," 11, ad finem.

length of time this rested in traditionary customs, observed in the domains of each prince or lord, without much regard to those of his neighbours. Laws were made occasionally by the emperor in Germany and Italy, which tended to fix the usages of those countries. About the year 1170, Girard and Obertus, two Milanese lawyers, published two books of the law of fiefs, which obtained a great authority, and have been regarded as the groundwork of that jurisprudence.[107] A number of subsequent commentators swelled this code with their glosses and opinions to enlighten or obscure the judgment of the imperial tribunals. These were chiefly civilians or canonists, who brought to the interpretation of old barbaric customs the principles of a very different school. Hence a manifest change was wrought in the law of feudal tenure, which they assimilated to the usufruct or the emphyteusis of the Roman code; modes of property somewhat analogous in appearance, but totally distinct in principle, from the legitimate fief. These Lombard lawyers propagated a doctrine which has been too readily received, that the feudal system originated in their country; and some writers upon jurisprudence, such as Duck and Sir James Craig, incline to give a preponderating authority to their code. But whatever weight it may have possessed within the limits of the empire, a different guide must be followed in the ancient customs of France and England.[108] These were fresh from the fountain of that curious polity with which the stream of Roman law had never mingled its waters. In England we know that the Norman system established between the conquest and the reign of Henry II was restrained by regular legislation, by paramount courts of justice, and by learned writings, from breaking into discordant local usages, except in a comparatively small number of places, and has become the principal source of our common law. But the independence of the French nobles produced a much greater variety of customs. The whole number collected and reduced to certainty in the sixteenth century amounted to two hundred and eighty-five, or, omitting those inconsiderable for extent or peculiarity, to sixty. The earliest written customary in France is that of Béarn, which is said to have been confirmed by Viscount Gaston IV in 1088.[109] Many others were written in the two subsequent ages, of which the customs of Beauvoisis, compiled by

[107] Giannone, " Ist. di Napoli," l. xiii, c. 3. The " Libri Feudorum " are printed in most editions of the " Corpus Juris Civilis."

[108] Giannone explicitly contrasts the French and Lombard laws respecting fiefs. The latter was the foundation of the " Libri Feudorum," and formed the common law of Italy. The former was introduced by Roger Guiscard into his dominions, in three books of constitutions, printed in Lindebrog's collection. There were several material differences, which Giannone enumerates, especially the Norman custom of primogeniture. (" Ist. di Nap." l. xi, c. 5.)

[109] There are two editions of this curious old code: one at Pau, in 1552, republished with a fresh title-page and permission of Henry IV in 1602; the other

Beaumanoir under Philip III, are the most celebrated, and contain a mass of information on the feudal constitution and manners. Under Charles VII an ordinance was made for the formation of a general code of customary law, by ascertaining forever in a written collection those of each district; but the work was not completed till the reign of Charles IX. This was what may be called the common law of the pays coutumiers, or northern division of France, and the rule of all their tribunals, unless where controlled by royal edicts.

The advocates of a Roman origin for most of the institutions which we find in the kingdoms erected on the ruins of the empire are naturally prone to magnify the analogies to feudal tenure which Rome presents to us, and even to deduce it either from the ancient relation of patron and client, and that of personal commendation, which was its representative in a later age, or from the frontier lands granted in the third century to the Læti, or barbarian soldiers, who held them, doubtless, subject to a condition of military service. The use of commendation especially, so frequent in the fifth century, before the conquest of Gaul, as well as afterward, does certainly bear a strong analogy to vassalage, and I have already pointed it out as one of its sources. It wanted, however, that definite relation to the tenure of land which distinguished the latter. The royal Antrustio (whether the word commendatus were applied to him or not) stood bound by gratitude and loyalty to his sovereign, and in a very different degree from a common subject; but he was not perhaps strictly a vassal till he had received a territorial benefice.[110] The complexity of subinfeudation could have no analogy in commendation. The grants to veterans and to the Læti are so far only analogous to fiefs, that they established the principle of holding lands on a condition of military service. But this service was no more than what, both under Charlemagne and in England, if not in other times and places, the allodial freeholder was bound to render for the defence of the realm; it was more commonly required, because the lands were on a barbarian frontier; but the duty was not even very analogous to that of a feudal tenant.[111] The es-

at Lescars, in 1633. These laws, as we read them, are subsequent to a revision made in the middle of the sixteenth century, in which they were more or less corrected. The basis, however, is unquestionably very ancient. We even find the composition for homicide preserved in them, so that murder was not a capital offence in Béarn, though robbery was such. ("Rubrica de Homicidis," art. xxxi; see, too, "Rubrica de Pœnis," art. i and ii.)

[110] This word "vassal" is used very indefinitely; it means, in its original sense, only a servant or dependent. But in the continental records of histories we commonly find it applied to feudal tenants.

[111] If Gothofred is right in his construction of the tenure of these Læti, they were not even generally liable to this part of our trinoda necessitas, but only to conscription for the legions. Et ea tamen conditione terras illis excolendas Læti consequebantur, ut delectibus quoque obnoxii essent et legionibus insererentur. ("Not. ad Cod. Theod.," l. vii, tit. 20, c. 12.) Sir Francis Palgrave, however, says, "The duty of bearing arms was inseparably connected with the

sence of a fief seems to be that its tenant owed fealty to a lord, and not to the state or the sovereign; the lord might be the latter, but it was not, feudally speaking, as a sovereign that he was obeyed. This is, therefore, sufficient to warrant us in tracing the real theory of feuds no higher than the Merovingian history in France; their full establishment, as has been seen, is considerably later. But the preparatory steps in the constitutions of the declining empire are of considerable importance, not merely as analogies, but as predisposing circumstances, and even germs to be subsequently developed. The beneficiary tenure of lands could not well be brought by the conquerors from Germany; but the donatives of arms or precious metals bestowed by the chiefs on their followers were also analogous to fiefs; and, as the Roman institutions were one source of the law of tenure, so these were another.

It is of great importance to be on our guard against seeming analogies which vanish away when they are closely observed. We should speak inaccurately if we were to use the word feudal for the service of the Irish or Highland clans to their chieftain; their tie was that of imagined kindred and respect for birth, not the spontaneous compact of vassalage. Much less can we extend the name of feud, though it is sometimes strangely misapplied, to the polity of Poland and Russia. All the Polish nobles were equal in rights, and independent of each other; all who were less than noble were in servitude. No government can be more opposite to the long gradations and mutual duties of the feudal system.[112]

The regular machinery and systematic establishment of feuds, in fact, may be considered as almost confined to the dominions of Charlemagne, and to those countries which afterward derived it from thence. In England it can hardly be thought to have existed in a complete state before the conquest. Scotland, it is supposed, borrowed it soon after from her neighbour. The Lombards of Benevento had introduced feudal customs into the Neapolitan provinces, which the Norman conquerors afterward perfected. Feudal tenures were so general in the kingdom of Aragon that I reckon it among the monarchies which were founded upon that basis.[113] Charlemagne's empire, it must be

property." ("English Commonwealth," i, 354.) This is too equivocal; but he certainly means more than Gothofred; he supposes a permanent universal obligation to render service in all public warfare.

[112] In civil history many instances might be found of feudal ceremonies in countries not regulated by the feudal law. Thus Selden has published an infeudation of a vayvod of Moldavia by the King of Poland, A. D. 1485, in the regular forms, vol. iii, p. 514. But these political fiefs have hardly any connection with the general system, and merely denote the subordination of one prince or people to another.

[113] It is probable that feudal tenure was as ancient in the north of Spain as in the contiguous provinces of France. But it seems to have chiefly prevailed in Aragon about the twelfth and thirteenth centuries, when the Moors south of the Ebro were subdued by the enter-

remembered, extended as far as the Ebro. But in Castile [114] and Portugal they were very rare, and certainly could produce no political effect. Benefices for life were sometimes granted in the kingdoms of Denmark and Bohemia. [115] Neither of these, however, nor Sweden, nor Hungary, come under the description of countries influenced by the feudal system. [116] That system, however, after all these limitations, was so extensively diffused that it might produce confusion as well as prolixity to pursue collateral branches of its history in all the countries where it prevailed. But this embarrassment may be avoided without any loss, I trust, of important information. The English constitution will find its place in another portion of these volumes; and the political condition of Italy, after the eleventh century, was not much affected, except in the kingdom of Naples, by the laws of feudal tenure. I shall confine myself, therefore, chiefly to France and Germany, and far more to the former than the latter country. But it may be expedient first to contemplate the state of society in its various classes during the prevalence of feudal principles before we trace their influence upon the national government.

prise of private nobles, who, after conquering estates for themselves, did homage for them to the king. James I, upon the reduction of Valencia, granted lands by way of fief, on condition of defending that kingdom against the Moors, and residing personally upon the estate. Many did not perform this engagement, and were deprived of the lands in consequence. It appears by the testament of this monarch that feudal tenures subsisted in every part of his dominions. (Martenne, " Thesaurus Anecdotorum," tome i, pp. 1141, 1155.) An edict of Peter II in 1210 prohibits the alienation of emphyteuses without the lord's consent. It is hard to say whether regular fiefs are meant by this word. (De Marca, " Marca Hispanica," p. 1396.) This author says that there were no arrière fiefs in Catalonia.

The Aragonese fiefs appear, however, to have differed from those of other countries in some respects. Zurita mentions fiefs according to the custom of Italy, which he explains to be such as were liable to the usual feudal aids for marrying the lord's daughter, and other occasions. We may infer, therefore, that these prestations were not customary in Aragon. (" Annals de Aragon," tome ii, p. 62.)

[114] What is said of vassalage in Alfonzo X's code, Las siete partidas, is short and obscure: nor am I certain that it meant anything more than voluntary commendation, the custom mentioned in the former part of this chapter, from which the vassal might depart at pleasure. See, however, Du Cange, v. Honour, where authorities are given for the

existence of Castilian fiefs; and I have met with occasional mention of them in history. I believe that tenures of this kind were introduced in the fourteenth and fifteenth centuries, but not to any great extent. (Marina, " Teoria de las Cortes," tome iii, p. 14.)

Tenures of a feudal nature, as I collect from " Freirii Institut. Juris Lusitani," tome ii, tit. 1 and 3, existed in Portugal, though the jealousy of the crown prevented the system from being established. There were even territorial jurisdictions in that kingdom, though not, at least originally, in Castile.

[115] Daniæ regni politicus status. Elzevir, 1629. Stransky, Respublica Bohemica, ib. In one of the oldest Danish historians, Sweno, I have noticed this expression: Waldemarus, patris tunc potitus feodo. (Langebek, " Scrip. Rerum Danic.," tome i, p. 62.) By this he means the duchy of Sleswick, not a fief, but an honour or government possessed by Waldemar. Saxo Grammaticus calls it, more classically, paternæ præfecturæ dignitas. Sleswick was, in later times, sometimes held as a fief; but this does not in the least imply that lands in Denmark proper were feudal, of which I find no evidence.

[116] Though there were no feudal tenures in Sweden, yet the nobility and others were exempt from taxes on condition of serving the king with a horse and arms at their own expense; and a distinction was taken between liber and tributarius. But any one of the latter might become of the former class, or vice versa.—Sueciæ descriptio. Elzevir, 1631, p. 92.

8

It has been laid down already as most probable that no proper aristocracy, except that of wealth, was known under the early kings of France; and it was hinted that hereditary bene- fices—or, in other words, fiefs—might supply the link that was wanting between personal privileges and those of descent. The possessors of beneficiary estates were usually the richest and most conspicuous individuals in the estate. They were immedi- ately connected with the crown, and partakers in the exercise of justice and royal counsels. Their sons now came to inherit this eminence; and, as fiefs were either inalienable, or at least not very frequently alienated, rich families were kept long in sight; and, whether engaged in public affairs, or living with magnificence and hospitality at home, naturally drew to them- selves popular estimation. The dukes and counts, who had changed their quality of governors into that of lords over the provinces intrusted to them, were at the head of this noble class. And in imitation of them their own vassals, as well as those of the crown, and even rich allodialists, assumed titles from their towns or castles, and thus arose a number of petty counts, barons, and viscounts. This distinct class of nobility became coextensive with the feudal tenures.[117] For the military tenant, however poor, was subject to no tribute; no prestation, but service in the field; he was the companion of his lord in the sports and feasting of his castle, the peer of his court; he fought on horseback, he was clad in the coat of mail, while the commonalty, if summoned at all to war, came on foot, and with no armour of defence. As everything in the habits of society conspired with that prejudice which, in spite of moral philosophers, will constantly raise the profession of arms above all others, it was a natural consequence that a new species of aristocracy, founded upon the mixed con- siderations of birth, tenure, and occupation, sprang out of the feudal system. Every possessor of a fief was a gentleman, though he owned but a few acres of land and furnished his slender con- tribution toward the equipment of a knight. In the " Libri Feudorum," indeed, those who were three degrees removed from the emperor in order of tenancy are considered as ignoble;[118] but this is restrained to modern investitures, and in France, where subinfeudation was carried the farthest, no such distinction has met my observation.[119]

[117] M. Guérard observes that in the Chartulary of Chartres, exhibiting the usages of the eleventh and beginning of the twelfth centuries, " La noblesse s'y montre complètement constituée; c'est à dire, privilégiée et héréditaire. Elle peut être divisée en haute, moyenne, et basse." By the first he understands those who held immediately of the crown; the middle nobility were mediate vassals, but had rights of jurisdiction, which the lower had not. (" Prolégomènes à la Cartulaire de Chartres," p. 30.)

[118] L. ii, tit. 10.

[119] The nobility of an allodial posses- sion, in France, depended upon its right to territorial jurisdiction. Hence there were franc-aleux nobles and franc-aleux roturiers; the latter of which were sub- ject to the jurisdiction of the neighbour-

There still, however, wanted something to ascertain gentility of blood where it was not marked by the actual tenure of land. This was supplied by two innovations devised in the eleventh and twelfth centuries—the adoption of surnames and of armorial bearings. The first are commonly referred to the former age, when the nobility began to add the names of their estates to their own, or, having any way acquired a distinctive appellation, transmitted it to their posterity.[120] As to armorial bearings, there is no doubt that emblems somewhat similar have been immemorially used both in war and peace. The shields of ancient warriors and devices upon coins or seals bear no distant resemblance to modern blazonry. But the general introduction of such bearings as hereditary distinctions has been sometimes attributed to tournaments, wherein the champions were distinguished by fanciful devices; sometimes to the crusades, where a multitude of all nations and languages stood in need of some visible token to denote the banners of their respective chiefs. In fact, the peculiar symbols of heraldry point to both these sources, and have been borrowed in part from each.[121] Hereditary arms were perhaps scarcely used by private families before the beginning of the thirteenth century.[122] From that time, however, they became very general, and have contributed to elucidate that branch of history which regards the descent of illustrious families.

When the privileges of birth had thus been rendered capable of legitimate proof, they were enhanced in a great degree, and a line drawn between the high-born and ignoble classes, almost as broad as that which separated liberty from servitude. All offices of trust and power were conferred on the former; those excepted which appertain to the legal profession. A plebeian

ing lord. (Loiseau, " Traité des Seigneuries," p. 76; Denisart, " Dictionnaire des Décisions," art. Franc-aleu.)

[120] Mabillon, " Traité de Diplomatique," l. ii, c. 7. The authors of the " Nouveau Traité de Diplomatique," tome ii, p. 563, trace the use of surnames in a few instances even to the beginning of the tenth century; but they did not become general, according to them, till the thirteenth.

M. Guérard finds a few hereditary surnames in the eleventh century and many that were personal. (" Cartulaire de Chartres," p. 93.) The latter are not surnames at all, in our usual sense. A good many may be found in " Doomsday," as that of Burdet in Leicestershire, Malet in Suffolk, Corbet in Shropshire, Colville in Yorkshire, besides those with de, which, of course, is a local designation, but became hereditary.

[121] " Mém. de l'Acad. des Inscriptions," tome xx, p. 579.

[122] I should be unwilling to make a negative assertion peremptorily in a matter of mere antiquarian research, but I am not aware of any decisive evidence that hereditary arms were borne in the twelfth century, except by a very few royal or almost royal families. (Mabillon, " Traité de Diplomatique," l. ii, c. 18.) Those of Geoffrey the Fair, Count of Anjou, who died in 1150, are extant on his shield; azure, four lions rampant or. (" Hist. Littéraire de la France," tome ix, p. 165.) If arms had been considered as hereditary at that time, this should be the bearing of England, which, as we all know, differs considerably. Louis VII sprinkled his seal and coin with fleurs-de-lis, a very ancient device, or rather ornament, and the same as what are sometimes called bees. The golden ornaments found in the tomb of Childeric I at Tournay, which may be seen in the Library of Paris, may pass either for fleurs-de-lis or bees. Charles V reduced the number to three, and thus fixed the arms of France. The Counts of Toulouse used their cross in the twelfth age; but no other arms, Vaissette tells us, can be traced in Languedoc so far back. (T. iii, p. 514.)

could not possess a fief.[123]   Such at least was the original strictness: but as the aristocratic principle grew weaker, an indulgence was extended to heirs, and afterward to purchasers.[124]
They were even permitted to become noble by the acquisition,
or at least by its possession for three generations.[125]   But notwithstanding this ennobling quality of the land, which seems
rather of an equivocal description, it became an established right
of the crown to take every twenty years, and on every change
of the vassal, a fine, known by the name of franc-fief, from plebeians in possession of land held by a noble tenure.[126]   A gentleman in France or Germany could not exercise any trade without derogating—that is, losing the advantages of—his rank.   A
few exceptions were made, at least in the former country, in
favour of some liberal arts and of foreign commerce.[127]   But in
nothing does the feudal haughtiness of birth more show itself
than in the disgrace which attended unequal marriages.   No
children could inherit a territory held immediately of the empire unless both their parents belonged to the higher class of
nobility.   In France the offspring of a gentleman by a plebeian
mother were reputed noble for the purposes of inheritance and
of exemption from tribute.[128]   But they could not be received

Armorial bearings were in use among
the Saracens during the latter crusades,
as appears by a passage in Joinville, tome
i, p. 88 (" Collect. des Mémoires "), and
Du Cange's note upon it.   Perhaps, however, they may have been adopted in
imitation of the Franks, like the ceremonies of knighthood.   Villaret ingeniously conjectures that the separation of
different branches of the same family by
their settlements in Palestine led to the
use of hereditary arms, in order to preserve the connection. (T. xi, p. 113.)
M. Sismondi, I observe, seems to entertain no doubt that the noble families
of Pisa, including that whose name he
bears, had their armorial distinctions in
the beginning of the twelfth century.
(" Hist. des Répub. Ital.," tome i, p.
373.)   It is at least probable that the
heraldic devices were as ancient in Italy
as in any part of Europe.   And the authors of " Nouveau Traité de Diplomatique," tome iv, p. 388, incline to refer
hereditary arms even in France to the
beginning of the twelfth century, though
without producing any evidence for this.
[123] We have no English word that conveys the full sense of roturier.   How
glorious is this deficiency in our political
language, and how different are the ideas
suggested by commoner!   Roturier, according to Du Cange, is derived from
rupturarius, a peasant, ab agrum rum-
pendo.
[124] The " Establishments of St. Louis "
forbid this innovation, but Beaumanoir
contends that the prohibition does not
extend to descent or marriage (c. 48).
The roturier who acquired a fief, if he

challenged any one, fought with ignoble
arms, but in all other respects was treated
as a gentleman.   (Ibid.)   Yet a knight
was not obliged to do homage to the
roturier who became his superior by the
acquisition of a fief on which he depended.   (Carpentier, Supplement. ad Du
Cange, voc. Homagium.)
[125] " Établissemens de St. Louis," c.
143, and note, in " Ordonnances des
Rois," tome i.   See also preface to the
same volume, p. xii.   According to Mably, the possession of a fief did not cease
to confer nobility (analogous to our
barony by tenure) till the " Ordonnances
des Blois " in 1579.   (" Observations sur
l'Hist. de France," l. iii, c. 1. note 6.)
But Laurière, author of the preface above
cited, refers to Bouteiller, a writer of the
fourteenth century, to prove that no one
could become noble without the king's
authority.   The contradiction will not
much perplex us when we reflect on the
disposition of lawyers to ascribe all prerogatives to the crown, at the expense
of territorial proprietors and of ancient
customary law.
[126] The right, originally perhaps usurpation, called franc fief, began under
Philip the Fair.   (" Ordonnances des
Rois," tome i, p. 324; Franc-fief.)
[127] Houard, " Dict. du Droit Normand.
Encyclopédie," art. Noblesse; Argou, l.
ii, c. 2.)
[128] Nobility, to a certain degree, was
communicated through the mother alone,
not only by the custom of Champagne,
but in all parts of France; that is, the
issue were " gentilhommes du fait de

into any order of chivalry, though capable of simple knighthood; nor were they considered as any better than a bastard class deeply tainted with the alloy of their maternal extraction. Many instances occur where letters of nobility have been granted to reinstate them in their rank.[129] For several purposes it was necessary to prove four, eight, sixteen, or a greater number of quarters—that is, of coats borne by paternal and maternal ancestors—and the same practice still subsists in Germany.[130]

It appears, therefore, that the original nobility of the Continent were what we may call self-created, and did not derive their rank from any such concessions of their respective sovereigns as have been necessary in subsequent ages. In England the baronies by tenure might belong to the same class if the lands upon which they depended had not been granted by the crown. But the Kings of France, before the end of the thirteenth century, began to assume a privilege of creating nobles by their own authority, and without regard to the tenure of land. Philip the Hardy, in 1271, was the first French king who granted letters of nobility; under the reigns of Philip the Fair and his children they gradually became frequent.[131] This effected a change in the character of nobility, and had as obvious a moral as other events of the same age had a political influence in diminishing the power and independence of the territorial aristocracy. The privileges originally connected with ancient lineage and extensive domains became common to the low-born creatures of a court, and lost consequently part of their title to respect. The lawyers, as I have observed above, pretended that nobility could not exist without a royal concession. They acquired themselves, in return for their exaltation of prerogative, an official nobility by the exercise of magistracy. The institutions of chivalry again gave rise to a vast increase of gentlemen, knighthood, on whomsoever conferred by the sovereign, being a sufficient passport to noble privileges. It was usual, perhaps, to grant previous letters of nobility to a plebeian for whom the honour of knighthood was designed.

In this noble or gentle class there were several gradations. All those in France who held lands immediately depending upon the crown, whatever titles they might bear, were comprised in the order of barons. These were originally the peers of the king's court; they possessed the higher territorial jurisdiction, and had

leur corps," and could possess fiefs; but, says Beaumanoir, " la gentilesse par laquelle on devient chevalier doit venir de par le père " (c. 45). There was a proverbial maxim in French law, rather emphatic than decent, to express the derivation of gentility from the father, and of freedom from the mother.

[129] Beaumanoir, c. 45; Du Cange, Dissert. 10, sur Joinville; Carpentier, voc. Nobilitatio.
[130] [Note XII.]
[131] Velly, tome vi, p. 432; Du Cange and Carpentier, voc. Nobilitaire, etc.; Boulainvilliers, " Hist. de l'Ancien Gouvernement de France," tome i, p. 317.

the right of carrying their own banner into the field.[132]   To these corresponded the Valvassores majores and Capitanei of the empire.   In a subordinate class were the vassals of this high nobility, who, upon the Continent, were usually termed Vavassors— an appellation not unknown, though rare, in England.[133]   The Châtelains belonged to the order of Vavassors, as they held only arrière fiefs; but, having fortified houses, from which they derived their name (a distinction very important in those times), and possessing ampler rights of territorial justice, they rose above the level of their fellows in the scale of tenure.[134]   But after the personal nobility of chivalry became the object of pride, the Vavassors who obtained knighthood were commonly styled bachelors; those who had not received that honour fell into the class of squires,[135] or damoiseaux.

[132] Beaumanoir, c. 34; Du Cange, v. Baro; "Établissemens de St. Louis," l. i, c. 24; l. ii, c. 36. The vassals of inferior lords were, however, called, improperly, barons, both in France and England. ("Recueil des Historiens," tome xi, p. 300; Madox, "Baronia Anglica," p. 133.) In perfect strictness, those only whose immediate tenure of the crown was older than the accession of Hugh Capet were barons of France; namely, Bourbon, Coucy, and Beaujeu, or Beaujolois. It appears, however, by a register in the reign of Philip Augustus, that fifty-nine were reckoned in that class; the feudatories of the Capetian fiefs, Paris and Orleans being confounded with the original vassals of the crown. (Du Cange, voc. Baro.)

[133] Du Cange, voc. Vavassor; Velly, tome vi, p. 151; Madox, "Baronia Anglica," p. 135. There is, perhaps, hardly any word more loosely used than vavassor. Bracton says, Sunt etiam Vavassores, magnæ dignitatis viri. In France and Germany they are sometimes named with much less honour. Je suis un chevalier né de c'est part, de vavasseurs et de basse gent, says a romance. This is to be explained by the poverty to which the subdivision of fiefs reduced idle gentlemen. Chaucer concludes his picturesque description of the Franklin, in the prologue to the "Canterbury Tales," thus: "Was never such a worthy vavassor." This has perplexed some of our commentators, who, not knowing well what was meant by a franklin or by a vavassor, fancied the latter to be of much higher quality than the former. The poet, however, was strictly correct; his acquaintance with French manners showed him that the country squire, for his franklin is no other, precisely corresponded to the vavassor in France. Those who, having been deceived, by comparatively modern law-books, into a notion that the word franklin denoted but a stout yeoman, in spite of the wealth and rank which Chaucer assigns to him, and believing also, on the authority of the loose phrase

in Bracton, that all vavassors were "magnæ dignitatis viri," might well be puzzled at seeing the words employed as synonyms. See Todd's "Illustrations of Gower and Chaucer" for an instance.

[134] Du Cange, voc. Castellanus; "Coûtumes de Poitou," tit. iii; Loiseau, "Traité des Seigneuries," p. 160. Whoever had a right to a castle had la haute justice, this being so incident to the castle that it was transferred along with it. There might, however, be a seigneur haut-justicier below the châtelain; and a ridiculous distinction was made as to the number of posts by which their gallows might be supported. A baron's instrument of execution stood on four posts; a châtelain's on three; while the inferior lord who happened to possess la haute justice was forced to hang his subjects on a two-legged machine. ("Coûtumes de Poitou"; Du Cange, voc. Furca.)

Laurière quotes from an old manuscript the following short scale of ranks: Duc est la première dignité, puis comtes, puis viscomtes, et puis baron, et puis châtelain, et puis vavasseur, et puis citaen, et puis villain. ("Ordonnances des Rois," tome i, p. 277.)

[135] The sons of knights, and gentlemen not yet knighted, took the appellation of squires in the twelfth century. (Vaissette, "Hist. de Lang.," tome ii, p. 513.) That of Damoiseau came into use in the thirteenth. (Id., tome iii, p. 529.) The latter was, I think, more usual in France. Du Cange gives little information as to the word squire (Scutifer). "Apud Anglos," he says, "penultima est nobilitatis descriptio, inter Equitem et Generosum. Quod et alibi in usu fuit." Squire was not used as a title of distinction in England till the reign of Edward III, and then but sparingly. Though by Henry VI's time it was grown more common, yet none assumed it but the sons and heirs of knights and some military men; except officers in courts of justice, who, by patent or prescription, had obtained that addition. (Spelman's Posthumous Works, p. 234.)

It will be needless to dwell upon the condition of the inferior clergy, whether secular or professed, as it bears little upon the general scheme of polity. The prelates and abbots, however, it must be understood, were completely feudal nobles. They swore fealty for their lands to the king or other superior, received the homage of their vassals, enjoyed the same immunities, exercised the same jurisdiction, maintained the same authority as the lay lords among whom they dwelt. Military service does not appear to have been reserved in the beneficiary grants made to cathedrals and monasteries. But when other vassals of the crown were called upon to repay the bounty of their sovereign by personal attendance in war, the ecclesiastical tenants were supposed to fall within the scope of this feudal duty, which men little less uneducated and violent than their compatriots were not reluctant to fulfil. Charlemagne exempted, or rather prohibited, them from personal service by several capitularies.[136] The practice, however, as every one who has some knowledge of history will be aware, prevailed in succeeding ages. Both in national and private warfare we find very frequent mention of martial prelates.[137] But, contrary as this actual service might be to the civil as well as ecclesiastical laws, the clergy who held military fiefs were of course bound to fulfil the chief obligation of that tenure and send their vassals into the field. We have many instances of their accompanying the army, though not mixing in the conflict; and even the parish priests headed the militia of their villages.[138] The prelates, however, sometimes contrived to avoid this military service, and the payments introduced in commutation for it, by holding lands in frank-almoigne, a tenure which exempted them from every species of obligation except that of saying masses for the benefit of the grantor's family.[139] But, notwithstanding the warlike disposition of some ecclesiastics, their more usual inability to protect the estates of their churches against rapacious neighbours suggested a new species of feudal relation and tenure. The rich abbeys elected an advocate, whose business it was to defend their interests both in secular courts and, if necessary, in the field. Pepin and Charlemagne are styled advocates of the Roman Church. This, indeed, was on a magnificent scale; but in ordinary practice the advocate of a monastery was some neighbouring lord, who, in return for

[136] Mably, l. i, c. 5; Baluze, tome i, pp. 410, 932, 987. Any bishop, priest, deacon, or subdeacon bearing arms was to be degraded and not even admitted to lay communion. (Id., p. 932.)
[137] One of the latest instances probably of a fighting bishop is Jean Montaigu, Archbishop of Sens, who was killed at Agincourt. Monstrelet says that he was "non pas en estat pontifical, car au lieu de mitre il portoit une bacinet, pour dalmatique portoit un haubergeon, pour chasuble la piece d'acier; et au lieu de crosse, portoit une hache." (Fol. 132.)
[138] Daniel, "Hist. de la Milice Françoise," tome i, p. 88.
[139] Du Cange, "Eleemosyna Libera"; Madox, "Baronia Angl.," p. 115; Coke on Littleton, and other English law-books.

his protection, possessed many lucrative privileges, and very frequently considerable estates by way of fief from his ecclesiastical clients. Some of these advocates are reproached with violating their obligation, and becoming the plunderers of those whom they had been retained to defend.[140]

The classes below the gentry may be divided into freemen and villains. Of the first were the inhabitants of chartered towns, the citizens and burghers, of whom more will be said presently. As to those who dwelt in the country, we can have no difficulty in recognising, so far as England is concerned, the socagers, whose tenure was free, though not so noble as knight's service, and a numerous body of tenants for term of life, who formed that ancient basis of our strength, the English yeomanry. But the mere freemen are not at first sight so distinguishable in other countries. In French records and law-books of feudal times, all besides the gentry are usually confounded under the names of villains or hommes de pooste (gens potestatis).[141] This proves the slight estimation in which all persons of ignoble birth were considered. For undoubtedly there existed a great many proprietors of land and others, as free, though not as privileged, as the nobility. In the south of France, and especially Provence, the number of freemen is remarked to have been greater than in the parts on the right bank of the Loire, where the feudal tenures were almost universal.[142] I shall quote part of a passage in Beaumanoir, which points out this distinction of ranks pretty fully. "It should be known," he says,[143] "that there are three conditions of men in this world: the first is that of gentlemen; and the second is that of such as are naturally free, being born of a free mother. All who have a right to be called gentlemen are free, but all who are free are not gentlemen. Gentility comes by the father, and not by the mother; but freedom is derived from the mother only; and whoever is born of a free mother is himself free, and has free power to do anything that is lawful." [144]

In every age and country until times comparatively recent, personal servitude appears to have been the lot of a large, perhaps the greater, portion of mankind. We lose a good deal of our sympathy with the spirit of freedom in Greece and Rome, when the importunate recollection occurs to us of the tasks which

---

[140] Du Cange, voc. Advocatus; a full and useful article. "Recueil des Historiens," tome xi, préface, p. 184.

[141] Homo potestatis, non nobilis—Ita nuncupantur, quod in potestate domini sunt—Opponuntur viris nobilibus; apud Butilerium Consuetudinarii vocantur, Coustumiers, prestationibus scilicet obnoxii et operis. (Du Cange, voc. Potestas.) As all these freemen were obliged, by the ancient laws of France, to live under the protection of some par-

ticular lord, and found great difficulty in choosing a new place of residence, as they were subject to many tributes and oppressive claims on the part of their territorial superiors, we can not be surprised that they are confounded, at this distance, with men in actual servitude.

[142] Heeren, "Essai sur les Croisades," p. 122.

[143] "Coûtumes de Beauvoisis," c. 45, p. 256.

[144] [Note XIII.]

might be enjoined, and the punishments which might be inflicted, without control either of law or opinion, by the keenest patriot of the Comitia, or the Council of Five Thousand. A similar, though less powerful, feeling will often force itself on the mind when we read the history of the middle ages. The Germans, in their primitive settlements, were accustomed to the notion of slavery, incurred not only by captivity, but by crimes, by debt, and especially by loss in gaming. When they invaded the Roman Empire they found the same condition established in all its provinces. Hence, from the beginning of the era now under review, servitude, under somewhat different modes, was extremely common. There is some difficulty in ascertaining its varieties and stages. In the Salic laws, and in the capitularies, we read not only of Servi, but of Tributarii, Lidi, and Coloni, who were cultivators of the earth and subject to residence upon their lord's estate, though not destitute of property or civil rights.[145] Those who appertained to the demesne lands of the crown were called Fiscalini. The composition for the murder of one of these was much less than that for a freeman.[146] The number of these servile cultivators was undoubtedly great, yet in those early times, I should conceive, much less than it afterward became. Property was for the most part in small divisions, and a Frank who could hardly support his family upon a petty allodial patrimony was not likely to encumber himself with many servants. But the accumulation of overgrown private wealth had a natural tendency to make slavery more frequent. Where the small proprietors lost their lands by mere rapine, we may believe that their liberty was hardly less endangered.[147] Even where this was not the case, yet, as the labour either of artisans or of free husbandmen was but sparingly in demand, they were often compelled to exchange their liberty for bread.[148] In seasons also of famine, and they were not infrequent, many freemen sold themselves to slavery. A capitulary of Charles the Bald in 864 permits their redemption at an equitable price.[149] Others became slaves, as

[145] These passages are too numerous for reference. In a very early charter in Martenne's "Thesaurus Anecdotorum," tome i, p. 20, lands are granted, cum hominibus ibidem permanentibus, quos colonario ordine vivere constituimus. Men of this class were called, in Italy, Aldiones. A Lombard capitulary of Charlemagne says, Aldiones eâ lege vivunt in Italiâ sub servitute dominorum suorum, quâ Fiscalini, vel Lidi vivunt in Franciâ. (Muratori, Dissert. 14.) [Note XIV.]

[146] Originally it was but 45 solidi ("Leges Salicæ," c. 43), but Charlemagne raised it to 100. ("Baluzii Capitularia," p. 402.) There are several provisions in the laws of this great and wise monarch in favour of liberty. If a lord claimed any one either as his villein or slave (colonus sive servus), who had escaped beyond his territory, he was not to be given up till strict inquiry had been made in the place to which he was asserted to belong, as to his condition and that of his family (p. 400). And if the villein showed a charter of enfranchisement, the proof of its forgery was to lie upon the lord. No man's liberty could be questioned in the Hundred-court.

[147] Montesquieu ascribes the increase of personal servitude in France to the continued revolts and commotions under the first two dynasties (l. xxx, c. 11).

[148] Du Cange, voc. Obnoxatio.

[149] "Baluzii Capitularia." The Greek

more fortunate men became vassals, to a powerful lord, for the sake of his protection. Many were reduced into this state through inability to pay those pecuniary compositions for offences which were numerous and sometimes heavy in the barbarian codes of law; and many more by neglect of attendance on military expeditions of the king, the penalty of which was a fine called Heribann, with the alternative of perpetual servitude.[150] A source of loss of liberty which may strike us as more extraordinary was superstition; men were infatuated enough to surrender themselves, as well as their properties, to churches and monasteries, in return for such benefits as they might reap by the prayers of their new masters.[151]

The characteristic distinction of a villein was his obligation to remain upon his lord's estate. He was not only precluded from selling the lands upon which he dwelt, but his person was bound, and the lord might reclaim him at any time, by suit in a court of justice, if he ventured to stray. But, equally liable to this confinement, there were two classes of villeins, whose condition was exceedingly different. In England, at least from the reign of Henry II, one only, and that the inferior species, existed; incapable of property, and destitute of redress, except against the most outrageous injuries.[152] The lord could seize whatever they acquired or inherited, or convey them, apart from the land, to a stranger. Their tenure bound them to what were called villein services, ignoble in their nature and indeterminate in their degree; the felling of timber, the carrying of manure, the repairing of roads for their lord, who seems to have possessed an equally unbounded right over their labour and its fruits. But by the customs of France and Germany, persons in this abject state seem to have been called serfs, and distinguished from villeins, who were only bound to fixed payments and duties in respect of their lord, though, as it seems, without any legal redress if injured by him.[153] "The third estate of men," says Beaumanoir, in the passage above quoted, "is that of such as are not free;

---

traders purchased famished wretches on the coasts of Italy, whom they sold to the Saracens. (Muratori, "Annalia d'Italia," A. D. 785.) Much more would persons in this extremity sell themselves to neighbouring lords.

[150] Du Cange, Heribannum. A full heribannum was 60 solidi, but it was sometimes assessed in proportion to the wealth of the party.

[151] Beaumanoir, c. 45. [Note XV.]

[152] Littleton, l. ii, c. 11. Non potest aliquis (says Glanvil), in villenagio positus, libertatem suam propriis denariis suis quærere—quia omnia catalla cujuslibet nativi intelliguntur esse in potestate domini sui (l. v, c. 5).

[153] This is clearly expressed in a French law-book of the thirteenth century, the "Conseil of Pierre des Fontaines," quoted by Du Cange, voc. Villanus. Et sache bien que selon Dieu tu n'as mie pleniero poesté sur ton vilain. Dont se tu prens du sien fors les droites redevances que te doit, tu les prens contre Dieu, et sur le peril de t'ame et come robierres. Et ce qu'on dit toutes les choses que vilains a, sont son Seigneur, c'est voir a garder. Car s'il estoient son seigneur propre, il n'avoit nule difference entre serf et vilain, mais par notre usage n'a entre toi et ton vilain juge fors Dieu, tant com il est tes couchans et tes levans, s'il n'a autre loi vers toi fors la commune. This seems to render the distinction little more than theoretical.

and these are not all of one condition, for some are so subject to their lord that he may take all they have, alive or dead, and imprison them, whenever he pleases, being accountable to none but God; while others are treated more gently, from whom the lord can take nothing but customary payments, though at their death all they have escheats to him." [154]

Under every denomination of servitude the children followed their mother's condition; except in England, where the father's state determined that of the children, on which account bastards of female villeins were born free, the law presuming the liberty of their father.[155] The proportion of freemen, therefore, would have been miserably diminished if there had been no reflux of the tide which ran so strongly toward slavery. But the usage of manumission made a sort of circulation between these two states of mankind. This, as is well known, was an exceedingly common practice with the Romans, and is mentioned, with certain ceremonies prescribed, in the Frankish and other early laws. The clergy, and especially several popes, enforced it as a duty upon laymen, and inveighed against the scandal of keeping Christians in bondage.[156] As society advanced in Europe, the manumission of slaves grew more frequent.[157] By the indulgence of custom in some places, or perhaps by original convention, villeins might possess property, and thus purchase their own redemption. Even where they had no legal title to property, it was accounted inhuman to divest them of their little possession (the peculium of Roman law), nor was their poverty, per-

---

[154] Beaumanoir, c. 45; Du Cange, Villanus, Servus, and several other articles; Schmidt, " Hist. des Allemands," tome ii, pp. 171, 435. By a law of the Lombards, a free woman who married a slave might be killed by her relations or sold; if they neglected to do so, the fisc might claim her as its own. (Muratori, Dissert. 14.) In France also she was liable to be treated as a slave. (" Marculfi Formulæ," l. ii, p. 29.) Even in the twelfth century it was the law of Flanders that whoever married a villein became one himself after he had lived with her a twelvemonth. (" Recueil des Historiens," tome xiii, p. 350.) And, by a capitulary of Pepin, if a man married a villein believing her to be free, he might repudiate her and marry another. (Baluze, p. 181.)

Villeins themselves could not marry without the lord's license, under penalty of forfeiting their goods, or at least of a mulct. (Du Cange, voc. Forismaritagium.) This seems to be the true origin of the famous mercheta mulierum, which has been ascribed to a very different custom. (Du Cange, voc. Mercheta Mulierum; Dalrymple's " Annals of Scotland," vol. i, p. 312; " Archæologia," vol. xii, p. 31.)

[155] Littleton, s. 188. Bracton, indeed, holds that the spurious issue of a neif, though by a free father, should be a villein, quia sequitur conditionem matris, quasi vulgo conceptus (l. i, c. 6). But the laws under the name of Henry I declare that a son should follow his father's condition, so that this peculiarity is very ancient in our law. (" Leges Hen. I," c. 75 and 77.)

[156] Enfranchisements by testament are very common. Thus in the will of Seniofred, Count of Barcelona, in 966, we find the following piece of corrupt Latin: De ipsos servos meos et ancillas, illi qui traditi fuerunt faciatis illos libros propter remedium animæ meæ; et alli qui fuerunt de parentorum meorum remaneant ad fratres meos. (" Marca Hispanica," p. 887.)

[157] No one could enfranchise his villein without the superior lord's consent; for this was to diminish the value of his land, apeticer le fief. (Beaumanoir, c. 15; " Établissemens de St. Louis," c. 34.) It was necessary, therefore, for the villein to obtain the suzerain's confirmation; otherwise he only changed masters and escheated, as it were, to the superior; for the lord who had granted the charter of franchise was estopped from claiming him again.

haps, less tolerable, upon the whole, than that of the modern peasantry in most countries of Europe. It was only in respect of his lord, it must be remembered, that the villein, at least in England, was without rights; [158] he might inherit, purchase, sue in the courts of law; though, as defendant in a real action or suit wherein land was claimed, he might shelter himself under the plea of villenage. The peasants of this condition were sometimes made use of in war, and rewarded with enfranchisement; especially in Italy, where the cities and petty states had often occasion to defend themselves with their own population, and in peace the industry of free labourers must have been found more productive and better directed. Hence the eleventh and twelfth centuries saw the number of slaves in Italy begin to decrease ; early in the fifteenth a writer quoted by Muratori speaks of them as no longer existing.[159] The greater part of the peasants in some countries of Germany had acquired their liberty before the end of the thirteenth century; in other parts, as well as in all the northern and eastern regions of Europe, they remained in a sort of villenage till the present age. Some very few instances of predial servitude have been discovered in England so late as the time of Elizabeth,[160] and perhaps they might be traced still lower. Louis Hutin, in France, after innumerable particular instances of manumission had taken place, by a general edict in 1315, reciting that his kingdom is denominated the kingdom of the Franks, that he would have the fact to correspond with the name, emancipates all persons in the royal domains upon paying a just composition, as an example for other lords possessing villeins to follow.[161] Philip the Lord renewed the same edict three years afterward; a proof that it had not been carried into execution.[162] Indeed, there are letters of the former prince, wherein, considering that many of his subjects are not apprised of the extent of the benefit conferred upon them, he directs his officers to tax them as high as their fortunes can well bear.[163]

[158] Littleton, s. 189. Perhaps this is not applicable to other countries. Villeins were incapable of being received as witnesses against freemen. (" Recueil des Historiens," tome xiv, préface, p. 65.) There are some charters of Kings of France admitting the serfs of particular monasteries to give evidence, or to engage in the judicial combat, against freemen. (" Ordonnances des Rois," tome i, p. 3.) But I do not know that their testimony, except against their lord, was ever refused in England; their state of servitude not being absolute, like that of negroes in the West Indies, but particular and relative, as that of an apprentice or hired servant. This subject, however, is not devoid of obscurity.

[159] Dissert. 14.
[160] Barrington's " Observations on the Ancient Statutes," p. 274.

[161] " Ordonnances des Rois," tome i, p. 583.
[162] Id., p. 653.
[163] Velly, tome viii, p. 38. Philip the Fair had emancipated the villeins in the royal domains throughout Languedoc, retaining only an annual rent for their lands, which thus became censives, or emphyteuses. It does not appear by the charter that he sold this enfranchisement, though there can be little doubt about it. He permitted his vassals to follow the example. (Vaissette, " Hist. de Languedoc," tome iv; appendix, pp. 3, 12.)
It is not generally known, I think, that predial servitude was not abolished in all parts of France till the revolution. In some places, says Pasquier, the peasants are taillables à volonté—that is, their contribution is not permanent, but assessed by the lord with the advice of

It is deserving of notice that a distinction existed from very early times in the nature of lands, collateral, as it were, to that of persons. Thus we find mansi ingenui and mansi serviles in the oldest charters, corresponding, as we may not unreasonably conjecture, to the liberum tenementum and villenagium, or freehold and copyhold of our own law. In France, all lands held in roture appear to be considered as villein tenements, and are so termed in Latin, though many of them rather answer to our socage freeholds. But although originally this servile quality of lands was founded on the state of their occupiers, yet there was this particularity, that lands never changed their character along with that of the possessor; so that a nobleman might, and often did, hold estates in roture, as well as a roturier acquire a fief. Thus in England the terre tenants in villenage, who occur in our old books, were not villeins, but freemen holding lands which had been from time immemorial of a villein quality.

At the final separation of the French from the German side of Charlemagne's empire by the Treaty of Verdun in 843, there was perhaps hardly any difference in the constitution of the two kingdoms. If any might be conjectured to have existed, it would be a greater independence and fuller rights of election in the nobility and people of Germany. But in the lapse of another century France had lost all her political unity, and her kings all their authority, while the Germanic Empire was entirely unbroken under an effectual, though not absolute, control of its sovereign. No comparison can be made between the power of Charles the Simple and Conrad I, though the former had the shadow of an hereditary right, and the latter was chosen from among his equals. A long succession of feeble princes or usurpers, and

prud' hommes, resseants sur les lieux, according to the peasant's ability. Others pay a fixed sum. Some are called serfs de poursuite, who can not leave their habitations, but may be followed by the lord into any part of France for the taille upon their goods. This was the case in part of Champagne and the Nivernois. Nor could these serfs, or gens de mainmorte, as they were sometimes called, be manumitted without letters-patent of the king, purchased by a fine. (" Recherches de la France," l. iv, c. 5.) Dubos informs us that, in 1615, the Tiers État prayed the king to cause all serfs (hommes de pooste) to be enfranchised on paying a composition; but this was not complied with, and they existed in many parts when he wrote. (" Histoire, Critique," tome iii, p. 298.) Argou, in his " Institutions du Droit François," confirms this, and refers to the customaries of Nivernois and Vitry (l. i, c. 1). And M. de Bréquigny, in his preface to the twelfth volume of the collection of " Ordonnances," p. 22, says that throughout almost the whole jurisdiction of the Parliament of Besançon the peasants were attached to the soil, not being capable of leaving it without the lord's consent; and that in some places he even inherited their goods in exclusion of the kindred. I recollect to have read in some part of Voltaire's correspondence an anecdote of his interference, with that zeal against oppression which is the shining side of his moral character, in behalf of some of these wretched slaves of Franche-comté.

About the middle of the fifteenth century, some Catalonian serfs who had escaped into France being claimed by their lords, the Parliament of Toulouse declared that every man who entered the kingdom en criant France should become free. The liberty of our kingdom is such, says Mezeray, that its air communicates freedom to those who breathe it, and our kings are too august to reign over any but freemen. (Villaret, tome xv, p. 348.) How much pretence Mezeray had for such a flourish may be decided by the former part of this note.

destructive incursions of the Normans, reduced France almost to a dissolution of society; while Germany, under Conrad, Henry, and the Othos, found their arms not less prompt and successful against revolted vassals than external enemies. The high dignities were less completely hereditary than they had become in France; they were granted, indeed, pretty regularly, but they were solicited as well as granted; while the chief vassals of the French crown assumed them as patrimonial sovereignties, to which a royal investiture gave more of ornament than sanction.

In the eleventh century these imperial prerogatives began to lose part of their lustre. The long struggles of the princes and clergy against Henry IV and his son, the revival of more effective rights of election on the extinction of the house of Franconia, the exhausting contests of the Swabian emperors in Italy, the intrinsic weakness produced by a law of the empire, according to which the reigning sovereign could not retain an imperial fief more than a year in his hands, gradually prepared that independence of the German aristocracy which reached its height about the middle of the thirteenth century. During this period the French crown had been insensibly gaining strength; and as one monarch degenerated into the mere head of a confederacy, the other acquired unlimited power over a solid kingdom.

It would be tedious, and not very instructive, to follow the details of German public law during the middle ages; nor are the more important parts of it easily separable from civil history. In this relation they will find a place in a subsequent chapter of the present work. France demands a more minute attention; and in tracing the character of the feudal system in that country, we shall find ourselves developing the progress of a very different polity.

To understand in what degree the peers and barons of France, during the prevalence of feudal principles, were independent of the crown, we must look at their leading privileges. These may be reckoned: 1. The right of coining money; 2. That of waging private war; 3. The exemption from all public tributes, except the feudal aids; 4. The freedom from legislative control; and 5. The exclusive exercise of original judicature in their dominions. Privileges so enormous, and so contrary to all principles of sovereignty, might lead us, in strictness, to account France rather a collection of states, partially allied to each other, than a single monarchy.

1. Silver and gold were not very scarce in the first ages of the French monarchy, but they passed more by weight than by tale. A lax and ignorant government, which had not learned the lucrative mysteries of a royal mint, was not particularly solicitous to give its subjects the security of a known stamp in their ex-

changes.[164] In some cities of France money appears to have been coined by private authority before the time of Charlemagne; at least one of his capitularies forbids the circulation of any that had not been stamped in the royal mint. His successors indulged some of their vassals with the privilege of coining money for the use of their own territories, but not without the royal stamp. About the beginning of the tenth century, however, the lords, among their other assumptions of independence, issued money with no marks but their own.[165] At the accession of Hugh Capet as many as a hundred and fifty are said to have exercised this power. Even under St. Louis it was possessed by about eighty, who, excluding as far as possible the royal coin from circulation, enriched themselves at their subjects' expense by high duties (seigniorages), which they imposed upon every new coinage, as well as by debasing its standard.[166] In 1185 Philip Augustus requests the Abbot of Corvey, who had desisted from using his own mint, to let the royal money of Paris circulate through his territories, promising that, when it should please the abbot to coin money afresh for himself, the king would not oppose its circulation.[167]

Several regulations were made by Louis IX to limit, as far as lay in his power, the exercise of this baronial privilege, and, in particular, by enacting that the royal money should circulate in the domains of those barons who had mints, concurrently with their own, and exclusively within the territories of those who did not enjoy that right. Philip the Fair established royal officers of inspection in every private mint. It was asserted in his reign, as a general truth, that no subject might coin silver money.[168] In fact, the adulteration practised in those baronial mints had reduced their pretended silver to a sort of black metal, as it was called (moneta nigra), into which little entered but copper. Sil-

---

[164] The practice of keeping fine gold and silver uncoined prevailed among private persons, as well as in the treasury, down to the time of Philip the Fair. Nothing is more common than to find, in the instruments of earlier time, payments or fines stipulated by weight of gold or silver. Le Blanc therefore thinks that little money was coined in France, and that only for small payments. ("Traité des Monnoyes.") It is curious that, though there are many gold coins extant of the first race of kings, yet few or none are preserved of the second or third before the reign of Philip the Fair. (Du Cange, voc. Moneta.)

[165] Vaissette, "Hist. de Languedoc," tome ii, p. 110; "Rec. des Historiens," tome xi, préface, p. 180; Du Cange, voc. Moneta.

[166] Le Blanc, "Traité des Monnoyes," p. 91.

[167] Du Cange, voc. Moneta ; Velly,

"Hist. de France," tome ii, p. 93; Villaret, tome xiv, p. 200.

[168] Du Cange, voc. Moneta. The right of debasing the coin was also claimed by this prince as a choice flower of his crown. Item, abaisser et amenuser la monnoye est privilege especial au roy de son droit royal, si que a luy appartient, et a non autre, et encore en un seul cas, c'est a scavoir en necessité, et lors ne vient pas les ganeg, ne convertit en son profit especial, mais en profit et en la defence du commun. This was in a process commenced by the king's procureur-general against the Comte de Nevers, for defacing his coin. (Le Blanc, "Traité des Monnoyes," p. 92.) In many places the lord took a sum from his tenants every three years, under the name of monetagium or focagium, in lieu of debasing his money. This was finally abolished in 1830. (Du Cange, voc. Monetagium.)

ver, however, and even gold, were coined by the Dukes of Brittany so long as that fief continued to exist. No subjects ever enjoyed the right of coining silver in England without the royal stamp and superintendence [169]—a remarkable proof of the restraint in which the feudal aristocracy was always held in this country.

2. The passion of revenge, always among the most ungovernable in human nature, acts with such violence upon barbarians that it is utterly beyond the control of their imperfect arrangements of polity. It seems to them no part of the social compact to sacrifice the privilege which Nature has placed in the arm of valour. Gradually, however, these fiercer feelings are blunted, and another passion, hardly less powerful than resentment, is brought to play in a contrary direction. The earlier object, accordingly, of jurisprudence is to establish a fixed atonement for injuries, as much for the preservation of tranquility as the prevention of crime. Such were the weregilds of the barbaric codes, which, for a different purpose, I have already mentioned.[170] But whether it were that the kindred did not always accept, or the criminal offer, the legal composition, or that other causes of quarrel occurred, private feuds (faida) were perpetually breaking out, and many of Charlemagne's capitularies are directed against them. After his time all hope of restraining so inveterate a practice was at an end; and every man who owned a castle to shelter him in case of defeat, and a sufficient number of dependents to take the field, was at liberty to retaliate upon his neighbours whenever he thought himself injured. It must be kept in mind that there was frequently either no jurisdiction to which he could appeal, or no power to enforce its awards; so that we may consider the higher nobility of France as in a state of Nature with respect to each other, and entitled to avail themselves of all legitimate grounds of hostility. The right of waging private war was moderated by Louis IX, checked by Philip IV, suppressed by Charles VI, but a few vestiges of its practice may be found still later.[171]

[169] I do not extend this to the fact, for in the anarchy of Stephen's reign both bishops and barons coined money for themselves. (Hoveden, p. 490.)

[170] The antiquity of compositions for murder is illustrated by Iliad xviii, 498, where, in the description of the shield of Achilles, two disputants are represented wrangling before the judge for the weregild or price of blood; εἵνεκα ποινῆς ἀνδρὸς ἀποφθιμένου.

[171] The subject of private warfare is treated so exactly and perspicuously by Robertson that I should only waste the reader's time by dwelling so long upon it as its extent and importance would otherwise demand. (See " Hist. of Charles V," vol. i, note 21.) Few leading passages in the monuments of the middle ages relative to this subject have escaped the penetrating eye of that historian, and they are arranged so well as to form a comprehensive treatise in small compass. I know not that I could add any much worthy of notice, unless it be the following: In the treaty between Philip Augustus and Richard Cœur de Lion (1194), the latter refused to admit the insertion of an article that none of the barons of either party should molest the other; lest he should infringe the customs of Poitou and his other dominions, in quibus consuetum erat ab antiquo, ut magnates causas proprias invicem gladiis allegarent. (Hoveden, p. 741, in Saville, " Script. Anglic.")

3. In the modern condition of governments, taxation is a chief engine of the well-compacted machinery which regulates the system. The payments, the prohibitions, the licenses, the watchfulness of collection, the evasions of fraud, the penalties and forfeitures, that attend a fiscal code of laws, present continually to the mind of the most remote and humble individual the notion of a supreme, vigilant, and coercive authority. But the early European kingdoms knew neither the necessities nor the ingenuity of modern finance. From their demesne lands the Kings of France and Lombardy supplied the common expenses of a barbarous court. Even Charlemagne regulated the economy of his farms with the minuteness of a steward, and a large portion of his capitularies are directed to this object. Their actual revenue was chiefly derived from free gifts, made, according to an ancient German custom, at the annual assemblies [172] of the nation, from amercements paid by allodial proprietors for default of military service, and from the freda, or fines, accruing to the judge out of compositions for murder.[173] These amounted to one third of the whole weregild; one third of this was paid over by the count to the royal exchequer. After the feudal government prevailed in France, and neither the heribannum nor the weregild continued in use, there seems to have been hardly any source of regular revenue besides the domanial estates of the crown; unless we may reckon as such that during a journey the king had a prescriptive right to be supplied with necessaries by the towns and abbeys through which he passed, commuted sometimes into petty regular payments, called droits de gist et de chevauché.[174] Hugh Capet was nearly indigent as King of France, though as Count of Paris and Orleans he might take the feudal aids and reliefs of his vassals. Several other small emoluments of himself and his successors, whatever they may since have been considered, were in that age rather seigniorial than royal. The rights of toll, of customs, of alienage (aubaine), generally even the regale or enjoyment of the temporalities of vacant episcopal sees and other ecclesiastical benefices,[175] were possessed within their own domains by the great feudatories of the crown. They, I apprehend, contributed nothing to their sovereign, not even those aids which the feudal customs enjoined.[176]

---

[172] Du Cange, Dissertation quatrième sur Joinville.

[173] Mably, l. i, c. 2, note 3; Du Cange, voc. Heribannum, Fredum.

[174] Velly, tome ii, p. 329; Villaret, tome xiv, pp. 174–195; " Recueil des Historiens," tome xiv, préface, p. 37. The last is a perspicuous account of the royal revenue in the twelfth century. But far the most luminous view of that subject, for the next three ages, is displayed by M. de Pastoret in his prefaces to the fifteenth and sixteenth volumes of the " Ordonnances des Rois."

[175] The Duke of Burgundy and Count of Champagne did not possess the regale. But it was enjoyed by all the other peers; by the Dukes of Normandy, Guienne, and Brittany; the Counts of Toulouse, Poitou, and Flanders. (Mably, l. iii, c. 4; " Recueil des Historiens," tome ii, p. 229, and tome xiv, p. 53; " Ordonnances des Rois," tome i, p. 621.)

[176] I have never met with any instance

The history of the royal revenue in France is, however, too important to be slightly passed over. As the necessities of government increased, partly through the love of magnificence and pageantry introduced by the crusades and the temper of chivalry, partly in consequence of employing hired troops instead of the feudal militia, it became impossible to defray its expenses by the ordinary means. Several devices, therefore, were tried, in order to replenish the exchequer. One of these was by extorting money from the Jews. It is almost incredible to what a length this was carried. Usury, forbidden by law and superstition to Christians, was confined to this industrious and covetous people.[177] It is now no secret that all regulations interfering with the interest of money render its terms more rigorous and burdensome. The children of Israel grew rich in despite of insult and oppression, and retaliated upon their Christian debtors. If a historian of Philip Augustus may be believed, they possessed almost one half of Paris. Unquestionably they must have had support both at the court and in the halls of justice. The policy of the Kings of France was to employ them as a sponge to suck their subjects' money, which they might afterward express with less odium than direct taxation would incur. Philip Augustus released all Christians in his dominions from their debts to the Jews, reserving a fifth part to himself.[178] He afterward expelled the whole nation from France. But they appear to have returned again—whether by stealth, or, as is more probable, by purchasing permission. St. Louis twice banished and twice recalled the Jews. A series of alternate persecution and tolerance was borne by this extraordinary people with an invincible perseverance, and a talent of accumulating riches which kept pace with their plunderers; till new schemes of finance supplying the turn, they were finally expelled under Charles VI, and never afterward obtained any legal establishment in France.[179]

A much more extensive plan of rapine was carried on by lowering the standard of coin. Originally the pound, a money of account, was equivalent to twelve ounces of silver;[180] and divided into twenty pieces of coin (sous), each equal consequently

[177] The Jews were celebrated for usury as early as the sixth century. (" Greg. Turon.," l. iv, c. 12, and l. vii, c. 23.)
[178] Rigord, in Du Chesne, "Hist. Franc. Script.," tome iii, p. 8.
[179] Villaret, tome ix, p. 433. Metz contained, and I suppose still contains, a great many Jews; but Metz was not part of the ancient kingdom.
[180] In every edition of this work, till that of 1846, a strange misprint has appeared of twenty instead of twelve ounces, as the division of the pound of silver. Most readers will correct this for themselves; but it is more material to observe that, according to what we find in the "Mémoires de l'Acad. des Inscriptions" (Nouvelle Série), vol. xiv, p. 234, the pound in the time of Charlemagne was not of 12 ounces, but of 13½. We must, therefore, add one ninth to the value of the sol, so long as this continued to be the case. I do not know the proofs upon which this assertion rests; but the fact seems not to have been much observed by those who had previously written upon the subject.

of a relief, aid, or other feudal contribution paid by the vassals of the French crown; but in this negative proposition it is possible that I may be deceived.

to nearly three shillings and fourpence of our new English money.[181] At the revolution the money of France had been depreciated in the proportion of seventy-three to one, and the sol was about equal to an English halfpenny. This was the effect of a long continuance of fraudulent and arbitrary government. The abuse began under Philip I in 1103, who alloyed his silver coin with a third of copper. So good an example was not lost upon subsequent princes; till, under St. Louis, the mark-weight of silver, or eight ounces, was equivalent to fifty sous of the debased coin. Nevertheless, these changes seem hitherto to have produced no discontent; whether it were that a people neither commercial nor enlightened did not readily perceive their tendency, or, as has been ingeniously conjectured, that these successive diminutions of the standard were nearly counterbalanced by an augmentation in the value of silver, occasioned by the drain of money during the crusades, with which they were about contemporaneous.[182] But the rapacity of Philip the Fair kept no measures with the public, and the mark in his reign had become equal to eight livres, or a hundred and sixty sous of money. Dissatisfaction, and even tumults, arose in consequence, and he was compelled to restore the coin to its standard under St. Louis.[183] His successors practised the same arts of enriching their treasury; under Philip of Valois the mark was again worth eight livres. But the film had now dropped from the eyes of the people; and these adulterations of money, rendered more vexatious by continued recoinages of the current pieces, upon which a fee was extorted by the moneyers, showed in their true light as mingled fraud and robbery.[184]

These resources of government, however, by no means super-

[181] Besides this silver coin, there was a golden sol, worth forty pence. Le Blanc thinks the solidi of the Salic law and capitularies mean the latter piece of money. The denarius, or penny, was worth two sous six deniers of modern French coin.

[182] Villaret, tome xiv, p. 198. The price of commodities, he asserts, did not rise till the time of St. Louis. If this be said on good authority, it is a remarkable fact; but in England we know very little of prices before that period, and I doubt if their history has been better traced in France.

[183] It is curious, and not perhaps unimportant, to learn the course pursued in adjusting payments upon the restoration of good coin, which happened pretty frequently in the fourteenth century, when the States-General, or popular clamour, forced the court to retract its fraudulent policy. Le Blanc has published several ordinances nearly to the same effect. One of Charles VI explains the method adopted rather more fully than the rest. All debts incurred since the depreciated coin began to circulate were to be paid in that coin, or according to its value. Those incurred previously to its commencement were to be paid according to the value of the money circulating at the time of the contract. Item, que tous les vrais emprunts faits en deniers sans fraude se payeront en telle monnoye comme l'on aura emprunté, si elle a plein cours au temps du payement, et sinon, ills payeront en monnoye coursable, lors selon la valeur et le prix du marc d'or ou d'argent (p. 32.)

[184] "Continuator Gul. de Nangis in Spicilegio," tome iii. For the successive changes in the value of French coins the reader may consult Le Blanc's treatise, or the "Ordonnances des Rois"; also a dissertation by Bonamy in the "Mém. de l'Acad. des Inscriptions," tome xxxii; or he may find a summary view of them in Du Cange, voc. Moneta. The bad consequences of these innovations are well treated by M. de Pastoret in his elaborate preface to the sixteenth volume of the "Ordonnances des Rois," p. 40.

seded the necessity of more direct taxation. The Kings of France exacted money from the roturiers, and particularly the inhabitants of towns, within their domains. In this they only acted as proprietors, or suzerains; and the barons took the same course in their own lands. Philip Augustus first ventured upon a stretch of prerogative, which, in the words of his biographer, disturbed all France. He deprived by force, says Rigord, both his own vassals, who had been accustomed to boast of their immunities, and their feudal tenants, of a third part of their goods.[185] Such arbitrary taxation of the nobility, who deemed that their military service discharged them from all pecuniary burdens, France was far too aristocratical a country to bear. It seems not to have been repeated, and his successors generally pursued more legitimate courses. Upon obtaining any contribution, it was usual to grant letters-patent, declaring that it had been freely given, and should not be turned into precedent in time to come. Several of these letters-patent of Philip the Fair are extant, and published in the general collection of ordinances.[186] But in the reign of this monarch a great innovation took place in the French constitution, which, though it principally affected the method of levying money, may seem to fall more naturally under the next head of consideration.

4. There is no part of the French feudal policy so remarkable as the entire absence of all supreme legislation. We find it difficult to conceive the existence of a political society, nominally one kingdom and under one head, in which, for more than three hundred years, there was wanting the most essential attribute of government. It will be requisite, however, to take this up a little higher, and inquire what was the original legislature of the French monarchy.

Arbitrary rule, at least in theory, was uncongenial to the character of the northern nations. Neither the power of making laws, nor that of applying them to the circumstances of particular cases, was left at the discretion of the sovereign. The Lombard kings held assemblies every year at Pavia, where the chief officers of the crown and proprietors of lands deliberated upon all legislative measures, in the presence, and nominally, at least, with the consent, of the multitude.[187] Frequent mention is made of similar public meetings in France by the historians of the

---

[185] Du Chesne, tome v, p. 43.

[186] Fasons scavoir et recognoissons que la derniere subvention que ils nous ont faite (les barons, vassaux, et nobles d'Auvergne) de pure grace sans ce que ils y fussent tenus que de grace: et voulons et leur octroyones que les autres subventions que ils nous ont faites ne leur facent nul prejudice, es choses esquelles ils n'étoient tenus, ne par ce nul nouveau droit ne nous soit acquis ne amenuisié (Or-donnance de 1304, apud Mably, l. iv, c. 3, note 5. See other authorities in the same place.)

[187] Liutprand, King of the Lombards, says that his laws sibi placuisse unà cum omnibus judicibus de Austriæ et Neustriæ partibus, et de Tusciæ finibus, cum reliquis fidelibus meis Langobardis, et omni populo assistente. (Muratori, Dissert. 22.)

Merovingian kings, and still more unequivocally by their statutes.[188] These assemblies have been called Parliaments of the Champ de Mars, having originally been held in the month of March. But they are supposed by many to have gone much into disuse under the later Merovingian kings. That of 615, the most important of which any traces remain, was at the close of the great revolution which punished Brunehaut for aspiring to despotic power. Whether these assemblies were composed of any except prelates, great landholders, or what we may call nobles, and the Antrustions of the king, is still an unsettled point. Some have even supposed, since bishops are only mentioned by name in the great statute of Clotaire II in 615, that they were then present for the first time; and Sismondi, forgetting this fact, has gone so far as to think that Pepin first admitted the prelates to national councils.[189] But the constitutions of the Merovingian kings frequently bear upon ecclesiastical regulations, and must have been prompted at least by the advice of the bishops. Their influence was immense; and though the Romans generally are not supposed to have been admitted by right of territorial property to the national assemblies, there can be no improbability in presuming that the chiefs of the Church, especially when some of them were barbarians, stood in a different position. We know this was so at least in 615, and nothing leads to a conclusion that it was for the first time.

It is far more difficult to determine the participation of the Frank people, the allodialists or Rachimburgii, in these assemblies of the Field of March. They could not, it is said, easily have repaired thither from all parts of France. But while the monarchy was divided, and all the left bank of the Loire, in consequence of the paucity of Franks settled there, was hardly connected politically with any section of it, there does not seem an improbability that the subjects of a King of Paris or Soissons might have been numerously present in those capitals. It is generally allowed that they attended with annual gifts to their

---

[188] Mably, l. i, c. i, note 1; Lindebrog., "Codex Legum Antiquarum," pp. 363, 360. The following passage, quoted by Mably (c. 2, note 6), from the preamble of the revised Salic law under Clotaire II, is explicit: Temporibus Clotairii regis unà cum principibus suis, id est 33 episcopis et 34 ducibus et 79 comitibus, vel cætero populo constituta est. A remarkable instance of the use of vel instead of et, which was not uncommon, and is noticed by Du Cange, under the word Vel. Another proof of it occurs in the very next quotation of Mably from the edict of 615: cum pontificibus, vel cum magnis viris optimatibus.
[189] Voltaire ("Essai sur l'Histoire Universelle") ascribes this to the elder Pe-pin, surnamed Héristal, and quotes the "Annals of Metz" for 692; but neither under that year nor any other do I find a word to the purpose. Yet he pompously announces this as "an epoch not regarded by historians, but that of the temporal power of the Church in France and Germany." Voltaire knew but superficially the early French history, and amused himself by questioning the most public as well as probable facts, such as the death of Brunehaut. The compliment which Robertson has paid to Voltaire's historical knowledge is much exaggerated relatively to the mediæval period; the latter history of his country he possessed very well.

sovereign; though perhaps these were chiefly brought by the beneficiary tenants and wealthy allodialists. We certainly find expressions, some of which I have quoted, indicating a popular assent to the resolutions taken or laws enacted in the Field of March. Perhaps the most probable hypothesis may be that the presence of the nation was traditionally required in conformity to the ancient German usage, which had not been formally abolished; while the difficulty of prevailing on a dispersed people to meet every year, as well as the enhanced influence of the king through his armed Antrustions, soon reduced the freemen to little more than spectators from the neighbouring districts. We find, indeed, that it was with reluctance, and by means of coercive fines, that they were induced to attend the mallus of their count for judicial purposes.[190]

Although no legislative proceedings of the Merovingian line are extant after 615, it is intimated by early writers that Pepin Héristal and his son, Charles Martel, restored the national council after some interruption; and if the language of certain historians be correct, they rendered it considerably popular.[191]

Pepin the younger, after his accession to the throne, changed the month of this annual assembly from March to May, and we have some traces of what took place at eight sessions during his reign.[192] Of his capitularies, however, one only is said to be made in generali populi conventu; the rest are enacted in synods of bishops, and all without exception relate merely to ecclesiastical affairs.[193] And it must be owned that, as in those of the first dynasty, we find generally mention of the optimates who met in these conventions, but rarely any word that can be construed of ordinary freemen.

Such, indeed, is the impression conveyed by a remarkable passage of Hincmar, Archbishop of Rheims, during the time of Charles the Bald, who has preserved, on the authority of a writer contemporary with Charlemagne, a sketch of the Frankish government under that great prince. Two assemblies (pla-

---

[190] Mably generally strives to make the most of any vestige of popular government, and Sismondi is not exempt from a similar bias. He overrates the liberties of the Franks. "Leurs ducs et leurs comtes étaient électifs: leurs généraux étaient choisis par les soldats, leurs grands juges ou maires par les hommes libres" (vol. ii, p. 87). But no part of these privileges can be inferred from the existing histories or other documents. The dukes and counts were, as we find by Marculfus and other evidence, solely appointed by the crown. A great deal of personal liberty may have been preserved by means of the local assemblies of the Franks; but we find in the general government only the preponderance of the kings during one period, and that of the aristocracy during another.

[191] The first of these Austrasian dukes, says the "Annals of Metz," "Singulis annis in Kalendis Martii generale cum omnibus Francis, secundum priscorum consuetudinem, concilium agebat." The second, according to the biographer of St. Salvian—"jussit campum magnum parari, sicut mos erat Francorum. Venerunt autem optimates et magistratus, omnisque populus." See the quotations in Guizot. ("Essai sur l'Hist. de France," p. 321.)

[192] "Essais sur l'Hist. de France," p. 324.

[193] "Rec. des Hist.," v, 637.

cita) were annually held. In the first, all regulations of importance to the public weal for the ensuing year were enacted; and to this, he says, the whole body of clergy and laity repaired; the greater, to deliberate upon what was fitting to be done; and the less, to confirm by their voluntary assent, not through deference to power, or sometimes even to discuss, the resolutions of their superiors.[194] In the second annual assembly the chief men and officers of state were alone admitted, to consult upon the most urgent affairs of government. They debated, in each of these, upon certain capitularies, or short proposals, laid before them by the king. The clergy and nobles met in separate chambers, though sometimes united for the purposes of deliberation. In these assemblies, principally, I presume, in the more numerous of the two annually summoned, that extensive body of laws, the capitularies of Charlemagne, were enacted. And though it would contradict the testimony just adduced from Hincmar to suppose that the lesser freeholders took a very effective share in public counsels, yet their presence, and the usage of requiring their assent, indicate the liberal principles upon which the system of Charlemagne was founded. It is continually expressed in his capitularies and those of his family that they were enacted by general consent.[195] In one of Louis the Debonair we even trace the first germ of representative legislation. Every count is directed to bring with him to the general assembly twelve Scabini, if there should be so many in his county; or, if not, should fill up the number out of the most respectable persons resident.[196] These Scabini were judicial assessors of the count, chosen by the allodial proprietors, in the county court, or mallus, though generally on his nomination.[197]

[194] Consuetudo tunc temporis talis erat, ut non sæpius, sed bis in anno placita duo tenerentur. Unum, quando ordinabatur status totius regni ad anni vertentis spatium; quod ordinatum nullus eventus rerum, nisi summa necessitas, quæ similiter toti regno incumbebat, mutabat. In quo placito generalitas universorum majorum, tam clericorum quam laicorum, conveniebat; seniores propter consilium ordinandum; minores, propter idem consilium suscipiendum, et interdum pariter tractandum, et non ex potestate, sed ex proprio mentis intellectu vel sententiâ, confirmandum. Hincmar, Epist. 5, de ordine palatii. I have not translated the word majorum in the above quotation, not apprehending its sense. [Note XVI.]
[195] Capitula quæ præterito anno legi Salicæ cum omnium consensu addenda esse censuimus. (A. D. 801.) Ut populus interrogetur de capitulis quæ in lege noviter addita sunt, et postquam omnes consenserint, subscriptiones et manufirmationes suas in ipsis capitulis faciant. (A. D. 513.) Capitularia patris nostri quæ Franci

pro lege tenenda judicaverunt. (A. D. 837.) I have borrowed these quotations from Mably, who remarks that the word populus is never used in the earlier laws. See, too, Du Cange, vv. Lex, Mallum, Pactum.
[196] Vult dominus Imperator ut in tale placitum quale ille nunc jusserit, veniat unusquisque comes, et adducat secum duodecim scabinos si tanti fuerint; sin autem, de melioribus hominibus illius comitatus suppleat numerum duodenarium. (Mably, l. ii, c. 2.)
[197] This seems to be sufficiently proved by Savigny (vol. i, pp. 192, 217, et post). His opinion is adopted by Meyer, Guizot, Grimm, and Troja. The last of these has found Scabini mentioned in Lombardy as early as 724, though Savigny had rejected all documents in which they are named anterior to Charlemagne.
The Scabini are not to be confounded, as sometimes has been the case, with the Rachimburgii, who were not chosen by the allodial proprietors, but were themselves such, or sometimes, perhaps, beneficiaries, summoned by the court as jurors were in England. They answered to

The circumstances, however, of the French Empire for several subsequent ages were exceedingly adverse to such enlarged schemes of polity. The nobles contemned the imbecile descendants of Charlemagne; and the people, or lesser freeholders, if they escaped absolute villenage, lost their immediate relation to the supreme government in the subordination to their lord established by the feudal law. Yet we may trace the shadow of ancient popular rights in one constitutional function of high importance, the choice of a sovereign. Historians who relate the election of an Emperor or King of France seldom omit to specify the consent of the multitude, as well as of the temporal and spiritual aristocracy, and even in solemn instruments that record such transactions we find a sort of importance attached to the popular suffrage.[198] It is surely less probable that a recognition of this elective right should have been introduced as a mere ceremony

the prud' hommes, boni homines, of later times; they formed the county or the hundred court, for the determination of civil and criminal causes. [Note XVI.]

[198] It has been intimated in another place (p. 156) that the French monarchy seems not to have been strictly hereditary under the later kings of the Merovingian race: at least expressions indicating a formal election are frequently employed by historians. Pepin, of course, came in by the choice of the nation. At his death he requested the consent of the counts and prelates to the succession of his sons (" Baluzii Capitularia," p. 187), though they had bound themselves by oath at his consecration never to elect a king out of another family. Ut nunquam de alterius lumbis regem eligere præsumant. (Formula Consecrationis Pippini in " Recueil des Historiens," tome v.) In the instrument of partition by Charlemagne among his descendants he provides for their immediate succession in absolute terms, without any mention of consent. But in the event of the decease of one of his sons leaving a child, whom the people shall choose, the other princes were to permit him to reign. (Baluze, p. 440.) This is repeated more perspicuously in the partition made by Louis I in 817. Si quis eorum decedens legitimos filios reliquerit, non inter eos potestas ipsa dividatur, sed potius populus pariter conveniens, unum ex iis, quem dominus voluerit, eligat, et hunc senior frater in loco fratris et filii recipiat. (Baluze, p. 577.) Proofs of popular consent given to the succession of kings during the next two centuries are frequent, but of less importance on account of the irregular condition of government. Even after Hugh Capet's accession, hereditary right was far from being established. The first six kings of this dynasty procured the co-optation of their sons by having them crowned during their own lives. And this was not done without the consent of the chief vassals. (" Recueil des Hist.," tome xi, p. 133.) In the reign of Robert it was a great question whether the elder son should be thus designated as heir in preference to his younger brother, whom the queen, Constance, was anxious to place upon the throne. Odolric, Bishop of Orleans, writes to Fulbert, Bishop of Chartres, in terms which lead one to think that neither hereditary succession nor primogeniture was settled on any fixed principle. (Id., tome x, p. 504.) And a writer in the same collection, about the year 1000, expresses himself in the following manner: Melius est electioni principis non subscribere, quàm post subscriptionem electum contemnere; in altero enim libertatis amor laudatur, in altero servilis contumacia probro datur. Tres namque generales electiones novimus; quarum una est regis vel imperatoris, altera pontificis, altera abbatis. Et primam quidem facit concordia totius regni; secundam vero unanimitas civium et cleri; tertiam sanius consilium cœnobiticæ congregationis. (Id., p. 626.) At the coronation of Philip I, in 1059, the nobility and people (milites et populi tam majores quàm minores) testified their consent by crying, Laudamus, volumus, fiat (tome xi, p. 33). I suppose, if search were made, that similar testimonies might be found still later: and perhaps hereditary succession can not be considered as a fundamental law till the reign of Philip Augustus, the era of many changes in the French constitution.

Sismondi has gone a great deal further down, and observes that, though John assumed the royal power immediately on the death of his father, in 1350, he did not take the name of king, nor any seal but that of Duke of Normandy, till his coronation. He says, however, " notre royaume " in his instruments (x, 375). Even Charles V called himself, or was called by some, Duke of Normandy until his coronation; but all the lawyers called him king (xi, 6). The lawyers had established their maxim that the king never dies, which, however, was unknown while any traces of elective monarchy remained.

than that the form should have survived after length of time and revolutions of government had almost obliterated the recollection of its meaning.

It must, however, be impossible to ascertain even the theoretical privileges of the subjects of Charlemagne, much more to decide how far they were substantial or illusory. We can only assert in general that there continued to be some mixture of democracy in the French constitution during the reigns of Charlemagne and his first successors. The primeval German institutions were not eradicated. In the capitularies the consent of the people is frequently expressed. Fifty years after Charlemagne his grandson, Charles the Bald, succinctly expresses the theory of legislative power. A law, he says, is made by the people's consent and the king's enactment.[199] It would hardly be warranted by analogy or precedent to interpret the word people so very narrowly as to exclude any allodial proprietors, among whom, however unequal in opulence, no legal inequality of rank is supposed to have yet arisen.

But by whatever authority laws were enacted, whoever were the constituent members of national assemblies, they ceased to be held in about seventy years from the death of Charlemagne. The latest capitularies are of Carloman in 882.[200] From this time there ensues a long blank in the history of French legislation. The kingdom was as a great fief, or rather as a bundle of fiefs, and the king little more than one of a number of feudal nobles, differing rather in dignity than in power from some of the rest. The royal council was composed only of barons, or tenants in chief, prelates, and household officers. These now probably deliberated in private, as we hear no more of the consenting multitude. Political functions were not in that age so clearly separated as we are taught to fancy they should be; this council advised the king in matters of government, confirmed and consented to his grants, and judged in all civil and criminal cases where any peers of their court were concerned.[201] The great vassals of the crown acted for themselves in their own territories, with the assistance of councils similar to that of the

[199] Lex consensu populi fit, constitutione regis. (" Recueil des Hist.," tome vii, p. 656.)

[200] It is generally said that the capitularies cease with Charles the Simple, who died in 921. But Baluze has published only two under the name of that prince: the first, a declaration of his queen's jointure; the second, an arbitration of disputes in the Church of Tongres; neither, surely, deserving the appellation of a law.

[201] Regali potentiâ in nullo abuti volentes, says Hugh Capet, omnia negotia reipublicæ in consultatione et sententiâ fidelium nostrorum disponimus. (" Re-

cueil des Hist.," tome x, p. 392.) The subscriptions of these royal councillors were necessary for the confirmation, or, at least, the authentication of charters, as was also the case in England, Spain, and Italy. This practice continued in England till the reign of John.

The Curia regis seems to have differed only in name from the Concilium regium. It is also called Curia parium, from the equality of the barons who composed it, standing in the same feudal degree of relation to the sovereign. But we are not yet arrived at the subject of jurisdiction, which it is very difficult to keep distinct from what is immediately before us.

king. Such, indeed, was the symmetry of feudal customs that the manorial court of every vavassor represented in miniature that of his sovereign.[202]

But, notwithstanding the want of any permanent legislation during so long a period, instances occur in which the Kings of France appear to have acted with the concurrence of an assembly more numerous and more particularly summoned than the royal council. At such a congress held in 1146 the crusade of Louis VII was undertaken.[203] We find also an ordinance of the same prince in some collections, reciting that he had convoked a general assembly at Soissons, where many prelates and barons then present had consented and requested that private wars might cease for the term of ten years.[204] The famous Saladine tithe was imposed upon lay as well as ecclesiastical revenues by a similar convention in 1188.[205] And when Innocent IV, during his contest with the Emperor Frederick, requested an asylum in France, St. Louis, though much inclined to favour him, ventured only to give a conditional permission, provided it were agreeable to his barons, whom, he said, a King of France was bound to consult in such circumstances. Accordingly, he assembled the French barons, who unanimously refused their consent.[206]

It was the ancient custom of the Kings of France, as well as of England, and, indeed, of all those vassals who affected a kind of sovereignty, to hold general meetings of their barons, called Cours Plénières, or Parliaments, at the great festivals of the year. These assemblies were principally intended to make a display of magnificence, and to keep the feudal tenants in good humour; nor is it easy to discover that they passed in anything but pageantry.[207] Some respectable antiquaries have, however, been of opinion that affairs of state were occasionally discussed in them; and this is certainly by no means inconsistent with probability, though not sufficiently established by evidence.[208]

Excepting a few instances, most of which have been men-

[202] "Recueil des Hist.," tome xi, p. 300, and préface, p. 179; Vaissette, "Hist. de Languedoc," tome ii, p. 508.

[203] Velly, tome iii, p. 119. This, he observes, is the first instance in which the word Parliament is used for a deliberative assembly.

[204] Ego Ludovicus Dei gratiâ Francorum rex, ad reprimendum fervorem malignantium, et compescendum violentas prædorum manus, postulationibus cleri et assensu baroniæ, toti regno pacem constituimus. Eâ causâ, anno Incarnati Verbi 1155, iv, idus Jun. Suessionense concilium celebre adunavimus, et effuerunt archiepiscopi Remensis, Senonensis et eorum suffraganei; item barones, comes Flandrensis, Trecensis, et Nivernensis et quamplures alii, et dux

Burgundiæ. Ex quorum beneplacito ordinavimus a veniente Paschâ ad decom annos, ut omnes ecclesiæ regni et omnes agricolæ, etc pacem habeant et securitatem.—In pacem istam juraverunt dux Burgundiæ, comes Flandriæ,—— et reliqui barones qui aderant.
This ordinance is published in Du Chesne, "Script. Rerum Gallicarum," tome iv, and in "Recueil des Histor.," tome xiv, p. 387; but not in the general collection.

[205] Velly, tome iii, p. 315.

[206] Velly, tome iv, p. 306.

[207] Du Cange, Dissert. 5, sur Joinville.

[208] "Mém. de l'Acad. des Inscript.," tome xli; "Recueil des Hist.," tome xi, préface, p. 155.

tioned, it does not appear that the kings of the house of Capet acted according to the advice and deliberation of any national assembly, such as assisted the Norman sovereigns of England: nor was any consent required for the validity of their edicts, except that of the ordinary council, chiefly formed of their household officers and less powerful vassals. This is at first sight very remarkable. For there can be no doubt that the government of Henry I or Henry II was incomparably stronger than that of Louis VI or Louis VII. But this apparent absoluteness of the latter was the result of their real weakness and the disorganization of the monarchy. The peers of France were infrequent in their attendance upon the king's council, because they denied its coercive authority. It was a fundamental principle that every feudal tenant was so far sovereign within the limits of his fief that he could not be bound by any law without his consent. The king, says St. Louis in his " Establishments," can not make proclamation—that is, declare any new law—in the territory of a baron, without his consent, nor can the baron do so in that of a vavassor.[209] Thus, if legislative power be essential to sovereignty, we can not in strictness assert the King of France to have been sovereign beyond the extent of his domanial territory. Nothing can more strikingly illustrate the dissimilitude of the French and English constitutions of government than the sentence above cited from the code of St. Louis.

Upon occasions when the necessity of common deliberation, or of giving to new provisions more extensive scope than the limits of a single fief, was too glaring to be overlooked, congresses of neighbouring lords met in order to agree upon resolutions which each of them undertook to execute within his own domains. The king was sometimes a contracting party, but without any coercive authority over the rest. Thus we have what is called an ordinance, but, in reality, an agreement, between the king (Philip Augustus), the Countess of Troyes or Champagne, and the Lord of Dampierre,[210] relating to the Jews in their domains; which agreement or ordinance, it is said, should endure " until ourselves, and the Countess of Troyes, and Guy de Dampierre, who make this contract, shall dissolve it with the consent of such of our barons as we shall summon for that purpose."[211]

[209] Ne li rois ne puet mettre ban en la terre au baron sans son assentment, ne li bers [baron] ne puet mettre ban en la terre au vavasor. (" Ordonnances des Rois," tome i, p. 126.)

[210] In former editions I have called the Lord of Dampierre Count of Flanders. But it has been suggested to me that the Lord of Dampierre was never Count of Flanders; his second brother married the younger sister of the heiress of that fief, who, after his death, inherited it from the elder. The ordinance related to the domains of Dampierre, in the Nivernois. This, however, makes the instance stronger against the legislative authority of the crown than as I had stated it.

[211] Quosque nos. et comitissa Trecensis, et Guido de Domnâ petrâ, qui hoc facimus, per nos, et illos de baronibus

Ecclesiastical councils were another substitute for a regular legislature; and this defect in the political constitution rendered their encroachments less obnoxious, and almost unavoidable. That of Troyes in 878, composed perhaps in part of laymen, imposed a fine upon the invaders of church property.[212] And the Council of Toulouse, in 1229, prohibited the erection of any new fortresses, or the entering into any leagues, except against the enemies of religion, and ordained that judges should administer justice gratuitously and publish the decrees of the council four times in the year.[213]

The first unequivocal attempt, for it was nothing more, at general legislation, was under Louis VIII in 1223, in an ordinance which, like several of that age, relates to the condition and usurious dealings of the Jews. It is declared in the preamble to have been enacted per assensum archiepiscoporum, episcoporum, comitum, baronum, et militum regni Franciæ, qui Judæos habent, et qui Judæos non habent. This recital is probably untrue, and intended to cloak the bold innovation contained in the last clause of the following provision: Sciendum, quod nos et barones nostri statuimus et ordinavimus de statu Judæorum quod nullus nostrûm alterius Judæos recipere potest vel retinere; et hoc intelligendum est tam de his qui stabilimentum juraverint, quam de illis qui non juraverint.[214] This was renewed with some alteration in 1230, de communi consilio baronum nostrorum.[215]

But whatever obedience the vassals of the crown might pay to this ordinance, their original exemption from legislative control remained, as we have seen, unimpaired at the date of the " Establishments " of St. Louis, about 1269; and their ill-judged confidence in this feudal privilege still led them to absent themselves from the royal council. It seems impossible to doubt that the barons of France might have asserted the same right which those of England had obtained, that of being duly summoned by special writ, and thus have rendered their consent necessary to every measure of legislation. But the fortunes of France were different. The " Establishments " of St. Louis are declared to be made " par grand conseil de sages hommes et de bons clers," but no mention is made of any consent given by the barons; nor does it often, if ever, occur in subsequent ordinances of the French kings.

The nobility did not long continue safe in their immunity from the king's legislative power. In the ensuing reign of Philip the Bold, Beaumanoir lays it down, though in very moderate and

nostris, quos ad hoc vocare volumus, illud diffaciamus. (" Ordonnances des Rois," tome i, p. 29.) This ordinance bears no date, but it was probably between 1218 and 1223, the year of Philip's death.

[212] Vaissette, " Hist. de Languedoc," tome ii, p. 6.
[213] Velly, tome iv, p. 132.
[214] " Ordonnances des Rois," tome i, p. 47.
[215] Id., p. 53.

doubtful terms, that " when the king makes any ordinance specially for his own domains, the barons do not cease to act in their territories according to the ancient usage; but when the ordinance is general, it ought to run through the whole kingdom, and we ought to believe that it is made with good advice, and for the common benefit." [216] In another place he says, with more positiveness, that " the king is sovereign above all, and has of right the general custody of the realm, for which cause he may make what ordinances he pleases for the common good, and what he ordains ought to be observed; nor is there any one so great but may be drawn into the king's court for default of right or for false judgment, or in matters that affect the sovereign." [217] These latter words give us a clew to the solution of the problem by what means an absolute monarchy was established in France. For though the barons would have been little influenced by the authority of a lawyer like Beaumanoir, they were much less able to resist the coercive logic of a judicial tribunal. It was in vain for them to deny the obligation of royal ordinances within their own domains when they were compelled to acknowledge the jurisdiction of the Parliament of Paris, which took a very different view of their privileges. This progress of the royal jurisdiction will fall under the next topic of inquiry, and is only now hinted at as the probable means of confirming the absolute legislative power of the French crown.

The ultimate source, however, of this increased authority will be found in the commanding attitude assumed by the Kings of France from the reign of Philip Augustus, and particularly in the annexation of the two great fiefs of Normandy and Toulouse. Though the châtelains and vavassors who had depended upon those fiefs before their reunion were, agreeably to the text of St. Louis's ordinance, fully sovereign, in respect of legislation, within their territories, yet they were little competent, and perhaps little disposed, to offer any opposition to the royal edicts; and the same relative superiority of force, which had given the first kings of the house of Capet a tolerably effective control over the vassals dependent on Paris and Orleans, while they hardly pretended to any over Normandy and Toulouse, was now extended to the greater part of the kingdom. St. Louis, in his scrupulous moderation, forbore to avail himself of all the advantages presented by the circumstances of his reign; and his " Establishments " bear testimony to a state of political society which,

[216] " Coûtumes de Beauvoisis," c. 48.
[217] C. 34. Beaumanoir uses in one place still stronger language about the royal authority. The king, he says, may annul the releases of debts made by any one who accompanies him in military service, so that he may enforce them again; " for what it pleases him to do ought to be held as law " (c. 35). This I owe to the new edition of the " Coûtumes de Beaumanoir," by M. Beugnot, 1842.

even at the moment of their promulgation, was passing away. The next thirty years after his death, with no marked crisis, and with little disturbance, silently demolished the feudal system, such as had been established in France during the dark confusion of the tenth century. Philip the Fair, by help of his lawyers and his financiers, found himself, at the beginning of the fourteenth century, the real master of his subjects.[218]

There was, however, one essential privilege which he could not hope to overturn by force, the immunity from taxation enjoyed by his barons. This, it will be remembered, embraced the whole extent of their fiefs, and their tenantry of every description, the king having no more right to impose a tallage upon the demesne towns of his vassals than upon themselves. Thus his resources, in point of taxation, were limited to his own domains; including certainly, under Philip the Fair, many of the noblest cities in France, but by no means sufficient to meet his increasing necessities. We have seen already the expedients employed by this rapacious monarch—a shameless depreciation of the coin, and, what was much more justifiable, the levying taxes within the territories of his vassals by their consent. Of these measures, the first was odious, the second slow and imperfect. Confiding in his sovereign authority—though recently, yet almost completely, established—and little apprehensive of the feudal principles, already grown obsolete and discountenanced, he was bold enough to make an extraordinary innovation in the French constitution. This was the convocation of the States-General, a representative body, composed of the three orders of the nation.[219] They were first convened in 1302, in order to give

[218] The reign of Philip the Fair has been very well discussed by Mably, Sismondi, and Guizot. "He changed," says the last, "monarchy into despotism; but he was not one of those despots who employ their absolute power for the public good." "On ne rencontre dans tout le cours de son règne aucune idée générale, et qui s'y rapporte au bien de ses sujets; c'est un despote égoïste, dévoué à lui-même qui règne pour lui seul." (Leçon 45.) The royal authority gained so much ascendency in his reign that, while we have only 50 ordonnances of St. Louis in forty-two years, we have 334 of Philip IV in about thirty.

[219] It is almost unanimously agreed among French writers that Philip the Fair first introduced a representation of the towns into his national assembly of States-General. Nevertheless, the "Chronicles of St. Denis," and other historians of rather a late date, assert that the deputies of towns were present at a Parliament in 1241, to advise the king what should be done in consequence of the Count of Angoulême's refusal of homage. (Boulainvilliers, "Hist. de l'Ancien Gouvernement de France," tome ii, p. 20;

Villaret, tome ix, p. 125.) The latter pretends even that they may be traced a century further back; on voit déjà les gens de bonnes villes assister aux états de 1145. (Ibid.) But he quotes no authority for this; and his vague language does not justify us in supposing that any representation of the three estates, properly so understood, did, or indeed could, early have been incorporated. If it be true that the deputies of some royal towns were summoned to the Parliament of 1241, the conclusion must not be inferred that they possessed any consenting voice, nor perhaps that they formed, strictly speaking, an integrant portion of the assembly. There is reason to believe that deputies from the royal burghs of Scotland occasionally appeared at the bar of Parliament long before they had any deliberative voice. (Pinkerton's "Hist. of Scotland," vol. i, p. 371.)

An ordinance of St. Louis, quoted in a very respectable book, Vaissette's "History of Languedoc," tome iii, p. 480, but not published in the "Recueil des Ordonnances," not only shows the exist-

more weight to the king's cause in his great quarrel with Boniface VIII, but their earliest grant of a subsidy is in 1314. Thus the nobility surrendered to the crown their last privilege of territorial independence; and, having first submitted to its appellant jurisdiction over their tribunals, next to its legislative supremacy, now suffered their own dependents to become, as it were, immediate, and a third estate to rise up almost co-ordinate with themselves, endowed with new franchises, and bearing a new relation to the monarchy.

It is impossible not to perceive the motives of Philip in embodying the deputies of towns as a separate estate in the national representation. He might, no question, have convoked a parliament of his barons, and obtained a pecuniary contribution, which they would have levied upon their burgesses and other tenants. But, besides the ulterior policy of diminishing the control of the barons over their dependents, he had good reason to expect more liberal aid from the immediate representatives of the people than through the concession of a dissatisfied aristocracy. "He must be blind, indeed," says Pasquier, "who does not see that the roturier was expressly summoned to this assembly, contrary to the ancient institutions of France, for no other reason than that, inasmuch as the burden was intended to fall principally upon him, he might engage himself so far by promise, that he could not afterward murmur or become refractory." [220] Nor would I deny the influence of more generous principles; the example

ence, in one instance, of a provincial legislative assembly, but is the earliest proof perhaps of the tiers état appearing as a constituent part of it. This relates to the seneschaussée, or county, of Beaucaire in Languedoc, and bears date in 1254. It provides that, if the seneschal shall think fit to prohibit the export of merchandise, he shall summon some of the prelates, barons, knights, and inhabitants of the chief towns, by whose advice he shall issue such prohibition, and not recall it, when made, without like advice. But though it is interesting to see the progressive importance of the citizens of towns, yet this temporary and insulated ordinance is not of itself sufficient to establish a constitutional right. Neither do we find therein any evidence of representation; it rather appears that the persons assisting in this assembly were notables, selected by the seneschal.

I am not aware of any instance of regular provincial estates being summoned with such full powers, although it was very common in the fourteenth century to ask their consent to grants of money, when the court was unwilling to convoke the States-General. Yet there is a passage in a book of considerable credit, the "Grand Customary," or "Somme Rurale" of Bouteiller, which seems to render general the particular case of the seneschaussée of Beaucaire.

Bouteiller wrote about the end of the fourteenth century. The great courts summoned from time to time by the baillis and seneschals were called assises. Their usual function was to administer justice, especially by way of appeal, and perhaps to redress abuses of inferior officers. But he seems to give them a more extended authority. En assise, he says, appellés, lec sages et seigneurs du pais, peuvent estre mises sus nouvelles constitutions, et ordonnances sur le pais et destruites autre que seront grevables, et en autre temps non, et doivent etre publiées safin que nul ne les pueust ignorer, et lors ne les peut ne doit jamais nul redarguer. ("Mém. de l'Acad. des Inscriptions," tome xxx, p. 606.

The taille was assessed by respectable persons chosen by the advice of the parish priests and others, which gave the people a sort of share in the repartition, to use a French term, of public burdens; a matter of no small importance where a tax is levied on visible property. ("Ordonnances des Rois," p. 291; Beaumanoir, p. 269.) This, however, continued, I believe, to be the practice in later times; I know it is so in the present system of France, and is perfectly distinguishable from a popular consent to taxation.

[220] "Recherches de la France," l. ii, c. 7.

of neighbouring countries, the respect due to the progressive civilization and opulence of the towns, and the application of that ancient maxim of the northern monarchies, that whoever was elevated to the perfect dignity of a freeman acquired a claim to participate in the imposition of public tributes.

It is very difficult to ascertain the constitutional rights of the States-General, claimed or admitted, during forty years after their first convocation. If, indeed, we could implicitly confide in a historian of the sixteenth century, who asserts that Louis Hutin bound himself and his successors not to levy any tax without the consent of the three estates, the problem would find its solution.[221] This ample charter does not appear in the French archives; and, though by no means to be rejected on that account, when we consider the strong motives for its destruction, can not fairly be adduced as an authentic fact. Nor can we altogether infer, perhaps, from the collection of ordinances, that the crown had ever intentionally divested itself of the right to impose tallages on its domanial tenants. All others, however, were certainly exempted from that prerogative; and there seems to have been a general sentiment that no tax whatever could be levied without free consent of the estates.[222] Louis Hutin, in a charter granted to the nobles and burgesses of Picardy, promises to abolish the unjust taxes (maltotes) imposed by his father;[223] and in another instrument, called the charter of Normandy, declares that he renounces for himself and his successors all undue tallages and exactions, except in case of evident utility.[224] This exception is doubtless of perilous ambiguity; yet, as the charter was literally wrested from the king by an insurrectionary league, it might be expected that the same spirit would rebel against his royal interpretation of state necessity. His successor, Philip the Long, tried the experiment of a gabelle, or excise upon salt. But it produced so much discontent that he was compelled to assemble the States-General, and to publish an ordinance, declaring that the impost was not designed to be perpetual, and that, if a sufficient supply for the existing war could be found elsewhere, it should instantly determine.[225] Whether this was done I do not discover; nor do I conceive that any of the sons of Philip the Fair, inheriting much of his rapacity and ambition, abstained from extorting money without consent.

---

[221] Boulainvilliers (" Hist. de l'Anc. Gouvernement," tome ii, p. 128) refers for this to Nicholas Gilles, a chronicler of no great repute.
[222] Mably (" Observat. sur l'Hist. de France," l. v, c. 1) is positive against the right of Philip the Fair and his successors to impose taxes. Montlosier (" Monarchie Française," tome i, p. 202) is of the same opinion. In fact, there is reason to believe that the kings in general did not claim that prerogative absolutely, whatever pretexts they might set up for occasional stretches of power.
[223] " Ordonnances des Rois," tome i, p. 566.
[224] " Ordonnances des Rois," tome i, p. 679.
[225] Idem, tome i, p. 589.

Philip of Valois renewed and augmented the duties on salt by his own prerogative, nor had the abuse of debasing the current coin been ever carried to such a height as during his reign and the first years of his successor. These exactions, aggravated by the smart of a hostile invasion, produced a very remarkable concussion in the government of France.

I have been obliged to advert, in another place, to the memorable resistance made by the States-General of 1355 and 1356 to the royal authority, on account of its inseparable connection with the civil history of France.[226] In the present chapter the assumption of political influence by those assemblies deserves particular notice. Not that they pretended to restore the ancient constitution of the northern nations, still flourishing in Spain and England, the participation of legislative power with the crown. Five hundred years of anarchy and ignorance had swept away all remembrance of those general Diets in which the capitularies of the Carlovingian dynasty had been established by common consent. Charlemagne himself was hardly known to the French of the fourteenth century, except as the hero of some silly romance or ballad. The States-General remonstrated, indeed, against abuses, and especially the most flagrant of all, the adulteration of money; but the ordinance granting redress emanated altogether from the king, and without the least reference to their consent, which sometimes appears to be studiously omitted.[227] But the privilege upon which the States under John solely relied for securing the redress of grievances was that of granting money and of regulating its collection. The latter, indeed, though for convenience it may be devolved upon the executive government, appears to be incident to every assembly in which the right of taxation resides. That, accordingly, which met in 1355 nominated a committee chosen out of the three orders, which was to sit after their separation, and which the king bound himself to consult, not only as to the internal arrangements of his administration, but upon every proposition of peace or armistice with England. Deputies were despatched into each district to superintend the collection and receive the produce of the subsidy granted by the States.[228] These

---

[226] Chap. i, p. 43.

[227] The proceedings of States-General held under Philip IV and his sons have left no trace in the French statute-book. Two ordonnances alone, out of some hundred enacted by Philip of Valois, appear to have been founded upon their suggestions.

It is absolutely certain that the States-General of France had at no period, and in no instance, a co-ordinate legislative authority with the crown, or even a consenting voice. Mably, Boulainvilliers,

and Montlosier are as decisive on this subject as the most courtly writers of that country. It follows as a just consequence that France never possessed a free constitution; nor had the monarchy any limitations in respect of enacting laws, save those which, until the reign of Philip the Fair, the feudal principles had imposed.

[228] "Ordonnances des Rois," tome iii, p. 21, and préface, p. 42. This preface by M. Sécousse, the editor, gives a very clear view of the general and provincial assem-

assumptions of power would not long, we may be certain, have
left the sole authority of legislation in the king, and might, perhaps, be censured as usurpation if the peculiar emergency in
which France was then placed did not furnish their defence.
But, if it be true that the kingdom was reduced to the utmost
danger and exhaustion, as much by malversation of its government as by the armies of Edward III, who shall deny to its representatives the right of ultimate sovereignty, and of suspending
at least the royal prerogatives, by the abuse of which they were
falling into destruction? [229]   I confess that it is exceedingly difficult, or perhaps impracticable, with such information as we possess, to decide upon the motives and conduct of the States-General in their several meetings before and after the battle of Poitiers. Arbitrary power prevailed; and its opponents became, of
course, the theme of obloquy with modern historians. Froissart,
however, does not seem to impute any fault to these famous
assemblies of the States-General; and still less a more contemporary historian, the anonymous continuator of Nangis. Their
notices, however, are very slight; and our chief knowledge of
the parliamentary history of France, if I may employ the expression, must be collected from the royal ordinances made upon
these occasions, or from unpublished accounts of their transactions. Some of these, which are quoted by the later historians,
are, of course, inaccessible to a writer in this country. But a
manuscript in the British Museum, containing the early proceedings of that assembly which met in October, 1356, immediately after the battle of Poitiers, by no means leads to an unfavourable estimate of its intentions.[230]   The tone of their representations to the Duke of Normandy (Charles V, not then called
dauphin) is full of loyal respect; their complaints of bad administration, though bold and pointed, not outrageous; their offers
of subsidy liberal. The necessity of restoring the coin is strongly

blies held in the reign of John. Boulainvilliers, " Hist. de l'Ancien Gouvernement de France," tome ii, or Villaret,
tome ix, may be perused with advantage.
    [229] The second continuator of Nangis
in the Spicilegium dwells on the heavy
taxes, diminution of money, and general
oppressiveness of government in this age
(tome iii, p. 108).
    [230] Cotton MSS. Titus, tome xii, fol.
58-74. This manuscript is noticed, as an
important document, in the preface to
the third volume of " Ordonnances," p.
48, by M. Sécousse, who had found it
mentioned in the " Bibliothèque Historique of Le Long," No. 11,242. No
French antiquary appears, at least before
that time, to have seen it; but Boulainvilliers conjectured that it related to the
assembly of states in February, 1356
(1357), and M. Sécousse supposed it

rather to be the original journal of the
preceding meeting in October, 1356, from
which a copy, found among the manuscripts of Dupuy, and frequently referred
to by Sécousse himself in his preface,
had been taken. M. Sécousse was perfectly right in supposing the manuscript
in question to relate to the proceedings
of October, and not of February; but it
is not an original instrument. It forms
part of a small volume written on vel-
lum, and containing several other treatises. It seems, however, as far as I
can judge, to be another copy of the account which Dupuy possessed, and which
Sécousse so often quotes, under the name
of Procès-verbal.
    It is singular that Sismondi says (x,
479), with Sécousse before his eyes, that
the procès-verbaux of the States-General,
in 1356, are not extant.

represented as the grand condition upon which they consented to tax the people, who had been long defrauded by the base money of Philip the Fair and his successors.[231]

But whatever opportunity might now be afforded for establishing a just and free constitution in France was entirely lost. Charles, inexperienced and surrounded by evil counsellors, thought the States-General inclined to encroach upon his rights, of which, in the best part of his life, he was always abundantly careful. He dismissed, therefore, the assembly, and had recourse to the easy but ruinous expedient of debasing the coin. This led to seditions at Paris, by which his authority, and even his life, were endangered. In February, 1357, three months after the last meeting had been dissolved, he was obliged to convoke the States again, and to enact an ordinance conformable to the petitions tendered by the former assembly.[232] This contained many excellent provisions, both for the redress of abuses and the vigorous prosecution of the war against Edward; and it is difficult to conceive that men who advised measures so conducive to the public weal could have been the blind instruments of the King of Navarre. But this, as I have already observed, is a problem in history that we can not hope to resolve. It appears, however, that, in a few weeks after the promulgation of this ordinance, the proceedings of the reformers fell into discredit, and their commission of thirty-six, to whom the collection of the new subsidy, the redress of grievances, and, in fact, the whole administration of government had been intrusted, became unpopular. The subsidy produced much less than they had led the people to expect: briefly, the usual consequence of democratical emotions in a monarchy took place. Disappointed by the failure of hopes unreasonably entertained and improvidently encouraged, and disgusted by the excesses of the violent demagogues, the nation, especially its privileged classes, who seem to have concurred in the original proceedings of the States-General, attached themselves to the party of Charles, and enabled him to quell opposi-

[231] Et estoit et est l'entente de ceulx qui a la ditte convocation estoient, que quelconque ottroy ou ayde qu'ils feissent, ils eussent bonne monnoye et estable selon l'advis des trois estats; et que les chartres et lettres faites pour les reformations du royaume par le roy Philippe le Bel, et toutes celles qui furent faites par le roy notre seigneur qui est a present, fussent confirmées, enterinées, tenues, et gardées de point en point ; et toutes les aides quelconques qui faites soient fussent recues et distribuées par ceulx qui soient a ce commis par les trois estats, et autorisées par M. le Duc, et sur certaines autres conditions et modifications justes et raissonables prouffitables, et semble que ceste aide eust été moult grant et moult prouffitable, et trop plus que aides de fait de monnoye. Car elle se feroit de volonté du peuple et consentement commun selon Dieu et selon conscience: Et le prouffit que on prent et veult on prendre sur le fait de la monnoye duquel on veult faire le fait de la guerre, et ce soit a la destruction, et a esté au temps passé, du roy et du royaume et des subjets; Et si se destruit le billon tant par fontures et blanchis comme autrement, ne le fait ne peust durer longuement qu'il ne vienne a destruction si on continue longuement; Et si est tout certain que les gens d'armes ne vouldroient estre contens de leurs gaiges par foible monnoye, etc.

[232] "Ordonnances des Rois," tome iii, p. 121.

tion by force.[233]   Marcel, provost of the traders, a municipal magistrate of Paris, detected in the overt execution of a traitorous conspiracy with the King of Navarre, was put to death by a private hand. Whatever there had been of real patriotism in the States-General, artfully confounded, according to the practice of courts, with these schemes of disaffected men, shared in the common obloquy; whatever substantial reforms had been projected the government threw aside as seditious innovations. Charles, who had assumed the title of regent, found in the States-General assembled at Paris, in 1359, a very different disposition from that which their predecessors had displayed, and publicly restored all counsellors whom in the former troubles he had been compelled to discard. Thus the monarchy resettled itself on its ancient basis, or, more properly, acquired additional stability.[234]

Both John, after the Peace of Bretigni, and Charles V imposed taxes without consent of the States-General.[235] The latter, indeed, hardly ever convoked that assembly. Upon his death the contention between the crown and representative body was renewed; and, in the first meeting held after the accession of Charles VI, the government was compelled to revoke all taxes illegally imposed since the reign of Philip IV. This is the most remedial ordinance, perhaps, in the history of French legislation. "We will, ordain, and grant," says the king, "that the aids, subsidies, and impositions, of whatever kind and however imposed, that have had course in the realm since the reign of our predecessor, Philip the Fair, shall be repealed and abolished; and we will and decree that, by the course which the said impositions have had, we or our successors shall not have acquired any right, nor shall any prejudice be wrought to our people, nor to their privileges and liberties, which shall be re-established in as full a manner as they enjoyed them in the reign of Philip the Fair or at any time since; and we will and decree that, if anything has been done contrary to them since that time to the present hour, neither we nor our successors shall take any advantage therefrom." [236] If circumstances had turned out favourably for the cause of liberty, this ordinance might have been the basis of a free constitution, in respect, at least, of immunity from arbitrary taxation. But the coercive measures of

---

[233] Discordiâ motâ, illi tres status ab incepto proposito cessaverunt. Ex tunc enim regni negotia male ire, etc. (Continuator Gul. de Nangis in Spicilegio, tome iii, p. 115.)
[234] A very full account of these transactions is given by Sécousse in his "History of Charles the Bad," p. 107, and in his preface to the third volume of the "Ordonnances des Rois." The reader must make allowance for the usual par-

tialities of a French historian, where an opposition to the reigning prince is his subject. A contrary bias is manifested by Boulainvilliers and Mably, whom, however, it is well worth while to hear.
[235] Mably, l. v, c. 5, note 5.
[236] "Ordonnances des Rois," tome vi, p. 564. The ordinance is long, containing frequent repetitions, and a great redundance of words, intended to give more force, or at least solemnity.

the court and tumultuous spirit of the Parisians produced an open quarrel, in which the popular party met with a decisive failure.

It seems, indeed, impossible that a number of deputies, elected merely for the purpose of granting money, can possess that weight, or be invested in the eyes of their constituents with that awfulness of station, which is required to withstand the royal authority. The States-General had no right of redressing abuses, except by petition; no share in the exercise of sovereignty, which is inseparable from the legislative power. Hence, even in their proper department of imposing taxes, they were supposed incapable of binding their constituents without their special assent. Whether it were the timidity of the deputies, or false notions of freedom, which produced this doctrine, it was evidently repugnant to the stability and dignity of a representative assembly. Nor was it less ruinous in practice than mistaken in theory. For as the necessary subsidies, after being provisionally granted by the States, were often rejected by their electors, the king found a reasonable pretence for dispensing with the concurrence of his subjects when he levied contributions upon them.

The States-General were convoked but rarely under Charles VI and VII, both of whom levied money without their concurrence. Yet there are remarkable testimonies under the latter of these princes that the sanction of national representatives was still esteemed strictly requisite to any ordinance imposing a general tax, however the emergency of circumstances might excuse a more arbitrary procedure. Thus Charles VII, in 1436, declares that he has set up again the aids which had been previously abolished by the consent of the three estates.[237] And in the important edict establishing the companies of ordonnance, which is recited to be done by the advice and counsel of the States-General assembled at Orleans, the forty-first section appears to bear a necessary construction that no tallage could lawfully be imposed without such consent.[238] It is maintained, indeed, by some writers, that the perpetual taille established about the same time was actually granted by these States of 1439, though it does not so appear upon the face of any ordinance.[239] And certainly this is consonant to the real and recognised constitution of that age.

But the crafty advisers of courts in the fifteenth century, enlightened by experience of past dangers, were averse to encountering these great political masses, from which there were, even in peaceful times, some disquieting interferences, some testimonies of

[237] " Ordonnances des Rois," tome xiii, p. 211.
[238] Ibid., p. 312. Boulainvilliers mentions other instances where the states granted money during this reign (tome iii, p. 70).

[239] Bréquigny, préface au treizième tome des " Ordonnances." (Boulainvilliers, tome iii, p. 108.)

public spirit, and recollections of liberty to apprehend. The Kings of France, indeed, had a resource, which generally enabled them to avoid a convocation of the States-General, without violating the national franchises. From provincial assemblies, composed of the three orders, they usually obtained more money than they could have extracted from the common representatives of the nation, and heard less of remonstrance and demand.[240] Languedoc in particular had her own assembly of States, and was rarely called upon to send deputies to the general body, or representatives of what was called the Languedoil. But Auvergne, Normandy, and other provinces belonging to the latter division, had frequent convocations of their respective estates during the intervals of the States-General—intervals which by this means were protracted far beyond that duration to which the exigencies of the crown would otherwise have confined them.[241] This was one of the essential differences between the constitutions of France and England, and arose out of the original disease of the former monarchy—the distraction and want of unity consequent upon the decline of Charlemagne's family, which separated the different provinces, in respect of their interests and domestic government, from each other.

But the formality of consent, whether by general or provincial States, now ceased to be reckoned indispensable. The lawyers had rarely seconded any efforts to restrain arbitrary power: in their hatred of feudal principles, especially those of territorial jurisdiction, every generous sentiment of freedom was proscribed; or, if they admitted that absolute prerogative might require some checks, it was such only as themselves, not the national representatives, should impose. Charles VII levied money by his own authority. Louis XI carried this encroachment to the highest pitch of exaction. It was the boast of courtiers that he first released the Kings of France from dependence (hors de page); or, in other words, that he effectually demolished those barriers which, however imperfect and ill placed, had imposed some impediment to the establishment of despotism.[242]

The exactions of Louis, however, though borne with patience, did not pass for legal with those upon whom they pressed. Men still remembered their ancient privileges, which they might see with mortification well preserved in England. " There is no

[240] Villaret, tome xi, p. 270.
[241] " Ordonnances des Rois," tome iii, préface.

[242] The preface to the sixteenth volume of " Ordonnances," before quoted, displays a lamentable picture of the internal situation of France in consequence of excessive taxation and other abuses. These evils, in a less aggravated degree, continued ever since to retard the improvement and diminish the intrinsic

prosperity of a country so extraordinarily endowed with natural advantages. Philip de Comines was forcibly struck with the different situation of England and the Netherlands. And Sir John Fortescue has a remarkable passage on the poverty and servitude of the French commons, contrasted with English freemen. (" Difference of Limited and Absolute Monarchy," p. 17.)

monarch or lord upon earth " (says Philip de Comines, himself bred in courts) " who can raise a farthing upon his subjects, beyond his own domains, without their free concession, except through tyranny and violence. It may be objected that in some cases there may not be time to assemble them, and that war will bear no delay; but I reply " (he proceeds) " that such haste ought not to be made, and there will be time enough; and I tell you that princes are more powerful, and more dreaded by their enemies, when they undertake anything with the consent of their subjects." [243]

The States-General met but twice during the reign of Louis XI, and on neither occasion for the purpose of granting money. But an assembly in the first year of Charles VIII, the states of Tours in 1484, is too important to be overlooked, as it marks the last struggle of the French nation by its legal representatives for immunity from arbitrary taxation.

A warm contention arose for the regency upon the accession of Charles VIII between his aunt, Anne de Beaujeu, whom the late king had appointed by testament, and the princes of the blood, at the head of whom stood the Duke of Orleans, afterward Louis XII. The latter combined to demand a convocation of the States-General, which accordingly took place. The king's minority and the factions at court seemed no unfavourable omens for liberty. But a scheme was artfully contrived which had the most direct tendency to break the force of a popular assembly. The deputies were classed in six nations, who debated in separate chambers, and consulted each other only upon the result of their respective deliberations. It was easy for the court to foment the jealousies natural to such a partition. Two nations, the Norman and Burgundian, asserted that the right of providing for the regency devolved, in the king's minority, upon the States-General; a claim of great boldness, and certainly not much founded upon precedents. In virtue of this, they proposed to form a council, not only of the princes, but of certain deputies to be elected by the six nations who composed the States. But the other four, those of Paris, Aquitaine, Languedoc, and Languedoil (which last comprised the central provinces), rejected this plan, from which the two former ultimately desisted, and the choice of councillors was left to the princes.

A firmer and more unanimous spirit was displayed upon the subject of public reformation. The tyranny of Louis XI had been so unbounded that all ranks agreed in calling for redress, and the new governors were desirous, at least by punishing his favourites, to show their inclination toward a change of system. They were very far, however, from approving the propositions

[243] " Mém. de Comines," l. iv, c. 19.

of the States-General. These went to points which no court can bear to feel touched, though there is seldom any other mode of redressing public abuses: the profuse expense of the royal household, the number of pensions and improvident grants, the excessive establishment of troops. The States explicitly demanded that the taille and all other arbitrary imposts should be abolished, and that from thenceforward, "according to the natural liberty of France," no tax should be levied in the kingdom without the consent of the States. It was with great difficulty, and through the skilful management of the court, that they consented to the collection of the taxes payable in the time of Charles VII, with the addition of one fourth as a gift to the king upon his accession. This subsidy they declare to be granted "by way of gift and concession, and not otherwise, and so as no one should from thenceforward call it a tax, but a gift and concession." And this was only to be in force for two years, after which they stipulated that another meeting should be convoked. But it was little likely that the government would encounter such a risk; and the princes, whose factious views the States had by no means seconded, felt no temptations to urge again their convocation. No assembly in the annals of France seems, notwithstanding some party selfishness arising out of the division into nations, to have conducted itself with so much public spirit and moderation, nor had that country perhaps ever so fair a prospect of establishing a legitimate constitution.[244]

5. The right of jurisdiction has undergone changes in France and in the adjacent countries still more remarkable than those of the legislative power; and passed through three very distinct stages, as the popular, aristocratic, or regal influence predominated in the political system. The Franks, Lombards, and Saxons seem alike to have been jealous of judicial authority, and averse to surrendering what concerned every man's private right out of the hands of his neighbours and his equals. Every ten families are supposed to have had a magistrate of their own election: the tithingman of England, the decanus of France and Lombardy.[245] Next in order was the Centenarius or Hundredary, whose name expresses the extent of his jurisdiction, and who, like the Decanus, was chosen by those subject to it.[246]

[244] I am altogether indebted to Garnier for the proceedings of the states of Tours. His account (" Hist. de France," tome xviii, pp. 154–348) is extremely copious, and derived from a manuscript journal. Comines alludes to them sometimes, but with little particularity. The above-mentioned manuscript was published in 1835, among the " Documens Inédits sur l'Histoire de France."
[245] The Decanus is mentioned by a writer of the ninth age as the lowest species of judge, immediately under the Centenarius. The latter is compared to the Plebanus, or priest, of a church where baptism was performed, and the former to an inferior presbyter. (Du Cange, voc. Decanus; and Muratori, " Antiq. Ital.," Dissert. 10.)
[246] It is evident from the capitularies of Charlemagne (Baluze, tome i, pp. 426, 466) that the Centenarii were elected by the people; that is, I suppose, the freeholders.

But the authority of these petty magistrates was gradually confined to the less important subjects of legal inquiry. No man, by a capitulary of Charlemagne, could be impleaded for his life, or liberty, or lands, or servants, in the hundred court.[247] In such weighty matters, or by way of appeal from the lower jurisdictions, the count of the district was judge. He, indeed, was appointed by the sovereign; but his power was checked by assessors, called Scabini, who held their office by the election, or at least the concurrence, of the people.[248] An ultimate appeal seems to have lain to the Count Palatine, an officer of the royal household, and sometimes causes were decided by the sovereign himself.[249] Such was the original model of judicature; but as complaints of injustice and neglect were frequently made against the counts, Charlemagne, desirous on every account to control them, appointed special judges, called Missi Regii, who held assizes from place to place, inquired into abuses and maladministration of justice, enforced its execution, and expelled inferior judges from their offices for misconduct.[250]

This judicial system was gradually superseded by one founded upon totally opposite principles, those of feudal privilege. It is difficult to ascertain the progress of territorial jurisdiction. In many early charters of the French kings, beginning with one of Dagobert I in 630, we find inserted in their grants of land an immunity from the entrance of the ordinary judges, either to hear causes or to exact certain dues accruing to the king and to themselves.[251] These charters, indeed, relate to church lands,

[247] Ut nullus homo in placito centenarii neque ad mortem, neque ad libertatem suam amittendam, aut ad res reddendas vel mancipia judicetur. Sed ista aut in presentiâ comitis vel missorum nostrorum judicentur. (Capit. A. D. 812; Baluz., p. 497.)
[248] "Baluzii Capitularia," p. 466; Muratori, Dissert. 10; Du Cange, voc. Scabini. These Scabini may be traced by the light of charters down to the eleventh century. (" Recueil des Historiens," tome vi, préface, p. 186.) There is, in particular, a decisive proof of their existence in 918, in a record which I have already had occasion to quote. (Vaissette, " Hist. de Languedoc," tome ii, appendix, p. 56.) Du Cange, Baluze, and other antiquaries have confounded the Scabini with the Rachimburgii, of whom we read in the oldest laws. But Savigny and Guizot have proved the latter were land-owners, acting in the county courts as judges under the presidency of the count, but wholly independent of him. The Scabini in Charlemagne's age superseded them. (" Essais sur l'Histoire de France," pp. 259, 272.)
[249] Du Cange, Dissertation 14, sur Joinville; and Glossary, v. Comites Palatini; " Mém. de l'Acad. des Inscript.,"

tome xxx, p. 590. Louis the Debonair gave one day in every week for hearing causes; but his subjects were required not to have recourse to him unless where the Missi or the counts had not done justice. (Baluze, tome i, p. 668.) Charles the Bald expressly reserves an appeal to himself from the inferior tribunals. (Capit., 869, tome ii, p. 215.) In his reign there was at least a claim to sovereignty preserved.
[250] For the jurisdiction of the Missi Regii, besides the capitularies themselves, see Muratori's eighth Dissertation. They went their circuits four times a year. (Capit. A. D. 812; A. D. 823.) A vestige of this institution long continued in the province of Auvergne, under the name of Grands Jours d'Auvergne; which Louis XI revived in 1479. (Garnier, " Hist. de France," tome xviii, p. 458.)
[251] If a charter of Clovis to a monastery called Reomaense, dated 496, is genuine, the same words of exemption occurring in it, we must refer territorial jurisdiction to the very infancy of the French monarchy. And M. Lehuerou (" Inst. Caroling.," p. 225 et post) has strongly contended for the right of lords to exercise jurisdiction in virtue of their ownership of the soil, and without re-

which, as it seems implied by a law of Charlemagne, universally possessed an exemption from ordinary jurisdiction. A precedent, however, in Marculfus leads us to infer a similar immunity to have been usual in gifts to private persons.[252] These rights of justice in the beneficiary tenants of the crown are attested in several passages of the capitularies. And a charter of Louis I to a private individual contains a full and exclusive concession of jurisdiction over all persons resident within the territory, though subject to the appellant control of the royal tribunals.[253] It is obvious, indeed, that an exemption from the regular judicial authorities implied or naturally led to a right of administering justice in their place. But this could at first hardly extend beyond the tributaries or villeins who cultivated their master's soil, or, at most, to free persons without property, resident in the territory. To determine their quarrels or chastise their offences was no very illustrious privilege. An allodial freeholder could own no jurisdiction but that of the king. It was the general prevalence of subinfeudation which gave importance to the territorial jurisdictions of the nobility. For now the military tenants, instead of repairing to the county court, sought justice in that of their immediate lord; or rather the count himself, become the suzerain instead of the governor of his district, altered the form of his tribunal upon the feudal model.[254] A system of procedure so congenial to the spirit of the age spread universally over France and Germany. The tribunals of the king were forgotten like his laws; the one retaining as little authority to correct, as the other to regulate, the decisions of a territorial judge. The rules of evidence were superseded by that monstrous birth of ferocity and superstition, the judicial combat, and the maxims of law reduced to a few capricious customs, which varied in almost every barony.

gard to the personal law of those coming within its scope by residence. This territorial right he deduces from the earliest times; it was an enlargement of the ancient mundium, or protection, among the Germans; which must have been solely personal before the establishment of separate property in land, but became local after the settlement in Gaul, to which that great civil revolution was due. The authority of M. Lehuerou is entitled to much respect; yet his theory seems to involve a more extensive development of the feudal system in the Merovingian period than we generally admit.

[252] "Marculfi Formulæ," l. i, c. 17.

[253] Et nullus comes, nec vicarius, nec juniores eorum, nec illus judex publicus illorum, homines qui super illorum aprisione habitant, aut in illorum proprio, distringere nec judicare præsumant; sed Johannes et filii sui, et posteritas illorum, illi eos judicent et distringant.

Et quicquid per legem judicaverint, stabilis permaneat. Et si extra legem fecerint, per legem emendent. ("Baluzii Capitularia," tome ii, p. 1405.) This appellant control was preserved by the capitulary of Charles the Bald, quoted already, over the territorial as well as royal tribunals. Si aliquis episcopus, vel comes ac vassus noster suo homini contra rectum et justitiam fecerit, et si inde ad nos reclamaverit, sciat quia, sicut ratio et lex est, hoc emendare faciemus.

[254] We may perhaps infer, from a capitulary of Charlemagne in 809, that the feudal tenants were already employed as assessors in the administration of justice, concurrently with the Scabini mentioned above. Ut nullus ad placitum venire cogatur, nisi qui causam habet ad quærendum, exceptis scabinis et vassallis comitum. ("Baluzii Capitularia," tome i, p. 465.)

These rights of administering justice were possessed by the owners of fiefs in very different degrees; and, in France, were divided into the high, the middle, and the low jurisdiction.[255] The first species alone (la haute justice) conveyed the power of life and death; it was inherent in the baron and the châtelain, and sometimes enjoyed by the simple vavassor. The lower jurisdictions were not competent to judge in capital cases, and consequently forced to send such criminals to the court of the superior. But in some places a thief taken in the fact might be punished with death by a lord who had only the low jurisdiction. In England this privilege was known by the uncouth terms of Infangthef and Outfangthef. The high jurisdiction, however, was not very common in this country, except in the chartered towns.[256]

Several customs rendered these rights of jurisdiction far less instrumental to tyranny than we might infer from their extent. While the counts were yet officers of the crown, they frequently appointed a deputy or viscount to administer justice. Ecclesiastical lords, who were prohibited by the canons from inflicting capital punishment, and supposed to be unacquainted with the law followed in civil courts, or unable to enforce it, had an officer by name of advocate, or vidame, whose tenure was often feudal and hereditary. The viguiers (vicarii), bailiffs, provosts, and seneschals of lay lords were similar ministers, though not in general of so permanent a right in their offices, or of such eminent station, as the advocates of monasteries. It seems to have been an established maxim, at least in later times, that the lord could not sit personally in judgment, but must intrust that function to his bailiff and vassals.[257] According to the feudal rules, the lord's vassals or peers of his court were to assist at all its proceedings. "There are some places," says Beaumanoir, "where the bailiff decides in judgment, and others where the vassals of the lord decide. But even where the bailiff is the judge, he ought to advise with the most prudent, and determine by their advice; since thus he shall be most secure if an appeal is made

[255] Velly, tome vi, p. 131; Denisart, Houard, and other law-books.
[256] A strangely cruel privilege was possessed in Aragon by the lords who had not the higher jurisdiction, and consequently could not publicly execute a criminal: that of starving him to death in prison. This was established by law in 1247. Si vassallus domini non habentis merum nec mixtum imperium, in loco occideret vassallum, dominus loci potest eum occidere fame, frigore et siti. Et quilibet dominus loci habet hanc jurisdictionum necandi fame, frigore et siti in suo loco, licet nullam aliam jurisdictionem criminalem habeat. (Du Cange, voc. Fame necare.)

It is remarkable that the Neapolitan barons had no criminal jurisdiction, at least of the higher kind, till the reign of Alfonso, in 1443, who sold this destructive privilege, at a time when it was almost abolished in other kingdoms. (Giannone, l. xxii, c. 5, and l. xxvi, c. 6.)
[257] Boutillier, in his "Somme Rurale," written near the end of the fourteenth century, asserts this positively. Il convient quilz facent jugier par aultre que par eulx, cest a savoir par leurs hommes feudaulx a leur semonce et conjuré [?] ou de leur bailiff ou lieutenant, et ont ressort a leur souverain. (Fol. 3.)

from his judgment." [258]   And indeed the presence of these assessors was so essential to all territorial jurisdiction that no lord, to whatever rights of justice his fief might entitle him, was qualified to exercise them, unless he had at least two vassals to sit as peers in his court.[259]

These courts of a feudal barony or manor required neither the knowledge of positive law nor the dictates of natural sagacity. In all doubtful cases, and especially where a crime not capable of notorious proof was charged, the combat was awarded; and God, as they deemed, was the judge.[260]   The nobleman fought on horseback, with all his arms of attack and defence; the plebeian on foot, with his club and target.   The same were the weapons of the champions to whom women and ecclesiastics were permitted to intrust their rights.[261]   If the combat was intended to ascertain a civil right, the vanquished party, of course, forfeited his claim and paid a fine.   If he fought by proxy, the champion was liable to have his hand struck off; a regulation necessary, perhaps, to obviate the corruption of these hired defenders.   In criminal cases the appellant suffered, in the event of defeat, the same punishment which the law awarded to the offence of which he accused his adversary.[262]   Even where the cause was more peaceably tried, and brought to a regular adjudication by the court, an appeal for false judgment might indeed be made to the suzerain, but it could only be tried by battle.[263]   And in this the appellant, if he would impeach the concurrent judgment of the court below, was compelled to meet successively in combat every one of its members; unless he should vanquish them all within the day, his life, if he escaped from so many hazards, was forfeited to the law.   If fortune or miracle should make him

[258] " Coûtumes de Beauvoisis," p. 11.
[259] It was lawful, in such case, to borrow the vassals of the superior lord. (" Thaumassière sur Beaumanoir," p. 375. See Du Cange, voc. Pares, an excellent article; and Placitum.)

In England a manor is extinguished, at least as to jurisdiction, when there are not two freeholders subject to escheat left as suitors to the court-baron. Their tenancy must therefore have been created before the statute of Quia Emptores, 18 Edw. I (1290), since which no new estate in fee simple can be held of the lord, nor consequently be liable to escheat to him.

[260] Trial by combat does not seem to have established itself completely in France till ordeals went into disuse, which Charlemagne rather encouraged, and which, in his age, the clergy for the most part approved.   The former species of decision may, however, be met with under the first Merovingian kings (Greg. Turon., l. vii, c. 19; l. x, c. 10), and seems to have prevailed in Burgundy.   It is established by the laws of the Alemanni

or Swabians. (Baluz., tome i, p. 80.) It was always popular in Lombardy.   Liutprand, King of the Lombards, says in one of his laws, Incerti sumus de judicio Dei, et quosdam audivimus per pugnam sine justâ causâ suam causam perdere.   Sed propter consuetudinem gentis nostræ Langobardorum legem impiam vetare non possumus. (Muratori, " Script. Rerum Italicarum," tome ii, p. 65.)   Otho II established it in all disputes concerning real property; and there is a famous case where the right of representation, or preference of the son of a deceased elder child to his uncle in succession to his grandfather's estate, was settled by this test.

[261] For the ceremonies of trial by combat, see Houard, " Anciennes Loix Françoises," tome i, p. 264; Velly, tome vi, p. 106; " Recueil des Historiens," tome xi, préface, p. 189; Du Cange, voc. Duellum.   The great original authorities are the " Assises de Jérusalem," c. 104, and Beaumanoir, c. 31.

[262] Beaumanoir, p. 315.
[263] Id., c. 61.   In England the appeal

conqueror in every contest, the judges were equally subject to death, and their court forfeited their jurisdiction forever. A less perilous mode of appeal was to call the first judge who pronounced a hostile sentence into the field. If the appellant came off victorious in this challenge, the decision was reversed, but the court was not impeached.[264] But for denial of justice—that is, for a refusal to try his suit—the plaintiff repaired to the court of the next superior lord, and supported his appeal by testimony.[265] Yet even here the witnesses might be defied, and the pure stream of justice turned at once into the torrent of barbarous contest.[266]

Such was the judicial system of France when St. Louis enacted that great code which bears the name of his " Establishments." The rules of civil and criminal procedure, as well as the principles of legal decisions, are there laid down with much detail. But that incomparable prince, unable to overthrow the judicial combat, confined himself to discourage it by the example of a wiser jurisprudence. It was abolished throughout the royal domains. The bailiffs and seneschals who rendered justice to the king's immediate subjects were bound to follow his own laws. He not only received appeals from their sentences in his own court of peers, but listened to all complaints with a kind of patriarchal simplicity. " Many times," says Joinville, " I have seen the good saint, after hearing mass, in the summer season, lay himself at the foot of an oak in the wood of Vincennes, and make us all sit round him; when those who would,

for false judgment to the king's court was not tried by battle. (Glanvil, l. xii, c. 7.)

[264] Id., c. 61.

[265] Id., p. 315. The practice was to challenge the second witness, since the testimony of one was insufficient. But this must be done before he completes his oath, says Beaumanoir, for after he has been sworn he must be heard and believed (p. 316). No one was bound, as we may well believe, to be a witness for another, in cases where such an appeal might be made from his testimony.

[266] Mably is certainly mistaken in his opinion that appeals for denial of justice were not older than the reign of Philip Augustus. (" Observations sur l'Hist. de France," l. iii, c. 3.) Before this time the vassal's remedy, he thinks, was to make war upon his lord. And this may probably have been frequently practised. Indeed, it is permitted, as we have seen by the code of St. Louis. But those who were not strong enough to adopt this dangerous means of redress would surely avail themselves of the assistance of the suzerain, which in general would be readily afforded. We find several instances of the king's interference for the redress of injuries in Suger's " Life of

Louis VI." That active and spirited prince, with the assistance of his enlightened biographer, recovered a great part of the royal authority, which had been reduced to the lowest ebb in the long and slothful reign of his father, Philip I. One passage especially contains a clear evidence of the appeal for denial of justice, and consequently refutes Mably's opinion. In 1105 the inhabitants of St. Sévère, in Berri, complain of their Lord Humbald, and request the king aut ad exequendam justitiam cogere, aut jure pro injuria castrum lege Salicâ amittere. I quote from the preface to the fourteenth volume of the " Recueil des Historiens," p. 44. It may be noticed, by the way, that lex Salica is here used for the feudal customs; in which sense I believe it not unfrequently occurs. Many proofs might be brought of the interposition of both Louis VI and VII in the diputes between their barons and arrière vassals. Thus the war between the latter and Henry II of England in 1166 was occasioned by his entertaining a complaint from the Count of Auvergne, without waiting for the decision of Henry, as Duke of Guienne. (Velly, tome ii, p. 190; Littleton's " Henry II," vol. ii, p. 448; " Recueil des Historiens," ubi supra, p. 49.

came and spake to him without let of any officer, and he would ask aloud if there were any present who had suits; and when they appeared, would bid two of his bailiffs determine their cause upon the spot."[267]

The influence of this new jurisprudence established by St. Louis, combined with the great enhancements of the royal prerogatives in every other respect, produced a rapid change in the legal administration of France. Though trial by combat occupies a considerable space in the work of Beaumanoir, written under Philip the Bold, it was already much limited. Appeals for false judgment might sometimes be tried, as he expresses it, par erremens de plait; that is, I presume, where the alleged error of the court below was in matter of law. For wager of battle was chiefly intended to ascertain controverted facts.[268] So where the suzerain saw clearly that the judgment of the inferior court was right, he ought not to permit the combat. Or if the plaintiff, even in the first instance, could produce a record or a written obligation, or if the fact before the court was notorious, there was no room for battle.[269] It would be a hard thing, says Beaumanoir, that if one had killed my near relation in open day before many credible persons, I should be compelled to fight in order to prove his death. This reflection is the dictate of common sense, and shows that the prejudice in favour of judicial combat was dying away. In the " Assises de Jérusalem," a monument of customs two hundred years earlier than the age of Beaumanoir, we find little mention of any other mode of decision. The compiler of that book thinks it would be very injurious if no wager of battle were to be allowed against witnesses in causes affecting succession; since otherwise every right heir might be disinherited, as it would be easy to find two persons who would perjure themselves for money if they had no fear of being challenged for their testimony.[270] This passage indicates the real cause of preserving the judicial combat, systematic perjury in witnesses, and want of legal discrimination in judges.

It was, in all civil suits, at the discretion of the litigant parties to adopt the law of the " Establishments," instead of resorting to combat.[271] As gentler manners prevailed, especially among those who did not make arms their profession, the wisdom and equity of the new code were naturally preferred. The superstition which had originally led to the latter lost its weight through experience and the uniform opposition of the clergy. The same

---

[267] " Collection des Mémoires," tome i, p. 25. Montesquieu supposes that the " Establishments of St. Louis " are not the original constitutions of that prince, but a work founded on them—a compilation of the old customs blended with his new provisions. (" Esprit des Loix,"

xxviii, 37, 38.) I do not know that any later inquirers have adopted this hypothesis.
[268] Beaumanoir, p. 22.
[269] Id., p. 314.
[270] C. 167.
[271] Beaumanoir, p. 309.

superiority of just and settled rules over fortune and violence, which had forwarded the encroachments of the ecclesiastical courts, was now manifested in those of the king. Philip Augustus, by a famous ordinance in 1190, first established royal courts of justice, held by the officers called bailiffs or seneschals, who acted as the king's lieutenants in his domains.[272] Every barony, as it became reunited to the crown, was subjected to the jurisdiction of one of these officers, and took the name of a bailliage or seneschaussée; the former name prevailing most in the northern, the latter in the southern, provinces. The vassals whose lands depended upon, or, in feudal language, moved, from the superiority of this fief, were obliged to submit to the ressort or supreme appellant jurisdiction of the royal court established in it.[273] This began rapidly to encroach upon the feudal rights of justice. In a variety of cases, termed royal, the territorial court was pronounced incompetent; they were reserved for the judges of the crown; and, in every case, unless the defendant excepted to the jurisdiction, the royal court might take cognizance of a suit, and decide it in exclusion of the feudal judicature.[274] The nature of cases reserved under the name of royal was kept in studied ambiguity, under cover of which the judges of the crown perpetually strove to multiply them. Louis X, when requested by the barons of Champagne to explain what was meant by royal causes, gave this mysterious definition: Everything which by right or custom ought exclusively to come under the cognizance of a sovereign prince.[275] Vassals were permitted to complain in the first instance to the king's court, of injuries committed by their lords. These rapid and violent encroachments left the nobility no alternative but armed combinations to support their remonstrances. Philip the Fair bequeathed to his successor the task of appeasing the storm which his own administration had excited. Leagues were formed in most of the northern provinces for the redress of grievances, in which the third estate, oppressed by taxation, united with the vassals, whose feudal privileges had been infringed. Separate charters were granted to each of these confederacies by Louis Hutin, which contain many remedial provisions against the grosser violations of ancient rights, though the crown persisted in restraining territorial jurisdiction.[276] Ap-

[272] " Ordonnances des Rois." tome i, p. 18.
[273] Du Cange, voc. Balivi. " Mém. de l'Acad. des Inscriptions," tome xxx, p. 603. Mably, l. iv, c. 4. Boulainvilliers, tome ii, p. 22.
[274] Mably, Boulainvilliers, Montlosier, tome i, p. 104.
[275] " Ordonnances des Rois," p. 606.
[276] Hoc perpetuo prohibemus edicto, ne subditi, seu justiciabiles prælatorum aut baronum nostrorum, aut aliorum sub-

jectorum nostrorum, trahantur in causam coram nostris officialibus, nec eorum causæ, nisi in casu ressorti, in nostris curiis audiantur, vel in alio casu ad nos pertinenti. (" Ordonnances des Rois," tome i, p. 362.) This ordinance is of Philip the Fair, in 1302; but those passed under Louis Hutin are to the same effect. They may be read at length in the " Ordonnances des Rois," or abridged by Boulainvilliers, tome ii, p. 94.

peals became more common for false judgment, as well as denial of right; and in neither was the combat permitted. It was still, however, preserved in accusations of heinous crimes, unsupported by any testimony but that of the prosecutor, and was never abolished by any positive law, either in France or England. But instances of its occurrence are not frequent even in the fourteenth century; and one of these, rather remarkable in its circumstances, must have had a tendency to explode the remaining superstition which had preserved this mode of decision.[277]

The supreme council, or court of peers, to whose deliberate functions I have already adverted, was also the great judicial tribunal of the French crown from the accession of Hugh Capet.[278] By this alone the barons of France, or tenants in chief of the king, could be judged. To this court appeals for denials of justice were referred. It was originally composed, as has been observed, of the feudal vassals, coequals of those who were to be tried by it; and also of the household officers, whose right of concurrence, however anomalous, was extremely ancient. But after the business of the court came to increase through the multiplicity of appeals, especially from the bailiffs established by Philip Augustus in the royal domains, the barons found neither leisure nor capacity for the ordinary administration of justice, and reserved their attendance for occasions where some of their own orders were implicated in a criminal process. St. Louis, anxious for regularity and enlightened decisions, made a considerable alteration by introducing some councillors of inferior rank, chiefly ecclesiastics, as advisers of the court, though, as is supposed, without any decisive suffrage. The court now became known by the name of Parliament. Registers of its proceedings were kept, of which the earliest extant are of the year 1254. It was still, perhaps, in some degree ambulatory; but by far the greater part of its sessions in the thirteenth century were at Paris. The councillors nominated by the king, some of them clerks, others of noble rank, but not peers of the ancient baronage, acquired insensibly a right of suffrage.[279]

An ordinance of Philip the Fair, in 1302, is generally supposed to have fixed the seat of Parliament at Paris, as well as altered its constituent parts.[280] Perhaps a series of progressive

[277] Philip IV restricted trial by combat to cases where four conditions were united. The crime must be capital; its commission certain; the accused greatly suspected; and no proof to be obtained by witnesses. Under these limitations, or at least some of them, for it appears that they were not all regarded, instances occur for some centuries.
See the singular story of Carouges and Le Gris, to which I allude in the text. (Villaret, tome xi, p. 412.) Trial by combat was allowed in Scotland exactly under the same conditions as in France. (Pinkerton's "Hist. of Scotland," vol. i, p. 66.)
[278] [Note XVII.]
[279] Boulainvilliers, tome ii, pp. 29, 44; Mably, l. iv, c. 2; Encyclopédie, art. Parlement; "Mém. de l'Acad. des Inscript.," tome xxx, p. 603. The great difficulty I have found in this investigation will plead my excuse if errors are detected.
[280] Pasquier ("Recherches de la

changes has been referred to a single epoch. But whether by virtue of this ordinance, or of more gradual events, the character of the whole feudal court was nearly obliterated in that of the Parliament of Paris. A systematic tribunal took the place of a loose aristocratic assembly. It was to hold two sittings in the year, each of two months' duration; it was composed of two prelates, two counts, thirteen clerks, and as many laymen. Great changes were made afterward in this constitution. The nobility, who originally sat there, grew weary of an attendance which detained them from war and from their favourite pursuits at home. The bishops were dismissed to their necessary residence upon their sees.[281] As they withdrew, a class of regular lawyers, originally employed, as it appears, in the preparatory business, without any decisive voice, came forward to the higher places, and established a complicated and tedious system of procedure, which was always characteristic of French jurisprudence.

They introduced at the same time a new theory of absolute power and unlimited obedience. All feudal privileges were treated as encroachments on the imprescriptible rights of monarchy. With the natural bias of lawyers in favour of prerogative conspired that of the clergy, who fled to the king for refuge against the tyranny of the barons. In the civil and canon laws a system of political maxims was found very uncongenial to the feudal customs. The French lawyers of the fourteenth and fifteenth centuries frequently give their king the title of emperor, and treat disobedience to him as sacrilege.[282]

But among these lawyers, although the general tenants of the crown by barony ceased to appear, there still continued to sit a more eminent body, the lay and spiritual peers of France, representatives, as it were, of that ancient baronial aristocracy. It is a very controverted question at what time this exclusive dignity of peerage, a word obviously applicable by the feudal law to all persons coequal in degree of tenure, was reserved to twelve vassals. At the coronation of Philip Augustus, in 1179, we first perceive the six great feudatories, Dukes of Burgundy, Normandy, Guienne, Counts of Toulouse, Flanders, Champagne, distinguished by the offices they performed in that ceremony. It was natural, indeed, that by their princely splendour and importance they should eclipse such petty lords as Bourbon and Coucy, however equal in quality of tenure. During the reign

France," l. ii, c. 3) published this ordinance, which, indeed, as the editor of " Ordonnances des Rois," tome i, p. 547, observes, is no ordinance, but a regulation for the execution of one previously made; nor does it establish the residence of the Parliament in Paris.
[281] Velly, " Hist. de France," tome vii,

p. 303, and Encyclopédie, art. Parlement, are the best authorities I have found. There may very possibly be superior works on this branch of the French constitution which have not fallen into my hands.
[282] Mably, l. iv, c. 2, note 10.

of Philip Augustus six ecclesiastical peers, the Duke-Bishops of
Rheims, Laon, and Langres, the Count-Bishops of Beauvais,
Châlons, and Noyon, were added as a sort of parallel or counterpoise.[283]   Their precedence does not, however, appear to have
carried with it any other privilege, at least in judicature, than
other barons enjoyed.   But their pre-eminence being fully confirmed, Philip the Fair set the precedent of augmenting their
original number by conferring the dignity of peerage on the
Duke of Brittany and the Count of Artois.[284]   Other creations
took place subsequently; but these were confined, during the
period comprised in this work, to princes of the royal blood.
The peers were constant members of the Parliament, from which
other vassals holding in chief were never, perhaps, excluded by
law, but their attendance was rare in the fourteenth century, and
soon afterward ceased altogether.[285]

A judicial body, composed of the greatest nobles in France,
as well as of learned and eminent lawyers, must naturally have
soon become politically important.   Notwithstanding their disposition to enhance every royal prerogative, as opposed to feudal
privileges, the Parliament was not disinclined to see its own
protection invoked by the subject.   It appears by an ordinance
of Charles V, in 1371, that the nobility of Languedoc had appealed to the Parliament of Paris against a tax imposed by the
king's authority; and this, at a time when the French constitution did not recognise the levying of money without consent
of the States-General, must have been a just ground of appeal,
though the present ordinance annuls and overturns it.[286]   During the tempests of Charles VI's unhappy reign the Parliament
acquired a more decided authority, and held, in some degree,
the balance between the contending factions of Orleans and
Burgundy.   This influence was partly owing to one remarkable
function attributed to the Parliament, which raised it much above
the level of a merely political tribunal, and has at various times
wrought striking effects in the French monarchy.

The few ordinances enacted by Kings of France in the twelfth
and thirteenth centuries were generally by the advice of their
royal council, in which probably they were solemnly declared as
well as agreed upon.   But after the gradual revolution of government, which took away from the feudal aristocracy all control over the king's edicts, and substituted a new magistracy
for the ancient baronial court, these legislative ordinances were
commonly drawn up by the interior council, or what we may
call the ministry.   They were in some instances promulgated by

[283] Velly, tome ii, p. 287; tome iii, p.
221; tome iv, p. 41.
[284] Id., tome vii, p. 97.

[285] Encyclopédie, art. Parlement, p. 6.
[286] Mably, l. v, c. 5, note 5.

the king in Parliament. Others were sent thither for registration or entry upon their records. This formality was by degrees, if not from the beginning, deemed essential to render them authentic and notorious, and therefore indirectly gave them the sanction and validity of a law.[287] Such, at least, appears to have been the received doctrine before the end of the fourteenth century. It has been contended by Mably, among other writers, that at so early an epoch the Parliament of Paris did not enjoy, nor even claim to itself, that anomalous right of judging the expediency of edicts proceeding from the king, which afterward so remarkably modified the absoluteness of his power. In the fifteenth century, however, it certainly manifested pretensions of this nature: first, by registering ordinances in such a manner as to testify its own unwillingness and disapprobation, of which one instance occurs as early as 1418, and another in 1443; and, afterward, by remonstrating against and delaying the registration of laws which it deemed inimical to the public interest. A conspicuous proof of this spirit was given in their opposition to Louis XI when repealing the Pragmatic Sanction of his father— an ordinance essential, in their opinion, to the liberties of the Gallican Church. In this instance they ultimately yielded; but at another time they persisted in a refusal to enregister letters containing an alienation of the royal domain.[288]

The counsellors of Parliament were originally appointed by the king, and they were even changed according to circumstances. Charles V made the first alteration, by permitting them to fill up vacancies by election, which usage continued during the next reign. Charles VII resumed the nomination of fresh members upon vacancies. Louis XI even displaced actual counsellors. But in 1468, from whatever motive, he published a most important ordinance, declaring the presidents and counsellors of Parliament immovable, except in case of legal forfeiture.[289] This extraordinary measure of conferring independence on a body which had already displayed a consciousness of its eminent privilege by opposing the registration of his edicts, is perhaps to be deemed a proof of that shortsightedness as to points of substantial interest so usually found in crafty men. But, be this as it may, there was formed in the Parliament of Paris an independent power not emanating from the royal will, nor liable, except through force, to be destroyed by it; which, in later times, became almost the sole depositary, if not of what we should call the love of freedom, yet of public spirit and attachment to justice. France, so fertile of great men in the sixteenth and

[287] Encyclopédie, art. Parlement.
[288] Mably, l. vi, c. 5, notes 19 and 21; Garnier, " Hist. de France," xvii, 219–380.

[289] Villaret, tome xiv, p. 231; Encyclopédie, art. Parlement.

seventeenth centuries, might better spare, perhaps, from her
annals any class and description of them than her lawyers.
Doubtless the Parliament of Paris, with its prejudices and narrow views, its high notions of loyal obedience so strangely mixed
up with remonstrances and resistance, its anomalous privilege
of objecting to edicts, hardly approved by the nation who did
not participate in it, and overturned with facility by the king
whenever he thought fit to exert the sinews of his prerogative,
was but an inadequate substitute for that co-ordinate sovereignty, that equal concurrence of national representatives in legislation, which has long been the exclusive pride of our government, and to which the States-General of France, in their best
days, had never aspired. No man of sane understanding would
desire to revive institutions both uncongenial to modern opinions and to the natural order of society. Yet the name of the
Parliament of Paris must ever be respectable. It exhibited upon
various occasions virtues from which human esteem is as inseparable as the shadow from the substance—a severe adherence to
principles, an unaccommodating sincerity, individual disinterestedness and consistency. Whether, indeed, these qualities have
been so generally characteristic of the French people as to afford
no peculiar commendation to the Parliament of Paris, it is rather
for the observer of the present day than the historian of past times
to decide.[290]

The principal causes that operated in subverting the feudal
system may be comprehended under three distinct heads—the
increasing power of the crown, the elevation of the lower ranks,
and the decay of the feudal principle.

[290] The province of Languedoc, with
its dependencies of Quercy and Rouergue, having belonged almost in full
sovereignty to the Counts of Toulouse,
was not perhaps subject to the feudal
resort or appellant jurisdiction of any
tribunal at Paris. Philip the Bold, after
its reunion to the crown, established the
Parliament of Toulouse, a tribunal without appeal, in 1280. This was, however,
suspended from 1291 to 1443, during
which interval the Parliament of Paris
exercised an appellant jurisdiction over
Languedoc. (Vaissette, "Hist. de
Lang.," tome iv, pp. 60, 71, 524.) Sovereign courts or Parliaments were established by Charles VII at Grenoble for
Dauphiné, and by Louis XI at Bordeaux and Dijon for Guienne and Burgundy. The Parliament of Rouen is not
so ancient. These institutions rather diminished the resort of the Parliament
of Paris, which had extended over Burgundy, and, in time of peace, over Guienne.

A work has appeared within a few
years which throws an abundant light on
the judicial system, and indeed on the
whole civil polity of France, as well as
other countries, during the middle ages.
I allude to "L'Esprit, Origine, et Progrès des Institutions judiciaires des
principaux Pays de l'Europe," by M.
Meyer, of Amsterdam, especially the first
and third volumes. It would have been
fortunate had its publication preceded
that of the first edition of the present
work, as I might have rendered this
chapter on the feudal system in many
respects more perspicuous and correct.
As it is, without availing myself of M.
Meyer's learning and acuteness to illustrate the obscurity of these researches,
or discussing the few questions upon
which I might venture, with deference,
to adhere to another opinion, neither
of which could conveniently be done on
the present occasion, I shall content myself with this general reference to a performance of singular diligence and ability, which no student of these antiquities
should neglect. In all essential points I
am happy to perceive that M. Meyer's
views of the middle ages are not far different from my own. (Note to the fourth
edition.)

It has been my object in the last pages to point out the acquisitions of power by the crown of France in respect of legislative and judicial authority. The principal augmentations of its domain have been historically mentioned in the last chapter, but the subject may here require further notice. The French kings naturally acted upon a system, in order to recover those possessions which the improvidence or necessities of the Carlovingian race had suffered almost to fall away from the monarchy. This course, pursued with tolerable steadiness for two or three centuries, restored their effective power. By escheat or forfeiture, by bequest or purchase, by marriage or succession, a number of fiefs were merged in their increasing domain.[291] It was part of their policy to obtain possession of arrière-fiefs, and thus to become tenants of their own barons. In such cases the king was obliged by the feudal duties to perform homage, by proxy, to his subjects, and engage himself to the service of his fief. But, for every political purpose, it is evident that the lord could have no command over so formidable a vassal.[292]

The reunion of so many fiefs was attempted to be secured by a legal principle, that the domain was inalienable and imprescriptible. This became at length a fundamental maxim in the law of France. But it does not seem to be much older than the reign of Philip V, who, in 1318, revoked the alienations of his predecessors, nor was it thoroughly established, even in the-

[291] The word domain is calculated, by a seeming ambiguity, to perplex the reader of French history. In its primary sense, the domain or demesne (dominicum) of any proprietor was confined to the lands in his immediate occupation; excluding those of which his tenants, whether in fief or villenage, whether for a certain estate or at will, had an actual possession, or, in our law language, pernancy of the profits. Thus the compilers of " Doomsday-Book " distinguish, in every manor, the lands held by the lord in demesne from those occupied by his villeins or other tenants. And in England the word, if not technically, yet in use, is still confined to this sense. But in a secondary acceptation, more usual in France, the domain comprehended all lands for which rent was paid (censives), and which contributed to the regular annual revenue of the proprietor. The great distinction was between lands in demesne and those in fief. A grant of territory, whether by the king or another lord, comprising as well domanial estates and tributary towns as feudal superiorities, was expressed to convey " in dominico quod est in dominico, et in feodo quod est in feodo." Since, therefore, fiefs, even those of the vavassors or inferior tenantry, were not part of the lord's domain, there is, as I said, an apparent

ambiguity in the language of historians who speak of the reunion of provinces to the royal domain. This ambiguity, however, is rather apparent than real. When the duchy of Normandy, for example, is said to have been united by Philip Augustus to his domain, we are not, of course, to suppose that the soil of that province became the private estate of the crown. It continued, as before, in the possession of the Norman barons and their sub-vassals, who had held their estates of the dukes. But it is meant only that the King of France stood exactly in the place of the Duke of Normandy, with the same rights of possession over lands absolutely in demesne, of rents and customary payments from the burgesses of towns and tenants in roture or villenage, and of feudal services from the military vassals. The immediate superiority, and the immediate resort, or jurisdiction, over these devolved to the crown; and thus the duchy of Normandy, considered as a fief, was reunited, or, more properly, merged in the royal domain, though a very small part of the territory might become truly domanial.

[292] See a memorial on the acquisition of arrière fiefs by the Kings of France, in " Mém. de l'Acad. des Inscript.," tome i, by M. Dacier.

ory, till the fifteenth century.[293]   Alienations, however, were certainly very repugnant to the policy of Philip Augustus and St. Louis.   But there was one species of infeudation so consonant to ancient usage and prejudice that it could not be avoided upon any suggestions of policy; this was the investiture of younger princes of the blood with considerable territorial appanages.   It is remarkable that the epoch of appanages on so great a scale was the reign of St. Louis, whose efforts were constantly directed against feudal independence.   Yet he invested his brothers with the counties of Poitou, Anjou, and Artois, and his sons with those of Clermont and Alençon.   This practice, in later times, produced very mischievous consequences.

Under a second class of events that contributed to destroy the spirit of the feudal system we may reckon the abolition of villenage, the increase of commerce and consequent opulence of merchants and artisans, and especially the institutions of free cities and boroughs.   This is one of the most important and interesting steps in the progress of society during the middle ages, and deserves particular consideration.

The provincial cities under the Roman Empire enjoyed, as is well known, a municipal magistracy and the right of internal regulation.   Nor was it repugnant to the spirit of the Frank or Gothic conquerors to leave them in possession of these privileges.   It was long believed, however, that little, if any, satisfactory proof of their preservation, either in France or Italy, could be found; or, at least, if they had ever existed, that they were wholly swept away in the former country during the confusion of the ninth century, which ended in the establishment of the feudal system.

Every town, except within the royal domains, was subject to some lord.   In episcopal cities the bishop possessed a considerable authority, and in many there was a class of resident nobility.   But this subject has been better elucidated of late years; and it has been made to appear that instances of municipal government were at least not rare, especially in the south of France, throughout the long period between the fall of the Western Empire and the beginning of the twelfth century,[294] though becoming far more common in its latter part.

The earliest charters of community granted to towns in France have been commonly referred to the time of Louis VI.   Noyon, St. Quentin, Laon, and Amiens appear to have been the first that received emancipation at the hands of this prince.[295]   The chief towns in the royal domains were successively admitted to

---

[293] Préface au 15me tome des " Ordonnances," par M. Pastoret.
[294] [Note XVIII.]

[295] " Ordonnances des Rois," ubi supra, p. 7.   These charters are as old as 1110, but the precise date is unknown.

the same privileges during the reigns of Louis VI, Louis VII, and Philip Augustus. This example was gradually followed by the peers and other barons; so that by the end of the thirteenth century the custom had prevailed over all France. It has been sometimes imagined that the crusades had a material influence in promoting the erection of communities. Those expeditions would have repaid Europe for the prodigality of crimes and miseries which attended them if this notion were founded in reality. But I confess that in this, as in most other respects, their beneficial consequences appear to me very much exaggerated. The cities of Italy obtained their internal liberties by gradual encroachments, and by the concessions of the Franconian emperors. Those upon the Rhine owed many of their privileges to the same monarchs, whose cause they had espoused in the rebellions of Germany. In France the charters granted by Louis the Fat could hardly be connected with the first crusade, in which the crown had taken no part, and were long prior to the second. It was not till fifty years afterward that the barons seem to have trod in his steps by granting charters to their vassals, and these do not appear to have been particularly related in time to any of the crusades. Still less can the corporations erected by Henry II in England be ascribed to these holy wars, in which our country had hitherto taken no considerable share.

The establishment of chartered towns in France has also been ascribed to deliberate policy. "Louis the Gross," says Robertson, "in order to create some power that might counterbalance those potent vassals who controlled or gave law to the crown, first adopted the plan of conferring new privileges on the towns situated within his own domain." Yet one does not immediately perceive what strength the king could acquire by granting these extensive privileges within his own domains, if the great vassals were only weakened, as he asserts afterward, by following his example. In what sense, besides, can it be meant that Noyon or Amiens, by obtaining certain franchises, became a power that could counterbalance the Duke of Normandy or Count of Champagne? It is more natural to impute this measure, both in the king and his barons, to their pecuniary exigencies; for we could hardly doubt that their concessions were sold at the highest price, even if the existing charters did not exhibit the fullest proof of it.[296] It is obvious, however, that the coarser methods of rapine must have grown obsolete, and the rights of the inhabitants of towns to property established, before they could enter into any compact with their lord for the purchase of liberty. Guibert, Abbot of St. Nogent, near Laon, relates the

[296] "Ordonnances des Rois," tome xi, préface, pp. 18 et 50.

establishment of a community in that city with circumstances that, in the main, might probably occur in any other place. Continual acts of violence and robbery having been committed, which there was no police adequate to prevent, the clergy and principal inhabitants agreed to enfranchise the populace for a sum of money, and to bind the whole society by regulations for general security. These conditions were gladly accepted; the money was paid, and the leading men swore to maintain the privileges of the inferior freemen. The Bishop of Laon, who happened to be absent, at first opposed this new institution, but was ultimately induced, by money, to take a similar oath, and the community was confirmed by the king. Unluckily for himself, the bishop afterward annulled the charter; when the inhabitants, in despair at seeing themselves reduced to servitude, rose and murdered him. This was in 1112; and Guibert's narrative certainly does not support the opinion that charters of community proceeded from the policy of government. He seems to have looked upon them with the jealousy of a feudal abbot, and blames the Bishop of Amiens for consenting to such an establishment in his city, from which, according to Guibert, many evils resulted. In his sermons, we are told, this abbot used to descant on "those execrable communities, where serfs, against law and justice, withdraw themselves from the power of their lords." [297]

In some cases they were indebted for success to their own courage and love of liberty. Oppressed by the exactions of their superiors, they had recourse to arms, and united themselves in a common league, confirmed by oath, for the sake of redress. One of these associations took place at Mans as early as 1067, and, though it did not produce any charter of privileges, is a proof of the spirit to which ultimately the superior classes were obliged to submit. [298] Several charters bear witness that this spirit of resistance was justified by oppression. Louis VII frequently declares the tyranny exercised over the towns to be his motive for enfranchising them. Thus the charter of Mantes, in 1150, is said to be given "pro nimiâ oppressione pauperum": that of Compiègne, in 1153, "propter enormitates clericorum": that of Dourlens, granted by the Count of Ponthieu in 1202, "propter injurias et molestias a potentibus terræ burgensibus frequenter illatas." [299]

The privileges which these towns of France derived from their charters were surprisingly extensive, especially if we do not suspect some of them to be merely in confirmation of previous usages. They were made capable of possessing common prop-

---

[297] " Hist. Littéraire de la France," tome x, p. 448; Du Cange, voc. Communia.

[298] " Recueil des Historiens," tome xiv, préface, p. 66.

[299] " Ordonnances des Rois," tome xi, préface, p. 17.

erty, and authorized to use a common seal as the symbol of their incorporation. The more oppressive and ignominious tokens of subjection, such as the fine paid to the lord for permission to marry their children, were abolished. Their payments of rent or tribute were limited both in amount and as to the occasions when they might be demanded: and these were levied by assessors of their own electing. Some obtained an exemption from assisting their lord in war; others were only bound to follow him when he personally commanded; and almost all limited their service to one, or, at the utmost, very few days. If they were persuaded to extend its duration, it was, like that of feudal tenants, at the cost of their superior. Their customs, as to succession and other matters of private right, were reduced to certainty, and, for the most part, laid down in the charter of incorporation. And the observation of these was secured by the most valuable privilege which the chartered towns obtained—that of exemption from the jurisdiction, as well of the royal as the territorial judges. They were subject only to that of magistrates, either wholly elected by themselves or, in some places, with a greater or less participation of choice in the lord. They were empowered to make special rules, or, as we call them, by-laws, so as not to contravene the provisions of their charter or the ordinances of the king.[300]

It was undoubtedly far from the intention of those barons who conferred such immunities upon their subjects to relinquish their own superiority and rights not expressly conceded. But a remarkable change took place in the beginning of the thirteenth century, which affected, in a high degree, the feudal constitution of France. Towns, distrustful of their lord's fidelity, sometimes called in the king as guarantee of his engagements. The first stage of royal interference led to a more extensive measure. Philip Augustus granted letters of safeguard to communities dependent upon the barons, assuring to them his own protection and patronage.[301] And this was followed up so quickly by the court, if we believe some writers, that in the next reign Louis VIII pretended to the immediate sovereignty over all chartered towns, in exclusion of their original lords.[302] Nothing, perhaps, had so decisive an effect in subverting the feudal aristocracy. The barons perceived too late

---

[300] " Ordonnances des Rois," préfaces aux tomes xi et xii; Du Cange, voc. Communia, Hostis; Carpentier, Suppl. ad Du Cange, voc. Hostis; Mably, " Observations sur l'Hist. de France," l. iii, c. 7.

[301] Mably, " Observations sur l'Hist. de France," l. iii, c. 7.

[302] Reputabat civitates omnes suas esse, in quibus communiæ essent. I mention this in deference to Du Cange,

Mably, and others, who assume the fact as incontrovertible; but the passage is only in a monkish chronicler, whose authority, were it even more explicit, would not weigh much in a matter of law. Beaumanoir, however, sixty years afterward, lays it down that no one can erect a commune without the king's consent (c. 50, p. 268). And this was an unquestionable maxim in the fourteenth century. (" Ordonnances," tome xi, p. 29.)

that, for a price long since lavished in prodigal magnificence
or useless warfare, they had suffered the source of their wealth
to be diverted and the nerves of their strength to be severed.
The government prudently respected the privileges secured by
charter. Philip the Long established an officer in all large towns
to preserve peace by an armed police; but though subject to
the orders of the crown, he was elected by the burgesses, and
they took a mutual oath of fidelity to each other. Thus shielded
under the king's mantle, they ventured to encroach upon the
neighbouring lords, and to retaliate for the long oppression of
the commonalty.[303] Every citizen was bound by oath to stand
by the common cause against all aggressors, and this obligation
was abundantly fulfilled. In order to swell their numbers, it
became the practice to admit all who came to reside within their
walls to the rights of burghership, even though they were villeins
appurtenant to the soil of a master from whom they had escaped.[304] Others, having obtained the same privileges, continued to dwell in the country; but, upon any dispute with their
lords, called in the assistance of their community. Philip the
Fair, erecting certain communes in Languedoc, gave to any who
would declare on oath that he was aggrieved by the lord or
his officers the right of being admitted a burgess of the next
town, upon paying one mark of silver to the king, and purchasing a tenement of a definite value. But the neglect of this condition and several other abuses are enumerated in an instrument
of Charles V, containing the complaints made by the nobility and
rich ecclesiastics of the neighbourhood.[305] In his reign the feudal
independence had so completely yielded that the court began

[303] In the charter of Philip Augustus
to the town of Roye in Picardy, we read,
If any stranger, whether noble or villein,
commits a wrong against the town, the
mayor shall summon him to answer for
it, and if he does not obey the summons
the mayor and inhabitants may go and
destroy his house, in which we (the
king) will lend them our assistance, if
the house be too strong for the burgesses
to pull down: except the case of one
of our vassals, whose house shall not
be destroyed; but he shall not be allowed
to enter the town till he has made
amends at the discretion of the mayor
and jurats. (" Ordonnances des Rois,"
tome xi, p. 228.) This summary process
could only, as I conceive, be employed
if the house was situated within the jurisdiction of the commune. (See Charter
of Crespy, id., p. 253.) In other cases
the application for redress was to be
made in the first instance to the lord of
the territory wherein the delinquent resided. But upon his failing to enforce
satisfaction, the mayor and jurats might
satisfy themselves; liceat justitiam quærere, prout poterunt; that is, might pull
down his house provided they could.

Mably positively maintains the communes to have had the right of levying
war (l. iii, c. 7). And Bréquigny seems
to coincide with him. (" Ordonnances,"
préface, p. 46; see also " Hist. de Languedoc," tome iii, p. 115.) The territory
of a commune was called Pax (p. 185);
an expressive word.

[304] One of the most remarkable privileges of chartered towns was that of conferring freedom on runaway serfs, if they
were not reclaimed by their masters
within a certain time. This was a pretty
general law. Si quis nativus quietè per
unum annum et unum diem in aliquâ
villâ privilegiatâ manserit, ita quod in
eorum communem gyldam tanquam civis
receptus fuerit, eo ipso à villenagio libe-
rabitur. (Glanvil, l. v, c. 5.) The cities
of Languedoc had the same privilege.
(Vaissette, tome iii, pp. 528, 530.) And
the editor of the " Ordonnances " speaks
of it as general (p. 44). A similar custom was established in Germany; but the
term of prescription was, in some places
at least, much longer than a year and a
day. (Pfeffel, tome i, p. 294.)

[305] Martenne, " Thesaur. Anecd.,"
tome i, p. 1515.

to give in to a new policy, which was ever after pursued: that of maintaining the dignity and privileges of the noble class against those attacks which wealth and liberty encouraged the plebeians to make upon them.

The maritime towns of the south of France entered into separate alliances with foreign states; as Narbonne with Genoa in 1166, and Montpellier in the next century. At the death of Raymond VII, Avignon, Arles, and Marseilles affected to set up republican governments, but they were soon brought into subjection.[306] The independent character of maritime towns was not peculiar to those of the southern provinces. Edward II and Edward III negotiated and entered into alliances with the towns of Flanders, to which neither their count nor the King of France were parties.[307] Even so late as the reign of Louis XI the Duke of Burgundy did not hesitate to address the citizens of Rouen, in consequence of the capture of some ships, as if they had formed an independent state.[308] This evidently arose out of the ancient customs of private warfare, which, long after they were repressed by a stricter police at home, continued with lawless violence on the ocean, and gave a character of piracy to the commercial enterprise of the middle ages.

Notwithstanding the forces which in opposite directions assailed the feudal system from the enhancement of royal prerogative, and the elevation of the chartered towns, its resistance would have been much longer but for an intrinsic decay. No political institution can endure which does not rivet itself to the hearts of men by ancient prejudice or acknowledged interest. The feudal compact had originally much of this character. Its principle of vitality was warm and active. In fulfilling the obligations of mutual assistance and fidelity by military service, the energies of friendship were awakened, and the ties of moral sympathy superadded to those of positive compact. While private wars were at their height, the connection of lord and vassal grew close and cordial, in proportion to the keenness of their enmity toward others. It was not the object of a baron to disgust and impoverish his vavassors by enhancing the profits of seigniory, for there was no rent of such price as blood, nor any labour so serviceable as that of the sword.

But the nature of feudal obligation was far better adapted to the partial quarrels of neighbouring lords than to the wars of kingdoms. Customs, founded upon the poverty of the smaller gentry, had limited their martial duties to a period never exceeding forty days, and diminished according to the subdivisions of the fief. They could undertake an expedition, but not a cam-

[306] Velly, tome iv, p. 446; tome v, p. 97. [308] Garnier, tome xvii, p. 396.
[307] Rymer, tome iv, passim.

paign; they could burn an open town, but had seldom leisure to besiege a fortress. Hence, when the Kings of France and England were engaged in wars which, on our side at least, might be termed national, the inefficiency of the feudal militia became evident. It was not easy to employ the military tenants of England upon the frontiers of Normandy and the Isle of France, within the limits of their term of service. When, under Henry II and Richard I, the scene of war was frequently transferred to the Garonne or the Charente, this was still more impracticable. The first remedy to which sovereigns had recourse was to keep their vassals in service after the expiration of their forty days at a stipulated rate of pay.[309]   But this was frequently neither convenient to the tenant, anxious to return back to his household, nor to the king, who could not readily defray the charges of an army.[310]   Something was to be devised more adequate to the exigency, though less suitable to the feudal spirit. By the feudal law the fief was, in strictness, forfeited by neglect of attendance upon the lord's expedition. A milder usage introduced a fine, which, however, was generally rather heavy, and assessed at discretion. An instance of this kind has been noticed in an earlier part of the present chapter, from the muster-roll of Philip the Bold's expedition against the Count de Foix. The first Norman Kings of England made these amercements very oppressive. But when a pecuniary payment became the regular course of redeeming personal service, which, under the name of escuage, may be referred to the reign of Henry II, it was essential to liberty that the military tenant should not lie at the mercy of the crown.[311]   Accordingly, one of the most important provisions contained in the Magna Charta of John secures the assessment of escuage in Parliament. This is not renewed in the charter of Henry III, but the practice during his reign was conformable to its spirit.

The feudal military tenures had superseded that earlier system of public defence which called upon every man, and especially every landholder, to protect his country.[312]   The relations

[309] Du Cange, et Carpentier, voc. Hostis.

[310] There are several instances where armies broke up, at the expiration of their limited term of service, in consequence of disagreement with the sovereign. Thus, at the siege of Avignon in 1226, Theobald, Count of Champagne, retired with his troops, that he might not promote the king's designs upon Languedoc. At that of Angers, in 1230, nearly the same thing occurred. (M. Paris, p. 308.)

[311] Madox, " Hist. of Exchequer," c. 16, conceives that escuage may have been levied by Henry I; the earliest mention of it, however, in a record, is under

Henry II in 1159. (Littleton's " Hist. of Henry II," vol. iv, p. 13.)

[312] Every citizen, however extensive may be his privileges, is naturally bound to repel invasion. A common rising of the people in arms, though not always the most convenient mode of resistance, is one to which all governments have a right to resort. Volumus, says Charles the Bald, ut cujuscunque nostrum homo, in cujuscunque regno sit, cum seniore suo in hostem, vel aliis suis utilitatibus pergat; nisi talis regni invasio, quam Lantweri dicunt (quod absit), acciderit ut omnis populus illius regni ad eam repellendam communiter pergat. (" Baluzii Capitularia," tome ii, p. 44.) This

of a vassal came in place of those of a subject and a citizen. This was the revolution of the ninth century. In the twelfth and thirteenth another innovation rather more gradually prevailed, and marks the third period in the military history of Europe. Mercenary troops were substituted for the feudal militia. Undoubtedly there could never have been a time when valour was not to be purchased with money; nor could any employment of surplus wealth be more natural either to the ambitious or the weak. But we can not expect to find numerous testimonies of facts of this description.[313] In public national history I am aware of no instance of what may be called a regular army more ancient than the body-guards, or huscarles, of Canute the Great. These select troops amounted to six thousand men, on whom he probably relied to insure the subjection of England. A code of martial law compiled for their regulation is extant in substance; and they are reported to have displayed a military spirit of mutual union, of which their master stood in awe.[314] Harold II is also

very ancient mention of the Landwehr, or insurrectional militia, so signally called forth in the present age, will strike the reader.

The obligation of bearing arms in defensive warfare was peculiarly incumbent on the freeholder or allodialist. It made part of the trinoda necessitas, in England, erroneously confounded by some writers with a feudal military tenure. But when these latter tenures became nearly universal, the original principles of public defence were almost obliterated, and I know not how far allodial proprietors, where they existed, were called upon for service. Kings did not, however, always dispense with such aid as the lower people could supply. Louis the Fat called out the militia of towns and parishes under their priests, who marched at their head, though they did not actually command them in battle. In the charters of incorporation which towns received the number of troops required was usually expressed. These formed the infantry of the French armies, perhaps more numerous than formidable to an enemy. In the war of the same prince with the Emperor Henry V all the population of the frontier provinces was called out, for the militia of the counties of Rheims and Châlons is said to have amounted to sixty thousand men. Philip IV summoned one foot soldier for every twenty hearths to take the field after the battle of Courtrai. (Daniel, " Hist. de la Milice Française "; Velly, tome iii, p. 62; tome vii, p. 287.) Commissions of array, either to call out the whole population, or, as was more common, to select the most serviceable by forced impressment, occur in English records from the reign of Edward I (Stuart's " View of Society," p. 400); and there are even several writs directed to the bishops, enjoining them to cause all ecclesiastical persons to be arrayed and

armed on account of an expected invasion. (Rymer, tome vi, p. 726 [46 E. III]; tome vii, p. 162 [1 R. II]; and tome viii, p. 270 [3 H. IV].)

[313] The preface to the eleventh volume of " Recueil des Historiens," p. 232, notices the word solidarii, for hired soldiers, as early as 1030. It was probably unusual at that time; though in Roger Hoveden, " Ordericus Vitalis," and other writers of the twelfth century, it occurs not very infrequently. We may perhaps conjecture the abbots, as both the richest and the most defenceless, to have been the first who availed themselves of mercenary valour.

[314] For these facts, of which I remember no mention in English history, I am indebted to the Danish collection of Langebek, " Scriptores Rerum Danicarum Medii Ævi." Though the " Leges Castrensis Canuti Magni," published by him (tome iii, p. 141), are not in their original statutory form, they proceed from the pen of Sweno, the earliest Danish historian, who lived under Waldemar I, less than a century and a half after Canute. I apply the word huscarle, familiar in Anglo-Saxon documents, to these military retainers, on the authority of Langebek, in another place (tome ii, p. 454). The object of Canute's institutions was to produce a uniformity of discipline and conduct among his soldiers, and thus to separate them more decidedly from the people. They were distinguished by their dress and golden ornaments. Their manners toward each other were regulated; quarrels and abusive words subjected to a penalty. All disputes, even respecting lands, were settled among themselves at their general Parliament. A singular story is told, which, if false, may still illustrate the traditionary character of these guards: that, Canute having killed one of their body in a fit of anger, it was debated

said to have had Danish soldiers in pay. But the most eminent example of a mercenary army is that by whose assistance William achieved the conquest of England. Historians concur in representing this force to have consisted of sixty thousand men. He afterward hired soldiers from various regions to resist an invasion from Norway. William Rufus pursued the same course. Hired troops did not, however, in general form a considerable portion of armies till the wars of Henry II and Philip Augustus. Each of these monarchs took into pay large bodies of mercenaries, chiefly, as we may infer from their appellation of Brabançons, enlisted from the Netherlands. These were always disbanded on cessation of hostilities; and, unfit for any habits but of idleness and license, oppressed the peasantry and ravaged the country without control. But their soldier-like principles of indiscriminate obedience, still more than their courage and field discipline, rendered them dear to kings, who dreaded the free spirit of a feudal army. It was by such a foreign force that John saw himself on the point of abrogating the Great Charter, and reduced his barons to the necessity of tendering his kingdom to a prince of France.[315]

It now became manifest that the probabilities of war inclined to the party who could take the field with selected and experienced soldiers. The command of money was the command of armed hirelings, more sure and steady in battle, as we must confess with shame, than the patriot citizen. Though the nobility still composed in a great degree the strength of an army, yet they served in a new character; their animating spirit was that of chivalry rather than of feudal tenure; their connection with a superior was personal rather than territorial. The crusades had probably a material tendency to effectuate this revolution by substituting, what was inevitable in those expeditions, a voluntary stipendiary service for one of absolute obligation.[316] It is the opinion of Daniel that in the thirteenth century all feudal tenants received pay, even during their prescribed term of service.[317] This does not appear consonant to the law of fiefs; yet their poverty may often have rendered it impossible to defray the cost of equipment on distant expeditions. A large propor-

whether the king should incur the legal penalty of death; and this was only compromised by his kneeling on a cushion before the assembly and awaiting their permission to rise (tome iii, p. 150).

[315] Matt. Paris.

[316] Joinville, in several passages, intimates that most of the knights serving in St. Louis's crusade received pay, either from their superior lord, if he were on the expedition, or from some other, into whose service they entered for the time. He set out himself with ten knights, whom he afterward found it difficult enough to maintain. (" Collection des Mémoires," tome i, p. 49, and tome ii, p. 53.)

[317] " Hist. de la Milice Française," p. 84. The use of mercenary troops prevailed much in Germany during the thirteenth century. (Schmidt, tome iv, p. 89.) In Italy it was also very common, though its general adoption is to be referred to the commencement of the succeeding age.

tion of the expense must in all cases have fallen upon the lord, and hence that perpetually increasing taxation, the effects whereof we have lately been investigating. A feudal army, however, composed of all tenants in chief and their vassals, still presented a formidable array. It is very long before the paradox is generally admitted that numbers do not necessarily contribute to the intrinsic efficiency of armies. Philip IV assembled a great force by publishing the arrière-ban, or feudal summons, for his unhappy expedition against the Flemings. A small and more disciplined body of troops would not, probably, have met with the discomfiture of Courtray. Edward I and Edward II frequently called upon those who owed military service in their invasions of Scotland.[318] But in the French wars of Edward III the whole, I think, of his army served for pay, and was raised by contract with men of rank and influence, who received wages for every soldier according to his station and the arms he bore. The rate of pay was so remarkably high that, unless we imagine a vast profit to have been intended for the contractors, the private lancers and even archers must have been chiefly taken from the middling classes, the smaller gentry, or rich yeomanry of England.[319] This part of Edward's military system was probably a leading cause of his superiority over the French, among whom the feudal tenantry were called into the field, and swelled their unwieldy armies at Crécy and Poitiers. Both parties, however, in this war employed mercenary troops. Philip had fifteen thousand Italian cross-bow-men at Crécy. It had for some time before become the trade of soldiers of fortune to enlist under leaders of the same description as themselves in companies of adventure, passing from one service to another, unconcerned as to the cause in which they were retained. These military adventurers played a more remarkable part in Italy than in France, though not a little troublesome to the latter country. The feudal tenures had at least furnished a loyal native militia, whose duties, though much limited in the extent, were defined by usage and enforced by principle. They gave place, in an evil hour for the people and eventually for sovereigns, to contracts with mutinous hirelings, generally strangers, whose valour in the day of battle inadequately redeemed their bad faith and vexatious rapacity. France, in her

---

[318] Rymer, tome iii, pp. 173, 189, 199, et alibi sæpius.

[319] Many proofs of this may be adduced from Rymer's collection. The following is from Brady's " History of England," vol. ii, appendix, p. 86: The wages allowed by contract in 1346 were: For an earl, 6s. 8d. per day; for barons and bannerets, 4s.; for knights, 2s.; for squires, 1s.; for archers and hobelers (light cavalry), 6d.; for archers on foot, 3d.; for Welshmen, 2d. These sums multiplied by about 24, to bring them on a level with the present value of money [1818], will show the pay to have been extremely high. The cavalry, of course, furnished themselves with horses and equipments, as well as arms, which were very expensive. (See, too, chap. i, p. 51, of this volume.)

calamitous period under Charles VI and Charles VII, experienced the full effects of military licentiousness. At tĥe expulsion of the English, robbery and disorder were substituted for the more specious plundering of war. Perhaps few measures have ever been more popular, as few certainly have been more politic, than the establishment of regular companies of troops by an ordinance of Charles VII in 1444.[320] These may justly pass for the earliest institution of a standing army in Europe, though some Italian princes had retained troops constantly in their pay, but prospectively to hostilities, which were seldom long intermitted. Fifteen companies were composed each of a hundred men at arms, or lancers; and, in the language of that age, the whole body was one thousand five hundred lances. But each lancer had three archers, a coutiller, or soldier armed with a knife, and a page or valet attached to him, all serving on horseback—so that the fifteen companies amounted to nine thousand cavalry.[321] From these small beginnings, as they must appear in modern times, arose the regular army of France, which every succeeding king was solicitous to augment. The ban was sometimes convoked—that is, the possessors of fiefs were called upon for military service in subsequent ages—but with more of ostentation than real efficiency.

The feudal compact, thus deprived of its original efficacy, soon lost the respect and attachment which had attended it. Homage and investiture became unmeaning ceremonies; the incidents of relief and aid were felt as burdensome exactions. And, indeed, the rapacity with which these were levied, especially by our Norman sovereigns and their barons, was of itself sufficient to extinguish all the generous feelings of vassalage. Thus galled, as it were, by the armour which he was compelled to wear, but not to use, the military tenant of England looked no longer with contempt upon the owner of lands in socage, who held his estate with almost the immunities of an allodial proprietor. But the profits which the crown reaped from wardships, and perhaps the prejudices of lawyers, prevented the abolition of military tenures till the restoration of Charles II. In France the fiefs of noblemen were very unjustly exempted from all territorial taxation, though the tailles of later times had, strictly speaking, only superseded the aids to which they had been always liable. The distinction, it is well known, was not annihilated till that

---

[320] The estates at Orleans in 1439 had advised this measure, as is recited in the preamble of the ordinance. (" Ordonnances des Rois," tome xii, p. 312.) Sismondi observes (vol. xiii, p. 352) that very little is to be found in historians about the establishment of these compagnies d'ordonnance, though the most important event in the reign of Charles VII. The old soldiers of fortune who pillaged the country either entered into these companies or were disbanded, and after their dispersion were readily made amenable to the law. This writer is exceedingly full on the subject.

[321] Daniel, " Hist. de la Milice Française," p. 266; Villaret, " Hist. de France," tome xv, p. 394.

event which annihilated all distinctions, the French Revolution.

It is remarkable that, although the feudal system established in England upon the conquest broke in very much upon our ancient Saxon liberties—though it was attended with harsher servitudes than in any other country, particularly those two intolerable burdens, wardship and marriage—yet it has in general been treated with more favour by English than French writers. The hardiness with which the ancient barons resisted their sovereign, and the noble struggles which they made for civil liberty, especially in that Great Charter, the baesment at least, if not the foundation, of our free constitution, have met with a kindred sympathy in the bosoms of Englishmen; while, from an opposite feeling, the French have been shocked at that aristocratic independence which cramped the prerogatives and obscured the lustre of their crown. Yet it is precisely to this feudal policy that France is indebted for that which is ever dearest to her children, their national splendour and power. That kingdom would have been irretrievably dismembered in the tenth century if the laws of feudal dependence had not preserved its integrity. Empires of unwieldy bulk, like that of Charlemagne, have several times been dissolved by the usurpation of provincial governors, as is recorded both in ancient history and in that of the Mohammedan dynasties in the East. What question can there be that the powerful Dukes of Guienne or Counts of Toulouse would have thrown off all connection with the crown of France, when usurped by one of their equals, if the slight dependence of vassalage had not been substituted for legitimate subjection to a sovereign?

It is the previous state of society, under the grandchildren of Charlemagne, which we must always keep in mind if we would appreciate the effects of the feudal system upon the welfare of mankind. The institutions of the eleventh century must be compared with those of the ninth, not with the advanced civilization of modern times. If the view that I have taken of those dark ages is correct, the state of anarchy which we usually term feudal was the natural result of a vast and barbarous empire feebly administered, and the cause rather than effect of the general establishment of feudal tenures. These, by preserving the mutual relations of the whole, kept alive the feeling of a common country and common duties, and settled, after the lapse of ages, into the free constitution of England, the firm monarchy of France, and the federal union of Germany.

The utility of any form of polity may be estimated by its effect upon national greatness and security, upon civil liberty and private rights, upon the tranquility and order of society,

12

upon the increase and diffusion of wealth, or upon the general tone of moral sentiment and energy. The feudal constitution was certainly, as has been observed already, little adapted for the defence of a mighty kingdom, far less for schemes of conquest. But as it prevailed alike in several adjacent countries, none had anything to fear from the military superiority of its neighbours. It was this inefficiency of the feudal militia, perhaps, that saved Europe during the middle ages from the danger of universal monarchy. In times when princes had little notion of confederacies for mutual protection, it is hard to say what might not have been the successes of an Otho the Great, a Frederick Barbarossa, or a Philip Augustus, if they could have wielded the whole force of their subjects whenever their ambition required. If an empire equally extensive with that of Charlemagne, and supported by military despotism, had been formed about the twelfth or thirteenth century, the seeds of commerce and liberty, just then beginning to shoot, would have perished, and Europe, reduced to a barbarous servitude, might have fallen before the free barbarians of Tartary.

If we look at the feudal polity as a scheme of civil freedom, it bears a noble countenance. To the feudal law it is owing that the very names of right and privilege were not swept away, as in Asia, by the desolating hand of power. The tyranny which, on every favourable moment, was breaking through all barriers, would have rioted without control if, when the people were poor and disunited, the nobility had not been brave and free. So far as the sphere of feudality extended, it diffused the spirit of liberty and the notions of private right. Every one, I think, will acknowledge this who considers the limitations of the services of vassalage, so cautiously marked in those law-books which are the records of customs, the reciprocity of obligation between the lord and his tenant, the consent required in every measure of a legislative or a general nature, the security, above all, which every vassal found in the administration of justice by his peers, and even (we may in this sense say) in the trial by combat. The bulk of the people, it is true, were degraded by servitude; but this had no connection with the feudal tenures.

The peace and good order of society were not promoted by this system. Though private wars did not originate in the feudal customs, it is impossible to doubt that they were perpetuated by so convenient an institution, which, indeed, owed its universal establishment to no other cause. And as predominant habits of warfare are totally irreconcilable with those of industry, not merely by the immediate works of destruction which render its efforts unavailing, but through that contempt of peaceful occupations which they produce, the feudal system must have been intrinsically adverse to the accumulation of wealth and the improvement of those arts which mitigate the evils or abridge the labours of mankind.

But as a school of moral discipline the feudal institutions were perhaps most to be valued. Society had sunk, for several centuries after the dissolution of the Roman Empire, into a condition of utter depravity, where, if any vices could be selected as more eminently characteristic than others, they were falsehood, treachery, and ingratitude. In slowly purging off the lees of this extreme corruption, the feudal spirit exerted its ameliorating influence. Violation of faith stood first in the catalogue of crimes, most repugnant to the very essence of a feudal tenure, most severely and promptly avenged, most branded by general infamy. The feudal law-books breathe throughout a spirit of honourable obligation. The feudal course of jurisdiction promoted, what trial by peers is peculiarly calculated to promote, a keener feeling and readier perception of moral as well as of legal distinctions. And as the judgment and sympathy of mankind are seldom mistaken, in these great points of veracity and justice, except through the temporary success of crimes, or the want of a definite standard of right, they gradually recovered themselves when law precluded the one and supplied the other. In the reciprocal services of lord and vassal there was ample scope for every magnanimous and disinterested energy. The heart of man, when placed in circumstances which have a tendency to excite them, will seldom be deficient in such sentiments. No occasions could be more favourable than the protection of a faithful supporter, or the defence of a beneficent suzerain, against such powerful aggression as left little prospect except of sharing in his ruin.

From these feelings engendered by the feudal relation has sprung up the peculiar sentiment of personal reverence and attachment toward a sovereign which we denominate loyalty; alike distinguishable from the stupid devotion of Eastern slaves, and from the abstract respect with which free citizens regard their chief magistrate. Men who had been used to swear fealty, to profess subjection, to follow, at home and in the field, a feudal superior and his family, easily transferred the same allegiance to the monarch. It was a very powerful feeling which could make the bravest men put up with slights and ill treatment at the hands of their sovereign; or call forth all the energies of disinterested exertion for one whom they never saw, and in whose character there was nothing to esteem. In ages when the rights of the community were unfelt this sentiment was one great preservative of society; and, though collateral or even subservient to more enlarged principles, it is still indispensable to the tranquility and permanence of every monarchy. In a moral view loyalty has scarcely perhaps less tendency to refine and elevate the heart than patriotism itself; and holds a middle place in the scale of human motives, as they ascend from the grosser inducements of self-interest to the furtherance of general happiness and conformity to the purposes of Infinite Wisdom.

CHAPTER III[1]

HISTORY OF ITALY, FROM THE EXTINCTION OF THE CARLOVINGIAN EMPERORS TO THE INVASION OF NAPLES BY CHARLES VIII

State of Italy after the death of Charles the Fat—Coronation of Otho the Great—State of Rome—Conrad II—Union of the kingdom of Italy with the empire—Establishment of the Normans in Naples and Sicily—Roger Guiscard—Rise of the Lombard cities—They gradually become more independent of the empire—Their internal wars—Frederick Barbarossa—Destruction of Milan—Lombard league—Battle of Legnano—Peace of Constance—Temporal principality of the popes—Guelf and Ghibelin factions—Otho IV—Frederick II—Arrangement of the Italian republics—Second Lombard war—Extinction of the house of Swabia—Causes of the success of Lombard republics—Their prosperity and forms of government—Contentions between the nobility and people—Civil wars—Story of Giovanni di Vicenza—State of Italy after the extinction of the house of Swabia—Conquest of Naples by Charles of Anjou—The Lombard republics become severally subject to princes or usurpers —The Visconti of Milan—Their aggrandizement—Decline of the imperial authority over Italy—Internal state of Rome—Rienzi—Florence—Her forms of government historically traced to the end of the fourteenth century—Conquest of Pisa—Pisa—Its commerce, naval wars with Genoa, and decay—Genoa—Her contentions with Venice—War of Chioggio—Government of Genoa—Venice—Her origin and prosperity—Venetian government—Its vices—Territorial conquests of Venice—Military system of Italy—Companies of adventure—1, foreign; Guarnieri, Hawkwood—and 2, native; Braccio, Sforza—Improvements in military service—Arms, offensive and defensive—Invention of gunpowder—Naples—First line of Anjou—Joanna I—Ladislaus —Joanna II—Francis Sforza becomes Duke of Milan—Alfonzo, King of Naples— State of Italy during the fifteenth century—Florence—Rise of the Medici and ruin of their adversaries—Pretensions of Charles VIII to Naples.

A
T the death of Charles the Fat in 888, that part of Italy which acknowledged the supremacy of the Western Empire was divided, like France and Germany, among a few powerful vassals, hereditary governors of provinces. The principal of these were the Dukes of Spoleto and Tuscany, the Marquises of Ivrea, Susa, and Friuli. The great Lombard duchy of Benevento, which had stood against the arms of Charlemagne, and comprised more than half the present kingdom of Naples, had now fallen into decay, and was straitened by the Greeks in Apulia, and by the principalities of Capua and Salerno, which had been severed from its own territory, on the opposite

[1] The authorities upon which this chapter is founded, and which do not always appear at the foot of the page, are chiefly the following: 1. Muratori's " Annals of Italy " (twelve volumes in 4to or eighteen in 8vo) comprehend a summary of its

history from the beginning of the Christian era to the Peace of Aix-la-Chapelle. The volumes relating to the middle ages, into which he has digested the original writers contained in his great collection, " Scriptores Rerum Italicarum," are by

coast.[2] Though princes of the Carlovingian line continued to reign in France, their character was too little distinguished to challenge the obedience of Italy, already separated by family partitions from the transalpine nations; and the only contest was among her native chiefs. One of these, Berenger, originally Marquis of Friuli, or the March of Treviso, reigned for thirty-six years, but with continually disputed pretensions; and after

much the best; and of these, the part which extends from the seventh or eighth to the end of the twelfth century is the fullest and most useful. Muratori's accuracy is in general almost implicitly to be trusted, and his plain integrity speaks in all his writings; but his mind was not philosophical enough to discriminate the wheat from the chaff, and his habits of life induced him to annex an imaginary importance to the dates of diplomas and other inconsiderable matters. His narrative presents a mere skeleton devoid of juices; and besides its intolerable aridity, it labours under that confusion which a merely chronological arrangement of concurrent and independent events must always produce. 2. The " Dissertations on Italian Antiquities," by the same writer, may be considered either as one or two works. In Latin they form six volumes in folio, enriched with a great number of original documents. In Italian they are freely translated by Muratori himself, abridged, no doubt, and without most of the original instruments, but well furnished with quotations, and abundantly sufficient for most purposes. They form three volumes in quarto. I have in general quoted only the number of the dissertation, on account of the variance between the Latin and Italian works: in cases where the page is referred to, I have indicated by the title which of the two I intend to vouch. 3. St. Marc, a learned and laborious Frenchman, has written a chronological abridgment of Italian history, somewhat in the manner of Hénault, but so strangely divided by several parallel columns in every page that I could hardly name a book more inconvenient to the reader. His knowledge, like Muratori's, lay a good deal in points of minute inquiry; and he is chiefly to be valued in ecclesiastical history. The work descends only to the thirteenth century. 4. Denina's " Rivoluzioni d'Italia," originally published in 1769, is a perspicuous and lively book, in which the principal circumstances are well selected. It is not perhaps free from errors in fact, and still less from those of opinion: but, till lately, I do not know from what source a general acquaintance with the history of Italy could have been so easily derived. 5. The publication of M. Sismondi's " Histoire des Républiques Italiennes " has thrown a blaze of light around the most interesting, at least in many respects, of European countries during the middle ages. I am happy to bear witness, so far as my own studies have enabled me,

to the learning and diligence of this writer—qualities which the world is sometimes apt not to suppose where they perceive so much eloquence and philosophy. I can not express my opinion of M. Sismondi in this respect more strongly than by saying that his work has almost superseded the " Annals " of Muratori; I mean from the twelfth century, before which period his labour hardly begins. Though doubtless not more accurate than Muratori, he has consulted a much more extensive list of authors; and, considered as a register of facts alone, his history is incomparably more useful. These are combined in so skilful a manner as to diminish, in a great degree, that inevitable confusion which arises from frequency of transition and want of general unity. It is much to be regretted that, from two redundant details of unnecessary circumstances, and sometimes, if I may take the liberty of saying so, from unnecessary reflections, M. Sismondi has run into a prolixity which will probably intimidate the languid students of our age. It is the more to be regretted, because the " History of Italian Republics " is calculated to produce a good far more important than storing the memory with historical facts, that of communicating to the reader's bosom some sparks of the dignified philosophy, the love for truth and virtue, which lives along its eloquent pages. 6. To Muratori's collection of original writers, the " Scriptores Rerum Italicarum," in twenty-four volumes in folio, I have paid considerable attention; perhaps there is no volume of it which I have not more or less consulted. But, after the " Annals " of the same writer, and the work of M. Sismondi, I have not thought myself bound to repeat a laborious search into all the authorities upon which those writers depend. The utility, for the most part, of perusing original and contemporary authors consists less in ascertaining mere facts than in acquiring that insight into the spirit and temper of their times which it is utterly impracticable for any compiler to impart. It would be impossible for me to distinguish what information I have derived from these higher sources; in cases, therefore, where no particular authority is named, I would refer to the writings of Muratori and Sismondi, especially the latter, as the substratum of the following chapter.

[2] Giannone, " Istoria Civile di Napoli," l. vii; Sismondi, " Hist. des Républiques Italiennes," tome i, p. 244.

his death the calamities of Italy were sometimes aggravated by tyranny, and sometimes by intestine war.[3] The Hungarians desolated Lombardy; the southern coasts were infested by the Saracens, now masters of Sicily. Plunged in an abyss, from which she saw no other means of extricating herself, Italy lost sight of her favourite independence, and called in the assistance of Otho I, King of Germany. Little opposition was made to this powerful monarch. Berenger II, the reigning sovereign of Italy, submitted to hold the kingdom of him as a fief.[4] But some years afterward, new disturbances arising, Otho descended from the Alps a second time, deposed Berenger, and received at the hands of Pope John XII the imperial dignity, which had been suspended for nearly forty years.

Every ancient prejudice, every recollection, whether of Augustus or of Charlemagne, had led the Italians to annex the notion of sovereignty to the name of Roman emperor; nor were Otho, or his two immediate descendants, by any means inclined to waive these supposed prerogatives, which they were well able to enforce. Most of the Lombard princes acquiesced without apparent repugnance in the new German government, which was conducted by Otho the Great with much prudence and vigour, and occasionally with severity. The citizens of Lombardy were still better satisfied with a change that insured a more tranquil and regular administration than they had experienced under the preceding kings. But in one, and that the chief of Italian cities, very different sentiments were prevalent. We find, indeed, a considerable obscurity spread over the internal history of Rome during the long period from the recovery of Italy by Belisarius to the end of the eleventh century. The popes appear to have possessed some measure of temporal power, even while the city was professedly governed by the exarchs of Ravenna, in the name of the Eastern Empire. This power became more extensive after her separation from Constantinople. It was, however, subordinate to the undeniable sovereignty of the new imperial family, who were supposed to enter upon all the rights of their predecessors. There was always an imperial officer, or prefect, in that city, to render criminal justice; an oath of

[3] Berenger, being grandson, by a daughter, of Louis the Debonair, may be reckoned of the Carlovingian family. He was a Frank by law, according to Troja, who denies to him and his son, Berenger II, the name of Italians. It was Otho I that put an end to the Frank dominion. ("Storia d' Italia," v. 357.) "Or già tutto all' apparir degli Ottoni si cangia da capo in Italia, nel modo stesso che tutto erasi cangiato alla venuta de' Franchi. Le città Longobarde prendono altra faccia, la possanza de' vescovi s' aumenta, i patti fra il sacerdozio e l' imperio guardano a più vasto scopo ed i pontifici Romano sono dalla forza delle cose chiamati a tenere il freno intellettuale della cività de' popoli di tutta Europa." Troja deduces the Italian communes "dopo il mille" from a German rather than a Roman origin. "Là sono veramente i comuni dov' è la spada per difendergli; ma nel regno Longobardico da lunga stagione la spada più non pendeva dal fianco del Romano" (p. 368).

[4] Muratori, A. D. 951; Denina, "Rivoluzioni d' Italia," l. ix, c. 6.

allegiance to the emperor was taken by the people; and upon any irregular election of a pope, a circumstance by no means unusual, the emperors held themselves entitled to interpose. But the spirit and even the institutions of the Romans were republican. Amid the darkness of the tenth century, which no contemporary historian dissipates, we faintly distinguish the awful names of senate, consuls, and tribunes, the domestic magistracy of Rome. These shadows of past glory strike us at first with surprise; yet there is no improbability in the supposition that a city so renowned and populous, and so happily sheltered from the usurpation of the Lombards, might have preserved, or might afterward establish, a kind of municipal government, which it would be natural to dignify with those august titles of antiquity.[5] During that anarchy which ensued upon the fall of the Carlovingian dynasty, the Romans acquired an independence which they did not deserve. The city became a prey to the most terrible disorders; the papal chair was sought for at best by bribery or controlling influence, often by violence and assassination; it was filled by such men as naturally rise by such means, whose sway was precarious, and generally ended either in their murder or degradation. For many years the supreme pontiffs were forced upon the Church by two women of high rank but infamous reputation, Theodora and her daughter Marozia. The Kings of Italy, whose election in a Diet of Lombard princes and bishops at Roncaglia was not conceived to convey any pretensions to the sovereignty of Rome, could never obtain any decided influence in papal elections, which were the object of struggling factions among the resident nobility. In this temper of the Romans, they were ill disposed to resume habits of obedience to a foreign sovereign. The next year after Otho's coronation they rebelled, the Pope at their head, but were, of course, subdued without difficulty. The same republican spirit broke out whenever the emperors were absent in Germany, especially during the minority of Otho III, and directed itself against the temporal superiority of the Pope. But when that emperor attained manhood he besieged and took the city, crushing all resistance by measures of severity; and especially by the execution of the Consul Crescentius, a leader of the popular faction, to whose instigation the tumultuous license of Rome was principally ascribed.[6]

At the death of Otho III without children, in 1002, the compact between Italy and the emperors of the house of Saxony was determined. Her engagement of fidelity was certainly not

[5] Muratori, A. D. 967, 987, 1015, 1087; Sismondi, tome i, p. 155.
[6] Sismondi, tome i, p. 164, makes a patriot hero of Crescentius. But we know so little of the man or the times that it seems better to follow the common tenor of history, without vouching for the accuracy of its representations.

applicable to every sovereign whom the princes of Germany might raise to their throne. Accordingly, Ardoin, Marquis of Ivrea, was elected King of Italy. But a German party existed among the Lombard princes and bishops, to which his insolent demeanour soon gave a pretext for inviting Henry II, the new King of Germany, collaterally related to their late sovereign. Ardoin was deserted by most of the Italians, but retained his former subjects in Piedmont, and disputed the crown for many years with Henry, who passed very little time in Italy. During this period there was hardly any recognised government; and the Lombards became more and more accustomed, through necessity, to protect themselves, and to provide for their own internal police. Meanwhile the German nation had become odious to the Italians. The rude soldiery, insolent and addicted to intoxication, were engaged in frequent disputes with the citizens, wherein the latter, as is usual in similar cases, were exposed first to the summary vengeance of the troops, and afterward to penal chastisement for sedition.[7] In one of these tumults, at the entry of Henry II in 1004, the city of Pavia was burned to the ground, which inspired its inhabitants with a constant animosity against that emperor. Upon his death in 1024, the Italians were disposed to break once more their connection with Germany, which had elected as sovereign Conrad, Duke of Franconia. They offered their crown to Robert, King of France, and to William, Duke of Guienne; but neither of them was imprudent enough to involve himself in the difficult and faithless politics of Italy. It may surprise us that no candidate appeared from among her native princes. But it had been the dexterous policy of the Othos to weaken the great Italian fiefs, which were still rather considered as hereditary governments than as absolute patrimonies, by separating districts from their jurisdiction, under inferior marquises and rural counts.[8] The bishops were incapable of becoming competitors, and generally attached to the German party. The cities already possessed material influence, but were disunited by mutual jealousies. Since ancient prejudices, therefore, precluded a federate league of independent principalities and republics, for which perhaps the actual condition of Italy unfitted her, Eribert, Archbishop of Milan, accompanied by some other chief men of Lombardy, repaired to Constance, and tendered the crown to Conrad, which he was already disposed to claim as a sort of dependency upon Germany. It does not appear that either Conrad or his successors were ever regularly elected to reign over Italy;[9] but whether this

[7] Muratori, A. D. 1027, 1037.
[8] Denina, l. ix, c. 11; Muratori, "Antiq. Ital.," Dissert. 8; "Annali d' Italia," A. D. 989.

[9] Muratori, A. D. 1026. It is said afterward (p. 367) that he was a Romanis ad Imperatorem electus. The people of Rome, therefore, preserved their nominal

ceremony took place or not, we may certainly date from that time the subjection of Italy to the Germanic body. It became an unquestionable maxim that the votes of a few German princes conferred a right to the sovereignty of a country which had never been conquered, and which had never formally recognised this superiority.[10] But it was an equally fundamental rule that the elected King of Germany could not assume the title of Roman emperor until his coronation by the Pope. The middle appellation of King of the Romans was invented as a sort of approximation to the imperial dignity. But it was not till the reign of Maximilian that the actual coronation at Rome was dispensed with, and the title of emperor taken immediately after the election.

The period between Conrad of Franconia and Frederick Barbarossa, or from about the middle of the eleventh to that of the twelfth century, is marked by three great events in Italian history: the struggle between the empire and the papacy for ecclesiastical investitures, the establishment of the Norman kingdom in Naples, and the formation of distinct and nearly independent republics among the cities of Lombardy. The first of these will find a more appropriate place in a subsequent chapter, where I shall trace the progress of ecclesiastical power. But it produced a long and almost incessant state of disturbance in Italy, and should be mentioned at present as one of the main causes which excited in that country a systematic opposition to the imperial authority.

The southern provinces of Italy, in the beginning of the eleventh century, were chiefly subject to the Greek Empire, which had latterly recovered part of its losses, and exhibited some ambition and enterprise, though without any intrinsic vigour. They were governed by a lieutenant, styled Catapan,[11] who resided at Bari, in Apulia. On the Mediterranean coast three duchies, or rather republics, of Naples, Gaeta, and Amalfi, had for several ages preserved their connection with the Greek Empire, and acknowledged its nominal sovereignty. The Lombard principalities of Benevento, Salerno, and Capua had much declined from their ancient splendour. The Greeks were, however, not likely to attempt any further conquests: the court of

right of concurring in the election of an emperor. Muratori, in another place (A. D. 1040), supposes that Henry III was chosen King of Italy, though he allows that no proof of it exists; and there seems no reason for the supposition.

[10] Gunther, the poet of Frederick Barbarossa, expresses this not inelegantly:
" Romani gloria regni
Nos penes est; quemcunque sibi Germania regem
Præficit, hunc dives submisso vertice Roma

Accipit, et verso Tiberim regit ordine Rhenus."
(Gunther, " Ligurinus ap. Struvium Corpus Hist. German.," p. 266.) Yet it appears from Otho of Frisingen, an unquestionable authority, that some Italian nobles concurred, or at least were present and assisting, in the election of Frederick himself (l. ii, c. 1).

[11] Catapanus, from κατὰ παν, one employed in the general administration of affairs.

Constantinople had relapsed into its usual indolence; nor had they much right to boast of successes rather due to the Saracen auxiliaries whom they hired from Sicily. No momentous revolution apparently threatened the south of Italy, and least of all could it be anticipated from what quarter the storm was about to gather.

The followers of Rollo, who rested from plunder and piracy in the quiet possession of Normandy, became devout professors of the Christian faith, and particularly addicted to the custom of pilgrimage, which gratified their curiosity and spirit of adventure. In small bodies, well armed on account of the lawless character of the countries through which they passed, the Norman pilgrims visited the shrines of Italy and even the Holy Land. Some of these, very early in the eleventh century, were engaged by a Lombard prince of Salerno against the Saracens, who had invaded his territory; and through that superiority of valour, and perhaps of corporal strength, which this singular people seem to have possessed above all other Europeans, they made surprising havoc among the enemy.[12] This exploit led to fresh engagements, and these engagements drew new adventurers from Normandy; they founded the little city of Aversa, near Capua, and were employed by the Greeks against the Saracens of Sicily. But, though performing splendid services in this war, they were ill repaid by their ungrateful employers, and, being by no means of a temper to bear with injury, they revenged themselves by a sudden invasion of Apulia. This province was speedily subdued, and divided among twelve Norman counts; but soon afterward Robert Guiscard, one of twelve brothers, many of whom were renowned in these Italian wars, acquired the sovereignty; and, adding Calabria to his conquests, put an end to the long dominion of the Eastern emperors in Italy.[13] He reduced the principalities of Salerno and Benevento, in the latter instance sharing the spoil with the Pope, who took the city to himself, while Robert retained the territory. His conquests in Greece, which he invaded with the magnificent design of overthrowing the Eastern Empire, were at least equally splendid, though less durable. Roger, his younger brother, undertook meanwhile the romantic enterprise, as it appeared, of conquering the island of Sicily with a small body of Norman volunteers. But the Saracens were broken into petty states, and discouraged by the bad success of their brethren in Spain and Sardinia. After many years of war, Robert became sole master of Sicily, and took the

---

[12] Giannone, tome ii, p. 7 [edit. 1753]. I should observe that St. Marc, a more critical writer in examination of facts than Giannone, treats this first adventure of the Normans as unauthenticated. (" Abrégé Chronologique," p. 990.)

[13] The final blow was given to the Greek domination over Italy by the capture of Bari in 1071, after a siege of four years. It had for some time been confined to this single city. (Muratori, St. Marc.)

title of count. The son of this prince, upon the extinction of
Robert Guiscard's posterity, united the two Norman sovereignties, and, subjugating the free republics of Naples and Amalfi,
and the principality of Capua, established a boundary which has
hardly been changed since his time.[14]

The first successes of these Norman leaders were viewed un-
favourably by the popes. Leo IX marched in person against
Robert Guiscard with an army of German mercenaries, but was
beaten and made prisoner in this unwise enterprise, the scandal
of which nothing but good fortune could have lightened. He
fell, however, into the hands of a devout people, who implored
his absolution for the crime of defending themselves; and,
whether through gratitude or as the price of his liberation, invested them with their recent conquests in Apulia, as fiefs of
the Holy See. This investiture was repeated and enlarged as
the popes, especially in their contention with Henry IV and
Henry V, found the advantage of using the Normans as faithful
auxiliaries. Finally, Innocent II, in 1139, conferred upon Roger
the title of King of Sicily. It is difficult to understand by what
pretence these countries could be claimed by the see of Rome
in sovereignty, unless by virtue of the pretended donation of
Constantine or that of Louis the Debonair, which is hardly less
suspicious; [15] and least of all how Innocent II could surrender
the liberties of the city of Naples, whether that was considered
as an independent republic or as a portion of the Greek Empire.
But the Normans, who had no title but their swords, were naturally glad to give an appearance of legitimacy to their conquest;
and the kingdom of Naples, even in the hands of the most powerful princes in Europe, never ceased to pay a feudal acknowledgment to the chair of St. Peter.

The revolutions which time brought forth on the opposite
side of Italy were still more interesting. Under the Lombard
and French princes every city with its adjacent district was subject to the government and jurisdiction of a count, who was himself subordinate to the duke or marquis of the province. From
these counties it was the practice of the first German emperors
to dismember particular towns or tracts of country, granting
them upon a feudal tenure to rural lords, by many of whom
also the same title was assumed. Thus by degrees the authority
of the original officers was confined almost to the walls of their

[14] M. Sismondi has excelled himself in
describing the conquest of Amalfi and
Naples by Roger Guiscard (tome i, c. 4),
warming his imagination with visions of
liberty and virtue in those obscure republics, which no real history survives
to dispel.
[15] Muratori presumes to suppose that
the interpolated, if not spurious, grants
of Louis the Debonair, Otho I, and
Henry II to the see of Rome were promulgated about the time of the first concessions to the Normans, in order to give
the popes a colourable pretext to dispose
of the southern provinces of Italy. (A. D.
1059.)

own cities; and in many cases the bishops obtained a grant of the temporal government, and exercised the functions which had belonged to the count.[16]

It is impossible to ascertain the time at which the cities of Lombardy began to assume a republican form of government, or to trace with precision the gradations of their progress. The last historian of Italy asserts that Otho the First erected them into municipal communities, and permitted the election of their magistrates; but of this he produces no evidence; and Muratori, from whose authority it is rash to depart without strong reasons, is not only silent about any charters, but discovers no express unequivocal testimonies of a popular government for the whole eleventh century.[17] The first appearance of the citizens acting for themselves is in a tumult at Milan in 991, when the archbishop was expelled from the city.[18] But this was a transitory ebullition, and we must descend lower for more specific proofs. It is possible that the disputed succession of Ardoin and Henry, at the beginning of the eleventh age, and the kind of interregnum which then took place, gave the inhabitants an opportunity of choosing magistrates and of sharing in public deliberations. A similar relaxation, indeed, of government in France had exposed the people to greater servitude, and established a feudal aristocracy. But the feudal tenures seem not to have produced in Italy that systematic and regular subordination which existed in France during the same period; nor were the mutual duties of the relation between lord and vassal so well understood or observed. Hence we find not only disputes, but actual civil war, between the lesser gentry, or vavassors, and the higher nobility, their immediate superiors. These differences were adjusted by Conrad the Salic, who published a remarkable edict in 1037, by which the feudal law of Italy was reduced to more certainty.[19] From this disunion among the members of the feudal confederacy, it was more easy for the citizens to render themselves secure against its dominion. The cities, too, of Lombardy were far more populous and better defended than those of France; they had learned to stand sieges in the Hungarian invasions of the tenth century, and had acquired the right of protecting themselves by strong fortifications. Those which had been placed under the temporal government of their bishops had peculiar advantages in struggling for emancipation.[20] This circumstance in the state of Lombardy

[16] Muratori, "Antiquit. Italiæ," Dissert. 8; "Annali d' Italia," A. D. 989; "Antichita Estensi," p. 26.
[17] Sismondi, tome i, pp. 97, 384; Muratori, Dissert. 49.
[18] Muratori, "Annali d' Italia."
[19] Muratori, "Annali d' Italia"; St. Marc.

[20] The bishops seem to have become counts, or temporal governors, of their sees, about the end of the tenth or before the middle of the eleventh century. (Muratori, Dissert. 8; Denina, l. ix, c. 11; St. Marc. A. D. 1041, 1047, 1070.) In Arnulf's "History of Milan," written before

I consider as highly important toward explaining the subsequent revolution. Notwithstanding several exceptions, a churchman was less likely to be bold and active in command than a soldier; and the sort of election which was always necessary, and sometimes more than nominal, on a vacancy of the see, kept up among the citizens a notion that the authority of their bishop and chief magistrate emanated in some degree from themselves. In many instances, especially in the Church of Milan, the earliest perhaps, and certainly the most famous of Lombard republics, there occurred a disputed election; two, or even three, competitors claimed the archiepiscopal functions, and were compelled, in the absence of the emperors, to obtain the exercise of them by means of their own faction among the citizens.[21]

These were the general causes which, operating at various times during the eleventh century, seem gradually to have produced a republican form of government in the Italian cities. But this part of history is very obscure. The archives of all cities before the reign of Frederick Barbarossa have perished. For many years there is a great deficiency of contemporary Lombard historians; and those of a later age, who endeavoured to search into the antiquities of their country, have found only some barren and insulated events to record. We perceive, however, throughout the eleventh century that the cities were continually in warfare with each other. This, indeed, was according to the manners of that age, and no inference can absolutely be drawn from it as to their internal freedom. But it is observable that their chronicles speak, in recording these transactions, of the people, and not of their leaders, which is the true republican tone of history. Thus, in the "Annals of Pisa," we read,

the close of the latter age, we have a contemporary evidence. And from the perusal of that work I should infer that the archbishop was, in the middle of the eleventh century, the chief magistrate of the city. But, at the same time, it appears highly probable that an assembly of the citizens, or at least a part of the citizens, partook in the administration of public affairs. (Muratori, "Scriptores Rerum Italicarum," tome iv, pp. 16, 22, 23, and particularly the last.) In most cities to the eastward of the Tesino, the bishops lost their temporal authority in the twelfth century, though the Archbishop of Milan had no small prerogatives while that city was governed as a republic. But in Piedmont they continued longer in the enjoyment of power. Vercelli, and even Turin, were almost subject to their respective prelates till the thirteenth century. For this reason, among others, the Piedmontese cities are hardly to be reckoned among the republics of Lombardy. (Denina, "Istoria dell' Italia Occidentale," tome i, p. 191.)

[21] Muratori, A. D. 1345. Sometimes the inhabitants of a city refused to acknowledge a bishop named by the emperor, as happened at Pavia and Asti about 1057. (Arnulf, p. 22.) This was, in other words, setting up themselves as republics. But the most remarkable instance of this kind occurred in 1070, when the Milanese absolutely rejected Godfrey, appointed by Henry IV, and, after a resistance of several years, obliged the emperor to fix upon another person. The city had been previously involved in long and violent tumults, which, though rather belonging to ecclesiastical than civil history, as they arose out of the endeavours made to reform the conduct and enforce the celibacy of the clergy, had a considerable tendency to diminish the archbishop's authority, and to give a republican character to the inhabitants. These proceedings are told at great length by St. Marc, tome iii, A. D. 1056–1077. Arnulf and Landulf are the original sources.

under the years 1002 and 1004, of victories gained by the Pisans over the people of Lucca; in 1006, that the Pisans and Genoese conquered Sardinia.[22]   These annals, indeed, are not by a contemporary writer, nor perhaps of much authority.   But we have an original account of a war that broke out in 1057, between Pavia and Milan, in which the citizens are said to have raised armies, made alliances, hired foreign troops, and in every respect acted like independent states.[23]   There was, in fact, no power left in the empire to control them.   The two Henrys IV and V were so much embarrassed during the quarrel concerning investitures, and the continual troubles of Germany, that they were less likely to interfere with the rising freedom of the Italian cities than to purchase their assistance by large concessions.   Henry IV granted a charter to Pisa in 1081, full of the most important privileges, promising even not to name any Marquis of Tuscany without the people's consent;[24] and it is possible that, although the instruments have perished, other places might obtain similar advantages.   However this may be, it is certain that before the death of Henry V, in 1125, almost all the cities of Lombardy, and many among those of Tuscany, were accustomed to elect their own magistrates, and to act as independent communities in waging war and in domestic government.[25]

The territory subjected originally to the count or bishop of these cities had been reduced, as I mentioned above, by numerous concessions to the rural nobility.   But the new republics, deeming themselves entitled to all which their former governors had once possessed, began to attack their nearest neighbours, and to recover the sovereignty of all their ancient territory.   They besieged the castles of the rural counts, and successively reduced them into subjection.   They suppressed some minor communities, which had been formed in imitation of themselves by little towns belonging to their district.   Sometimes they purchased feudal superiorities or territorial jurisdictions, and, according to a policy not unusual with the stronger party, converted the rights of property into those of government.[26]   Hence, at the

---

[22] Murat., Dissert. 45. Arnulfus, the historian of Milan, makes no mention of any temporal counts, which seems to be a proof that there were none in any authority. He speaks always of Mediolanenses, Papienses, Ravenates, etc. This history was written about 1085, but relates to the earlier part of that century. That of Landulphus corroborates this supposition, which, indeed, is capable of proof as to Milan and several other cities in which the temporal government had been legally vested in the bishops.
[23] Murat., Dissert. 45; Arnulf., " Hist. Mediolan.," p. 22.

[24] Murat., Dissert. 45.
[25] Murat., " Annali d' Ital.," A. D. 1107.
[26] Il dominio utile delle città e de' villaggi era talvolta diviso fra due o più padroni, ossia che s' assegnassero a ciascuno diversi quartieri, o si dividessoro i proventi della gabelle, ovvero che l'uno signore godesse d'una spezie della giurisdizione, e l' altro d' un' altra. (Denina, l. xii, c. 3.) This produced a vast intricacy of titles, which was, of course, advantageous to those who wanted a pretext for robbing their neighbours.

middle of the twelfth century, we are assured by a contemporary writer that hardly any nobleman could be found, except the Marquis of Montferrat, who had not submitted to some city.[27] We may except, also, I should presume, the families of Este and Malaspina, as well as that of Savoy. Muratori produces many charters of mutual compact between the nobles and the neighbouring cities; whereof one invariable article is, that the former should reside within the walls a certain number of months in the year.[28] The rural nobility, thus deprived of the independence which had endeared their castles, imbibed a new ambition of directing the municipal government of the cities, which consequently, during this period of the republic, fell chiefly into the hands of the superior families. It was the sagacious policy of the Lombards to invite settlers by throwing open to them the privileges of citizenship, and sometimes they even bestowed them by compulsion. Sometimes a city, imitating the wisdom of ancient Rome, granted these privileges to all the inhabitants of another.[29] Thus the principal cities, and especially Milan, reached, before the middle of the twelfth century, a degree of population very far beyond that of the capitals of the great kingdoms. Within their strong walls and deep trenches, and in the midst of their well-peopled streets, the industrious dwelt secure from the license of armed pillagers and the oppression of feudal tyrants. Artisans, whom the military landholders contemned, acquired and deserved the right of bearing arms for their own and the public defence.[30] Their occupations became liberal, because they were the foundation of their political franchises; the citizens were classed in companies according to their respective crafts, each of which had its tribune or standard-bearer (gonfalonier), at whose command, when any tumult arose or enemy threatened, they rushed in arms to muster in the market-place.

But, unhappily, we can not extend the sympathy which institutions so full of liberty create to the national conduct of these little republics. Their love of freedom was alloyed by that restless spirit, from which a democracy is seldom exempt, of tyrannizing over weaker neighbours. They played over again the tragedy of ancient Greece, with all its circumstances of inveterate hatred, unjust ambition, and atrocious retaliation, though with less consummate actors upon the scene. Among all the Lombard cities, Milan was the most conspicuous, as well for power

[27] " Otho Frisingens.," l. ii, c. 13.
[28] Murat., Dissert. 49.
[29] Murat., Dissert. 49.
[30] Otho Frisingensis ap. Murat., " Scr. Rer. Ital.," tome vi, p. 708. Ut etiam ad comprimendos vicinos materiâ non careant, inferioris ordinis juvenes, vel quoslibet contemptibilium etiam mechanicarum artium opifices, quos cæteræ gentes ab honestioribus et liberioribus studiis tanquam pestem propellunt, ad militiæ cingulum, vel dignitatum gradus assumere non dedignantur. Ex quo factum est, ut cæteris orbis civitatibus, divitiis et potentiâ præemineant.

and population as for the abuse of those resources by arbitrary and ambitious conduct. Thus, in 1111, they razed the town of Lodi to the ground, distributing the inhabitants among six villages, and subjecting them to an unrelenting despotism.[31] Thus, in 1118, they commenced a war of ten years' duration with the little city of Como; but the surprising perseverance of its inhabitants procured for them better terms of capitulation, though they lost their original independence. The Cremonese treated so harshly the town of Crema that it revolted from them, and put itself under the protection of Milan. Cities of more equal forces carried on interminable hostilities by wasting each other's territory, destroying the harvests, and burning the villages.

The sovereignty of the emperors, meanwhile, though not very effective, was in theory always admitted. Their name was used in public acts, and appeared upon the coin. When they came into Italy they had certain customary supplies of provisions, called fodrum regale, at the expense of the city where they resided; during their presence all inferior magistracies were suspended, and the right of jurisdiction devolved upon them alone. But such was the jealousy of the Lombards that they built the royal palaces outside their gates; a precaution to which the emperors were compelled to submit. This was at a very early time a subject of contention between the inhabitants of Pavia and Conrad II, whose palace, seated in the heart of the city, they had demolished in a sedition, and were unwilling to rebuild in that situation.[32]

Such was the condition of Italy when Frederick Barbarossa, Duke of Swabia, and nephew of the last emperor, Conrad III, ascended the throne of Germany. His accession forms the commencement of a new period, the duration of which is about one hundred years, and which is terminated by the death of Conrad IV, the last emperor of the house of Swabia. It is characterized, like the former, by three distinguishing features in Italian history: the victorious struggle of the Lombard and other cities for independence, the final establishment of a temporal sovereignty over the middle provinces by the popes, and the union of the kingdom of Naples to the dominions of the house of Swabia.

In Frederick Barbarossa the Italians found a very different sovereign from the last two emperors, Lothaire and Conrad III,

[31] The animosity between Milan and Lodi was of very old standing. It originated, according to Arnulf, in the resistance made by the inhabitants of the latter city to an attempt made by Archbishop Eribert to force a bishop of his own nomination upon them. The bloodshed, plunder, and conflagrations which had ensued, would, he says, fill a volume if they were related at length. (" Scriptores Rerum Italic.," tome iv, p. 16.) And this is the testimony of a writer who did not live beyond 1085. Seventy years more either of hostility or servitude elapsed before Lodi was permitted to respire.

[32] " Otho Frisingens.," p. 710; Muratori, A. D. 1027.

13

who had seldom appeared in Italy, and with forces quite inadequate to control such insubordinate subjects. The distinguished valour and ability of this prince rendered a severe and arbitrary temper and a haughty conceit of his imperial rights more formidable. He believed, or professed to believe, the magnificent absurdity that, as successor of Augustus, he inherited the kingdoms of the world. In the same right, he more powerfully, if not more rationally, laid claim to the entire prerogatives of the Roman emperors over their own subjects; and in this the professors of the civil law, which was now diligently studied, lent him their aid with the utmost servility. To such a disposition the self-government of the Lombard cities appeared mere rebellion. Milan especially, the most renowned of them all, drew down upon herself his inveterate resentment. He found, unfortunately, too good a pretence in her behaviour toward Lodi. Two natives of that ruined city threw themselves at the emperor's feet, imploring him, as the ultimate source of justice, to redress the wrongs of their country. It is a striking proof of the terror inspired by Milan that the consuls of Lodi disavowed the complaints of their countrymen, and the inhabitants trembled at the danger of provoking a summary vengeance, against which the imperial arms seemed no protection.[33] The Milanese, however, abstained from attacking the people of Lodi, though they treated with contempt the emperor's order to leave them at liberty. Frederick meanwhile came into Italy and held a Diet at Roncaglia, where complaints poured in from many quarters against the Milanese. Pavia and Cremona, their ancient enemies, were impatient to renew hostilities under the imperial auspices. Brescia, Tortona, and Crema were allies, or rather dependents, of Milan. Frederick soon took occasion to attack the latter confederacy. Tortona was compelled to surrender and levelled to the ground. But a feudal army was soon dissolved; the emperor had much to demand his attention at Rome, where he was on ill terms with Adrian IV; and when the imperial troops were withdrawn from Lombardy, the Milanese rebuilt Tortona, and expelled the citizens of Lodi from their dwellings. Frederick assembled a fresh army, to which almost every city of Lombardy, willingly or by force, contributed its militia. It is said to have exceeded a hundred thousand men. The Milanese shut themselves up within their walls; and perhaps might have defied the imperial forces if their immense population, which gave them confidence in arms, had not exposed them

[33] See an interesting account of these circumstances in the narrative of Otho Morena, a citizen of Lodi. (" Script. Rer. Ital.," tome vi, p. 966.) M. Sismondi, who reproaches Morena for par- tiality toward Frederick in the Milanese war, should have remembered the provocations of Lodi. (" Hist. des Répub. Ital.," tome ii, p. 102.)

to a different enemy. Milan was obliged by hunger to capitulate, upon conditions not very severe, if a vanquished people could ever safely rely upon the convention that testifies their submission.

Frederick, after the surrender of Milan, held a Diet at Roncaglia, where the effect of his victories was fatally perceived. The bishops, the higher nobility, the lawyers, vied with one another in exalting his prerogatives. He defined the regalian rights, as they were called, in such a manner as to exclude the cities and private proprietors from coining money, and from tolls or territorial dues, which they had for many years possessed. These, however, he permitted them to retain for a pecuniary stipulation. A more important innovation was the appointment of magistrates, with the title of podestà, to administer justice concurrently with the consuls; but he soon proceeded to abolish the latter office in many cities, and to throw the whole government into the hands of his own magistrates. He prohibited the cities from levying war against each other. It may be presumed that he showed no favour to Milan. The capitulation was set at naught in its most express provisions; a podestà was sent to supersede the consuls, and part of the territory taken away. Whatever might be the risk of resistance, and the Milanese had experience enough not to undervalue it, they were determined rather to see their liberties at once overthrown than gradually destroyed by a faithless tyrant. They availed themselves of the absence of his army to renew the war. Its issue was more calamitous than that of the last. Almost all Lombardy lay patient under subjection. The small town of Crema, always the faithful ally of Milan, stood a memorable siege against the imperial army; but the inhabitants were ultimately compelled to capitulate for their lives, and the vindictive Cremonese razed their dwellings to the ground.[34] But all smaller calamities were forgotten when the great city of Milan, worn out by famine rather than subdued by force, was reduced to surrender at discretion. Lombardy stood in anxious suspense to know the determination of Frederick respecting this ancient metropolis, the seat of the early Christian emperors, and second only to Rome in the hierarchy of the Latin Church. A delay of three weeks excited fallacious hopes; but at the end of that time an order was given to the Milanese to evacuate their habitations. The deserted streets were instantly occupied by the imperial army; the people of Pavia and Cremona, of Lodi and Como, were commissioned

---

[34] The siege of Crema is told at great length by Otto Morena; it is interesting, not only as a display of extraordinary, though unsuccessful, perseverance and intrepidity, but as the most detailed account of the methods used in the attack and defence of fortified places before the introduction of artillery. ("Scrip. Rer. Ital.," tome vi, pp. 1032–1052.)

to revenge themselves on the respective quarters of the city assigned to them, and in a few days the pillaged churches stood alone amid the ruins of what had been Milan.

There was now little left of that freedom to which Lombardy had aspired: it was gone like a pleasant dream, and she awoke to the fears and miseries of servitude. Frederick obeyed the dictates of his vindictive temper, and of the policy usual among statesmen. He abrogated the consular regimen in some even of the cities which had supported him, and established his podestà in their place. This magistrate was always a stranger, frequently not even an Italian; and he came to his office with all those prejudices against the people he was to govern which cut off every hope of justice and humanity. The citizens of Lombardy, especially the Milanese, who had been dispersed in the villages adjoining their ruined capital, were unable to meet the perpetual demands of tribute. In some parts, it is said, two thirds of the produce of their lands, the only wealth that remained, were extorted from them by the imperial officers. It was in vain that they prostrated themselves at the feet of Frederick. He gave at the best only vague promises of redress; they were in his eyes rebels; his delegates had acted as faithful officers, whom, even if they had gone a little beyond his intentions, he could not be expected to punish.

But there still remained at the heart of Lombardy the strong principle of national liberty, imperishable among the perishing armies of her patriots, inconsumable in the conflagration of her cities.[35] Those whom private animosities had led to assist the German conqueror blushed at the degradation of their country, and at the share they had taken in it. A league was secretly formed, in which Cremona, one of the chief cities on the imperial side, took a prominent part. Those beyond the Adige, hitherto not much engaged in the disputes of central Lombardy, had already formed a separate confederacy to secure themselves from encroachments, which appeared the more unjust as they had never borne arms against the emperor. Their first successes corresponded to the justice of their cause; Frederick was repulsed from the territory of Verona, a fortunate augury for the rest of Lombardy. These two clusters of cities on the east and west of the Adige now united themselves into the famous Lombard league, the terms of which were settled in a general Diet, Their alliance was to last twenty years, during which they pledged themselves to mutual assistance against any one who should exact more from them than they had been used to perform from the time of Henry to the first coming of Frederick into Italy;

[35] " Quæ neque Dardaniis campis potuere perire,
Nec cum capta capi, nec cum combusta cremari."—Ennius.

implying in this the recovery of their elective magistracies, their rights of war and peace, and those lucrative privileges which, under the name of regalian, had been wrested from them in the Diet of Roncaglia.[36]
This union of the Lombard cities was formed at a very favourable juncture. Frederick had almost ever since his accession been engaged in open hostility with the see of Rome, and was pursuing the fruitless policy of Henry IV, who had endeavoured to substitute an antipope of his own faction for the legitimate pontiff. In the prosecution of this scheme he had besieged Rome with a great army, which, the citizens resisting longer than he expected, fell a prey to the autumnal pestilence which visits the neighbourhood of that capital. The flower of German nobility was cut off by this calamity, and the emperor recrossed the Alps, entirely unable for the present to withstand the Lombard confederacy. Their first overt act of insurrection was the rebuilding of Milan; the confederate troops all joined in this undertaking, and the Milanese, still numerous, though dispersed and persecuted, revived as a powerful republic. Lodi was compelled to enter into the league; Pavia alone continued on the imperial side. As a check to Pavia and to the Marquis of Montferrat, the most potent of the independent nobility, the Lombards planned the erection of a new city between the confines of these two enemies, in a rich plain to the south of the Po, and bestowed upon it, in compliment to the Pope, Alexander III, the name of Alessandria. Though, from its hasty construction, Alessandria was even in that age deemed rude in appearance, it rapidly became a thriving and populous city.[37] The intrinsic energy and resources of Lombardy were now made manifest. Frederick, who had triumphed by their disunion, was unequal to contend against their league. After several years of indecisive war the emperor invaded the Milanese territory; but the confederates gave him battle, and gained a complete victory at Legnano. Frederick escaped alone and disguised from the field, with little hope of raising a fresh army, though still reluctant from shame to acquiesce in the freedom of Lombardy. He was at length persuaded, through the mediation of the republic of

---

[36] For the nature and conditions of the Lombard league, besides the usual authorities, see Muratori's forty-eighth dissertation. The words, a tempore Henrici Regis usque ad introitum imperatoris Frederici, leave it ambiguous which of the Henrys was intended. Muratori thinks it was Henry IV, because the cities then began to be independent. It seems, however, natural, when a king is mentioned without any numerical designation, to interpret it of the last bearing that name; as we say King William for William III. And certainly the liberties of Lombardy were more perfect under Henry V than his father; besides which, the one reign might still be remembered, and the other rested in tradition. The question, however, is of little moment.

[37] Alessandria was surnamed, in derision, della paglia, from the thatch with which the houses were covered. Frederick was very desirous to change its name to Cæsarea, as it is actually called in the Peace of Constance, being at that time on the imperial side. But it soon recovered its former appellation.

Venice, to consent to a truce of six years, the provisional terms of which were all favourable to the league. It was weakened, however, by the defection of some of its own members; Cremona, which had never cordially united with her ancient enemies, made separate conditions with Frederick, and suffered herself to be named among the cities on the imperial side in the armistice. Tortona and even Alessandria followed the same course during the six years of its duration; a fatal testimony of unsubdued animosities, and omen of the calamities of Italy. At the expiration of the truce, Frederick's anxiety to secure the crown for his son overcame his pride, and the famous Peace of Constance established the Lombard republics in real independence.

By the Treaty of Constance the cities were maintained in the enjoyment of all the regalian rights, whether within their walls or in their district, which they could claim by usage. Those of levying war, of erecting fortifications, and of administering civil and criminal justice were specially mentioned. The nomination of their consuls or other magistrates was left absolutely to the citizens; but they were to receive the investiture of their office from an imperial legate. The customary tributes of provision during the emperor's residence in Italy were preserved, and he was authorized to appoint in every city a judge of appeal in civil causes. The Lombard league was confirmed, and the cities were permitted to renew it at their own discretion, but they were to take every ten years an oath of fidelity to the emperor. This just compact preserved, along with every security for the liberties and welfare of the cities, as much of the imperial prerogatives as could be exercised by a foreign sovereign consistently with the people's happiness.[38]

The successful insurrection of Lombardy is a memorable refutation of that system of policy to which its advocates give the appellation of vigorous, and which they perpetually hold forth as the only means through which a disaffected people are to be restrained. By a certain class of statesmen, and by all men of harsh and violent disposition, measures of conciliation, adherence to the spirit of treaties, regard to ancient privileges, or to those rules of moral justice which are paramount to all positive right, are always treated with derision. Terror is their only specific, and the physical inability to rebel their only security for allegiance. But if the razing of cities, the abrogation of privileges, the impoverishment and oppression of a nation could assure its constant submission, Frederick Barbarossa would never have seen the militia of Lombardy arrayed against him at Legnano. Whatever may be the pressure upon a conquered people, there will come a moment of their recoil. Nor is it material

<hr/>

[38] Muratori, " Antiquitates Italiæ," Dissert. 50.

to allege, in answer to the present instance, that the accidental destruction of Frederick's army by disease enabled the cities of Lombardy to succeed in their resistance. The fact may well be disputed, since Lombardy, when united, appears to have been more than equal to a contest with any German force that could have been brought against her; but even if we admit the effect of this circumstance, it only exhibits the precariousness of a policy which collateral events are always liable to disturb. Providence reserves to itself various means by which the bonds of the oppressor may be broken; and it is not for human sagacity to anticipate whether the army of a conqueror shall moulder in the unwholesome marshes of Rome or stiffen with frost in a Russian winter.

The Peace of Constance presented a noble opportunity to the Lombards of establishing a permanent federal union of small republics; a form of government congenial from the earliest ages to Italy, and that, perhaps, under which she is again destined one day to flourish. They were entitled by the provisions of that treaty to preserve their league, the basis of a more perfect confederacy, which the course of events would have emancipated from every kind of subjection to Germany.[39] But dark, long-cherished hatreds, and that implacable vindictiveness which, at least in former ages, distinguished the private manners of Italy, deformed her national character, which can only be the aggregate of individual passions. For revenge she threw away the pearl of great price, and sacrificed even the recollection of that liberty which had stalked like a majestic spirit among the ruins of Milan.[40] It passed away, that high disdain of absolute power, that steadiness and self-devotion, which raised the half-civilized Lombards of the twelfth century to the level of those ancient republics from whose history our first notions of freedom and virtue are derived. The victim by turns of selfish and sanguinary factions, of petty tyrants, and of foreign invaders, Italy has fallen like a star from its place in heaven; she has seen her harvests trodden down by the horses of the stranger, and the blood of her children wasted in quarrels not their own: Conquering or conquered, in the indignant language of her poet, still alike a slave,[41] a long retribution for the tyranny of Rome.

[39] Though there was no permanent Diet of the Lombard league, the consuls and podestàs of the respective cities composing it occasionally met in congress to deliberate upon measures of general safety. Thus assembled, they were called Rectores Societatis Lombardiæ. It is evident that, if Lombardy had continued in any degree to preserve the spirit of union, this congress might readily have become a permanent body, like the Helvetic Diet, with as extensive powers as are necessary in a federal constitution. (Muratori, "Antichità Italiane," tome iii, p. 126; Dissert. 50; Sismondi, tome ii, p. 189.)

[40] "Anzi girar la libertà mirai,
        E baciar lieta ogni ruina, e dire,
        Ruine sì, ma servitù non mai."
(Gaetana Passerini [ossia piutosto Giovan Battista Pastorini] in Mathias, "Componimenti Lirici," vol. iii, p. 331.)

[41] Per servir sempre, o vincitrice o vinta. (Filicaja.)

Frederick did not attempt to molest the cities of Lombardy in the enjoyment of those privileges conceded by the Treaty of Constance. His ambition was diverted to a new scheme for aggrandizing the house of Swabia by the marriage of his eldest son, Henry, with Constance, the aunt and heiress of William II, King of Sicily. That kingdom, which the first monarch Roger had elevated to a high pitch of renown and power, fell into decay through the misconduct of his son William, surnamed the Bad, and did not recover much of its lustre under the second William, though styled the Good. His death without issue was apparently no remote event, and Constance was the sole legitimate survivor of the royal family. It is a curious circumstance that no hereditary kingdom appears absolutely to have excluded females from its throne, except that which from its magnitude was of all the most secure from falling into the condition of a province. The Sicilians felt too late the defect of their constitution, which permitted an independent people to be transferred, as the dowry of a woman, to a foreign prince, by whose ministers they might justly expect to be insulted and oppressed. Henry, whose marriage with Constance took place in 1186, and who succeeded in her right to the throne of Sicily three years afterward, was exasperated by a courageous but unsuccessful effort of the Norman barons to preserve the crown for an illegitimate branch of the royal family, and his reign is disgraced by a series of atrocious cruelties. The power of the house of Swabia was now at its zenith on each side of the Alps; Henry received the imperial crown the year after his father's death in the third crusade, and even prevailed upon the princes of Germany to elect his infant son Frederick as his successor. But his own premature decease clouded the prospects of his family: Constance survived him but a year; and a child of four years old was left with the inheritance of a kingdom which his father's severity had rendered disaffected, and which the leaders of German mercenaries in his service desolated and disputed.

During the minority of Frederick II, from 1198 to 1216, the papal chair was filled by Innocent III, a name second only, and hardly second, to that of Gregory VII. Young, noble, and intrepid, he united with the accustomed spirit of ecclesiastical usurpation, which no one had ever carried to so high a point, the more worldly ambition of consolidating a separate principality for the Holy See in the centre of Italy. The real or spurious donations of Constantine, Pepin, Charlemagne, and Louis had given rise to a perpetual claim, on the part of the popes, to very extensive dominions; but little of this had been effectuated, and in Rome itself they were thwarted by the prefect, an officer who swore fidelity to the emperor, and by the insubordinate spirit of the people. In the very neighbourhood the small cities owned no subjection to the capital, and were probably as much self-governed as those of Lombardy. One is transported back to the earliest times of the republic in reading of the desperate wars between Rome and Tibur or Tusculum; neither of which was subjugated till the latter part of the twelfth century. At a farther distance were the duchy of Spoleto, the march of Ancona, and what had been the exarchate of Ravenna, to all of which the popes had more or less grounded pretensions. Early in the last-mentioned age the famous Countess Matilda, to whose zealous protection Gregory VII had been eminently indebted during his long dispute with the emperor, granted the reversion of all her possessions to the Holy See, first in the lifetime of Gregory, and again under the pontificate of Paschal III. These were very extensive, and held by different titles. Of her vast imperial fiefs, Mantua, Modena, and Tuscany, she certainly could not dispose. The duchy of Spoleto and march of Ancona were supposed to rest upon a different footing. I confess myself not distinctly to comprehend the nature of this part of her succession. These had been formerly among the great fiefs of the kingdom of Italy. But if I understand it rightly, they had tacitly ceased to be subject to the emperors some years before they were seized by Godfrey of Lorraine, father-in-law and stepfather of Matilda. To his son, her husband, she succeeded in the possession of those countries. They are commonly considered as her allodial or patrimonial property; yet it is not easy to see how, being herself a subject of the empire, she could transfer even her allodial estates from its sovereignty. Nor, on the other hand, can it apparently be maintained that she was lawful sovereign of countries which had not long since been imperial fiefs, and the suzerainty over which had never been renounced. The original title of the Holy See, therefore, does not seem incontestable even as to this part of Matilda's donation. But I state with hesitation a difficulty to which the authors I have consulted do not advert.[42] It is certain, however, that the emperors kept possession of the whole during the twelfth century, and treated both Spoleto and Ancona as parts of the empire, notwithstanding continual remonstrances from the Roman pontiffs. Frederick Barbarossa, at the negotiations of Venice in 1177, promised to restore the patrimony of Matilda in fifteen years; but

---

[42] It is almost hopeless to look for explicit information upon the rights and pretensions of the Roman See in Italian writers even of the eighteenth century. Muratori, the most learned, and upon the whole the fairest of them all, moves cautiously over this ground; except when the claims of Rome happen to clash with those of the house of Este. But I have not been able to satisfy myself by the perusal of some dry and tedious dissertations in St. Marc ("Abrégé Chronologique de l'Hist. de l'Italie," tome iv), who, with learning scarcely inferior to that of Muratori, possessed more opportunity and inclination to speak out.

at the close of that period Henry VI was not disposed to execute this arrangement, and granted the county in fief to some of his German followers. Upon his death the circumstances were favourable to Innocent III. The infant King of Sicily had been intrusted by Constance to his guardianship. A double election of Philip, brother of Henry VI, and of Otho, Duke of Bruns- wick, engaged the princes of Germany, who had entirely over- looked the claims of young Frederick, in a doubtful civil war. Neither party was in a condition to enter Italy; and the imperial dignity was vacant for several years, till, the death of Philip removing one competitor, Otho IV, whom the Pope had con- stantly favoured, was crowned emperor. During this interval the Italians had no superior; and Innocent availed himself of it to maintain the pretensions of the see. These he backed by the production of rather a questionable document, the will of Henry VI, said to have been found among the baggage of Marquard, one of the German soldiers who had been invested with fiefs by the late emperor. The cities of what we now call the eccle- siastical state had in the twelfth century their own municipal government like those of Lombardy, but they were far less able to assert a complete independence. They gladly, therefore, put themselves under the protection of the Holy See, which held out some prospect of securing them from Marquard and other rapacious partisans, without disturbing their internal regula- tions. Thus the duchy of Spoleto and march of Ancona sub- mitted to Innocent III; but he was not strong enough to keep constant possession of such extensive territories, and some years afterward adopted the prudent course of granting Ancona in fief to the Marquis of Este. He did not, as may be supposed, neg- lect his authority at home; the Prefect of Rome was now com- pelled to swear allegiance to the Pope, which put an end to the regular imperial supremacy over that city, and the privileges of the citizens were abridged. This is the proper era of that temporal sovereignty which the bishops of Rome possess over their own city, though still prevented by various causes for nearly three centuries from becoming unquestioned and unlimited.

The policy of Rome was now more clearly defined than ever. In order to preserve what she had thus suddenly gained rather by opportunity than strength, it was her interest to enfeeble the imperial power, and consequently to maintain the freedom of the Italian republics. Tuscany had hitherto been ruled by a marquis of the emperor's appointment, though her cities were flourishing and, within themselves, independent. In imitation of the Lombard confederacy, and impelled by Innocent III, they now (with the exception of Pisa, which was always strongly at- tached to the empire) formed a similar league for the preservation of their rights. In this league the influence of the Pope was far more strongly manifested than in that of Lombardy. Although the latter had been in alliance with Alexander III, and was formed during the height of his dispute with Frederick, this ecclesiastical quarrel mingled so little in their struggle for liberty that no allusion to it is found in the act of their confederacy. But the Tuscan union was expressly established "for the honour and aggrandizement of the apostolic see." The members bound themselves to defend the possessions and rights of the Church, and not to acknowledge any king or emperor without the approbation of the supreme pontiff.[43] The Tuscans, accordingly, were more thoroughly attached to the Church party than the Lombards, whose principle was animosity toward the house of Swabia. Hence, when Innocent III, some time after, supported Frederick II against the Emperor Otho IV, the Milanese and their allies were arranged on the imperial side, but the Tuscans continued to adhere to the Pope.

In the wars of Frederick Barbarossa against Milan and its allies, we have seen the cities of Lombardy divided, and a considerable number of them firmly attached to the imperial interest. It does not appear, I believe, from history, though it is by no means improbable, that the citizens were at so early a time divided among themselves, as to their line of public policy, and that the adherence of a particular city to the emperor, or to the Lombard league, was only, as proved afterward the case, that one faction or another acquired an ascendency in its councils. But jealousies long existing between the different classes, and only suspended by the national struggle which terminated at Constance, gave rise to new modifications of interests, and new relations toward the empire. About the year 1200, or perhaps a little later, the two leading parties which divided the cities of Lombardy, and whose mutual animosity, having no general subject of contention, required the association of a name to direct as well as invigorate its prejudices, became distinguished by the celebrated appellations of Guelfs and Ghibelins, the former adhering to the papal side, the latter to that of the emperor. These names were derived from Germany, and had been the rallying word of faction for more than half a century in that country before they were transported to a still more favourable soil. The Guelfs took their name from a very illustrious family, several of whom had successively been Dukes of Bavaria in the tenth and eleventh centuries. The heiress of the last of these intermarried with a younger son of the house of Este, a noble family settled

---

[43] Quod possessiones et jura sacrosanctæ ecclesiæ bonâ fide defenderent; et quod nullum in regem aut imperatorem reciperent, nisi quem Romanus pontifex approbaret. (Muratori, Dissert. 48; Latin, tome iv, p. 320; Italian, tome iii, p. 112.)

near Padua, and possessed of great estates on each bank of the lower Po. They gave birth to a second line of Guelfs, from whom the royal house of Brunswick is descended. The name of Ghibelin is derived from a village in Franconia, whence Conrad the Salic came, the progenitor, through females, of the Swabian emperors. At the election of Lothaire in 1125, the Swabian family were disappointed of what they considered almost an hereditary possession; and at this time a hostility appears to have commenced between them and the house of Guelf, who were nearly related to Lothaire. Henry the Proud and his son, Henry the Lion, representatives of the latter family, were frequently persecuted by the Swabian emperors, but their fortunes belong to the history of Germany.[44] Meanwhile the elder branch, though not reserved for such glorious destinies as the Guelfs, continued to flourish in Italy; the Marquises of Este were by far the most powerful nobles in eastern Lombardy, and about the end of the twelfth century began to be considered as the heads of the Church party in their neighbourhood. They were frequently chosen to the office of podestà, or chief magistrate, by the cities of Romagna; and in 1208 the people of Ferrara set the fatal example of sacrificing their freedom for tranquility by electing Azzo VII, Marquis of Este, as their lord or sovereign.[45]

Otho IV was son of Henry the Lion, and consequently head of the Guelfs. On his obtaining the imperial crown, the prejudices of Italian factions were diverted out of their usual channel. He was soon engaged in a quarrel with the Pope, whose hostility to the empire was certain, into whatever hands it might fall. In Milan, however, and generally in the cities which had belonged to the Lombard league against Frederick I, hatred of the house of Swabia prevailed more than jealousy of the imperial prerogatives; they adhered to names rather than to principles, and supported a Guelf emperor even against the Pope. Terms of this description, having no definite relation to principles which it might be troublesome to learn and defend, are always acceptable to mankind, and have the peculiar advantage of precluding altogether that spirit of compromise and accommodation by which it is sometimes endeavoured to obstruct their tendency to hate and injure each other. From this time every city, and almost every citizen, gloried in one of these barbarous denominations. In several cities the imperial party predominated through hatred of their neighbours, who espoused that of the Church. Thus the inveterate feuds between Pisa and Florence, Modena and Bologna, Cremona and Milan, threw

[44] The German origin of these celebrated factions is clearly proved by a passage in Otho of Frisingen, who lived half a century before we find the de-

nomination transferred to Italy. (Struvius, " Corpus Hist. German.," p. 378, and Muratori, A. D. 1152.)
[45] Sismondi, tome ii, p. 329.

them into opposite factions. But there was in every one of these a strong party against that which prevailed, and consequently a Guelf city frequently became Ghibelin, or conversely, according to the fluctuations of the time.[46]

The change to which we have adverted in the politics of the Guelf party lasted only during the reign of Otho IV. When the heir of the house of Swabia grew up to manhood, Innocent, who, though his guardian, had taken little care of his interests, as long as he flattered himself with the hope of finding a Guelf emperor obedient, placed the young Frederick at the head of an opposition, composed of cities always attached to his family, and of such as implicitly followed the see of Rome. He met with considerable success both in Italy and Germany, and after the death of Otho received the imperial crown. But he had no longer to expect any assistance from the Pope who conferred it. Innocent was dead, and Honorius III, his successor, could not behold without apprehension the vast power of Frederick, supported in Lombardy by a faction which balanced that of the Church, and menacing the ecclesiastical territories on the other side by the possession of Naples and Sicily. This kingdom, feudatory to Rome, and long her firmest ally, was now, by a fatal connection which she had not been able to prevent, thrown into the scale of her most dangerous enemy. Hence the temporal dominion which Innocent III had taken so much pains to establish became a very precarious possession, exposed on each side to the attacks of a power that had legitimate pretensions to almost every province composing it. The life of Frederick II was wasted in an unceasing contention with the Church and with his Italian subjects, whom she excited to rebellions against him. Without inveighing, like the popish writers, against this prince, certainly an encourager of letters, and endowed with many eminent qualities, we may lay to his charge a good deal of dissimulation; I will not add ambition, because I am not aware of any period in the reign of Frederick when he was not obliged to act on his

[46] For the Guelf and Ghibelin factions, besides the historians, the fifty-first dissertation of Muratori should be read. There is some degree of inaccuracy in his language, where he speaks of these distractions expiring at the beginning of the fifteenth century. Quel secolo, e vero, abbondò anch' esso di molte guerre, ma nulla si operò sotto nome o pretesto delle fazioni suddette. Solamente ritennero esse piede in alcune private famiglie. (" Antichità Italiane," tome iii, p. 148.) But certainly the names of Guelf and Ghibelin, as party distinctions, may be traced all through the fifteenth century. The former faction showed itself distinctly in the insurrection of the cities subject to Milan, upon the death of Gian Galeazzo Visconti in 1404. It appeared again in the attempt of the Milanese to re-establish their republic in 1447. (Sismondi, tome ix, p. 334.) So, in 1477, Ludovico Sforza made use of Ghibelin prejudices to exclude the regent Bonne of Savoy as a Guelf. (Sismondi, tome xi, p. 79.) In the ecclesiastical state the same distinctions appear to have been preserved still later. Stefano Infessura, in 1487, speaks familiarly of them. (" Script. Rer. Ital.," tome iii, p. 1221.) And even in the conquest of Milan by Louis XII, in 1500, the Guelfs of that city are represented as attached to the French party, while the Ghibelins abetted Ludovico Sforza and Maximilian. (Guicciardini, p. 399.) Other passages in the same historian show these factions to have been alive in various parts of Italy.

defence against the aggression of others. But if he had been a model of virtues, such men as Honorius III, Gregory IX, and Innocent IV, the popes with whom he had successively to contend, would not have given him respite while he remained master of Naples, as well as the empire.[47]

It was the custom of every Pope to urge princes into a crusade, which the condition of Palestine rendered indispensable, or, more properly, desperate. But this great piece of supererogatory devotion had never yet been raised into an absolute duty of their station, nor had even private persons been ever required to take up the cross by compulsion. Honorius III, however, exacted a vow from Frederick, before he conferred upon him the imperial crown, that he would undertake a crusade for the deliverance of Jerusalem. Frederick submitted to this engagement, which perhaps he never designed to keep, and certainly endeavoured afterward to evade. Though he became by marriage nominal King of Jerusalem,[48] his excellent understanding was not captivated with so barren a prospect, and at length his delays in the performance of his vow provoked Gregory IX to issue against him a sentence of excommunication. Such a thunderbolt was not to be lightly regarded; and Frederick sailed the next year for Palestine. But having disdained to solicit absolution for what he considered as no crime, the court of Rome was excited to still fiercer indignation against this profanation of a crusade by an excommunicated sovereign. Upon his arrival in Palestine, he received intelligence that the papal troops had broken into the kingdom of Naples. No one could rationally have blamed Frederick if he had quitted the Holy Land as he found it; but he made a treaty with the Saracens, which, though by no means so disadvantageous as under all the circumstances

[47] The rancour of bigoted Catholics against Frederick has hardly subsided at the present day. A very moderate commendation of him in "Tiraboschi," vol. iv, t. 7, was not suffered to pass uncontradicted by the Roman editor. And though Muratori shows quite enough prejudice against that emperor's character, a fierce Roman bigot, whose animadversions are printed in the seventeenth volume of his "Annals" (8vo edition), flies into paroxysms of fury at every syllable that looks like moderation. It is well known that, although the public policy of Rome has long displayed the pacific temper of weakness, the thermometer of ecclesiastical sentiment in that city stands very nearly as high as in the thirteenth century [1810]. Giannone, who suffered for his boldness, has drawn Frederick II very favourably, perhaps too favourably, in the sixteenth and seventeenth books of the "Istoria Civile di Napoli."

[48] The second wife of Frederick was Iolante, or Violante, daughter of John, Count of Brienne, by Maria, eldest daughter and heiress of Isabella, wife of Conrad, Marquis of Montferrat. This Isabella was the youngest daughter of Almaric or Amaury, King of Jerusalem, and by the deaths of her brother, Baldwin IV, of her eldest sister Sibilla, wife of Guy de Lusignan, and that sister's child, Baldwin V, succeeded to a claim upon Jerusalem, which, since the victories of Saladin, was not very profitable. It is said that the Kings of Naples deduce their title to that sounding inheritance from this marriage of Frederick (Giannone, l. xvi, c. 2); but the extinction of Frederick's posterity must have, strictly speaking, put an end to any right derived from him; and Giannone himself indicates a better title by the cession of Maria, a princess of Antioch, and legitimate heiress of Jerusalem, to Charles of Anjou in 1272. How far, indeed, this may have been regularly transmitted to the present King of Naples I do not know, and am sure that it is not worth while to inquire.

might have been expected, served as a pretext for new calumnies against him in Europe. The charge of irreligion, eagerly and successfully propagated, he repelled by persecuting edicts against heresy that do no great honour to his memory, and availed him little at the time. Over his Neapolitan dominions he exercised a rigorous government, rendered perhaps necessary by the levity and insubordination characteristic of the inhabitants, but which tended, through the artful representations of Honorius and Gregory, to alarm and alienate the Italian republics.

A new generation had risen up in Lombardy since the Peace of Constance, and the prerogatives reserved by that treaty to the empire were so seldom called into action that few cities were disposed to recollect their existence. They denominated themselves Guelfs or Ghibelins, according to habit, and out of their mutual opposition, but without much reference to the empire. Those, however, of the former party, and especially Milan, retained their antipathy to the house of Swabia. Though Frederick II was entitled, as far as established usage can create a right, to the sovereignty of Italy, the Milanese would never acknowledge him, nor permit his coronation at Monza, according to ancient ceremony, with the iron crown of the Lombard kings. The Pope fomented to the utmost of his power this disaffected spirit, and encouraged the Lombard cities to renew their former league. This, although conformable to a provision in the Treaty of Constance, was manifestly hostile to Frederick, and may be considered as the commencement of a second contest between the republican cities of Lombardy and the empire. But there was a striking difference between this and the former confederacy against Frederick Barbarossa. In the league of 1167 almost every city, forgetting all smaller animosities in the great cause of defending the national privileges, contributed its share of exertion to sustain that perilous conflict; and this transient unanimity in a people so distracted by internal faction as the Lombards is the surest witness to the justice of their undertaking. Sixty years afterward, their war against the second Frederick had less of provocation and less of public spirit. It was, in fact, a party struggle of Guelf and Ghibelin cities, to which the names of the Church and the empire gave more of dignity and consistence.

The republics of Italy in the thirteenth century were so numerous and independent, and their revolutions so frequent, that it is a difficult matter to avoid confusion in following their history. It will give more arrangement to our ideas, and at the same time illustrate the changes that took place in these little states, if we consider them as divided into four clusters or constellations, not, indeed, unconnected one with another, yet each having its own centre of motion and its own boundaries. The first of these we may suppose formed of the cities in central Lombardy, between the Sessia and the Adige, the Alps and the Ligurian Mountains; it comprehends Milan, Cremona, Pavia, Brescia, Bergamo, Parma, Piacenza, Mantua, Lodi, Alessandria, and several others less distinguished. These were the original seats of Italian liberty, the great movers in the wars of the elder Frederick. Milan was at the head of this cluster of cities, and her influence gave an ascendency to the Guelf party; she had, since the Treaty of Constance, rendered Lodi and Pavia almost her subjects, and was in strict union with Brescia and Piacenza. Parma, however, and Cremona, were unshaken defenders of the empire. In the second class we may place the cities of the march of Verona, between the Adige and the frontiers of Germany. Of these, there were but four worth mentioning: Verona, Vicenza, Padua, and Treviso. The citizens of all the four were inclined to the Guelf interests; but a powerful body of rural nobility, who had never been compelled, like those upon the upper Po, to quit their fortresses in the hilly country, or reside within the walls, attached themselves to the opposite denomination.[49]   Some of them obtained very great authority in the civil feuds of these four republics; and especially two brothers, Eccelin and Alberic da Romano, of a rich and distinguished family, known for its devotion to the empire. By extraordinary vigour and decision of character, by dissimulation and breach of oaths, by the intimidating effects of almost unparalleled cruelty, Eccelin da Romano became after some years the absolute master of three cities, Padua, Verona, and Vicenza; and the Guelf party, in consequence, was entirely subverted beyond the Adige during the continuance of his tyranny.[50]   Another cluster was composed of the cities in Romagna—Bologna, Imola, Faenza, Ferrara, and several others. Of these, Bologna was far the most powerful, and, as no city was more steadily for the interests of the Church, the Guelfs usually predominated in this class, to which also the influence of the house of Este not a little contributed. Modena, though not geographically within the limits of this division, may be classed along with it from her constant wars with Bologna. A fourth class will comprehend the whole of Tuscany, separated almost entirely from

[49] Sismondi, tome ii, p. 222.
[50] The cruelties of Eccelin excited universal horror in an age when inhumanity toward enemies was as common as fear and revenge could make it. It was a usual trick of beggars, all over Italy, to pretend that they had been deprived of their eyes or limbs by the Veronese tyrant. There is hardly an instance in European history of so sanguinary a government subsisting for more than twenty years. The crimes of Eccelin are remarkably well authenticated by the testimony of several contemporary writers, who enter into great details. Most of these are found in the seventh volume of "Scriptores Rerum Italicarum." Sismondi, tome iii, pp. 33, 111, 203, is more full than any of the moderns.

the politics of Lombardy and Romagna. Florence headed the Guelf cities in this province, Pisa the Ghibelin. The Tuscan union was formed, as has been said above, by Innocent III, and was strongly inclined to the popes; but gradually the Ghibelin party acquired its share of influence, and the cities of Siena, Arezzo, and Lucca shifted their policy, according to external circumstances or the fluctuations of their internal factions. The petty cities in the region of Spoleto and Ancona hardly perhaps deserve the name of republics; and Genoa does not readily fall into any of our four classes, unless her wars with Pisa may be thought to connect her with Tuscany.[51]

After several years of transient hostility and precarious truce, the Guelf cities of Lombardy engaged in a regular and protracted war with Frederick II, or, more properly, with their Ghibelin adversaries. Few events of this contest deserve particular notice. Neither party ever obtained such decisive advantages as had alternately belonged to Frederick Barbarossa and the Lombard confederacy, during the war of the preceding century. A defeat of the Milanese by the emperor at Corte Nuova, in 1237, was balanced by his unsuccessful siege at Brescia the next year. The Pisans assisted Frederick to gain a great naval victory over the Genoese fleet in 1241, but he was obliged to rise from the blockade of Parma, which had left the standard of Ghibelinism, in 1248. Ultimately, however, the strength of the house of Swabia was exhausted by so tedious a struggle; the Ghibelins of Italy had their vicissitudes of success, but their country, and even themselves, lost more and more of the ancient connection with Germany.

In this resistance to Frederick II the Lombards were much indebted to the constant support of Gregory IX and his successor, Innocent IV; and the Guelf, or the Church party, were used as synonymous terms. These pontiffs bore an unquenchable hatred to the house of Swabia. No concessions mitigated their animosity; no reconciliation was sincere. Whatever faults may be imputed to Frederick, it is impossible for any one not blindly devoted to the court of Rome to deny that he was iniquitously proscribed by her unprincipled ambition. His real crime was the inheritance of his ancestors, and the name of the house of Swabia. In 1239 he was excommunicated by Gregory IX.

[51] I have taken no notice of Piedmont in this division. The history of that country seems to be less elucidated by ancient or modern writers than that of other parts of Italy. It was at this time divided between the Counts of Savoy and Marquises of Montferrat. But Asti, Chieri, and Turin, especially the two former, appear to have had a republican form of government. They were, however, not absolutely independent. The only Piedmontese city that can properly be considered as a separate state, in the thirteenth century, was Vercelli; and even there the bishop seems to have possessed a sort of temporal sovereignty. Denina, author of the " Rivoluzioni d' Italia," first printed in 1769, lived to publish in his old age a history of western Italy, or Piedmont, from which I have gleaned a few facts. (" Istoria dell' Italia Occidentale," Torino, 1809, 6 vols., 8vo.)

14

To this he was tolerably accustomed by former experience; but
the sentence was attended by an absolution of his subjects from
their allegiance, and a formal deposition. These sentences were
not very effective upon men of vigorous minds, or upon those
whose passions were engaged in their cause; but they influenced
both those who feared the threatenings of the clergy and those
who wavered already as to their line of political conduct. In
the fluctuating state of Lombardy the excommunication of Frederick undermined his interests even in cities like Parma, that
had been friendly, and seemed to identify the cause of his enemies with that of religion—a prejudice artfully fomented by
means of calumnies propagated against himself, and which the
conduct of such leading Ghibelins as Eccelin, who lived in an
open defiance of God and man, did not contribute to lessen. In
1240 Gregory proceeded to publish a crusade against Frederick,
as if he had been an open enemy to religion; which he revenged
by putting to death all the prisoners he made who wore the
cross. There was one thing wanting to make the expulsion of
the emperor from the Christian commonwealth more complete.
Gregory IX accordingly projected, and Innocent IV carried
into effect, the convocation of a general council. This was held
at Lyons, an imperial city, but over which Frederick could no
longer retain his supremacy. In this assembly, where one hundred and forty prelates appeared, the question whether Frederick ought to be deposed was solemnly discussed; he submitted to defend himself by his advocates: and the Pope in the
presence, though without formally collecting the suffrages of
the council, pronounced a sentence, by which Frederick's excommunication was renewed, the empire and all his kingdoms
taken away, and his subjects absolved from their fidelity. This
is the most pompous act of usurpation in all the records of
the Church of Rome; and the tacit approbation of a general
council seemed to incorporate the pretended right of deposing
kings, which might have passed as a mad vaunt of Gregory
VII and his successors, with the established faith of Christendom.

Upon the death of Frederick II in 1250, he left to his son
Conrad a contest to maintain for every part of his inheritance,
as well as for the imperial crown. But the vigour of the house
of Swabia was gone; Conrad was reduced to fight for the kingdom of Naples, the only succession which he could hope to secure
against the troops of Innocent IV, who still pursued his family
with implacable hatred, and claimed that kingdom as forfeited
to its feudal superior, the Holy See. After Conrad's premature
death, which happened in 1254, the throne was filled by his illegitimate brother Manfred, who retained it by his bravery and

address, in despite of the popes, till they were compelled to call in the assistance of a more powerful arm.

The death of Conrad brings to a termination that period in Italian history which we have described as nearly coextensive with the greatness of the house of Swabia. It is perhaps, upon the whole, the most honourable to Italy; that in which she displayed the most of national energy and patriotism. A Florentine or Venetian may dwell with pleasure upon later times, but a Lombard will cast back his eye across the desert of centuries till it reposes on the field of Legnano. Great changes followed in the foreign and internal policy, in the moral and military character of Italy. But before we descend to the next period, it will be necessary to remark some material circumstances in that which has just passed under our review.

The successful resistance of the Lombard cities to such princes as both the Fredericks must astonish a reader who brings to the story of these middle ages notions derived from modern times. But when we consider not only the ineffectual control which could be exerted over a feudal army, bound only to a short term of service, and reluctantly kept in the field at its own cost, but the peculiar distrust and disaffection with which many German princes regarded the house of Swabia, less reason will appear for surprise. Nor did the kingdom of Naples, almost always in agitation, yield any material aid to the second Frederick. The main cause, however, of that triumph which attended Lombardy was the intrinsic energy of a free government. From the eleventh century, when the cities became virtually republican, they put out those vigorous shoots which are the growth of freedom alone. Their domestic feuds, their mutual wars, the fierce assaults of their national enemies, checked not their strength, their wealth, or their population; but rather as the limbs are nerved by labour and hardship, the republic of Italy grew in vigour and courage through the conflicts they sustained. If we but remember what savage license prevailed during the ages that preceded their rise, the rapine of public robbers, or of feudal nobles little differing from robbers, the contempt of industrious arts, the inadequacy of penal laws and the impossibility of carrying them into effect, we shall form some notion of the change which was wrought in the condition of Italy by the growth of its cities. In comparison with the blessings of industry protected, injustice controlled, emulation awakened, the disorders which ruffled their surface appear slight and momentary. I speak only of this first stage of their independence, and chiefly of the twelfth century, before those civil dissensions had reached their height, by which the glory and prosperity of Lombardy were soon to be subverted.

We have few authentic testimonies as to the domestic improvement of the free Italian cities, while they still deserve the name. But we may perceive by history that their power and population, according to their extent of territory, were almost incredible. In Galvaneus Flamma, a Milanese writer, we find a curious statistical account of that city in 1288, which, though of a date about thirty years after its liberties had been overthrown by usurpation, must be considered as implying a high degree of previous advancement, even if we make allowance, as probably we should, for some exaggeration. The inhabitants are reckoned at two hundred thousand; the private houses, thirteen thousand; the nobility alone dwelt in sixty streets; eight thousand gentlemen or heavy cavalry (milites) might be mustered from the city and its district, and two hundred and forty thousand men capable of arms: a force sufficient, the writer observes, to crush all the Saracens. There were in Milan six hundred notaries, two hundred physicians, eighty schoolmasters, and fifty transcribers of manuscripts. In the district were one hundred and fifty castles with adjoining villages. Such was the state of Milan, Flamma concludes, in 1288; it is not for me to say whether it has gained or lost ground since that time.[52] At this period the territory of Milan was not perhaps more extensive than the county of Surrey; it was bounded at a little distance, on almost every side, by Lodi, or Pavia, or Bergamo, or Como. It is possible, however, that Flamma may have meant to include some of these as dependencies of Milan, though not strictly united with it. How flourishing must the state of cultivation have been in such a country, which not only drew no supplies from any foreign land, but exported part of her own produce! It was in the best age of their liberties, immediately after the battle of Legnano, that the Milanese commenced the great canal which conducts the waters of the Tesino to their capital, a work very extraordinary for that time. During the same period the cities gave proofs of internal prosperity that in many instances have descended to our own observation in the solidity and magnificence of their architecture. Ecclesiastical structures were perhaps more splendid in France and England; but neither country could pretend to match the palaces and public buildings, the streets flagged with stone, the bridges of the same material, or the commodious private houses of Italy.[53]

[52] Muratori, " Script. Rerum Italic.," tome xi. This expression of Flamma may seem to intimate that Milan had declined in his time, which was about 1340. Yet as she had been continually advancing in power, and had not yet experienced any tyrannical government, I can not imagine this to have been the case; and the same Flamma, who is a great flatterer of the Visconti, and has dedicated a particular work to the praises of Azzo, asserts therein that he had greatly improved the beauty and convenience of the city, though Brescia, Cremona, and other places had declined. Azarius, too, a writer of the same age, makes a similar representation. (" Script. Rer. Ital.," tome xvi, pp. 314, 317.) Of Luchino Visconti he says, Statum Mediolani reintegravit in tantum, quod non civitas, sed provincia videbatur.

[53] Sismondi, tome iv, p. 176; Tirabos-

The courage of these cities was wrought sometimes to a tone of insolent defiance through the security inspired by their means of defence. From the time of the Romans to that when the use of gunpowder came to prevail little change was made, or perhaps could be made, in that part of military science which relates to the attack and defence of fortified places. We find precisely the same engines of offence: the cumbrous towers, from which arrows were shot at the besieged, the machines from which stones were discharged, the battering-rams which assailed the walls, and the basket-work covering (the vinea or testudo of the ancients, and the gattus or chat-chateil of the middle ages) under which those who pushed the battering engines were protected from the enemy. On the other hand, a city was fortified with a strong wall of brick or marble, with towers raised upon it at intervals, and a deep moat in front. Sometimes the antemural or barbacan was added; a rampart of less height, which impeded the approach of the hostile engines. The gates were guarded with a portcullis; an invention which, as well as the barbacan, was borrowed from the Saracens.[54] With such advantages for defence, a numerous and intrepid body of burghers might not unreasonably stand at bay against a powerful army; and as the consequences of capture were most terrible, while resistance was seldom hopeless, we can not wonder at the desperate bravery of so many besieged towns. Indeed, it seldom happened that one of considerable size was taken except by famine or treachery. Tortona did not submit to Frederick Barbarossa till the besiegers had corrupted with sulphur the only fountain that supplied the citizens; nor Crema till her walls were overtopped by the battering engines. Ancona held out a noble example of sustaining the pressure of extreme famine. Brescia tried all the resources of a skilful engineer against the second Frederick; and swerved not from her steadiness when that prince, imitating an atrocious precedent of his grandfather at the siege of Crema, exposed his prisoners upon his battering engines to the stones that were hurled by their fellow-citizens upon the walls.[55]

Of the government which existed in the republics of Italy during the twelfth and thirteenth centuries no definite sketch can be traced. The chroniclers of those times are few and jejune; and, as is usual with contemporaries, rather intimate than describe the civil polity of their respective countries. It would, indeed, be a weary task, if it were even possible, to delineate

chi, tome iv, p. 426. See also the observations of Denina on the population and agriculture of Italy (l. xiv, c. 9, 10), chiefly, indeed, applicable to a period rather later than that of her free republics.

[54] Muratori, "Antiquit. Ital.," Dissert. 26.

[55] See these sieges in the second and third volumes of Sismondi. That of Ancona, tome ii, pp. 145–206, is told with remarkable elegance, and several interesting circumstances.

the constitutions of thirty or forty little states which were in perpetual fluctuation. The magistrates elected in almost all of them,
when they first began to shake off the jurisdiction of their count
or bishop, were styled consuls; a word very expressive to an
Italian ear, since in the darkest ages tradition must have preserved some acquaintance with the republican government of
Rome.[56] The consuls were always annual; and their office comprehended the command of the national militia in war, as well
as the administration of justice and preservation of public order;
but their number was various—two, four, six, or even twelve.
In their legislative and deliberative councils the Lombards still
copied the Roman constitution, or perhaps fell naturally into the
form most calculated to unite sound discretion with the exercise
of popular sovereignty. A council of trust and secrecy (della
credenza) was composed of a small number of persons, who took
the management of public affairs, and may be called the ministers of the state. But the decision upon matters of general
importance, treaties of alliance or declarations of war, the choice
of consuls, or ambassadors, belonged to the general council.
This appears not to have been uniformly constituted in every
city, and according to its composition the government was more
or less democratical. An ultimate sovereignty, however, was reserved to the mass of the people, and a parliament or general
assembly was held to deliberate on any change in the form of
constitution.[57]

About the end of the twelfth century a new and singular species of magistracy was introduced into the Lombard cities. During the tyranny of Frederick I he had appointed officers of his
own, called podestàs, instead of the elective consuls. It is remarkable that this memorial of despotic power should not have
excited insuperable alarm and disgust in the free republics. But,
on the contrary, they almost universally, after the Peace of Constance, revived an office which had been abrogated when they
first rose in rebellion against Frederick. From experience, as
we must presume, of the partiality which their domestic factions
carried into the administration of justice, it became a general
practice to elect, by the name of podestà, a citizen of some neighbouring state as their general, their criminal judge, and pre-
server of the peace. The last duty was frequently arduous, and
required a vigorous as well as an upright magistrate. Offences
against the laws and security of the commonwealth were during
the middle ages as often, perhaps more often, committed by the

[56] Landulf, the younger, whose history
of Milan extends from 1094 to 1133, calls
himself publicorum officiorum particeps
et   consulum   epistolarum   dictator.
("Script. Rer. Ital.," tome v, p. 486.)

This is, I believe, the earliest mention
of those magistrates. (Muratori, "Annali d' Italia," A. D. 1107.)
[57] Muratori, Dissert. 46 and 52; Sismondi, tome i, p. 385.

rich and powerful than by the inferior class of society. Rude and licentious manners, family feuds and private revenge, or the mere insolence of strength, rendered the execution of criminal justice practically and in every day's experience, what is now little required, a necessary protection to the poor against oppression. The sentence of a magistrate against a powerful offender was not pronounced without danger of tumult; it was seldom executed without force. A convicted criminal was not, as at present, the stricken deer of society, whose disgrace his kindred shrink from participating, and whose memory they strive to forget. Imputing his sentence to iniquity, or glorying in an act which the laws of his fellow-citizens, but not their sentiments, condemned, he stood upon his defence amid a circle of friends. The law was to be enforced not against an individual, but a family —not against a family, but a faction—not perhaps against a local faction, but the whole Guelf or Ghibelin name, which might become interested in the quarrel. The podestà was to arm the republic against her refractory citizen; his house was to be besieged and razed to the ground, his defenders to be quelled by violence: and thus the people, become familiar with outrage and homicide under the command of their magistrates, were more disposed to repeat such scenes at the instigation of their passions.[58]

The podestà was sometimes chosen in a general assembly, sometimes by a select number of citizens. His office was annual, though prolonged in peculiar emergencies. He was invariably a man of noble family, even in those cities which excluded their own nobility from any share in the government. He received a fixed salary, and was compelled to remain in the city after the expiration of his office for the purpose of answering such charges as might be adduced against his conduct. He could neither marry a native of the city, nor have any relation resident within the district, nor even, so great was their jealousy, eat or drink in the house of any citizen. The authority of these foreign magistrates was not by any means alike in all cities. In some he seems to have superseded the consuls, and commanded the armies in war. In others, as Milan and Florence, his authority was merely judicial. We find in some of the old annals the years headed by the names of the podestàs, as by those of the consuls in the history of Rome.[59]

The effects of the evil spirit of discord that had so fatally breathed upon the republics of Lombardy were by no means confined to national interests, or to the grand distinction of Guelf

[58] Sismondi, tome iii, p. 258, from whom the substance of these observations is borrowed. They may be copiously illus-

trated by Villani's history of Florence and Stella's annals of Genoa.
[59] Muratori, Dissert. 46.

and Ghibelin. Dissensions glowed in the heart of every city, and as the danger of foreign war became distant, these grew more fierce and unappeasable. The feudal system had been established upon the principle of territorial aristocracy; it maintained the authority, it encouraged the pride of rank. Hence, when the rural nobility were compelled to take up their residence in cities, they preserved the ascendency of birth and riches. From the natural respect which is shown to these advantages, all offices of trust and command were shared among them; it is not material whether this were by positive right or continual usage. A limited aristocracy of this description, where the inferior citizens possess the right of selecting their magistrates by free suffrage from a numerous body of nobles, is not among the worst forms of government, and affords no contemptible security against oppression and anarchy. This regimen appears to have prevailed in most of the Lombard cities during the eleventh and twelfth centuries; though, in so great a deficiency of authentic materials, it would be too peremptory to assert this as an unequivocal truth. There is one very early instance, in the year 1041, of a civil war at Milan between the capitanei, or vassals of the empire, and the plebeian burgesses, which was appeased by the mediation of Henry III. This is ascribed to the ill treatment which the latter experienced—as was usual, indeed, in all parts of Europe, but which was endured with inevitable submission everywhere else. In this civil war, which lasted three years, the nobility were obliged to leave Milan and carry on the contest in the adjacent plains; and one of their class, by name Lanzon, whether moved by ambition or by virtuous indignation against tyranny, put himself at the head of the people.[60]

From this time we scarcely find any mention of dissensions among the two orders till after the Peace of Constance—a proof, however defective the contemporary annals may be, that such disturbances had neither been frequent nor serious. A schism between the nobles and people is noticed to have occurred at Faenza in 1185. A serious civil war of some duration broke out between them at Brescia in 1200. From this time mutual jealousies interrupted the domestic tranquility of other cities, but it is about 1220 that they appear to have taken a decided aspect of civil war; within a few years of that epoch the question of aristocratical or popular command was tried by arms in Milan, Piacenza, Modena, Cremona, and Bologna.[61]

It would be in vain to enter upon the merits of these feuds, which the meagre historians of the time are seldom much dis-

---

[60] Landulfus, "Hist. Mediolan.," in "Script. Rerum Ital.," tome iv, p. 86; Muratori, Dissert. 52; "Annali d' Italia," A. D. 1041; St Marc, tome iii, p. 94.

[61] Sismondi, tome ii, p. 444; Muratori, "Annali d' Italia," A. D. 1185, etc.

posed to elucidate, and which they saw with their own prejudices. A writer of the present age would show little philosophy if he were to heat his passions by the reflection, as it were, of those forgotten animosities, and aggravate, like a partial contemporary, the failings of one or another faction. We have no need of positive testimony to acquaint us with the general tenor of their history. We know that a nobility is always insolent, that a populace is always intemperate; and may safely presume that the former began, as the latter ended, by injustice and abuse of power. At one time the aristocracy, not content with seeing the annual magistrates selected from their body, would endeavour by usurpation to exclude the bulk of the citizens from suffrage. At another, the merchants, grown proud by riches, and confident of their strength, would aim at obtaining the honours of the state, which had been reserved to the nobility. This is the inevitable consequence of commercial wealth, and, indeed, of freedom and social order, which are the parents of wealth. There is in the progress of civilization a term at which exclusive privileges must be relaxed, or the possessors must perish along with them. In one or two cities a temporary compromise was made through the intervention of the Pope, whereby offices of public trust, from the highest to the lowest, were divided, in equal proportions, or otherwise, between the nobles and the people. This also is no bad expedient, and proved singularly efficacious in appeasing the dissensions of ancient Rome.

There is, however, a natural preponderance in the popular scale, which, in a fair trial, invariably gains on that of the less numerous class. The artisans, who composed the bulk of the populations, were arranged in companies according to their occupations. Sometimes, as at Milan, they formed separate associations, with rules for their internal government.[62] The clubs, called at Milan La Motta and La Credenza, obtained a degree of weight not at all surprising to those who consider the spirit of mutual attachment which belongs to such fraternities, and we shall see a more striking instance of this hereafter in the republic of Florence. To so formidable and organized a democracy the nobles opposed their numerous families, the generous spirit that belongs to high birth, the influence of wealth and established name. The members of each distinguished family appear to have lived in the same street; their houses were fortified with square massive towers of commanding height, and wore the semblance of castles within the walls of a city. Brancaleon, the famous senator of Rome, destroyed one hundred and forty of these domestic intrenchments, which were constantly serving the purpose of civil broils and outrage. Expelled, as frequently

---

[62] Muratori, Dissert. 52; Sismondi, tome iii, p. 262.

happened, from the city, it was in the power of the nobles to
avail themselves of their superiority in the use of cavalry, and
to lay waste the district, till weariness of an unprofitable contention reduced the citizens to terms of compromise. But when
all these resources were ineffectual, they were tempted or forced
to sacrifice the public liberty to their own welfare, and lent their
aid to a foreign master or a domestic usurper.

In all these scenes of turbulence, whether the contest was
between the nobles and people or the Guelf or Ghibelin factions, no mercy was shown by the conquerors. The vanquished
lost their homes and fortunes, and, retiring to other cities of
their own party, waited for the opportunity of revenge. In a
popular tumult the houses of the beaten side were frequently
levelled to the ground—not perhaps from a sort of senseless
fury, which Muratori inveighs against, but on account of the
injury which these fortified houses inflicted upon the lower citizens. The most deadly hatred is that which men exasperated by
proscription and forfeiture bear to their country; nor have we
need to ask any other cause for the calamities of Italy than the
bitterness with which an unsuccessful faction was thus pursued
into banishment. When the Ghibelins were returning to Florence, after a defeat given to the prevailing party in 1260, it was
proposed among them to demolish the city itself which had cast
them out; and but for the persuasion of one man, Farinata degl'
Uberti, their revenge would have thus extinguished all patriotism.[63] It is to this that we must ascribe their proneness to call
in assistance from every side, and to invite any servitude for
the sake of retaliating upon their adversaries. The simple love
of public liberty is in general, I fear, too abstract a passion to
glow warmly in the human breast; and, though often invigorated
as well as determined by personal animosities and predilections,
is as frequently extinguished by the same cause.

Independently of the two leading differences which embattled
the citizens of an Italian state, their form of government and
their relation to the empire, there were others more contemptible
though not less mischievous. In every city the quarrels of private families became the foundation of general schism, sedition,
and proscription. Sometimes these blended themselves with the
grand distinctions of Guelf and Ghibelin; sometimes they were
more nakedly conspicuous. This may be illustrated by one or
two prominent examples. Imilda de' Lambertazzi, a noble young
lady at Bologna, was surprised by her brothers in a secret interview with Boniface Gieremei, whose family had long been sepa-

[63] G. Villani, l. vi, c. 82; Sismondi.
I can not forgive Dante for placing this
patriot trà l' anime più nere, in one of
the worst regions of his " Inferno." The
conversation of the poet with Farinata,
canto 10, is very fine, and illustrative of
Florentine history.

rated by the most inveterate enmity from her own. She had just time to escape, while the Lambertazzi despatched her lover with their poisoned daggers. On her return she found his body still warm, and a faint hope suggested the remedy of sucking the venom from his wounds. But it only communicated itself to her own veins, and they were found by her attendants stretched lifeless by each other's side. So cruel an outrage wrought the Gieremei to madness; they formed alliances with some neighbouring republics; the Lambertazzi took the same measures; and after a fight in the streets of Bologna, of forty days' duration, the latter were driven out of the city, with all the Ghibelins, their political associates. Twelve thousand citizens were condemned to banishment, their houses razed, and their estates confiscated.[64] Florence was at rest till, in 1215, the assassination of an individual produced a mortal feud between the families Buondelmonti and Uberti, in which all the city took a part. An outrage committed at Pistoja in 1300 split the inhabitants into the parties of Bianchi and Neri; and these, spreading to Florence, created one of the most virulent divisions which annoyed that republic. In one of the changes which attended this little ramification of faction, Florence expelled a young citizen who had borne offices of magistracy, and espoused the cause of the Bianchi. Dante Alighieri retired to the courts of some Ghibelin princes, where his sublime and inventive mind, in the gloom of exile, completed that original combination of vast and extravagant conceptions with keen political satire, which has given immortality to his name, and even lustre to the petty contests of his time.[65]

In the earlier stages of the Lombard republics their differences, as well mutual as domestic, had been frequently appeased by the mediation of the emperors; and the loss of this salutary influence may be considered as no slight evil attached to that absolute emancipation which Italy attained in the thirteenth century. The popes sometimes endeavoured to interpose an authority which, though not quite so direct, was held in greater veneration; and if their own tempers had been always pure from the selfish and vindictive passions of those whom they influenced, might have produced more general and permanent good. But they considered the Ghibelins as their own peculiar enemies, and the triumph of the opposite faction as the Church's best security. Gregory X and Nicholas III, whether from benevolent motives, or because their jealousy of Charles of Anjou, while at the head of the Guelfs, suggested the revival of a Ghibelin party as a coun-

[64] Sismondi, tome iii, p. 442. This story may suggest that of Romeo and Juliet, itself founded upon an Italian novel, and not an unnatural picture of manners.

[65] Dino Compagni, in " Scr. Rer. Ital.," tome ix; Villani, " Ist. Fiorent.," l. viii; Dante, passim.

terpoise to his power, distinguished their pontificate by enforcing measures of reconciliation in all Italian cities; but their successors returned to the ancient policy and prejudices of Rome.

The singular history of an individual far less elevated in station than popes or emperors, Fra Giovanni di Vicenza, belongs to these times and to this subject. This Dominican friar began his career at Bologna in 1233, preaching the cessation of war and forgiveness of injuries. He repaired from thence to Padua, to Verona, and the neighbouring cities. At his command men laid down their instruments of war and embraced their enemies. With that susceptibility of transient impulse natural to popular governments, several republics implored him to reform their laws and to settle their differences. A general meeting was summoned in the plain of Paquara, upon the banks of the Adige. The Lombards poured themselves forth from Romagna and the cities of the March; Guelfs and Ghibelins, nobles and burghers, free citizens and tenantry of feudal lords, marshalled around their carroccios, caught from the lips of the preacher the allusive promise of universal peace. They submitted to agreements dictated by Fra Giovanni, which contain little else than a mutual amnesty; whether it were that their quarrels had been really without object, or that he had dexterously avoided to determine the real points of contention. But power and reputation suddenly acquired are transitory. Not satisfied with being the legislator and arbiter of Italian cities, he aimed at becoming their master, and abused the enthusiasm of Vicenza and Verona to obtain a grant of absolute sovereignty. Changed from an apostle to a usurper, the fate of Fra Giovanni might be predicted; and he speedily gave place to those who, though they made a worse use of their power, had, in the eyes of mankind, more natural pretensions to possess it.[66]

From the death of Frederick II in 1250 to the invasion of Charles VIII in 1494 a long and undistinguished period occurs, which it is impossible to break into any natural divisions. It is an age in many respects highly brilliant: the age of poetry and letters, of art, and of continual improvement. Italy displayed an intellectual superiority in this period over the transalpine nations which certainly had not appeared since the destruction of the Roman Empire. But her political history presents a labyrinth of petty facts so obscure and of so little influence as not to arrest the attention, so intricate and incapable of classification as to leave only confusion in the memory. The general events that are worthy of notice, and give a character to this long period, are the establishment of small tyrannies upon the

[66] Tiraboschi, "Storia della Letteratura," tome iv, page 214 (a very well- written account); Sismondi, tome ii, page 484.

ruins of republican government in most of the cities, the gradual
rise of three considerable states—Milan, Florence, and Venice—
the naval and commercial rivalry between the last city and Genoa,
the final acquisition by the popes of their present territorial
sovereignty, and the revolutions in the kingdom of Naples under
the lines of Anjou and Aragon.

After the death of Frederick II the distinctions of Guelf and
Ghibelin became destitute of all rational meaning. The most
odious crimes were constantly perpetrated, and the utmost miseries endured, for an echo and a shade that mocked the deluded
enthusiasts of faction. None of the Guelfs denied the nominal
but indefinite sovereignty of the empire; and beyond a name the
Ghibelins themselves would have been little disposed to carry it.
But the virulent hatred attached to these words grew continually
more implacable, till ages of ignominy and tyrannical government had extinguished every energetic passion in the bosoms
of a degraded people.

In the fall of the house of Swabia Rome appeared to have
consummated her triumph; and, although the Ghibelin party
was for a little time able to maintain itself, and even to gain
ground in the north of Italy, yet two events that occurred not
long afterward restored the ascendency of their adversaries. The
first of these was the fall of Eccelin da Romano, whose rapid
successes in Lombardy appeared to threaten the establishment
of a tremendous despotism, and induced a temporary union of
Guelf and Ghibelin states, by which he was overthrown. The
next and far more important was the change of dynasty in Naples.
This kingdom had been occupied, after the death of Conrad,
by his illegitimate brother, Manfred, in the behalf, as he at
first pretended, of young Conradin the heir, but in fact as his
own acquisition. He was a prince of an active and firm mind,
well fitted for his difficult post, to whom the Ghibelins looked
up as their head and as the representative of his father. It was
a natural object with the popes, independently of their ill will
toward a son of Frederick II, to see a sovereign on whom they
could better rely placed upon so neighbouring a throne. Charles,
Count of Anjou, brother of St. Louis, was tempted by them to
lead a crusade (for as such all wars for the interest of Rome were
now considered) against the Neapolitan usurper. The chance
of a battle decided the fate of Naples, and had a striking influence upon the history of Europe for several centuries. Manfred
was killed in the field: but there remained the legitimate heir
of the Fredericks, a boy of seventeen years old, Conradin, son
of Conrad, who rashly, as we say at least after the event, attempted to regain his inheritance. He fell into the hands of
Charles; and the voice of those rude ages, as well as of a more

enlightened posterity, has united in branding with everlasting infamy the name of that prince, who did not hesitate to purchase the security of his own title by the public execution of an honourable competitor, or rather a rightful claimant of the throne he had usurped. With Conradin the house of Swabia was extinguished; but Constance, the daughter of Manfred, had transported his right to Sicily and Naples into the house of Aragon, by her marriage with Peter III.

This success of a monarch selected by the Roman pontiffs as their particular champion turned the tide of faction over all Italy. He expelled the Ghibelins from Florence, of which they had a few years before obtained a complete command by means of their memorable victory upon the river Arbia. After the fall of Conradin, that party was everywhere discouraged. Germany held out small hopes of support, even when the imperial throne, which had long been vacant, should be filled by one of her princes. The populace were in almost every city attached to the Church and to the name of Guelf; the Kings of Naples employed their arms, and the popes their excommunications, so that for the remainder of the thirteenth century the name of Ghibelin was a term of proscription in the majority of Lombard and Tuscan republics. Charles was constituted by the Pope vicar-general in Tuscany. This was a new pretension of the Roman pontiffs, to name the lieutenants of the empire during its vacancy, which, indeed, could not be completely filled up without their consent. It soon, however, became evident that he aimed at the sovereignty of Italy. Some of the popes themselves, Gregory X and Nicholas IV, grew jealous of their own creature. At the Congress of Cremona, in 1269, it was proposed to confer upon Charles the seigniory of all the Guelf cities, but the greater part were prudent enough to choose him rather as a friend than a master.[67]

The cities of Lombardy, however, of either denomination, were no longer influenced by that generous disdain of one man's will which is to republican governments what chastity is to women—a conservative principle, never to be reasoned upon or subjected to calculations of utility. By force, or stratagem, or free consent, almost all the Lombard republics had already fallen under the yoke of some leading citizen, who became the lord (signore), or, in the German sense, tyrant of his country. The

[67] Sismondi, tome iii, p. 417. Several, however, including Milan, took an oath of fidelity to Charles the same year. (Ibid.) In 1273 he was Lord of Alessandria and Piacenza, and received tribute from Milan, Bologna, and most Lombard cities. (Muratori.) It was evidently his intention to avail himself of the vacancy of the empire, and either to acquire that title himself or at least to stand in the same relation as the emperors had done to the Italian states; which, according to the usage of the twelfth and thirteenth centuries, left them in possession of everything that we call independence, with the reservation of a nominal allegiance.

first instance of a voluntary delegation of sovereignty was that above mentioned of Ferrara, which placed itself under the Lord of Este. Eccelin made himself truly the tyrant of the cities beyond the Adige; and such experience ought naturally to have inspired the Italians with more universal abhorrence of despotism. But every danger appeared trivial in the eyes of exasperated factions when compared with the ascendency of their adversaries. Weary of unceasing and useless contests, in which ruin fell with an alternate but equal hand upon either party, Liberty withdrew from a people who disgraced her name; and the tumultuous, the brave, the intractable Lombards became eager to submit themselves to a master, and patient under the heaviest oppression. Or, if tyranny sometimes overstepped the limits of forbearance, and a seditious rising expelled the reigning prince, it was only to produce a change of hands, and transfer the impotent people to a different, and perhaps a worse, despotism.[68] In many cities not a conspiracy was planned, not a sigh was breathed, in favour of republican government after once they had passed under the sway of a single person. The progress, indeed, was gradual, though sure, from limited to absolute, from temporary to hereditary power, from a just and conciliating rule to extortion and cruelty. But before the middle of the fourteenth century, at the latest, all those cities which had spurned at the faintest mark of submission to the emperors lost even the recollection of self-government, and were bequeathed, like an undoubted patrimony, among the children of their new lords. Such is the progress of usurpation; and such the vengeance that Heaven reserves for those who waste in license and faction its first of social blessings, liberty.[69]

The city most distinguished in both wars against the house of Swabia, for an unconquerable attachment to republican institutions, was the first to sacrifice them in a few years after the death of Frederick II. Milan had for a considerable time been agitated by civil dissensions between the nobility and inferior

[68] See an instance of the manner in which one tyrant was exchanged for another in the fate of Passerino Bonaccorsi, Lord of Mantua, in 1328. Luigi di Gonzaga surprised him, rode the city (corse la città) with a troop of horse, crying, "Viva il popolo, e muoja Messer Passerino e le sue gabelle!" killed Passerino upon the spot, put his son to death in cold blood, e poi si fece signore della terra. Villani, l. x, c. 99, observes, like a good republican, that God had fulfilled in this the words of his Gospel (query, what Gospel?), I will slay my enemy by my enemy — abbattendo l'uno tiranno per l'altro.
[69] See the observations of Sismondi, tome iv, p. 212, on the conduct of the

Lombard signori (I know not of any English word that characterizes them, except tyrant in its primitive sense) during the first period of their dominion. They were generally chosen in an assembly of the people, sometimes for a short term, prolonged in the same manner. The people was consulted upon several occasions. At Milan there was a council of 900 nobles, not permanent or representative, but selected and convened at the discretion of the government, throughout the reigns of the Visconti. (Corio, pp. 519, 583.) Thus, as Sismondi remarks, they respected the sovereignty of the people, while they destroyed its liberty.

citizens. These parties were pretty equally balanced, and their success was consequently alternate. Each had its own podestà, as a party leader, distinct from the legitimate magistrate of the city. At the head of the nobility was their archbishop, Fra Leon Perego; the people chose Martin della Torre, one of a noble family which had ambitiously sided with the democratic faction. In consequence of the crime of a nobleman, who had murdered one of his creditors, the two parties took up arms in 1257. A civil war, of various success, and interrupted by several pacifications, which in that unhappy temper could not be durable, was terminated in about two years by the entire discomfiture of the aristocracy, and by the election of Martin della Torre as chief and lord (capitano e signore) of the people. Though the Milanese did not probably intend to renounce the sovereignty resident in their general assemblies, yet they soon lost the republican spirit; five in succession of the family Della Torre might be said to reign in Milan, each, indeed, by a formal election, but with an implied recognition of a sort of hereditary title. Twenty years afterward the Visconti, a family of opposite interests, supplanted the Torriani at Milan, and the rivalry between these great houses was not at an end till the final establishment of Matteo Visconti in 1313; but the people were not otherwise considered than as aiding by force the one or other party, and at most deciding between the pretensions of their masters.

The vigour and concert infused into the Guelf party by the successes of Charles of Anjou were not very durable. That prince was soon involved in a protracted and unfortunate quarrel with the Kings of Aragon, to whose protection his revolted subjects in Italy had recurred. On the other hand, several men of energetic character retrieved the Ghibelin interests in Lombardy, and even in the Tuscan cities. The Visconti were acknowledged heads of that faction. A family early established as Lords of Verona, the Della Scala, maintained the credit of the same denomination between the Adige and the Adriatic. Castruccio Castrucani, an adventurer of remarkable ability, rendered himself Prince of Lucca, and drew over a formidable accession to the imperial side from the heart of the Church party in Tuscany, though his death restored the ancient order of things. The inferior tyrants were partly Guelf, partly Ghibelin, according to local revolutions; but, upon the whole, the latter acquired a gradual ascendency. Those, indeed, who cared for the independence of Italy, or for their own power, had far less to fear from the phantom of imperial prerogatives, long intermitted and incapable of being enforced, than from the new race of foreign princes whom the Church had substituted for the house of Swabia.

The Angevin Kings of Naples were sovereigns of Provence, and from thence easily encroached upon Piedmont, and threatened the Milanese. Robert, the third of this line, almost openly aspired, like his grandfather, Charles I, to a real sovereignty over Italy. His offers of assistance to Guelf cities in war were always coupled with a demand of the sovereignty. Many yielded to his ambition; and even Florence twice bestowed upon him a temporary dictatorship. In 1314 he was acknowledged Lord of Lucca, Florence, Pavia, Alessandria, Bergamo, and the cities of Romagna. In 1318 the Guelfs of Genoa found no other resource against the Ghibelin emigrants who were under their walls than to resign their liberties to the King of Naples for the term of ten years, which he procured to be renewed for six more. The Avignon popes, especially John XXII, out of blind hatred to the Emperor Louis of Bavaria and the Visconti family, abetted all these measures of ambition. But they were rendered abortive by Robert's death and the subsequent disturbances of his kingdom.

At the latter end of the thirteenth century there were almost as many princes in the north of Italy as there had been free cities in the preceding age. Their equality, and the frequent domestic revolutions which made their seat unsteady, kept them for a while from encroaching on each other. Gradually, however, they became less numerous: a number of obscure tyrants were swept away from the smaller cities; and the people, careless or hopeless of liberty, were glad to exchange the rule of despicable petty usurpers for that of more distinguished and powerful families. About the year 1350 the central parts of Lombardy had fallen under the dominion of the Visconti. Four other houses occupied the second rank: that of Este at Ferrara and Modena; of Scala at Verona, which under Cane and Mastino della Scala had seemed likely to contest with the Lords of Milan the supremacy over Lombardy; of Carrara at Padua, which later than any Lombard city had resigned her liberty; and of Gonzaga at Mantua, which, without ever obtaining any material extension of territory, continued, probably for that reason, to reign undisturbed till the eighteenth century. But these united were hardly a match, as they sometimes experienced, for the Visconti. That family, the object of every league formed in Italy for more than fifty years, in constant hostility to the Church, and well inured to interdicts and excommunications, producing no one man of military talents, but fertile of tyrants detested for their perfidiousness and cruelty, was nevertheless enabled, with almost uninterrupted success, to add city after city to the dominion of Milan till it absorbed all the north of Italy. Under Gian Galeazzo, whose reign began in 1385, the viper (their armorial bearing)

15

assumed, indeed, a menacing attitude: [70] he overturned the great family of Scala, and annexed their extensive possessions to his own; no power intervened from Vercelli in Piedmont to Feltre and Belluno, while the free cities of Tuscany, Pisa, Siena, Perugia, and even Bologna, as if by a kind of witchcraft, voluntarily called in a dissembling tyrant as their master.

Powerful as the Visconti were in Italy, they were long in washing out the tinge of recent usurpation which humbled them before the legitimate dynasties of Europe. At the siege of Genoa, in 1318, Robert, King of Naples, rejected with contempt the challenge of Marco Visconti to decide their quarrel in single combat.[71] But the pride of sovereigns, like that of private men, is easily set aside for their interest. Galeazzo Visconti purchased with one hundred thousand florins a daughter of France for his son, which the French historians mention as a deplorable humiliation for their crown. A few years afterward, Lionel, Duke of Clarence, second son of Edward III, certainly not an inferior match, espoused Galeazzo's daughter. Both these connections were short-lived; but the union of Valentine, daughter of Gian Galeazzo, with the Duke of Orleans, in 1389, produced far more important consequences, and served to transmit a claim to her descendants, Louis XII and Francis I, from which the long calamities of Italy at the beginning of the sixteenth century were chiefly derived. Not long after this marriage the Visconti were tacitly admitted among the reigning princes by the erection of Milan into a duchy under letters-patent of the Emperor Wenceslaus.[72]

The imperial authority over Italy was almost entirely suspended after the death of Frederick II. A long interregnum followed in Germany; and when the vacancy was supplied by Rodolph of Hapsburg, he was too prudent to dissipate his moderate resources where the great house of Swabia had failed. About forty years afterward the Emperor Henry of Luxemburg, a prince, like Rodolph, of small hereditary possessions, but active and discreet, availed himself of the ancient respect borne to the imperial name and the mutual jealousies of the Italians, to recover for a very short time a remarkable influence. But, though professing neutrality and desire of union between the Guelfs and Ghibelins, he could not succeed in removing the distrust of the former; his exigencies impelled him to large demands of money, and the Italians, when they counted his scanty German cavalry,

---

[70] Allusions to heraldry are very common in the Italian writers. All the historians of the fourteenth century habitually use the viper, il biscione, as a synonym for the power of Milan.

[71] Della qual cosa il Rè molto sdegne ne prese. (Villani, l. ix, c. 93.) It was reckoned a misalliance, as Dante tells us, in the widow of Nino di Gallura, a nobleman of Pisa, though a sort of prince in Sardinia, to marry one of the Visconti. ("Purgatorio," canto viii.)

[72] Corio, p. 538.

perceived that obedience was altogether a matter of their own choice. Henry died, however, in time to save himself from any decisive reverse. His successors, Louis of Bavaria and Charles IV, descended from the Alps with similar motives, but after some temporary good fortune were obliged to return, not without discredit. Yet the Italians never broke that almost invisible thread which connected them with Germany; the fallacious name of Roman emperor still challenged their allegiance, though conferred by seven Teutonic electors without their concurrence. Even Florence, the most independent and high-spirited of republics, was induced to make a treaty with Charles IV in 1355, which, while it confirmed all her actual liberties, not a little, by that very confirmation, affected her sovereignty.[73] This deference to the supposed prerogatives of the empire, even while they were least formidable, was partly owing to jealousy of French or Neapolitan interference, partly by the national hatred of the popes who had seceded to Avignon, and in some degree to a misplaced respect for antiquity, to which the revival of letters had given birth. The great civilians, and the much greater poets, of the fourteenth century, taught Italy to consider her emperor as a dormant sovereign, to whom her various principalities and republics were subordinate, and during whose absence alone they had legitimate authority.

In one part, however, of that country the empire had, soon after the commencement of this period, spontaneously renounced its sovereignty. From the era of Pepin's donation, confirmed and extended by many subsequent charters, the Holy See had tolerably just pretensions to the province entitled Romagna, or the exarchate of Ravenna. But the popes, whose menaces were dreaded at the extremities of Europe, were still very weak as temporal princes. Even Innocent III had never been able to obtain possession of this part of St. Peter's patrimony. The circumstances of Rodolph's accession inspired Nicholas III with more confidence. That emperor granted a confirmation of every-

[73] The republic of Florence was at this time in considerable peril from a coalition of the Tuscan cities against her, which rendered the protection of the emperor convenient. But it was very reluctantly that she acquiesced in even a nominal submission to his authority. The Florentine envoys, in their first address, would only use the words, Santa Corona, or Serenissimo Principe; senza ricordarlo imperadore, o dimostrargli alcuna reverenza di suggezzione, domandando che il commune di Firenze volea essendogli ubbidiente, le cotali e le cotali franchigie per mantenere il suo popolo nell' usata libertade. (Mat. Villani, p. 274; "Script. Rer. Ital.," tome xiv.) This style made Charles angry; and the city soon atoned for it by accepting his privi-

lege. In this, it must be owned, he assumes a decided tone of sovereignty. The gonfalonier and priors are declared to be his vicars. The deputies of the city did homage and swore obedience. Circumstances induced the principal citizens to make this submission, which they knew to be merely nominal. But the high-spirited people, not so indifferent about names, came into it very unwillingly. The treaty was seven times proposed, and as often rejected, in the consiglio dei popolo, before their feelings were subdued. Its publication was received with no marks of joy. The public buildings alone were illuminated: but a sad silence indicated the wounded pride of every private citizen. (M. Villani, pp. 286, 290; Sismondi, tome vi, p. 238.)

thing included in the donations of Louis I, Otho, and his other predecessors, but was still reluctant or ashamed to renounce his imperial rights. Accordingly, his charter is expressed to be granted without diminution of the empire (sine demembratione imperii), and his chancellor received an oath of fidelity from the cities of Romagna. But the Pope insisting firmly on his own claim, Rodolph discreetly avoided involving himself in a fatal quarrel, and in 1278 absolutely released the imperial supremacy over all the dominions already granted to the Holy See.[74]

This is a leading epoch in the temporal monarchy of Rome. But she stood only in the place of the emperor; and her ultimate sovereignty was compatible with the practicable independence of the free cities, or of the usurpers who had risen up among them. Bologna, Faenza, Rimini, and Ravenna, with many others less considerable, took an oath indeed to the Pope, but continued to regulate both their internal concerns and foreign relations at their own discretion. The first of these cities was far preeminent above the rest for population and renown, and, though not without several intermissions, preserved a republican character till the end of the fourteenth century. The rest were soon enslaved by petty tyrants, more obscure than those of Lombardy. It was not easy for the pontiffs of Avignon to reinstate themselves in a dominion which they seemed to have abandoned; but they made several attempts to recover it, sometimes with spiritual arms, sometimes with the more efficacious aid of mercenary troops. The annals of this part of Italy are peculiarly uninteresting.

Rome itself was, throughout the middle ages, very little disposed to acquiesce in the government of her bishop. His rights were indefinite and unconfirmed by positive law; the emperor was long sovereign, the people always meant to be free. Besides the common causes of insubordination and anarchy among the Italians, which applied equally to the capital city, other sentiments more peculiar to Rome preserved a continual, though not uniform, influence for many centuries. There still remained enough in the wreck of that vast inheritance to swell the bosoms of her citizens with a consciousness of their own dignity. They bore the venerable name, they contemplated the monuments of art and empire, and forgot, in the illusions of national pride, that the tutelar gods of the building were departed forever. About the middle of the twelfth century these recollections were heightened by the eloquence of Arnold of Brescia, a political heretic who preached against the temporal jurisdiction of the hierarchy. In a temporary intoxication of fancy, they were led to make a ridiculous show of self-importance toward Frederick

<hr>

[74] Muratori, ad ann. 1274, 1275, 1278; Sismondi, tome iii, p. 461.

Barbarossa when he came to receive the imperial crown; but the German sternly chided their ostentation, and chastised their resistance.[75] With the popes they could deal more securely. Several of them were expelled from Rome during that age by the seditious citizens. Lucius II died of hurts received in a tumult. The government was vested in fifty-six senators, annually chosen by the people, through the intervention of an electoral body, ten delegates from each of the thirteen districts of the city.[76] This constitution lasted not quite fifty years. In 1192 Rome imitated the prevailing fashion by the appointment of an annual foreign magistrate.[77] Except in name, the senator of Rome appears to have perfectly resembled the podestà of other cities. This magistrate superseded the representative senate, who had proved by no means adequate to control the most lawless aristocracy of Italy. I shall not repeat the story of Brancaleon's rigorous and inflexible justice, which a great historian has already drawn from obscurity. It illustrates not the annals of Rome alone, but the general state of Italian society, the nature of a podestà's duty, and the difficulties of its execution. The office of senator survives after more than six hundred years; but he no longer wields the " iron flail " [78] of Brancaleon, and his nomination proceeds, of course, from the supreme pontiff, not from the people. In the twelfth and thirteenth centuries the senate, and the senator who succeeded them, exercised one distinguishing attribute of sovereignty, that of coining gold and silver money. Some of their coins still exist, with legends in a very republican tone.[79] Doubtless the temporal authority of the popes varied according to their personal character. Innocent III had much more than his predecessors for almost a century, or than some of his successors. He made the senator take an oath of fealty to him, which, though not very comprehensive, must have passed in those times as a recognition of his superiority.[80]

Though there was much less obedience to any legitimate power at Rome than anywhere else in Italy, even during the thirteenth century, yet, after the secession of the popes to Avignon, their own city was left in a far worse condition than before. Disorders of every kind, tumult, and robbery prevailed in the streets. The Roman nobility were engaged in perpetual war with each

[75] The impertinent address of a Roman orator to Frederick, and his answer, are preserved in Otho of Frisingen, l. ii, c. 22; but so much at length that we may suspect some exaggeration. Otho is rather rhetorical. They may be read in Gibbon, c. 69.

[76] Sismondi, tome ii, p. 36. Besides Sismondi and Muratori, I would refer for the history of Rome during the middle ages to the last chapters of Gibbon's " Decline and Fall."

[77] Sismondi, tome ii, p. 308.

[78] The readers of Spenser will recollect the iron flail of Talus, the attendant of Arthegal, emblematic of the severe justice of the lord deputy of Ireland, Sir Arthur Grey, shadowed under that allegory.

[79] Gibbon, " Decline and Fall," vol. xii, p. 289; Muratori, " Antiquit. Ital.," Dissert. 27.

[80] Sismondi, p. 309.

other. Not content with their own fortified palaces, they turned the sacred monuments of antiquity into strongholds, and consummated the destruction of time and conquest. At no period has the city endured such irreparable injuries; nor was the downfall of the Western Empire so fatal to its capital as the contemptible feud of the Orsini and Colonna families. Whatever there was of government, whether administered by a legate from Avignon or by the municipal authorities, had lost all hold on these powerful barons. In the midst of this degradation and wretchedness an obscure man, Nicola di Rienzi, conceived the project of restoring Rome not only to good order, but even to her ancient greatness. He had received an education beyond his birth, and nourished his mind with the study of the best writers. After many harangues to the people, which the nobility, blinded by their self-confidence, did not attempt to repress, Rienzi suddenly excited an insurrection and obtained complete success. He was placed at the head of a new government, with the title of tribune, and with almost unlimited power. The first effects of this revolution were wonderful. All the nobles submitted, though with great reluctance; the roads were cleared of robbers; tranquility was restored at home; some severe examples of justice intimidated offenders; and the tribune was regarded by all the people as the destined restorer of Rome and Italy. Though the court of Avignon could not approve of such a usurpation, it temporized enough not directly to oppose it. Most of the Italian republics, and some of the princes, sent ambassadors, and seemed to recognise pretensions which were tolerably ostentatious. The King of Hungary and Queen of Naples submitted their quarrel to the arbitration of Rienzi, who did not, however, undertake to decide upon it. But this sudden exaltation intoxicated his understanding, and exhibited failings entirely incompatible with his elevated condition. If Rienzi had lived in our own age, his talents, which were really great, would have found their proper orbit. For his character was one not unusual among literary politicians—a combination of knowledge, eloquence, and enthusiasm for ideal excellence, with vanity, inexperience of mankind, unsteadiness, and physical timidity. As these latter qualities became conspicuous, they eclipsed his virtues and caused his benefits to be forgotten; he was compelled to abdicate his government, and retire into exile. After several years, some of which he passed in the prisons of Avignon, Rienzi was brought back to Rome, with the title of senator, and under the command of the legate. It was supposed that the Romans, who had returned to their habits of insubordination, would gladly submit to their favourite tribune. And this proved the case for a few months; but after that time they ceased altogether to respect a man who so little respected himself in accepting a station where he could no longer be free, and Rienzi was killed in a sedition.[81]

Once more, not long after the death of Rienzi, the freedom of Rome seems to have revived in republican institutions, though with names less calculated to inspire peculiar recollections. Magistrates, called bannerets, chosen from the thirteen districts of the city, with a militia of three thousand citizens at their command, were placed at the head of this commonwealth. The great object of this new organization was to intimidate the Roman nobility, whose outrages, in the total absence of government, had grown intolerable. Several of them were hanged the first year by order of the bannerets. The citizens, however, had no serious intention of throwing off their allegiance to the popes. They provided for their own security, on account of the lamentable secession and neglect of those who claim allegiance while they denied protection. But they were ready to acknowledge and welcome back their bishop as their sovereign. Even without this they surrendered their republican constitution in 1362, it does not appear for what reason, and permitted the legate of Innocent VI to assume the government.[82] We find, however, the institution of bannerets revived and in full authority some years afterward. But the internal history of Rome appears to be obscure, and I have not had opportunities of examining it minutely. Some degree of political freedom the city probably enjoyed during the schism of the Church; but it is not easy to discriminate the assertion of legitimate privileges from the licentious tumults of the barons or populace. In 1435 the Romans formally took away the government from Eugenius IV, and elected seven signiors, or chief magistrates, like the priors of Florence.[83] But this revolution was not of long continuance. On the death of Eugenius the citizens deliberated upon proposing a constitutional charter to the future Pope. Stephen Porcaro, a man of good family and inflamed by a strong spirit of liberty, was one of their principal instigators. But the people did not sufficiently partake of that

[81] Sismondi, tome v, c. 37; tome vi, p. 201; Gibbon, c. 70; De Sade, "Vie de Pétrarque," tome ii, passim; Tiraboschi, tome vi, p. 339. It is difficult to resist the admiration which all the romantic circumstances of Rienzi's history tend to excite, and to which Petrarch so blindly gave way. That great man's characteristic excellence was not good common sense. He had imbibed two notions, of which it is hard to say which was the more absurd: that Rome had a legitimate right to all her ancient authority over the rest of the world, and that she was likely to recover this authority in consequence of the revolution produced by Rienzi. Giovanni Villani, living at Florence, and a stanch republican, formed

a very different estimate, which weighs more than the enthusiastic panegyrics of Petrarch. La detta impresa del tribuno era un' opera fantastica, e di poco durare (l. xii, c. 90). An illustrious female writer has drawn with a single stroke the character of Rienzi, Crescentius, and Arnold of Brescia, the fond restorers of Roman liberty, qui ont pris les souvenirs pour les espérances. (Corinne, tome i, p. 159.) Could Tacitus have excelled this?

[82] Matt. Villani, pp. 576, 604, 709; Sismondi, tome v, p. 92. He seems to have overlooked the former period of government by bannerets, and refers their institution to 1375.

[83] "Script. Rerum Italic.," tome iii, pars 2, p. 1128.

spirit. No measures were taken upon this occasion; and Porcaro, whose ardent imagination disguised the hopelessness of his enterprise, tampering in a fresh conspiracy, was put to death under the pontificate of Nicholas V.[84]

The province of Tuscany continued longer than Lombardy under the government of an imperial lieutenant. It was not till about the middle of the twelfth century that the cities of Florence, Lucca, Pisa, Siena, Arezzo, Pistoja, and several less considerable, which might, perhaps, have already their own elected magistrates, became independent republics. Their history is, with the exception of Pisa, very scanty till the death of Frederick II. The earliest fact of any importance recorded of Florence occurs in 1184, when it is said that Frederick Barbarossa took from her the dominion over the district or county, and restored it to the rural nobility, on account of her attachment to the Church.[85] This I chiefly mention to illustrate the system pursued by the cities of bringing the territorial proprietors in their neighbourhood under subjection. During the reign of Frederick II Florence became, as far as she was able, an ally of the popes. There was, indeed, a strong Ghibelin party, comprehending many of the greatest families, which occasionally predominated through the assistance of the emperor. It seems, however, to have existed chiefly among the nobility; the spirit of the people was thoroughly Guelf. After several revolutions, accompanied by alternate proscription and demolition of houses, the Guelf party, through the assistance of Charles of Anjou, obtained a final ascendency in 1266; and after one or two unavailing schemes of accommodation, it was established as a fundamental law in the Florentine constitution that no person of Ghibelin ancestry could be admitted to offices of public trust which, in such a government, was in effect an exclusion from the privileges of citizenship.

The changes of internal government and vicissitudes of success among factions were so frequent at Florence for many years after this time that she is compared by her great banished poet to one in sickness, who, unable to rest, gives herself momentary ease by continual change of posture in her bed.[86] They did not become much less numerous after the age of Dante. Yet the revolutions of Florence should, perhaps, be considered as no more than a necessary price of her liberty. It was her boast and her happiness to have escaped, except for one short period, that odious rule of vile usurpers, under which so many other

---

[84] Id., pp. 1131, 1134; Sismondi, tome x, p. 18.
[85] Villani, l. v, c. 12.
[86] " E se ben ti ricordi, e vedi il lume,
Vedrai te somigliante a quella inferma,

Che non può trovar posa in sù le piume,
Ma con dar volta suo dolore scherma."

(" Purgatorio," canto vi.)

free cities had been crushed. A sketch of the constitution of so famous a republic ought not to be omitted in this place. Nothing else in the history of Italy after Frederick II is so worthy of our attention.[87]

The basis of the Florentine polity was a division of the citizens exercising commerce into their several companies or arts. These were at first twelve: seven called the greater arts, and five lesser, but the latter were gradually increased to fourteen. The seven greater arts were those of lawyers and notaries, of dealers in foreign cloth, called sometimes calimala, of bankers or money-changers, of woollen-drapers, of physicians and druggists, of dealers in silk, and of furriers. The inferior arts were those of retailers of cloth, butchers, smiths, shoemakers, and builders. This division, so far at least as regarded the greater arts, was as old as the beginning of the thirteenth century.[88] But it was fully established and rendered essential to the constitution in 1266. By the provisions made in that year, each of the seven greater arts had a council of its own, a chief magistrate or consul, who administered justice in civil causes to all members of his company, and a banneret (gonfaloniere), or military officer, to whose standard they repaired when any attempt was made to disturb the peace of the city.

The administration of criminal justice belonged at Florence, as at other cities, to a foreign podestà, or rather to two foreign magistrates, the podestà and the capitano del popolo, whose jurisdiction, so far as I can trace it, appears to have been concurrent.[89] In the first part of the thirteenth century the authority of the podestà may have been more extensive than afterward. These offices were preserved till the innovations of the Medici. The domestic magistracies underwent more changes. Instead of consuls, which had been the first denomination of the chief magistrates of Florence, a college of twelve or fourteen persons called Anziani or Buonuomini, but varying in name as well as number, according to revolutions of party, was established about the middle of the thirteenth century to direct public affairs.[90] This order was entirely changed in 1282, and gave place to a new form of supreme magistracy, which lasted till the extinction of the republic. Six priors, elected every two months, one from each of the six quarters of the city, and from

---

[87] I have found considerable difficulties in this part of my task; no author with whom I am acquainted giving a tolerable view of the Florentine government, except M. Sismondi, who is himself not always satisfactory.

[88] Ammirato, ad ann. 1204 et 1235. Villani intimates (l. vii, c. 13) that the arts existed as commercial companies before 1266. Machiavelli and Sismondi express

themselves rather inaccurately, as if they had been erected at that time, which indeed is the era of their political importance.

[89] Matteo Villani, p. 194. G. Villani places the institution of the podestà in 1207; we find it, however, as early as 1184. (Ammirato.)

[90] G. Villani, l. vi, c. 39.

each of the greater arts, except that of lawyers, constituted an
executive magistracy. They lived during their continuance in
office in a palace belonging to the city, and were maintained
at the public cost. The actual priors, jointly with the chiefs
and councils (usually called la capitudine) of the seven greater
arts, and with certain adjuncts (arroti) named by themselves,
elected by ballot their successors. Such was the practice for
about forty years after this government was established. But
an innovation, begun in 1324, and perfected four years afterward, gave a peculiar character to the constitution of Florence.
A lively and ambitious people, not merely jealous of their public
sovereignty, but deeming its exercise a matter of personal enjoyment, aware at the same time that the will of the whole body
could neither be immediately expressed on all occasions, nor
even through chosen representatives, without the risk of violence
and partiality, fell upon the singular idea of admitting all citizens
not unworthy by their station or conduct to offices of magistracy
by rotation. Lists were separately made out by the priors, the
twelve buonuomini, the chiefs and councils of arts, the bannerets
and other respectable persons, of all citizens, Guelfs by origin,
turned of thirty years of age, and, in their judgment, worthy of
public trust. The lists thus formed were then united, and those
who had composed them, meeting together, in number ninety-
seven, proceeded to ballot upon every name. Whoever obtained
sixty-eight black balls was placed upon the reformed list; and
all the names it contained, being put on separate tickets into a
bag or purse (imborsati), were drawn successively as the magistracies were renewed. As there were above fifty of these, none
of which could be held for more than four months, several hundred citizens were called in rotation to bear their share in the
government within two years. But at the expiration of every
two years the scrutiny was renewed, and fresh names were mingled with those which still continued undrawn, so that accident
might deprive a man for life of his portion of magistracy.[91]

Four councils had been established by the constitution of
1266 for the decision of all propositions laid before them by
the executive magistrates, whether of a legislative nature or
relating to public policy. These were now abrogated; and in
their places were substituted one of three hundred members, all
plebeians, called consiglio di popolo, and one of two hundred
and fifty, called consiglio di commune, into which the nobles
might enter. These were changed by the same rotation as the

[91] Villani, l. ix, c. 27; l. x, c. 110; l. xi,
c. 105; Sismondi, tome v, p. 174. This
species of lottery, recommending itself by
an apparent fairness and incompatibil-
ity with undue influence, was speedily
adopted in all the neighbouring republics, and has always continued, according
to Sismondi, in Lucca, and in those cities
of the ecclesiastical state which preserved
the privilege of choosing their municipal
officers (p. 95).

magistracies, every four months.[92]   A parliament, or general assembly of the Florentine people, was rarely convoked; but the leading principle of a democratical republic, the ultimate sovereignty of the multitude, was not forgotten.   This constitution of 1324 was fixed by the citizens at large in a parliament; and the same sanction was given to those temporary delegations of the signiory to a prince, which occasionally took place.   What is technically called by their historians farsi popolo was the assembly of a parliament, or a resolution of all derivative powers into the immediate operation of the popular will.

The ancient government of this republic appears to have been chiefly in the hands of its nobility.   These were very numerous, and possessed large estates in the district.   But by the constitution of 1266, which was nearly coincident with the triumph of the Guelf faction, the essential powers of magistracy, as well as of legislation, were thrown into the scale of the commons. The colleges of arts, whose functions became so eminent, were altogether commercial.   Many, indeed, of the nobles enrolled themselves in these companies, and were among the most conspicuous merchants of Florence.   These were not excluded from the executive college of the priors at its first institution in 1282. It was necessary, however, to belong to one or other of the greater arts in order to reach that magistracy.   The majority, therefore, of the ancient families saw themselves pushed aside from the helm, which was intrusted to a class whom they had habitually held in contempt.

It does not appear that the nobility made any overt opposition to these democratical institutions.   Confident in a force beyond the law, they cared less for what the law might provide against them.   They still retained the proud spirit of personal independence which had belonged to their ancestors in the fastnesses of the Apennines.   Though the laws of Florence and a change in Italian customs had transplanted their residence to the city, it was in strong and lofty houses that they dwelt, among their kindred, and among the fellows of their rank.   Notwithstanding the tenor of the constitution, Florence was for some years after the establishment of priors incapable of resisting the violence of her nobility.   Her historians all attest the outrages and assassinations committed by them on the inferior people. It was in vain that justice was offered by the podestà and the capitano del popolo.   Witnesses dared not to appear against a noble offender; or if, on a complaint, the officer of justice arrested the accused, his family made common cause to rescue their kinsman, and the populace rose in defence of the laws, till the city was a scene of tumult and bloodshed.   I have already

[92] Villani, l. ix, c. 27; l. x, c. 110; l. xi, c. 105; Sismondi, tome v, p. 174.

alluded to this insubordination of the higher classes as general in the Italian republics; but the Florentine writers, being fuller than the rest, are our best specific testimonies.[93]

The dissensions between the patrician and plebeian orders ran very high when Giano della Bella, a man of ancient lineage, but attached, without ambitious views, so far as appears, though not without passion, to the popular side, introduced a series of enactments exceedingly disadvantageous to the ancient aristocracy. The first of these was the appointment of an executive officer, the gonfalonier of justice, whose duty it was to enforce the sentences of the podestà and capitano del popolo in cases where the ordinary officers were insufficient. A thousand citizens, afterward increased to four times that number, were bound to obey his commands. They were distributed into companies, the gonfaloniers or captains of which became a sort of corporation or college, and a constituent part of the government. This new militia seems to have superseded that of the companies of arts, which I have not observed to be mentioned at any later period. The gonfalonier of justice was part of the signiory along with the priors, of whom he was reckoned the president, and changed, like them, every two months. He was, in fact, the first magistrate of Florence.[94] If Giano della Bella had trusted to the efficacy of this new security for justice, his fame would have been beyond reproach. But he followed it up by harsher provisions. The nobility were now made absolutely ineligible to the office of prior. For an offence committed by one of a noble family, his relations were declared responsible in a penalty of three thousand pounds. And, to obviate the difficulty arising from the frequent intimidation of witnesses, it was provided that common fame, attested by two credible persons, should be sufficient for the condemnation of a nobleman.[95]

These are the famous ordinances of justice which passed at Florence for the great charter of her democracy. They have been reprobated in later times as scandalously unjust, and I have little inclination to defend them. The last, especially, was a violation of those eternal principles which forbid us, for any calculations of advantage, to risk the sacrifice of innocent blood.

[93] Villani, l. vii, c. 113; l. viii, c. 8; Ammirato, " Storia Fiorentina," l. iv in cominciamento.
[94] It is to be regretted that the accomplished biographer of Lorenzo de' Medici should have taken no pains to inform himself of the most ordinary particulars in the constitution of Florence. Among many other errors, he says (vol. ii, p. 51, fifth edit.) that the gonfalonier of justice was subordinate to the delegated mechanics (a bad expression), or priori dell' arti, whose number, too, he

augments to ten. The proper style of the republic seems to run thus: I priori dell' arti e gonfaloniere di giustizia, il popolo e 'l comune della città di Firenze. (G. Villani, l. xii, c. 109.)
[95] Villani, l. viii, c. 1; Ammirato, p. 188, edit. 1647. A magistrate, called l' esecutor della giustizia, was appointed with authority equal to that of the podestà for the special purpose of watching over the observation of the ordinances of justice. (Ammirato, p. 666.)

But it is impossible not to perceive that the same unjust severity has sometimes, under a like pretext of necessity, been applied to the weaker classes of the people, which they were in this instance able to exercise toward their natural superiors.

The nobility were soon aware of the position in which they stood. For half a century their great object was to procure the relaxation of the ordinances of justice. But they had no success with an elated enemy. In three years' time, indeed, Giano della Bella, the author of these institutions, was driven into exile; a conspicuous, though by no means singular, proof of Florentine ingratitude.[96] The wealth and physical strength of the nobles were, however, untouched, and their influence must always have been considerable. In the great feuds of the Bianchi and Neri the ancient families were most distinguished. No man plays a greater part in the annals of Florence at the beginning of the fourteenth century than Corso Donati, chief of the latter faction, who might pass as representative of the turbulent, intrepid, ambitious citizen-noble of an Italian republic.[97] But the laws gradually became more sure of obedience; the sort of proscription which attended the ancient nobles lowered their spirit; while a new aristocracy began to raise its head, the aristocracy of families who, after filling the highest magistracies for two or three generations, obtained an hereditary importance, which answered the purpose of more unequivocal nobility; just as in ancient Rome plebeian families, by admission to curule offices, acquired the character and appellation of nobility, and were only distinguishable by their genealogy from the original patricians.[98] Florence had her plebeian nobles (popolani grandi), as well as Rome; the Peruzzi, the Ricci, the Albizi, the Medici, correspond to the Catos, the Pompeys, the Brutuses, and the Antonies. But at Rome the two orders, after an equal partition of the highest offices, were content to respect their mutual privileges; at Florence the commoner preserved a rigorous monopoly, and the distinction of high birth was that it debarred men from political franchises and civil justice.[99]

This second aristocracy did not obtain much more of the popular affection than that which it superseded. Public outrage and violation of law became less frequent; but the new leaders of Florence are accused of continual misgovernment at home and abroad, and sometimes of peculation. There was, of course, a

[96] Villani, 1. viii, c. 8.
[97] Dino Compagni; Villani.
[98] La nobilità civile, se bene non in baronaggi, è capace di grandissimi honori, percioche esercitando i supremi magistrati della sua patria, viene spesso a comandare a capitani d' eserciti e ella stessa per se ò in mare, ò in terra, molte vota i supremi carichi adopera. E tale è la Fiorentina nobilità. (Ammirato delle Famiglie Fiorentine. Firenze, 1614, p. 25.)
[99] Quello, che all' altre città suolo recare splendore, in Firenze era dannoso, o veramente vano e inutile, says Ammirato of nobility. (" Storia Fiorentina," p. 161.)

strong antipathy between the leading commoners and the ancient nobles; both were disliked by the people. In order to keep the nobles under more control, the governing party more than once introduced a new foreign magistrate, with the title of captain of defence (della guardia), whom they invested with an almost unbounded criminal jurisdiction. One Gabrielli of Agobbio was twice fetched for this purpose; and in each case he behaved in so tyrannical a manner as to occasion a tumult.[100] His office, however, was of short duration, and the title at least did not import a sovereign command. But very soon afterward Florence had to experience one taste of a cup which her neighbours had drunk off to the dregs, and to animate her magnanimous love of freedom by a knowledge of the calamities of tyranny.

A war with Pisa, unsuccessfully if not unskilfully conducted, gave rise to such dissatisfaction in the city that the leading commoners had recourse to an appointment something like that of Gabrielli, and from similar motives. Walter de Brienne, Duke of Athens, was descended from one of the French crusaders who had dismembered the Grecian Empire in the preceding century; but his father, defeated in battle, had lost the principality along with his life, and the titular duke was an adventurer in the court of France. He had been, however, slightly known at Florence on a former occasion. There was a uniform maxim among the Italian republics that extraordinary powers should be conferred upon none but strangers. The Duke of Athens was accordingly pitched upon for the military command, which was united with domestic jurisdiction. This appears to have been promoted by the governing party in order to curb the nobility; but they were soon undeceived in their expectations. The first act of the Duke of Athens was to bring four of the most eminent commoners to capital punishment for military offences. These sentences, whether just or otherwise, gave much pleasure to the nobles, who had so frequently been exposed to similar severity, and to the populace, who are naturally pleased with the humiliation of their superiors. Both of these were caressed by the duke, and both conspired, with blind passion, to second his ambitious views. It was proposed and carried in a full Parliament, or assembly of the people, to bestow upon him the signiory for life. The real friends of their country, as well as the oligarchy, shuddered at this measure. Throughout all the vicissitudes of party Florence had never yet lost sight of republican institutions. Not that she had never accommodated herself to temporary circumstances by naming a signior. Charles of Anjou had been invested with that dignity for the

[100] Villani, l. xi, c. 39 and 117.

term of ten years; Robert, King of Naples, for five; and his
son, the Duke of Calabria, was at his death signior of Florence.
These princes named the podestà, if not the priors; and were
certainly pretty absolute in their executive powers, though bound
by oath not to alter the statutes of the city.[101] But their office
had always been temporary. Like the dictatorship of Rome,
it was a confessed, unavoidable evil; a suspension, but not ex-
tinguishment, of rights. Like that, too, it was a dangerous
precedent, through which crafty ambition and popular rashness
might ultimately subvert the republic. If Walter de Brienne
had possessed the subtle prudence of a Matteo Visconti or a
Cane della Scala, there appears no reason to suppose that Florence would have escaped the fate of other cities; and her history might have become as useless a record of perfidy and assassination as that of Mantua or Verona.[102]

But, happily for Florence, the reign of tyranny was very
short. The Duke of Athens had neither judgment nor activity
for so difficult a station. He launched out at once into excesses
which it would be desirable that arbitrary power should always
commit at the outset. The taxes were considerably increased;
their produce was dissipated. The honour of the state was sacrificed by an inglorious treaty with Pisa; her territory was diminished by some towns throwing off their dependence. Severe
and multiplied punishments spread terror through the city. The
noble families, who had on the duke's election destroyed the
ordinances of justice, now found themselves exposed to the more
partial caprice of a despot. He filled the magistracies with low
creatures from the inferior artificers, a class which he continued
to flatter.[103] Ten months passed in this manner, when three
separate conspiracies, embracing most of the nobility and of
the great commoners, were planned for the recovery of freedom.
The duke was protected by a strong body of hired cavalry.
Revolutions in an Italian city were generally effected by surprise. The streets were so narrow and so easily secured by barricades that, if a people had time to stand on its defence, no cavalry was of any avail. On the other hand, a body of lancers in
plate-armour might dissipate any number of a disorderly populace. Accordingly, if a prince or usurper would get possession
by surprise, he, as it was called, rode the city—that is, galloped
with his cavalry along the streets, so as to prevent the people
from collecting to erect barricades. This expression is very
usual with historians of the fourteenth century.[104] The conspirators at Florence were too quick for the Duke of Athens.

[101] Villani, l. ix, c. 55, 60, 135, 328.
[102] Id., l. xii, c. 1, 2, 3.
[103] Villani, c. 8.

[104] Villani, l. x, c. 81; Castruccio . . .
corse la città di Pisa due volte. (Sismondi, tome v, p. 105.)

The city was barricaded in every direction, and, after a contest of some duration, he consented to abdicate his signiory. Thus Florence recovered her liberty. Her constitutional laws now seemed to revive of themselves. But the nobility, who had taken a very active part in the recent liberation of their country, thought it hard to be still placed under the rigorous ordinances of justice. Many of the richer commoners acquiesced in an equitable partition of magistracies, which was established through the influence of the bishop. But the populace of Florence, with its characteristic forgetfulness of benefits, was tenacious of those proscriptive ordinances. The nobles, too, elated by their success, began again to strike and injure the inferior citizens. A new civil war in the city streets decided their quarrel; after a desperate resistance many of the principal houses were pillaged and burned, and the perpetual exclusion of the nobility was confirmed by fresh laws. But the people, now sure of their triumph, relaxed a little upon this occasion the ordinances of justice, and, to make some distinction in favour of merit or innocence, effaced certain families from the list of nobility. Five hundred and thirty persons were thus elevated, as we may call it, to the rank of commoners.[105] As it was beyond the competence of the republic of Florence to change a man's ancestors, this nominal alteration left all the real advantages of birth as they were, and was undoubtedly an enhancement of dignity, though, in appearance, a very singular one. Conversely, several unpopular commoners were ennobled in order to disfranchise them. Nothing was more usual in subsequent times than such an arbitrary change of rank, as a penalty or a benefit.[106] Those nobles who were rendered plebeian by favour were obliged to change their name and arms.[107] The constitution now underwent some change. From six the priors were increased to eight; and instead of being chosen from each of the greater arts, they were taken from the four quarters of the city, the lesser artisans, as I conceive, being admissible. The gonfaloniers of companies were reduced to sixteen. And these, along with the signiory, and the twelve buonuomini, formed the college, where every proposition was discussed before it could be offered to the councils for their legislative sanction. But it could only originate, strictly speaking, in the signiory—that is, the gonfalonier of justice, and eight

[105] Villani, l. xii, c. 18–23. Sismondi says, by a momentary oversight, cinq cent trente familles (tome v, p. 377). There were but thirty-seven noble families at Florence, as M. Sismondi himself informs us (tome iv, p. 66), though Villani reckons the number of individuals at 1,500. Nobles, or grandi as they are more strictly called, were such as had been inscribed, or rather proscribed, as such in the ordinances of justice; at least I do not know what other definition there was.

[106] Messer Antonio di Baldinaccio degli Adimari, tutto che fosse de più grandi e nobili, per grazia era messo tra 'l popolo. (Villani, l. xii, c. 108.)

[107] Ammirato, p. 748. There were several exceptions to this rule in later times. The Pazzi were made popolani, plebeians, by favour of Cosmo de' Medici. (Machiavelli.)

priors, the rest of the college having merely the function of advice and assistance.[108]

Several years elapsed before any material disturbance arose at Florence. Her contemporary historian complains, indeed, that mean and ignorant persons obtained the office of prior, and ascribes some errors in her external policy to this cause.[109] Besides the natural effects of the established rotation, a particular law, called the divieto, tended to throw the better families out of public office. By this law two of the same name could not be drawn for any magistracy : which, as the ancient families were extremely numerous, rendered it difficult for their members to succeed, especially as a ticket once drawn was not replaced in the purse, so that an individual liable to the divieto was excluded until the next biennial revolution.[110] This created dissatisfaction among the leading families. They were likewise divided by a new faction, entirely founded, as far as appears, on personal animosity between two prominent houses, the Albizi and the Ricci. The city was, however, tranquil, when in 1357 a spring was set in motion which gave quite a different character to the domestic history of Florence.

At the time when the Guelfs, with the assistance of Charles of Anjou, acquired an exclusive domination in the republic, the estates of the Ghibelins were confiscated. One third of these confiscations was allotted to the state; another went to repair the losses of Guelf citizens ; but the remainder became the property of a new corporate society, denominated the Guelf party (parte Guelfa), with a regular internal organization. The Guelf party had two councils, one of fourteen and one of sixty members; three, or afterward four, captains, elected by scrutiny every two months, a treasury, and common seal; a little republic within the republic of Florence. Their primary duty was to watch over the Guelf interest; and for this purpose they had a particular officer for the accusation of suspected Ghibelins.[111] We hear not much, however, of the Guelf society for nearly a century after their establishment. The Ghibelins hardly ventured to show themselves after the fall of the White Guelfs in 1304, with whom they had been connected, and confiscation had almost annihilated that unfortunate faction. But as the oligarchy of Guelf families lost part of its influence through the divieto and system of lottery, some persons of Ghibelin descent crept into public offices ; and this was exaggerated by the zealots of an opposite party, as if the fundamental policy of the city was put into danger.

The Guelf society had begun as early as 1346 to manifest

[108] Nardi. " Storia di Firenze," p. 7, edit. 1584; Villani, loc. cit.
[109] "Script. Rer. Italic.," xiv, pp. 89, 244.
[110] Sismondi, tome vi, p. 338.
[111] G. Villani, l. vii, c. 16.

some disquietude at the foreign artisans, who, settling at Florence and becoming members of some of the trading corporations, pretended to superior offices. They procured, accordingly, a law excluding from public trust and magistracy all persons not being natives of the city or its territory. Next year they advanced a step further; and, with a view to prevent disorder, which seemed to threaten the city, a law was passed declaring every one whose ancestors at any time since 1300 had been known Ghibelins, or who had not the reputation of sound Guelf principles, incapable of being drawn or elected to offices.[112] It is manifest from the language of the historian who relates these circumstances, and whose testimony is more remarkable from his having died several years before the politics of the Guelf corporation more decidedly showed themselves, that the real cause of their jealousy was not the increase of Ghibelinism, a merely plausible pretext, but the democratical character which the government had assumed since the revolution of 1343, which raised the fourteen inferior arts to the level of those which the great merchants of Florence exercised. In the Guelf society the ancient nobles retained a considerable influence. The laws of exclusion had never been applied to that corporation. Two of the captains were always noble, two were commoners. The people, in debarring the nobility from ordinary privileges, were little aware of the more dangerous channel which had been left open to their ambition. With the nobility some of the great commoners acted in concert, and especially the family and faction of the Albizi. The introduction of obscure persons into office still continued, and some measures more vigorous than the law of 1347 seemed necessary to restore the influence of their aristocracy. They proposed, and, notwithstanding the reluctance of the priors, carried by violence, both in the preliminary deliberations of the signiory and in the two councils, a law by which every person accepting an office who should be convicted of Ghibelinism or of Ghibelin descent, upon testimony of public fame, became liable to punishment, capital or pecuniary, at the discretion of the priors. To this law they gave a retrospective effect, and, indeed, it appears to have been little more than a revival of the provisions made in 1347, which had probably been disregarded. Many citizens who had been magistrates within a few years were cast in heavy fines on this indefinite charge. But the more usual practice was to warn (ammonire) men beforehand against undertaking public trust. If they neglected this hint, they were sure to be treated as convicted Ghibelins. Thus a very numerous class, called Ammoniti, was formed of proscribed and discontented persons, eager to throw off the intolerable yoke of the Guelf society. For the imputation of Ghibelin connections was generally an unfounded pretext for crushing the enemies of the governing faction.[113]   Men of approved Guelf principles and origin were every day warned from their natural privileges of sharing in magistracy. This spread a universal alarm through the city; but the great advantage of union and secret confederacy rendered the Guelf society, who had also the law on their side, irresistible by their opponents. Meanwhile the public honour was well supported abroad; Florence had never before been so distinguished as during the prevalence of this oligarchy.[114]

The Guelf society had governed with more or less absoluteness for nearly twenty years when the republic became involved, through the perfidious conduct of the papal legate, in a war with the Holy See. Though the Florentines were by no means superstitious, this hostility to the Church appeared almost an absurdity to determined Guelfs, and shocked those prejudices about names which make up the politics of vulgar minds. The Guelf society, though it could not openly resist the popular indignation against Gregory XI, was not heartily inclined to this war. Its management fell, therefore, into the hands of eight commissioners, some of them not well affected to the society, whose administration was so successful and popular as to excite the utmost jealousy in the Guelfs. They began to renew their warnings, and in eight months excluded fourscore citizens.[115]

The tyranny of a court may endure for ages, but that of a faction is seldom permanent. In June, 1378, the gonfalonier of justice was Salvestro de' Medici, a man of approved patriotism, whose family had been so notoriously of Guelf principles that it was impossible to warn him from office. He proposed to mitigate the severity of the existing law. His proposition did not succeed; but its rejection provoked an insurrection, the forerunner of still more alarming tumults. The populace of Florence, like that of other cities, was terrible in the moment of sedition, and a party so long dreaded shrank before the physical strength of the multitude. Many leaders of the Guelf society had their houses destroyed, and some fled from the city. But instead of annulling their acts, a middle course was adopted by the committee of magistrates who had been empowered to

<hr />

[113] Besides the effect of ancient prejudice, Ghibelinism was considered at Florence, in the fourteenth century, as immediately connected with tyrannical usurpation. The Guelf party, says Matteo Villani, is the foundation rock of liberty in Italy; so that, if any Guelf becomes a tyrant, he must of necessity turn to the Ghibelin side, and of this there have been many instances (p. 481). So Giovanni

Villani says of Passerino, Lord of Mantua, that his ancestors had been Guelfs, ma per essere signore e tiranno si fece Ghibellino (l. x, c. 99). And Matteo Villani of the Pepoli at Bologna; essendo di natura Guelfi, per la tirannia erano quasi alienati della parte (p. 69).

[114] M. Villani, pp. 531, 637, 731. Ammirato; Machiavelli; Sismondi.

[115] Ammirato, p. 709.

reform the state; the Ammoniti were suspended three years longer from office, and the Guelf society preserved with some limitations. This temporizing course did not satisfy either the Ammoniti or the populace. The greater arts were generally attached to the Guelf society. Between them and the lesser arts, composed of retail and mechanical traders, there was a strong jealousy. The latter were adverse to the prevailing oligarchy and to the Guelf society, by whose influence it was maintained. They were eager to make Florence a democracy in fact as well as in name by participating in the executive government.

But every political institution appears to rest on too confined a basis to those whose point of view is from beneath it. While the lesser arts were murmuring at the exclusive privileges of the commercial aristocracy, there was yet an inferior class of citizens who thought their own claims to equal privileges irrefragable. The arrangement of twenty-one trading companies had still left several kinds of artisans unincorporated, and consequently unprivileged. These had been attached to the art with which their craft had most connection in a sort of dependent relation. Thus to the company of drapers, the most wealthy of all, the various occupations instrumental in the manufacture, as woolcombers, dyers, and weavers, were appendant.[116] Besides the sense of political exclusion, these artisans alleged that they were oppressed by their employers of the art, and that, when they complained to the consul, their judge in civil matters, no redress could be procured. A still lower order of the community was the mere populace, who did not practise any regular trade, or who only worked for daily hire. These were called Ciompi, a corruption, it is said, of the French compère.

"Let no one," says Machiavel in this place, "who begins an innovation in a state expect that he shall stop it at his pleasure or regulate it according to his intention." After about a month from the first sedition another broke out, in which the ciompi, or lowest populace, were alone concerned. Through the surprise, or cowardice, or disaffection of the superior citizens, this was suffered to get ahead, and for three days the city was in the hand of a tumultuous rabble. It was vain to withstand their propositions had they even been more unreasonable than they were. But they only demanded the establishment of two new arts for the trades hitherto dependent, and one for the lower people; and that three of the priors should be chosen from the greater arts, three from the fourteen lesser, and two from those just created. Some delay, however, occurring to prevent the sanction of these innovations by the councils, a new fury took

---

[116] Before the year 1340, according to Villani's calculation, the woollen trade occupied 30,000 persons (l. xi, c. 93).

possession of the populace; the gates of the palace belonging to the signiory were forced open, the priors compelled to fly, and no appearance of a constitutional magistracy remained to throw the veil of law over the excesses of anarchy. The republic seemed to rock from its foundations; and the circumstance to which historians ascribe its salvation is not the least singular in this critical epoch. One Michel di Lando, a woolcomber, half dressed and without shoes, happened to hold the standard of justice wrested from the proper officer when the populace burst into the palace. Whether he was previously conspicuous in the tumult is not recorded; but the wild, capricious mob, who had destroyed what they had no conception how to rebuild, suddenly cried out that Lando should be gonfalonier or signior, and reform the city at his pleasure.

A choice, arising probably from wanton folly, could not have been better made by wisdom. Lando was a man of courage, moderation, and integrity. He gave immediate proofs of these qualities by causing his office to be respected. The eight commissioners of the war, who, though not instigators of the sedition, were well pleased to see the Guelf party so entirely prostrated, now fancied themselves masters, and began to nominate priors. But Lando sent a message to them that he was elected by the people, and that he could dispense with their assistance. He then proceeded to the choice of priors. Three were taken from the greater arts, three from the lesser, and three from the two new arts and the lower people. This eccentric college lost no time in restoring tranquility, and compelled the populace, by threat of punishment, to return to their occupations. But the ciompi were not disposed to give up the pleasures of anarchy so readily. They were dissatisfied at the small share allotted to them in the new distribution of offices, and murmured at their gonfalonier as a traitor to the popular cause. Lando was aware that an insurrection was projected; he took measures with the most respectable citizens; the insurgents, when they showed themselves, were quelled by force, and the gonfalonier retired from office with an approbation which all historians of Florence have agreed to perpetuate. Part of this has undoubtedly been founded on a consideration of the mischief which it was in his power to inflict. The ciompi, once checked, were soon defeated. The next gonfalonier was, like Lando, a woolcomber; but, wanting the intrinsic merit of Lando, his mean station excited universal contempt. None of the arts could endure their low coadjutors; a short struggle was made by the populace, but they were entirely overpowered with considerable slaughter, and the government was divided between the seven greater and sixteen lesser arts, in nearly equal proportions.

The party of the lesser arts, or inferior tradesmen, which had begun this confusion, were left winners when it ceased. Three men of distinguished families who had instigated the revolution became the leaders of Florence—Benedetto Alberti, Tomaso Strozzi, and Georgio Scali. Their government had at first to contend with the ciompi, smarting under loss and disappointment. But a populace which is beneath the inferior mechanics may with ordinary prudence be kept in subjection by a government that has a well-organized militia at its command. The Guelf aristocracy was far more to be dreaded. Some of them had been banished, some fined, some ennobled: the usual consequences of revolution which they had too often practised to complain. A more iniquitous proceeding disgraces the new administration. Under pretence of conspiracy, the chief of the house of Albizi, and several of his most eminent associates, were thrown into prison. So little evidence of the charge appeared that the podestà refused to condemn them; but the people were clamorous for blood, and half with, half without the forms of justice, these noble citizens were led to execution. The part he took in this murder sullies the fame of Benedetto Alberti, who in his general conduct had been more uniformly influenced by honest principles than most of his contemporaries. Those who shared with him the ascendency in the existing government, Strozzi and Scali, abused their power by oppression toward their enemies, and insolence toward all. Their popularity was, of course, soon at an end. Alberti, a sincere lover of freedom, separated himself from men who seemed to emulate the arbitrary government they had overthrown. An outrage of Scali, in rescuing a criminal from justice, brought the discontent to a crisis; he was arrested, and lost his head on the scaffold, while Strozzi, his colleague, fled from the city. But this event was instantly followed by a reaction, which Alberti, perhaps, did not anticipate. Armed men filled the streets; the cry of " Live the Guelfs! " was heard. After a three years' depression, the aristocratical party regained its ascendency. They did not revive the severity practised toward the Ammoniti; but the two new arts, created for the small trades, were abolished, and the lesser arts reduced to a third part, instead of something more than one half, of public offices. Several persons who had favoured the plebeians were sent into exile; and among these Michel di Lando, whose great services in subduing anarchy ought to have secured the protection of every government. Benedetto Alberti, the enemy by turns of every faction—because every faction was in its turn oppressive—experienced some years afterward the same fate. For half a century after this time no revolution took place at Florence. The Guelf aristocracy, strong in opulence and antiquity, and rendered prudent by experience, under the guidance of the Albizi family, maintained a preponderating influence without much departing, the times considered, from moderation and respect for the laws.[117]

It is sufficiently manifest, from this sketch of the domestic history of Florence, how far that famous republic was from affording a perfect security for civil rights or general tranquility. They who hate the name of free constitutions may exult in her internal dissensions, as in those of Athens or Rome. But the calm philosopher will not take his standard of comparison from ideal excellence, nor even from that practical good which has been reached in our own unequalled constitution, and in some of the republics of modern Europe. The men and the institutions of the fourteenth century are to be measured by their contemporaries. Who would not rather have been a citizen of Florence than a subject of the Visconti? In a superficial review of history we are sometimes apt to exaggerate the vices of free states, and to lose sight of those inherent in tyrannical power. The bold censoriousness of republican historians, and the cautious servility of writers under an absolute monarchy, conspire to mislead us as to the relative prosperity of nations. Acts of outrage and tumultuous excesses in a free state are blazoned in minute detail, and descend to posterity; the deeds of tyranny are studiously and perpetually suppressed. Even those historians who have no particular motives for concealment turn away from the monotonous and disgusting crimes of tyrants. " Deeds of cruelty," it is well observed by Matteo Villani, after relating an action of Bernabo Visconti, " are little worthy of remembrance; yet let me be excused for having recounted one out of many as an example of the peril to which men are exposed under the yoke of an unbounded tyranny." [118]   The reign of Bernabo afforded abundant instances of a like kind. Second only to Eccelin among the tyrants of Italy, he rested the security of his dominion upon tortures and death, and his laws themselves enact the protraction of capital punishment through forty days of suffering.[119]   His nephew, Giovanni Maria, is said, with a madness like that of Nero or Commodus, to have coursed the streets of Milan by night with bloodhounds, ready to chase and tear any unlucky passenger.[120]   Nor were other Italian principalities free from similar tyrants, though none, perhaps, upon the

---

[117] For this part of Florentine history, besides Ammirato, Machiavel, and Sismondi, I have read an interesting narrative of the sedition of the ciompi, by Gino Capponi, in the eighteenth volume of Muratori's collection. It has an air of liveliness and truth which is very pleasing, but it breaks off rather too soon, at the instant of Lando's assuming

the office of banneret. Another contemporary writer, Melchione de Stefani, who seems to have furnished the materials of the three historians above mentioned, has not fallen in my way.

[118] P. 434.

[119] Sismondi, tome vi, p. 316; Corio, " Ist. di Milano," p. 486.

[120] Corio, p. 595.

whole, so odious as the Visconti. The private history of many families—such, for instance, as the Scala and the Gonzaga—is but a series of assassinations. The ordinary vices of mankind assumed a tint of portentous guilt in the palaces of Italian princes. Their revenge was fratricide, and their lust was incest.

Though fertile and populous, the proper district of Florence was by no means extensive. An independent nobility occupied the Tuscan Apennines with their castles. Of these, the most conspicuous were the Counts of Guidi, a numerous and powerful family, who possessed a material influence in the affairs of Florence and of all Tuscany till the middle of the fourteenth century, and some of whom preserved their independence much longer.[121] To the south, the republics of Arezzo, Perugia, and Siena; to the west, those of Volterra, Pisa, and Lucca; Prato and Pistoja to the north, limited the Florentine territory. It was late before these boundaries were removed. During the usurpations of Uguccione at Pisa, and of Castruccio at Lucca, the republic of Florence was always unsuccessful in the field. After the death of Castruccio she began to act more vigorously, and engaged in several confederacies with the powers of Lombardy, especially in a league with Venice against Mastino della Scala. But the republic made no acquisition of territory till 1351, when she annexed the small city of Prato, not ten miles from her walls.[122] Pistoja, though still nominally independent, received a Florentine garrison about the same time. Several additions were made to the district by fair purchase from the nobility of the Apennines, and a few by main force. The territory was still very little proportioned to the fame and power of Florence. The latter was founded upon her vast commercial opulence. Every Italian state employed mercenary troops, and the richest was, of course, the most powerful. In the war against Mestino della Scala in 1336 the revenues of Florence are reckoned by Villani at three hundred thousand florins, which, as he observes, is more than the King of Naples or of Aragon possesses.[123] The expenditure went at that time very much beyond the receipt, and was defrayed by loans from the principal mercantile firms, which were secured by public funds, the earliest instance, I believe, of that financial resource.[124] Her population was computed at

[121] G. Villani, l. v, c. 37, 41, et alibi. The last of the Counts Guidi, having unwisely embarked in a confederacy against Florence, was obliged to give up his ancient patrimony in 1440.
[122] M. Villani, p. 72. This was rather a measure of usurpation; but the republic had some reason to apprehend that Prato might fall into the hands of the Visconti. Their conduct toward Pistoja was influenced by the same motive; but it was still further removed from absolute justice (p. 91).

[123] G. Villani, l. ix, c. 90-93. These chapters contain a very full and interesting statement of the revenues, expenses, population, and internal condition of Florence at that time. Part of them is extracted by M. Sismondi (tome v, p. 365). The gold florin was worth about ten shillings of our money. The district of Florence was not then much larger than Middlesex.
[124] G. Villani, l. xi, c. 49.

ninety thousand souls. Villani reckons the district at eighty thousand men, I suppose those only of military age; but this calculation must have been too large, even though he included, as we may presume, the city in his estimate.[125] Tuscany, though well cultivated and flourishing, does not contain by any means so great a number of inhabitants in that space at present. The first eminent conquest made by Florence was that of Pisa, early in the fifteenth century. Pisa had been distinguished as a commercial city ever since the age of the Othos. From her ports, and those of Genoa, the earliest naval armaments of the western nations were fitted out against the Saracen corsairs who infested the Mediterranean coasts. In the eleventh century she undertook, and, after a pretty long struggle, completed, the important, or at least the splendid, conquest of Sardinia, an island long subject to a Moorish chieftain. Several noble families of Pisa, who had defrayed the chief cost of this expedition, shared the island in districts, which they held in fief of the republic.[126] At a later period the Balearic Isles were subjected, but not long retained, by Pisa. Her naval prowess was supported by her commerce. A writer of the twelfth century reproaches her with the Jews, the Arabians, and other " monsters of the sea," who thronged in her streets.[127] The crusades poured fresh wealth into the lap of the maritime Italian cities. In some of those

[125] C. 93. Troviamo diligentemente, che in questi tempi avea in Firenze circa a 25 mila uomini da portare arme da 15 in 70 anni—Stimavasi avere in Firenze da 90 mila bocche tra uomini e femine e fanciulli, per l' avviso del pane bisognava al continuo alla città. These proportions of 25,000 men between fifteen and seventy, and of 90,000 souls, are as nearly as possible consonant to modern calculation, of which Villani knew nothing. which confirms his accuracy; though M. Sismondi asserts (p. 369) that the city contained 150,000 inhabitants, on no better authority, as far as appears, than that of Boccaccio, who says that 100,000 perished in the great plague of 1348, which was generally supposed to destroy two out of three. But surely two vague suppositions are not to be combined, in order to overthrow such a testimony as that of Villani, who seems to have consulted all registers and other authentic documents in his reach.

What Villani says of the population of the district may lead us to reckon it, perhaps, at about 180,000 souls, allowing the baptisms to be one in thirty of the population. Ragionavasi in questi tempi avere nel contado e distretto di Firenze de 80 mila uomini. Troviamo del piovano, che battezzava i fanciulli, impe-roche per ogni maschio, che battezzava in San Giovanni, per avere il novero, metea una fava nera, e per ogni femina una bianca, trovò, ch' erano l' anno in questi tempi dalle 5,800 in sei mila, avan-zando le più volte il sesso masculino da 300 in 500 per anno. Baptisms could only be performed in one public font, at Florence, Pisa, and some other cities. The building that contained this font was called the Baptistery. The baptisteries of Florence and Pisa still remain, and are well known. (Du Cange, voc. Baptisterium.) But there were fifty-seven parishes and one hundred and ten churches within the city. (Villani, ibid.) Mr. Roscoe has published a manuscript, evidently written after the taking of Pisa in 1406, though, as I should guess, not long after that event, containing a proposition for an income tax of ten per cent throughout the Florentine dominions. Among its other calculations, the population is reckoned at 400,000; assuming that to be the proportion to 80,000 men of military age, though certainly beyond the mark. It is singular that the district of Florence in 1343 is estimated by Villani to contain as great a number, before Pisa, Volterra, or even Prato and Pistoja, had been annexed to it. (Roscoe's " Life of Lorenzo." Appendix, No. 16.)

[126] Sismondi, tome i, pp. 345, 372.
[127] " Qui pergit Pisas, videt illic mon-
    stra marina;
Hæc urbs, Paganis, Turchis, Liby-
    cis quoque, Parthis,
Sordida; Chaldæi sua lustrant mœ-
    nia tetri."
(Donizo, Vita Comitissæ Mathildis, apud Muratori, Dissert. 31.)

expeditions a great portion of the armament was conveyed by
sea to Palestine, and freighted the vessels of Pisa, Genoa, and
Venice. When the Christians had bought with their blood the
sea-coast of Syria, these republics procured the most extensive
privileges in the new states that were formed out of their slender
conquests, and became the conduits through which the produce
of the East flowed in upon the ruder nations of Europe. Pisa
maintained a large share of this commerce, as well as of maritime
greatness, till near the end of the thirteenth century. In 1282,
we are told by Villani, she was in great power, possessing Sardinia, Corsica, and Elba, from whence the republic, as well as
private persons, derived large revenues, and almost ruled the
sea with their ships and merchandises, and beyond sea were very
powerful in the city of Acre, and much connected with its principal citizens.[128] The prosperous era of Pisa is marked by her
public edifices. She was the first Italian city that took a pride
in architectural magnificence. Her cathedral is of the eleventh
century; the baptistery, the famous inclined tower, or belfry,
the arcades that surround the Campo Santo, or cemetery of Pisa,
are of the twelfth, or, at latest, of the thirteenth.[129]

It would have been no slight anomaly in the annals of Italy,
or, we might say, of mankind, if two neighbouring cities, competitors in every mercantile occupation and every naval enterprise, had not been perpetual enemies to each other. One is
more surprised, if the fact be true, that no war broke out between
Pisa and Genoa till 1119.[130] From this time at least they continually recurred. An equality of forces and of courage kept
the conflict uncertain for the greater part of two centuries. Their
battles were numerous, and sometimes, taken separately, decisive; but the public spirit and resources of each city were called
out by defeat, and we generally find a new armament replace the
losses of an unsuccessful combat. In this respect the naval contest between Pisa and Genoa, though much longer protracted,
resembles that of Rome and Carthage in the first Punic war.
But Pisa was reserved for her Ægades. In one fatal battle, off
the little isle of Meloria, in 1284, her whole navy was destroyed.
Several unfortunate and expensive armaments had almost exhausted the state, and this was the last effort, by private sacrifices, to equip one more fleet. After this defeat it was in vain
to contend for empire. Eleven thousand Pisans languished for
many years in prison; it was a current saying that whoever
would see Pisa should seek her at Genoa. A treacherous chief,
that Count Ugolino whose guilt was so terribly avenged, is said

[128] Villani, l. vi, c. 83.
[129] Sismondi, tome iv, p. 178; Tiraboschi, tome iii, p. 406.
[130] Muratori, ad ann., 1119.

to have purposely lost the battle, and prevented the ransom of
the captives, to secure his power: accusations that obtain easy
credit with an unsuccessful people.

From the epoch of the battle of Meloria, Pisa ceased to
be a maritime power. Forty years afterward she was stripped
of her ancient colony, the island of Sardinia. The four Pisan
families who had been invested with that conquest had been
apt to consider it as their absolute property; their appellation
of judge seemed to indicate deputed power, but they sometimes
assumed that of king, and several attempts had been made to
establish an immediate dependence on the empire, or even on
the Pope. A new potentate had now come forward on the stage.
The malcontent feudatories of Sardinia made overtures to the
King of Aragon, who had no scruples about attacking the indis-
putable possession of a declining republic. Pisa made a few unavailing efforts to defend Sardinia; but the nominal superiority
was hardly worth a contest, and she surrendered her rights to
the crown of Aragon. Her commerce now dwindled with her
greatness. During the fourteenth century Pisa almost renounced
the ocean and directed her main attention to the politics of Tuscany. Ghibelin by invariable predilection, she was in constant
opposition to the Guelf cities which looked up to Florence. But
in the fourteenth century the names of freeman and Ghibelin
were not easily united, and a city in that interest stood insulated
between the republics of an opposite faction and the tyrants of
her own. Pisa fell several times under the yoke of usurpers; she
was included in the wide-spreading acquisitions of Gian Galeazzo
Visconti. At his death one of his family seized the dominion,
and finally the Florentines purchased for four hundred thousand
florins a rival and once equal city. The Pisans made a resistance
more according to what they had been than what they were.

The early history of Genoa, in all her foreign relations, is
involved in that of Pisa. As allies against the Saracens of Africa,
Spain, and the Mediterranean islands, as corrivals in commerce
with these very Saracens or with the Christians of the East, as
co-operators in the great expeditions under the banner of the
cross, or as engaged in deadly warfare with each other, the two
republics stand in continual parallel. From the beginning of
the thirteenth century Genoa was, I think, the more prominent
and flourishing of the two. She had conquered the island of
Corsica at the same time that Pisa reduced Sardinia; and her
acquisition, though less considerable, was longer preserved. Her
territory at home, the ancient Liguria, was much more extensive,
and, what was most important, contained a greater range of sea-
coast than that of Pisa. But the commercial and maritime prosperity of Genoa may be dated from the recovery of Constantinople

by the Greeks in 1261. Jealous of the Venetians, by whose arms the Latin emperors had been placed, and were still maintained, on their throne, the Genoese assisted Palæologus in overturning that usurpation. They obtained in consequence the suburb of Pera or Galata, over against Constantinople, as an exclusive settlement, where their colony was ruled by a magistrate sent from home, and frequently defied the Greek capital with its armed galleys and intrepid seamen. From this convenient station Genoa extended her commerce into the Black Sea, and established her principal factory at Caffa, in the Crimean peninsula. This commercial monopoly, for such she endeavoured to render it, aggravated the animosity of Venice. As Pisa retired from the field of waters, a new enemy appeared upon the horizon to dispute the maritime dominion of Genoa. Her first war with Venice was in 1258. The second was not till after the victory of Meloria had crushed her more ancient enemy. It broke out in 1293, and was prosecuted with determined fury and a great display of naval strength on both sides. One Genoese armament, as we are assured by a historian, consisted of one hundred and fifty-five galleys, each manned with from two hundred and twenty to three hundred sailors; [131] a force astonishing to those who know the more slender resources of Italy in modern times, but which is rendered credible by several analogous facts of good authority. It was, however, beyond any other exertion. The usual fleets of Genoa and Venice were of seventy to ninety galleys.

Perhaps the naval exploits of these two republics may afford a more interesting spectacle to some minds than any other part of Italian history. Compared with military transactions of the same age, they are more sanguinary, more brilliant, and exhibit full as much skill and intrepidity. But maritime warfare is scanty in circumstances, and the indefiniteness of its locality prevents it from resting in the memory. And though the wars of Genoa and Venice were not always so unconnected with territorial politics as those of the former city with Pisa, yet, from the alternation of success and equality of forces, they did not often produce any decisive effect. One memorable encounter in the Sea of Marmora, where the Genoese fought and conquered single-handed against the Venetians, the Catalans, and the Greeks, hardly belongs to Italian history.[132]

But the most remarkable war, and that productive of the greatest consequences, was one that commenced in 1378, after several acts of hostility in the Levant, wherein the Venetians appear to have been the principal aggressors. Genoa did not stand alone in this war. A formidable confederacy was raised

[131] Muratori, A. D. 1295.   [132] Gibbon, c. 63.

against Venice, who had given provocation to many enemies.
Of this Francis Carrara, Signor of Padua, and the King of
Hungary were the leaders. But the principal struggle was, as
usual, upon the waves. During the winter of 1378 a Genoese
fleet kept the sea, and ravaged the shores of Dalmatia. The
Venetian armament had been weakened by an epidemic disease,
and when Vittor Pisani, their admiral, gave battle to the enemy,
he was compelled to fight with a hasty conscription of lands-
men against the best sailors in the world. Entirely defeated,
and taking refuge at Venice with only seven galleys, Pisani was
cast into prison, as if his ill fortune had been his crime. Meanwhile the Genoese fleet, augmented by a strong re-enforcement,
rode before the long natural ramparts that separate the lagoons
of Venice from the Adriatic. Six passages intersect the islands
which constitute this barrier, besides the broader outlets of Brondolo and Fossone, through which the waters of the Brenta and
the Adige are discharged. The lagoon itself, as is well known,
consists of extremely shallow water, unnavigable for any vessel
except along the course of artificial and intricate passages. Notwithstanding the apparent difficulties of such an enterprise,
Pietro Doria, the Genoese admiral, determined to reduce the
city. His first successes gave him reason to hope. He forced
the passage and stormed the little town of Chioggia,[133] built upon
the inside of the isle bearing that name, about twenty-five miles
south of Venice. Nearly four thousand prisoners fell here into
his hands: an augury, as it seemed, of a more splendid triumph.
In the consternation this misfortune inspired at Venice the first
impulse was to ask for peace. The ambassadors carried with
them seven Genoese prisoners, as a sort of peace-offering to the
admiral, and were empowered to make large and humiliating
concessions, reserving nothing but the liberty of Venice. Francis
Carrara strongly urged his allies to treat for peace. But the
Genoese were stimulated by long hatred, and intoxicated by this
unexpected opportunity of revenge. Doria, calling the ambassadors into council, thus addressed them: "Ye shall obtain no
peace from us, I swear to you, nor from the Lord of Padua, till
first we have put a curb in the mouths of those wild horses that
stand upon the place of St. Mark. When they are bridled you
shall have enough of peace. Take back with you your Genoese
captives, for I am coming within a few days to release both them
and their companions from your prisons." When this answer
was reported to the senate, they prepared to defend themselves
with the characteristic firmness of their government. Every eye
was turned toward a great man unjustly punished, their Admiral

[133] Chioggia, known at Venice by the name of Chioza, according to the usage of the Venetian dialect, which changes the g into z.

Vittor Pisani. He was called out of prison to defend his country amid general acclamations; but, equal in magnanimity and simple republican patriotism to the noblest characters of antiquity, Pisani repressed the favouring voices of the multitude, and bade them reserve their enthusiasm for St. Mark, the symbol and war cry of Venice. Under the vigorous command of Pisani the canals were fortified or occupied by large vessels armed with artillery; thirty-four galleys were equipped; every citizen contributed according to his power; in the entire want of commercial resources (for Venice had not a merchant ship during this war) private plate was melted; and the senate held out the promise of ennobling thirty families who should be most forward in this strife of patriotism.

The new fleet was so ill provided with seamen that for some months the admiral employed them only in manœuvring along and canals. From some unaccountable supineness, or more probably from the insuperable difficulties of the undertaking, the Genoese made no assault upon the city. They had, indeed, fair grounds to hope its reduction by famine or despair. Every access to the continent was cut off by the troops of Padua; and the King of Hungary had mastered almost all the Venetian towns in Istria and along the Dalmatian coast. The Doge Contarini, taking the chief command, appeared at length with his fleet near Chioggia, before the Genoese were aware. They were still less aware of his secret design. He pushed one of the large round vessels, then called cocche, into the narrow passage of Chioggia which connects the lagoon with the sea, and, mooring her athwart the channel, interrupted that communication. Attacked with fury by the enemy, this vessel went down on the spot, and the doge improved his advantage by sinking loads of stones until the passage became absolutely unnavigable. It was still possible for the Genoese fleet to follow the principal canal of the lagoon toward Venice and the northern passages, or to sail out of it by the harbour of Brondolo; but, whether from confusion or from miscalculating the dangers of their position, they suffered the Venetians to close the canal upon them by the same means they had used at Chioggia, and even to place their fleet in the entrance of Brondolo so near to the lagoon that the Genoese could not form their ships in line of battle. The circumstances of the two combatants were thus entirely changed. But the Genoese fleet, though besieged in Chioggia, was impregnable, and their command of the land secured them from famine. Venice, notwithstanding her unexpected success, was still very far from secure; it was difficult for the doge to keep his position through the winter, and, if the enemy could appear in open sea, the risks of combat were extremely hazardous. It is said that

the senate deliberated upon transporting the seat of their liberty
to Candia, and that the doge had announced his intention to
raise the siege of Chioggia if expected succours did not arrive
by the 1st of January, 1380. On that very day Carlo Zeno,
an admiral who, ignorant of the dangers of his country, had
been supporting the honour of her flag in the Levant and on
the coast of Liguria, appeared with a re-enforcement of eighteen
galleys and a store of provisions. From that moment the confidence of Venice revived. The fleet, now superior in strength
to the enemy, began to attack them with vivacity. After several months of obstinate resistance the Genoese, whom their
republic had ineffectually attempted to relieve by a fresh armament, blocked up in the town of Chioggia, and pressed by hunger, were obliged to surrender. Nineteen galleys only out of
forty-eight were in good condition, and the crews were equally
diminished in the ten months of their occupation of Chioggia.
The pride of Genoa was deemed to be justly humbled; and even
her own historian confesses that God would not suffer so noble
a city as Venice to become the spoil of a conqueror.[134]

Each of the two republics had sufficient reason to lament
their mutual prejudices, and the selfish cupidity of their merchants, which usurps in all maritime countries the name of
patriotism. Though the capture of Chioggia did not terminate
the war, both parties were exhausted and willing next year to
accept the mediation of the Duke of Savoy. By the Peace of
Turin, Venice surrendered most of her territorial possessions to
the King of Hungary. That prince and Francis Carrara were
the only gainers. Genoa obtained the isle of Tenedos, one of
the original subjects of dispute—a poor indemnity for her losses.
Though, upon a hasty view, the result of this war appears more
unfavourable to Venice, yet in fact it is the epoch of the decline
of Genoa. From this time she never commanded the ocean
with such navies as before; her commerce gradually went into
decay; and the fifteenth century, the most splendid in the annals
of Venice, is, till recent times, the most ignominious in those of
Genoa. But this was partly owing to internal dissensions, by
which her liberty, as well as glory, was for a while suspended.

At Genoa, as in other cities of Lombardy, the principal
magistrates of the republic were originally styled consuls. A
chronicle drawn up under the inspection of the senate perpetuates the names of these early magistrates. It appears that their
number varied from four to six, annually elected by the people
in their full Parliament. These consuls presided over the repub-

[134] G. Stella, "Annales Genuenses";
Gataro, "Istoria Padovana." Both these
contemporary works, of which the latter
gives the best relation, are in the seventeenth volume of Muratori's collection.
Sismondi's narrative is very clear and
spirited. ("Hist. des Républ. Ital.,"
tome vii, pp. 205-232.)

lic and commanded the forces by land and sea; while another class of magistrates, bearing the same title, were annually elected by the several companies into which the people were divided for the administration of civil justice.[135] This was the regimen of the twelfth century; but in the next Genoa fell into the fashion of intrusting the executive power to a foreign podestà. The podestà was assisted by a council of eight, chosen by the eight companies of nobility. This institution, if indeed it were anything more than a custom or usurpation, originated probably not much later than the beginning of the thirteenth century. It gave not only an aristocratic, but almost an oligarchical character to the constitution, since many of the nobility were not members of these eight societies. Of the senate or councils we hardly know more than their existence; they are very little mentioned by historians. Everything of a general nature, everything that required the expression of public will, was reserved for the entire and unrepresented sovereignty of the people. In no city was the Parliament so often convened: for war, for peace, for alliance, for change of government.[136] These very dissonant elements were not likely to harmonize. The people, sufficiently accustomed to the forms of democracy to imbibe its spirit, repined at the practical influence which was thrown into the scale of the nobles. Nor did some of the latter class scruple to enter that path of ambition which leads to power by flattery of the populace. Two or three times within the thirteenth century a high-born demagogue had nearly overturned the general liberty, like the Torriani at Milan, through the pretence of defending that of individuals.[137] Among the nobility themselves four houses were distinguished beyond all the rest—the Grimaldi, the Fieschi, the Doria, the Spinola; the two former of Guelf politics, the latter adherents of the empire.[138] Perhaps their equality of forces, and a jealousy which even the families of the same faction entertained of each other, prevented any one from usurping the signiory at Genoa. Neither the Guelf nor Ghibelin party obtaining a decided preponderance, continual revolutions occurred in the city. The most celebrated was the expulsion of the Ghibelins under the Doria and Spinola in 1318. They had recourse to the Visconti of Milan, and their own resources were not unequal to cope with their country. The Guelfs thought it necessary to call in Robert, King of Naples, always ready to give assistance as the price of dominion, and conferred upon him the temporary sovereignty of Genoa. A siege of several years' duration, if we believe a historian of that age, produced as many remarkable exploits as that of Troy. They have not proved so

---

[135] Sismondi, tome i, p. 353.
[136] Id., tome i, p. 324.
[137] Id., tome iii, p. 310.
[138] Id., tome iii, p. 328.

interesting to posterity. The Ghibelins continued for a length of time excluded from the city, but in possession of the seaport of Savona, whence they traded and equipped fleets, as a rival republic, and even entered into a separate war with Venice.[139] Experience of the uselessness of hostility, and the loss to which they exposed their common country, produced a reconciliation, or rather a compromise, in 1331, when the Ghibelins returned to Genoa. But the people felt that many years of misfortune had been owing to the private enmities of four overbearing families. An opportunity soon offered of reducing their influence within very narrow bounds.

The Ghibelin faction was at the head of affairs in 1339, a Doria and a Spinola being its leaders, when the discontent of a large fleet in want of pay broke out in open insurrection. Savona and the neighbouring towns took arms avowedly against the aristocratical tyranny, and the capital was itself on the point of joining the insurgents. There was, by the Genoese constitution, a magistrate named the abbot of the people, acting as a kind of tribune for their protection against the oppression of the nobility. His functions are not, however, in any book I have seen, very clearly defined. This office had been abolished by the present government, and it was the first demand of the malcontents that it should be restored. This was acceded to, and twenty delegates were appointed to make the choice. While they delayed, and the populace was grown weary with waiting, a nameless artisan called out from an elevated station that he could direct them to a fit person. When the people, in jest, bade him speak on, he uttered the name of Simon Boccanegra. This was a man of noble birth, and well esteemed, who was then present among the crowd. The word was suddenly taken up; a cry was heard that Boccanegra should be abbot; he was instantly brought forward, and the sword of justice forced into his hand. As soon as silence could be obtained, he modestly thanked them for their favour, but declined an office which his nobility disqualified him from exercising. At this a single voice out of the crowd exclaimed, " Signior!" and this title was reverberated from every side. Fearful of worse consequences, the actual magistrates urged him to comply with the people and accept the office of abbot. But Boccanegra, addressing the assembly, declared his readiness to become their abbot, signior, or whatever they would. The cry of " Signior!" was now louder than before; while others cried out, " Let him be duke!" The latter title was received with greater approbation; and Boccanegra was conducted to the palace, the first duke, or doge, of Genoa.[140]

[139] Villani, l. ix, passim.

[140] G. Stella, " Annal. Genuenses," in " Script. Rer. Ital.," tome xvii, p. 1072.

17

Caprice alone, or an idea of more pomp and dignity, led the populace, we may conjecture, to prefer this title to that of signior; but it produced important and highly beneficial consequences. In all neighbouring cities an arbitrary government had been already established under their respective signiors; the name was associated with indefinite power, while that of doge had only been taken by the elective and very limited chief magistrate of another maritime republic. Neither Boccanegra nor his successors ever rendered their authority unlimited or hereditary. The constitution of Genoa, from an oppressive aristocracy, became a mixture of the two other forms, with an exclusion of the nobles from power. Those four great families who had domineered alternately for almost a century lost their influence at home after the revolution of 1339. Yet, what is remarkable enough, they were still selected in preference for the highest of trusts; their names are still identified with the glory of Genoa; her fleets hardly sailed but under a Doria, a Spinola, or a Grimaldi; such confidence could the republic bestow upon their patriotism, or that of those whom they commanded. Meanwhile two or three new families, a plebeian oligarchy, filled their place in domestic honours; the Adorni, the Fregosi, the Montalti, contended for the ascendant. From their competition ensued revolutions too numerous almost for a separate history; in four years, from 1390 to 1394, the doge was ten times changed—swept away or brought back in the fluctuations of popular tumult. Antoniotto Adorno, four times Doge of Genoa, had sought the friendship of Gian Galeazzo Visconti; but that crafty tyrant meditated the subjugation of the republic, and played her factions against one another to render her fall secure. Adorno perceived that there was no hope for ultimate independence but by making a temporary sacrifice of it. His own power, ambitious as he had been, he voluntarily resigned, and placed the republic under the protection or signiory of the King of France. Terms were stipulated very favourable to her liberties; but, with a French garrison once received into the city, they were not always sure of observance.[141]

While Genoa lost even her political independence, Venice became more conspicuous and powerful than before. That famous republic deduces its origin, and even its liberty, from an era beyond the commencement of the middle ages. The Venetians boast of a perpetual emancipation from the yoke of barbarians. From that ignominious servitude some natives, or, as their historians will have it, nobles, of Aquileja and neighbouring towns,[142] fled to the small cluster of islands that rise

<hr/>

[141] Sismondi, tome vii, pp. 237, 367.
[142] Ebbe principio, says Sanuto haugh-   tily, non da pastori, come ebbe Roma, ma da potenti, e nobili.

amid the shoals at the mouth of the Brenta. Here they built
the town of Rivoalto, the modern Venice, in 421; but their chief
settlement was, till the beginning of the ninth century, at Mala-
mocco. A living writer has, in a passage of remarkable eloquence, described the sovereign republic, immovable upon the
bosom of the waters from which her palaces emerge, contem-
plating the successive tides of continental invasion, the rise and
fall of empires, the change of dynasties, the whole moving scene
of human revolution, till, in her own turn, the last surviving
witness of antiquity, the common link between two periods of
civilization, has submitted to the destroying hand of time.[143]
Some part of this renown must, on a cold-blooded scrutiny, be
detracted from Venice. Her independence was, at the best, the
fruit of her obscurity. Neglected upon their islands, a people
of fishermen might without molestation elect their own magistrates; a very equivocal proof of sovereignty in cities much more
considerable than Venice. But both the Western and the Eastern Empire alternately pretended to exercise dominion over her;
she was conquered by Pepin, son of Charlemagne, and restored
by him, as the chronicles say, to the Greek emperor Nicephorus.
There is every appearance that the Venetians had always considered themselves as subject, in a large sense not exclusive
of their municipal self-government, to the Eastern Empire.[144]
And this connection was not broken, in the early part, at least,
of the tenth century. But, for every essential purpose, Venice
might long before be deemed an independent state. Her doge
was not confirmed at Constantinople, she paid no tribute, and
lent no assistance in war. Her own navies, in the ninth century,
encountered the Normans, the Saracens, and the Slavonians in
the Adriatic Sea. Upon the coast of Dalmatia were several Greek
cities, which the empire had ceased to protect, and which, like
Venice itself, became republics for want of a master. Ragusa
was one of these, and, more fortunate than the rest, survived
as an independent city till our own age. In return for the assistance of Venice, these little seaports put themselves under
her government; the Slavonian pirates were repressed; and after
acquiring, partly by consent, partly by arms, a large tract of
maritime territory, the doge took the title of Duke of Dalmatia,
which is said by Dandolo to have been confirmed at Constantinople. Three or four centuries, however, elapsed before the republic became secure of these conquests, which were frequently
wrested from her by rebellions of the inhabitants, or by her powerful neighbour, the King of Hungary.

[143] Sismondi, tome i, p. 309.
[144] Nicephorus stipulates with Charlemagne for his faithful city of Venice,
Quæ in devotione imperii illibatæ ste-
terant. (Danduli Chronicon, in Muratori, " Script. Rer. Ital.," tome xii, p.

A more important source of Venetian greatness was commerce. In the darkest and most barbarous period, before Genoa
or even Pisa had entered into mercantile pursuits, Venice carried
on an extensive traffic both with the Greek and Saracen regions
of the Levant. The crusades enriched and aggrandized Venice
more, perhaps, than any other city. Her splendour may, however, be dated from the taking of Constantinople by the Latins
in 1204. In this famous enterprise, which diverted a great armament destined for the recovery of Jerusalem, the French and
Venetian nations were alone engaged; but the former only as
private adventurers, the latter with the whole strength of their
republic under its doge, Henry Dandolo. Three eighths of the
city of Constantinople, and an equal proportion of the provinces,
were allotted to them in the partition of the spoil, and the doge
took the singular but accurate title, duke of three eighths of
the Roman Empire. Their share was increased by purchases
from less opulent crusaders, especially one of much importance,
the island of Candia, which they retained till the middle of the
seventeenth century. These foreign acquisitions were generally
granted out in fief to private Venetian nobles under the supremacy of the republic.[145] It was thus that the Ionian Islands, to
adopt the vocabulary of our day, came under the dominion of
Venice, and guaranteed that sovereignty which she now began
to affect over the Adriatic. Those of the archipelago were lost
in the sixteenth century. This political greatness was sustained
by an increasing commerce. No Christian state preserved so
considerable an intercourse with the Mohammedans. While
Genoa kept the keys of the Black Sea by her colonies of Pera
and Caffa, Venice directed her vessels to Acre and Alexandria.
These connections, as is the natural effect of trade, deadened the
sense of religious antipathy; and the Venetians were sometimes
charged with obstructing all efforts toward a new crusade, or
even any partial attacks upon the Mohammedan nations.

The earliest form of government at Venice, as we collect from
an epistle of Cassiodorus in the sixth century, was by twelve
annual tribunes. Perhaps the union of the different islanders
was merely federative. However, in 697, they resolved to elect
a chief magistrate by name of Duke, or, in their dialect, Doge

156.) In the tenth century Constantine
Porphyrogenitus, in his book " De Ad-
ministratione Imperii," claims the Venetians as his subjects, though he admits
that they had, for peace sake, paid tribute
to Pepin and his successors as Kings of
Italy (p. 71). I have not read the famous
" Squittinio della libertà Veneta," which
gave the republic so much offence in the
seventeenth century; but a very strong
case is made out against their early independence in Giannone's history, tome

ii, p. 283, edit. Haia, 1753. Muratori informs us that so late as 1084 the doge
obtained the title of Imperialis Protose-
vastos from the court of Constantinople;
a title which he continued always to use.
(" Annali d' Italia," ad ann.) But I
should lay no stress on this circumstance.
The Greek, like the German emperors in
modern times, had a mint of specious
titles, which passed for ready money over
Christendom.
    [145] Sismondi, tome ii, p. 431.

of Venice. No councils appear to have limited his power or represented the national will. The doge was general and judge; he was sometimes permitted to associate his son with him, and thus to prepare the road for hereditary power; his government had all the prerogatives, and, as far as in such a state of manners was possible, the pomp, of a monarchy. But he acted in important matters with the concurrence of a general assembly, though, from the want of positive restraints, his executive government might be considered as nearly absolute. Time, however, demonstrated to the Venetians the imperfections of such a constitution. Limitations were accordingly imposed on the doge in 1032; he was prohibited from associating a son in the government, and obliged to act with the consent of two elected counsellors, and, on important occasions, to call in some of the principal citizens. No other change appears to have taken place till 1172, long after every other Italian city had provided for its liberty by constitutional laws, more or less successful, but always manifesting a good deal of contrivance and complication. Venice was, however, dissatisfied with her existing institutions. General assemblies were found, in practice, inconvenient and unsatisfactory. Yet some adequate safeguard against a magistrate of indefinite powers was required by freemen. A representative council, as in other republics, justly appeared the best innovation that could be introduced.[146]

The great council of Venice, as established in 1172, was to consist of four hundred and eighty citizens, equally taken from the six districts of the city, and annually renewed. But the election was not made immediately by the people. Two electors, called tribunes, from each of the six districts, appointed the members of the council by separate nomination. These tribunes at first were themselves chosen by the people, so that the intervention of this electoral body did not apparently trespass upon the democratical character of the constitution. But the great council, principally composed of men of high birth, and invested by the law with the appointment of the doge, and of all the councils of magistracy, seem, early in the thirteenth century, to have assumed the right of naming their own constituents. Besides appointing the tribunes, they took upon themselves another privilege, that of confirming or rejecting their successors before they resigned their functions. These usurpations rendered the annual election almost nugatory; the same members were usually

[146] Sismondi, tome iii, p. 287. As I have never read the "Storia civile Veneta," by Vettor Sandi, in nine volumes, 4to, or even Laugier's "History of Venice," my reliance has chiefly been placed on M. Sismondi, who has made use of Sandi, the latest, and probably the most accurate, historian. To avoid frequent reference, the principal passages in Sismondi relative to the domestic revolutions of Venice are tome i, p. 323; tome iii, pp. 287-300; tome iv, pp. 349-370. The history of Daru had not been published when this was written.

renewed; and though the dignity of councillor was not yet hereditary, it remained, upon the whole, in the same families. In this transitional state the Venetian government continued during the thirteenth century; the people actually debarred of power, but an hereditary aristocracy not completely or legally confirmed. The right of electing, or rather of re-electing, the great council was transferred, in 1297, from the tribunes, whose office was abolished, to the council of forty; they balloted upon the names of the members who already sat; and whoever obtained twelve favouring balls out of forty retained his place. The vacancies occasioned by rejection or death were filled up by a supplemental list formed by three electors nominated in the great council. But they were expressly prohibited, by laws of 1298 and 1300, from inserting the name of any one whose paternal ancestors had not enjoyed the same honour. Thus an exclusive hereditary aristocracy was finally established. And the personal rights of noble descent were rendered complete in 1319 by the abolition of all elective forms. By the constitution of Venice as it was then settled every descendant of a member of the great council, on attaining twenty-five years of age, entered as of right into that body, which, of course, became unlimited in its numbers.[147]

But an assembly so numerous as the great council, even before it was thus thrown open to all the nobility, could never have conducted the public affairs with that secrecy and steadiness which were characteristic of Venice; and without an intermediary power between the doge and the patrician multitude, the constitution would have gained nothing in stability to compensate for the loss of popular freedom. The great council had proceeded very soon after its institution to limit the ducal prerogatives. That of exercising criminal justice, a trust of vast importance, was transferred in 1179 to a council of forty members annually chosen. The executive government itself was thought too considerable for the doge without some material limitations. Instead of naming his own assistants or pregadi, he was only to preside in a council of sixty members, to whom the care of the state in all domestic and foreign relations, and the previous deliberation upon proposals submitted to the great council, was confided. This council of pregadi, generally called in later times the senate, was enlarged in the fourteenth century

[147] These gradual changes between 1297 and 1319 were first made known by Sandi, from whom M. Sismondi has introduced the facts into his own history. I notice this, because all former writers, both ancient and modern, fix the complete and final establishment of the Venetian aristocracy in 1297.

Twenty-five years complete was the statutable age at which every Venetian noble had a right to take his seat in the great council. But the names of those who had passed the age of twenty were annually put into an urn, and one fifth drawn out by lot, who were thereupon admitted. On an average, therefore, the age of admission was about twenty-three. (Janotus de Rep. Venet. ; Contarini ; Amelot de la Houssaye.)

by sixty additional members; and as a great part of the magistrates had also seats in it, the whole number amounted to between two and three hundred. Though the legislative power, properly speaking, remained with the great council, the senate used to impose taxes, and had the exclusive right of making peace and war. It was annually renewed, like almost all other councils at Venice, by the great council. But since even this body was too numerous for the preliminary discussion of business, six councillors, forming, along with the doge, the signiory, or visible representative of the republic, were empowered to despatch orders, to correspond with ambassadors, to treat with foreign states, to convoke and preside in the councils, and perform other duties of an administration. In part of these they were obliged to act with the concurrence of what was termed the college, comprising, besides themselves, certain select councillors, from different constituted authorities.[148]

It might be imagined that a dignity so shorn of its lustre as that of doge would not excite an overweening ambition. But the Venetians were still jealous of extinguished power; and while their constitution was yet immature, the great council planned new methods of restricting their chief magistrate. An oath was taken by the doge on his election, so comprehensive as to embrace every possible check upon undue influence. He was bound not to correspond with foreign states, or to open their letters, except in the presence of the signiory; to acquire no property beyond the Venetian dominions, and to resign what he might already possess; to interpose, directly or indirectly, in no judicial process; and not to permit any citizen to use tokens of subjection in saluting him. As a further security, they devised a remarkably complicated mode of supplying the vacancy of his office. Election by open suffrage is always liable to tumult or corruption; nor does the method of secret ballot, while it prevents the one, afford in practice any adequate security against the other. Election by lot incurs the risk of placing incapable persons in situations of arduous trust. The Venetian scheme was intended to combine the two modes without their evils, by leaving the absolute choice of their doge to electors taken by lot. It was presumed that, among a competent number of persons, though taken promiscuously, good sense and right principles would gain such an ascendency as to prevent any flagrantly improper nomination if undue influence could be excluded. For this purpose the ballot was rendered exceedingly complicated,

148 The college of Savj consisted of sixteen persons; and it possessed the initiative in all public measures that required the assent of the senate. For no single senator, much less any noble of the great council, could propose anything for debate. The signiory had the same privilege. Thus the virtual powers even of the senate were far more limited than they appear at first sight; and no possibility remained of innovation in the fundamental principles of the constitution.

that no possible ingenuity or stratagem might ascertain the electoral body before the last moment. A single lottery, if fairly conducted, is certainly sufficient for this end. At Venice as, many balls as there were members of the great council present were placed in an urn. Thirty of these were gilt. The holders of gilt balls were reduced by a second ballot to nine. The nine elected forty, whom lot reduced to twelve. The twelve chose twenty-five by separate nomination.[149] The twenty-five were reduced by lot to nine; and each of the nine chose five. These forty-five were reduced to eleven as before; the eleven elected forty-one, who were the ultimate voters for a doge. This intricacy appears useless, and consequently absurd; but the original principle of a Venetian election (for something of the same kind was applied to all their councils and magistrates) may not always be unworthy of imitation. In one of our best modern statutes, that for regulating the trials of contested elections, we have seen this mixture of chance and selection very happily introduced.[150]

An hereditary prince could never have remained quiet in such trammels as were imposed upon the Doge of Venice. But early prejudice accustoms men to consider restraint, even upon themselves, as advantageous; and the limitations of ducal power appeared to every Venetian as fundamental as the great laws of the English constitution do to ourselves. Many doges of Venice, especially in the middle ages, were considerable men; but they were content with the functions assigned to them, which, if they could avoid the tantalizing comparison of sovereign princes, were enough for the ambition of republicans. For life the chief magistrates of their country, her noble citizens forever, they might thank her in their own name for what she gave, and in that of their posterity for what she withheld. Once only a Doge of Venice was tempted to betray the freedom of the republic. Marin Falieri, a man far advanced in life, engaged, from some petty resentment, in a wild intrigue to overturn the government. The conspiracy was soon discovered, and the doge avowed his guilt. An aristocracy so firm and so severe did not hesitate to order his execution in the ducal palace.

For some years after what was called the closing of the great council by the law of 1296, which excluded all but the families actually in possession, a good deal of discontent showed itself among the commonalty. Several commotions took place about the beginning of the fourteenth century, with the object of restoring a more popular regimen. Upon the suppression of the

[149] Amelot de la Houssaye asserts this: but, according to Contarini, the method was by ballot.
[150] This was written about 1810. The statute to which I allude grew out of favour afterward. But there is too much reason to doubt whether grosser instances of partial or unjust, or at best erroneous, determination have not taken place since a new tribunal was erected, than could be imputed to the celebrated Grenville act. [1850.]

last, in 1310, the aristocracy sacrificed their own individual freedom, along with that of the people, to the preservation of an
imaginary privilege. They established the famous Council of
Ten, that most remarkable part of the Venetian constitution.
This council, it should be observed, consisted, in fact, of seventeen, comprising the signiory, or the doge and his six councillors,
as well as the ten properly so called. The Council of Ten had
by usage, if not by right, a controlling and dictatorial power
over the senate and other magistrates, rescinding their decisions,
and treating separately with foreign princes. Their vast influence strengthened the executive government, of which they
formed a part, and gave a vigour to its movements which the
jealousy of the councils would possibly have impeded. But they
are chiefly known as an arbitrary and inquisitorial tribunal, the
standing tyranny of Venice. Excluding the old Council of Forty,
a regular court of criminal judicature, not only from the investigation of treasonable charges, but of several other crimes of
magnitude, they inquired, they judged, they punished, according to what they called reason of state. The public eye never
penetrated the mystery of their proceedings; the accused was
sometimes not heard, never confronted with witnesses; the condemnation was secret as the inquiry, the punishment undivulged
like both.[151] The terrible and odious machinery of a police, the
insidious spy, the stipendiary informer, unknown to the care-
lessness of feudal governments, found their natural soil in the
republic of Venice. Tumultuous assemblies were scarcely possible in so peculiar a city; and private conspiracies never failed
to be detected by the vigilance of the Council of Ten. Compared
with the Tuscan republics, the tranquility of Venice is truly striking. The names of Guelf and Ghibelin hardly raised any emotion
in her streets, though the government was considered in the first
part of the fourteenth century as rather inclined toward the latter
party.[152] But the wildest excesses of faction are less dishonour-
ing than the stillness and moral degradation of servitude.[153]

[151] Illum etiam morem observant, ne reum, cum de eo judicium laturi sunt, in collegium admittant, neque cognitorem, aut oratorem quempiam, qui ejus causam agat. (" Contarini de Rep. Venet.")
[152] Villani several times speaks of the Venetians as regular Ghibelins (l. ix, c. 2; l. x, c. 89, etc.). But this is put much too strongly: though their government may have had a slight bias toward that faction, they were in reality neutral, and far enough removed from any domestic feuds upon that score.
[153] By the modern law of Venice a no-bleman could not engage in trade with-out derogating from his rank: I do not find this peculiarity observed by Jannotti and Contarini, the oldest writers on the

Venetian government: but Daru informs us it was by a law enacted in 1400. (" Hist. de Venise," l. 589.) It is noticed by Amelot de la Houssaye, who tells us also, as Daru does, that the nobility evaded the law by secret partnership with the privileged merchants or cittadini, who formed a separate class at Venice. This was the custom in modern times. But I have never understood the principle or common sense of such a restriction, especially combined with that other fun-damental law which disqualified a Vene-tian nobleman from possessing a landed estate on the terra firma of the republic. The latter, however, did not extend, as I have been informed, to Dalmatia, or the Ionian Islands.

It was a very common theme with political writers till about
the beginning of the last century, when Venice fell almost into
oblivion, to descant upon the wisdom of this government. And,
indeed, if the preservation of ancient institutions be, as some
appear to consider it, not a means but an end, and an end for
which the rights of man and laws of God may at any time be
set aside, we must acknowledge that it was a wisely constructed
system. Formed to compress the two opposite forces from which
resistance might be expected, it kept both the doge and the people in perfect subordination. Even the coalition of an executive magistrate with the multitude, so fatal to most aristocracies,
never endangered that of Venice. It is most remarkable that a
part of the constitution which destroyed every man's security,
and incurred general hatred, was still maintained by a sense of
its necessity. The Council of Ten, annually renewed, might annually have been annihilated. The great council had only to
withhold their suffrages from the new candidates, and the tyranny
expired of itself. This was several times attempted (I speak
now of more modern ages); but the nobles, though detesting
the Council of Ten, never steadily persevered in refusing to re-
elect it. It was, in fact, become essential to Venice. So great
were the vices of her constitution that she could not endure
their remedies. If the Council of Ten had been abolished at any
time since the fifteenth century, if the removal of that jealous
despotism had given scope to the corruption of a poor and debased aristocracy, to the license of a people unworthy of freedom, the republic would have soon lost her territorial possessions, if not her own independence. If, indeed, it be true, as reported, that during the last hundred years this formidable tribunal
had sensibly relaxed its vigilance, if the Venetian government
had become less tyrannical through sloth or decline of national
spirit, our conjecture will have acquired the confirmation of experience. Experience has recently shown that a worse calamity
than domestic tyranny might befall the Queen of the Adriatic.
In the Place of St. Mark, among the monuments of extinguished
greatness, a traveller may regret to think that an insolent German soldiery has replaced even the senators of Venice. Her
ancient liberty, her bright and romantic career of glory in countries so dear to the imagination, her magnanimous defence in
the war of Chioggia, a few thinly scattered names of illustrious
men, will rise upon his mind and mingle with his indignation
at the treachery which robbed her of her independence. But if
he has learned the true attributes of wisdom in civil policy, he
will not easily prostitute that word to a constitution formed
without reference to property or to population, that vested sovereign power partly in a body of impoverished nobles, partly

in an overruling despotism; or to a practical system of government that made vice the ally of tyranny, and sought impunity for its own assassinations by encouraging dissoluteness of private life. Perhaps, too, the wisdom so often imputed to the senate in its foreign policy has been greatly exaggerated. The balance of power established in Europe, and, above all, in Italy, maintained for the last two centuries states of small intrinsic resources, without any efforts of their own. In the ultimate crisis, at least, of Venetian liberty, that solemn mockery of statesmanship was exhibited to contempt; too blind to avert danger, too cowardly to withstand it, the most ancient government of Europe made not an instant's resistance; the peasants of Underwald died upon their mountains; the nobles of Venice clung only to their lives.[154]

Until almost the middle of the fourteenth century Venice had been content without any territorial possessions in Italy; unless we reckon a very narrow strip of sea-coast, bordering on her lagoons, called the Dogato. Neutral in the great contests between the Church and the empire, between the free cities and their sovereigns, she was respected by both parties, while neither ventured to claim her as an ally. But the rapid progress of Mastino della Scala, Lord of Verona, with some particular injuries, led the senate to form a league with Florence against him. Villani mentions it as a singular honour for his country to have become the confederate of the Venetians, " who, for their great excellence and power, had never allied themselves with any state or prince, except at their ancient conquest of Constantinople and Romania." [155] The result of this combination was to annex the district of Treviso to the Venetian dominions. But they made no further conquests in that age. On the contrary, they lost Treviso in the unfortunate war of Chioggia, and did not regain it till 1389. Nor did they seriously attempt to withstand the progress of Gian Galeazzo Visconti, who, after overthrowing the family of Scala, stretched almost to the Adriatic, and altogether subverted for a time the balance of power in Lombardy.

<hr/>

[154] The circumstances to which Venice was reduced in her last agony by the violence and treachery of Napoleon, and the apparent impossibility of an effective resistance, so fully described by Daru, and still better by Botta, induce me to modify the severity of this remark. In former editions I have by mistake said that the last Doge of Venice, Manini, is buried in the Church of the Scalzi, with the inscription on the stone, Manini Cineres. This church was indeed built by the contributions of several noble families, among them the Manini, most of whom are interred there; but the last doge himself lies in that of the Jesuits. The words Manini Cineres may be read in both, which probably was the cause of my forgetfulness. [1850.]

See in the " Edinburgh Review," vol. xii, p. 379, an account of a book which is, perhaps, little known, though interesting to the history of our own age: a collection of documents illustrating the fall of the republic of Venice. The article is well written, and, I presume, contains a faithful account of the work, the author of which, Signor Barzoni, is respected as a patriotic writer in Italy.

[155] L. xi, c. 49.

But upon the death of this prince, in 1404, a remarkable crisis took place in that country. He left two sons, Giovanni Maria and Filippo Maria, both young, and under the care of a mother who was little fitted for her situation. Through her misconduct and the selfish ambition of some military leaders, who had commanded Gian Galeazzo's mercenaries, that extensive dominion was soon broken into fragments. Bergamo, Como, Lodi, Cremona, and other cities revolted, submitting themselves in general to the families of their former princes, the earlier race of usurpers, who had for nearly a century been crushed by the Visconti. A Guelf faction revived after the name had long been proscribed in Lombardy. Francesco da Carrara, Lord of Padua, availed himself of this revolution to get possession of Verona, and seemed likely to unite all the cities beyond the Adige. No family was so odious to the Venetians as that of Carrara. Though they had seemed indifferent to the more real danger in Gian Galeazzo's lifetime, they took up arms against this inferior enemy. Both Padua and Verona were reduced, and, the Duke of Milan ceding Vicenza, the republic of Venice came suddenly into the possession of an extensive territory. Francesco da Carrara, who had surrendered in his capital, was put to death in prison at Venice.

Notwithstanding the deranged condition of the Milanese, no further attempts were made by the senate of Venice for twenty years. They had not yet acquired that decided love of war and conquest which soon began to influence them against all the rules of their ancient policy. There were still left some wary statesmen of the old school to check ambitious designs. Sanuto has preserved an interesting account of the wealth and commerce of Venice in those days. This is thrown into the mouth of the Doge Mocenigo, whom he represents as dissuading his country, with his dying words, from undertaking a war against Milan. " Through peace our city has every year," he said, " ten millions of ducats employed as mercantile capital in different parts of the world; the annual profit of our traders upon this sum amounts to four millions. Our housing is valued at seven million ducats; its annual rental at five hundred thousand. Three thousand merchant ships carry on our trade; forty-three galleys and three hundred smaller vessels, manned by nineteen thousand sailors, secure our naval power. Our mint has coined one million ducats within the year. From the Milanese dominions alone we draw one million six hundred and fifty-four thousand ducats in coin, and the value of nine hundred thousand more in cloths; our profit upon this traffic may be reckoned at six hundred thousand ducats. Proceeding as you have done to acquire this wealth, you will become masters of all the gold in Christendom; but war, and especially unjust war, will lead infallibly to ruin. Already you have spent nine hundred thousand ducats in the acquisition of Verona and Padua; yet the expense of protecting these places absorbs all the revenue which they yield. You have many among you, men of probity and experience; choose one of these to succeed me, but beware of Francesco Foscari. If he is doge, you will soon have war, and war will bring poverty and loss of honour." [156] Mocenigo died, and Foscari became doge: the prophecies of the former were neglected, and it can not wholly be affirmed that they were fulfilled. Yet Venice is described by a writer thirty years later as somewhat impaired in opulence by her long warfare with the Dukes of Milan.

The latter had recovered a great part of their dominions as rapidly as they had lost them. Giovanni Maria, the elder brother, a monster of guilt even among the Visconti, having been assassinated, Filippo Maria assumed the government of Milan and Pavia, almost his only possessions. But though weak and unwarlike himself, he had the good fortune to employ Carmagnola, one of the greatest generals of that military age. Most of the revolted cities were tired of their new masters, and, their inclinations conspiring with Carmagnola's eminent talents and activity, the house of Visconti reassumed its former ascendency from the Sessia to the Adige. Its fortunes might have been still more prosperous if Filippo Maria had not rashly as well as ungratefully offended Carmagnola. That great captain retired to Venice, and inflamed a disposition toward war which the Florentines and the Duke of Savoy had already excited. The Venetians had previously gained some important advantages in another quarter by reducing the country of Friuli, with part of Istria, which had for many centuries depended on the temporal authority of a neighbouring prelate, the Patriarch of Aquileia. They entered into this new alliance. No undertaking of the republic had been more successful. Carmagnola led on their armies, and in about two years Venice acquired Brescia and Bergamo, and extended her boundary to the river Adda, which she was destined never to pass.

Such conquests could only be made by a city so peculiarly maritime as Venice through the help of mercenary troops. But, in employing them, she merely conformed to a fashion which

---

[156] Sanuto, " Vite di Duchi di Venezia," in " Script. Rer. Ital.," tome xxii, p. 958. Mocenigo's harangue is very long in Sanuto. I have endeavoured to preserve the substance. But the calculations are so strange and manifestly inexact that they deserve little regard. Daru has given them more at length. (" Hist. de Venise," vol. ii, p. 205.) The revenues of Venice, which had amounted to 996,290 ducats in 1423, were but 945,- 750 in 1460, notwithstanding her acquisition, in the meantime, of Brescia, Bergamo, Ravenna, and Crema. (Id., ii, 462.) They increased considerably in the next twenty years. The taxes, however, were light in the Venetian dominions; and Daru conceives the revenues of the republic, reduced to a corn price, to have not exceeded the value of 11,000,000 francs at the present day (p. 542).

states to whom it was less indispensable had long since established. A great revolution had taken place in the system of military service through most parts of Europe, but especially in Italy. During the twelfth and thirteenth centuries, whether the Italian cities were engaged in their contest with the emperors or in less arduous and general hostilities among each other, they seem to have poured out almost their whole population as an armed and loosely organized militia. A single city, with its adjacent district, sometimes brought twenty or thirty thousand men into the field. Every man, according to the trade he practised, or quarter of the city wherein he dwelt, knew his own banner and the captain he was to obey.[157] In battle the carroccio formed one common rallying point, the pivot of every movement. This was a chariot, or rather wagon, painted with vermilion, and bearing the city standard elevated upon it. That of Milan required four pair of oxen to drag it forward.[158] To defend this sacred emblem of his country, which Muratori compares to the ark of the covenant among the Jews, was the constant object, that, giving a sort of concentration and uniformity to the army, supplied in some degree the want of more regular tactics. This militia was, of course, principally composed of infantry. At the famous battle of the Arbia, in 1260, the Guelf Florentines had thirty thousand foot and three thousand horse;[159] and the usual proportion was five, six, or ten to one. Gentlemen, however, were always mounted; and the superiority of a heavy cavalry must have been prodigiously great over an undisciplined and ill-armed populace. In the thirteenth and following centuries armies seem to have been considered as formidable nearly in proportion to the number of men at arms or lancers. A charge of cavalry was irresistible; battles were continually won by inferior numbers, and vast slaughter was made among the fugitives.[160]

As the comparative inefficiency of foot soldiers became evident, a greater proportion of cavalry was employed, and armies, though better equipped and disciplined, were less numerous. This we find in the early part of the fourteenth century. The main point for a state at war was to obtain a sufficient force of men at arms. As few Italian cities could muster a large body of cavalry from their own population, the obvious resource was to hire mercenary troops. This had been practised in some in-

[157] Muratori. "Antiq. Ital.," Dissert. 26; Denina, "Rivoluzoni d' Italia," l. xii, c. 4.
[158] The carroccio was invented by Eribert, a celebrated Archbishop of Milan, about 1039. ("Annali di Murat."; "Antiq. Ital.," Dissert. 26.) The carroccio of Milan was taken by Frederick II in 1237, and sent to Rome. Parma and Cre-

mona lost their carroccios to each other, and exchanged them some years afterward with great exultation. In the fourteenth century this custom had gone into disuse. (Id., ibid.; Denina, l. xii, c. 4.)
[159] Villani, l. vi, c. 79.
[160] Sismondi, tome iii, p. 263, etc., has some judicious observations on this subject.

stances much earlier. The city of Genoa took the Count of
Savoy into pay with two hundred horse in 1225.[161] Florence
retained five hundred French lances in 1282.[162] But it became
much more general in the fourteenth century, chiefly after the
expedition of the Emperor Henry VII in 1310. Many German
soldiers of fortune, remaining in Italy upon this occasion, engaged in the service of Milan, Florence, or some other state.
The subsequent expeditions of Louis of Bavaria in 1326, and
of John, King of Bohemia, in 1331, brought a fresh accession
of adventurers from the same country. Others, again, came from
France, and some from Hungary. All preferred to continue in
the richest country and finest climate of Europe, where their
services were anxiously solicited and abundantly repaid. An
unfortunate prejudice in favour of strangers prevailed among
the Italians of that age. They ceded to them, one knows not
why, certainly without having been vanquished, the palm of military skill and valour. The word transalpine (oltramontani) is
frequently applied to hired cavalry by the two Villani as an epi-
thet of excellence.

The experience of every fresh campaign now told more and
more against the ordinary militia. It has been usual for modern
writers to lament the degeneracy of martial spirit among the
Italians of that age. But the contest was too unequal between
an absolutely invulnerable body of cuirassiers and an infantry
of peasants or citizens. The bravest men have little appetite
for receiving wounds and death without the hope of inflicting
any in return. The parochial militia of France had proved
equally unserviceable; though, as the life of a French peasant
was of much less account in the eyes of his government than
that of an Italian citizen, they were still led forward like sheep
to the slaughter against the disciplined forces of Edward III.
The cavalry had about this time laid aside the hauberk, or coat
of mail, their ancient distinction from the unprotected populace;
which, though incapable of being cut through by the sabre, afforded no defence against the pointed sword introduced in the
thirteenth century,[163] nor repelled the impulse of a lance or the
crushing blow of a battle-axe. Plate-armour was substituted
in its place; and the man at arms, cased in entire steel, the several pieces firmly riveted, and proof against every stroke, his
charger protected on the face, chest, and shoulders, or, as it was

[161] Muratori, Dissert. 26.
[162] Ammirato, " Ist. Fiorent.," p. 159.
The same was done in 1297 (p. 200). A
lance, in the technical language of those
ages, included the lighter cavalry attached to the man at arms as well as
himself. In France the full complement
of a lance (lance fournie) was five or six
horses; thus the 1,500 lances who composed the original companies of ordonnance raised by Charles VI amounted to
9,000 cavalry. But in Italy the number
was smaller. We read frequently of bar-
buti, which are defined lanze de due
cavalli. (Corio, p. 437.) Lances of three
horses were introduced about the middle
of the fourteenth century. (Id., p. 466.)
[163] Muratori, ad ann., 1226.

called, barded, with plates of steel, fought with a security of success against enemies inferior perhaps only in these adventitious sources of courage to himself.[164]

Nor was the new system of conducting hostilities less inconvenient to the citizens than the tactics of a battle. Instead of rapid and predatory invasions, terminated instantly by a single action, and not extending more than a few days' march from the soldier's home, the more skilful combinations usual in the fourteenth century frequently protracted an indecisive contest for a whole summer.[165] As wealth and civilization made evident the advantages of agriculture and mercantile industry, this loss of productive labour could no longer be endured. Azzo Visconti, who died in 1339, dispensed with the personal service of his Milanese subjects. "Another of his laws," says Galvaneo Fiamma, "was that the people should not go to war, but remain at home for their own business. For they had hitherto been kept with much danger and expense every year, and especially in time of harvest and vintage, when princes are wont to go to war, in besieging cities, and incurred numberless losses, and chiefly on account of the long time that they were so detained."[166] This law of Azzo Visconti, taken separately, might be ascribed to the usual policy of an absolute government. But we find a similar innovation not long afterward at Florence. In the war carried on by that republic against Giovanni Visconti in 1351, the younger Villani informs us that "the useless and mischievous personal service of the inhabitants of the district was commuted into a money payment."[167] This change, indeed, was necessarily accompanied by a vast increase of taxation. The Italian states, republics as well as principalities, levied very heavy contributions. Mastino della Scala had a revenue of seven hundred thousand florins, more, says John Villani, than the king of any European country, except France, possesses.[168] Yet this arose from only nine cities of Lombardy. Considered with reference to economy, almost any taxes must be a cheap commutation for personal service. But economy may be regarded too exclusively, and can never counterbalance that degradation of a national

---

[164] The earliest plate-armour, engraved in Montfaucon's "Monumens de la Monarchie Française," tome ii, is of the reign of Philip the Long, about 1315; but it does not appear generally till that of Philip of Valois, or even later. Before the complete harness of steel was adopted, plated caps were sometimes worn on the knees and elbows, and even greaves on the legs. This is represented in a statue of Charles I, King of Naples, who died in 1285. Possibly the statue may not be quite so ancient. (Montfaucon, passim ; Daniel, "Hist. de la Milice Française," p. 395.)

[165] This tedious warfare à la Fabius is called by Villani guerra guereggiata (l. viii, c. 49); at least I can annex no other meaning to the expression.
[166] Muratori, "Antiquit. Ital.," Dissert. 26.
[167] Matt. Villani, p. 135.
[168] L. xi, c. 45. I can not imagine why Sismondi asserts (tome iv, p. 432) that the lords of cities in Lombardy did not venture to augment the taxes imposed while they had been free. Complaints of heavy taxation are certainly often made against the Visconti and other tyrants in the fourteenth century.

character which proceeds from intrusting the public defence to foreigners.

It could hardly be expected that stipendiary troops, chiefly composed of Germans, would conduct themselves without insolence and contempt of the effeminacy which courted their services. Indifferent to the cause they supported, the highest pay and the richest plunder were their constant motives. As Italy was generally the theatre of war in some of her numerous states, a soldier of fortune, with his lance and charger for an inheritance, passed from one service to another without regret and without discredit. But if peace happened to be pretty universal, he might be thrown out of his only occupation, and reduced to a very inferior condition, in a country of which he was not a native. It naturally occurred to men of their feelings that, if money and honour could only be had while they retained their arms, it was their own fault if they ever relinquished them. Upon this principle they first acted in 1343, when the republic of Pisa disbanded a large body of German cavalry which had been employed in a war with Florence.[169] A partisan, whom the Italians call the Duke Guarnieri, engaged these dissatisfied mercenaries to remain united under his command. His plan was to levy contributions on all countries which he entered with his company, without aiming at any conquests. No Italian army, he well knew, could be raised to oppose him, and he trusted that other mercenaries would not be ready to fight against men who had devised a scheme so advantageous to the profession. This was the first of the companies of adventure which continued for many years to be the scourge and disgrace of Italy. Guarnieri, after some time, withdrew his troops, satiated with plunder, into Germany; but he served in the invasion of Naples by Louis, King of Hungary, in 1348, and, forming a new company, ravaged the ecclesiastical state. A still more formidable band of disciplined robbers appeared in 1353, under the command of Fra Moriale, and afterward of Conrad Lando. This was denominated the Great Company, and consisted of several thousand regular troops, besides a multitude of half-armed ruffians, who assisted as spies, pioneers, and plunderers. The rich cities of Tuscany and Romagna paid large sums that the Great Company, which was perpetually in motion, might not march through their territory. Florence alone magnanimously resolved not to offer this ignominious tribute. Upon two occasions, once in 1358, and

---

[169] Sismondi, tome v, p. 380. The dangerous aspect which these German mercenaries might assume had appeared four years before, when Lodrisio, one of the Visconti, having quarrelled with the Lord of Milan, led a large body of troops who had just been disbanded against the city. After some desperate battles the mercenaries were defeated and Lodrisio taken (tome v, p. 278). In this instance, however, they acted for another; Guarnieri was the first who taught them to preserve the impartiality of general robbers.

18

still more conspicuously the next year, she refused either to give a passage to the company or to redeem herself by money; and in each instance the German robbers were compelled to retire. At this time they consisted of five thousand cuirassiers, and their whole body was not less than twenty thousand men; a terrible proof of the evils which an erroneous system had entailed upon Italy. Nor were they repulsed on this occasion by the actual exertions of Florence. The courage of that republic was in her councils, not in her arms; the resistance made to Lando's demand was a burst of national feeling, and rather against the advice of the leading Florentines; [170] but the army employed was entirely composed of mercenary troops, and probably for the greater part of foreigners.

None of the foreign partisans who entered into the service of Italian states acquired such renown in that career as an Englishman whom contemporary writers call Aucud or Agutus, but to whom we may restore his national appellation of Sir John Hawkwood. This very eminent man had served in the war of Edward III, and obtained his knighthood from that sovereign, though originally, if we may trust common fame, bred to the trade of a tailor. After the Peace of Bretigni, France was ravaged by the disbanded troops, whose devastations Edward was accused, perhaps unjustly, of secretly instigating. A large body of these, under the name of the White Company, passed into the service of the Marquis of Montferrat. They were some time afterward employed by the Pisans against Florence, and during this latter war Hawkwood appears as their commander. For thirty years he was continually engaged in the service of the Visconti, of the Pope, or of the Florentines, to whom he devoted himself for the latter part of his life with more fidelity and steadiness than he had shown in his first campaigns. The republic testified her gratitude by a public funeral, and by a monument in the Duomo, which still perpetuates his memory.

The name of Sir John Hawkwood is worthy to be remembered as that of the first distinguished commander who had appeared in Europe since the destruction of the Roman Empire. It would be absurd to suppose that any of the constituent elements of military genius which Nature furnishes to energetic characters were wanting to the leaders of a barbarian or feudal army: untroubled perspicacity in confusion, firm decision, rapid execution, providence against attack, fertility of resource and stratagem—these are in quality as much required from the chief of an Indian tribe as from the accomplished commander. But we do not find them in any instance so consummated by habitual skill as to challenge the name of generalship. No one at least

[170] Matt. Villani, p. 537.

occurs to me, previously to the middle of the fourteenth century, to whom history has unequivocally assigned that character. It is very rarely that we find even the order ot battle specially noticed. The monks, indeed, our only chroniclers, were poor judges of martial excellence; yet, as war is the main topic of all annals, we could hardly remain ignorant of any distinguished skill in its operations. This neglect of military science certainly did not proceed from any predilection for the arts of peace. It arose out of the general manners of society, and out of the nature and composition of armies in the middle ages. The insubordinate spirit of feudal tenants and the emulous equality of chivalry were alike hostile to that gradation of rank, that punctual observance of irksome duties, that prompt obedience to a supreme command, through which a single soul is infused into the active mass, and the rays of individual merit converge to the head of the general.

In the fourteenth century we begin to perceive something of a more scientific character in military proceedings, and historians for the first time discover that success does not entirely depend upon intrepidity and physical prowess. The victory of Mühldorf over the Austrian princes in 1322, that decided a civil war in the empire, is ascribed to the ability of the Bavarian commander.[171] Many distinguished officers were formed in the school of Edward III. Yet their excellences were perhaps rather those of active partisans than of experienced generals. Their successes are still due rather to daring enthusiasm than to wary and calculating combination. Like inexpert chess players, they surprise us by happy sallies against rule, or display their talents in rescuing themselves from the consequence of their own mistakes. Thus the admirable arrangements of the Black Prince at Poitiers hardly redeem the temerity which placed him in a situation where the egregious folly of his adversary alone could have permitted him to triumph. Hawkwood therefore appears to me the first real general of modern times; the earliest master, however imperfect, in the science of Turenne and Wellington. Every contemporary Italian historian speaks with admiration of his skilful tactics in battle, his stratagems, his well-conducted retreats. Praise of this description, as I have observed, is hardly bestowed, certainly not so continually, on any former captain.

Hawkwood was not only the greatest but the last of the foreign condottieri, or captains of mercenary bands. While he was yet living a new military school had been formed in Italy, which not only superseded, but eclipsed, all the strangers. This important reform was ascribed to Alberic di Barbiano, lord of some

[171] Struvius, " Corpus Hist. German.," p. 585. Schwepperman, the Bavarian general, is called by a contemporary writer clarus militari scientiâ vir.

petty territories near Bologna. He formed a company altogether
of Italians about the year 1379. It is not to be supposed that
natives of Italy had before been absolutely excluded from service.
We find several Italians, such as the Malatesta family, Lords of
Rimini, and the Rossi of Parma, commanding the armies of
Florence much earlier. But this was the first trading company,
if I may borrow the analogy, the first regular body of Italian
mercenaries, attached only to their commander without any consideration of party, like the Germans and English of Lando and
Hawkwood. Alberic di Barbiano, though himself no doubt a
man of military talents, is principally distinguished by the school
of great generals which the company of St. George under his
command produced, and which may be deduced, by regular
succession, to the sixteenth century. The first in order of time,
and immediate contemporaries of Barbiano, were Jacopo del
Verme, Facino Cane, and Ottobon Terzo. Among an intelligent
and educated people, little inclined to servile imitation, the military art made great progress. The most eminent condottieri
being divided, in general, between belligerents, each of them had
his genius excited and kept in tension by that of a rival in glory.
Every resource of science as well as experience, every improvement in tactical arrangements, and the use of arms, were required
to obtain an advantage over such equal enemies. In the first
year of the fifteenth century the Italians brought their newly
acquired superiority to a test. The Emperor Robert, in alliance
with Florence, invaded Gian Galeazzo's dominions with a considerable army. From old reputation, which so frequently survives the intrinsic qualities upon which it was founded, an impression appears to have been excited in Italy that the native
troops were still unequal to meet the charge of German cuirassiers. The Duke of Milan gave orders to his general, Jacopo
del Verme, to avoid a combat. But that able leader was aware
of a great relative change in the two armies. The Germans had
neglected to improve their discipline; their arms were less easily
wielded, their horses less obedient to the bit. A single skirmish
was enough to open their eyes; they found themselves decidedly
inferior; and having engaged in the war with the expectation
of easy success, were readily disheartened.[172] This victory, or
rather this decisive proof that victory might be achieved, set
Italy at rest for almost a century from any apprehensions on the
side of her ancient masters.

Whatever evils might be derived, and they were not trifling,
from the employment of foreign or native mercenaries, it was
impossible to discontinue the system without general consent;
and too many states found their own advantage in it for such an

[172] Sismondi, tome vii, p. 439.

agreement. The condottieri were indeed all notorious for contempt of engagements. Their rapacity was equal to their bad faith. Besides an enormous pay, for every private cuirassier received much more in value than a subaltern officer at present, they exacted gratifications for every success.[173] But everything was endured by ambitious governments who wanted their aid. Florence and Venice were the two states which owed most to the companies of adventure. The one loved war without its perils; the other could never have obtained an inch of territory with a population of sailors. But they were both almost inexhaustibly rich by commercial industry; and, as the surest paymasters, were best served by those they employed. The Visconti might perhaps have extended their conquest over Lombardy with the militia of Milan; but without a Jacopo del Verme or a Carmagnola, the banner of St. Mark would never have floated at Verona and Bergamo.

The Italian armies of the fifteenth century have been remarked for one striking peculiarity. War has never been conducted at so little personal hazard to the soldier. Combats frequently occur, in the annals of that age, wherein success, though warmly contested, costs very few lives even to the vanquished.[174] This innocence of blood, which some historians turn into ridicule, was no doubt owing in a great degree to the rapacity of the companies of adventure, who, in expectation of enriching themselves by the ransom of prisoners, were anxious to save their lives. Much of the humanity of modern warfare was originally due to this motive. But it was rendered more practicable by the nature of their arms. For once, and for once only in the history of mankind, the art of defence had outstripped that of

---

[173] Paga doppia, e mese compiuto, of which we frequently read, sometimes granted improvidently, and more often demanded unreasonably. The first speaks for itself; the second was the reckoning a month's service as completed when it was begun, in calculating their pay. (Matt. Villani, p. 62; Sismondi, tome v, p. 412.)

Gian Galeazzo Visconti promised constant half pay to the condottieri whom he disbanded in 1396. This, perhaps, is the first instance of half pay. (Sismondi, tome vii, p. 379.)

[174] Instances of this are very frequent. Thus at the action of Zagonara, in 1423, but three persons, according to Machiavel, lost their lives, and these by suffocation in the mud. (" Ist. Fiorent.," l. iv.) At that of Molinella, in 1467, he says that no one was killed (l. vii). Ammirato reproves him for this, as all the authors of the time represent it to have been sanguinary (tome ii, p. 102), and insinuates that Machiavel ridicules the inoffensiveness of those armies more than they de-

serve, schernendo, come egli suol far, quella milizia. Certainly some few battles of the fifteenth century were not only obstinately contested, but attended with considerable loss. (Sismondi, tome x, pp. 126, 137.) But, in general, the slaughter must appear very trifling. Ammirato himself says that in an action between the Neapolitan and papal troops in 1486, which lasted all day, not only no one was killed, but it is not recorded that any one was wounded. (Roscoe's " Lorenzo de' Medici," vol. ii, p. 37.) Guicciardini's general testimony to the character of these combats is unequivocal. He speaks of the battle of Fornova, between the confederates of Lombardy and the army of Charles VIII returning from Naples in 1495, as very remarkable on account of the slaughter, which amounted on the Italian side to 3,000 men: perchè fù la prima, che da lunghissimo tempo in quà si combattesse con uccisione e con sangue in Italia, perchè innanzi à questa morivano pochissimi uomini in un fatto d'arme (l. ii, p. 175).

destruction. In a charge of lancers many fell, unhorsed by the shock, and might be suffocated or bruised to death by the pressure of their own armour; but the lance's point could not penetrate the breastplate, the sword fell harmless upon the helmet, the conqueror, in the first impulse of passion, could not assail any vital part of a prostrate but not exposed enemy. Still less was to be dreaded from the archers or cross-bowmen, who composed a large part of the infantry. The bow, indeed, as drawn by an English foot soldier, was the most formidable of arms before the invention of gunpowder. That ancient weapon, though not perhaps common among the northern nations, nor for several centuries after their settlement, was occasionally in use before the crusades. William employed archers in the battle of Hastings.[175] Intercourse with the East, its natural soil, during the twelfth and thirteenth ages, rendered the bow better known. But the Europeans improved on the Eastern method of confining its use to cavalry. By employing infantry as archers, they gained increased size, more steady position, and surer aim for the bow. Much, however, depended on the strength and skill of the archer. It was a peculiarly English weapon, and none of the other principal nations adopted it so generally or so successfully. The cross-bow, which brought the strong and weak to a level, was more in favour upon the continent. This instrument is said by some writers to have been introduced after the first crusade in the reign of Louis the Fat.[176] But, if we may trust William of Poitou, it was employed, as well as the long-bow, at the battle of Hastings. Several of the popes prohibited it as a treacherous weapon; and the restriction was so far regarded that, in the time of Philip Augustus, its use is said to have been unknown in France.[177] By degrees it became more general; and cross-bowmen were considered as a very necessary part of a well-organized army. But both the arrow and the quarrel glanced away from plate-armour, such as it became in the fifteenth century, impervious in every point, except when the visor was raised from the face, or some part of the body accidentally exposed. The horse, indeed, was less completely protected.

Many disadvantages attended the security against wounds for which this armour had been devised. The enormous weight exhausted the force and crippled the limbs. It rendered the heat of a southern climate insupportable. In some circumstances it increased the danger of death, as in the passage of a river or

---

[175] Pedites in fronte locavit, sagittis armatos et balistis, item pedites in ordine secundo firmiores et loricatos, ultimo turmas equitum. ("Gul. Pictaviensis," in Du Chesne, p. 201.) Several archers are represented in the tapestry of Bayeux.

[176] Le Grand, "Vie privée des Français," tome i, p. 349.

[177] Du Cange, voc. Balista: Muratori, Dissert. 26, tome i, p. 462 (Ital.).

morass. It was impossible to compel an enemy to fight, because
the least intrenchment or natural obstacle could stop such unwieldy assailants. The troops might be kept in constant alarm
at night, and either compelled to sleep under arms or run the
risk of being surprised before they could rivet their plates of
steel.[178] Neither the Italians, however, nor the transalpines,
would surrender a mode of defence which they ought to have
deemed inglorious. But in order to obviate some of its military
inconveniences, as well as to give a concentration in attack, which
lancers impetuously charging in a single line, according to the
practice at least of France in the middle ages, did not preserve,
it became usual for the cavalry to dismount, and, leaving their
horses at some distance, to combat on foot with the lance. This
practice, which must have been singularly embarrassing with the
plate-armour of the fifteenth century, was introduced before it
became so ponderous. It is mentioned by historians of the
twelfth century both as a German and an English custom.[179]
We find it in the wars of Edward III. Hawkwood, the disciple
of that school, introduced it into Italy.[180] And it was practised
by the English in their second wars with France, especially at
the battles of Crevant and Verneuil.[181]

Meanwhile a discovery accidentally made, perhaps, in some
remote age and distant region, and whose importance was but
slowly perceived by Europe, had prepared the way not only for
a change in her military system, but for political effects still
more extensive. If we consider gunpowder as an instrument
of human destruction, incalculably more powerful than any that
skill had devised or accident presented before, acquiring, as experience shows us, a more sanguinary dominion in every succeeding age, and borrowing all the progressive resources of science and civilization for the extermination of mankind, we shall
be appalled at the future prospects of the species, and feel perhaps in no other instance so much difficulty in reconciling the
mysterious dispensation with the benevolent order of Providence.
As the great security for established governments, the surest
preservation against popular tumult, it assumes a more equivocal
character, depending upon the solution of a doubtful problem,
whether the sum of general happiness has lost more in the last

---

[178] Sismondi, tome ix, p. 158.
[179] The Emperor Conrad's cavalry in
the second crusade are said by William
of Tyre to have dismounted on one occasion and fought on foot, de equis de-
scendentes, et facti pedites; sicut mos est
Teutonicis in summis necessitatibus bel-
lica tractare negotia (l. xvii, c. 4). And
the same was done by the English in
their engagement with the Scotch near
North Allerton, commonly called the bat-

tle of the Standard, in 1138. (Twysden,
" Decem Script.," p. 342.)
[180] Sismondi, tome vi, p. 429; Azarius,
in " Script. Rer. Ital.," tome xvi; Matt.
Villani.
[181] Monstrelet, tome ii, fol. 7, 14, 76;
Villaret, tome xvii, p. 89. It was a Burgundian as well as English fashion. Entre les Bourguignons, says Comines, lors
estoient les plus honorez ceux que des-
cendoient avec les archers (l. i, c. 3).

three centuries through arbitrary power than it has gained
through regular police and suppression of disorder.

There seems little reason to doubt that gunpowder was introduced through the means of the Saracens into Europe. Its
use in engines of war, though they may seem to have been rather
like our fireworks than artillery, is mentioned by an Arabic
writer in the Escurial collection about the year 1249.[182] It was
known not long afterward to our philosopher, Roger Bacon,
though he concealed, in some degree, the secret of its composition. In the first part of the fourteenth century cannon, or rather
mortars, were invented, and the applicability of gunpowder to
purposes of war was understood. Edward III employed some
pieces of artillery with considerable effect at Crécy.[183] But its
use was still not very frequent; a circumstance which will surprise us less when we consider the unscientific construction of
artillery; the slowness with which it could be loaded; its stone
balls, of uncertain aim and imperfect force, being commonly fired
at a considerable elevation; and especially the difficulty of removing it from place to place during an action. In sieges and
in naval engagements—as, for example, in the war of Chioggia—
it was more frequently employed.[184] Gradually, however, the
new artifice of evil gained ground. The French made the principal improvements. They cast their cannon smaller, placed
them on lighter carriages, and used balls of iron.[185] They invented portable arms for a single soldier, which, though clumsy
in comparison with their present state, gave an augury of a

[182] Casiri, " Bibl. Arab. Hispan.," tome
ii, p. 7, thus renders the original description of certain missiles used by the
Moors: Serpunt, susurrantque scorpiones
circumligati ac pulvere nitrato incensi,
unde explosi fulgurant ac incendunt.
Jam videre erat manganum excussum
veluti nubem per aera extendi ac tonitrus
instar horrendum edere fragorem, ig-
nemque undequàque vomens, omnia di-
rumpere, incendere, in cineres redigere.
The Arabic passage is at the bottom
of the page; and one would be glad to
know whether pulvis nitratus is a fair
translation. But I think there can, on
the whole, be no doubt that gunpowder
is meant. Another Arabian writer seems
to describe the use of cannon in the years
1312 and 1323. (Id., ibid.) And the
chronicle of Alphonso XI, King of Castile, distinctly mentions them at the siege
of Algeciras in 1342. But before this they
were sufficiently known in France. Gunpowder and cannon are both mentioned
in registers of accounts under 1338 (Du
Cange, voc. Bombarda), and in another
document of 1345. (" Hist. du Languedoc," tome iv, p. 204.) But the strongest
evidence is a passage of Petrarch, written
before 1344, and quoted in Muratori,
" Antich. Ital.," Dissert. 26, p. 456, where
he speaks of the art, nuper rara, nunc
communis.

[183] G. Villani, l. xii, c. 67. Gibbon has
thrown out a sort of objection to the certainty of this fact, on account of Froissart's silence. But the positive testimony
of Villani, who died within two years
afterward, and had manifestly obtained
much information as to the great events
passing in France, can not be rejected.
He ascribes a material effect to the cannon of Edward, colpi delle bombarde,
which I suspect, from his strong expressions, had not been employed before,
except against stone walls. It seemed,
he says, as if God thundered con grande
uccisione di genti, e sfondamento di
cavalli.

[184] Gattaro, " Ist. Padovana," in
" Script. Rer. Ital.," tome xvii, p. 360.
Several proofs of the employment of artillery in French sieges during the reign
of Charles V occur in Villaret. See the
word Artillerie in the index.
Gian Galeazzo had, according to Corio,
thirty-four pieces of cannon, small and
great, in the Milanese army, about 1397.

[185] Guicciardini, l. i, p. 75, has a remarkable passage on the superiority of
the French over the Italian artillery in
consequence of these improvements.

prodigious revolution in the military art. John, Duke of Burgundy, in 1411, had four thousand hand cannons, as they were called, in his army.[186] They are found, under different names and modifications of form—for which I refer the reader to professed writers on tactics—in most of the wars that historians of the fifteenth century record, but less in Italy than beyond the Alps. The Milanese, in 1449, are said to have armed their militia with twenty thousand muskets, which struck terror into the old generals.[187] But these muskets, supported on a rest, and charged with great delay, did less execution than our sanguinary science would require; and, uncombined with the admirable invention of the bayonet, could not in any degree resist a charge of cavalry. The pike had a greater tendency to subvert the military system of the middle ages, and to demonstrate the efficiency of disciplined infantry. Two free nations had already discomfited, by the help of such infantry, those arrogant knights on whom the fate of battles had depended—the Bohemians, instructed in the art of war by their great master, John Zisca; and the Swiss, who, after winning their independence inch by inch from the house of Austria, had lately established their renown by a splendid victory over Charles of Burgundy. Louis XI took a body of mercenaries from the United Cantons into pay. Maximilian had recourse to the same assistance.[188] And though the importance of infantry was not perhaps decidedly established till the Milanese wars of Louis XII and Francis I, in the sixteenth century, yet the last years of the middle ages, according to our division, indicated the commencement of that military revolution in the general employment of pikemen and musketeers.

Soon after the beginning of the fifteenth century, to return from this digression, two illustrious captains, educated under Alberic di Barbiano, turned upon themselves the eyes of Italy. These were Braccio di Montone, a noble Perugian, and Sforza Attendolo, originally a peasant in the village of Cotignuola. Nearly equal in reputation, unless perhaps Braccio may be reckoned the more consummate general, they were divided by a long rivalry, which descended to the next generation, and involved all the distinguished leaders of Italy. The distractions of Naples, and the anarchy of the ecclesiastical state, gave scope not only to their military but political ambition. Sforza was invested with extensive fiefs in the kingdom of Naples, and with the office of

[186] Villaret, tome xiii, page 176 and page 310.
[187] Sismondi, tome ix, p. 341. He says that it required a quarter of an hour to charge and fire a musket. I must confess that I very much doubt the fact of so many muskets having been collected. In 1432 that arm was seen for the first time in Tuscany. (Muratori, Dissert. 26, p. 457.)
[188] See Guicciardini's character of the Swiss troops (p. 192). The French, he says, had no native infantry; il regno di Francia era debolissimo di fanteria propria, the nobility monopolizing all warlike occupations. (Ibid.)

great constable. Braccio aimed at independent acquisitions, and formed a sort of principality around Perugia. This, however, was entirely dissipated at his death. When Sforza and Braccio were no more, their respective parties were headed by the son of the former, Francesco Sforza, and by Nicholas Piccinino, who for more than twenty years fought, with few exceptions, under opposite banners. Piccinino was constantly in the service of Milan. Sforza, whose political talents fully equalled his military skill, never lost sight of the splendid prospects that opened to his ambition. From Eugenius IV he obtained the march of Ancona as a fief of the Roman see. Thus rendered more independent than the ordinary condottieri, he mingled as a sovereign prince in the politics of Italy. He was generally in alliance with Venice and Florence, throwing his weight into their scale to preserve the balance of power against Milan and Naples. But his ultimate designs rested upon Milan. Filippo Maria, duke of that city, the last of his family, had only a natural daughter, whose hand he sometimes offered and sometimes withheld from Sforza. Even after he had consented to their union, his suspicious temper was incapable of admitting such a son-in-law into confidence, and he joined in a confederacy with the Pope and King of Naples to strip Sforza of the march. At the death of Filippo Maria, in 1447, that general had nothing left but his glory and a very disputable claim to the Milanese succession. This, however, was set aside by the citizens, who revived their republican government. A republic in that part of Lombardy might, with the help of Venice and Florence, have withstood any domestic or foreign usurpation. But Venice was hostile, and Florence indifferent. Sforza became the general of this new state, aware that such would be the probable means of becoming its master. No politician of that age scrupled any breach of faith for his interest. Nothing, says Machiavel, was thought shameful but to fail. Sforza, with his army, deserted to the Venetians; and the republic of Milan, being both incapable of defending itself and distracted by civil dissensions, soon fell a prey to his ambition. In 1450 he was proclaimed duke, rather by right of election, or of conquest, than in virtue of his marriage with Bianca, whose sex, as well as illegitimacy, seemed to preclude her from inheriting.

I have not alluded for some time to the domestic history of a kingdom which bore a considerable part, during the fourteenth and fifteenth centuries, in the general combinations of Italian policy, not wishing to interrupt the reader's attention by too frequent transitions. We must return again to a more remote age in order to take up the history of Naples. Charles of Anjou, after the deaths of Manfred and Conradin had left him without a competitor, might be ranked in the first class of European sovereigns. Master of Provence and Naples, and at the head of the Guelf faction in Italy, he had already prepared a formidable attack on the Greek Empire, when a memorable revolution in Sicily brought humiliation on his latter years. John of Procida, a Neapolitan, whose patrimony had been confiscated for his adherence to the party of Manfred, retained during long years of exile an implacable resentment against the house of Anjou. From the dominions of Peter III, King of Aragon, who had bestowed estates upon him in Valencia, he kept his eye continually fixed on Naples and Sicily. The former held out no favourable prospects; the Ghibelin party had been entirely subdued, and the principal barons were of French extraction or inclinations. But the island was in a very different state. Unused to any strong government, it was now treated as a conquered country. A large body of French soldiers garrisoned the fortified towns, and the systematic oppression was aggravated by those insults upon the honour of families which are most intolerable to an Italian temperament. John of Procida, travelling in disguise through the island, animated the barons with a hope of deliverance. In like disguise he repaired to the Pope, Nicolas III, who was jealous of the new Neapolitan dynasty, and obtained his sanction to the projected insurrection; to the court of Constantinople, from which he readily obtained money; and to the King of Aragon, who employed that money in fitting out an armament, that hovered upon the coast of Africa, under pretext of attacking the Moors. It is, however, difficult at this time to distinguish the effects of preconcerted conspiracy from those of casual resentment. Before the intrigues so skilfully conducted had taken effect, yet after they were ripe for development, an outrage committed upon a lady at Palermo, during a procession on the vigil of Easter, provoked the people to that terrible massacre of all the French in their island, which has obtained the name of Sicilian Vespers. Unpremeditated as such an ebullition of popular fury must appear, it fell in, by the happiest coincidence, with the previous conspiracy. The King of Aragon's fleet was at hand; the Sicilians soon called in his assistance; he sailed to Palermo, and accepted the crown. John of Procida is a remarkable witness to a truth which the pride of governments will seldom permit them to acknowledge: that an individual, obscure and apparently insignificant, may sometimes, by perseverance and energy, shake the foundations of established states; while the perfect concealment of his intrigues proves also, against a popular maxim, that a political secret may be preserved by a number of persons during a considerable length of time.[189]

[189] Giannone, though he has well described the schemes of John of Procida, yet, as is too often his custom, or rather that of Costanzo, whom he implicitly fol-

The long war that ensued upon this revolution involved or interested the greater part of civilized Europe. Philip III of France adhered to his uncle, and the King of Aragon was compelled to fight for Sicily within his native dominions. This, indeed, was the more vulnerable point of attack. Upon the sea he was lord of the ascendant. His Catalans, the most intrepid of Mediterranean sailors, were led to victory by a Calabrian refugee, Roger di Loria, the most illustrious and successful admiral whom Europe produced till the age of Blake and De Ruyter. In one of Loria's battles the eldest son of the King of Naples was made prisoner, and the first years of his own reign were spent in confinement. But notwithstanding these advantages, it was found impracticable for Aragon to contend against the arms of France, and latterly of Castile, sustained by the rolling thunders of the Vatican. Peter III had bequeathed Sicily to his second son, James; Alfonso, the eldest, King of Aragon, could not fairly be expected to ruin his inheritance for his brother's cause; nor were the barons of that free country disposed to carry on a war without national objects. He made peace, accordingly, in 1295, and engaged to withdraw all his subjects from the Sicilian service. Upon his own death, which followed very soon, James succeeded to the kingdom of Aragon, and ratified the renunciation of Sicily. But the natives of that island had received too deeply the spirit of independence to be thus assigned over by the letter of a treaty. After solemnly abjuring, by their ambassadors, their allegiance to the King of Aragon, they placed the crown upon the head of his brother Frederick. They maintained the war against Charles II of Naples, against James of Aragon, their former king, who had bound himself to enforce their submission, and even against the great Roger di Loria, who, upon some discontent with Frederick, deserted their banner and entered into the Neapolitan service. Peace was at length made in 1300, upon condition that Frederick should retain during his life the kingdom, which was afterward to revert to the crown of Naples: a condition not likely to be fulfilled.

Upon the death of Charles II, King of Naples, in 1305, a question arose as to the succession. His eldest son, Charles

lows, drops or slides over leading facts; and thus, omitting entirely, or misrepresenting, the circumstances of the Sicilian Vespers, treats the whole insurrection as the result of a deliberate conspiracy. On the other hand, Nicolas Specialis, a contemporary writer, in the seventh volume of Muratori's collection, represents the Sicilian Vespers as proceeding entirely from the casual outrage in the streets of Palermo. The thought of calling in Peter, he asserts, did not occur to the Sicilians till Charles had actually commenced the siege of Messina. But this is equally removed from the truth. Gibbon has made more errors than are usual with so accurate a historian in his account of this revolution, such as calling Constance, the queen of Peter, sister instead of daughter of Manfred. A good narrative of the Sicilian Vespers may be found in Velly's "History of France," tome vi.

Martel, had been called by maternal inheritance to the throne
of Hungary, and had left at his decease a son, Carobert, the
reigning sovereign of that country. According to the laws of
representative succession, which were at this time tolerably settled in private inheritance, the crown of Naples ought to have
regularly devolved upon that prince. But it was contested by
his uncle Robert, the eldest living son of Charles II, and the
cause was pleaded by civilians at Avignon before Pope Clement
V, the feudal superior of the Neapolitan kingdom. Reasons of
public utility, rather than of legal analogy, seem to have prevailed
in the decision which was made in favour of Robert.[190] The
course of his reign evinced the wisdom of this determination.
Robert, a wise and active though not personally a martial prince,
maintained the ascendency of the Guelf faction, and the papal
influence connected with it, against the formidable combination
of Ghibelin usurpers in Lombardy and the two emperors, Henry
VII and Louis of Bavaria. No male issue survived Robert,
whose crown descended to his granddaughter Joanna. She had
been espoused, while a child, to her cousin Andrew, son of
Carobert, King of Hungary, who was educated with her in the
court of Naples. Auspiciously contrived as this union might
seem to silence a subsisting claim upon the kingdom, it proved
eventually the source of civil war and calamity for a hundred
and fifty years. Andrew's manners were barbarous, more worthy
of his native country than of that polished court wherein he had
been bred. He gave himself up to the society of Hungarians,
who taught him to believe that a matrimonial crown and derivative royalty were derogatory to a prince who claimed by a paramount hereditary right. In fact, he was pressing the court of
Avignon to permit his own coronation, which would have placed
in a very hazardous condition the rights of the queen, with whom
he was living on ill terms, when one night he was seized, stran-
gled, and thrown out of a window. Public rumour, in the absence of notorious proof, imputed the guilt of this mysterious
assassination to Joanna. Whether historians are authorized to
assume her participation in it so confidently as they have generally done may perhaps be doubted, though I can not venture
positively to rescind their sentence. The circumstances of Andrew's death were undoubtedly pregnant with strong suspicions.[191] Louis, King of Hungary, his brother, a just and stern

[190] Giannone, l. xxii; Summonte, tome
ii, p. 370. Some of the civilians of that
age, however, approved the decision.
[191] The " Chronicle of Dominic di Gravina " (" Script. Rer. Ital.," tome xii)
seems to be our best testimony for the
circumstances connected with Andrew's
death; and after reading his narrative
more than once, I find myself undecided
as to this perplexed and mysterious story.
Gravina's opinion, it should be observed,
is extremely hostile to the queen.
Nevertheless there are not wanting presumptions that Charles, first Duke of
Durazzo, who had married the sister of
Andrew, was concerned in his murder,
for which, in fact, he was afterward put
to death by the King of Hungary. But,

prince, invaded Naples, partly as an avenger, partly as a conqueror. The queen and her second husband, Louis of Tarento, fled to Provence, where her acquittal, after a solemn, if not an impartial, investigation, was pronounced by Clement VI. Louis meanwhile found it more difficult to retain than to acquire the kingdom of Naples; his own dominion required his presence, and Joanna soon recovered her crown. She reigned for thirty years more without the attack of any enemy, but not intermeddling, like her progenitors, in the general concerns of Italy. Childless by four husbands, the succession of Joanna began to excite ambitious speculations. Of all the male descendants of Charles I, none remained but the King of Hungary and Charles, Duke of Durazzo, who had married the queen's niece, and was regarded by her as the presumptive heir to the crown. But, offended by her marriage with Otho of Brunswick, he procured the assistance of a Hungarian army to invade the kingdom, and, getting the queen into his power, took possession of the throne. In this enterprise he was seconded by Urban VI, against whom Joanna had unfortunately declared in the great schism of the Church. She was smothered with a pillow in prison by the order of Charles. The name of Joan of Naples has suffered by the lax repetition of calumnies. Whatever share she may have had in her husband's death, and certainly under circumstances of extenuation, her subsequent life was not open to any flagrant reproach. The charge of dissolute manners, so frequently made, is not warranted by any specific proof or contemporary testimony.

In the extremity of Joanna's distress she had sought assistance from a quarter too remote to afford it in time for her relief. She adopted Louis, Duke of Anjou, eldest uncle of the young King of France, Charles VI, as her heir in the kingdom of Naples and county of Provence. This bequest took effect without difficulty in the latter country. Naples was entirely in the possession of Charles of Durazzo. Louis, however, entered Italy with a very large army, consisting at least of thirty thousand cavalry, and, according to some writers, more than double that number.[192] He was joined by many Neapolitan barons attached to the late queen. But, by a fate not unusual in so imperfect a state of military science, this armament produced no adequate

if the Duke of Durazzo was guilty, it is unlikely that Joanna should be so too; because she was on very bad terms with him, and indeed the chief proofs against her are founded on the investigation which Durazzo himself professed to institute. Confessions obtained through torture are as little credible in history as they ought to be in judicature; even if we could be positively sure, which is not the case in this instance, that such confessions were ever made. However, I do not pretend to acquit Joanna, but merely to notice the uncertainty that rests over her story, on account of the positiveness with which all historians, except those of Naples and the Abbé de Sade, whose vindication ("Vie de Pétrarque," tome ii, notes) does her more harm than good, have assumed the murder of Andrew to have been her own act, as if she had ordered his execution in open day.

[192] Muratori; Summonte; Costanzo.

effect, and mouldered away through disease and want of provisions. Louis himself dying not long afterward, the government of Charles III appeared secure, and he was tempted to accept an offer of the crown of Hungary. This enterprise, equally unjust and injudicious, terminated in his assassination. Ladislaus, his son, a child ten years old, succeeded to the throne of Naples, under the guardianship of his mother Margaret, whose exactions of money producing discontent, the party which had supported the late Duke of Anjou became powerful enough to call in his son. Louis II, as he was called, reigned at Naples, and possessed most part of the kingdom, for several years; the young King Ladislaus, who retained some of the northern provinces, fixing his residence at Gaeta. If Louis had prosecuted the war with activity, it seems probable that he would have subdued his adversary. But his character was not very energetic; and Ladislaus, as he advanced to manhood, displaying much superior qualities, gained ground by degrees, till the Angevin barons, perceiving the turn of the tide, came over to his banner, and he recovered his whole dominions.

The kingdom of Naples, at the close of the fourteenth century, was still altogether a feudal government. This had been introduced by the first Norman kings, and the system had rather been strengthened than impaired under the Angevin line. The princes of the blood, who were at one time numerous, obtained extensive domains by way of appanage. The principality of Tarento was a large portion of the kingdom.[193] The rest was occupied by some great families, whose strength, as well as pride, was shown in the number of men at arms whom they could muster under their banner. At the coronation of Louis II, in 1390, the Sanseverini appeared with eighteen hundred cavalry completely equipped.[194] This illustrious house, which had filled all the high offices of state, and changed kings at its pleasure, was crushed by Ladislaus, whose bold and unrelenting spirit well fitted him to bruise the heads of the aristocratic hydra. After thoroughly establishing his government at home, this ambitious monarch directed his powerful resources toward foreign conquests. The ecclesiastical territories had never been secure from rebellion or usurpation, but legitimate sovereigns had hitherto respected the patrimony of the head of the Church. It was reserved for Ladislaus, a feudal vassal of the Holy See, to seize upon Rome itself as his spoil. For several years, while the disordered state of the Church, in consequence of the schism

[193] It comprehended the provinces now called Terra d'Otranto and Terra di Bari, besides part of those adjoining. (Summonte, "Istoria di Napoli," tome iii, p. 537.) Orsini, Prince of Tarento, who died in 1463, had 4,000 troops in arms, and the value of 1,000,000 florins in movables. (Sismondi, tome x, p. 151.)

[194] Summonte, tome iii, p. 517; Giannone, l. xxiv, c. 4.

and the means taken to extinguish it, gave him an opportunity, the King of Naples occupied great part of the papal territories. He was disposed to have carried his arms farther north, and attacked the republic of Florence, if not the states of Lombardy, when his death relieved Italy from the danger of this new tyranny.

An elder sister, Joanna II, reigned at Naples after Ladislaus. Under this queen, destitute of courage and understanding, and the slave of appetites which her age rendered doubly disgraceful, the kingdom relapsed into that state of anarchy from which its late sovereign had rescued it. I shall only refer the reader to more enlarged histories for the first years of Joanna's reign. In 1421 the two most powerful individuals were Sforza Attendolo, great constable, and Ser Gianni Caraccioli, the queen's minion, who governed the palace with unlimited sway. Sforza, aware that the favourite was contriving his ruin, and remembering the prison in which he had lain more than once since the accession of Joanna, determined to anticipate his enemies by calling in a pretender to the crown, another Louis of Anjou, third in descent of that unsuccessful dynasty. The Angevin party, though proscribed and oppressed, was not extinct, and the populace of Naples in particular had always been on that side. Caraccioli's influence and the queen's dishonourable weakness rendered the nobility disaffected. Louis III, therefore, had no remote prospect of success. But Caraccioli was more prudent than favourites, selected from such motives, have usually proved. Joanna was old and childless; the reversion to her dominions was a valuable object to any prince in Europe. None was so competent to assist her, or so likely to be influenced by the hope of succession, as Alfonso, King of Aragon and Sicily. That island, after the reign of its deliverer, Frederick I, had unfortunately devolved upon weak or infant princes. One great family, the Chiaramonti, had possessed itself of half Sicily; not by a feudal title, as in other kingdoms, but as a kind of counter-sovereignty, in opposition to the crown, though affecting rather to bear arms against the advisers of their kings than against themselves. The marriage of Maria, Queen of Sicily, with Martin, son of the King of Aragon, put an end to the national independence of her country. Dying without issue, she left the crown to her husband. This was consonant, perhaps, to the received law of some European kingdoms. But, upon the death of Martin, in 1409, his father, also named Martin, King of Aragon, took possession as heir to his son, without any election by the Sicilian Parliament. The Chiaramonti had been destroyed by the younger Martin, and no party remained to make opposition. Thus was Sicily united to the crown of Aragon. Alfonso, who now enjoyed those two crowns, gladly embraced the proposals of the

Queen of Naples. They were founded, indeed, on the most substantial basis, mutual interest. She adopted Alfonso as her son and successor, while he bound himself to employ his forces in delivering a kingdom that was to become his own. Louis of Anjou, though acknowledged in several provinces, was chiefly to depend upon the army of Sforza, and an army of Italian mercenaries could only be kept by means which he was not able to apply. The King of Aragon, therefore, had far the better prospects in the war, when one of the many revolutions of this reign defeated his immediate expectations. Whether it were that Alfonso's noble and affable nature afforded a contrast which Joanna was afraid of exhibiting to the people, or that he had really formed a plan to anticipate his succession to the throne, she became more and more distrustful of her adopted son, till, an open rupture having taken place, she entered into a treaty with her hereditary competitor, Louis of Anjou, and, revoking the adoption of Alfonso, substituted the French prince in his room. The King of Aragon was disappointed by this unforeseen stroke, which, uniting the Angevin faction with that of the reigning family, made it impracticable for him to maintain his ground for any length of time in the kingdom. Joanna reigned for more than ten years without experiencing any inquietude from the pacific spirit of Louis, who, content with his reversionary hopes, lived as a sort of exile in Calabria.[195] Upon his death, the queen, who did not long survive him, settled the kingdom on his brother Regnier. The Neapolitans were generally disposed to execute this bequest. But Regnier was unluckily at that time a prisoner to the Duke of Burgundy; and though his wife maintained the cause with great spirit, it was difficult for her, or even for himself, to contend against the King of Aragon, who immediately laid claim to the kingdom. After a contest of several years, Regnier, having experienced the treacherous and selfish abandonment of his friends, yielded the game to his adversary; and Alfonso founded the Aragonese line of sovereigns at Naples, deriving pretensions more splendid than just from Manfred, from the house of Swabia, and from Roger Guiscard.[196]

[195] Joanna's great favourite, Caraccioli, fell a victim some time before his mistress's death to an intrigue of the palace; the Duchess of Sessia, a new favourite, having prevailed on the feeble old queen to permit him to be assassinated. About this time Alfonso had every reason to hope for the renewal of the settlement in his favour. Caraccioli had himself opened a negotiation with the King of Aragon; and after his death the Duchess of Sessia embarked in the same cause. Joan even revoked secretly the adoption of the Duke of Anjou. This circumstance might appear doubtful : but the historian to whom I refer has published the act of revocation itself, which bears date April 11, 1433. Zurita (" Annales de Aragon," tome iv, p. 217) admits that no other writer, either contemporary or subsequent, has mentioned any part of the transaction, which must have been kept very secret; but his authority is so respectable that I thought it worth notice, however uninteresting these remote intrigues may appear to most readers. Joanna soon changed her mind again, and took no overt steps in favour of Alfonso.
[196] According to a treaty between Frederick III, King of Sicily, and Joanna I

19

In the first year of Alfonso's Neapolitan war he was defeated and taken prisoner by a fleet of the Genoese, who, as constant enemies of the Catalans in all the naval warfare of the Mediterranean, had willingly lent their aid to the Angevin party. Genoa was at this time subject to Filippo Maria, Duke of Milan, and her royal captive was transmitted to his court. But here the brilliant graces of Alfonso's character won over his conqueror, who had no reason to consider the war as his own concern. The king persuaded him, on the contrary, that a strict alliance with an Aragonese dynasty in Naples against the pretensions of any French claimant would be the true policy and best security of Milan. That city, which he had entered as a prisoner, he left as a friend and ally. From this time Filippo Maria Visconti and Alfonso were firmly united in their Italian politics, and formed one weight of the balance which the republics of Venice and Florence kept in equipoise. After the succession of Sforza to the duchy of Milan the same alliance was generally preserved. Sforza had still more powerful reasons than his predecessor for excluding the French from Italy, his own title being contested by the Duke of Orleans, who derived a claim from his mother Valentine, a daughter of Gian Galeazzo Visconti. But the two republics were no longer disposed toward war. Florence had spent a great deal without any advantage in her contest with Filippo Maria,[197] and the new Duke of Milan had been the constant personal friend of Cosmo de' Medici, who altogether influenced that republic. At Venice, indeed, he had been regarded with very different sentiments; the senate had prolonged their war against Milan with redoubled animosity after his elevation, deeming him a not less ambitious and more formidable neighbour than the Visconti. But they were deceived in the character of Sforza. Conscious that he had reached an eminence beyond his early hopes, he had no care but to secure for his family the possession of Milan without disturbing the balance of Lombardy. No one better knew than Sforza the faithless temper and destructive politics of the condottieri, whose interest was placed in the oscillations of interminable war, and whose defection might shake the stability of any government. Without peace it was impossible to break that ruinous system, and accustom states to rely upon their natural resources. Venice had little reason

of Naples, in 1363, the former monarch was to assume the title of King of Trinacria, leaving the original style to the Neapolitan line. But neither he nor his successors in the island ever complied with this condition, or entitled themselves otherwise than Kings of Sicily ultra Pharum, in contradistinction to the other kingdom, which they denominated Sicily citra Pharum. Alfonso of Aragon, when he united both these, was the first who took the title King of the Two Sicilies, which his successors have retained ever since. (Giannone, tome iii, p. 234.)

[197] The war ending with the Peace of Ferrara, in 1428, is said to have cost the republic of Florence 3,500,000 florins. (Ammirato, p. 1043.)

to expect further conquests in Lombardy; and if her ambition had inspired the hope of them, she was summoned by a stronger call—that of self-preservation—to defend her numerous and dispersed possessions in the Levant against the arms of Mohammed II. All Italy, indeed, felt the peril that impended from that side; and these various motions occasioned a quadruple league in 1455, between the King of Naples, the Duke of Milan, and the two republics, for the preservation of peace in Italy. One object of this alliance, and the prevailing object with Alfonso, was the implied guarantee of his succession in the kingdom of Naples to his illegitimate son Ferdinand. He had no lawful issue, and there seemed no reason why an acquisition of his own valour should pass against his will to collateral heirs. The Pope, as feudal superior of the kingdom, and the Neapolitan Parliament, the sole competent tribunal, confirmed the inheritance of Ferdinand.[198] Whatever may be thought of the claims subsisting in the house of Anjou, there can be no question that the reigning family of Aragon were legitimately excluded from the throne of Naples, though force and treachery enabled them ultimately to obtain it.

Alfonso, surnamed the Magnanimous, was by far the most accomplished sovereign whom the fifteenth century produced. The virtues of chivalry were combined in him with the patronage of letters, and with more than their patronage, a real enthusiasm for learning, seldom found in a king, and especially in one so active and ambitious.[199] This devotion to literature was, among the Italians of that age, almost as sure a passport to general admiration as his more chivalrous perfection. Magnificence in architecture and the pageantry of a splendid court gave fresh lustre to his reign. The Neapolitans perceived with grateful pride that he lived almost entirely among them, in preference to his patrimonial kingdom, and forgave the heavy taxes which faults nearly allied to his virtues, profuseness and ambition, compelled him to impose.[200] But they remarked a very different character in his son. Ferdinand was as dark and vindictive as his father was affable and generous. The barons, who had many opportunities of ascertaining his disposition, began, immediately upon Alfonso's death, to cabal against his succession, turning their eyes first to the legitimate branch of the family, and, on finding that prospect not favourable, to John, titular Duke of Calabria, son of Regnier of Anjou, who survived to protest against the revolution that had dethroned him. John was easily prevailed upon to undertake an invasion of Naples. Notwith-

[198] Giannone, l. xxvi, c. 2.
[199] A story is told, true or false, that his delight in hearing Quintus Curtius read, without any other medicine, cured the king of an illness. (See other proofs of his love of letters in Tiraboschi, tome vi, p. 40.)
[200] Giannone, l. xxvi.

standing the treaty concluded in 1455, Florence assisted him
with money, and Venice at least with her wishes; but Sforza
remained unshaken in that alliance with Ferdinand which his
clear-sighted policy discerned to be the best safeguard for his
own dynasty. A large proportion of the Neapolitan nobility,
including Orsini, Prince of Tarento, the most powerful vassal
of the crown, raised the banner of Anjou, which was sustained
also by the youngest Piccinino, the last of the great condottieri,
under whose command the veterans of former warfare rejoiced
to serve. But John underwent the fate that had always attended
his family in their long competition for that throne. After some
brilliant successes, his want of resources, aggravated by the defection of Genoa, on whose ancient enmity to the house of Aragon he had relied, was perceived by the barons of his party, who,
according to the practice of their ancestors, returned one by
one to the allegiance of Ferdinand.

The peace of Italy was little disturbed, except by a few domestic revolutions, for several years after this Neapolitan war.[201]
Even the most short-sighted politicians were sometimes withdrawn from selfish objects by the appalling progress of the Turks,
though there was not energy enough in their councils to form
any concerted plans for their own security. Venice maintained
a long but ultimately an unsuccessful contest with Mohammed II

[201] The following distribution of a tax
of 458,000 florins, imposed, or rather proposed, in 1464, to defray the expense of
a general war against the Turks, will
give a notion of the relative wealth and
resources of the Italian powers; but it is
probable that the Pope rated himself
above his fair contingent. He was to
pay 100,000 florins; the Venetians, 100,000;
Ferdinand of Naples, 80,000; the Duke
of Milan, 70,000; Florence, 50,000; the
Duke of Modena, 20,000; Siena, 15,000;
the Marquis of Mantua, 10,000; Lucca,
8,000; the Marquis of Montferrat, 5,000.
(Sismondi, tome x, p. 229.) A similar
assessment occurs (p. 307) where the proportions are not quite the same.

Perhaps it may be worth while to extract an estimate of the force of all
Christian powers, written about 1454,
from Sanuto's "Lives of the Doges of
Venice," p. 963. Some parts, however,
appear very questionable. The King of
France, it is said, can raise 30,000 men
at arms, but for any foreign enterprise
only 15,000. The King of England can
do the same. These powers are exactly
equal; otherwise one of the two would
be destroyed. The King of Scotland,
"ch' è signore di grandi paesi e popoli
con grande povertà," can raise 10,000
men at arms; the King of Norway the
same; the King of Spain (Castile), 30,-
000; the King of Portugal, 6,000; the
Duke of Savoy, 8,000; the Duke of Milan,
10,000. The republic of Venice can pay

from her revenues 10,000; that of Florence, 4,000; the Pope, 6,000. The emperor
and empire can raise 60,000; the King
of Hungary, 80,000 (not men at arms,
certainly).

The King of France, in 1414, had
2,000,000 ducats of revenue, but now
only half. The King of England had
then as much; now only 700,000. The
King of Spain's revenue also is reduced
by the wars from 3,000,000 to 800,000. The
Duke of Burgundy had 3,000,000; now
900,000. The Duke of Milan had sunk
from 1,000,000 to 500,000; Venice from
1,100,000, which she possessed in 1423, to
800,000; Florence from 400,000 to 200,000.
These statistical calculations, which
are not quite accurate as to Venice, and
probably much less so as to some other
states, are chiefly remarkable as they
manifest that comprehensive spirit of
treating all the powers of Europe as parts
of a common system which began to actu-
ate the Italians of the fifteenth century.
Of these enlarged views of policy, the
writings of Æneas Sylvius afford an eminent instance. Besides the more general
and insensible causes, the increase of
navigation and revival of literature, this
may be ascribed to the continual danger
from the progress of the Ottoman arms,
which led the politicians of that part of
Europe most exposed to them into more
extensive views as to the resources and
dispositions of Christian states.

for her maritime acquisitions in Greece and Albania; and it was
not till after his death relieved Italy from its immediate terror
that the ambitious republic endeavoured to extend its territories
by encroaching on the house of Este. Nor had Milan shown
much disposition toward aggrandizement. Francesco Sforza had
been succeeded, such is the condition of despotic governments,
by his son Galeazzo, a tyrant more execrable than the worst of
the Visconti. His extreme cruelties, and the insolence of a de-
bauchery that gloried in the public dishonour of families, excited
a few daring spirits to assassinate him. The Milanese profited
by a tyrannicide the perpetrators of which they had not courage
or gratitude to protect. The regency of Bonne of Savoy, mother
of the infant Duke Gian Galeazzo, deserved the praise of wisdom
and moderation. But it was overthrown in a few years by Ludovico Sforza, surnamed the Moor, her husband's brother, who,
while he proclaimed his nephew's majority and affected to treat
him as a sovereign, hardly disguised in his conduct toward foreign states that he had usurped for himself the sole direction
of government.

The annals of one of the few surviving republics, that of
Genoa, present to us, during the fifteenth as well as the preceding century, an unceasing series of revolutions, the shortest enumeration of which would occupy several pages. Torn by the
factions of Adorni and Fregosi, equal and eternal rivals, to whom
the whole patrician families of Doria and Fieschi were content
to become secondary, sometimes sinking from weariness of civil
tumult into the grasp of Milan or France, and again, from impatience of foreign subjection, starting back from servitude to
anarchy, the Genoa of those ages exhibits a singular contrast to
the calm and regular aristocracy of the next three centuries.
The latest revolution within the compass of this work was in
1488, when the Duke of Milan became sovereign, and Adorno
holding the office of doge as his lieutenant.

Florence, the most illustrious and fortunate of Italian republics, was now rapidly descending from her rank among free
commonwealths, though surrounded with more than usual lustre
in the eyes of Europe. We must take up the story of that city
from the revolution of 1382, which restored the ancient Guelf
aristocracy, or party of the Albizi, to the ascendency of which
a popular insurrection had stripped them. Fifty years elapsed
during which this party retained the government in its own
hands with few attempts at disturbance. Their principal adversaries had been exiled, according to the invariable and perhaps
necessary custom of a republic; the populace and inferior artisans were dispirited by their ill success. Compared with the
leaders of other factions, Maso degl' Albizi and Nicola di Uzzano,

who succeeded him in the management of his party, were attached to a constitutional liberty. Yet so difficult is it for any government which does not rest on a broad basis of public consent to avoid injustice that they twice deemed it necessary to violate the ancient constitution. In 1393, after a partial movement in behalf of the vanquished faction, they assembled a Parliament, and established what was technically called at Florence a Balia.[202] This was a temporary delegation of sovereignty to a number, generally a considerable number, of citizens, who during the period of their dictatorship named the magistrates, instead of drawing them by lot, and banished suspected individuals. A precedent so dangerous was eventually fatal to themselves and to the freedom of their country. Besides this temporary balia, the regular scrutinies periodically made in order to replenish the bags out of which the names of all magistrates were drawn by lot, according to the constitution established in 1328, were so managed as to exclude all persons disaffected to the dominant faction. But, for still greater security, a council of two hundred was formed in 1411, out of those alone who had enjoyed some of the higher offices within the last thirty years, the period of the aristocratical ascendency, through which every proposition was to pass before it could be submitted to the two legislative councils.[203] These precautions indicate a government conscious of public enmity; and if the Albizi had continued to sway the republic of Florence, their jealousy of the people would have suggested still more innovations, till the constitution had acquired, in legal form as well as substance, an absolutely aristocratical character.

But, while crushing with deliberate severity their avowed adversaries, the ruling party had left one family whose prudence gave no reasonable excuse for persecuting them, and whose popularity as well as wealth rendered the experiment hazardous. The Medici were among the most considerable of the new or plebeian nobility. From the first years of the fourteenth century their name not very infrequently occurs in the domestic and military annals of Florence.[204] Salvestro de' Medici, who had been partially implicated in the democratical revolution that lasted from 1378 to 1382, escaped proscription on the revival of the Guelf party, though some of his family were afterward banished. Throughout the long depression of the popular faction the house of Medici was always regarded as their consola-

[202] Ammirato, p. 840.
[203] Ib., p. 961.
[204] The Medici are enumerated by Villani among the chiefs of the Black faction in 1304 (l. viii, c. 71). One of that family was beheaded by order of the Duke of Athens in 1343 (l. xii, c. 2). It is singular that Mr. Roscoe should refer their first appearance in history, as he seems to do, to the siege of Scarperia in 1351.

tion and their hope. That house was now represented by Giovanni,[205] whose immense wealth, honourably acquired by commercial dealings, which had already rendered the name celebrated in Europe, was expended with liberality and magnificence. Of a mild temper and averse to cabals, Giovanni de' Medici did not attempt to set up a party, and contented himself with repressing some fresh encroachments on the popular part of the constitution which the Albizi were disposed to make.[206] They, in their turn, freely admitted him to that share in public councils to which he was entitled by his eminence and virtues—a proof that the spirit of their administration was not illiberally exclusive. But, on the death of Giovanni, his son, Cosmo de' Medici, inheriting his father's riches and estimation, with more talents and more ambition, thought it time to avail himself of the popularity belonging to his name. By extensive connections with the most eminent men in Italy, especially with Sforza, he came to be considered as the first citizen of Florence. The oligarchy were more than ever unpopular. Their administration since 1382 had indeed been in general eminently successful; the acquisition of Pisa and of other Tuscan cities had aggrandized the republic, while from the port of Leghorn her ships had begun to trade with Alexandria, and sometimes to contend with the Genoese.[207] But an unprosperous war with Lucca diminished a reputation which was never sustained by public affection. Cosmo and his friends aggravated the errors of the government, which having lost its wise and temperate leader, Nicola di Uzzano, had fallen into the rasher hands of Rinaldo degl' Albizi. He incurred the blame of being the first aggressor in a struggle which had become inevitable. Cosmo was arrested by command of a gonfalonier devoted to the Albizi, and condemned to banishment. But the oligarchy had done too much or too little. The city was full of his friends; the honours conferred upon him in his exile attested the sentiments of Italy. Next year he was recalled in triumph to Florence, and the Albizi were completely overthrown.

It is vain to expect that a victorious faction will scruple to retaliate upon its enemies a still greater measure of injustice

[205] Giovanni was not nearly related to Salvestro de' Medici. Their families are said per lungo tratto allontanarsi. (Ammirato, p. 992.) Nevertheless, his being drawn gonfalonier in 1421 created a great sensation in the city, and prepared the way to the subsequent revolution. (Ibid.; Machiavelli, l. iv.)

[206] Machiavelli, " Istoria Fiorent.," l. iv.

[207] The Florentines sent their first merchant ship to Alexandria in 1422, with great and anxious hopes. Prayers were ordered for the success of the republic by sea, and an embassy despatched with presents to conciliate the Sultan of Baby-lon—that is, of Grand Cairo. (Ammirato, p. 997.) Florence had never before been so wealthy. The circulating money was reckoned (perhaps extravagantly) at 4,000,000 florins. The manufactures of silk and cloth of gold had never flourished so much. Architecture shone under Brunelleschi; literature under Leonard Aretin and Filelfo (p. 977). There is some truth in M. Sismondi's remark that the Medici have derived part of their glory from their predecessors in government, whom they subverted, and whom they have rendered obscure. But the Milanese war, breaking out in 1423, tended a good deal to impoverish the city.

than it experienced at their hands. The vanquished have no
rights in the eyes of a conqueror. The sword of returning exiles,
flushed by victory and incensed by suffering, falls successively
upon their enemies, upon those whom they suspect of being
enemies, upon those who may hereafter become such. The
Albizi had in general respected the legal forms of their free republic, which good citizens, and perhaps themselves, might hope
one day to see more effective. The Medici made all their government conducive to hereditary monarchy. A multitude of
noble citizens were driven from their country; some were even
put to death. A balia was appointed for ten years to exclude
all the Albizi from magistracy, and, for the sake of this security
to the ruling faction, to supersede the legitimate institutions of
the republic. After the expiration of this period the dictatorial
power was renewed on pretence of fresh danger, and this was
repeated six times in twenty-one years.[208] In 1455 the constitutional mode of drawing magistrates was permitted to revive,
against the wishes of some of the leading party. They had good
reason to be jealous of a liberty which was incompatible with
their usurpation. The gonfaloniers, drawn at random from
among respectable citizens, began to act with an independence
to which the new oligarchy was little accustomed. Cosmo, indeed, the acknowledged chief of the party, perceiving that some
who had acted in subordination to him were looking forward
to the opportunity of becoming themselves its leaders, was not
unwilling to throw upon them the unpopularity attached to a
usurpation by which he had maintained his influence. Without
his apparent participation, though not against his will, the free
constitution was again suspended by a balia appointed for the
nomination of magistrates, and the regular drawing of names
by lot seems never to have been restored.[209] Cosmo died at an
advanced age in 1464. His son, Piero de' Medici, though not
deficient in either virtues or abilities, seemed too infirm in health
for the administration of public affairs. At least, he could only
be chosen by a sort of hereditary title, which the party above
mentioned, some from patriotic, more from selfish motives, were
reluctant to admit. A strong opposition was raised to the family
pretensions of the Medici. Like all Florentine factions, it trusted
to violence, and the chance of arms was not in its favour. From
this revolution in 1466, when some of the most considerable citizens were banished, we may date an acknowledged supremacy
in the house of Medici, the chief of which nominated the regular
magistrates, and drew to himself the whole conduct of the republic.[210]

[208] Machiavelli, l. v; Ammirato.
[209] Ammirato, tome ii, pp. 82-87.

[210] Ammirato, p. 93; Roscoe's " Lorenzo de' Medici," ch. 2; Machiavelli;

The two sons of Piero, Lorenzo and Julian, especially the former, though young at their father's death, assumed, by the request of their friends, the reins of government. It was impossible that, among a people who had so many recollections to attach to the name of liberty, among so many citizens whom their ancient constitution invited to public trust, the control of a single family should excite no dissatisfaction; and perhaps their want of any positive authority heightened the appearance of usurpation in their influence. But, if the people's wish to resign their freedom gives a title to accept the government of a country, the Medici were no usurpers. That family never lost the affections of the populace. The cry of " Palle, Palle!" (their armorial distinction), would at any time rouse the Florentines to defend the chosen patrons of the republic. If their substantial influence could before be questioned, the conspiracy of the Pazzi, wherein Julian perished, excited an enthusiasm for the surviving brother that never ceased during his life. Nor was this anything unnatural, or any severe reproach to Florence. All around, in Lombardy and Romagna, the lamp of liberty had long since been extinguished in blood. The freedom of Siena and Genoa was dearly purchased by revolutionary proscriptions; that of Venice was only a name. The republic which had preserved longest, and with greatest purity, that vestal fire, had at least no relative degradation to fear in surrendering herself to Lorenzo de' Medici. I need not in this place expatiate upon what the name instantly suggests, the patronage of science and art, and the constellation of scholars and poets, of architects and painters, whose reflected beams cast their radiance around his head. His political reputation, though far less durable, was in his own age as conspicuous as that which he acquired in the history of letters. Equally active and sagacious, he held his way through the varying combinations of Italian policy, always with credit, and generally with success. Florence, if not enriched, was upon the whole aggrandized during his administration, which was exposed to some severe storms from the unscrupulous adversaries, Sixtus IV and Ferdinand of Naples, whom he was compelled to resist. As a patriot, indeed, we never can bestow upon Lorenzo de' Medici the meed of disinterested virtue. He completed that subversion of the Florentine republic which his two immediate ancestors had so well prepared. The two councils, her regular legislature, he superseded by a permanent senate of seventy persons; [211] while the gonfalonier and priors, become a mockery and pageant to keep up the illusion of liberty, were

---

Sismondi. The two latter are perpetual references in this part of history, where no other is made.

[211] Ammirato, p. 145. Machiavel says (l. viii) that this was done ristringere il governo, e che le deliberazioni impor-

taught that in exercising a legitimate authority without the sanction of their prince, a name now first heard at Florence, they incurred the risk of punishment for their audacity.[212] Even the total dilapidation of his commercial wealth was repaired at the cost of the state, and the republic disgracefully screened the bankruptcy of the Medici by her own.[213] But compared with the statesmen of his age, we can reproach Lorenzo with no heinous crime. He had many enemies; his descendants had many more; but no unequivocal charge of treachery or assassination has been substantiated against his memory. By the side of Galeazzo or Ludovico Sforza, of Ferdinand or his son, Alfonso of Naples, of the Pope Sixtus IV, he shines with unspotted lustre. So much was Lorenzo esteemed by his contemporaries that his premature death has frequently been considered as the cause of those unhappy revolutions that speedily ensued, and which his foresight would, it was imagined, have been able to prevent—an opinion which, whether founded in probability or otherwise, attests the common sentiment about his character.

If, indeed, Lorenzo de' Medici could not have changed the destinies of Italy, however premature his death may appear if we consider the ordinary duration of human existence, it must be admitted that for his own welfare, perhaps for his glory, he had lived out the full measure of his time. An age of new and uncommon revolutions was about to arise, among the earliest of which the temporary downfall of his family was to be reckoned. The long-contested succession of Naples was again to involve

tanti si riducessero in minore numero. But though it rather appears from Ammirato's expressions that the two councils were now abolished, yet from M. Sismondi, tome xi, p. 186, who quotes an author I have not seen, and from Nardi, p. 7, I should infer that they still formally subsisted.

[212] Cambi, a gonfalonier of justice, had, in concert with the priors, admonished some public officers for a breach of duty. Fu giudicato questo atto molto superbo, says Ammirato, che senza participazione di Lorenzo de' Medici, principe del governo, fosse seguito, che in Pisa in quel tempo si ritrovava (p. 184). The gonfalonier was fined for executing his constitutional functions. This was a downright confession that the republic was at an end; and all it provokes M. Sismondi to say is not too much (tome xi, p. 345).

[213] Since the Medici took on themselves the character of princes, they had forgotten how to be merchants. But, imprudently enough, they had not discontinued their commerce, which was, of course, mismanaged by agents whom they did not overlook. The consequence was the complete dilapidation of their vast fortune. The public revenues had been for some years applied to make up its deficiencies. But from the measures adopted by the republic, if we may still use that name, she should appear to have considered herself, rather than Lorenzo, as the debtor. The interest of the public debt was diminished one half. Many charitable foundations were suppressed. The circulating specie was taken at one fifth below its nominal value in payment of taxes, while the government continued to issue it at its former rate. Thus was Lorenzo reimbursed a part of his loss at the expense of all his fellow-citizens. (Sismondi, tome xi, p. 347.) It is slightly alluded to by Machiavel.

The vast expenditure of the Medici for the sake of political influence would of itself have absorbed all their profits. Cosmo is said by Guicciardini to have spent 400,000 ducats in building churches, monasteries, and other public works (l. i, p. 91). The expenses of the family between 1434 and 1471, in buildings, charities, and taxes alone, amounted to 663,755 florins; equal in value, according to Sismondi, to 32,000,000 francs at present. (" Hist. des Républ.," tome x, p. 173.) They seem to have advanced moneys imprudently, through their agents, to Edward IV, who was not the best of debtors. (Comines, " Mém. de Charles VIII," l. vii, c. 6.)

Italy in war. The ambition of strangers was once more to desolate her plains. Ferdinand, King of Naples, had reigned for
thirty years after the discomfiture of his competitor with success
and ability, but with a degree of ill faith as well as tyranny toward
his subjects that rendered his government deservedly odious.
His son Alfonso, whose succession seemed now near at hand,
was still more marked by these vices than himself.[214] Meanwhile the pretensions of the house of Anjou had legally descended, after the death of old Regnier, to Regnier, Duke of
Lorraine, his grandson by a daughter; whose marriage into the
house of Lorraine had, however, so displeased her father that
he bequeathed his Neapolitan title, along with his real patrimony, the county of Provence, to a Count of Maine, by whose
testament they became vested in the crown of France. Louis
XI, while he took possession of Provence, gave himself no trouble about Naples. But Charles VIII, inheriting his father's ambition without that cool sagacity which restrained it in general
from impracticable attempts, and far better circumstanced at home
than Louis had ever been, was ripe for an expedition to vindicate his pretensions upon Naples, or even for more extensive
projects. It was now two centuries since the Kings of France
had begun to aim, by intervals, at conquests in Italy. Philip
the Fair and his successors were anxious to keep up a connection
with the Guelf party, and to be considered its natural heads,
as the German emperors were of the Ghibelins. The long English wars changed all views of the court of France to self-defence.
But in the fifteenth century its plans of aggrandizement beyond
the Alps began to revive. Several times, as I have mentioned,
the republic of Genoa put itself under the dominion of France.
The Dukes of Savoy, possessing most part of Piedmont, and
masters of the mountain passes, were, by birth, intermarriage,
and habitual policy, completely dedicated to the French interests.[215] In the former wars of Ferdinand against the house of
Anjou, Pope Pius II, a very enlightened statesman, foresaw the
danger of Italy from the prevailing influence of France, and
deprecated the introduction of her armies.[216] But at that time

[214] Comines, who speaks sufficiently ill
of the father, sums up the son's character
very concisely: Nul homme n'a este plus
cruel que lui, ne plus mauvais, ne plus
vicieux et plus infect, ne plus gourmand
que lui (l. vii, c. 13).
[215] Denina, " Storia dell' Italia Occidentale," tome ii, passim. Louis XI
treated Savoy as a fief of France, interfering in all its affairs, and even taking on
himself the regency after the death of
Philibert I, under pretence of preventing
disorders (p. 185). The Marquis of Sa-
luzzo, who possessed considerable territories in the south of Piedmont, had done

homage to France ever since 1353 (p. 40),
though to the injury of his real superior,
the Duke of Savoy. This gave France
another pretext for interference in Italy
(p. 187).
[216] Cosmo de' Medici, in a conference
with Pius II at Florence, having expressed his surprise that the Pope should
support Ferdinand : Pontifex haud fe-
rendum fuisse ait, regem a se constitu-
tum, armis ejici, neque id Italiæ libertati
conducere; Gallos, si regnum obtinuis-
sent, Senas haud dubiè subacturos; Flor-
entinos adversus lilia nihil acturos; Bor-
sium Mutinæ ducem Gallis galliorem

the central parts of Lombardy were held by a man equally renowned as a soldier and a politician, Francesco Sforza. Conscious that a claim upon his own dominions subsisted in the
house of Orleans, he maintained a strict alliance with the Aragonese dynasty at Naples, as having a common interest against
France. But after his death the connection between Milan and
Naples came to be weakened. In the new system of alliances
Milan and Florence, sometimes including Venice, were combined against Ferdinand and Sixtus IV, an unprincipled and
restless pontiff. Ludovico Sforza, who had usurped the guardianship of his nephew, the Duke of Milan, found, as that young
man advanced to maturity, that one crime required to be completed by another. To depose and murder his ward was, however, a scheme that prudence, though not conscience, bade him
hesitate to execute. He had rendered Ferdinand of Naples and
Piero de' Medici, Lorenzo's heir, his decided enemies. A revolution at Milan would be the probable result of his continuing
in usurpation. In these circumstances Ludovico Sforza excited
the King of France to undertake the conquest of Naples.[217]

So long as the three great nations of Europe were unable
to put forth their natural strength through internal separation
or foreign war, the Italians had so little dread for their independence that their policy was altogether directed to regulating
the domestic balance of power among themselves. In the latter
part of the fifteenth century a more enlarged view of Europe
would have manifested the necessity of reconciling petty animosities and sacrificing petty ambition, in order to preserve the
nationality of their governments; not by attempting to melt
down Lombards and Neapolitans, principalities and republics,
into a single monarchy, but by the more just and rational scheme
of a common federation. The politicians of Italy were abundantly competent, as far as cool and clear understandings could
render them, to perceive the interests of their country. But it is
the will of Providence that the highest and surest wisdom, even
in matters of policy, should never be unconnected with virtue.
In relieving himself from an immediate danger, Ludovico Sforza
overlooked the consideration that the presumptive heir of the
King of France claimed by an ancient title that principality of
Milan which he was compassing by usurpation and murder. But
neither Milan nor Naples was free from other claimants than
France, nor was she reserved to enjoy unmolested the spoil of
Italy. A louder and a louder strain of warlike dissonance will

videri; Flaminiæ regulos ad Francos in-
clinare; Genuam Francis subesse, et
civitatem Astensem; si pontifex Romanus
aliquando Francorum amicus assumatur,
nihil reliqui in Italiâ remanere quod non
transeat in Gallorum nomen; tueri se
Italiam, dum Ferdinandum tueretur.
(Commentar. Pii Secundi, l. iv, p. 96.)
Spondamus, who led me to this passage,
is very angry; but the year 1494 proved
Pius II to be a wary statesman.
[217] Guicciardini, l. i.

be heard from the banks of the Danube and from the Mediterranean Gulf. The dark and wily Ferdinand, the rash and lively Maximilian, are preparing to hasten into the lists; the schemes of ambition are assuming a more comprehensive aspect; and the controversy of Neapolitan succession is to expand into the long rivalry between the houses of France and Austria. But here, while Italy is still untouched, and before as yet the first lances of France gleam along the defiles of the Alps, we close the history of the middle ages.

CHAPTER IV

HISTORY OF SPAIN TO THE CONQUEST OF GRANADA

Kingdom of the Visigoths—Conquest of Spain by the Moors—Gradual revival of the Spanish nation—Kingdoms of Leon, Aragon, Navarre, and Castile successively formed—Chartered towns of Castile—Military orders—Conquest of Ferdinand III and James of Aragon—Causes of the delay in expelling the Moors—History of Castile continued—Character of the government—Peter the Cruel—House of Trastamare—John II—Henry IV—Constitution of Castile—National assemblies or Cortes—Their constituent parts—Right of taxation—Legislation—Privy council of Castile—Laws for the protection of liberty—Imperfections of the constitution—Aragon—Its history in the fourteenth and fifteenth centuries—Disputed succession—Constitution of Aragon—Free spirit of its aristocracy—Privilege of union—Powers of the Justiza—Legal securities—Illustrations—Other constitutional laws—Valencia and Catalonia—Union of two crowns by the marriage of Ferdinand and Isabella—Conquest of Granada.

THE history of Spain during the middle ages ought to commence with the dynasty of the Visigoths; a nation among the first that assaulted and overthrew the Roman Empire, and whose establishment preceded by nearly half a century the invasion of Clovis. Vanquished by that conqueror in the battle of Poitiers, the Gothic monarchs lost their extensive dominions in Gaul, and transferred their residence from Toulouse to Toledo. But I will not detain the reader by naming one sovereign of that obscure race. It may suffice to mention that the Visigothic monarchy differed in several respects from that of the Franks during the same period. The crown was less hereditary, or at least the regular succession was more frequently disturbed. The prelates had a still more commanding influence in temporal government. The distinction of Romans and barbarians was less marked, the laws more uniform, and approaching nearly to the imperial code. The power of the sovereign was perhaps more limited by an aristocratical council than in France, but it never yielded to the dangerous influence of mayors of the palace. Civil wars and disputed successions were very frequent, but the integrity of the kingdom was not violated by the custom of partition.

Spain, after remaining for nearly three centuries in the possession of the Visigoths, fell under the yoke of the Saracens in 712. The fervid and irresistible enthusiasm which distinguished the youthful period of Mohammedism might sufficiently account for this conquest, even if we could not assign additional causes—the factions which divided the Goths, the resentment of disappointed pretenders to the throne, the provocations, as has been generally believed, of Count Julian, and the temerity that risked the fate of an empire on the chances of a single battle.[1] It is more surprising that a remnant of this ancient monarchy should not only have preserved its national liberty and name in the northern mountains, but waged for some centuries a successful and generally an offensive warfare against the conquerors, till the balance was completely turned in its favour, and the Moors were compelled to maintain almost as obstinate and protracted a contest for a small portion of the peninsula. But the Arabian monarchs of Cordova found in their success and imagined security a pretext for indolence; even in the cultivation of science and contemplation of the magnificent architecture of their mosques and palaces they forgot their poor but daring enemies in the Asturias; while, according to the nature of despotism, the fruits of wisdom or bravery in one generation were lost in the follies and effeminacy of the next. Their kingdom was dismembered by successful rebels, who formed the states of Toledo, Huesca, Saragossa, and others less eminent; and these, in their own mutual contests, not only relaxed their natural enmity toward the Christian princes, but sometimes sought their alliance.[2]

The last attack which seemed to endanger the reviving monarchy of Spain was that of Almanzor, the illustrious vizier of Haccham II, toward the end of the tenth century, wherein the city of Leon, and even the shrine of Compostella, were burned to the ground. For some ages before this transient reflux, gradual encroachments had been made upon the Saracens, and the kingdom originally styled of Oviedo, the seat of which was removed to Leon in 914, had extended its boundary to the Douro, and even to the mountainous chain of the Guadarrama. The province of Old Castile, thus denominated, as is generally supposed, from the castles erected while it remained a march or frontier against the Moors, was governed by hereditary counts, elected originally by the provincial aristocracy, and virtually independent, it seems probable, of the Kings of Leon, though commonly serving them in war as brethren of the same faith and nation.[3]

---

[1] [Note.]

[2] Cardonne, " Histoire de l'Afrique et de l'Espagne."

[3] According to Roderic of Toledo, one of the earliest Spanish historians, though not older than the beginning of the thirteenth century, the nobles of Castile, in

the reign of Froila, about the year 924, sibi et posteris providerunt, et duos milites non de potentioribus, sed de prudentioribus elegerunt, quos et judices statuerunt, ut dissensiones patriæ et querelantium causæ suo judicio sopirentur (l. v, c. 1). Several other passages in the

While the Kings of Leon were thus occupied in recovering the western provinces, another race of Christian princes grew up silently under the shadow of the Pyrenean Mountains. Nothing can be more obscure than the beginnings of those little states which were formed in Navarre and the country of Soprarbe. They might perhaps be almost contemporaneous with the Moorish conquests. On both sides of the Pyrenees dwelt an aboriginal people, the last to undergo the yoke, and who had never acquired the language, of Rome. We know little of these intrepid mountaineers in the dark period which elapsed under the Gothic and Frank dynasties till we find them cutting off the rear guard of Charlemagne in Roncesvalles, and maintaining at least their independence, though seldom, like the Kings of Asturias, waging offensive war against the Saracens. The town of Jaca, situated among long, narrow valleys that intersect the southern ridges of the Pyrenees, was the capital of a little free state, which afterward expanded into the monarchy of Aragon.[4] A territory rather more extensive belonged to Navarre, the kings of which fixed their seat at Pampeluna. Biscay seems to have been divided between this kingdom and that of Leon. The connection of Aragon or Soprarbe and Navarre was very intimate, and they were often united under a single chief.

At the beginning of the eleventh century, Sancho the Great, King of Navarre and Aragon, was enabled to render his second son, Ferdinand, count, or, as he assumed the title, King of Castile. This effectually dismembered that province from the kingdom of Leon; but their union soon became more complete than ever, though with a reversed supremacy. Bermudo III, King of Leon, fell in an engagement with the new King of Castile, who had married his sister; and Ferdinand, in her right, or in that of conquest, became master of the united monarchy.

same writer prove that the Counts of Castile were nearly independent of Leon, at least from the time of Ferdinand Gonsalvo about the middle of the tenth century. Ex quo iste suscepit suæ patriæ comitatum, cessaverunt reges Asturiarum insolescere in Castellam, et a flumine Pisoricâ nihil amplius vindicârunt (l. v, c. 2). Marina, in his "Ensayo Historico-Critico," is disposed to controvert this fact.

[4] The Fueros, or written laws of Jaca, were perhaps more ancient than any local customary in Europe. Alfonso III confirms them by name of the ancient usages of Jaca. They prescribe the descent of lands and movables, as well as the election of municipal magistrates. The following law, which enjoins the rising in arms on a sudden emergency, illustrates, with a sort of romantic wildness, the manners of a pastoral but warlike people, and reminds us of a well-known passage

in the "Lady of the Lake": De appellitis ita statuimus. Cum homines de villis, vel qui stant in montanis cum suis ganatis [gregibus], audierint appellitum; omnes capiant arma, et dimissis ganatis, et omnibus aliis suis faziendis [negotiis] sequantur appellitum. Et si illi qui fuerint magis remoti, invenerint in villâ magis proximâ appellito [deest aliquid?], omnes qui nondum fuerint egressi tunc villam illam, quæ tardius secuta est appellitum, pecent [solvant] unam baccam [vaccam]; et unusquisque homo ex illis qui tardius secutus est appellitum, et quem magis remoti præcesserint, pecet tres solidos, quomodo nobis videbitur, partiendos. Tamen in Jacâ et in aliis villis, sint aliqui nominati et certi, quos elegerint consules, qui remaneant ad villas custodiendas et defendendas. (" Biancæ Commentaria," in " Schotti Hispania Illustrata," p. 595.)

THE DAY AFTER THE VICTORY.

Photogravure from a painting by Benjamin Constant.

Goupil&ravure

This cessation of hostilities between the Christian states enabled them to direct a more unremitting energy against their ancient enemies, who were now sensibly weakened by the various causes of decline to which I have already alluded. During the eleventh century the Spaniards were almost always superior in the field; the towns which they began by pillaging they gradually possessed; their valour was heightened by the customs of chivalry and inspired by the example of the Cid; and before the end of this age Alfonso VI recovered the ancient metropolis of the monarchy, the city of Toledo. This was the severest blow which the Moors had endured, and an unequivocal symptom of that change in their relative strength which, from being so gradual, was the more irretrievable. Calamities scarcely inferior fell upon them in a different quarter. The Kings of Aragon (a title belonging originally to a little district upon the river of that name) had been cooped up almost in the mountains by the small Moorish states north of the Ebro, especially that of Huesca. About the middle of the eleventh century they began to attack their neighbours with success; the Moors lost one town after another, till, in 1118, exposed and weakened by the reduction of all these places, the city of Saragossa, in which a line of Mohammedan princes had flourished for several ages, became the prize of Alfonso I and the capital of his kingdom. The southern parts of what is now the province of Aragon were successively reduced during the twelfth century, while all new Castile and Estremadura became annexed in the same gradual manner to the dominion of the descendants of Alfonso VI.

Although the feudal system can not be said to have obtained in the kingdoms of Leon and Castile, their peculiar situation gave the aristocracy a great deal of the same power and independence which resulted in France and Germany from that institution. The territory successively recovered from the Moors, like waste lands reclaimed, could have no proprietor but the conquerors, and the prospect of such acquisitions was a constant incitement to the nobility of Spain, especially to those who had settled themselves on the Castilian frontier. In their new conquests they built towns and invited Christian settlers, the Saracen inhabitants being commonly expelled or voluntarily retreating to the safer provinces of the south. Thus Burgos was settled by a Count of Castile about 880; another fixed his seat at Osma; a third at Sepulveda; a fourth at Salamanca. These cities were not free from incessant peril of a sudden attack till the union of the two kingdoms under Ferdinand I, and consequently the necessity of keeping in exercise a numerous and armed population gave a character of personal freedom and privilege to the inferior classes which they hardly possessed at so early a period in any other

20

monarchy. Villenage seems never to have been established in
the Hispano-Gothic kingdoms, Leon and Castile; though I confess it was far from being unknown in that of Aragon, which had
formed its institutions on a different pattern. Since nothing makes
us forget the arbitrary distinctions of rank so much as participation in any common calamity, every man who had escaped
the great shipwreck of liberty and religion in the mountains
of Asturias was invested with a personal dignity, which gave him
value in his own eyes and those of his country. It is probably
this sentiment transmitted to posterity, and gradually fixing the
national character, that has produced the elevation of manner
remarked by travellers in the Castilian peasant. But while these
acquisitions of the nobility promoted the grand object of winning back the peninsula from its invaders, they by no means invigorated the government or tended to domestic tranquility.

A more interesting method of securing the public defence
was by the institution of chartered towns or communities. These
were established at an earlier period than in France and England, and were, in some degree, of a peculiar description. Instead of purchasing their immunities, and almost their personal
freedom, at the hands of a master, the burgesses of Castilian
towns were invested with civil rights and extensive property
on the more liberal condition of protecting their country. The
earliest instance of the erection of a community is in 1020, when
Alfonso V in the Cortes at Leon established the privileges of
that city with a regular code of laws, by which its magistrates
should be governed. The citizens of Carrion, Llanes, and other
towns were incorporated by the same prince. Sancho the Great
gave a similar constitution to Naxara. Sepulveda had its code
of laws in 1076 from Alfonso VI; in the same reign Logroño
and Sahagun acquired their privileges, and Salamanca not long
afterward. The fuero, or original charter of a Spanish community, was properly a compact, by which the king or lord granted
a town and adjacent district to the burgesses, with various privileges, and especially that of choosing magistrates and a common
council, who were bound to conform themselves to the laws prescribed by the founder. These laws, civil as well as criminal,
though essentially derived from the ancient code of the Visigoths,
which continued to be the common law of Castile till the fourteenth or fifteenth century, varied from each other in particular
usages, which had probably grown up and been established in
these districts before their legal confirmation. The territory
held by chartered towns was frequently very extensive, far beyond any comparison with corporations in our own country or
in France; including the estates of private landholders, subject
to the jurisdiction and control of the municipality as well as its

inalienable demesnes, allotted to the maintenance of the magistrates and other public expenses. In every town the king appointed a governor to receive the usual tributes and watch over the police and the fortified places within the district, but the administration of justice was exclusively reserved to the inhabitants and their elected judges. Even the executive power of the royal officer was regarded with jealousy; he was forbidden to use violence toward any one without legal process; and, by the fuero of Logroño, if he attempted to enter forcibly into a private house he might be killed with impunity. These democratical customs were altered in the fourteenth century by Alfonso XI, who vested the municipal administration in a small number of jurats, or regidors. A pretext for this was found in some disorders to which popular elections had led; but the real motive, of course, must have been to secure a greater influence for the crown, as in similar innovations of some English kings.

In recompense for such liberal concessions the incorporated towns were bound to certain money payments and to military service. This was absolutely due from every inhabitant, without dispensation or substitution, unless in case of infirmity. The royal governor and the magistrates, as in the simple times of primitive Rome, raised and commanded the militia; who, in a service always short, and for the most part necessary, preserved that delightful consciousness of freedom, under the standard of their fellow-citizens and chosen leaders, which no mere soldier can enjoy. Every man of a certain property was bound to serve on horseback, and was exempted in return from the payment of taxes. This produced a distinction between the caballeros, or noble class, and the pecheros, or payers of tribute. But the distinction appears to have been founded only upon wealth, as in the Roman equites, and not upon hereditary rank, though it most likely prepared the way for the latter. The horses of these caballeros could not be seized for debt; in some cases they were exclusively eligible to magistracy, and their honour was protected by laws which rendered it highly penal to insult or molest them. But the civil rights of rich and poor in courts of justice were as equal as in England.[5]

The progress of the Christian arms in Spain may in part be ascribed to another remarkable feature in the constitution of that country, the military orders. These had already been

[5] I am indebted for this account of municipal towns in Castile to a book published at Madrid in 1808, immediately after the revolution, by the Doctor Marina, a canon of the Church of St. Isidor, entitled "Ensayo Historico-Critico" sobre la antigua legislación y principales cuerpos legales de los reynos de Lyon y Castilla, especialmente sobre el codigo de D. Alonso el Sabio, conocido con el nombre de las "Siete Partidas." This work is perhaps not readily to be procured in England; but an article in the "Edinburgh Review," No. XLIII, will convey a sufficient notion of its contents.

tried with signal effect in Palestine, and the similar circumstances of Spain easily led to an adoption of the same policy. In a very few years after the first institution of the Knights Templars, they were endowed with great estates, or rather districts, won from the Moors, on condition of defending their own and the national territory. These lay chiefly in the parts of Aragon beyond the Ebro, the conquest of which was then recent and insecure.[6] So extraordinary was the respect for this order and that of St. John, and so powerful the conviction that the hope of Christendom rested upon their valour, that Alfonso I, King of Aragon, dying childless, bequeathed to them his whole kingdom; an example of liberality, says Mariana, to surprise future times and displease his own.[7] The states of Aragon annulled, as may be supposed, this strange testament; but the successor of Alfonso was obliged to pacify the ambitious knights by immense concessions of money and territory, stipulating even not to make peace with the Moors against their will.[8] In imitation of these great military orders common to all Christendom, there arose three Spanish institutions of a similar kind, the orders of Calatrava, Santiago, and Alcantara. The first of these was established in 1158; the second and most famous had its charter from the Pope in 1175, though it seems to have existed previously; the third branched off from that of Calatrava at a subsequent time.[9] These were military colleges, having their walled towns in different parts of Castile, and governed by an elective grand master, whose influence in the state was at least equal to that of any of the nobility. In the civil dissensions of the fourteenth and fifteenth centuries, the chiefs of these incorporated knights were often very prominent.

The kingdoms of Leon and Castile were unwisely divided anew by Alfonso VII between his sons, Sancho and Ferdinand, and this produced not only a separation but a revival of the ancient jealousy, with frequent wars, for nearly a century. At length, in 1238, Ferdinand III, King of Castile, reunited forever the two branches of the Gothic monarchy. He employed their joint strength against the Moors, whose dominion, though it still embraced the finest provinces of the peninsula, was sinking by internal weakness, and had never recovered a tremendous defeat at Banos di Toloso, a few miles from Baylen, in 1210.[10] Ferdinand, bursting into Andalusia, took its great capital, the city of Cordova, not less ennobled by the cultivation of Arabian science, and by the names of Avicenna and Averroes, than by

6 Mariana, " Hist. Hispan.," l. x, c. 10.
7 L. x, c. 15.
8 L. x, c. 18.
9 L. xi, c. 6, 13; l. xii, c. 3.
10 A letter of Alfonso IX, who gained this victory, to Pope Innocent III, puts the loss of the Moors at 180,000 men. The Arabian historians, though without specifying numbers, seem to confirm this immense slaughter, which nevertheless it

the splendid works of a rich and munificent dynasty.[11]   In a few years more Seville was added to his conquests, and the Moors lost their favourite regions on the banks of the Guadalquivir. James I of Aragon, the victories of whose long reign gave him the surname of Conqueror, reduced the city and kingdom of Valencia, the Balearic Isles, and the kingdom of Murcia; but the last was annexed, according to compact, to the crown of Castile.

It could hardly have been expected about the middle of the thirteenth century, when the splendid conquests of Ferdinand and James had planted the Christian banner on the three principal Moorish cities, that two hundred and fifty years were yet to elapse before the rescue of Spain from their yoke should be completed.   Ambition, religious zeal, national enmity, could not be supposed to pause in a career which now seemed to be obstructed by such moderate difficulties; yet we find, on the contrary, the exertions of the Spaniards begin from this time to relax, and their acquisitions of territory to become more slow.   One of the causes, undoubtedly, that produced this unexpected protraction of the contest was the superior means of resistance which the Moors found in retreating.   Their population, spread originally over the whole of Spain, was now condensed, and, if I may so say, become no further compressible, in a single province.   It had been mingled, in the northern and central parts, with the Mozarabic Christians, their subjects and tributaries, not perhaps treated with much injustice, yet naturally and irremediably their enemies.   Toledo and Saragossa, when they fell under a Christian sovereign, were full of these inferior Christians, whose long intercourse with their masters has infused the tones and dialect of Arabia into the language of Castile.[12]   But in the twelfth century the Moors, exasperated by defeat and jealous of secret disaffection, began to persecute their Christian subjects, till they renounced or fled for their religion, so that in the southern provinces scarcely any professors of Christianity were left at the time of Ferdinand's invasion.   An equally severe policy was adopted on the other side.   The Moors had been permitted to dwell in Saragossa as the Christians had dwelt before, sub-

is difficult to conceive before the invention of gunpowder, or indeed since. (Cardonne, tome ii, p. 327.)

[11] If we could rely on a Moorish author quoted by Cardonne (tome i, p. 337), the city of Cordova contained, I know not exactly in what century, 200,000 houses, 600 mosques, and 900 public baths. There were 12,000 towns and villages on the banks of the Guadalquivir. This, however, must be greatly exaggerated, as numerical statements generally are. The mines of gold and silver were very productive. And the revenues of the khalifs of Cordova are said to have amounted to 130,000,000 of French money; besides large contributions that, according to the practice of Oriental governments, were paid in the fruits of the earth. Other proofs of the extraordinary opulence and splendour of this monarchy are dispersed in Cardonne's work, from which they have been chiefly borrowed by later writers. The splendid engravings in Murphy's "Moorish Antiquities of Spain" illustrate this subject.

[12] Mariana, l. xi, c. 1; Gibbon, c. 51.

jects, not slaves; but on the capture of Seville they were entirely expelled, and new settlers invited from every part of Spain. The strong fortified towns of Andalusia, such as Gibraltar, Algeciras, Tarifa, maintained also a more formidable resistance than had been experienced in Castile; they cost tedious sieges, were sometimes recovered by the enemy, and were always liable to his attacks. But the great protection of the Spanish Mohammedans was found in the alliance and ready aid of their kindred beyond the straits. Accustomed to hear of the African Moors only as pirates, we can not easily conceive the powerful dynasties, the warlike chiefs, the vast armies, which for seven or eight centuries illustrate the annals of that people. Their assistance was always afforded to the true believers in Spain, though their ambition was generally dreaded by those who stood in need of their valour.[13]

Probably, however, the Kings of Granada were most indebted to the indolence which gradually became characteristic of their enemies. By the cession of Murcia to Castile, the kingdom of Aragon shut itself out from the possibility of extending those conquests which had ennobled her earlier sovereigns; and their successors, not less ambitious and enterprising, diverted their attention toward objects beyond the peninsula. The Castilian, patient and undesponding in bad success, loses his energy as the pressure becomes less heavy, and puts no ordinary evil in comparison with the exertions by which it must be removed. The greater part of his country freed by his arms, he was content to leave the enemy in a single province rather than undergo the labour of making his triumph complete.

If a similar spirit of insubordination had not been found compatible in earlier ages with the aggrandizement of the Castilian monarchy, we might ascribe its want of splendid successes against the Moors to the continued rebellions which disturbed that government for more than a century after the death of Ferdinand III. His son, Alfonso X, might justly acquire the surname of Wise for his general proficiency in learning, and especially in astronomical science, if these attainments deserve praise in a king who was incapable of preserving his subjects in their duty. As a legislator, Alfonso, by his code of the " Siete Partidas," sacrificed the ecclesiastical rights of his crown to the usurpation of Rome;[14] and his philosophy sunk below the level of ordinary prudence when he permitted the phantom of an imperial crown in Germany to seduce his hopes for almost twenty years. For the sake of such an illusion he would even have withdrawn himself from Castile if the states had not remonstrated against an

[13] Cardonne, tomes ii and iii, passim.
[14] Marina, " Ensayo Historico-Critico," p. 272, etc.

expedition that would probably have cost him the kingdom. In the latter years of his turbulent reign Alfonso had to contend against his son. The right of representation was hitherto unknown in Castile, which had borrowed little from the customs of feudal nations. By the received law of succession the nearer was always preferred to the more remote, the son to the grandson. Alfonso X had established the different maxim of representation by his code of the " Siete Partidas," the authority of which, however, was not universally acknowledged. The question soon came to an issue: on the death of his elder son, Ferdinand, leaving two male children, Sancho, their uncle, asserted his claim, founded upon the ancient Castilian right of succession; and this, chiefly, no doubt, through fear of arms, though it did not want plausible arguments, was ratified by an assembly of the Cortes, and secured, notwithstanding the king's reluctance, by the courage of Sancho. But the descendants of Ferdinand, generally called the infants of La Cerda, by the protection of France, to whose royal family they were closely allied, and of Aragon, always prompt to interfere in the disputes of a rival people, continued to assert their pretensions for more than half a century, and, though they were not very successful, did not fail to aggravate the troubles of their country.

The annals of Sancho IV and his two immediate successors, Ferdinand IV and Alfonso XI, present a series of unhappy and dishonourable civil dissensions with too much rapidity to be remembered or even understood. Although the Castilian nobility had no pretence to the original independence of the French peers, or to the liberties of feudal tenure, they assumed the same privilege of rebelling upon any provocation from their sovereign. When such occurred, they seem to have been permitted, by legal custom, to renounce their allegiance by a solemn instrument, which exempted them from the penalties of treason.[15] A very few families composed an oligarchy, the worst and most ruinous condition of political society, alternately the favourites and ministers of the prince or in arms against him. If unable to protect themselves in their walled towns, and by the aid of their faction, these Christian patriots retired to Aragon or Granada, and excited a hostile power against their country, and perhaps their religion. Nothing is more common in the Castilian history than instances of such defection. Mariana remarks coolly of the family of Castro that they were much in the habit of revolting to the Moors.[16] This house and that of Lara were at one time the great rivals for power; but from the time of Alfonso X the

15 Mariana, l. xiii, c. 11.
16 Alvarus Castrius patriâ aliquanto antea, uti moris erat, renunciatâ.—Castria gens per hæc tempora ad Mauros sæpe defecisse visa est. (L. xii, c. 12; see also chapters 17 and 19.)

former seems to have declined, and the sole family that came in
competition with the Laras during the tempestuous period that
followed was that of Haro, which possessed the lordship of Biscay by a hereditary title. The evils of a weak government were
aggravated by the unfortunate circumstances in which Ferdinand
IV and Alfonso XI ascended the throne; both minors, with a
disputed regency, and the interval too short to give ambitious
spirits leisure to subside. There is, indeed, some apology for the
conduct of the Laras and Haros in the character of their sovereigns, who had but one favourite method of avenging a dissem-
bled injury or anticipating a suspected treason. Sancho IV as-
sassinates Don Lope Haro in his palace at Valladolid. Alfonso
XI invites to court the infant Don Juan, his first cousin, and
commits a similar violence. Such crimes may be found in the
history of other countries, but they were nowhere so usual as
in Spain, which was far behind France, England, and even Germany in civilization.

But whatever violence and arbitrary spirit might be imputed
to Sancho and Alfonso was forgotten in the unexampled tyranny
of Peter the Cruel. A suspicion is frequently intimated by Mariana, which seems, in more modern times, to have gained some
credit, that party malevolence has at least grossly exaggerated
the enormities of this prince.[17] It is difficult, however, to believe
that a number of atrocious acts unconnected with each other, and
generally notorious enough in their circumstances, have been
ascribed to any innocent man. The history of his reign, chiefly
derived, it is admitted, from the pen of an inveterate enemy, Lope
de Ayala, charges him with the murder of his wife, Blanche of
Bourbon, most of his brothers and sisters, with Eleanor Gus-
man, their mother, many Castilian nobles, and multitudes of the
commonalty; besides continual outrages of licentiousness, and
especially a pretended marriage with a noble lady of the Castrian
family. At length a rebellion was headed by his illegitimate
brother, Henry, Count of Trastamare, with the assistance of
Aragon and Portugal. This, however, would probably have
failed of dethroning Peter, a resolute prince, and certainly not

---

[17] There is in general room enough for
scepticism as to the characters of men
who are only known to us through their
enemies. History is full of calumnies,
and of calumnies that can never be
effaced. But I really see no ground for
thinking charitably of Peter the Cruel.
Froissart (part i, c. 230) and Matteo Villani (in " Script. Rerum Italic.," tome
xiv, p. 53), the latter of whom died before the rebellion of Henry of Trastamare,
speak of him much in the same terms
as the Spanish historians. And why
should Ayala be doubted, when he gives
a long list of murders committed in the
face of day, within the recollection of
many persons living when he wrote?
There may be a question whether Richard III smothered his nephews in the
Tower, but nobody can dispute that
Henry VIII cut off Anna Boleyn's head.
The passage from Matteo Villani above
mentioned is as follows: Cominciò aspra-
mente a se far ubbidire, perchè temendo
de' suoi baroni, trovò modo di far in-
famare l' uno l' altro, e prendendo cagi-
one, gli cominciò ad uccidere con le sue
mani. E in brieve tempo ne fece morire
25 e tre suoi fratelli fece morire, etc.

destitute of many faithful supporters, if Henry had not invoked the more powerful succour of Bertrand du Guesclin, and the companies of adventure, who, after the pacification between France and England, had lost the occupation of war, and retained only that of plunder. With mercenaries so disciplined it was in vain for Peter to contend; but, abandoning Spain for a moment, he had recourse to a more powerful weapon from the same armory. Edward, the Black Prince, then resident at Bordeaux, was induced by the promise of Biscay to enter Spain as the ally of Castile; and at the great battle of Navarette he continued lord of the ascendant over those who had so often already been foiled by his prowess. Du Guesclin was made prisoner; Henry fled to Aragon, and Peter remounted the throne. But a second revolution was at hand: the Black Prince, whom he had ungratefully offended, withdrew into Guienne; and he lost his kingdom and life in a second short contest with his brother.

A more fortunate period began with the accession of Henry. His own reign was hardly disturbed by any rebellion; and though his successors, John I and Henry III, were not altogether so unmolested, especially the latter, who ascended the throne in his minority, yet the troubles of their time were slight in comparison with those formerly excited by the houses of Lara and Haro, both of which were now happily extinct. Though Henry II's illegitimacy left him no title but popular choice, his queen was sole representative of the Cerdas, the offspring, as has been mentioned above, of Sancho IV's elder brother, and, by the extinction of the younger branch, unquestioned heiress of the royal line. Some years afterward, by the marriage of Henry III with Catherine, daughter of John of Gaunt and Constance, an illegitimate child of Peter the Cruel, her pretensions, such as they were, became merged in the crown.

No kingdom could be worse prepared to meet the disorders of a minority than Castile, and in none did the circumstances so frequently recur. John II was but fourteen months old at his accession; and but for the disinterestedness of his uncle Ferdinand, the nobility would have been inclined to avert the danger by placing that prince upon the throne. In this instance, however, Castile suffered less from faction during the infancy of her sovereign than in his maturity. The queen dowager, at first jointly with Ferdinand, and solely after his accession to the crown of Aragon, administered the government with credit. Fifty years had elapsed at her death in 1418 since the elevation of the house of Trastamare, who had entitled themselves to public affection by conforming themselves more strictly than their predecessors to the constitutional laws of Castile, which were never so well established as during this period. In external affairs their reigns were not what is considered as glorious. They were generally at peace with Aragon and Granada; but one memorable defeat by the Portuguese at Aljubarrota disgraces the annals of John I, whose cause was as unjust as his arms were unsuccessful. This comparatively golden period ceases at the majority of John II. His reign was filled up by a series of conspiracies and civil wars, headed by his cousins, John and Henry, the Infants of Aragon, who enjoyed very extensive territories in Castile by the testament of their father Ferdinand. Their brother, the King of Aragon, frequently lent the assistance of his arms. John himself, the elder of these two princes, by marriage with the heiress of the kingdom of Navarre, stood in a double relation to Castile, as a neighbouring sovereign, and as a member of the native oligarchy. These conspiracies were all ostensibly directed against the favourite of John II, Alvaro de Luna, who retained for five-and-thirty years an absolute control over his feeble master. The adverse faction naturally ascribed to this powerful minister every criminal intention and all public mischiefs. He was certainly not more scrupulous than the generality of statesmen, and appears to have been rapacious in accumulating wealth. But there was an energy and courage about Alvaro de Luna which distinguishes him from the cowardly sycophants who usually rise by the favour of weak princes; and Castile probably would not have been happier under the administration of his enemies. His fate is among the memorable lessons of history. After a life of troubles endured for the sake of this favourite, sometimes a fugitive, sometimes a prisoner, his son heading rebellions against him, John II suddenly yielded to an intrigue of the palace, and adopted sentiments of dislike toward the man he had so long loved. No substantial charge appears to have been brought against Alvaro de Luna, except that general malversation which it was too late for the king to object to him. The real cause of John's change of affection was, most probably, the insupportable restraint which the weak are apt to find in that spell of a commanding understanding which they dare not break: the torment of living subject to the ascendant of an inferior, which has produced so many examples of fickleness in sovereigns. That of John II is not the least conspicuous. Alvaro de Luna was brought to a summary trial and beheaded; his estates were confiscated. He met his death with the intrepidity of Strafford, to whom he seems to have borne some resemblance in character.

John II did not long survive his minister, dying in 1454, after a reign that may be considered as inglorious, compared with any except that of his successor. If the father was not respected, the son fell completely into contempt. He had been

governed by Pacheco, Marquis of Villena, as implicitly as John
by Alvaro de Luna. This influence lasted for some time afterward. But the king inclining to transfer his confidence to the
Queen Joanna of Portugal, and to one Bertrand de Cueva, upon
whom common fame had fixed as her paramour, a powerful
confederacy of disaffected nobles was formed against the royal
authority. In what degree Henry IV's government had been
improvident or oppressive toward the people it is hard to determine. The chiefs of that rebellion, Carillo, Archbishop of Toledo, the admiral of Castile, a veteran leader of faction, and the
Marquis of Villena, so lately the king's favourite, were undoubtedly actuated only by selfish ambition and revenge. They deposed Henry in an assembly of their faction at Avila with a sort
of theatrical pageantry which has often been described. But
modern historians, struck by the appearance of judicial solemnity
in this proceeding, are sometimes apt to speak of it as a national
act; while, on the contrary, it seems to have been reprobated
by the majority of the Castilians as an audacious outrage upon
a sovereign who, with many defects, had not been guilty of any
excessive tyranny. The confederates set up Alfonso, the king's
brother, and a civil war of some duration ensued, in which they
had the support of Aragon. The Queen of Castile had at this time
borne a daughter, whom the enemies of Henry IV, and indeed
no small part of his adherents, were determined to treat as spurious. Accordingly, after the death of Alfonso, his sister Isabel
was considered as heiress of the kingdom. She might have
aspired, with the assistance of the confederates, to its immediate
possession; but, avoiding the odium of a contest with her brother,
Isabel agreed to a treaty, by which the succession was absolutely settled upon her. This arrangement was not long afterward followed by the union of that princess with Ferdinand,
son of the King of Aragon. This marriage was by no means
acceptable to a part of the Castilian oligarchy, who had preferred a connection with Portugal. And as Henry had never
lost sight of the interests of one whom he considered, or pretended to consider, as his daughter, he took the first opportunity
of revoking his forced disposition of the crown and restoring
the direct line of succession in favour of the Princess Joanna.
Upon his death, in 1474, the right was to be decided by arms.
Joanna had on her side the common presumptions of law, the
testamentary disposition of the late king, the support of Alfonso,
King of Portugal, to whom she was betrothed, and of several
considerable leaders among the nobility, as the young Marquis
of Villena, the family of Mendoza, and the Archbishop of Toledo,
who, charging Ferdinand with ingratitude, had quitted a party
which he had above all men contributed to strengthen. For

Isabella were the general belief of Joanna's illegitimacy, the assistance of Aragon, the adherence of a majority both among the nobles and people, and, more than all, the reputation of ability which both she and her husband had deservedly acquired. The scale was, however, pretty equally balanced till, the King of Portugal having been defeated at Toro in 1476, Joanna's party discovered their inability to prosecute the war by themselves, and successively made their submission to Ferdinand and Isabella.

The Castilians always considered themselves as subject to a legal and limited monarchy. For several ages the crown was elective, as in most nations of German origin, within the limits of one royal family.[18]   In general, of course, the public choice fell upon the nearest heir; and it became a prevailing usage to elect a son during the lifetime of his father, till about the eleventh century a right of hereditary succession was clearly established. But the form of recognising the heir apparent's title in an assembly of the Cortes has subsisted until our own time.[19]

In the original Gothic monarchy of Spain, civil as well as ecclesiastical affairs were decided in national councils, the acts of many of which are still extant, and have been published in ecclesiastical collections. To these assemblies the dukes and other provincial governors, and, in general, the principal individuals of the realm, were summoned along with spiritual persons. This double aristocracy of Church and State continued to form the great council of advice and consent in the first ages of the new kingdoms of Leon and Castile. The prelates and nobility, or rather some of the more distinguished nobility, appear to have concurred in all general measures of legislation, as we infer from the preamble of their statutes. It would be against analogy, as well as without evidence, to suppose that any representation of the commons had been formed in the earlier period of the monarchy. In the preamble of laws passed in 1020, and at several subsequent times during that and the ensuing century, we find only the bishops and magnates recited as present. According to the " General Chronicle " of Spain, deputies from the Castilian towns formed a part of the Cortes in 1169, a date not to be rejected as incompatible with their absence in 1178. However, in 1188, the first year of the reign of Alfonso IX, they are

---

[18] Defuncto in pace principe, primates totius regni unà cum sacerdotibus successorum regni concilio communi constituant.   Concil.   Toletan. IV,, c. 75; apud Marina, " Teoria de las Cortes," tome ii, p. 2.   This important work, by the author of the " Ensayo Historico-Critico," quoted above, contains an ample digest of the parliamentary law of Castile, drawn from original and, in a great degree, unpublished records.   I have been

favoured with the use of a copy, from which I am the more disposed to make extracts, as the book is likely, through its liberal principles, to become almost as scarce in Spain as in England.   Marina's former work (the " Ensayo Hist.-Crit.") furnishes a series of testimonies (c. 66) to the elective character of the monarchy from Pelayo downward to the twelfth century.

[19] " Teoria de las Cortes," tome ii, p. 7.

expressly mentioned, and from that era were constant and necessary parts of those general assemblies.[20] It has been seen already
that the corporate towns or districts of Castile had early acquired
considerable importance, arising less from commercial wealth,
to which the towns of other kingdoms were indebted for their
liberties, than from their utility in keeping up a military organization among the people. To this they probably owe their early
reception into the Cortes as integrant portions of the legislature,
since we do not read that taxes were frequently demanded, till
the extravagance of later kings, and their alienation of the domain, compelled them to have recourse to the national representatives.

Every chief town of a concejo or corporation ought perhaps,
by the constitution of Castile, to have received its regular writ
for the election of deputies to the Cortes.[21] But there does not
appear to have been, in the best times, any uniform practice in
this respect. At the Cortes of Burgos, in 1315, we find one hundred and ninety-two representatives from more than ninety
towns; at those of Madrid, in 1391, one hundred and twenty-six
were sent from fifty towns; and the latter list contains names
of several places which do not appear in the former.[22] No deputies were present from the kingdom of Leon in the Cortes of
Alcala in 1348, where, among many important enactments, the
code of the " Siete Partidas " first obtained a legislative recognition.[23] We find, in short, a good deal more irregularity than
during the same period in England, where the number of electing boroughs varied pretty considerably at every Parliament.
Yet the Cortes of Castile did not cease to be a numerous body
and a fair representation of the people till the reign of John II.
The first princes of the house of Trastamare had acted in all
points with the advice of their Cortes. But John II, and still
more his son Henry IV, being conscious of their own unpopularity, did not venture to meet a full assembly of the nation.
Their writs were directed only to certain towns—an abuse for
which the looseness of preceding usage had given a pretence.[24]
It must be owned that the people bore it in general very patiently. Many of the corporate towns, impoverished by civil

[20] " Ensayo Hist-Crit.," p. 77; " Teoria
de las Cortes," tome i, p. 66. Marina
seems to have somewhat changed his
opinion since the publication of the former work, where he inclines to assert
that the commons were from the earliest
times admitted into the legislature. In
1188, the first year of the reign of Alfonso IX, we find positive mention of
la muchedumbre de las cibdades è em-
biados de cada cibdat.
[21] " Teoria de las Cortes," p. 130.
[22] Id., p. 148. Geddes gives a list of

one hundred and twenty-seven deputies
from forty-eight towns to the Cortes at
Madrid in 1390. (" Miscellaneous Tracts,"
vol. iii.)
[23] Id., p. 154.
[24] Sepades (says John II in 1442) que
en el ayuntamiento que yo fice en la
noble villa de Valladolid . . . los procuradores de ciertas cibdades é villas de
mis reynos que por mi mandado fueron
llamados. This language is repeated as
to subsequent meetings (p. 156).

warfare and other causes, were glad to save the cost of defraying their deputies' expenses. Thus, by the year 1480, only seventeen cities had retained privilege of representation. A vote was afterward added for Granada, and three more in later times for Palencia and the provinces of Estremadura and Galicia.[25] It might have been easy perhaps to redress this grievance while the exclusion was yet fresh and recent. But the privileged towns, with a mean and preposterous selfishness, although their zeal for liberty was at its height, could not endure the only means of effectually securing it, by a restoration of elective franchises to their fellow-citizens. The Cortes of 1506 assert, with one of those bold falsifications upon which a popular body sometimes ventures, that "it is established by some laws and by immemorial usage that eighteen cities of these kingdoms have the right of sending deputies to the Cortes, and no more"; remonstrating against the attempts made by some other towns to obtain the same privilege, which they request may not be conceded. This remonstrance is repeated in 1512.[26]

From the reign of Alfonso XI, who restrained the government of corporations to an oligarchy of magistrates, the right of electing members of the Cortes was confined to the ruling body, the bailiffs or regidores, whose number seldom exceeded twenty-four, and whose succession was kept up by close election among themselves.[27] The people, therefore, had no direct share in the choice of representatives. Experience proved, as several instances in these pages will show, that even upon this narrow basis the deputies of Castile were not deficient in zeal for their country and its liberties. But it must be confessed that a small body of electors is always liable to corrupt influence and to intimidation. John II and Henry IV often invaded the freedom of election; the latter even named some of the deputies.[28] Several energetic remonstrances were made in the Cortes against this flagrant grievance. Laws were enacted and other precautions devised to secure the due return of deputies. In the sixteenth century the evil, of course, was aggravated. Charles and Philip corrupted the members by bribery.[29] Even in 1573 the Cortes are bold enough to complain that creatures of government were sent thither, "who are always held for suspected by the other deputies, and cause disagreement among them."[30]

[25] The cities which retained their representation in the Cortes were Burgos, Toledo (there was a constant dispute for precedence between these two), Leon, Granada, Cordova, Murcia, Jaen, Zamora, Toro, Soria, Valladolid, Salamanca, Segovia, Avila, Madrid, Guadalaxara, and Cuenca. The representatives of these were supposed to vote not only for their immediate constituents, but for other adjacent towns. Thus Toro voted for Pa-lencia and the kingdom of Galicia, before they obtained separate votes; Salamanca for most of Estremadura; Guadalaxara for Siguenza and four hundred other towns. ("Teoria de las Cortes," pp. 160, 268.)
[26] Idem, p. 161.
[27] Idem, pp. 86, 197.
[28] Idem, p. 199.
[29] Idem, p. 213.
[30] Idem, p. 202.

There seems to be a considerable obscurity about the constitution of the Cortes, so far as relates to the two higher estates, the spiritual and temporal nobility. It is admitted that down to the latter part of the thirteenth century, and especially before the introduction of representatives from the commons, they were summoned in considerable numbers. But the writer to whom I must almost exclusively refer for the constitutional history of Castile contends that from the reign of Sancho IV they took much less share and retained much less influence in the deliberation of the Cortes.[31] There is a remarkable protest of the Archbishop of Toledo, in 1295, against the acts done in the Cortes, because neither he nor the other prelates had been admitted to their discussions, nor given any consent to their resolutions, although such consent was falsely recited in the laws enacted therein.[32] This protestation is at least a testimony to the constitutional rights of the prelacy, which, indeed, all the early history of Castile, as well as the analogy of other governments, conspires to demonstrate. In the fourteenth and fifteenth centuries, however, they were more and more excluded. None of the prelates were summoned to the Cortes of 1299 and 1301; none either of the prelates or nobles to those of 1370 and 1373, of 1480 and 1505. In all the latter cases, indeed, such members of both orders as happened to be present in the court attended the Cortes—a fact which seems to be established by the language of the statutes.[33] Other instances of a similar kind may be adduced. Nevertheless, the more usual expression in the preamble of laws reciting those summoned to and present at the Cortes, though subject to considerable variation, seems to imply that all the three estates were, at least nominally and according to legitimate forms, constituent members of the national assembly. And a chronicle mentions, under the year 1406, the nobility and clergy as deliberating separately, and with some difference of judgment, from the deputies of the commons.[34] A theory, indeed, which should exclude the

[31] " Teoria de las Cortes," p. 67.

[32] Protestamos que desde aquí venimos non fuemos llamados á consejo, ni á los tratados soore los fechos del reyno, ni sobre las otras cosas que hí fueren tractadas et fechas, et sennaladamente sobre los fechos de los consejos de las hermandades et de las peticiones que fueron fechas de su parte, et sobre los otorgamentos que les ficieron, et sobre los previlegios que por esta nazon les fueron otorgados; mas ante fuemos ende apartados et estrannados et secados expresamente nos et los otros perlados et ricos homes et los fijosdalgo; et non fue hí cosa fecha con nuestro consejo. Otrosi protestamos por razon de aquello que dice en los previlegios que les otorgaron, que fueren los perlados llamados, et que eran otorgados de consentimiento et de voluntad dellos, que non fuemos hí presentes ni llamados nin fué fecho con nuestra voluntad, nin consentimos, nin consentimos en ellos, etc. (p. 72).

[33] " Teoria de las Cortes." p. 74.

[34] Tome ii, p. 234. Marina is influenced by a prejudice in favour of the abortive Spanish constitution of 1812, which excluded the temporal and spiritual aristocracy from a place in the legislature, to imagine a similar form of government in ancient times. But his own work furnishes abundant reasons, if I am not mistaken, to modify this opinion very essentially. A few out of many instances may be adduced from the enacting words of statutes, which we consider in England as good evidences to establish a constitutional theory. Sepades que yo hube mio acuerdo é mio consejo con mios her-

great territorial aristocracy from their place in the Cortes, would expose the dignity and legislative rights of that body to unfavourable inferences. But it is manifest that the king exercised very freely a prerogative of calling or omitting persons of both the higher orders at his discretion. The bishops were numerous, and many of their sees not rich; while the same objections of inconvenience applied perhaps to the ricoshombres, but far more forcibly to the lower nobility, the hijosdalgo or caballeros. Castile never adopted the institution of deputies from this order, as in the States-General of France and some other countries, much less that liberal system of landed representation which forms one of the most admirable peculiarities in our own constitution. It will be seen hereafter that spiritual and even temporal peers were summoned by our kings with much irregularity, and the disordered state of Castile through almost every reign was likely to prevent the establishment of any fixed usage in this and most other points.

The primary and most essential characteristic of a limited monarchy is that money can only be levied upon the people through the consent of their representatives. This principle was thoroughly established in Castile; and the statutes which enforce it, the remonstrances which protest against its violation, bear a lively analogy to corresponding circumstances in the history of our constitution. The lands of the nobility and clergy were, I believe, always exempted from direct taxation—an immunity which, perhaps, rendered the attendance of the members of those estates in the Cortes less regular. The corporate districts or concejos, which, as I have observed already, differed from the communities of France and England by possessing a large extent of territory subordinate to the principal town, were bound by their charter to a stipulated annual payment, the price of their franchises, called moneda forera.[35] Beyond this sum nothing

manos é los arzobispos, é los obispos, é con los ricos homes de Castella, é de Leon, é con homes buenos de las villas de Castella, é de Leon, que fueron conmigo en Valladolit, sobre muchas cosas, etc. (Alfonso X in 1258.) Mandamos enviar llama por cartas del rei é nuestras á los infantes é perlados é ricos homes é infanzones é caballeros é homes buenos de las cibdades é de las villas de los reynos de Castilia et de Toledo é de Leon é de las Estramaduras, é de Gallicia é de las Asturias é del Andalusia. (Writ of summons to Cortes of Burgos in 1315.) Con acuerdo de los perlados é de los ricos homes é procuradores de las cibdades é villas é logares de los nuestros reynos. (Ordinances of Toro in 1371.) Estanho hí con él el infante Don Ferrando, etc., é otros perlados é condes é ricos homes é otros caballeros é escuderos, é los procuradores de las cibdades é villas é logares de sus reynos. (Cortes of 1391.) Los tres estados que deben venir á las Cortes

é ayuntamientos segunt se debe facer é es de buena costumbre antigua. (Cortes of 1393.) This last passage is apparently conclusive to prove that three estates, the superior clergy, the nobility, and the commons, were essential members of the legislature in Castile, as they were in France and England; and one is astonished to read in Marina that no faltaron á ninguna de las formalidades de derecho los monarcas que no tuvieron por oportuno llamar á Cortes para semejantes actos ni al clero ni á la nobleza ni á las personas singulares de uno y otro estado. (Tome i, p. 69.) That great citizen, Jovellanos, appears to have had much wiser notions of the ancient government of his country, as well as of the sort of reformation which she wanted, as we may infer from passages in his " Memoria " á sus compatriotas, Coruña, 1811, quoted by Marina for the purpose of censure.
    [35] Marina, " Ensayo Hist.-Crit.," cap. 158; " Teoria de las Cortes," tome ii, p.

could be demanded without the consent of the Cortes. Alfonso
VIII, in 1177, applied for a subsidy toward carrying on the siege
of Cuenca. Demands of money do not, however, seem to have
been very usual before the prodigal reign of Alfonso X. That
prince and his immediate successors were not much inclined to
respect the rights of their subjects; but they encountered a steady
and insuperable resistance. Ferdinand IV, in 1307, promises
to raise no money beyond his legal and customary dues. A more
explicit law was enacted by Alfonso XI in 1328, who bound
himself not to exact from his people, or cause them to pay any
tax, either partial or general, not hitherto established by law,
without the previous grant of all the deputies convened to the
Cortes.[36] This abolition of illegal impositions was several times
confirmed by the same prince. The Cortes, in 1393, having made
a grant to Henry III, annexed this condition, that " since they
had granted him enough for his present necessities, and even to
lay up a part for a future exigency, he should swear before one
of the archbishops not to take or demand any money, service,
or loan, or anything else, of the cities and towns, nor of individuals belonging to them, on any pretence of necessity, until
the three estates of the kingdom should first be duly summoned
and assembled in Cortes according to ancient usage. And if
any such letters requiring money have been written, that they
shall be obeyed and not complied with." [37]   His son, John II,
having violated this constitutional privilege on the allegation of
a pressing necessity, the Cortes, in 1420, presented a long remonstrance, couched in very respectful but equally firm language,
wherein they assert " the good custom, founded in reason and
in justice, that the cities and towns of your kingdoms shall not
be compelled to pay taxes or requisitions, or other new tribute,
unless your Highness order it by advice and with the grant of
the said cities and towns, and of their deputies for them." And
they express their apprehension lest this right should be infringed, because, as they say, " there remains no other privilege
or liberty which can be profitable to subjects if this be shaken." [38]

387. This is expressed in one of their
fueros, or charters: Liberi et ingenui semper maneatis, reddendo mihi et succes-
soribus meis in unoquoque anno in die
Pentecostes de unaquaque domo 12 de-
narios; et, mihi cum bonâ voluntate vestrâ
feceritis, nullum servitium faciatis.
[36] De los con echar nin mandar pagar
pecho desaforado ninguno, especial nin
general, en toda mi tierra, sin ser llamados primeramente á Cortes é otorgado
por todos los procuradores que hí veni-
eren (p. 388).
[37] Obedecidas é non cumplidas. This
expression occurs frequently in provisions made against illegal acts of the
crown; and is characteristic of the singular respect with which the Spaniards
always thought it right to treat their
sovereign, while they were resisting the
abuses of his authority.
[38] La buena costumbre é possession
fundada en razon é en justicia que las
cibdades é villas de vuestros reinos tenian
de no ser mandado coger monedas é pedidos nin otro tributo nuevo alguno en
los vuestros reinos sin que la vuestra se-
ñoria lo faga é ordene de consejo é con
otorgamiento de las cibdades é villas de
los vuestros reinos é de sus procuradores
en su nombre . . . no queda otro pre-
vilegio ni libertad de que los subditos
puedan gozar ni aprovechar quebrantado
el sobre dicho (tome iii, p. 30).

The king gave them as full satisfaction as they desired that his encroachment should not be drawn into precedent. Some fresh abuses during the unfortunate reign of Henry IV produced another declaration in equally explicit language, forming part of the sentence awarded by the arbitrators to whom the differences between the king and his people had been referred at Medina del Campo in 1465.[39] The Catholic kings, as they are eminently called, Ferdinand and Isabella, never violated this part of the constitution; nor did even Charles I, although sometimes refused money by the Cortes, attempt to exact it without their consent.[40] In the "Recopilación," or code of Castilian law published by Philip II, we read a positive declaration against arbitrary imposition of taxes, which remained unaltered on the face of the statute-book till the present age.[41] The law was indeed frequently broken by Philip II; but the Cortes, who retained throughout the sixteenth century a degree of steadiness and courage truly admirable when we consider their political weakness, did not cease to remonstrate with that suspicious tyrant, and recorded their unavailing appeal to the law of Alfonso XI, " so ancient and just, and which so long time has been used and observed." [42]

The free assent of the people by their representatives to grants of money was by no means a mere matter of form. It was connected with other essential rights indispensable to its effectual exercise, those of examining public accounts and checking the expenditure. The Cortes, in the best times at least, were careful to grant no money until they were assured that what had been already levied on their constituents had been properly employed.[43] They refused a subsidy in 1390 because they had

39 Declaramos é ordenamos, que el dicho señor rei nin los otros reyes que despues del fueren non echan nin repartan nin pidan pedidos nin monedas en sus reynos, salvo por gran necessidad, é seyendo primero accordado con los perlados é grandes de sus reynos, é con los otros que á la sazon residieren en su consejo, é seyendo para ello llamados los procuradores de las cibdades é villas de sus reynos, que para las tales cosas se suelen é acostumbran llamar, é seyendo per los dichos procuradores otorgado el dicho pedimento é monedas (tome ii, p. 391).

40 Marina has published two letters from Charles to the city of Toledo, in 1542 and 1548, requesting them to instruct their deputies to consent to a further grant of money, which they had refused to do without leave of their constituents (tome iii, pp. 180, 187).

41 Tome ii, p. 393.

42 En las Cortes de ano de 70 y en las de 76 pedimos á v. m. fuese servide de no poner nuevos impuestos, rentas, pechos, ni derechos ni otros tributos particulares ni generales sin junta del reyno en Cortes,

como está dispuesto por lei del señor rei Don Alonso, y se significó á v. m. el daño grande que con las nuevas rentas habia rescibido el reino, suplicando á v. m. fuese servido de mandarle aliviar y descargar, y que en lo de adelante se les hiciesse merced de guardar las dichas leyes reales, y que ne se impuiessen nuevas rentas sin su asistencia ; pues podria v. m. estar satisfecho de que el reino sirve en las cosas necessarias con toda lealtad y hasta ahora no se ha proveido lo susodicho; y el reino por la obligacion que tiene á pedir á v. m. guarde la dicha lei, y que no solamente han cessado las necessidades de los subditos y naturales de v. m. pero antes crecen de cada dia: vuelve á suplicar á v. m. sea servido concederle lo susodicho, y que las nuevas rentas pechos y derechos se quiten, y que de aquí adelante se guarde la dicha lei del señor rei Don Alonso, como tan antigua y justa y que tanto tiempo se usó y guardó (p. 395). This petition was in 1579.

43 Marina, tome ii, pp. 404, 406.

already given so much, and, "not knowing how so great a sum had been expended, it would be a great dishonour and mischief to promise any more." In 1406 they stood out a long time, and at length gave only half of what was demanded.[44] Charles I attempted to obtain money in 1527 from the nobility as well as commons. But the former protested that "their obligation was to follow the king in war, wherefore to contribute money was totally against their privilege, and for that reason they could not acquiesce in his Majesty's request."[45] The commons also refused on this occasion. In 1538, on a similar proposition, the superior and lower nobility (los grandes y caballeros) "begged with all humility that they might never hear any more of that matter."[46]

The contributions granted by the Cortes were assessed and collected by respectable individuals (hombres buenos) of the several towns and villages.[47] This repartition, as the French call it, of direct taxes is a matter of the highest importance in those countries where they are imposed by means of a gross assessment on a district. The produce was paid to the royal council. It could not be applied to any other purpose than that to which the tax had been appropriated. Thus the Cortes of Segovia, in 1407, granted a subsidy for the war against Granada, on condition that "it should not be laid out on any other service except this war"; which they requested the queen and Ferdinand, both regents in John II's minority, to confirm by oath. Part, however, of the money remaining unexpended, Ferdinand wished to apply it to his own object of procuring the crown of Aragon; but the queen first obtained not only a release from her oath by the Pope, but the consent of the Cortes. They continued to insist upon this appropriation, though ineffectually, under the reign of Charles I.[48]

The Cortes did not consider it beyond the line of their duty, notwithstanding the respectful manner in which they always addressed the sovereign, to remonstrate against profuse expenditure even in his own household. They told Alfonso X in 1258, in the homely style of that age, that they thought it fitting that the king and his wife should eat at the rate of a hundred and fifty maravedis a day, and no more, and that the king should order his attendants to eat more moderately than they did.[49] They remonstrated more forcibly against the podigality of John II. Even in 1559 they spoke with an undaunted Castilian spirit to Philip II: "Sir, the expenses of your royal establishment and

[44] Marina, tome ii, p. 409.
[45] Pero que contribuir á la guerra con ciertas sumas era totalmente opuesto á sus previlegios, é asi que no podrian acomodarse á lo que s. m. deseaba (p. 411).
[46] Marina, tome ii, p. 411.
[47] P. 398.
[48] P. 412.
[49] P. 417.

household are much increased; and we conceive it would much redound to the good of these kingdoms that your Majesty should direct them to be lowered, both as a relief to your wants and that all the great men and other subjects of your Majesty may take example therefrom to restrain the great disorder and excess they commit in that respect." [50]

The forms of a Castilian Cortes were analogous to those of an English Parliament in the fourteenth century. They were summoned by a writ almost exactly coincident in expression with that in use among us.[51] The session was opened by a speech from the chancellor or other chief officer of the court. The deputies were invited to consider certain special business, and commonly to grant money.[52] After the principal affairs were despatched, they conferred together, and, having examined the instructions of their respective constituents, drew up a schedule of petitions. These were duly answered one by one; and from the petition and answer, if favourable, laws were afterward drawn up where the matter required a new law, or promises of redress were given if the petition related to an abuse or grievance. In the struggling condition of Spanish liberty under Charles I, the crown began to neglect answering the petitions of the Cortes, or to use unsatisfactory generalities of expression. This gave rise to many remonstrances. The deputies insisted in 1523 on having answers before they granted money. They repeated the same contention in 1525, and obtained a general law inserted in the " Recopilación " enacting that the king should answer all their petitions before he dissolved the assembly.[53] This, however, was disregarded as before; but the Cortes, whose intrepid honesty under Philip II so often attracts our admiration, continued as late as 1586 to appeal to the written statute and lament its violation.[54]

According to the ancient fundamental constitution of Castile, the king did not legislate for his subjects without their consent. The code of the Visigoths, called in Spain the " Fuero Jusgo," was enacted in public councils, as were also the laws of the early Kings of Leon, which appears by the reciting words of their preambles.[55] This consent was originally given only by

[50] Senhor, los gastos de vuestro real estado y mesa son muy crescidos, y entendemos que convernia mucho al bien de estos reinos que v. m. los mandasse moderar, así para algun remedio de sus necessidades, como para que de v. m. tomen egempló totos los grandes y caballeros y otros subditos de v. m. en la grandesorden y excessos que hacen en las cosas sobredichas (p. 437).
[51] Marina, tome i, p. 175; tome iii, p. 103.
[52] Tome i, p. 278.
[53] P. 301.

[54] Pp. 288–304.
[55] Tome ii, p. 202. The acts of the Cortes of Leon in 1020 run thus: Omnes pontifices et abbates et optimates regni Hispaniæ jussu ipsius regis talia decreta decrevimus quæ firmiter teneantur futuris temporibus. So those of Salamanca, in 1178: Ego rex Fernandus inter cætera quæ cum episcopis et abbatibus regni nostri et quamplurimis aliis religiosis, cum comitibus terrarum et principibus et rectoribus provinciarum, toto posse tenenda statuimus apud Salamancam.

the higher estates, who might be considered, in a large sense, as representing the nation, though not chosen by it, but from the end of the twelfth century by the elected deputies of the commons in the Cortes. The laws of Alfonso X in 1258, those of the same prince in 1274, and many others in subsequent times, are declared to be made with the consent (con acuerdo) of the several orders of the kingdom. More commonly, indeed, the preamble of Castilian statutes only recites their advice (consejo); but I do not know that any stress is to be laid on this circumstance. The laws of the " Siete Partidas," compiled by Alfonso X, did not obtain any direct sanction till the famous Cortes of Alcala, in 1348, when they were confirmed along with several others, forming altogether the basis of the statute law of Spain.[56] Whether they were, in fact, received before that time has been a matter controverted among Spanish antiquaries, and upon the question of their legal validity at the time of their promulgation depends an important point in Castilian history, the disputed right of succession between Sancho IV and the Infants of La Cerda; the former claiming under the ancient customary law, the latter under the new dispositions of the " Siete Partidas." If the king could not legally change the established laws without consent of his Cortes, as seems most probable, the right of representative succession did not exist in favour of his grandchildren, and Sancho IV can not be considered as a usurper.

It appears, upon the whole, to have been a constitutional principle that laws could neither be made nor annulled except in the Cortes. In 1506 this is claimed by the deputies as an established right.[57] John I had long before admitted that what was done by the Cortes and general assemblies could not be undone by letters missive, but by such Cortes and assemblies alone.[58] For the Kings of Castile had adopted the English practice of dispensing with statutes by a non-obstante clause in their grants. But the Cortes remonstrated more steadily against this abuse than our own Parliament, who suffered it to remain in a certain degree till the Revolution. It was several times enacted upon their petition, especially by an explicit statute of Henry II, that grants and letters-patent dispensing with statutes should not be obeyed.[59] Nevertheless, John II, trusting to force or the

[56] " Ensayo Hist.-Crit.," p. 353; " Teoria de las Cortes," tome ii, p. 77. Marina seems to have changed his opinion between the publication of these two works, in the former of which he contends for the previous authority of the " Siete Partidas," and in favour of the Infants of La Cerda.
[57] Los reyes establecieron que cuando hubiesen de hacer leyes, para que fuesen provechosas á sus reynos y cada provincias fuesen proveidas, se llamasen Cortes y procuradores que entendiesen en ellas, y por esto se establecio lei que no se hiciesen ni renovasen leyes sino en Cortes. (" Teoria de las Cortes," tome ii, p. 218.)
[58] Lo que es fecho por Cortes é por ayuntamientos que non se pueda disfacer por las tales cartas, salvo por ayuntamientos é Cortes. (" Teoria de las Cortes," tome ii, p. 215.)
[59] P. 215.

servility of the judges, had the assurance to dispense explicitly with this very law.[60] The Cortes of Valladolid, in 1442, obtained fresh promises and enactments against such an abuse. Philip I and Charles I began to legislate without asking the consent of the Cortes; this grew much worse under Philip II, and reached its height under his successors, who entirely abolished all constitutional privileges.[61] In 1555 we find a petition that laws made in the Cortes should be revoked nowhere else. The reply was such as became that age: " To this we answer that we shall do what best suits our government." But even in 1619, and still afterward, the patriot representatives of Castile continued to lift an unavailing voice against illegal ordinances, though in the form of very humble petition; perhaps the latest testimonies to the expiring liberties of their country.[62] The denial of exclusive legislative authority to the crown must, however, be understood to admit the legality of particular ordinances designed to strengthen the king's executive government.[63] These, no doubt, like the royal proclamations in England, extended sometimes very far, and subjected the people to a sort of arbitrary coercion much beyond what our enlightened notions of freedom would consider as reconcilable to it. But in the middle ages such temporary commands and prohibitions were not reckoned strictly legislative, and passed, perhaps rightly, for inevitable consequences of a scanty code and short sessions of the national council.

The kings were obliged to swear to the observance of laws enacted in the Cortes, besides their general coronation oath to keep the laws and preserve the liberties of their people. Of this we find several instances from the middle of the thirteenth century, and the practice continued till the time of John II, who, in 1433, on being requested to swear to the laws then enacted, answered that he intended to maintain them, and consequently no oath was necessary; an evasion in which the Cortes seem unaccountably to have acquiesced.[64] The guardians of Alfonso XI not only swore to observe all that had been agreed on at Burgos in 1315, but consented that, if any one of them did not keep his oath, the people should no longer be obliged to regard or obey him as regent.[65]

It was customary to assemble the Cortes of Castile for many purposes besides those of granting money and concurring in legislation. They were summoned in every reign to acknowledge and confirm the succession of the heir apparent, and upon his

[60] " Teoria de las Cortes," p. 216; tome iii, p. 40.
[61] Tome ii, p. 218.
[62] Ha suplicado el reino á v. m. no se promulguen nuevas leyes, ni en todo ni en parte las antiguas se alteren, sin que

sea por Cortes . . . y por ser de tanta importancia vuelve el reino á suplicarlo humilmente á v. m. (p. 220).
[63] P. 207.
[64] Tome i, p. 306.
[65] Tome iii, p. 62.

accession to swear allegiance.[66]   These acts were, however, little more than formal, and accordingly have been preserved for the sake of parade after all the real dignity of the Cortes was annihilated.   In the fourteenth and fifteenth centuries they claimed and exercised very ample powers.   They assumed the right, when questions of regency occurred, to limit the prerogative, as well as to designate the persons who were to use it.[67]   And the frequent minorities of Castilian kings, which were unfavourable enough to tranquility and subordination, served to confirm these parliamentary privileges.   The Cortes were usually consulted upon all material business.   A law of Alfonso XI in 1328, printed in the " Recopilación " or code published by Philip II, declares, " Since in the arduous affairs of our kingdom the counsel of our natural subjects is necessary, especially of the deputies from our cities and towns, therefore we ordain and command that on such great occasions the Cortes shall be assembled, and counsel shall be taken of the three estates of our kingdoms, as the kings our forefathers have been used to do." [68]   A Cortes of John II, in 1419, claimed this right of being consulted in all matters of importance, with a warm remonstrance against the alleged violation of so wholesome a law by the reigning prince; who answered that in weighty matters he had acted, and would continue to act, in conformity to it.[69]   What should be intended by great and weighty affairs might be not at all agreed upon by the two parties, to each of whose interpretations these words gave pretty full scope.   However, the current usage of the monarchy certainly permitted much authority in public deliberations to the Cortes.   Among other instances, which, indeed, will continually be found in the common civil histories, the Cortes of Ocana, in 1469, remonstrate with Henry IV for allying himself with England rather than France, and give, as the first reason of complaint, that, " according to the laws of your kingdom, when the kings have anything of great importance in hand, they ought not to undertake it without advice and knowledge of the chief towns and cities of your kingdom." [70]   This privilege of general interference was asserted, like other ancient rights, under Charles, whom they strongly urged, in 1548, not to permit his son Philip to depart out of the realm.[71]   It is hardly necessary to observe that, in such times, they had little chance of being regarded.

The Kings of Leon and Castile acted, during the interval of the Cortes, by the advice of a smaller council, answering, as it seems, almost exactly to the king's ordinary council in Eng-

[66] Tome i, p. 33; tome ii, p. 24.
[67] P. 230.
[68] Tome i, p. 31.
[69] P. 34.
[70] Porque, segunt leyes de nuestros reynos, cuando los reyes han de facer alguna cosa de gran importancia, non lo deben facer sin consejo é sabiduria de las cibdades e villas principales de vuestros reynos. (" Teoria de las Cortes," tome ii, p. 241.)
[71] Tome iii, p. 183.

land. In early ages, before the introduction of the commons, it is sometimes difficult to distinguish this body from the general council of the nation, being composed, in fact, of the same class of persons, though in smaller numbers. A similar difficulty applies to the English history. The nature of their proceedings seems best to ascertain the distinction. All executive acts, including those ordinances which may appear rather of a legislative nature, all grants and charters, are declared to be with the assent of the court (curia), or of the magnates of the palace, or of the chiefs or nobles.[72] This privy council was an essential part of all European monarchies; and, though the sovereign might be considered as free to call in the advice of whomsoever he pleased, yet, in fact, the princes of the blood and most powerful nobility had anciently a constitutional right to be members of such a council, so that it formed a very material check upon his personal authority.

The council underwent several changes in progress of time, which it is not necessary to enumerate. It was justly deemed an important member of the constitution, and the Cortes showed a laudable anxiety to procure its composition in such a manner as to form a guarantee for the due execution of laws after their own dissolution. Several times, especially in minorities, they even named its members or a part of them; and in the reigns of Henry III and John II they obtained the privilege of adding a permanent deputation, consisting of four persons elected out of their own body, annexed, as it were, to the council, who were to continue at the court during the interval of the Cortes and watch over the due observance of the laws.[73] This deputation continued as an empty formality in the sixteenth century. In the council the king was bound to sit personally three days in the week. Their business, which included the whole executive government, was distributed with considerable accuracy into what might be despatched by the council alone, under their own seals and signatures, and what required the royal seal.[74] The consent of this body was necessary for almost every act of the crown: for pensions or grants of money, ecclesiastical and political promotions, and for charters of pardon, the easy concession of which was a great encouragement to the homicides so usual in those ages, and was restrained by some of our own laws.[75] But the council did not exercise any judicial authority, if we may believe the well-informed author from whom I have learned these particulars; unlike, in this, to the ordinary council of the Kings of Eng-

[72] Cum assensu magnatum palatii: Cum consilio curiæ meæ: Cum consilio et beneplacito omnium principum meorum, nullo contradicente nec reclamente. ("Teoria de las Cortes," tome iii, p. 325.)

[73] "Teoria de las Cortes," tome ii, p. 346.
[74] P. 354.
[75] Pp. 360, 362, 372.

land. It was not until the days of Ferdinand and Isabella that this, among other innovations, was introduced.[76]

Civil and criminal justice was administered, in the first instance, by the alcaldes, or municipal judges of towns; elected within themselves originally by the community at large, but in subsequent times by the governing body. In other places a lord possessed the right of jurisdiction by grant from the crown, not, what we find in countries where the feudal system was more thoroughly established, as incident to his own territorial superiority. The kings, however, began in the thirteenth century to appoint judges of their own, called corregidores, a name which seems to express concurrent jurisdiction with the regidores, or ordinary magistrates.[77] The Cortes frequently remonstrated against this encroachment. Alfonso XI consented to withdraw his judges from all corporations by which he had not been requested to appoint them.[78] Some attempts to interfere with the municipal authorities of Toledo produced serious disturbances under Henry III and John II.[79] Even where the king appointed magistrates at a city's request, he was bound to select them from among the citizens.[80] From this immediate jurisdiction an appeal lay to the adelantado or governor of the province, and thence to the tribunal of royal alcades.[81] The latter, however, could not take cognizance of any cause depending before the ordinary judges; a contrast to the practice of Aragon, where the justiciary's right of evocation (juris firma) was considered as a principal safeguard of public liberty.[82] As a court of appeal, the royal alcaldes had the supreme jurisdiction. The king could only cause their sentence to be revised, but neither alter nor revoke it.[83] They have continued to the present day as a criminal tribunal; but civil appeals were transferred by the ordinances of Toro in 1371 to a new court, styled the king's audience, which, though deprived under Ferdinand and his successors of part of its jurisdiction, still remains one of the principal judicatures in Castile.[84]

No people in a half-civilized state of society have a full practical security against particular acts of arbitrary power. They were more common perhaps in Castile than in any other European monarchy which professed to be free. Laws, indeed, were not wanting to protect men's lives and liberties, as well as their properties. Ferdinand IV, in 1299, agreed to a petition that

[76] Tome ii, pp. 375, 379.
[77] Alfonso X says, Ningun ome sea osado juzgar pleytos, se no fuere alcalde puesto pol el rey. (Id., fol. 27.) This seems an encroachment on the municipal magistrates.
[78] " Teoria de las Cortes," tome ii, p. 251.
[79] P. 255; Mariana, l. xx, c. 13.

[80] P. 255.
[81] P. 266.
[82] P. 260.
[83] Pp. 287, 304.
[84] " Teoria de las Cortes," tome ii, pp. 292–302. The use of the present tense, in this and many other passages, will not confuse the attentive reader.

"justice shall be executed impartially according to law and right; and that no one shall be put to death or imprisoned, or deprived of his possessions, without trial, and that this be better observed than heretofore."[85] He renewed the same law in 1307. Nevertheless, the most remarkable circumstance of this monarch's history was a violation of so sacred and apparently so well-established a law. Two gentlemen having been accused of murder, Ferdinand, without waiting for any process, ordered them to instant execution. They summoned him with their last words to appear before the tribunal of God in thirty days; and his death within the time, which has given him the surname of the Summoned, might, we may hope, deter succeeding sovereigns from iniquity so flagrant. But from the practice of causing their enemies to be assassinated, neither law nor conscience could withhold them. Alfonso XI was more than once guilty of this crime. Yet he, too, passed an ordinance in 1325 that no warrant should issue for putting any one to death, or seizing his property, till he should be duly tried by course of law. Henry II repeats the same law in very explicit language.[86] But the civil history of Spain displays several violations of it. An extraordinary prerogative of committing murder appears to have been admitted in early times by several nations who did not acknowledge unlimited power in their sovereign.[87] Before any regular police was established, a powerful criminal might have been secure from all punishment but for a notion, as barbarous as any which it served to counteract, that he could be lawfully killed by the personal mandate of the king. And the frequent attendance of sovereigns in their courts of judicature might lead men not accustomed to consider the indispensable necessity of legal forms to confound an act of assassination with the execution of justice.

Though it is very improbable that the nobility were not considered as essential members of the Cortes, they certainly attended in smaller numbers than we should expect to find from the great legislative and deliberative authority of that assembly. This arose chiefly from the lawless spirit of that martial aristocracy which placed less confidence in the constitutional methods of resisting arbitrary encroachment than in its own armed com-

[85] Que mandase facer la justicia en aquellos que la merecen comunalmente con fuero é con derecho é los homes que non sean muertos nin presos nin tomados lo que han sin ser oidos por derecho ó por fuero de aquel logar do acaesciere, é que sea guardado mejor que se guardó fasta aquí. (Marina, " Ensayo Hist.-Critico," p. 148.)
[86] Que non mandemos matar nin prender nin lisiar nin despechar nin tomar á alguno ninguna cosa de lo suyo, sin ser

anté llamado é oido é vencido por fuero é por derecho, por querella nin por querellas que á nos fuesen dadas, segunt que esto está ordenado por el rei Don Alonso nuestro padre. (" Teoria de las Cortes," tome ii, p. 287.)
[87] Si quis hominem per jussionem regis vel ducis sui occiderit, non requiratur ei, nec sit faidosus, quia jussio domini sui fuit, et non potuit contradicere jussionem. (" Leges Bajuvariorum," tit. 2 in " Baluz. Capitularibus."

binations.[88] Such confederacies to obtain redress of grievances by force, of which there were five or six remarkable instances, were called Hermandad (brotherhood or union), and, though not so explicitly sanctioned as they were by the celebrated Privilege of Union in Aragon, found countenance in a law of Alfonso X, which can not be deemed so much to have voluntarily emanated from that prince as to be a record of original rights possessed by the Castilian nobility. " The duty of subjects toward their king," he says, " enjoins them not to permit him knowingly to endanger his salvation, nor to incur dishonour and inconvenience in his person or family, nor to produce mischief to his kingdom. And this may be fulfilled in two ways: one by good advice, showing him the reason wherefore he ought not to act thus; the other by deeds, seeking means to prevent his going on to his own ruin, and putting a stop to those who give him ill counsel: forasmuch as his errors are of worse consequence than those of other men, it is the bounden duty of subjects to prevent his committing them.[89] To this law the insurgents appealed in their coalition against Alvaro de Luna; and, indeed, we must confess that, however just and admirable the principles which it breathes, so general a license of rebellion was not likely to preserve the tranquility of a kingdom. The deputies of towns in a Cortes of 1445 petitioned the king to declare that no construction should be put on this law inconsistent with the obedience of subjects toward their sovereign—a request to which, of course, he willingly acceded.

Castile, it will be apparent, bore a closer analogy to England in its form of civil polity than France or even Aragon. But the frequent disorders of its government and a barbarous state of manners rendered violations of law much more continual and flagrant than they were in England under the Plantagenet dynasty. And, besides these practical mischiefs, there were two essential defects in the constitution of Castile, through which perhaps it was ultimately subverted. It wanted those two brilliants in the coronet of British liberty, the representation of freeholders among the commons and trial by jury. The Cortes of Castile became a congress of deputies from a few cities, public-spirited, indeed, and intrepid, as we find them in bad times, to an eminent degree, but too much limited in number, and too unconnected with the territorial aristocracy, to maintain a just balance against the crown. Yet, with every disadvantage, that country possessed a liberal form of government, and was animated with a noble spirit for its defence. Spain, in her late memorable though short resuscitation, might well have gone

[88] " Teoria de las Cortes," tome ii, p. 465.
[89] " Ensayo Hist.-Critico," p. 312.

back to her ancient institutions, and perfected a scheme of policy which the great example of England would have shown to be well adapted to the security of freedom. What she did, or rather attempted, instead, I need not recall. May her next effort be more wisely planned and more happily terminated![90]

Though the kingdom of Aragon was very inferior in extent to that of Castile, yet the advantages of a better form of government and wiser sovereigns, with those of industry and commerce along a line of sea-coast, rendered it almost equal in importance. Castile rarely intermeddled in the civil dissensions of Aragon; the Kings of Aragon frequently carried their arms into the heart of Castile. During the sanguinary outrages of Peter the Cruel, and the stormy revolutions which ended in establishing the house of Trastamare, Aragon was not indeed at peace, nor altogether well governed; but her political consequence rose in the eyes of Europe through the long reign of the ambitious and wily Peter IV, whose sagacity and good fortune redeemed, according to the common notions of mankind, the iniquity with which he stripped his relation, the King of Majorca, of the Balearic Islands, and the constant perfidiousness of his character. I have mentioned in another place the Sicilian war, prosecuted with so much eagerness for many years by Peter III and his son, Alfonso III. After this object was relinquished, James II undertook an enterprise less splendid, but not much less difficult—the conquest of Sardinia. That island, long accustomed to independence, cost an incredible expense of blood and treasure to the Kings of Aragon during the whole fourteenth century. It was not fully subdued till the commencement of the next, under the reign of Martin.

At the death of Martin, King of Aragon, in 1410, a memorable question arose as to the right of succession. Though Petronilla, daughter of Ramiro II, had reigned in her own right from 1137 to 1172, an opinion seems to have gained ground from the thirteenth century that females could not inherit the crown of Aragon. Peter IV had excited a civil war by attempting to settle the succession upon his daughter, to the exclusion of his next brother. The birth of a son about the same time suspended the ultimate decision of this question; but it was tacitly understood that what is called the Salic law ought to prevail.[91] Accordingly, on the death of John I in 1395, his two daughters were set aside in favour of his brother Martin, though not without opposition on the part of the elder, whose husband, the Count of Foix, invaded the kingdom, and desisted from his pretension

[90] The first edition of this work was published in 1818.
[91] Zurita, tome ii, f. 188. It was pretended that women were excluded from the crown in England as well as France: and this analogy seems to have had some influence in determining the Aragonese to adopt a Salic law.

only through want of force. Martin's son, the King of Sicily, dying in his father's lifetime, the nation was anxious that the king should fix upon his successor, and would probably have acquiesced in his choice. But his dissolution occurring more rapidly than was expected, the throne remained absolutely vacant. The Count of Urgel had obtained a grant of the lieutenancy, which was the right of the heir apparent. This nobleman possessed an extensive territory in Catalonia, bordering on the Pyrenees. He was grandson of James, next brother to Peter IV, and, according to our rules of inheritance, certainly stood in the first place. The other claimants were the Duke of Gandia, grandson of James II, who, though descended from a more distant ancestor, set up a claim founded on proximity to the royal stock, which in some countries was preferred to a representative title; the Duke of Calabria, son of Violante, younger daughter of John I (the Countess of Foix being childless); Frederick, Count of Luna, a natural son of the younger Martin, King of Sicily, legitimated by the Pope, but with a reservation excluding him from royal succession; and, finally, Ferdinand, Infant of Castile, son of the late king's sister.[92] The Count of Urgel was favoured in general by the Catalans, and he seemed to have a powerful support in Antonio de Luna, a baron of Aragon, so rich that he might go through his own estate from France to Castile. But this apparent superiority frustrated his hopes. The justiciary and other leading Aragonese were determined not to suffer this great constitutional question to be decided by an appeal to force, which might sweep away their liberties in the struggle. Urgel, confident of his right, and surrounded by men of ruined fortunes, was unwilling to submit his pretensions to a civil tribunal. His adherent, Antonio de Luna, committed an

[92] The subjoined pedigree will show more clearly the respective titles of the competitors:

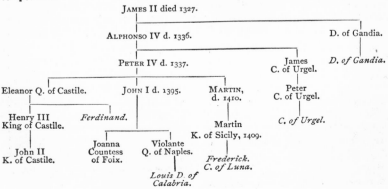

extraordinary outrage, the assassination of the Archbishop of Saragossa, which alienated the minds of good citizens from his cause. On the other hand, neither the Duke of Gandia, who was very old,[93] nor the Count of Luna, seemed fit to succeed. The party of Ferdinand, therefore, gained ground by degrees. It was determined, however, to render a legal sentence. The Cortes of each nation agreed upon the nomination of nine persons, three Aragonese, three Catalans, and three Valencians, who were to discuss the pretensions of the several competitors, and by a plurality of six votes to adjudge the crown. Nothing could be more solemn, more peaceful, nor, in appearance, more equitable than the proceedings of this tribunal. They summoned the claimants before them, and heard them by counsel. One of these, Frederick of Luna, being ill defended, the court took charge of his interests, and named other advocates to maintain them. A month was passed in hearing arguments; a second was allotted to considering them; and at the expiration of the prescribed time it was announced to the people, by the mouth of St. Vincent Ferrier, that Ferdinand of Castile had ascended the throne.[94]

In this decision it is impossible not to suspect that the judges were swayed rather by politic considerations than a strict sense of hereditary right. It was, therefore, by no means universally popular, especially in Catalonia, of which principality the Count of Urgel was a native; and perhaps the great rebellion of the Catalans fifty years afterward may be traced to the disaffection which this breach, as they thought, of the lawful succession had excited. Ferdinand, however, was well received in Aragon. The Cortes generously recommended the Count of Urgel to his favour, on account of the great expenses he had incurred in prosecuting his claim. But Urgel did not wait the effect of this recommendation. Unwisely attempting a rebellion with very inadequate means, he lost his estates, and was thrown for life into prison. Ferdinand's successor was his son, Alfonso V, more distinguished in the history of Italy than of Spain. For all the

[93] This Duke of Gandia died during the interregnum. His son, though not so objectionable on the score of age, seemed to have a worse claim; yet he became a competitor.

[94] " Biancæ Commentaria," in " Schotti Hispania Illustrata," tome ii ; Zurita, tome iii. f. 1-74. Vincent Ferrier was the most distinguished churchman of his time in Spain. His influence, as one of the nine judges, is said to have been very instrumental in procuring the crown for Ferdinand. Five others voted the same way; one for the Count of Urgel; one doubtfully between the Count of Urgel and Duke of Gandia; the ninth declined to vote. (Zurita, tome iii, f. 71.)

It is curious enough that John, King of Castile, was altogether disregarded, though his claim was at least as plausible as that of his uncle Ferdinand. Indeed, upon the principles of inheritance to which we are accustomed, Louis, Duke of Calabria, had a prior right to Ferdinand, admitting the rule which it was necessary for both of them to establish; namely, that a right of succession might be transmitted through females, which females could not personally enjoy. This, as is well known, had been advanced in the preceding age by Edward III as the foundation of his claim to the crown of France.

latter years of his life he never quitted the kingdom that he had acquired by his arms; and, enchanted by the delicious air of Naples, intrusted the government of his patrimonial territories to the care of a brother and an heir. John II, upon whom they devolved by the death of Alfonso without legitimate progeny, had been engaged during his youth in the turbulent revolutions of Castile, as the head of a strong party that opposed the domination of Alvaro de Luna. By marriage with the heiress of Navarre he was entitled, according to the usage of those times, to assume the title of king, and administration of government, during her life. But his ambitious retention of power still longer produced events which are the chief stain on his memory. Charles, Prince of Viana, was, by the constitution of Navarre, entitled to succeed his mother. She had requested him in her testament not to assume the government without his father's consent. That consent was always withheld. The prince raised what we ought not to call a rebellion; but was made prisoner, and remained for some time in captivity. John's ill disposition toward his son was exasperated by a stepmother, who scarcely disguised her intention of placing her own child on the throne of Aragon at the expense of the eldest born. After a life of perpetual oppression, chiefly passed in exile or captivity, the Prince of Viana died in Catalonia, at a moment when that province was in open insurrection upon his account. Though it hardly seems that the Catalans had any more general provocations, they persevered for more than ten years with inveterate obstinacy in their rebellion, offering the sovereignty first to a prince of Portugal, and afterward to Regnier, Duke of Anjou, who was destined to pass his life in unsuccessful competition for kingdoms. The King of Aragon behaved with great clemency toward these insurgents on their final submission.

It is consonant to the principle of this work to pass lightly over the common details of history, in order to fix the reader's attention more fully on subjects of philosophical inquiry. Perhaps in no European monarchy except our own was the form of government more interesting than in Aragon, as a fortunate temperament of law and justice with the royal authority. So far as anything can be pronounced of its earlier period before the capture of Saragossa in 1118, it was a kind of regal aristocracy, where a small number of powerful barons elected their sovereign on every vacancy, though, as usual in other countries, out of one family, and considered him as little more than the chief of their confederacy.[95] These were the ricoshombres or

---

[95] Alfonso III complained that his barons wanted to bring back old times, quando havia en el reyno tantos reyes como ricos hombres. ("Biancæ Commentaria," p. 787.) The form of election supposed to have been used by these bold barons is well known. "We, who are as good as you, choose you for our king

barons, the first order of the state. Among these the Kings of Aragon, in subsequent times, as they extended their dominions, shared the conquered territory in grants of honours on a feudal tenure.[96] For this system was fully established in the kingdom of Aragon. A ricohombre, as we read in Vitalis, Bishop of Huesca, about the middle of the thirteenth century,[97] must hold of the king an honour or barony capable of supporting more than three knights; and this he was bound to distribute among his vassals in military fiefs. Once in the year he might be summoned with his feudatories to serve the sovereign for two months (Zurita says three); and he was to attend the royal court, or general assembly, as a counsellor, whenever called upon, assisting in its judicial as well as deliberative business. In the towns and villages of his barony he might appoint bailiffs to administer justice and receive penalties; but the higher criminal jurisdiction seems to have been reserved to the crown. According to Vitalis, the king could divest these ricoshombres of their honours at pleasure, after which they fell into the class of mesnadaries, or mere tenants in chief. But if this were constitutional in the reign of James I, which Blancas denies, it was not long permitted by that high-spirited aristocracy. By the General Privilege or Charter of Peter III it is declared that no barony can be taken away without a just cause and legal sentence of the justiciary and council of barons.[98] And the same protection was extended to the vassals of the ricoshombres.

Below these superior nobles were the mesnadaries, corresponding to our mere tenants in chief, holding estates not baronial immediately from the crown; and the military vassals of the high nobility, the knights and infanzones; a word which may be rendered by gentlemen. These had considerable privileges in that aristocratic government; they were exempted from all taxes, they could only be tried by the royal judges for any crime; and offences committed against them were punished with additional severity.[99] The ignoble classes were, as in other countries, the burgesses of towns and the villeins, or peasantry. The peasantry seem to have been subject to territorial servitude, as in France and England. Vitalis says that some villeins were originally so

and lord, provided that you observe our laws and privileges; and if not, not." But I do not much believe the authenticity of this form of words. (See Robertson's "Charles V," vol. i, note 31.) It is, however, sufficiently agreeable to the spirit of the old government.

[96] Los ricos hombres, por los feudos que tenian del rey, eran obligados de seguir al rey, si yva en persona á la guerra, y residir en ella tres meses en cadaun ano. (Zurita, tome i, fol. 43; Saragossa, 1610.) A fief was usually called in Aragon an honour, que en Castilla llamavan tierra, y en el principado de Cataluna feudo (fol. 46).

[97] I do not know whether this work of Vitalis has been printed; but there are large extracts from it in Blanca's history, and also in Du Cange, under the words Infancia, Mesnadarius, etc. Several illustrations of these military tenures may be found in the "Fueros de Aragon," especially lib. 7.

[98] "Biancæ Comm.," p. 730.

[99] P. 732.

unprotected that, as he expresses it, they might be divided into pieces by sword among the sons of their masters, till they were provoked to an insurrection, which ended in establishing certain stipulations, whence they obtained the denomination of villeins de parada, or of convention.[100]

Though from the twelfth century the principle of hereditary succession to the throne superseded, in Aragon as well as Castile, the original right of choosing a sovereign within the royal family, it was still founded upon one more sacred and fundamental, that of compact. No King of Aragon was entitled to assume that name until he had taken a coronation oath, administered by the justiciary at Saragossa, to observe the laws and liberties of the realm.[101] Alfonso III, in 1285, being in France at the time of his father's death, named himself king in addressing the states, who immediately remonstrated on this premature assumption of his title, and obtained an apology.[102] Thus, too, Martin, having been called to the crown of Aragon by the Cortes in 1395, was specially required not to exercise any authority before his coronation.[103]

Blancas quotes a noble passage from the acts of the Cortes in 1451 : " We have always heard of old time, and it is found by experience that, seeing the great barrenness of this land, and the poverty of the realm, if it were not for the liberties thereof, the folk would go hence to live and abide in other realms and lands more fruitful." [104] This high spirit of freedom had long animated the Aragonese. After several contests with the crown in the reign of James I, not to go back to earlier times, they compelled Peter III in 1283 to grant a law, called the General Privilege, the Magna Charta of Aragon, and perhaps a more full and satisfactory basis of civil liberty than our own. It contains a series of provisions against arbitrary tallages, spoliations of property, secret process after the manner of the Inquisition in criminal charges, sentences of the justiciary without assent of the Cortes, appointment of foreigners or Jews to judicial

---

[100] " Biancæ Comm.," p. 729.
[101] Zurita, " Anales de Aragon," tome i, fol. 104; tome iii, fol. 76.
[102] Biancæ Comm.," p. 661. They acknowledged, at the same time, that he was their natural lord, and entitled to reign as lawful heir to his father—so oddly were the hereditary and elective titles jumbled together. (Zurita, tome i, fol. 303.)
[103] Zurita, tome ii, fol. 424.
[104] Siempre havemos oydo dezir antigament, é se troba por esperiencia, que attendida la grand sterilidad de aquesta tierra, é pobreza de aqueste regno, si non fues por las libertades de aquel, se yrian á bivir, y habitar las gentes á otros regnos, é tierras mas frutieras (p. 571).

Aragon was, in fact, a poor country, barren and ill peopled. The kings were forced to go to Catalonia for money, and indeed were little able to maintain expensive contests. The wars of Peter IV in Sardinia, and of Alfonso V with Genoa and Naples, impoverished their people. A hearth tax having been imposed in 1404, it was found that there were 42,683 houses in Aragon, which, according to most calculations, will give less than 300,000 inhabitants. In 1429, a similar tax being laid on, it is said that the number of houses was diminished in consequence of war. (Zurita, tome iii, fol. 189.) It contains at present between 600,000 and 700,000 inhabitants.

22

offices; trials of accused persons in places beyond the kingdom, the use of torture, except in charges of falsifying the coin, and the bribery of judges. These are claimed as the ancient liberties of their country. "Absolute power (mero imperio è mixto)," it is declared, "never was the constitution of Aragon, nor of Valencia, nor yet of Ribagorça, nor shall there be in time to come any innovation made; but only the law, custom, and privilege which has been anciently used in the aforesaid kingdoms." [105]

The concessions extorted by our ancestors from John, Henry III, and Edward I were secured by the only guarantee those times could afford, the determination of the barons to enforce them by armed confederacies. These, however, were formed according to emergencies, and, except in the famous commission of twenty-five conservators of Magna Charta, in the last year of John, were certainly unwarranted by law. But the Aragonese established a positive right of maintaining their liberties by arms. This was contained in the Privilege of Union granted by Alfonso III in 1287, after a violent conflict with his subjects; but which was afterward so completely abolished, and even eradicated from the records of the kingdom, that its precise words have never been recovered.[106] According to Zurita, it consisted of two articles: First, that in the case of the king's proceeding forcibly against any member of the union without previous sentence of the justiciary, the rest should be absolved from their allegiance; secondly, that he should hold a Cortes every year in Saragossa.[107] During the two subsequent reigns of James II and Alfonso IV little pretence seems to have been given for the exercise of this right. But dissensions breaking out under Peter IV in 1347, rather on account of his attempt to settle the crown upon his daughter than of any specific public grievances, the nobles had recourse to the Union, that last voice, says Blancas, of an almost expiring state, full of weight and dignity, to chastise the presumption of kings.[108] They assembled at Saragossa, and used a remarkable seal for all their public instruments, an engraving from which may be seen in the historian I have just quoted. It represents the king sitting on his throne, with the confederates kneeling in a suppliant attitude around, to denote their loyalty and unwillingness to offend. But in the background tents and lines of spears are discovered, as a hint of their ability and resolution to

---

[105] "Fueros de Aragon," fol. 9; Zurita, tome i, fol. 265.
[106] Blancas says that he had discovered a copy of the "Privilege of Union" in the archives of the see of Tarragona, and would gladly have published it but for his deference to the wisdom of former ages, which had studiously endeavoured to destroy all recollection of that dangerous law (p. 662).

[107] Zurita, tome i, fol. 322.
[108] Priscam illam Unionis, quasi morientis reipublicæ extremam vocem, auctoritatis et gravitatis plenam, regum insolentiæ apertum vindicem excitârunt, summâ ac singulari bonorum omnium consensione (p. 669). It is remarkable that such strong language should have been tolerated under Philip II.

defend themselves. The legend is "Sigillum Unionis Aragonum."
This respectful demeanour toward a sovereign against whom
they were waging war reminds us of the language held out by
our Long Parliament before the Presbyterian party was overthrown. And although it has been lightly censured as inconsistent and hypocritical, this tone is the safest that men can adopt,
who, deeming themselves under the necessity of withstanding
the reigning monarch, are anxious to avoid a change of dynasty
or subversion of their constitution. These confederates were
defeated by the king at Epila in 1348.[109] But his prudence and
the remaining strength of his opponents inducing him to pursue
a moderate course, there ensued a more legitimate and permanent balance of the constitution from this victory of the royalists.
The Privilege of Union was abrogated, Peter himself cutting
to pieces with his sword the original instrument. But in return
many excellent laws for the security of the subject were enacted;[110] and their preservation was intrusted to the greatest
officer of the kingdom, the justiciary, whose authority and pre-
eminence may in a great degree be dated from this period.[111]
That watchfulness over public liberty, which originally belonged
to the aristocracy of ricoshombres, always apt to thwart the crown
or to oppress the people, and which was afterward maintained
by the dangerous Privilege of Union, became the duty of a civil
magistrate, accustomed to legal rules and responsible for his
actions, whose office and functions are the most pleasing feature
in the constitutional history of Aragon.

The justiza or justiciary of Aragon has been treated by some
writers as a sort of anomalous magistrate, created originally as
an intermediate power between the king and people, to watch
over the exercise of royal authority. But I do not perceive that
his functions were, in any essential respect, different from those
of the Chief Justice of England, divided, from the time of Edward I, among the judges of the King's Bench. We should
undervalue our own constitution by supposing that there did
not reside in that court as perfect an authority to redress the
subject's injuries as was possessed by the Aragonese magistrate.
In the practical exercise, indeed, of this power there was an
abundant difference. Our English judges, more timid and pli-
ant, left to the remonstrances of Parliament that redress of griev-

[109] Zurita observes that the battle of
Epila was the last fought in defence of
public liberty, for which it was held lawful of old to take up arms, and resist the
king, by virtue of the " Privileges of
Union." For the authority of the justiciary being afterward established, the former contentions and wars came to an end,
means being found to put the weak on a
level with the powerful, in which consists
the peace and tranquility of all states;
and from thence the name of union was,
by common consent, proscribed (tome ii,
fol. 226). Blancas also remarks that nothing could have turned out more advantageous to the Aragonese than their ill
fortune at Epila.
[110] " Fueros de Aragon." De iis, quæ
Dominus rex (fol. 14, et alibi passim).
[111] " Bianc. Comm.," pp. 671, 811; Zurita, tome ii, fol. 229.

ances which very frequently lay within the sphere of their jurisdiction. There is, I believe, no recorded instance of a habeas
corpus granted in any case of illegal imprisonment by the crown
or its officers during the continuance of the Plantagenet dynasty.
We shall speedily take notice of a very different conduct in
Aragon.

The office of justiciary, whatever conjectural antiquity some
have assigned to it, is not to be traced beyond the capture of
Saragossa in 1118, when the series of magistrates commences.[112]
But for a great length of time they do not appear to have been
particularly important; the judicial authority residing in the
council of ricoshombres, whose suffrages the justiciary collected,
in order to pronounce their sentence rather than his own. A
passage in Vitalis, Bishop of Huesca, whom I have already mentioned, shows this to have been the practice during the reign
of James I.[113] Gradually, as notions of liberty became more
definite, and laws more numerous, the reverence paid to their
permanent interpreter grew stronger, and there was fortunately
a succession of prudent and just men in that high office, through
whom it acquired dignity and stable influence. Soon after the
accession of James II, on some dissensions arising between the
king and his barons, he called in the justiciary as a mediator
whose sentence, says Blancas, all obeyed.[114] At a subsequent
time in the same reign the military orders, pretending that some
of their privileges were violated, raised a confederacy or union
against the king. James offered to refer the dispute to the justiciary, Ximenes Salanova, a man of eminent legal knowledge.
The knights resisted his jurisdiction, alleging the question to
be of spiritual cognizance. He decided it, however, against them
in full Cortes at Saragossa, annulled their league, and sentenced
the leaders to punishment.[115] It was adjudged also that no appeal
could lie to the spiritual court from a sentence of the justiciary
passed with assent of the Cortes. James II is said to have frequently sued his subjects in the justiciary's court, to show his
regard for legal measures, and during the reign of this good
prince its authority became more established.[116] Yet it was not

[112] " Biancæ Comment.," p. 638.
[113] Id., p. 772. Zurita, indeed, refers
the justiciary's pre-eminence to an earlier
date—namely, the reign of Peter II, who
took away a great part of the local jurisdictions of the ricoshombres (tome i, fol.
102). But if I do not misunderstand the
meaning of Vitalis, his testimony seems
to be beyond dispute. By the General
Privilege of 1283, the justiciary was to
advise with the ricoshombres in all cases
where the king was a party against any
of his subjects. (Zurita, fol. 281. See
also fol. 180.)
[114] Zurita, p. 663.

[115] Zurita, tome i, fol. 403; tome ii, fol.
34; Bian., p. 666. The assent of the Cortes seems to render this in the nature of
a legislative, rather than a judicial, proceeding; but it is difficult to pronounce
anything about a transaction so remote
in time and in a foreign country, the
native historians writing rather concisely.
[116] Bianc., p. 663. James acquired the
surname of Just, el Justiciero, by his fair
dealings toward his subjects. (Zurita,
tome ii, fol. 82.) El Justiciero properly
denotes his exercise of civil and criminal
justice.

perhaps looked upon as fully equal to maintain public liberty against the crown till, in the Cortes of 1348, after the Privilege of Union was forever abolished, such laws were enacted, and such authority given to the justiciary, as proved eventually a more adequate barrier against oppression than any other country could boast. All the royal as well as territorial judges were bound to apply for his opinion in case of legal difficulties arising in their courts, which he was to certify within eight days. By subsequent statutes of the same reign it was made penal for any one to obtain letters from the king impeding the execution of the justiza's process, and they were declared null. Inferior courts were forbidden to proceed in any business after his prohibition.[117] Many other laws might be cited, corroborating the authority of this great magistrate, but there are two parts of his remedial jurisdiction which deserve special notice.

These are the processes of jurisfirma, or firma del derecho, and of manifestation. The former bears some analogy to the writs of pone and certiorari in England, through which the Court of King's Bench exercises its right of withdrawing a suit from the jurisdiction of inferior tribunals. But the Aragonese jurisfirma was of more extensive operation. Its object was not only to bring a cause commenced in an inferior court before the justiciary, but to prevent or inhibit any process from issuing against the person who applied for its benefit, or any molestation from being offered to him; so that, as Blancas expresses it, when we have entered into a recognisance (firmè et graviter asseveremus) before the justiciary of Aragon to abide the decision of law, our fortunes shall be protected, by the interposition of his prohibition, from the intolerable iniquity of the royal judges.[118] The process termed manifestation afforded as ample security for personal liberty as that of jurisfirma did for property. "To manifest any one," says the writer so often quoted, "is to wrest him from the hands of the royal officers, that he may not suffer any illegal violence; not that he is at liberty by this process, because the merits of his case are still to be inquired into, but because he is now detained publicly, instead of being, as it were, concealed, and the charge against him is investigated, not suddenly or with passion, but in calmness and according to law, therefore this is called manifestation."[119] The power of this writ

[117] " Fueros de Aragon ": Quod in dubiis non crassis. (A. D. 1348.) Quod impetrans (1372), etc. (Zurita, tome ii, fol. 229; Bian., pp. 671 and 811.)
[118] P. 751. " Fueros de Aragon," f. 137.
[119] Est apud nos manifestare, reum subito sumere, atque è regiis manibus extorquere, ne qua ipsi contra jus vis inferatur. Non quod tunc reus judicio liberetur; nihilominus tamen, ut loquimur, de meritis causæ ad plenum cognoscitur. Sed quod deinceps manifesto teneatur, quasi antea celatus extitisset; necesseque deinde sit de ipsius culpâ, non impetu et cum furore, sed sedatis prorsus animis, et juxta constitutas leges judicari. Ex eo autem, quod hujusmodi judicium manifesto deprehensum, omnibus jam patere debeat, Manifestationis sibi nomen arripuit (p. 675).
Ipsius Manifestationis potestas tam solida est et repentina, ut homini jam

(if I may apply our term) was such, as he elsewhere asserts, that it would rescue a man whose neck was in the halter. A particular prison was allotted to those detained for trial under this process. Several proofs that such admirable provisions did not remain a dead letter in the law of Aragon appear in the two historians, Blancas and Zurita, whose noble attachment to liberties, of which they had either witnessed or might foretell the extinction, continually displays itself. I can not help illustrating this subject by two remarkable instances. The heir apparent of the kingdom of Aragon had a constitutional right to the lieutenancy or regency during the sovereign's absence from the realm. The title and office, indeed, were permanent, though the functions must, of course, have been superseded during the personal exercise of royal authority. But as neither Catalonia nor Valencia, which often demanded the king's presence, were considered as parts of the kingdom, there were pretty frequent occasions for this

collum in laqueum inserenti subveniat. Illius enim præsidio, damnatus, dum per leges licet, quasi experiendi juris gratiâ, de manibus judicum confestim extorquetur, et in carcerem ducitur ad id ædificatum, ibidemque asservatur tamdiu, quamdiu jurene, an injuriâ, quid in eâ causâ factum fuerit, judicatur. Propterea carcer hic vulgari linguâ, la carcel de los manifestados nuncupatur (p. 751). "Fueros de Aragon," fol. 60. De Manifestationibus personarum. Independently of this right of manifestation by writ of the justiciary, there are several statutes in the "Fueros" against illegal detention, or unnecessary severity toward prisoners. ("De Custodiâ reorum," fol. 163.) No judge could proceed secretly in a criminal process; an indispensable safeguard to public liberty, and one of the most salutary, as well as most ancient provisions in our own constitution. (De judiciis.) Torture was abolished, except in cases of coining false money, and then only in respect of vagabonds. (General Privilege of 1283.)

Zurita has explained the two processes of jurisfirma and manifestation so perspicuously that, as the subject is very interesting, and rather out of the common way, I shall both quote and translate the passage: Con firmar de derecho, que es dar caution á estar á justicia, se conseden literas inhibitorias por el justicia de Aragon, para que no puedan sur presos, ni privados, ni despojados de su possession, hasta que judicialmente se conozca, y declare sobre la pretension, y justicia de las partes, y parezca por processo legitimo, que se deve revocar la tal inhibition. Esta fué la suprema y principal autoridad del Justicia de Aragond esde que este magistrado tuvo origen, y lo que llama manifestation; porque assi como la firma de derecho por privilegio general del reyno impide, que no puede ninguno ser preso, ó agraviado contra razon y justicia, de la misma manera la manifesta-

cion, que es otro privilegio, y remedia muy principal, tiene fuerca, quando alguno es preso sin preceder processo legitimo, ó quando lo prenden de hecho sin orden de justiciâ; y en estos casos solo el Justicia de Aragon, quando se tiene recurso al el, se interpone, manifestando il preso, que es tomarlo á su mano, de poder de qualquiera juez, aunque sea el mas supremo; y es obligado el Justicia de Aragon, y sus lugartenientes de proveer la manifestacion en el mismo instante, que les es pedida sin preceder informacion; y basta que se pida por qualquiere persona que se diga procurador del que quiere que lo tengan por manifesto (tome ii, fol. 386). "Upon a firma de derecho, which is to give security for abiding the decision of the law, the Justiciary of Aragon issues letters inhibiting all persons to arrest the party, or deprive him of his possession, until the matter shall be judicially inquired into, and it shall appear that such inhibition ought to be revoked. This process and that which is called manifestation have been the chief powers of the justiciary, ever since the commencement of that magistracy. And as the firma de derecho by the general privilege of the realm secures every man from being arrested or molested against reason and justice, so the manifestation, which is another principal and remedial right takes place when any one is actually arrested without lawful process; and in such cases only the Justiciary of Aragon, when recourse is had to him, interposes by manifesting the person arrested—that is, by taking him into his own hands, out of the power of any judge, however high in authority—and this manifestation the justiciary, or his deputies in his absence, are bound to issue at the same instant it is demanded, without further inquiry; and it may be demanded by any one as attorney of the party requiring to be manifested."

anticipated reign of the eldest prince. Such a regulation was not likely to diminish the mutual and almost inevitable jealousies between kings and their heirs apparent, which have so often disturbed the tranquility of a court and a nation. Peter IV removed his eldest son, afterward John I, from the lieutenancy of the kingdom. The prince entered into a firma del derecho before the justiciary, Dominic de Cerda, who, pronouncing in his favour, enjoined the king to replace his son in the lieutenancy as the undoubted right of the eldest born. Peter obeyed, not only in fact, to which, as Blancas observes, the law compelled him, but with apparent cheerfulness.[120] There are, indeed, no private persons who have so strong an interest in maintaining a free constitution and the civil liberties of their countrymen as the members of royal families, since none are so much exposed, in absolute governments, to the resentment and suspicion of a reigning monarch.

John I, who had experienced the protection of law in his weakness, had afterward occasion to find it interposed against his power. This king had sent some citizens of Saragossa to prison without form of law. They applied to Juan de Cerda, the justiciary, for a manifestation. He issued his writ accordingly; nor, says Blancas, could he do otherwise without being subject to a heavy fine. The king, pretending that the justiciary was partial, named one of his own judges, the vice-chancellor, as coadjutor. This raised a constitutional question, whether, on suspicion of partiality, a coadjutor to the justiciary could be appointed. The king sent a private order to the justiciary not to proceed to sentence upon this interlocutory point until he should receive instructions in the council, to which he was directed to repair. But he instantly pronounced sentence in favour of his exclusive jurisdiction without a coadjutor. He then repaired to the palace. Here the vice-chancellor, in a long harangue, enjoined him to suspend sentence till he had heard the decision of the council. Juan de Cerda answered that, the case being clear, he had already pronounced upon it. This produced some expressions of anger from the king, who began to enter into an argument on the merits of the question. But the justiciary answered that, with all deference to his Majesty, he was bound to defend his conduct before the Cortes, and not elsewhere. On a subsequent day the king, having drawn the justiciary to his country palace on pretence of hunting, renewed the conversation with the assistance of his ally, the vice-chancellor; but no impression was made on the venerable magistrate, whom John at length, though much pressed by his advisers to violent courses, dismissed with civility. The king was probably misled through-

---

[120] Zurita, ubi supra; Blancas, p. 673.

out this transaction, which I have thought fit to draw from obscurity, not only in order to illustrate the privilege of manifestation, but as exhibiting an instance of judicial firmness and integrity, to which, in the fourteenth century, no country perhaps in Europe could offer a parallel.[121]

Before the Cortes of 1348 it seems as if the justiciary might have been displaced at the king's pleasure. From that time he held his station for life. But in order to evade this law, the king sometimes exacted a promise to resign upon request. Ximenes Cerdan, the justiciary in 1420, having refused to fulfil this engagement, Alfonso V gave notice to all his subjects not to obey him, and, notwithstanding the alarm which this encroachment created, eventually succeeded in compelling him to quit his office. In 1439 Alfonso insisted with still greater severity upon the execution of a promise to resign made by another justiciary, detaining him in prison until his death. But the Cortes of 1442 proposed a law, to which the king reluctantly acceded, that the justiciary should not be compelled to resign his office on account of any previous engagement he might have made.[122]

But lest these high powers, imparted for the prevention of abuses, should themselves be abused, the justiciary was responsible, in case of an unjust sentence, to the extent of the injury inflicted;[123] and was also subjected, by a statute of 1390, to a court of inquiry, composed of four persons chosen by the king out of eight named by the Cortes, whose office appears to have been that of examining and reporting to the four estates in the Cortes, by whom he was ultimately to be acquitted or condemned. This superintendence of the Cortes, however, being thought dilatory and inconvenient, a court of seventeen persons was appointed in 1461 to hear complaints against the justiciary. Some alterations were afterward made in this tribunal.[124] The justiciary was always a knight, chosen from the second order of nobility, the barons not being liable to personal punishment. He administered the coronation oath to the king; and in the Cortes of Aragon the justiciary acted as a sort of royal commissioner, opening or proroguing the assembly by the king's direction.

No laws could be enacted or repealed, nor any tax imposed, without the consent of the estates duly assembled.[125] Even as

[121] " Biancæ Commentar.," ubi supra. Zurita relates the story, but not so fully.
[122] " Fueros de Aragon," fol. 22; Zurita, tome iii, fols. 140, 255, 272; " Bianc. Comment.," p. 701.
[123] " Fueros de Aragon," fol. 25.
[124] Blancas; Zurita, tome iii, fol. 321; tome iv, fol. 103. These regulations were very acceptable to the nation. In fact, the justiza of Aragon had possessed much more unlimited powers than ought to be intrusted to any single magistrate. The

Court of King's Bench in England, besides its consisting of four co-ordinate judges, is checked by the appellant jurisdictions of the Exchequer Chamber and House of Lords, and still more importantly by the rights of juries.
[125] Majores nostri, quæ de omnibus statuenda essent, noluerunt juberi, vetarive posse, nisi vocatis, descriptisque ordinibus, ac cunctis eorum adhibitis suffragiis, re ipsâ cognitâ et promulgatâ. Unde perpetuum illud nobis comparatum

early as the reign of Peter II, in 1205, that prince having attempted to impose a general tallage, the nobility and commons united for the preservation of their franchises, and the tax, was afterward granted in part by the Cortes.[126] It may easily be supposed that the Aragonese were not behind other nations in statutes to secure these privileges, which, upon the whole, appear to have been more respected than in any other monarchy.[127] The General Privilege of 1283 formed a sort of groundwork for this legislation, like the Great Charter in England. By a clause in this law, Cortes were to be held every year at Saragossa. But under James II their time of meeting was reduced to once in two years, and the place was left to the king's discretion.[128] Nor were the Cortes of Aragon less vigilant than those of Castile in claiming a right to be consulted in all important deliberations of the executive power, or in remonstrating against abuses of government, or in superintending the proper expenditure of public money.[129] A variety of provisions, intended to secure these parliamentary privileges and the civil liberties of the subject, will be found dispersed in the collection of Aragonese laws,[130] which may be favourably compared with those of our own statute-book.

Four estates, or, as they were called, arms (brazos), formed the Cortes of Aragon—the prelates and commanders of military orders, who passed for ecclesiastics;[131] the barons or

est jus, ut communes et publicæ leges neque tolli, neque rogari possint, nisi prius universus populus una voce comitiis institutis suum eâ de re liberum suffragium ferat; idque postea ipsius regis assensu comprobetur. (Biancæ, p. 761.)
[126] Zurita, tome i, fol. 92.
[127] " Fueros de Aragon ": Quod sissæ in Aragoniâ removeantur. (A. D. 1372.) De prohibitione sissarum. (1398.) De conservatione patrimonii. (1461.) I have only remarked two instances of arbitrary taxation in Zurita's history, which is singularly full of information; one, in 1343, when Peter IV collected money from various cities, though not without opposition; and the other a remonstrance of the Cortes in 1383 against heavy taxes; and it is not clear that this refers to general unauthorized taxation. (Zurita, tome ii, fols. 168 and 382.) Blancas mentions that Alfonso V set a tallage upon his towns for the marriage of his natural daughters, which he might have done had they been legitimate; but they appealed to the justiciary's tribunal, and the king receded from his demand (p. 701).

Some instances of tyrannical conduct in violation of the constitutional laws occur, as will naturally be supposed, in the annals of Zurita. The execution of Bernard Cabrera under Peter IV (tome ii, fol. 336), and the severities inflicted on Queen Forcia by her son-in-law, John

I, (fol. 391), are perhaps as remarkable as any.
[128] Zurita, tome i, fol. 426. In general the session lasted from four to six months. One assembly was prorogued from time to time, and continued six years, from 1446 to 1452, which was complained of as a violation of the law for their biennial renewal (tome iv, fol. 6).
[129] The Sicilian war of Peter III was very unpopular, because it had been undertaken without consent of the barons, contrary to the practice of the kingdom; porque ningun negocio arduo emprendian, sin acuerdo y consejo de sus ricoshombres. (Zurita, tome i, fol. 264.) The Cortes, he tells us. were usually divided into two parties, Whigs and Tories; estava ordinariamente dividida en dos partas, la una que pensava procurar el beneficio del reyno, y la otra que el servicio del rey (tome iii, fol. 321).
[130] " Fueros y Observancias del Reyno de Aragon," 2 vols., in fol. Saragossa, 1667. The most important of these are collected by Blancas, p. 750.
[131] It is said by some writers that the ecclesiastical arm was not added to the Cortes of Aragon till about the year 1300. But I do not find mention in Zurita of any such constitutional change at that time; and the prelates, as we might expect from the analogy of other countries, appear as members of the national council long before. Queen Petronilla, in 1142,

ricoshombres; the equestrian order or infanzones; and the deputies of royal towns.[132] The two former had a right of appearing by proxy. There was no representation of the infanzones, or lower nobility. But it must be remembered that they were not numerous, nor was the kingdom large. Thirty-five are reckoned by Zurita as present in the Cortes of 1395, and thirty-three in those of 1412; and as upon both occasions an oath of fealty to a new monarch was to be taken, I presume that nearly all the nobility of the kingdom were present.[133] The ricoshombres do not seem to have exceeded twelve or fourteen in number. The ecclesiastical estate was not much, if at all, more numerous. A few principal towns alone sent deputies to the Cortes, but their representation was very full; eight or ten, and sometimes more, sat for Saragossa, and no town appears to have had less than four representatives. During the interval of the Cortes a permanent commission, varying a good deal as to numbers, but chosen out of the four estates, was empowered to sit with very considerable authority, receiving and managing the public revenue, and protecting the justiciary in his functions.[134]

The kingdom of Valencia, and principality of Catalonia, having been annexed to Aragon, the one by conquest, the other by marriage, were always kept distinct from it in their laws and government. Each had its Cortes, composed of three estates, for the division of the nobility into two orders did not exist in either country. The Catalans were tenacious of their ancient usages, and averse to incorporation with any other people of Spain. Their national character was high-spirited and independent; in no part of the peninsula did the territorial aristocracy retain, or at least pretend to, such extensive privileges,[135] and the citizens were justly proud of wealth acquired by industry, and of renown achieved by valour. At the accession of Ferdinand I, which they had not much desired, the Catalans obliged him to swear three times successively to maintain their liberties before they would take the reciprocal oath of allegiance.[136] For Valencia it seems to have been a politic design of James the Conqueror to establish a constitution nearly analogous to that

summoned á los perlados, ricoshombres, y cavalleros, y procuradores de las ciudades y villas, que le juntassen á Cortes generales en la ciudad de Huesca. (Zurita, tome i, fol. 71.) So in the Cortes of 1275, and on other occasions.
[132] Popular representation was more ancient in Aragon than in any other monarchy. The deputies of towns appear in the Cortes of 1133, as Robertson has remarked form Zurita. ("Hist. of Charles V," note 32.) And this can not well be called in question, or treated as an anomaly; for we find them mentioned in 1142 (the passage cited in the last note), and

again in 1164, when Zurita enumerates many of their names (fol. 74). The institution of consejos, or corporate districts under a presiding town, prevailed in Aragon as it did in Castile.
[133] Zurita, tome ii, fol. 490; tome iii, fol. 76.
[134] Biancæ, p. 762; Zurita, tome iii, fol. 76, fol. 182 et alibi.
[135] Zurita, tome ii, fol. 360. The villenage of the peasantry in some parts of Catalonia was very severe, even near the end of the fifteenth century (tome iv, fol. 327).
[136] Zurita, tome iii, fol. 81.

of Aragon, but with such limitations as he should impose, taking care that the nobles of the two kingdoms should not acquire strength by union. In the reigns of Peter III and Alfonso III, one of the principal objects contended for by the barons of Aragon was the establishment of their own laws in Valencia, to which the kings never acceded.[137] They permitted, however, the possessions of the natives of Aragon in the latter kingdom to be governed by the law of Aragon.[138] These three states—Aragon, Valencia, and Catalonia—were perpetually united by a law of Alfonso III, and every king on his accession was bound to swear that he would never separate them.[139] Sometimes general Cortes of the kingdoms and principality were convened; but the members did not, even in this case, sit together, and were not otherwise united than as they met in the same city.[140]

I do not mean to represent the actual condition of society in Aragon as equally excellent with the constitutional laws. Relatively to other monarchies, as I have already observed, there seem to have been fewer excesses of the royal prerogative in that kingdom. But the licentious habits of a feudal aristocracy prevailed very long. We find in history instances of private war between the great families, so as to disturb the peace of the whole nation, even near the close of the fifteenth century.[141] The right of avenging injuries by arms, and the ceremony of diffidation, or solemn defiance of an enemy, are preserved by the laws. We even meet with the ancient barbarous usage of paying a composition to the kindred of a murdered man.[142] The citizens of Saragossa were sometimes turbulent, and a refractory nobleman sometimes defied the ministers of justice. But owing to the remarkable copiousness of the principal Aragonese historian, we find more frequent details of this nature than in the scantier annals of some countries. The internal condition of society was certainly far from peaceable in other parts of Europe.

By the marriage of Ferdinand with Isabella, and by the death of John II, in 1479, the two ancient and rival kingdoms of Castile and Aragon were forever consolidated in the monarchy of Spain. There had been some difficulty in adjusting the respective rights of the husband and wife over Castile. In the middle ages it was customary for the more powerful sex to exercise all the rights which it derived from the weaker, as much in sovereignties as in private possessions. But the Castilians were determined to maintain the positive and distinct prerogatives of their queen, to which they attached the independence of their nation.

[137] Zurita, tome i, fols. 281, 310, 333. There was originally a justiciary in the kingdom of Valencia (fol. 281), but this, I believe, did not long continue.
[138] Tome ii, fol. 433.
[139] Tome ii, fol. 91.
[140] " Biancæ Comment.," p. 760; Zurita, tome iii, fol. 239.
[141] Zurita, tome iv, fol. 189.
[142] " Fueros de Aragon," fol. 1660, etc.

A compromise, therefore, was concluded, by which, though, according to our notions, Ferdinand obtained more than a due share, he might consider himself as more strictly limited than his father had been in Navarre. The names of both were to appear jointly in their style and upon the coin, the king's taking the precedence in respect of his sex. But in the royal scutcheon the arms of Castile were preferred on account of the kingdom's dignity. Isabella had the appointment to all civil offices in Castile; the nomination to spiritual benefices ran in the name of both. The government was to be conducted by the two conjointly when they were together, or by either singly in the province where one or other might happen to reside.[143] This partition was well preserved throughout the life of Isabel without mutual encroachments or jealousies. So rare a unanimity between persons thus circumstanced must be attributed to the superior qualities of that princess, who, while she maintained a constant good understanding with a very ambitious husband, never relaxed in the exercise of her paternal authority over the kingdoms of her ancestors.

Ferdinand and Isabella had no sooner quenched the flames of civil discord in Castile than they determined to give an unequivocal proof to Europe of the vigour which the Spanish monarchy was to display under their government. For many years an armistice with the Moors of Granada had been uninterrupted. Neither John II nor Henry IV had been at leisure to think of aggressive hostilities; and the Moors themselves, a prey, like their Christian enemies, to civil war and the feuds of their royal family, were content with the unmolested enjoyment of the finest province in the peninsula. If we may trust historians, the sovereigns of Granada were generally usurpers and tyrants. But I know not how to account for that vast populousness, that grandeur and magnificence, which distinguished the Mohammedan kingdom of Spain, without ascribing some measure of wisdom and beneficence to their governments. These southern provinces have dwindled in later times; and, in fact, Spain itself is chiefly interesting to many travellers for the monuments which a foreign and odious race of conquerors have left behind them. Granada was, however, disturbed by a series of revolutions about the time of Ferdinand's accession, which naturally encouraged his designs. The Moors, contrary to what might have been expected from their relative strength, were the aggressors by attacking a town in Andalusia.[144] Predatory inroads of this nature had hitherto been only retaliated by the Christians. But Ferdinand was conscious that his resources extended to the con-

143 Zurita, tome iv, fol. 224; Mariana, l. xxiv, c. 5.
144 Zurita, tome iv, fol. 314.

quest of Granada, the consummation of a struggle protracted through nearly eight centuries. Even in the last stage of the Moorish dominion, exposed on every side to invasion, enfeebled by civil dissension that led one party to abet the common enemy, Granada was not subdued without ten years of sanguinary and unremitting contest. Fertile beyond all the rest of Spain, that kingdom contained seventy walled towns ; and the capital is said, almost two centuries before, to have been peopled by two hundred thousand inhabitants.[145] Its resistance to such a force as that of Ferdinand is perhaps the best justification of the apparent negligence of earlier monarchs. But Granada was ultimately to undergo the yoke. The city surrendered on the 2d of January, 1492—an event glorious not only to Spain but to Christendom—and which, in the political combat of the two religions, seemed almost to counterbalance the loss of Constantinople. It raised the name of Ferdinand and of the new monarchy which he governed to high estimation throughout Europe. Spain appeared an equal competitor with France in the lists of ambition. These great kingdoms had for some time felt the jealousy natural to emulous neighbours. The house of Aragon loudly complained of the treacherous policy of Louis XI. He had fomented the troubles of Castile, and given, not, indeed, an effectual aid, but all promises of support, to the Princess Joanna, the competitor of Isabel. Rousillon, a province belonging to Aragon, had been pledged to France by John II for a sum of money. It would be tedious to relate the subsequent events, or to discuss their respective claims to its possession.[146] At the accession of Ferdinand, Louis XI still held Rousillon, and showed little intention to resign it. But Charles VIII, eager to smooth every impediment to his Italian expedition, restored the province to Ferdinand in 1493. Whether by such a sacrifice he was able to lull the King of Aragon into acquiescence, while he dethroned his relation at Naples, and alarmed for a moment all Italy with the apprehension of French dominion, it is not within the limits of the present work to inquire.

[145] Zurita, tome iv, fol. 314.
[146] For these transactions see Garnier, " Hist. de France," or Gaillard, " Rivalité de France et d'Espagne," tome iii.

The latter is the most impartial French writer I have ever read in matters where his own country is concerned.

CHAPTER V

HISTORY OF GERMANY TO THE DIET OF WORMS IN 1495

Sketch of German history under the emperors of the house of Saxony—House of Franconia—Henry IV—House of Swabia—Frederick Barbarossa—Fall of Henry the Lion—Frederick II—Extinction of house of Swabia—Changes in the Germanic constitution—Electors—Territorial sovereignty of the princes—Rodolph of Hapsburg—State of the empire after his time—Causes of decline of imperial power—House of Luxemburg—Charles IV—Golden bull—House of Austria—Frederick III—Imperial cities—Provincial states—Maximilian—Diet of Worms—Abolition of private wars—Imperial chamber—Aulic Council—Bohemia—Hungary—Switzerland.

A FTER the deposition of Charles the Fat in 888, which finally severed the connection between France and Germany,[1] Arnulf, an illegitimate descendant of Charlemagne, obtained the throne of the latter country, in which he was succeeded by his son Louis.[2] But upon the death of this prince in 911, the German branch of that dynasty became extinct. There remained, indeed, Charles the Simple, acknowledged as king in some parts of France, but rejected in others, and possessing no personal claims to respect. The Germans, therefore, wisely determined to choose a sovereign from among themselves. They were at this time divided into five nations, each under its own duke, and distinguished by difference of laws, as well as of origin; the Franks, whose territory, comprising Franconia and the modern Palatinate, was considered as the cradle of the empire, and who seem to have arrogated some superiority over the rest, the Swabians, the Bavarians, the Saxons, under which name the inhabitants of Lower Saxony alone and Westphalia

[1] There can be no question about this in a general sense. But several German writers of the time assert that both Eudes and Charles the Simple, rival Kings of France, acknowledged the feudal superiority of Arnulf. Charles, says Regino, regnum quod usurpaverit ex manu ejus percepit. (Struvius, " Corpus Hist. German.," pp. 202, 203.) This acknowledgment of sovereignty in Arnulf, King of Germany, who did not even pretend to be emperor, by both the claimants of the throne of France, for such it virtually was, though they do not appear to have rendered homage, can not affect

the independence of the crown in that age, which had been established by the Treaty of Verdun in 843, but proves the weakness of the competitors and their want of patriotism. In Eudes it is more remarkable than in Charles the Simple, a man of feeble character, and a Carlovingian by birth.

[2] The German princes had some hesitation about the choice of Louis, but their partiality to the Carlovingian line prevailed. Struvius, p. 208: quia reges Francorum semper ex uno genere procedebant, says an Archbishop Hatto in writing to the Pope.

350

were included, and the Lorrainers, who occupied the left bank of the Rhine as far as its termination. The choice of these nations in their general assembly fell upon Conrad, Duke of Franconia, according to some writers, or at least a man of high rank, and descended through females from Charlemagne.[3]

Conrad dying without male issue, the crown of Germany was bestowed upon Henry the Fowler, Duke of Saxony, ancestor of the three Othos, who followed him in direct succession. To Henry, and to the first Otho, Germany was more indebted than to any sovereign since Charlemagne. The conquest of Italy and recovery of the imperial title are indeed the most brilliant trophies of Otho the Great; but he conferred far more unequivocal benefits upon his own country by completing what his father had begun, her liberation from the inroads of the Hungarians. Two marches, that of Misnia, erected by Henry the Fowler, and that of Austria, by Otho, were added to the Germanic territories by their victories.[4]

A lineal succession of four descents without the least opposition seems to show that the Germans were disposed to consider their monarchy as fixed in the Saxon family. Otho II and III had been chosen each in his father's lifetime, and during legal infancy. The formality of election subsisted at that time in every European kingdom, and the imperfect rights of birth required a ratification by public assent. If, at least, France and England were hereditary monarchies in the tenth century, the same may surely be said of Germany, since we find the lineal succession fully as well observed in the last as in the former. But upon the early and unexpected decease of Otho III a momentary opposition was offered to Henry, Duke of Bavaria, a collateral branch of the reigning family. He obtained the crown, however, by what contemporary historians call an hereditary title,[5] and it was not until his death in 1024 that the house of Saxony was deemed to be extinguished.

No person had now any pretensions that could interfere with the unbiassed suffrages of the nation; and, accordingly, a general assembly was determined by merit to elect Conrad, surnamed the Salic, a nobleman of Franconia.[6] From this prince sprang

---

[3] Schmidt, "Hist. des Allemands," tome ii, p. 288; Struvius, "Corpus Historiæ Germanicæ," p. 210. The former of these writers does not consider Conrad as Duke of Franconia.

[4] Many towns in Germany, especially on the Saxon frontier, were built by Henry I, who is said to have compelled every ninth man to take up his residence in them. This had a remarkable tendency to promote the improvement of that territory, and, combined with the discovery of the gold and silver mines of Goslar under Otho I, rendered it the richest and most important part of the em-

pire. (Struvius, pp. 225 and 251; Schmidt, tome ii, p. 322; Putter, "Historical Development of the German Constitution," vol. i, p. 115.)

[5] A maximâ multitudine vox una respondit; Henricum, Christi adjutorio, et jure hæreditario, regnaturum. (Ditmar apud Struvium, p. 273. See other passages quoted in the same place. Schmidt, tome ii, p. 410.)

[6] Conrad was descended from a daughter of Otho the Great, and also from Conrad I. His first cousin was Duke of Franconia. (Struvius; Schmidt; Pfeffel.)

three successive emperors, Henry III, IV, and V. Perhaps the imperial prerogatives over that insubordinate confederacy never reached so high a point as in the reign of Henry III, the second emperor of the house of Franconia. It had been, as was natural, the object of all his predecessors not only to render their throne hereditary, which, in effect, the nation was willing to concede, but to surround it with authority sufficient to control the leading vassals. These were the dukes of the four nations of Germany, Saxony, Bavaria, Swabia, and Franconia, and the three archbishops of the Rhenish cities, Mentz, Treves, and Cologne. Originally, as has been more fully shown in another place, duchies, like counties, were temporary governments, bestowed at the pleasure of the crown. From this first stage they advanced to hereditary offices, and finally to patrimonial fiefs. But their progress was much slower in Germany than in France. Under the Saxon line of emperors, it appears probable that, although it was usual, and consonant to the prevailing notions of equity, to confer a duchy upon the nearest heir, yet no positive rule enforced this upon the emperor, and some instances of a contrary proceeding occurred.[7] But, if the royal prerogative in this respect stood higher than in France, there was a countervailing principle that prohibited the emperor from uniting a fief to his domain, or even retaining one which he had possessed before his accession. Thus Otho the Great granted away his duchy of Saxony, and Henry II that of Bavaria. Otho the Great endeavoured to counteract the effects of this custom by conferring the duchies that fell into his hands upon members of his own family. This policy, though apparently well conceived, proved of no advantage to Otho, his son and brother having mixed in several rebellions against him. It was revived, however, by Conrad II and Henry III. The latter was invested by his father with the two duchies of Swabia and Bavaria. Upon his own accession he retained the former for six years, and even the latter for a short time. The duchy of Franconia, which became vacant, he did not regrant, but endeavoured to set a precedent of uniting fiefs to the domain. At another time, after sentence of forfeiture against the Duke of Bavaria, he bestowed that great province on his wife, the Empress Agnes.[8] He put an end altogether to the form of popular concurrence, which had been usual when the investiture of a duchy was conferred, and even deposed dukes by the sentence of a few princes, without the consent of the Diet.[9] If we combine with these proofs of authority in the do-

[7] Schmidt, tome ii, pp. 393, 403. Struvius (p. 214) supposes the hereditary rights of dukes to have commenced under Conrad I, but Schmidt is perhaps a better authority; and Struvius afterward mentions the refusal of Otho I to grant the duchy of Bavaria to the sons of the last duke, which, however, excited a rebellion (p. 235).
[8] Schmidt, tome iii, pp. 25, 37.
[9] Id., p. 207.

RETURN OF VICTORIOUS GERMANS.

Photogravure from a painting by Paul Thumann.

mestic administration of Henry III his almost unlimited control over papal elections, or rather the right of nomination that he acquired, we must consider him as the most absolute monarch in the annals of Germany.

These ambitious measures of Henry III prepared fifty years of calamity for his son. It is easy to perceive that the misfortunes of Henry IV were primarily occasioned by the jealousy with which repeated violations of their constitutional usages had inspired the nobility.[10] The mere circumstance of Henry IV's minority, under the guardianship of a woman, was enough to dissipate whatever power his father had acquired. Hanno, Archbishop of Mentz, carried the young king away by force from his mother, and governed Germany in his name, till another archbishop, Adalbert of Bremen, obtained greater influence over him. Through the neglect of his education, Henry grew up with a character not well fitted to retrieve the mischief of so unprotected a minority; brave, indeed, well-natured, and affable, but dissolute beyond measure, and addicted to low and debauched company. He was soon involved in a desperate war with the Saxons, a nation valuing itself on its populousness and riches, jealous of the house of Franconia, who wore a crown that had belonged to their own dukes, and indignant at Henry's conduct in erecting fortresses throughout their country.

In the progress of this war many of the chief princes evinced an unwillingness to support the emperor.[11] Notwithstanding this, it would probably have terminated, as other rebellions had done, with no permanent loss to either party. But in the middle of this contest another far more memorable broke out with the Roman See, concerning ecclesiastical investitures. The motives of this famous quarrel will be explained in a different chapter of the present work. Its effect in Germany was ruinous to Henry. A sentence, not only of excommunication, but of deposition, which Gregory VII pronounced against him, gave a pretence to all his enemies, secret as well as avowed, to withdraw their allegiance.[12] At the head of these was Rodolph, Duke of Swabia, whom an assembly of revolted princes raised to the throne. We may perceive, in the conditions of Rodolph's elec-

[10] In the very first year of Henry's reign, while he was but six years old, the Princes of Saxony are said by Lambert of Aschaffenburg to have formed a conspiracy to depose him, out of resentment for the injuries they had sustained from his father. (Struvius, p. 306; St. Marc, tome iii, p. 248.)

[11] Struvius; Schmidt.

[12] A party had been already formed, who were meditating to depose Henry. His excommunication came just in time to confirm their resolutions. It appears clearly, upon a little consideration of Henry IV's reign, that the ecclesiastical quarrel was only secondary in the eyes of Germany. The contest against him was a struggle of the aristocracy, jealous of the imperial prerogatives which Conrad II and Henry III had strained to the utmost. Those who were in rebellion against Henry were not pleased with Gregory VII. Bruno, author of a history of the Saxon war, a furious invective, manifests great dissatisfaction with the court of Rome, which he reproaches with dissimulation and venality.

23

tion, a symptom of the real principle that animated the German aristocracy against Henry IV. It was agreed that the kingdom should no longer be hereditary, not conferred on the son of a reigning monarch unless his merit should challenge the popular approbation.[13] The Pope strongly encouraged this plan of rendering the empire elective, by which he hoped either eventually to secure the nomination of its chief for the Holy See, or at least, by sowing the seed of civil dissensions in Germany, to render Italy more independent. Henry IV, however, displayed greater abilities in his adversity than his early conduct had promised. In the last of several decisive battles, Rodolph, though victorious, was mortally wounded, and no one cared to take up a gauntlet which was to be won with so much trouble and uncertainty. The Germans were sufficiently disposed to submit, but Rome persevered in her unrelenting hatred. At the close of Henry's long reign she excited against him his eldest son, and, after more than thirty years of hostility, had the satisfaction of wearing him down with misfortune, and casting out his body, as excommunicated, from its sepulchre.

In the reign of his son, Henry V, there is no event worthy of much attention, except the termination of the great contest about investitures. At his death, in 1125, the male line of the Franconian emperors was at an end. Frederick, Duke of Swabia, grandson by his mother of Henry IV, had inherited their patrimonial estates, and seemed to represent their dynasty. But both the last emperors had so many enemies, and a disposition to render the crown elective prevailed so strongly among the leading princes, that Lothaire, Duke of Saxony, was elevated to the throne, though rather in a tumultuous and irregular manner.[14] Lothaire, who had been engaged in a revolt against Henry V, and the chief of a nation that bore an inveterate hatred to the house of Franconia, was the natural enemy of the new family that derived its importance and pretensions from that stock. It was the object of his reign, accordingly, to oppress the two brothers, Frederick and Conrad, of the Hohenstauffen or Swabian family. By this means he expected to secure the succession of the empire for his son-in-law. Henry, surnamed the Proud,

---

[13] Hoc etiam ibi consensu communi comprobatum, Romani pontificis auctoritate est corroboratum, ut regia potestas nulli per hæreditatem, sicut antea fuit consuetudo, cederet, sed filius regis, etiamsi valde dignus esset, per electionem spontaneam, non per successionis lineam, rex proveniret: si vero non esset dignus regis filius, vel si nollet eum populus, quem regem facere vellet, haberet in potestate populus. (" Bruno de Bello Saxonico," apud Struvium, p. 327.)

[14] See an account of Lothaire's election by a contemporary writer in Struvius,

p. 357. See also proofs of the dissatisfaction of the aristocracy at the Franconian government. (Schmidt, tome iii, p. 328.) It was evidently their determination to render the empire truly elective (id., p. 335): and perhaps we may date that fundamental principle of the Germanic constitution from the accession of Lothaire. Previously to that era, birth seems to have given not only a fair title to preference, but a sort of inchoate right, as in France, Spain, and England. Lothaire signed a capitulation at his accession.

who married Lothaire's only child, was fourth in descent from Welf, son of Azon, Marquis of Este, by Cunegonda, heiress of a distinguished family, the Welfs of Altorf, in Swabia. Her son was invested with the duchy of Bavaria in 1071. His descendant, Henry the Proud, represented also, through his mother, the ancient Dukes of Saxony, surnamed Billung, from whom he derived the duchy of Luneburg. The wife of Lothaire transmitted to her daughter the patrimony of Henry the Fowler, consisting of Hanover and Brunswick. Besides this great dowry, Lothaire bestowed upon his son-in-law the duchy of Saxony in addition to that of Bavaria.[15]

This amazing preponderance, however, tended to alienate the princes of Germany from Lothaire's views in favour of Henry, and the latter does not seem to have possessed abilities adequate to his eminent station. On the death of Lothaire in 1138, the partisans of the house of Swabia made a hasty and irregular election of Conrad, in which the Saxon faction found itself obliged to acquiesce.[16] The new emperor availed himself of the jealousy which Henry the Proud's aggrandizement had excited. Under pretence that two duchies could not legally be held by the same person, Henry was summoned to resign one of them; and on his refusal, the Diet pronounced that he had incurred the forfeiture of both. Henry made but little resistance, and before his death, which happened soon afterward, saw himself stripped of all his hereditary as well as acquired possessions. Upon this occasion the famous names of Guelf and Ghibelin were first heard, which were destined to keep alive the flame of civil dissension in far-distant countries, and after their meaning had been forgotten. The Guelfs, or Welfs, were, as I have said, the ancestors of Henry, and the name has become a sort of patronymic in his family. The word Ghibelin is derived from Wibelung, a town in Franconia, whence the emperors of that line are said to have sprung. The house of Swabia were considered in Germany as representing that of Franconia; as the Guelfs may, without much impropriety, be deemed to represent the Saxon line.[17]

Though Conrad III left a son, the choice of the electors fell, at his own request, upon his nephew, Frederick Barbarossa.[18] The most conspicuous events of this great emperor's life belong to the history of Italy. At home he was feared and respected; the imperial prerogatives stood as high during his reign as, after their previous decline, it was possible for a single man to carry them.[19] But the only circumstance which appears memorable enough for the present sketch is the second fall of the Guelfs.

---

[15] Pfeffel, "Abrégé Chronologique de l'Histoire d'Allemagne," tome i, p. 269. (Paris, 1777.) Gibbon's "Antiquities of the House of Brunswick."

[16] Schmidt.
[17] Struvius, pp. 370 and 378.
[18] Struvius.
[19] Pfeffel, p. 341.

Henry the Lion, son of Henry the Proud, had been restored by
Conrad III to his father's duchy of Saxony, resigning his claim
to that of Bavaria, which had been conferred on the Margrave of
Austria. This renunciation, which indeed was only made in his
name during childhood, did not prevent him from urging the Emperor Frederick to restore the whole of his birthright; and Frederick, his first cousin, whose life he had saved in a sedition at
Rome, was induced to comply with this request in 1156. Far from
evincing that political jealousy which some writers impute to him,
the emperor seems to have carried his generosity beyond the
limits of prudence. For many years their union was apparently
cordial. But, whether it was that Henry took umbrage at part of
Frederick's conduct,[20] or that mere ambition rendered him ungrateful, he certainly abandoned his sovereign in a moment of
distress, refusing to give any assistance in that expedition into
Lombardy which ended in the unsuccessful battle of Legnano.
Frederick could not forgive this injury, and, taking advantage of
complaints, which Henry's power and haughtiness had produced,
summoned him to answer charges in a general Diet. The duke
refused to appear, and, being adjudged contumacious, a sentence
of confiscation, similar to that which ruined his father, fell upon
his head; and the vast imperial fiefs that he possessed were shared
among some potent enemies.[21] He made an ineffectual resistance; like his father, he appears to have owed more to fortune
than to nature; and, after three years' exile, was obliged to remain
content with the restoration of his allodial estates in Saxony.
These, fifty years afterward, were converted into imperial fiefs, and
became the two duchies of the house of Brunswick, the lineal representatives of Henry the Lion, and inheritors of the name of
Guelf.[22]

Notwithstanding the prevailing spirit of the German oligarchy,
Frederick Barbarossa had found no difficulty in procuring the
election of his son Henry, even during infancy, as his successor.[23]
The fall of Henry the Lion had greatly weakened the ducal authority in Saxony and Bavaria; the princes who acquired that title,
especially in the former country, finding that the secular and spiritual nobility of the first class had taken the opportunity to raise
themselves into an immediate dependence upon the empire.
Henry VI came, therefore, to the crown with considerable advan-

[20] Frederick had obtained the succession of Wolf, Marquis of Tuscany, uncle
of Henry the Lion, who probably considered himself as entitled to expect it.
(Schmidt, p. 427.)
[21] Putter, in his "Historical Development of the Constitution of the German
Empire," is inclined to consider Henry
the Lion as sacrificed to the emperor's
jealousy of the Guelfs, and as illegally
proscribed by the Diet. But the provo-

cations he had given Frederick are undeniable; and, without pretending to decide on a question of German history, I
do not see that there was any precipi-
tancy or manifest breach of justice in
the course of proceedings against him.
Schmidt, Pfeffel, and Struvius do not
represent the condemnation of Henry as
unjust.
[22] Putter, p. 220.
[23] Struvius, p. 418.

1125-1274] HOUSE OF SWABIA 357

tages in respect of prerogative; and these inspired him with the bold scheme of declaring the empire hereditary. One is more surprised to find that he had no contemptible prospect of success in this attempt: fifty-two princes, and even what appears hardly credible, the See of Rome, under Clement III, having been induced to concur in it. But the Saxons made so vigorous an opposition that Henry did not think it advisable to persevere.[24] He procured, however, the election of his son Frederick, an infant only two years old. But the emperor dying almost immediately, a powerful body of princes, supported by Pope Innocent III, were desirous to withdraw their consent. Philip, Duke of Swabia, the late king's brother, unable to secure his nephew's succession, brought about his own election by one party, while another chose Otho, of Brunswick, younger son of Henry the Lion. This double election renewed the rivalry between the Guelfs and Ghibelins, and threw Germany into confusion for several years. Philip, whose pretensions appear to be the more legitimate of the two, gained ground upon his adversary, notwithstanding the opposition of the Pope, till he was assassinated in consequence of a private resentment. Otho IV reaped the benefit of a crime in which he did not participate, and became for some years undisputed sovereign. But, having offended the Pope by not entirely abandoning his imperial rights over Italy, he had, in the latter part of his reign, to contend against Frederick, son of Henry VI, who, having grown up to manhood, came into Germany as heir of the house of Swabia, and, what was not very usual in his history, or that of his family, the favoured candidate of the Holy See. Otho IV had been almost entirely deserted except by his natural subjects when his death, in 1218, removed every difficulty, and left Frederick II in the peaceable possession of Germany.

The eventful life of Frederick II was chiefly passed in Italy. To preserve his hereditary dominions and chastise the Lombard cities were the leading objects of his political and military career. He paid therefore but little attention to Germany, from which it was in vain for any emperor to expect effectual assistance toward objects of his own. Careless of prerogatives which it seemed hardly worth an effort to preserve, he sanctioned the independence of the princes, which may be properly dated from his reign. In return, they readily elected his son Henry King of the Romans; and on his being implicated in a rebellion, deposed him with equal readiness, and substituted his brother Conrad at the emperor's request.[25] But in the latter part of Frederick's reign the deadly hatred of Rome penetrated beyond the Alps. After his solemn

---

[24] Struvius, p. 424. Impetravit a subditis, ut cessante pristinâ Palatinorum electione, imperium in ipsius posteritatem, distinctâ proximorum successione, transiret, et sic in ipso terminus esset electionis, principiumque successivæ dignitatis. (" Gervas. Tilburiens.," ibidem.)
[25] Struvius, p. 457.

deposition in the council of Lyons, he was incapable, in ecclesiastical eyes, of holding the imperial sceptre. Innocent IV found, however, some difficulty in setting up a rival emperor. Henry, Landgrave of Thuringia, made an indifferent figure in this character. Upon his death, William, Count of Holland, was chosen by the party adverse to Frederick and his son Conrad; and after the emperor's death he had some success against the latter. It is hard, indeed, to say that any one was actually sovereign for twenty-two years that followed the death of Frederick II: a period of contested title and universal anarchy, which is usually denominated the grand interregnum. On the decease of William of Holland, in 1256, a schism among the electors produced the double choice of Richard, Earl of Cornwall, and Alfonso X, King of Castile. It seems not easy to determine which of these candidates had a legal majority of votes;[26] but the subsequent recognition of almost all Germany, and a sort of possession evidenced by public acts, which have been held valid, as well as the general consent of contemporaries, may justify us in adding Richard to the imperial list. The choice indeed was ridiculous, as he possessed no talents which could compensate for his want of power; but the electors attained their objects, to perpetuate a state of confusion by which their own independence was consolidated, and to plunder without scruple a man, like Didius at Rome, rich and foolish enough to purchase the first place upon earth.

That place indeed was now become a mockery of greatness. For more than two centuries, notwithstanding the temporary influence of Frederick Barbarossa and his son, the imperial authority had been in a state of gradual decay. From the time of Frederick II it had bordered upon absolute insignificance; and the more prudent German princes were slow to canvass for a dignity so little accompanied by respect. The changes wrought in the Germanic constitution during the period of the Swabian emperors chiefly consist in the establishment of an oligarchy of electors, and of the territorial sovereignty of the princes.

1. At the extinction of the Franconian line by the death of Henry V it was determined by the German nobility to make their empire practically elective, admitting no right, or even natural

[26] The election ought legally to have been made at Frankfort. But the Elector of Treves, having got possession of the town, shut out the Archbishops of Mentz and Cologne and the count palatine, on pretence of apprehending violence. They met under the walls, and there elected Richard. Afterward Alfonso was chosen by the votes of Treves, Saxony, and Brandenburg. Historians differ about the vote of Ottocar, King of Bohemia, which would turn the scale. Some time after the election it is certain that he was on the side of Richard. Perhaps we may collect from the opposite statements in Struvius (p. 504) that the proxies of Ottocar had voted for Alfonso, and that he did not think fit to recognise their act.

There can be no doubt that Richard was de facto sovereign of Germany; and it is singular that Struvius should assert the contrary, on the authority of an instrument of Rodolph, which expressly designates him king, per quondam Richardum regem illustrem. (Struv., p. 502.)

pretension, in the eldest son of a reigning sovereign. Their choice upon former occasions had been made by free and general suffrage. But it may be presumed that each nation voted unanimously, and according to the disposition of its duke. It is probable, too, that the leaders, after discussing in previous deliberations the merits of the several candidates, submitted their own resolutions to the assembly, which would generally concur in them without hesitation. At the election of Lothaire, in 1124, we find an evident instance of this previous choice, or, as it was called, pretaxation, from which the electoral college of Germany has been derived. The princes, it is said, trusted the choice of an emperor to ten persons, in whose judgment they promised to acquiesce.[27] This precedent was, in all likelihood, followed at all subsequent elections. The proofs indeed are not perfectly clear. But in the famous privilege of Austria, granted by Frederick I in 1156, he bestows a rank upon the newly created duke of that country, immediately after the electing princes (post principes electores);[28] a strong presumption that the right of pretaxation was not only established, but limited, to a few definite persons. In a letter of Innocent III, concerning the double election of Philip and Otho in 1198, he asserts the latter to have had a majority in his favour of those to whom the right of election chiefly belongs (ad quos principaliter spectat electio).[29] And a law of Otho in 1208, if it be genuine, appears to fix the exclusive privilege of the seven electors.[30] Nevertheless, so obscure is this important part of the Germanic system, that we find four ecclesiastical and two secular princes concurring with the regular electors in the act, as reported by a contemporary writer, that creates Conrad, son of Frederick II, King of the Romans.[31] This, however, may have been an irregular deviation from the principle already established. But it is admitted that all the princes retained, at least during the twelfth century, their consenting suffrage; like the laity in an episcopal election, whose approbation continued to be necessary long after the real power of choice had been withdrawn from them.[32]

It is not easy to account for all the circumstances that gave to seven spiritual and temporal princes this distinguished pre-eminence. The three archbishops, Mentz, Treves, and Cologne, were always indeed at the head of the German church. But the secular electors should naturally have been the dukes of four nations:

---

[27] Struvius, p. 357; Schmidt, tome iii, p. 331.
[28] Schmidt, tome iii, p. 390.
[29] Pfeffel, p. 360.
[30] Schmidt, tome iv, p. 80.
[31] This is not mentioned in Struvius or the other German writers. But Denina ("Rivoluzioni d' Italia," l. ix, c. 9) quotes the style of the act of election from the "Chronicle of Francis Pippin."
[32] This is manifest by the various passages relating to the elections of Philip and Otho, quoted by Struvius, pp. 428, 430. See, too, Pfeffel, ubi supra; Schmidt, tome iv, p. 79.

Saxony, Franconia, Swabia, and Bavaria. We find, however, only the first of these in the undisputed exercise of a vote. It seems probable that, when the electoral princes came to be distinguished from the rest, their privilege was considered as peculiarly connected with the discharge of one of the great offices in the imperial court. These were attached, as early as the Diet of Mentz in 1184, to the four electors, who ever afterward possessed them: the Duke of Saxony having then officiated as arch-marshal, the Count Palatine of the Rhine as arch-steward, the King of Bohemia as arch-cupbearer, and the Margrave of Brandenburg as arch-chamberlain of the empire.[33] But it still continues a problem why the three latter offices, with the electoral capacity as their incident, should not rather have been granted to the Dukes of Franconia, Swabia, and Bavaria. I have seen no adequate explanation of this circumstance; which may perhaps lead us to presume that the right of pre-election was not quite so soon confined to the precise number of seven princes. The final extinction of two great original duchies, Franconia and Swabia, in the thirteenth century, left the electoral rights of the Count Palatine and the Margrave of Brandenburg beyond dispute. But the Dukes of Bavaria continued to claim a vote in opposition to the Kings of Bohemia. At the election of Rodolph, in 1272, the two brothers of the house of Wittelsbach voted separately, as Count Palatine and Duke of Lower Bavaria. Ottocar was excluded upon this occasion; and it was not till 1290 that the suffrage of Bohemia was fully recognized. The Palatine and Bavarian branches, however, continued to enjoy their family vote conjointly, by a determination of Rodolph; upon which Louis of Bavaria slightly innovated, by rendering the suffrage alternate. But the Golden Bull of Charles IV put an end to all doubts on the rights of electoral houses, and absolutely excluded Bavaria from voting. The limitation to seven electors, first perhaps fixed by accident, came to be invested with a sort of mysterious importance, and certainly was considered, until times comparatively recent, as a fundamental law of the empire.[34]

2. It might appear natural to expect that an oligarchy of seven persons, who had thus excluded their equals from all share in the election of a sovereign, would assume still greater authority, and trespass further upon the less powerful vassals of the empire. But while the electors were establishing their peculiar privilege, the class immediately inferior raised itself by important acquisitions of power. The German dukes, even after they became hereditary, did not succeed in compelling the chief nobility within their limits to hold their lands in fief so completely as the peers of

[33] Schmidt, tome iv, p. 78.
[34] Ibid., pages 78, 568, Putter, page 274; Pfeffel, pages 435, 565; Struvius, page 511.

France had done. The nobles of Swabia refused to follow their duke into the field against the Emperor Conrad II.[35] Of this aristocracy the superior class were denominated princes; an appellation which, after the eleventh century, distinguished them from the untitled nobility, most of whom were their vassals. They were constituent parts of all Diets; and though gradually deprived of their original participation in electing an emperor, possessed in all other respects the same rights as the dukes or electors. Some of them were fully equal to the electors in birth as well as extent of dominions, such as the princely houses of Austria, Hesse, Brunswick, and Misnia. By the division of Henry the Lion's vast territories,[36] and by the absolute extinction of the Swabian family in the following century, a great many princes acquired additional weight. Of the ancient duchies, only Saxony and Bavaria remained, the former of which especially was so dismembered that it was vain to attempt any renewal of the ducal jurisdiction. That of the emperor, formerly exercised by the counts palatine, went almost equally into disuse during the contest between Philip and Otho IV. The princes accordingly had acted with sovereign independence within their own fiefs before the reign of Frederick II, but the legal recognition of their immunities was reserved for two edicts of that emperor; one, in 1220, relating to ecclesiastical, and the other, in 1232, to secular princes. By these he engaged neither to levy the customary imperial dues, nor to permit the jurisdiction of the palatine judges, within the limits of a state of the empire,[37] concessions that amounted to little less than an abdication of his own sovereignty. From this epoch the territorial independence of the states may be dated.

A class of titled nobility, inferior to the princes, were the counts of the empire, who seem to have been separated from the former in the twelfth century, and to have lost at the same time their right of voting in the Diets.[38] In some parts of Germany, chiefly in Franconia and upon the Rhine, there always existed a very numerous body of lower nobility, untitled at least till modern times, but subject to no superior except the emperor. These are supposed to have become immediate after the destruction of the house of Swabia, within whose duchies they had been comprehended.[39]

A short interval elapsed after the death of Richard of Cornwall before the electors could be induced, by the deplorable state of confusion into which Germany had fallen, to fill the imperial

[35] Pfeffel, p. 209.
[36] See the arrangements made in consequence of Henry's forfeiture, which gave quite a new face to Germany, in Pfeffel, p. 234; also p. 437.
[37] Pfeffel, p. 384; Putter, p. 233.
[38] In the instruments relating to the election of Otho IV the princes sign their names, Ego N. elegi et subscripsi. But the counts only as follows, Ego N. consensi et subscripsi. (Pfeffel, p. 360.)
[39] Pfeffel, p. 455; Putter, p. 254; Struvius, p. 511.

throne. Their choice was, however, the best that could have been made. It fell upon Rodolph, Count of Hapsburg, a prince of very ancient family and of considerable possessions as well in Switzerland as upon each bank of the Upper Rhine, but not sufficiently powerful to alarm the electoral oligarchy. Rodolph was brave, active, and just, but his characteristic quality appears to have been good sense, and judgment of the circumstances in which he was placed. Of this he gave a signal proof in relinquishing the favourite project of so many preceding emperors, and leaving Italy altogether to itself. At home he manifested a vigilant spirit in administering justice, and is said to have destroyed seventy strongholds of noble robbers in Thuringia and other parts, bringing many of the criminals to capital punishment.[40] But he wisely avoided giving offence to the more powerful princes, and during his reign there were hardly any rebellions in Germany.

It was a very reasonable object of every emperor to aggrandize his family by investing his near kindred with vacant fiefs, but no one was so fortunate in his opportunities as Rodolph. At his accession, Austria, Styria, and Carniola were in the hands of Ottocar, King of Bohemia. These extensive and fertile countries had been formed into a march or margraviate, after the victories of Otho the Great over the Hungarians. Frederick Barbarossa erected them into a duchy, with many distinguished privileges, especially that of female succession, hitherto unknown in the feudal principalities of Germany.[41] Upon the extinction of the house of Bamberg, which had enjoyed this duchy, it was granted by Frederick II to a cousin of his own name, after whose death a disputed succession gave rise to several changes, and ultimately enabled Ottocar to gain possession of the country. Against this King of Bohemia Rodolph waged two successful wars, and recovered the Austrian provinces, which, as vacant fiefs, he conferred, with the consent of the Diet, upon his son Albert.[42]

Notwithstanding the merit and popularity of Rodolph, the electors refused to choose his son King of the Romans in his life-

[40] Struvius, p. 530; Coxe's "Hist. of House of Austria," p. 57. This valuable work contains a full and interesting account of Rodolph's reign.

[41] The privileges of Austria were granted to the Margrave Henry in 1156, by way of indemnity for his restitution of Bavaria to Henry the Lion. The territory between the Inn and the Ems was separated from the latter province and annexed to Austria at this time. The Dukes of Austria are declared equal in rank to the palatine archdukes (archiducibus palatinis). This expression gave a hint to the Duke Rodolph IV to assume the title of Archduke of Austria. (Schmidt, tome iii, p. 390.) Frederick II even created the Duke of Austria king:

a very curious fact, though neither he nor his successors ever assumed the title. (Struvius, p. 463.) The instrument runs as follows: Ducatus Austriæ et Styriæ, cum pertinentiis et terminis suis quot hactenus habuit, ad nomen et honorem regium transferentes, te hactenus ducatuum prædictorum ducem, de potestatis nostræ plenitudine et magnificentiâ speciali promovemus in regem, per libertates et jura prædictum regnum tuum præsentis epigrammatis auctoritate donantes, quæ regiam deceant dignitatem; ut tamen ex honore quem tibi libenter addimus, nihil honoris et juris nostri diadematis aut imperii subtrahatur.

[42] Struvius, p. 525; Schmidt; Coxe.

time; and, after his death, determined to avoid the appearance of hereditary succession, put Adolphus of Nassau upon the throne. There is very little to attract notice in the domestic history of the empire during the next two centuries. From Adolphus to Sigismund every emperor had either to struggle against a competitor claiming the majority of votes at his election or against a combination of the electors to dethrone him. The imperial authority became more and more ineffective; yet it was frequently made a subject of reproach against the emperors that they did not maintain a sovereignty to which no one was disposed to submit.

It may appear surprising that the Germanic confederacy under the nominal supremacy of an emperor should have been preserved in circumstances apparently so calculated to dissolve it. But, besides the natural effect of prejudice and a famous name, there were sufficient reasons to induce the electors to preserve a form of government in which they bore so decided a sway. Accident had in a considerable degree restricted the electoral suffrages to seven princes. Without the college there were houses more substantially powerful than any within it. The duchy of Saxony had been subdivided by repeated partitions among children till the electoral right was vested in a prince who possessed only the small territory of Wittenberg. The great families of Austria, Bavaria, and Luxemburg, though not electoral, were the real heads of the German body; and though the two former lost much of their influence for a time through the pernicious custom of partition, the empire seldom looked for its head to any other house than one of these three.

While the duchies and counties of Germany retained their original character of offices or governments, they were of course, even though considered as hereditary, not subject to partition among children. When they acquired the nature of fiefs, it was still consonant to the principles of a feudal tenure that the eldest son should inherit according to the law of primogeniture, an inferior provision or appanage, at most, being reserved for the younger children. The law of England favoured the eldest exclusively, that of France gave him great advantages. But in Germany a different rule began to prevail about the thirteenth century.[43] An equal partition of the inheritance, without the least regard to priority of birth, was the general law of its principalities. Sometimes this was effected by undivided possession, or tenancy in common, the brothers residing together and reigning jointly. This tended to preserve the integrity of dominion; but as it was frequently incommodious, a more usual practice was to divide the territory. From such partitions are derived those numerous in-

---

[43] Schmidt, tome iv, p. 66. Pfeffel (p. 280) maintains that partitions were not introduced till the latter end of the thirteenth century. This may be true as a general rule; but I find the house of Baden divided into two branches, Baden and Hochberg, in 1190, with rights of mutual reversion.

dependent principalities of the same house, many of which still
subsist in Germany. In 1589 there were eight reigning princes
of the Palatine family, and fourteen, in 1675, of that of Saxony.[44]
Originally these partitions were in general absolute and without
reversion; but, as their effect in weakening families became evident, a practice was introduced of making compacts of reciprocal
succession, by which a fief was prevented from escheating to the
empire until all the male posterity of the first feudatory should be
extinct. Thus, while the German Empire survived, all the princes
of Hesse or of Saxony had reciprocal contingencies of succession,
or what our lawyers call cross-remainders, to each other's dominions. A different system was gradually adopted. By the Golden
Bull of Charles IV the electoral territory—that is, the particular
district to which the electoral suffrage was inseparably attached—
became incapable of partition, and was to descend to the eldest
son. In the fifteenth century the present house of Brandenburg
set the first example of establishing primogeniture by law; the
principalities of Anspach and Bayreuth were dismembered from
it for the benefit of younger branches; but it was declared that all
the other dominions of the family should for the future belong
exclusively to the reigning elector. This politic measure was
adopted in several other families; but, even in the sixteenth century, the prejudice was not removed, and some German princes
denounced curses on their posterity if they should introduce the
impious custom of primogeniture.[45] Notwithstanding these subdivisions, and the most remarkable of those which I have mentioned are of a date rather subsequent to the middle ages, the
antagonist principle of consolidation by various means of acquisition was so actively at work that several princely houses, especially those of Hohenzollern or Brandenburg, of Hesse, Würtem-
berg, and the Palatinate, derive their importance from the same
era, the fourteenth and fifteenth centuries, in which the prejudice
against primogeniture was the strongest. And thus it will often
be found in private patrimonies; the tendency to consolidation of
property works more rapidly than that to its disintegration by a
law of gavelkind.

Weakened by these subdivisions, the principalities of Germany
in the fourteenth and fifteenth centuries shrink to a more and more
diminutive size in the scale of nations. But one family, the most
illustrious of the former age, was less exposed to this enfeebling
system. Henry VII, Count of Luxemburg, a man of much more
personal merit than hereditary importance, was elevated to the
empire in 1308. Most part of his short reign he passed in Italy;
but he had a fortunate opportunity of obtaining the crown of Bohemia for his son. John, King of Bohemia, did not himself wear

[44] Pfeffel, p. 289; Putter, p. 189.   [45] Pfeffel, p. 280.

the imperial crown, but three of his descendants possessed it, with less interruption than could have been expected. His son Charles IV succeeded Louis of Bavaria in 1347, not indeed without opposition, for a double election and a civil war were matters of course in Germany. Charles IV has been treated with more derision by his contemporaries, and consequently by later writers, than almost any prince in history; yet he was remarkably successful in the only objects that he seriously pursued. Deficient in personal courage, insensible of humiliation, bending without shame to the Pope, to the Italians, to the electors, so poor and so little reverenced as to be arrested by a butcher at Worms for want of paying his demand, Charles IV affords a proof that a certain dexterity and cold-blooded perseverance may occasionally supply in a sovereign the want of more respectable qualities. He has been reproached with neglecting the empire. But he never designed to trouble himself about the empire, except for his private ends. He did not neglect the kingdom of Bohemia, to which he almost seemed to render Germany a province. Bohemia had been long considered as a fief of the empire, and indeed could pretend to an electoral vote by no other title. Charles, however, gave the states by law the right of choosing a king, on the extinction of the royal family, which seems derogatory to the imperial prerogative.[46] It was much more material that, upon acquiring Brandenburg, partly by conquest and partly by a compact of succession in 1373, he not only invested his sons with it, which was conformable to usage, but tried to annex that electorate forever to the kingdom of Bohemia.[47] He constantly resided at Prague, where he founded a celebrated university, and embellished the city with buildings. This kingdom, augmented also during his reign by the acquisition of Silesia, he bequeathed to his son Wenceslaus, for whom, by pliancy toward the electors and the court of Rome, he had procured, against all recent example, the imperial succession.[48]

The reign of Charles IV is distinguished in the constitutional history of the empire by his Golden Bull, an instrument which finally ascertained the prerogatives of the electoral college. The Golden Bull terminated the disputes which had arisen between different members of the same house as to their right of suffrage, which was declared inherent in certain definite territories. The number was absolutely restrained to seven. The place of legal imperial elections was fixed at Frankfort; of coronations, at Aix-la-Chapelle; and the latter ceremony was to be performed by the Archbishop of Cologne. These regulations, though consonant to ancient usage, had not always been observed, and their neglect had sometimes excited questions as to the validity of elections.

[46] Struvius, p. 641.
[47] Pfeffel, p. 575; Schmidt, tome iv, p. 595.
[48] Struvius, p. 637.

The dignity of elector was enhanced by the Golden Bull as highly as an imperial edict could carry it; they were declared equal to kings, and conspiracy against their persons incurred the penalty of high treason.[49] Many other privileges are granted to render them more completely sovereign within their dominions. It seems extraordinary that Charles should have voluntarily elevated an oligarchy, from whose pretensions his predecessors had frequently suffered injury. But he had more to apprehend from the two great families of Bavaria and Austria, whom he relatively depressed by giving such a preponderance to the seven electors, than from any members of the college. By his compact with Brandenburg he had a fair prospect of adding a second vote to his own; and there was more room for intrigue and management, which Charles always preferred to arms, with a small number, than with the whole body of princes.

The next reign, nevertheless, evinced the danger of investing the electors with such preponderating authority. Wenceslaus, a supine and voluptuous man, less respected, and more negligent of Germany, if possible, than his father, was regularly deposed by a majority of the electoral college in 1400. This right, if it is to be considered as a right, they had already used against Adolphus of Nassau in 1298, and against Louis of Bavaria in 1346. They chose Robert Count Palatine instead of Wenceslaus; and though the latter did not cease to have some adherents, Robert has generally been counted among the lawful emperors.[50] Upon his death the empire returned to the house of Luxemburg, Wenceslaus himself waiving his rights in favour of his brother Sigismund of Hungary.[51]

The house of Austria had hitherto given but two emperors to Germany—Rodolph, its founder, and his son Albert, whom a successful rebellion elevated in the place of Adolphus. Upon the death of Henry of Luxemburg, in 1313, Frederick, son of Albert, disputed the election of Louis, Duke of Bavaria, alleging a majority of genuine votes. This produced a civil war, in which the Austrian party were entirely worsted. Though they advanced no pretensions to the imperial dignity during the rest of the fourteenth century, the princes of that line added to their possessions

[49] Pfeffel, p. 565; Putter, p. 271; Schmidt, tome iv, p. 566. The Golden Bull not only fixed the palatine vote, in absolute exclusion of Bavaria, but settled a controversy of long standing between the two branches of the house of Saxony, Wittenberg and Lauenburg, in favour of the former.

[50] Many of the cities, besides some princes, continued to recognise Wenceslaus throughout the life of Robert; and the latter was so much considered as a usurper by foreign states that his ambassadors were refused admittance at the Council of Pisa. (Struvius, p. 658.)

[51] This election of Sigismund was not uncontested: Josse, or Jodocus, Margrave of Moravia, having been chosen, as far as appears, by a legal majority. However, his death within three months removed the difficulty; and Josse, who was not crowned at Frankfort, has never been reckoned among the emperors, though modern critics agree that his title was legitimate. (Struvius, p. 684; Pfeffel, p. 612.)

Carinthia, Istria, and the Tyrol. As a counterbalance to these acquisitions, they lost a great part of their ancient inheritance by unsuccessful wars with the Swiss. According to the custom of partition, so injurious to princely houses, their dominions were divided among three branches: one reigning in Austria, a second in Styria and the adjacent provinces, a third in the Tyrol and Alsace. This had in a considerable degree eclipsed the glory of the house of Hapsburg. But it was now its destiny to revive, and to enter upon a career of prosperity which has never since been permanently interrupted. Albert, Duke of Austria, who had married Sigismund's only daughter, the Queen of Hungary and Bohemia, was raised to the imperial throne upon the death of his father-in-law in 1437. He died in two years, leaving his wife pregnant with a son, Ladislaus Posthumus, who afterward reigned in the two kingdoms just mentioned; and the choice of the electors fell upon Frederick, Duke of Styria, second cousin of the last emperor, from whose posterity it never departed, except in a single instance, upon the extinction of his male line in 1740.

Frederick III reigned fifty-three years, a longer period than any of his predecessors; and his personal character was more insignificant. With better fortune than could be expected, considering both these circumstances, he escaped any overt attempt to depose him, though such a project was sometimes in agitation. He reigned during an interesting age, full of remarkable events, and big with others of more leading importance. The destruction of the Greek Empire and appearance of the victorious Crescent upon the Danube gave an unhappy distinction to the earlier years of his reign, and displayed his mean and pusillanimous character in circumstances which demanded a hero. At a later season he was drawn into contentions with France and Burgundy, which ultimately produced a new and more general combination of European politics. Frederick, always poor, and scarcely able to protect himself in Austria from the seditions of his subjects or the inroads of the King of Hungary, was yet another founder of his family, and left their fortunes incomparably more prosperous than at his accession.[52] The marriage of his son Maximilian

---

[52] Ranke has drawn the character of Frederick III more favourably, on the whole, than preceding historians, and with a discrimination which enables us to account better for his success in the objects which he had at heart. " From his youth he had been inured to trouble and adversity. When compelled to yield, he never gave up a point, and always gained the mastery in the end. The maintenance of his prerogatives was the governing principle of all his actions, the more because they acquired an ideal value from their connection with the imperial dignity. It cost him a long and severe struggle to allow his son to be crowned King of the Romans; he wished to take the supreme authority undivided with him to the grave: in no case would he grant Maximilian any independent share in the administration of government; but kept him, even after he was king, still as 'son of the house'; nor would he ever give him anything but the countship of Cilli; 'for the rest he would have time enough.' His frugality

with the heiress of Burgundy began that aggrandizement of the house of Austria which Frederick seems to have anticipated.[53] The electors, who had lost a good deal of their former spirit, and were grown sensible of the necessity of choosing a powerful sovereign, made no opposition to Maximilian's becoming king of the Romans in his father's lifetime. The Austrian provinces were reunited either under Frederick or in the first years of Maximilian; so that at the close of that period which we denominate the middle ages the German Empire, sustained by the patrimonial dominions of its chief, became again considerable in the scale of nations, and capable of preserving a balance between the ambitious monarchies of France and Spain.

The period between Rodolph and Frederick III is distinguished by no circumstance so interesting as the prosperous state of the free imperial cities, which had attained their maturity about the commencement of that interval. We find the cities of Germany in the tenth century divided into such as depended immediately upon the empire, which were usually governed by their bishop as imperial vicar, and such as were included in the territories of the dukes and counts.[54] Some of the former, lying principally upon the Rhine and in Franconia, acquired a certain degree of importance before the expiration of the eleventh century. Worms and Cologne manifested a zealous attachment to Henry IV, whom they supported in despite of their bishops.[55] His son Henry V granted privileges of enfranchisement to the inferior townsmen or artisans who had hitherto been distinguished from the upper class of freemen, and particularly relieved them from oppressive usages, which either gave the whole of their movable

bordered on avarice, his slowness on inertness, his stubbornness on the most determined selfishness ; yet all these faults are removed from vulgarity by high qualities. He had at bottom a sober depth of judgment, a sedate and inflexible honour; the aged prince, even when a fugitive imploring succour, had a personal bearing which never allowed the majesty of the empire to sink." (" Hist. Reformation," translation, vol. ii, p. 103.)

A character of such obstinate passive resistance was well fitted for his station in that age; spite of his poverty and weakness, he was hereditary sovereign of extensive and fertile territories; he was not loved, feared, or respected, but he was necessary; he was a German, and therefore not to be exchanged for a king of Hungary or Bohemia; he was, not as Frederick of Austria, but as elected emperor, the sole hope for a more settled rule, for public peace, for the maintenance of a confederacy so ill held together by any other tie. Hence he succeeded in what seemed so difficult—in procuring the election of Maximilian as King of the Romans; and interested the German Diet

in maintaining the Burgundian inheritance, the western provinces of the Netherlands, which the latter's marriage brought into the house of Austria.

[53] The famous device of Austria, A. E. I. O. U., was first used by Frederick III, who adopted it on his plate, books, and buildings. These initials stand for Austriæ Est Imperare Orbi Universo; or, in German, Alles Erdreich Ist Osterreich Unterthan: a bold assumption for a man who was not safe in an inch of his dominions. (Struvius, p. 722.) He confirmed the archducal title of his family, which might seem implied in the original grant of Frederick I, and bestowed other high privileges above all princes of the empire. These are enumerated in Coxe's " House of Austria," vol. i, p. 263.

[54] Pfeffel, p. 187. The Othos adopted the same policy in Germany which they had introduced in Italy, conferring the temporal government of cities upon the bishops; probably as a counterbalance to the lay aristocracy. (Putter, p. 136 ; Struvius, p. 252.)

[55] Schmidt, tome iii, p. 239.

goods to the lord upon their decease or at least enabled him to seize the best chattel as his heriot.[56]   He took away the temporal authority of the bishop at least in several instances, and restored the cities to a more immediate dependence upon the empire.   The citizens were classed in companies, according to their several occupations, an institution which was speedily adopted in other commercial countries.   It does not appear that any German city had obtained under this emperor those privileges of choosing its own magistrates which were conceded about the same time, in a few instances, to those of France.[57]   Gradually, however, they began to elect councils of citizens, as a sort of senate or magistracy. This innovation might perhaps take place as early as the reign of Frederick I;[58] at least, it was fully established in that of his grandson.   They were at first only assistants to the imperial or episcopal bailiff, who probably continued to administer criminal justice.   But in the thirteenth century the citizens, grown richer and stronger, either purchased the jurisdiction or usurped it through the lord's neglect, or drove out the bailiff by force.[59]   The great revolution in Franconia and Swabia, occasioned by the fall of the Hohenstauffen family, completed the victory of the cities.   Those which had depended upon mediate lords became immediately connected with the empire; and with the empire in its state of feebleness, when an occasional present of money would easily induce its chief to acquiesce in any claims of immunity which the citizens might prefer.

It was a natural consequence of the importance which the free citizens had reached, and of their immediacy, that they were admitted to a place in the Diets or general meetings of the confederacy.   They were tacitly acknowledged to be equally sovereign with the electors and princes.   No proof exists of any law by which they were adopted into the Diet.   We find it said that Rodolph of Hapsburg, in 1291, renewed his oath with the princes, lords, and cities.   Under the Emperor Henry VII there is unequivocal mention of the three orders composing the Diet—electors, princes, and deputies from cities.[60]   And in 1344 they appear as a third distinct college in the Diet of Frankfort.[61]

The inhabitants of these free cities always preserved their respect for the emperor, and gave him much less vexation than his

---

[56] Schmidt, p. 242; Pfeffel, p. 293; Dumont, "Corps Diplomatique," tome i, p. 64.
[57] Schmidt, p. 245.
[58] In the charter granted by Frederick I to Spire in 1182, confirming and enlarging that of Henry V, though no express mention is made of any municipal jurisdiction, yet it seems implied in the following words: Causam in civitate jam lite contestatam non episcopus aut alia potestas extra civitatem determinari compellet. (Dumont, p. 108.)
[59] Schmidt, tome iv, p. 96; Pfeffel, p. 441.
[60] Mansit ibi rex sex hebdom adibus cum principibus electoribus et aliis principibus et civitatum nuntiis, de suo transitu et de praestandis servitiis in Italiam disponendo. (Auctor apud Schmidt, tome vi, p. 31.)
[61] Pfeffel, p. 552.

24

other subjects. He was indeed their natural friend. But the nobility and prelates were their natural enemies; and the western
parts of Germany were the scenes of irreconcilable warfare between the possessors of fortified castles and the inhabitants of
fortified cities. Each party was frequently the aggressor. The
nobles were too often mere robbers, who lived upon the plunder
of travellers. But the citizens were almost equally inattentive to
the rights of others. It was their policy to offer the privileges of
burghership to all strangers. The peasantry of feudal lords, flying
to a neighbouring town, found an asylum constantly open. A
multitude of aliens, thus seeking as it were sanctuary, dwelt in the
suburbs or liberties, between the city walls and the palisades
which bounded the territory. Hence they were called Pfahlbürger,
or burgesses of the palisades; and this encroachment on the rights
of the nobility was positively but vainly prohibited by several imperial edicts, especially the Golden Bull. Another class were the
Ausbürger, or outburghers, who had been admitted to privileges
of citizenship, though resident at a distance, and pretended in
consequence to be exempted from all dues to their original feudal
superiors. If a lord resisted so unreasonable a claim he incurred
the danger of bringing down upon himself the vengeance of the
citizens. These outburghers are in general classed under the
general name of Pfahlbürger by contemporary writers.[62]

As the towns were conscious of the hatred which the nobility
bore toward them, it was their interest to make a common cause,
and render mutual assistance. From this necessity of maintaining by united exertions their general liberty, the German cities
never suffered the petty jealousies which might no doubt exist
among them, to ripen into such deadly feuds as sullied the glory,
and ultimately destroyed the freedom, of Lombardy. They withstood the bishops and barons by confederacies of their own,
framed expressly to secure their commerce against rapine or unjust exactions of toll. More than sixty cities, with three ecclesiastical electors at their head, formed the League of the Rhine, in
1255, to repel the inferior nobility who, having now become immediate, abused that independence by perpetual robberies.[63] The
Hanseatic Union owes its origin to no other cause, and may be
traced perhaps to rather a higher date. About the year 1370 a
league was formed which, though it did not continue so long,
seems to have produced more striking effects in Germany. The
cities of Swabia and the Rhine united themselves in a strict confederacy against the princes, and especially the families of Wür-
temberg and Bavaria. It is said that the Emperor Wenceslaus

[62] Schmidt, tome iv, p. 98; tome vi, p.
76; Pfeffel, p. 402; Du Cange, Gloss.,
voc. Pfahlbürger. Faubourg is derived
from this word.

[63] Struvius, p. 498; Schmidt, tome iv,
p. 101; Pfeffel, p. 416.

secretly abetted their projects. The recent successes of the Swiss, who had now almost established their republic, inspired their neighbours in the empire with expectations which the event did not realize; for they were defeated in this war, and ultimately compelled to relinquish their league. Counter-associations were formed by the nobles, styled Society of St. George, St. William, the Lion, or the Panther.[64]

The spirit of political liberty was not confined to the free immediate cities. In all the German principalities a form of limited monarchy prevailed, reflecting on a reduced scale the general constitution of the empire. As the emperors shared their legislative sovereignty with the Diet, so all the princes who belonged to that assembly had their own provincial states, composed of their feudal vassals and of their mediate towns within their territory. No tax could be imposed without consent of the states, and in some countries the prince was obliged to account for the proper disposition of the money granted. In all matters of importance affecting the principality, and especially in cases of partition, it was necessary to consult them; and they sometimes decided between competitors in a disputed succession, though this indeed more strictly belonged to the emperor. The provincial states concurred with the prince in making laws, except such as were enacted by the general Diet. The city of Würzburg, in the fourteenth century, tells its bishop that, if a lord would make any new ordinance, the custom is that he must consult the citizens, who have always opposed his innovating upon the ancient laws without their consent.[65]

The ancient imperial domain, or possessions which belonged to the chief of the empire as such, had originally been very extensive. Besides large estates in every province, the territory upon each bank of the Rhine, afterward occupied by the counts palatine and ecclesiastical electors, was, until the thirteenth century, an exclusive property of the emperor. This imperial domain was deemed so adequate to the support of his dignity that it was usual, if not obligatory, for him to grant away his patrimonial domains upon his election. But the necessities of Frederick II, and the long confusion that ensued upon his death, caused the domain to be almost entirely dissipated. Rodolph made some efforts to retrieve it, but too late; and the poor remains of what had belonged to Charlemagne and Otho were alienated by Charles IV.[66] This produced a necessary change in that part of the constitution which deprived an emperor of hereditary possessions. It was, however, some time before it took place. Even Albert I

[64] Struvius, p. 649 ; Pfeffel, p. 586 ; Schmidt, tome v, p. 10; tome vi, p. 78; Putter, p. 293.

[65] Schmidt, tome vi, p. 8; Putter, p. 236.

[66] Pfeffel, p. 580.

conferred the Duchy of Austria upon his son when he was chosen emperor.[67] Louis of Bavaria was the first who retained his hereditary dominions, and made them his residence.[68] Charles IV and Wenceslaus lived almost wholly in Bohemia, Sigismund chiefly in Hungary, Frederick III in Austria. This residence in their hereditary countries, while it seemed rather to lower the imperial dignity and to lessen their connection with the general confederacy, gave them intrinsic power and influence. If the emperors of the houses of Luxemburg and Austria were not like the Conrads and Fredericks, they were at least very superior in importance to the Williams and Adolphuses of the thirteenth century.

The accession of Maximilian nearly coincides with the expedition of Charles VIII against Naples; and I should here close the German history of the middle age were it not for the great epoch which is made by the Diet of Worms in 1495. This assembly is celebrated for the establishment of a perpetual public peace, and of a paramount court of justice, the Imperial Chamber.

The same causes which produced continual hostilities among the French nobility were not likely to operate less powerfully on the Germans, equally warlike with their neighbours and rather less civilized. But while the imperial government was still vigorous, they were kept under some restraint. We find Henry III, the most powerful of the Franconian emperors, forbidding all private defiances, and establishing solemnly a general peace.[69] After his time the natural tendency of manners overpowered all attempts to coerce it, and private war waged without limits in the empire. Frederick I endeavoured to repress it by a regulation which admitted its legality. This was the law of defiance (jus diffidationis), which required a solemn declaration of war and three days' notice before the commencement of hostile measures. All persons contravening this provision were deemed robbers and not legitimate enemies.[70] Frederick II carried the restraint further and limited the right of self-redress to cases where justice could not be obtained. Unfortunately, there was, in later times, no sufficient provision for rendering justice. The German Empire indeed had now assumed so peculiar a character, and the mass of states which composed it were in so many respects sovereign within their own territories, that wars, unless in themselves unjust, could not be made a subject of reproach against them, nor considered, strictly speaking, as private. It was certainly most desirable to put an

---

[67] Pfeffel, p. 494; Struvius, p. 546.

[68] Struvius, p. 611. In the capitulation of Robert it was expressly provided that he should retain any escheated fief for the domain, instead of granting it away, so completely was the public policy of the empire reversed. (Schmidt, tome v, p. 44.)

[69] Pfeffel, p. 212.

[70] Schmidt, tome iv, p. 108, et infra; Pfeffel, p. 340; Putter, p. 205.

end to them by common agreement, and by the only means that could render war unnecessary—the establishment of a supreme jurisdiction. War indeed, legally undertaken, was not the only nor the severest grievance. A very large proportion of the rural nobility lived by robbery.[71] Their castles, as the ruins still bear witness, were erected upon inaccessible hills, and in defiles that command the public road. An Archbishop of Cologne having built a fortress of this kind, the governor inquired how he was to maintain himself, no revenue having been assigned for that purpose: the prelate only desired him to remark that the castle was situated near the junction of four roads.[72] As commerce increased, and the example of French and Italian civilization rendered the Germans more sensible to their own rudeness, the preservation of public peace was loudly demanded. Every Diet under Frederick III professed to occupy itself with the two great objects of domestic reformation, peace and law. Temporary cessations, during which all private hostility was illegal, were sometimes enacted; and, if observed, which may well be doubted, might contribute to accustom men to habits of greater tranquility. The leagues of the cities were probably more efficacious checks upon the disturbers of order. In 1486 a ten years' peace was proclaimed, and before the expiration of this period the perpetual abolition of the right of defiance was happily accomplished in the Diet of Worms.[73]

These wars, incessantly waged by the states of Germany, seldom ended in conquest. Very few princely houses of the middle ages were aggrandized by such means. That small and independent nobility, the counts and knights of the empire whom the revolutions of our own age have annihilated, stood through the storms of centuries with little diminution of their numbers. An incursion into the enemy's territory, a pitched battle, a siege, a treaty, are the general circumstances of the minor wars of the middle ages, as far as they appear in history. Before the invention of artillery, a strongly fortified castle or walled city was hardly reduced except by famine, which a besieging army, wasting improvidently its means of subsistence, was full as likely to feel. That invention altered the condition of society, and introduced an inequality of forces that rendered war more inevitably ruinous to the inferior party. Its first and most beneficial effect was to bring the plundering class of the nobility into control; their castles were more easily taken, and it became their interest to deserve

[71] Germani atque Alemanni, quibus census patrimonii ad victum suppetit, et hos qui procul urbibus, aut qui castellis et oppidulis dominantur, quorum magna pars latrocinio deditur, nobiles censent. (Pet. de Andlo. apud Schmidt, tome v, p. 490.)

[72] Quem cum officiatus suus inter-rogans, de quo castrum deberet retinere, cum annuis careret reditibus, dicitur respondisse ; Quatuor viæ sunt trans castrum situatæ. (Auctor apud Schmidt, p. 492.)

[73] Schmidt, tome iv, p. 116; tome v, pp. 338, 371; tome vi, p. 34; Putter, pp. 292, 348.

the protection of law. A few of these continued to follow their old profession after the Diet of Worms; but they were soon over-powered by the more efficient police established under Maxi-milian.

The next object of the Diet was to provide an effectual remedy for private wrongs which might supersede all pretence for taking up arms. The administration of justice had always been a high prerogative as well as bounden duty of the emperors. It was ex-ercised originally by themselves in person, or by the count pala-tine, the judge who always attended their court. In the provinces of Germany the dukes were intrusted with this duty; but, in order to control their influence, Otho the Great appointed provincial counts palatine, whose jurisdiction was in some respects exclu-sive of that still possessed by the dukes. As the latter became more independent of the empire, the provincial counts palatine lost the importance of their office, though their name may be traced to the twelfth and thirteenth centuries.[74] The ordinary adminis-tration of justice by the emperors went into disuse; in cases where states of the empire were concerned, it appertained to the Diet or to a special court of princes. The first attempt to re-establish an imperial tribunal was made by Frederick II in a Diet held at Mentz in 1235. A judge of the court was appointed to sit daily, with certain assessors, half nobles, half lawyers, and with juris-diction over all causes where princes of the empire were not con-cerned.[75] Rodolph of Hapsburg endeavoured to give efficacy to this judicature; but after his reign it underwent the fate of all those parts of the Germanic constitution which maintained the prerogatives of the emperors. Sigismund endeavoured to revive this tribunal; but as he did not render it permanent, nor fix the place of its sittings, it produced little other good than as it excited an earnest anxiety for a regular system. This system, delayed throughout the reign of Frederick III, was reserved for the first Diet of his son.[76]

The Imperial Chamber—such was the name of the new tri-bunal—consisted at its original institution of a chief judge, who was to be chosen among the princes or counts, and of sixteen assessors, partly of noble or equestrian rank, partly professors of law. They were named by the emperor with the approbation of the Diet. The functions of the Imperial Chamber were chiefly the two following. They exercised an appellant jurisdiction over causes that had been decided by the tribunals established in states of the empire. But their jurisdiction in private causes was merely appellant. According to the original law of Germany, no man could be sued except in the nation or province to which he be-

---

[74] Pfeffel, p. 180.
[75] Idem, p. 386; Schmidt, tome iv, p. 56.
[76] Pfeffel, tome ii, p. 66.

longed. The early emperors travelled from one part of their dominions to another in order to render justice consistently with
this fundamental privilege.   When the Luxemburg emperors
fixed their residence in Bohemia, the jurisdiction of the imperial
court in the first instance would have ceased of itself by the operation of this ancient rule.   It was not, however, strictly complied
with; and it is said that the emperors had a concurrent jurisdiction with the provincial tribunals even in private causes.   They
divested themselves, nevertheless, of this right by granting privileges de non evocando; so that no subject of a state which enjoyed such a privilege could be summoned into the imperial court.
All the electors possessed this exemption by the terms of the
Golden Bull; and it was specially granted to the burgraves of
Nuremberg and some other princes.   This matter was finally settled at the Diet of Worms; and the Imperial Chamber was positively restricted from taking cognizance of any causes in the first
instance, even where a state of the empire was one of the parties.
It was enacted, to obviate the denial of justice that appeared likely
to result from the regulation in the latter case, that every elector
and prince should establish a tribunal in his own dominions, where
suits against himself might be entertained.[77]

The second part of the chamber's jurisdiction related to disputes between two states of the empire.   But these two could
only come before it by way of appeal.   During the period of anarchy which preceded the establishment of its jurisdiction, a custom was introduced, in order to prevent the constant recurrence
of hostilities, of referring the quarrels of states to certain arbitrators called Austregues, chosen among states of the same rank.
This conventional reference became so popular that the princes
would not consent to abandon it on the institution of the Imperial
Chamber; but, on the contrary, it was changed into an invariable and universal law, that all disputes between different states
must, in the first instance, be submitted to the arbitration of
Austregues.[78]

The sentences of the chamber would have been very idly pronounced if means had not been devised to carry them into execution.   In earlier times the want of coercive process had been more
felt than that of actual jurisdiction.   For a few years after the
establishment of the chamber this deficiency was not supplied.
But in 1501 an institution, originally planned under Wenceslaus,
and attempted by Albert II, was carried into effect.   The empire,
with the exception of the electorates and the Austrian dominions,
was divided into six circles, each of which had its council of states,
its director whose province it was to convoke them, and its mili-

[77] Schmidt, tome v, p. 373; Putter, p. 372.
[78] Putter, p. 361; Pfeffel, p. 452.

tary force to compel obedience. In 1512 four more circles were added, comprehending those states which had been excluded in the first division. It was the business of the police of the circles to enforce the execution of sentences pronounced by the Imperial Chamber against refractory states of the empire.[79]

As the judges of the Imperial Chamber were appointed with the consent of the Diet, and held their sittings in a free imperial city, its establishment seemed rather to encroach on the ancient prerogatives of the emperors. Maximilian expressly reserved these in consenting to the new tribunal. And, in order to revive them, he soon afterward instituted an Aulic Council at Vienna, composed of judges appointed by himself, and under the political control of the Austrian government. Though some German patriots regarded this tribunal with jealousy, it continued until the dissolution of the empire. The Aulic Council had, in all cases, a concurrent jurisdiction with the Imperial Chamber; an exclusive one in feudal and some other causes. But it was equally confined to cases of appeal; and these, by multiplied privileges de non appellando, granted to the electoral and superior princely houses, were gradually reduced into moderate compass.[80]

The Germanic constitution may be reckoned complete, as to all its essential characteristics, in the reign of Maximilian. In later times, and especially by the Treaty of Westphalia, it underwent several modifications. Whatever might be its defects, and many of them seem to have been susceptible of reformation without destroying the system of government, it had one invaluable excellence: it protected the rights of the weaker against the stronger powers. The law of nations was first taught in Germany, and grew out of the public law of the empire. To narrow, as far as possible, the rights of war and of conquest, was a natural principle of those who belonged to petty states, and had nothing to tempt them in ambition. No revolution of our own eventful age, except the fall of the ancient French system of government, has been so extensive, or so likely to produce important consequences, as the spontaneous dissolution of the German Empire. Whether the new confederacy that has been substituted for that venerable constitution will be equally favourable to peace, justice, and liberty, is among the most interesting and difficult problems that can occupy a philosophical observer.[81]

At the accession of Conrad I Germany had by no means reached its present extent on the eastern frontier. Henry the Fowler and the Othos made great acquisitions upon that side. But tribes of Slavonian origin, generally called Venedic, or less properly Vandal, occupied the northern coast from the Elbe to the

[79] Putter, p. 355; tome ii, p. 100.
[80] Putter, p. 357; Pfeffel, p. 102.

[81] The first edition of this work was published early in 1818.

Vistula. These were independent, and formidable both to the Kings of Denmark and princes of Germany, till, in the reign of Frederick Barbarossa, two of the latter, Henry the Lion, Duke of Saxony, and Albert the Bear, Margrave of Brandenburg, subdued Mecklenburg and Pomerania, which afterward became duchies of the empire. Bohemia was undoubtedly subject, in a feudal sense, to Frederick I and his successors, though its connection with Germany was always slight. The emperors sometimes assumed a sovereignty over Denmark, Hungary, and Poland. But what they gained upon this quarter was compensated by the gradual separation of the Netherlands from their dominion, and by the still more complete loss of the kingdom of Arles. The house of Burgundy possessed most part of the former, and paid as little regard as possible to the imperial supremacy, though the German Diets in the reign of Maximilian still continued to treat the Netherlands as equally subject to their lawful control with the states on the right bank of the Rhine. But the provinces between the Rhône and the Alps were absolutely separated; Switzerland had completely succeeded in establishing her own independence; and the Kings of France no longer sought even the ceremony of an imperial investiture for Dauphiné and Provence.

Bohemia, which received the Christian faith in the tenth century, was elevated to the rank of a kingdom near the end of the twelfth. The dukes and Kings of Bohemia were feudally dependent upon the emperors, from whom they received investiture. They possessed, in return, a suffrage among the seven electors, and held one of the great offices in the imperial court. But separated by a rampart of mountains, by a difference of origin and language, and perhaps by national prejudices from Germany, the Bohemians withdrew as far as possible from the general politics of the confederacy. The kings obtained dispensations from attending the Diets of the empire, nor were they able to reinstate themselves in the privilege thus abandoned till the beginning of the last century.[82] The government of this kingdom, in a very slight degree partaking of the feudal character,[83] bore rather a resemblance to that of Poland; but the nobility were divided into two classes, the baronial and the equestrian, and the burghers formed a third state in the national Diet. For the peasantry, they were in a condition of servitude, or predial villenage. The royal authority was restrained by a coronation oath, by a permanent senate, and by frequent assemblies of the Diet, where a numerous and armed nobility appeared to secure their liberties by law or

[82] Pfeffel, tome ii, p. 497.
[83] Bona ipsorum totâ Bohemiâ pleraque omnia hæreditaria sunt seu alodialia, perpauca feudalia. (Stransky, " Resp. Bohemica," p. 392.) Stransky was a Bohemian Protestant, who fled to Holland after the subversion of the civil and religious liberties of his country by the fatal battle of Prague in 1621.

force.[84]   The sceptre passed, in ordinary times, to the nearest heir of the royal blood; but the right of election was only suspended and no King of Bohemia ventured to boast of it as his inheritance.[85]   This mixture of elective and hereditary monarchy was common, as we have seen, to most European kingdoms in their original constitution, though few continued so long to admit the participation of popular suffrages.

The reigning dynasty having become extinct in 1306, by the death of Wenceslaus, son of that Ottocar who, after extending his conquests to the Baltic Sea, and almost to the Adriatic, had lost his life in an unsuccessful contention with the Emperor Rodolph, the Bohemians chose John of Luxemburg, son of Henry VII.   Under the kings of this family in the fourteenth century, and especially Charles IV, whose character appeared in a far more advantageous light in his native domains than in the empire, Bohemia imbibed some portion of refinement and science.[86]   A university erected by Charles at Prague became one of the most celebrated in Europe.   John Huss, rector of the university, who had distinguished himself by opposition to many abuses then prevailing in the Church, repaired to the Council of Constance, under a safe-conduct from the Emperor Sigismund.   In violation of this pledge, to the indelible infamy of that prince and of the council, he was condemned to be burned; and his disciple, Jerome of Prague, underwent afterward the same fate.   His countrymen, aroused by this atrocity, flew to arms.   They found at their head one of those extraordinary men whose genius, created by nature and called into action by fortuitous events, appears to borrow no reflected light from that of others.   John Ziska had not been trained in any school which could have initiated him in the science of war; that indeed, except in Italy, was still rude, and nowhere more so than in Bohemia.   But, self-taught, he became one of the greatest captains who had appeared hitherto in Europe.   It renders his exploits more marvellous that he was totally deprived of sight.   Ziska has been called the inventor of the modern art of fortification; the famous mountain near Prague, fanatically called Tabor, became by his skill an impregnable intrenchment.   For his stratagems he has been compared to Hannibal.   In battle, being destitute of cavalry, he disposed at intervals ramparts of carriages filled with soldiers, to defend his troops from the enemy's horse.   His own station was by the chief standard, where,

[84] Dubravius, the Bohemian historian, relates (lib. xviii) that, the kingdom having no written laws, Wenceslaus, one of the kings, about the year 1300, sent for an Italian lawyer to compile a code. But the nobility refused to consent to this, aware, probably, of the consequences of letting in the prerogative doctrines of the civilians. They opposed, at the same time, the institution of a university at Prague; which, however, took place afterward under Charles IV.

[85] Stransky, " Resp. Bohem."; Coxe's " House of Austria," p. 487.
[86] Schmidt; Coxe.

after hearing the circumstances of the situation explained, he gave his orders for the disposition of the army. Ziska was never defeated; and his genius inspired the Hussites with such enthusiastic affection, that some of those who had served under him refused to obey any other general, and denominated themselves Orphans in commemoration of his loss. He was indeed a ferocious enemy, though some of his cruelties might, perhaps, be extenuated by the law of retaliation; but to his soldiers affable and generous, dividing among them all the spoil.[87]

Even during the lifetime of Ziska the Hussite sect was disunited, the citizens of Prague and many of the nobility contenting themselves with moderate demands, while the Taborites, his peculiar followers, were actuated by a most fanatical frenzy. The former took the name of Calixtins, from their retention of the sacramental cup, of which the priests had latterly thought fit to debar laymen; an abuse so totally without pretence or apology that nothing less than the determined obstinancy of the Romish Church could have maintained it to this time. The Taborites, though no longer led by Ziska, gained some remarkable victories, but were at last wholly defeated, while the Catholic and Calixtin parties came to an accommodation by which Sigismund was acknowledged as King of Bohemia, which he had claimed by the title of heir to his brother Wenceslaus, and a few indulgences, especially the use of the sacramental cup, conceded to the moderate Hussites. But this compact, though concluded by the Council of Basle, being ill observed, through the perfidious bigotry of the See of Rome, the reformers armed again to defend their religious liberties, and ultimately elected a nobleman of their own party, by name George Podiebrad, to the throne of Bohemia, which he maintained during his life with great vigour and prudence.[88] Upon his death they chose Uladislaus, son of Casimir, King of Poland, who afterward obtained also the kingdom of Hungary. Both these crowns were conferred on his son Louis, after whose death, in the unfortunate battle of Mohacz, Ferdinand of Austria became sovereign of the two kingdoms.

The Hungarians, that terrible people who laid waste the Italian and German provinces of the empire in the tenth century, became proselytes soon afterward to the religion of Europe, and their sovereign, St. Stephen, was admitted by the Pope into the list of Christian kings. Though the Hungarians were of a race perfectly distinct from either the Gothic or the Slavonian tribes, their system of government was in a great measure analogous. None indeed could be more natural to rude nations who had but recently accustomed themselves to settled possessions, than a ter-

[87] Lenfant, " Hist. de la Guerre des Hussites "; Schmidt; Coxe.
[88] Lenfant; Schmidt; Coxe.

ritorial aristocracy, jealous of unlimited or even hereditary power in their chieftain, and subjugating the inferior people to that servitude which, in such a state of society, is the unavoidable consequences of poverty.

The marriage of a Hungarian princess with Charles II, King of Naples, eventually connected her country far more·than it had been with the affairs of Italy. I have mentioned in a different place the circumstances which led to the invasion of Naples by Louis, King of Hungary, and the wars of that powerful monarch with Venice. By marrying the eldest daughter of Louis, Sigismund, afterward emperor, acquired the crown of Hungary, which upon her death without issue he retained in his own right, and was even able to transmit to the child of a second marriage, and to her husband Albert, Duke of Austria. From this commencement is deduced the connection between Hungary and Austria. In two years, however, Albert, dying, left his widow pregnant; but the states of Hungary, jealous of Austrian influence, and of the intrigues of a minority, without waiting for her delivery, bestowed the crown upon Uladislaus, King of Poland. The birth of Albert's posthumous son Ladislaus produced an opposition in behalf of the infant's right; but the Austrian party turned out the weaker, and Uladislaus, after a civil war of some duration, became undisputed king. Meanwhile a more formidable enemy drew near. The Turkish arms had subdued all Servia, and excited a just alarm throughout Christendom. Uladislaus led a considerable force, to which the presence of the Cardinal Julian gave the appearance of a crusade, into Bulgaria, and, after several successes, concluded an honourable treaty with Amurath II. But this he was unhappily persuaded to violate, at the instigation of the cardinal, who abhorred the impiety of keeping faith with infidels.[89] Heaven judged of this otherwise, if the judgment of Heaven was pronounced upon the field of Warna. In that fatal battle Uladislaus was killed, and the Hungarians' utterly routed. The crown was now permitted to rest on the head of young Ladislaus; but the regency was allotted by the states of Hungary to a native warrior, John Hunniades.[90] This hero stood in the

[89] Æneas Sylvius lays this perfidy on Pope Eugenius IV. Scripsit cardinali, nullum valere fœdus, quod *se inconsulto* cum hostibus religionis percussum esset, (p. 397). The words in italics are slipped in, to give a slight pretext for breaking the treaty.

[90] Hunniades was a Wallachian, of a small family. The Poles charged him with cowardice at Warna. (Æneas Sylvius, p. 398.) And the Greeks impute the same to him, or at least desertion of his troops, at Cossova, where he was defeated in 1448. (Spondanus, ad ann. 1448.) Probably he was one of those

prudently brave men who, when victory is out of their power, reserve themselves to fight another day; which is the character of all partisans accustomed to desultory warfare. This is the apology made for him by Æneas Sylvius: fortasse rei militaris perito nulla in pugnā salus visa, et salvare aliquos quàm omnes perire maluit. Poloni acceptam eo prælio cladem Hunniadis vecordiæ atque ignaviæ tradiderunt; ipse sua concilia spreta conquestus est. I observe that all the writers upon Hungarian affairs have a party bias one way or other. The best and most authentic account of Hunniades seems to

breach for twelve years against the Turkish power, frequently defeated but unconquered in defeat. If the renown of Hunniades may seem exaggerated by the partiality of writers who lived under the reign of his son, it is confirmed by more unequivocal evidence, by the dread and hatred of the Turks, whose children were taught obedience by threatening them with his name, and by the deference of a jealous aristocracy to a man of no distinguished birth. He surrendered to young Ladislaus a trust that he had exercised with perfect fidelity; but his merit was too great to be forgiven, and the court never treated him with cordiality. The last and the most splendid service of Hunniades was the relief of Belgrade. That strong city was besieged by Mohammed II three years after the fall of Constantinople; its capture would have laid open all Hungary. A tumultuary army, chiefly collected by the preaching of a friar, was intrusted to Hunniades: he penetrated into the city, and, having repulsed the Turks in a fortunate sally wherein Mohammed was wounded, had the honour of compelling him to raise the siege in confusion. The relief of Belgrade was more important in its effect than in its immediate circumstances. It revived the spirits of Europe, which had been appalled by the unceasing victories of the infidels. Mohammed himself seemed to acknowledge the importance of the blow, and seldom afterward attacked the Hungarians. Hunniades died soon after this achievement, and was followed by the King Ladislaus.[91] The states of Hungary, although the Emperor Frederick III had secured to himself, as he thought, the reversion, were justly averse to his character, and to Austrian connections. They conferred their crown on Matthias Corvinus, son of their great Hunniades. This prince reigned above thirty years with considerable reputation, to which his patronage of learned men, who repaid his munificence with very profuse eulogies, did not a little contribute.[92] Hungary, at least in his time, was undoubtedly formidable to her neighbours, and held a respectable rank as an independent power in the republic of Europe.

The kingdom of Burgundy or Arles comprehended the whole mountainous region which we now call Switzerland. It was ac-

be, still allowing for this partiality, in the chronicle of John Thwrocz, who lived under Matthias. Bonfinius, an Italian compiler of the same age, has amplified this original authority in his three decades of Hungarian history.

[91] Ladislaus died at Prague, at the age of twenty-two, with great suspicion of poison, which fell chiefly on George Podiebrad and the Bohemians. Æneas Sylvius was with him at the time, and in a letter written immediately after plainly hints this; and his manner carries with it more persuasion than if he had spoken out. (Epist. 324.) Mr. Coxe, however, informs us that the Bohemian historians have fully disproved the charge.

[92] Spondanus frequently blames the Italians, who received pensions from Matthias, or wrote at his court, for exaggerating his virtues, or dissembling his misfortunes. And this was probably the case. However, Spondanus has rather contracted a prejudice against the Corvini. A treatise of Galeotus Martius, an Italian littérateur, De dictis et factis Mathiæ, though it often notices an ordinary saying as jocosè or facetè dictum, gives a favourable impression of Matthias's ability, and also of his integrity.

cordingly reunited to the Germanic Empire by the bequest of Rodolph along with the rest of his dominions.   A numerous and
ancient nobility, vassals one to another or to the empire, divided
the possession with ecclesiastical lords hardly less powerful than
themselves.   Of the former we find the Counts of Zahringen, Kyburg, Hapsburg, and Tokenburg most conspicuous; of the latter,
the Bishop of Coire, the Abbot of St. Gall, and Abbess of Seck-
ingen.   Every variety of feudal rights was early found and long
preserved in Helvetia; nor is there any country whose history
better illustrates that ambiguous relation, half property and half
dominion, in which the territorial aristocracy, under the feudal
system, stood with respect to their dependents.   In the twelfth
century the Swiss towns rise into some degree of importance.
Zurich was eminent for commercial activity, and seems to have
had no lord but the emperor.   Basle, though subject to its bishop,
possessed the usual privileges of municipal government.   Berne
and Freiburg, founded only in that century, made a rapid progress,
and the latter was raised, along with Zurich, by Frederick II in
1218, to the rank of a free imperial city.   Several changes in the
principal Helvetian families took place in the thirteenth century,
before the end of which the house of Hapsburg, under the politic
and enterprising Rodolph and his son Albert, became possessed
through various titles of a great ascendency in Switzerland.[93]
   Of these titles none was more tempting to an ambitious chief
than that of advocate to a convent.   That specious name conveyed
with it a kind of indefinite guardianship and right of interference
which frequently ended in reversing the conditions of the ecclesiastical sovereign and its vassal.   But during times of feudal anarchy there was perhaps no other means to secure the rich abbeys
from absolute spoliation; and the free cities in their early stage
sometimes adopted the same policy.   Among other advocacies,
Albert obtained that of some convents which had estates in the
valleys of Schweitz and Underwald.   These sequestered regions
in the heart of the Alps had been for ages the habitation of a
pastoral race, so happily forgotten or so inaccessible in their fastnesses as to have acquired a virtual independence, regulating their
own affairs in their general assembly with a perfect equality,
though they acknowledged the sovereignty of the empire.[94]   The
people of Schweitz had made Rodolph their advocate.   They distrusted Albert, whose succession to his father's inheritance spread
alarm through Helvetia.   It soon appeared that their suspicions
were well founded.   Besides the local rights which his ecclesiastical advocacies gave him over part of the forest cantons, he pretended, after his election to the empire, to send imperial bailiffs

into their valleys as administrators of criminal justice. Their oppression of a people unused to control, whom it was plainly the design of Albert to reduce into servitude, excited those generous emotions of resentment which a brave and simple race have seldom the discretion to repress. Three men—Stauffacher of Schweitz, Furst of Uri, Melchthal of Underwald—each with ten chosen associates, met by night in a sequestered field, and swore to assert the common cause of their liberties, without bloodshed or injury to the rights of others. Their success was answerable to the justice of their undertaking; the three cantons unanimously took up arms, and expelled their oppressors without a contest. Albert's assassination by his nephew, which followed soon afterward, fortunately gave them leisure to consolidate their union.[95] He was succeeded in the empire by Henry VII, jealous of the Austrian family, and not at all displeased at proceedings which had been accompanied with so little violence or disrespect for the empire. But Leopold, Duke of Austria, resolved to humble the peasants who had rebelled against his father, led a considerable force into their country. The Swiss, commending themselves to Heaven, and determined rather to perish than undergo that yoke a second time, though ignorant of regular discipline, and unprovided with defensive armour, utterly discomfited the assailants at Morgarten.[96]

This great victory, the Marathon of Switzerland, confirmed the independence of the three original cantons. After some years, Lucerne, contiguous in situation and alike in interests, was incorporated into their confederacy. It was far more materially enlarged about the middle of the fourteenth century by the accession of Zurich, Glaris, Zug, and Berne, all which took place within two years. The first and last of these cities had already been engaged in frequent wars with the Helvetian nobility, and their internal polity was altogether republican.[97] They acquired, not independence, which they already enjoyed, but additional security, by this union with the Swiss, properly so called, who in deference to their power and reputation ceded to them the first rank in the league. The eight already enumerated are called the ancient cantons, and continued, till the late reformation of the Helvetic system, to possess several distinctive privileges and even rights of sovereignty over subject territories, in which the five cantons of Freiburg, Soleure, Basle, Schaffhausen, and Appenzell did not participate. From this time the united cantons, but especially those of Berne and Zurich, began to extend their territories at the expense of the rural nobility. The same contest between these parties, with the same termination which we know generally to have taken place in Lombardy during the eleventh and twelfth centuries, may be

[95] Planta, c. 6.   [96] Id., c. 7.   [97] Id., chaps. 8, 9.

traced with more minuteness in the annals of Switzerland.[98]
Like the Lombards, too, the Helvetic cities acted with policy and
moderation toward the nobles whom they overcame, admitting
them to the franchises of their community as co-burghers (a
privilege which virtually implied a defensive alliance against any
assailant), and uniformly respecting the legal rights of property.
Many feudal superiorities they obtained from the owners in a
more peaceable manner, through purchase or mortgage.   Thus
the house of Austria, to which the extensive domains of the
Counts of Kyburg had devolved, abandoning, after repeated de-
feats, its hopes of subduing the forest cantons, alienated a great
part of its possessions to Zurich and Berne.[99]   And the last remnant of their ancient Helvetic territories in Argovia was wrested
in 1417 from Frederick, Count of Tyrol, who, imprudently supporting Pope John XXIII against the Council of Constance, had
been put to the ban of the empire.   These conquests Berne could
not be induced to restore, and thus completed the independence
of the confederate republics.[100]   The other free cities, though not
yet incorporated, and the few remaining nobles, whether lay or
spiritual, of whom the Abbot of St. Gaul was the principal, entered into separate leagues with different cantons.   Switzerland
became, therefore, in the first part of the fifteenth century a free
country, acknowledged as such by neighbouring states, and subject to no external control, though still comprehended within the
nominal sovereignty of the empire.

The affairs of Switzerland occupy a very small space in the
great chart of European history.   But in some respects they are
more interesting than the revolutions of mighty kingdoms.   Nowhere besides do we find so many titles to our sympathy, or the
union of so much virtue with so complete success.   In the Italian
republics a more splendid temple may seem to have been erected
to liberty, but, as we approach, the serpents of faction hiss around
her altar, and the form of tyranny flits among the distant shadows
behind the shrine.   Switzerland, not absolutely blameless (for what
republic has been so?) but comparatively exempt from turbulence, usurpation, and injustice, has well deserved to employ the
native pen of a historian accounted the most eloquent of the last
age.[101]   Other nations displayed an insuperable resolution in the

---

[98] Planta, c. 10.
[99] Id., c. 11.
[100] Id., vol. ii, c. 1.
[101] I am unacquainted with Muller's
history in the original language; but,
presuming the first volume of Mr. Planta's " History of the Helvetic Confederacy " to be a free translation or abridgment of it, I can well conceive that it
deserves the encomiums of Madame de
Staël and other foreign critics.   It is very
rare to meet with such picturesque and
lively delineation in a modern historian of
distant times.   But I must observe that,
if the authentic chronicles of Switzerland
have enabled Müller to embellish his narration with so much circumstantial detail, he has been remarkably fortunate
in his authorities.   No man could write
the annals of England or France in the
fourteenth century with such particularity if he was scrupulous not to fill up

defence of walled towns; but the steadiness of the Swiss in the field of battle was without a parallel, unless we recall the memory of Lacedæmon. It was even established as a law, that whoever returned from battle after a defeat should forfeit his life by the hands of the executioner. Sixteen hundred men, who had been sent to oppose a predatory invasion of the French in 1444, though they might have retreated without loss, determined rather to perish on the spot, and fell amid a far greater heap of the hostile slain.[102] At the famous battle of Sempach, in 1385, the last which Austria presumed to try against the foreign cantons, the enemy's knights, dismounted from their horses, presented an impregnable barrier of lances, which disconcerted the Swiss, till Winkelried, a gentleman of Underwald, commending his wife and children to his countrymen, threw himself upon the opposite ranks, and, collecting as many lances as he could grasp, forced a passage for his followers by burying them in his bosom.[103]

The burghers and peasants of Switzerland, ill provided with cavalry, and better able to dispense with it than the natives of champaign countries, may be deemed the principal restorers of the Greek and Roman tactics, which place the strength of armies in a steady mass of infantry. Besides their splendid victories over the Dukes of Austria and their own neighbouring nobility, they had repulsed, in the year 1375, one of those predatory bodies of troops, the scourge of Europe in that age, and to whose licentiousness kingdoms and free states yielded alike a passive submission. They gave the dauphin, afterward Louis XI, who entered their country in 1444 with a similar body of ruffians called Armagnacs, the disbanded mercenaries of the English war, sufficient reason to desist from his invasion and to respect their valour. That able prince formed indeed so high a notion of the Swiss that he sedulously cultivated their alliance during the rest of his life. He was made abundantly sensible of the wisdom of this policy when he saw his greatest enemy, the Duke of Burgundy, routed at Granson and Morat, and his affairs irrecoverably ruined, by these hardy republicans. The ensuing age is the most conspicuous, though not the most essentially glorious, in the history of Switzerland. Courted for the excellence of their troops by the rival sovereigns of Europe, and themselves too sensible both to ambitious schemes of dominion and to the thirst of money, the united cantons came to play a very prominent part in the wars of Lombardy, with great military renown, but not without some impeachment of that sterling probity which had distinguished their earlier efforts for independence. These events, however, do not fall within my lim-

---

the meagre sketch of chroniclers from the stores of his invention. The striking scenery of Switzerland, and Müller's exact acquaintance with it, have given him another advantage as a painter of history.

[102] Planta, vol. ii, c. 2.
[103] Id., vol. i, c. 10.

its; but the last year of the fifteenth century is a leading epoch, with which I shall close this sketch. Though the house of Austria had ceased to menace the liberties of Helvetia, and had even been for many years its ally, the Emperor Maximilian, aware of the important service he might derive from the cantons in his projects upon Italy, as well as of the disadvantage he sustained by their partiality to French interest, endeavoured to revive the unextinguished supremacy of the empire. That supremacy had just been restored in Germany by the establishment of the Imperial Chamber, and of a regular pecuniary contribution for its support as well as for other purposes, in the Diet of Worms. The Helvetic cantons were summoned to yield obedience to these imperial laws; an innovation, for such the revival of obsolete prerogatives must be considered, exceedingly hostile to their republican independence, and involving consequences not less material in their eyes, the abandonment of a line of policy, which tended to enrich if not to aggrandize them. Their refusal to comply brought on a war, wherein the Tyrolese subjects of Maximilian, and the Swabian league, a confederacy of cities in that province lately formed under the emperor's auspices, were principally engaged against the Swiss. But the success of the latter was decisive; and after a terrible devastation of the frontiers of Germany, peace was concluded upon terms very honourable for Switzerland. The cantons were declared free from the jurisdiction of the Imperial Chamber, and from all contributions imposed by the Diet. Their right to enter into foreign alliance, even hostile to the empire, if it was not expressly recognised, continued unimpaired in practice; nor am I aware that they were at any time afterward supposed to incur the crime of rebellion by such proceedings. Though, perhaps, in the strictest letter of public law, the Swiss cantons were not absolutely released from their subjection to the empire until the Treaty of Westphalia, their real sovereignty must be dated by an historian from the year when every prerogative which a government can exercise was finally abandoned.[104]

[104] Planta, vol. ii, c. 4.

CHAPTER VI

THE GREEKS AND SARACENS

Rise of Mohammedism—Causes of its success—Progress of Saracen arms—Greek Empire—Decline of the Khalifs—The Greeks recover part of their losses—The Turks—The crusades—Capture of Constantinople by the Latins—Its recovery by the Greeks—The Moguls—The Ottomans—Danger at Constantinople—Timur—Capture of Constantinople by Mohammed II—Alarm of Europe.

THE difficulty which occurs to us in endeavouring to fix a natural commencement of modern history even in the western countries of Europe is much enhanced when we direct our attention to the Eastern Empire. In tracing the long series of the Byzantine annals we never lose sight of antiquity; the Greek language, the Roman name, the titles, the laws, all the shadowy circumstance of ancient greatness, attend us throughout the progress from the first to the last of the Constantines; and it is only when we observe the external condition and relations of their empire that we perceive ourselves to be embarked in a new sea, and are compelled to deduce, from points of bearing to the history of other nations, a line of separation which the domestic revolutions of Constantinople would not satisfactorily afford. The appearance of Mohammed, and the conquests of his disciples, present an epoch in the history of Asia still more important and more definite than the subversion of the Roman Empire in Europe; and hence the boundary line between the ancient and modern divisions of Byzantine history will intersect the reign of Heraclius. That prince may be said to have stood on the verge of both hemispheres of time, whose youth was crowned with the last victories over the successors of Artaxerxes, and whose age was clouded by the first calamities of Mohammedan invasion.

Of all the revolutions which have had a permanent influence upon the civil history of mankind, none could so little be anticipated by human prudence as that effected by the religion of Arabia. As the seeds of invisible disease grow up sometimes in silence to maturity, till they manifest themselves hopeless and irresistible, the gradual propagation of a new faith in a barbarous country beyond the limits of the empire was hardly known perhaps, and certainly disregarded, in the court of Constantinople. Arabia, in the age of Mohammed, was divided into many small states, most of which, however, seem to have looked up to Mecca as the capital of their nation and the chief seat of their religious worship. The capture of that city, accordingly, and the subjugation of its powerful and numerous aristocracy, readily drew after it the submission of the minor tribes, who transferred to the conqueror the reverence they were used to show to those he had subdued. If we consider Mohammed only as a military usurper, there is nothing more explicable or more analogous, especially to the course of Oriental history, than his success. But as the author of a religious imposture, upon which, though avowedly unattested by miraculous powers, and though originally discountenanced by the civil magistrate, he had the boldness to found a scheme of universal dominion, which his followers were half enabled to realize, it is a curious speculation by what means he could inspire so sincere, so ardent, so energetic, and so permanent a belief.

A full explanation of the causes which contributed to the progress of Mohammedism is not perhaps, at present, attainable by those most conversant with this department of literature.[1] But we may point out several of leading importance: In the first place, those just and elevated notions of the divine nature and of moral duties, the gold ore that pervades the dross of the Koran, which were calculated to strike a serious and reflecting people, already perhaps disinclined, by intermixture with their Jewish and Christian fellow-citizens, to the superstitions of their ancient idolatry;[2] next, the artful incorporation of tenets, usages, and traditions from the various religions that existed in Arabia;[3] and, thirdly, the extensive application of the pre-

[1] We are very destitute of satisfactory materials for the history of Mohammed himself. Abulfeda, the most judicious of his biographers, lived in the fourteenth century, when it must have been morally impossible to discriminate the truth amid the torrent of fabulous tradition. Al Jannabi, whom Gagnier translated, is a mere legend writer; it would be as rational to rely on the "Acta Sanctorum" as his romance. It is therefore difficult to ascertain the real character of the Prophet, except as it is deducible from the Koran.

[2] The very curious romance of Antar, written, perhaps, before the appearance of Mohammed, seems to render it probable that, however idolatry, as we are told by Sale, might prevail in some parts of Arabia, yet the genuine religion of the descendants of Ishmael was a belief in the unity of God as strict as is laid down in the Koran itself, and accompanied by the same antipathy, partly religious, partly national, toward the fire-worshippers which Mohammed inculcated. This corroborates what I had said in the text before the publication of that work.

[3] I am very much disposed to believe, notwithstanding what seems to be the general opinion, that Mohammed had never read any part of the New Testament. His knowledge of Christianity appears to be wholly derived from the apocryphal gospels and similar works. He admitted the miraculous conception and prophetic character of Jesus, but not his divinity or pre-existence. Hence it is rather surprising to read, in a popular book of sermons by a living prelate, that all the heresies of the Christian Church (I quote the substance from memory) are to be found in the Koran, but especially that of Arianism. No one who

cepts in the Koran, a book confessedly written with much elegance and purity, to all legal transactions and all the business of life. It may be expected that I should add to these what is commonly considered as a distinguishing mark of Mohammedism, its indulgence to voluptuousness. But this appears to be greatly exaggerated. Although the character of its founder may have been tainted by sensuality as well as ferociousness, I do not think that he relied upon inducements of the former kind for the diffusion of his system. We are not to judge of this by rules of Christian purity or of European practice. If polygamy was a prevailing usage in Arabia, as is not questioned, its permission gave no additional license to the proselytes of Mohammed, who will be found rather to have narrowed the unbounded liberty of Oriental manners in this respect; while his decided condemnation of adultery, and of incestuous connection, so frequent among barbarous nations, does not argue a very lax and accommodating morality. A devout Mussulman exhibits much more of the Stoical than the Epicurean character. Nor can any one read the Koran without being sensible that it breathes an austere and scrupulous spirit. And, in fact, the founder of a new religion or sect is little likely to obtain permanent success by indulging the vices and luxuries of mankind. I should rather be disposed to reckon the severity of Mohammed's discipline among the causes of its influence. Precepts of ritual observance, being always definite and unequivocal, are less likely to be neglected, after their obligation has been acknowledged, than those of moral virtue. Thus the long fasting, the pilgrimages, the regular prayers and ablutions, the constant alms-giving, the abstinence from stimulating liquors, enjoined by the Koran, created a visible standard of practice among its followers, and preserved a continual recollection of their law.

But the prevalence of Islam in the lifetime of its prophet, and during the first ages of its existence, was chiefly owing to the spirit of martial energy that he infused into it. The religion of Mohammed is as essentially a military system as the institution of chivalry in the west of Europe. The people of Arabia, a race of strong passions and sanguinary temper, inured to habits of pillage and murder, found in the law of their native prophet not a license, but a command, to desolate the world, and the promise of all that their glowing imaginations could anticipate

knows what Arianism is, and what Mohammedism is, could possibly fall into so strange an error. The misfortune has been that the learned writer, while accumulating a mass of reading upon this part of his subject, neglected what should have been the nucelus of the whole, a perusal of the single book which contains the doctrine of the Arabian impostor. In this strange chimera about the Arianism of Mohammed, he has been led away by a misplaced trust in Whitaker; a writer almost invariably in the wrong, and whose bad reasoning upon all the points of historical criticism which he attempted to discuss is quite notorious.

of paradise annexed to all in which they most delighted upon earth. It is difficult for us in the calmness of our closets to conceive that feverish intensity of excitement to which man may be wrought, when the animal and intellectual energies of his nature converge to a point, and the buoyancy of strength and courage reciprocates the influence of moral sentiment or religious hope. The effect of this union I have formerly remarked in the crusades; a phenomenon perfectly analogous to the early history of the Saracens. In each, one hardly knows whether most to admire the prodigious exertions of heroism or to revolt from the ferocious bigotry that attended them. But the crusades were a temporary effort, not thoroughly congenial to the spirit of Christendom, which, even in the darkest and most superstitious ages, was not susceptible of the solitary and overruling fanaticism of the Moslem. They needed no excitement from pontiffs and preachers to achieve the work to which they were called; the precept was in their law, the principle was in their hearts, the assurance of success was in their swords. " O Prophet! " exclaimed Ali, when Mohammed, in the first years of his mission, sought among the scanty and hesitating assembly of his friends a vizier and lieutenant in command, " I am the man; whoever rises against thee, I will dash out his teeth, tear out his eyes, break his legs, rip up his belly. O Prophet! I will be thy vizier over them." [4] These words of Mohammed's early and illustrious disciple are, as it were, a text, upon which the commentary expands into the whole Saracenic history. They contain the vital essence of his religion, implicit faith and ferocious energy. Death, slavery, tribute to unbelievers, were the glad tidings of the Arabian Prophet. To the idolaters, indeed, or those who acknowledged no special revelation, one alternative only was proposed—conversion or the sword. The people of the book, as they are termed in the Koran, or four sects of Christians, Jews, Magians, and Sabians, were permitted to redeem their adherence to their ancient law by the payment of tribute, and other marks of humiliation and servitude. But the limits which Mohammedan intolerance had prescribed to itself were seldom transgressed; the word pledged to unbelievers was seldom forfeited; and with all their insolence and oppression, the Moslem conquerors were mild and liberal in comparison with those who obeyed the pontiffs of Rome or Constantinople.

At the death of Mohammed, in 632, his temporal and religious sovereignty embraced and was limited by the Arabian peninsula. The Roman and Persian Empires, engaged in tedious and indecisive hostility upon the rivers of Mesopotamia and the Armenian mountains, were viewed by the ambitious fanatics of

[4] Gibbon, vol. ix, p. 284.

his creed as their quarry. In the very first year of Mohammed's immediate successor, Abubeker, each of these mighty empires was invaded. The latter opposed but a short resistance. The crumbling fabric of Eastern despotism is never secure against rapid and total subversion; a few victories, a few sieges, carried the Arabian arms from the Tigris to the Oxus, and overthrew, with the Sassanian dynasty, the ancient and famous religion they had professed. Seven years of active and unceasing warfare sufficed to subjugate the rich province of Syria, though defended by numerous armies and fortified cities; and the Khalif Omar had scarcely returned thanks for the accomplishment of this conquest when Amrou, his lieutenant, announced to him the entire reduction of Egypt. After some interval the Saracens won their way along the coast of Africa as far as the Pillars of Hercules, and a third province was irretrievably torn from the Greek Empire. These Western conquests introduced them to fresh enemies, and ushered in more splendid successes; encouraged by the disunion of the Visigoths, and perhaps invited by treachery, Musa, the general of a master who sat beyond the opposite extremity of the Mediterranean Sea, passed over into Spain, and within about two years the name of Mohammed was invoked under the Pyrenees.[5]

These conquests, which astonish the careless and superficial, are less perplexing to a calm inquirer than their cessation; the loss of half the Roman Empire than the preservation of the rest. A glance from Medina to Constantinople in the middle of the seventh century would probably have induced an indifferent spectator, if such a being may be imagined, to anticipate by eight hundred years the establishment of a Mohammedan dominion upon the shores of the Hellespont. The fame of Heraclius had withered in the Syrian war, and his successors appeared as incapable to resist as they were unworthy to govern. Their despotism, unchecked by law, was often punished by successful rebellion; but not a whisper of civil liberty was ever heard, and the vicissitudes of servitude and anarchy consummated the moral degeneracy of the nation. Less ignorant than the Western barbarians, the Greeks abused their ingenuity in theological controversies, those especially which related to the nature and incarnation of our Saviour; wherein the disputants, as is usual, became more positive and rancorous as their creed receded from

[5] Ockley's " History of the Saracens "; Cardonne, " Révolutions de l'Afrique et de l'Espagne." The former of these works is well known and justly admired for its simplicity and picturesque details. Scarcely any narrative has ever excelled in beauty that of the death of Hossein. But these do not tend to render it more deserving of confidence. On the contrary, it may be laid down as a pretty general rule that circumstantiality, which enhances the credibility of a witness, diminishes that of a historian remote in time or situation. And I observe that Reiske, in his preface to Abulfeda, speaks of Wakidi, from whom Ockley's book is but a translation, as a mere fabulist.

the possibility of human apprehension. Nor were these confined to the clergy, who had not, in the East, obtained the prerogative of guiding the national faith; the sovereigns sided alternately with opposing factions; Heraclius was not too brave, nor Theodora too infamous, for discussions of theology; and the dissenters from an imperial decision were involved in the double proscription of treason and heresy. But the persecutors of their opponents at home pretended to cowardly scrupulousness in the field; nor was the Greek Church ashamed to require the lustration of a canonical penance from the soldier who shed the blood of his enemies in a national war.

But this depraved people were preserved from destruction by the vices of their enemies, still more than by some intrinsic resources which they yet possessed. A rapid degeneracy enfeebled the victorious Moslem in their career. That irresistible enthusiasm, that earnest and disinterested zeal of the companions of Mohammed, was in a great measure lost even before the first generation had passed away. In the fruitful valleys of Damascus and Bassora the Arabs of the desert forgot their abstemious habits. Rich from the tributes of an enslaved people, the Mohammedan sovereigns knew no employment of riches but in sensual luxury, and paid the price of voluptuous indulgence in the relaxation of their strength and energy. Under the reign of Moawiah, the fifth khalif, an hereditary succession was substituted for the free choice of the faithful, by which the first representatives of the Prophet had been elevated to power; and this regulation, necessary as it plainly was to avert in some degree the dangers of schism and civil war, exposed the kingdom to the certainty of being often governed by feeble tyrants. But no regulation could be more than a temporary preservative against civil war. The dissensions which still separate and render hostile the followers of Mohammed may be traced to the first events that ensued upon his death, to the rejection of his son-in-law Ali by the electors of Medina. Two reigns, those of Abubeker and Omar, passed in external glory and domestic reverence; but the old age of Othman was weak and imprudent, and the conspirators against him established the first among a hundred precedents of rebellion and regicide. Ali was now chosen; but a strong faction disputed his right; and the Saracen Empire was for many years distracted with civil war, among competitors who appealed in reality to no other decision than that of the sword. The family of Ommiyah succeeded at last in establishing an unresisted, if not an undoubted, title. But rebellions were perpetually afterward breaking out in that vast extent of dominion, till one of these revolters acquired by success a better name than rebel, and founded the dynasty of the Abbassides.

Damascus had been the seat of empire under the Ommiades; it was removed by the succeeding family to their new city of Bagdad. There are not any names in the long line of khalifs, after the companions of Mohammed, more renowned in history than some of the earlier sovereigns who reigned in this capital— Almansor, Haroun Alraschid, and Almamùn. Their splendid palaces, their numerous guards, their treasures of gold and silver, the populousness and wealth of their cities, formed a striking contrast to the rudeness and poverty of the Western nations in the same age. In their court learning, which the first Moslem had despised as unwarlike or rejected as profane, was held in honour.[6] The Khalif Almamùn especially was distinguished for his patronage of letters; the philosophical writings of Greece were eagerly sought and translated; the stars were numbered, the course of the planets was measured. The Arabians improved upon the science they borrowed, and returned it with abundant interest to Europe in the communication of numeral figures and the intellectual language of algebra.[7] Yet the merit of the Abbassides has been exaggerated by adulation or gratitude. After all the vague praises of hireling poets, which have sometimes been repeated in Europe, it is very rare to read the history of an Eastern sovereign unstained by atrocious crimes. No Christian government, except, perhaps, that of Constantinople, exhibits such a series of tyrants as the Khalifs of Bagdad; if deeds of blood, wrought through unbridled passion or jealous policy, may challenge the name of tyranny. These are ill redeemed by ceremonious devotion and acts of trifling, perhaps ostentatious, humility, or even by the best attribute of Mohammedan princes —a rigorous justice in chastising the offences of others. Anecdotes of this description give as imperfect a sketch of an Oriental sovereign as monkish chroniclers sometimes draw of one in Europe who founded monasteries and obeyed the clergy, though it must be owned that the former are in much better taste.

Though the Abbassides have acquired more celebrity, they never attained the real strength of their predecessors. Under the last of the house of Ommiyah, one command was obeyed almost along the whole diameter of the known world, from the banks of the Sihon to the utmost promontory of Portugal. But the revolution which changed the succession of khalifs pro-

[6] The Arabian writers date the origin of their literature (except those works of fiction which had always been popular) from the reign of Almansor, A. D. 758. (Abulpharagius, p. 160; Gibbon, c. 52.)
[7] Several very recent publications contain interesting details on Saracen literature: Berington's " Literary History of the Middle Ages," Mill's " History of Mohammedanism," chap. vi, Turner's " History of England," vol. i. Harris's " Philological Arrangement " is perhaps a book better known; and though it has since been much excelled, was one of the first contributions in our own language to this department, in which a great deal yet remains for the Oriental scholars of Europe. Casiri's admirable catalogue of Arabic MSS. in the Escurial ought before this to have been followed up by a more accurate examination of their contents than it was possible for him to give.

duced another not less important. A fugitive of the vanquished family, by name Abdalrahman, arrived in Spain, and the Moslem of that country, not sharing in the prejudices which had stirred up the Persians in favour of the line of Abbas, and conscious that their remote situation entitled them to independence, proclaimed him Khalif of Cordova. There could be little hope of reducing so distant a dependency; and the example was not unlikely to be imitated. In the reign of Haroun Alraschid two principalities were formed in Africa—of the Aglabites, who reigned over Tunis and Tripoli; and of the Edrisites, in the western parts of Barbary. These yielded in about a century to the Fatimites, a more powerful dynasty, who afterward established an empire in Egypt.[8]

The loss, however, of Spain and Africa was the inevitable effect of that immensely extended dominion, which their separation alone would not have enfeebled. But other revolutions awaited it at home. In the history of the Abbassides of Bagdad we read over again the decline of European monarchies, through their various symptoms of ruin; and find successive analogies to the insults of the barbarians toward imperial Rome in the fifth century, to the personal insignificance of the Merovingian kings, and to the feudal usurpations that dismembered the inheritance of Charlemagne. 1. Beyond the northeastern frontier of the Saracen Empire dwelt a warlike and powerful nation of the Tartar family, who defended the independence of Turkestan from the Sea of Aral to the great central chain of mountains. In the wars which the khalifs or their lieutenants waged against them many of these Turks were led into captivity and dispersed over the empire. Their strength and courage distinguished them among a people grown effeminate by luxury; and that jealousy of disaffection among his subjects so natural to an Eastern monarch might be an additional motive with the Khalif Motassem to form bodies of guards out of these prisoners. But his policy was fatally erroneous. More rude and even more ferocious than the Arabs, they contemned the feebleness of the khalifate, while they grasped at its riches. The son of Motassem, Motawakkel, was murdered in his palace by the barbarians of the north; and his fate revealed the secret of the empire, that the choice of its sovereign had passed to their slaves. Degradation and death were frequently the lot of succeeding khalifs; but in the East the son leaps boldly on the throne which the blood of his father has stained, and the pretorian guards of Bagdad rarely failed to render a fallacious obedience to the nearest heir of the house of Abbas. 2. In about one hundred years after the introduction

---

[8] For these revolutions, which it is not very easy to fix in the memory, consult Cardonne, who has made as much of them as the subject would bear.

of the Turkish soldiers the sovereigns of Bagdad sunk almost
into oblivion. Al Radi, who died in 940, was the last of these
that officiated in the mosque, that commanded the forces in
person, that addressed the people from the pulpit, that enjoyed
the pomp and splendour of royalty.[9] But he was the first who
appointed, instead of a vizier, a new officer—a mayor, as it were,
of the palace—with the title of Emir al Omra, commander of
commanders, to whom he delegated by compulsion the functions
of his office. This title was usually seized by active and martial
spirits; it was sometimes hereditary, and in effect irrevocable
by the khalifs, whose names hardly appear after this time in
Oriental annals. 3. During these revolutions of the palace every
province successively shook off its allegiance; new principalities
were formed in Syria and Mesopotamia, as well as in Khorasan
and Persia, till the dominion of the Commander of the Faithful
was literally confined to the city of Bagdad and its adjacent territory. For a time some of these princes, who had been appointed as governors by the khalifs, professed to respect his
supremacy by naming him in the public prayers and upon the
coin, but these tokens of dependence were gradually obliterated.[10]

Such is the outline of Saracenic history for three centuries
after Mohammed: one age of glorious conquest; a second of
stationary but rather precarious greatness; a third of rapid decline. The Greek Empire meanwhile survived, and almost recovered from the shock it had sustained. Besides the decline of its
enemies, several circumstances may be enumerated tending to its
preservation. The maritime province of Cilicia had been overrun by the Mohammedans; but between this and the Lesser
Asia Mount Taurus raises its massy buckler, spreading as a natural bulwark from the sea-coast of the ancient Pamphylia to the
hilly district of Isauria, whence it extends in an easterly direction, separating the Cappadocian and Cilician plains, and, after
throwing off considerable ridges to the north and south, connects itself with other chains of mountains that penetrate far
into the Asiatic continent. Beyond this barrier the Saracens
formed no durable settlement, though the armies of Alraschid
wasted the country as far as the Hellespont, and the city of
Amorium, in Phrygia, was razed to the ground by Al Motassem.
The position of Constantinople, chosen with a sagacity to which
the course of events almost gave the appearance of prescience,
secured her from any immediate danger on the side of Asia, and
rendered her as little accessible to an enemy as any city which

---

[9] Abulfeda, p. 261 ; Gibbon, c. 52 ;
" Modern Univ. Hist.," vol. ii. Al Radi's
command of the army is only mentioned
by the last.
[10] The decline of the Saracens is fully
discussed in the fifty-second chapter of
Gibbon, which is, in itself, a complete
philosophical dissertation upon this part
of history.

valour and patriotism did not protect. Yet in the days of Arabian energy she was twice attacked by great naval armaments. The first siege, or rather blockade, continued for seven years; the second, though shorter, was more terrible, and her walls, as well as her port, were actually invested by the combined forces of the Khalif Waled, under his brother Moslema.[11] The final discomfiture of these assailants showed the resisting force of the empire, or rather of its capital; but perhaps the abandonment of such maritime enterprises by the Saracens may be in some measure ascribed to the removal of their metropolis from Damascus to Bagdad. But the Greeks in their turn determined to dispute the command of the sea. By possessing the secret of an inextinguishable fire, they fought on superior terms; their wealth, perhaps their skill, enabled them to employ larger and better appointed vessels; and they ultimately expelled their enemies from the islands of Crete and Cyprus. By land they were less desirous of encountering the Moslem. The science of tactics is studied by the pusillanimous, like that of medicine by the sick; and the Byzantine emperors, Leo and Constantine, have left written treatises on the art of avoiding defeat, of protracting contest, of resisting attack.[12] But this timid policy, and even the purchase of armistices from the Saracens, were not ill calculated for the state of both nations. While Constantinople temporized, Bagdad shook to her foundations; and the heirs of the Roman name might boast the immortality of their own empire when they contemplated the dissolution of that which had so rapidly sprung up and perished. Amid all the crimes and revolutions of the Byzantine Government—and its history is but a series of crimes and revolutions—it was never dismembered by intestine war. A sedition in the army, a tumult in the theatre, a conspiracy in the palace, precipitated a monarch from the throne; but the allegiance of Constantinople was instantly transferred to his successor, and the provinces implicitly obeyed the voice of the capital. The custom, too, of partition, so baneful to the Latin kingdoms, and which was not altogether unknown to the Saracens, never prevailed in the Greek Empire. It stood in the middle of the tenth century, as vicious, indeed, and cowardly, but more wealthy, more enlightened, and far more secure from its enemies than under the first successors of Heraclius. For about one hundred years preceding there had been only partial wars with the Mohammedan potentates; and in these the emperors seem gradually to have gained the advantage, and to have become more frequently the aggressors. But the increasing distractions

[11] Gibbon, c. 52.
[12] Gibbon, c. 53. Constantine Porphyrogenitus, in his advice to his son as to the administration of the empire, betrays a mind not ashamed to confess weakness and cowardice, and pleasing itself in petty arts to elude the rapacity or divide the power of its enemies.

of the East encouraged two brave usurpers, Nicephorus Phocas and John Zimisces, to attempt the actual recovery of the lost provinces. They carried the Roman arms (one may use the term with less reluctance than usual) over Syria; Antioch and Aleppo were taken by storm; Damascus submitted; even the cities of Mesopotamia, beyond the ancient boundary of the Euphrates, were added to the trophies of Zimisces, who unwillingly spared the capital of the khalifate. From such distant conquests it was expedient, and indeed necessary, to withdraw; but Cilicia and Antioch were permanently restored to the empire. At the close of the tenth century the Emperors of Constantinople possessed the best and greatest portion of the modern kingdom of Naples, a part of Sicily, the whole European dominions of the Ottomans, the province of Anatolia or Asia Minor, with some part of Syria and Armenia.[13]

These successes of the Greek Empire were certainly much rather due to the weakness of its enemies than to any revival of national courage and vigour; yet they would probably have been more durable if the contest had been only with the khalifate, or the kingdoms derived from it. But a new actor was to appear on the stage of Asiatic tragedy. The same Turkish nation, the slaves and captives from which had become arbiters of the sceptre of Bagdad, passed their original limits of the Iaxartes or Sihon. The Sultans of Ghazna, a dynasty whose splendid conquests were of very short duration, had deemed it politic to divide the strength of these formidable allies by inviting a part of them into Khorasan. They covered that fertile province with their pastoral tents, and beckoned their compatriots to share the riches of the south. The Ghaznevides fell the earliest victims; but Persia, violated in turn by every conqueror, was a tempting and unresisting prey. Togrol Bek, the founder of the Seljukian dynasty of Turks, overthrew the family of Bowides, who had long reigned at Ispahan, respected the pageant of Mohammedan sovereignty in the Khalif of Bagdad, embraced with all his tribes the religion of the vanquished, and commenced the attack upon Christendom by an irruption into Armenia. His nephew and successor, Alp Arslan, defeated and took prisoner the Emperor Romanus Diogenes; and the conquest of Asia Minor was almost completed by princes of the same family, the Seljukians of Rûm,[14] who were permitted by Malek Shah, the third Sultan of the Turks, to form an independent kingdom. Through their own exertions, and the selfish impolicy of rival competitors for the throne

---

[13] Gibbon, chaps. 52 and 53. The latter of these chapters contains as luminous a sketch of the condition of Greece as the former does of Saracenic history. In each the facts are not grouped historically, according to the order of time, but philosophically, according to their relations.

[14] Rûm, i. e., country of the Romans.

of Constantinople, who bartered the strength of the empire for
assistance, the Turks became masters of the Asiatic cities and
fortified passes; nor did there seem any obstacle to the invasion
of Europe.[15]

In this state of jeopardy the Greek Empire looked for aid
to the nations of the West, and received it in fuller measure than
was expected, or perhaps desired. The deliverance of Constantinople was indeed a very secondary object with the crusaders.
But it was necessarily included in their scheme of operations,
which, though they all tended to the recovery of Jerusalem, must
commence with the first enemies that lay on their line of march.
The Turks were entirely defeated, their capital of Nice restored
to the empire. As the Franks passed onward, the Emperor
Alexius Comnenus trod on their footsteps, and secured to himself the fruits for which their enthusiasm disdained to wait. He
regained possession of the strong places on the Ægean shores,
of the defiles of Bithynia, and of the entire coast of Asia Minor,
both on the Euxine and Mediterranean Seas, which the Turkish armies, composed of cavalry and unused to regular warfare,
could not recover.[16] So much must undoubtedly be ascribed
to the first crusade. But I think that the general effect of these
expeditions has been overrated by those who consider them as
having permanently retarded the progress of the Turkish power.
The Christians in Palestine and Syria were hardly in contact
with the Seljukian kingdom of Rûm, the only enemies of the
empire; and it is not easy to perceive that their small and feeble
principalities, engaged commonly in defending themselves against
the Mohammedan princes of Mesopotamia or the Fatimite khalifs
of Egypt, could obstruct the arms of a sovereign of Iconium
upon the Mæander or the Halys. Other causes are adequate to
explain the equipoise in which the balance of dominion in Anatolia was kept during the twelfth century: the valour and activity
of the two Comneni, John and Manuel, especially the former;
and the frequent partitions and internal feuds, through which
the Seljukians of Iconium, like all other Oriental governments,
became incapable of foreign aggression.

But whatever obligation might be due to the first crusaders
from the Eastern Empire was cancelled by their descendants
one hundred years afterward, when the fourth in number of those
expeditions was turned to the subjugation of Constantinople
itself. One of those domestic revolutions which occur perpetually in Byzantine history had placed a usurper on the imperial
throne. The lawful monarch was condemned to blindness and

---

[15] Gibbon, c. 57; De Guignes, "Hist.
des Huns," tome ii, l. 2.

[16] It does not seem perfectly clear
whether the sea-coast, north and south,

was reannexed to the empire during the
reign of Alexius or of his gallant son,
John Comnenus. But the doubt is hardly worth noticing.

a prison, but the heir escaped to recount his misfortunes to the fleet and army of crusaders assembled in the Dalmatian port of Zara. This armament had been collected for the usual purposes, and through the usual motives, temporal and spiritual, of a crusade; the military force chiefly consisted of French nobles; the naval was supplied by the republic of Venice, whose doge commanded personally in the expedition. It was not apparently consistent with the primary object of retrieving the Christian affairs in Palestine to interfere in the government of a Christian empire; but the temptation of punishing a faithless people, and the hope of assistance in their subsequent operations, prevailed. They turned their prows up the Archipelago; and, notwithstanding the vast population and defensible strength of Constantinople, compelled the usurper to fly and the citizens to surrender. But animosities springing from religious schism and national jealousy were not likely to be allayed by such remedies; the Greeks, wounded in their pride and bigotry, regarded the legitimate emperor as a creature of their enemies, ready to sacrifice their church, a stipulated condition of his restoration, to that of Rome. In a few months a new sedition and conspiracy raised another usurper in defiance of the crusaders' army encamped without the walls. The siege instantly recommenced, and after three months the city of Constantinople was taken by storm. The tale of pillage and murder is always uniform; but the calamities of ancient capitals, like those of the great, impress us more forcibly. Even now we sympathize with the virgin majesty of Constantinople, decked with the accumulated wealth of ages, and resplendent with the monuments of Roman Empire and of Grecian art. Her populousness is estimated beyond credibility: ten, twenty, thirtyfold that of London or Paris; certainly far beyond the united capitals of all European kingdoms in that age.[17] In magnificence she excelled them more than in numbers; instead of the thatched roofs, the mud walls, the narrow streets, the pitiful buildings of those cities, she had marble and gilded palaces, churches, and monasteries, the works of skilful architects, through nine centuries, gradually sliding from the severity of ancient taste into the more various and brilliant combinations of Eastern fancy.[18] In the libraries of Constantinople were collected the remains of Grecian learning; her forum and

---

[17] Ville Hardouin reckons the inhabitants of Constantinople at quatre cens mil nommes ou plus, by which Gibbon understands him to mean men of a military age. Le Beau allows a million for the whole population. (Gibbon, vol. xi, p. 213.) We should probably rate London, in 1204, too high at 60,000 souls. Paris had been enlarged by Philip Augustus, and stood on more ground than London. ("Delamare sur la Police," tome i, p. 76.)

[18] O quanta civitas, exclaims Fulk of Chartres a hundred years before, nobilis et decora! quot monasteria quotque palatia sunt in eâ, opere mero fabrefacta! quo etiam in plateis vel in vicis opera ad spectandum mirabilia! Tædium est quidem magnum recitare, quanta sit ibi opulentia bonorum omnium, auri et

hippodrome were decorated with those of Grecian sculpture; but neither would be spared by undistinguishing rapine; nor were the chiefs of the crusaders more able to appreciate the loss than their soldiery. Four horses, that breathe in the brass of Lysippus, were removed from Constantinople to the square of St. Mark at Venice, destined again to become the trophies of war and to follow the alternate revolutions of conquest. But we learn from a contemporary Greek to deplore the fate of many other pieces of sculpture, which were destroyed in wantonness, or even coined into brass money.[19]

The lawful emperor and his son had perished in the rebellion that gave occasion to this catastrophe, and there remained no right to interfere with that of conquest. But the Latins were a promiscuous multitude, and what their independent valour had earned was not to be transferred to a single master. Though the name of emperor seemed necessary for the government of Constantinople, the unity of despotic power was very foreign to the principles and the interests of the crusaders. In their selfish schemes of aggrandizement they tore in pieces the Greek Empire. One fourth only was allotted to the emperor, three eighths were the share of the republic of Venice, and the remainder was divided among the chiefs. Baldwin, Count of Flanders, obtained the imperial title, with the feudal sovereignty over the minor principalities. A monarchy thus dismembered had little prospect of honour or durability. The Latin emperors of Constantinople were more contemptible and unfortunate, not so much from personal character as political weakness, than their predecessors; their vassals rebelled against sovereigns not more powerful than themselves; the Bulgarians, a nation who, after being long formidable, had been subdued by the imperial arms, and only recovered independence on the eve of the Latin conquest, insulted their capital; the Greeks viewed them with silent hatred, and hailed the dawning deliverance from the Asiatic coast. On that side of the Bosporus the Latin usurpation was scarcely for a moment acknowledged; Nice became the seat of a Greek dynasty, who reigned with honour as far as the Mæander; and crossing into Europe, after having established their dominion throughout Roumania and other provinces, expelled the last Latin emperors from Constantinople in less than sixty years from its capture.

During the reign of these Greeks at Nice they had fortunately little to dread on the side of their former enemies, and were generally on terms of friendship with the Seljukians of Iconium.

argenti palliorum multiformium, sacra-rumque reliquiarum. Omni etiam tempore, navigio frequenti cuncta hominum necessaria illuc afferuntur. (Du Chesne,

" Scrip. Rerum Gallicarum," tome iv, p. 822.)

[19] Gibbon, c. 60.

That monarchy, indeed, had sufficient objects of apprehension for itself. Their own example in changing the upland plains of Tartary for the cultivated valleys of the south was imitated in the thirteenth century by two successive hordes of northern barbarians. The Karismians, whose tents had been pitched on the lower Oxus and Caspian Sea, availed themselves of the decline of the Turkish power to establish their dominion in Persia, and menaced, though they did not overthrow, the kingdom of Iconium. A more tremendous storm ensued in the eruption of Moguls under the sons of Zingis Khan. From the farthest regions of Chinese Tartary issued a race more fierce and destitute of civilization than those who had preceded, whose numbers were told by hundreds of thousands, and whose only test of victory was devastation. All Asia, from the sea of China to the Euxine, wasted beneath the locusts of the north. They annihilated the phantom of authority which still lingered with the name of Khalif at Bagdad. They reduced into dependence and finally subverted the Seljukian dynasties of Persia, Syria, and Iconium. The Turks of the latter kingdom betook themselves to the mountainous country, where they formed several petty principalities, which subsisted by incursions into the territory of the Moguls or the Greeks. The chief of one of these, named Othman, at the end of the thirteenth century, penetrated into the province of Bithynia, from which his posterity were never withdrawn.[20]

The empire of Constantinople had never recovered the blow it received at the hands of the Latins. Most of the islands in the Archipelago, and the provinces of proper Greece from Thessaly southward, were still possessed by those invaders. The wealth and naval power of the empire had passed into the hands of the maritime republics; Venice, Genoa, Pisa, and Barcelona were enriched by a commerce which they carried on as independent states within the precincts of Constantinople, scarcely deigning to solicit the permission or recognise the supremacy of its master. In a great battle fought under the walls of the city between the Venetian and Genoese fleets, the weight of the Roman Empire, in Gibbon's expression, was scarcely felt in the balance of these opulent and powerful republics. Eight galleys were the contribution of the Emperor Cantacuzene to his Venetian allies; and upon their defeat he submitted to the ignominy of excluding them forever from trading in his dominions. Meantime the remains of the empire in Asia were seized by the independent Turkish dynasties, of which the most illustrious, that of the Ottomans, occupied the province of Bithynia. Invited by a Byzantine faction into Europe, about the middle of the four-

[20] De Guignes, " Hist. des Huns," tome iii, l. 15; Gibbon, c. 64.
26

teenth century, they fixed themselves in the neighbourhood of
the capital, and in the thirty years' reign of Amurath I subdued,
with little resistance, the province of Roumania and the small
Christian kingdoms that had been formed on the lower Danube.
Bajazet, the successor of Amurath, reduced the independent
Emirs of Anatolia to subjection, and, after long threatening Constantinople, invested it by sea and land. The Greeks called
loudly upon their brethren of the West for aid against the common enemy of Christendom; but the flower of French chivalry
had been slain or taken in the battle of Nicopolis in Bulgaria,[21]
where the King of Hungary, notwithstanding the heroism of
these volunteers, was entirely defeated by Bajazet. The Emperor Manuel left his capital with a faint hope of exciting the
courts of Europe to some decided efforts by personal representations of the danger; and during his absence Constantinople
was saved, not by a friend, indeed, but by a power more formidable to her enemies than to herself.

The loose masses of mankind that, without laws, agriculture,
or fixed dwellings, overspread the vast central regions of Asia,
have, at various times, been impelled by necessity of subsistence,
or through the casual appearance of a commanding genius, upon
the domain of culture and civilization. Two principal roads
connect the nations of Tartary with those of the west and south:
the one into Europe along the sea of Azof and northern coast
of the Euxine; the other across the interval between the Bu-
kharian mountains and the Caspian into Persia. Four times at
least within the period of authentic history the Scythian tribes
have taken the former course and poured themselves into Europe, but each wave was less effectual than the preceding. The
first of these was in the fourth and fifth centuries, for we may
range those rapidly successive migrations of the Goths and Huns
together when the Roman Empire fell to the ground, and the
only boundary of barbarian conquest was the Atlantic Ocean
upon the shores of Portugal. The second wave came on with
the Hungarians in the tenth century, whose ravages extended
as far as the southern provinces of France. A third attack was
sustained from the Moguls under the children of Zingis at the
same period as that which overwhelmed Persia. The Russian
monarchy was destroyed in this invasion, and for two hundred

---

[21] The Hungarians fled in this battle
and deserted their allies, according to
the "Mémoires de Boucicaut," c. 25.
But Froissart, who seems a fairer authority, imputes the defeat to the rashness of the French. (Part iv, c. 79.)
The Count de Nevers (Jean Sans Peur,
afterward Duke of Burgundy), who commanded the French, was made prisoner
with others of the royal blood, and ran-
somed at a very high price. Many of
eminent birth and merit were put to
death; a fate from which Boucicaut was
saved by the interference of the Count
de Nevers, who might better himself
have perished with honour on that occasion than survived to plunge his country into civil war and his name into
infamy.

years that great country lay prostrate under the yoke of the
Tartars. As they advanced, Poland and Hungary gave little
opposition, and the farthest nations of Europe were appalled
by the tempest. But Germany was no longer as she had been
in the anarchy of the tenth century; the Moguls were unused
to resistance, and still less inclined to regular warfare; they retired before the Emperor Frederick II, and the utmost points
of their western invasion were the cities of Lignitz in Silesia and
Neustadt in Austria. In the fourth and last aggression of the
Tartars their progress in Europe is hardly perceptible; the
Moguls of Timur's army could only boast the destruction of
Azof and the pillage of some Russian provinces. Timur, the
sovereign of these Moguls and founder of their second dynasty,
which has been more permanent and celebrated than that of
Zingis, had been the prince of a small tribe in Transoxiana, between the Gihon and Sirr, the doubtful frontier of settled and
pastoral nations. His own energy and the weakness of his neighbours are sufficient to explain the revolution he effected. Like
former conquerors, Togrol Bek and Zingis, he chose the road
through Persia; and, meeting little resistance from the disordered governments of Asia, extended his empire on one side
to the Syrian coast, while by successes still more renowned,
though not belonging to this place, it reached on the other to
the heart of Hindostan. In his old age the restlessness of ambition impelled him against the Turks of Anatolia. Bajazet
hastened from the siege of Constantinople to a more perilous
contest: his defeat and captivity in the plains of Angora clouded
for a time the Ottoman crescent, and preserved the wreck of
the Greek Empire for fifty years longer.

The Moguls did not improve their victory; in the western
parts of Asia, as in Hindostan, Timur was but a barbarian de-
stroyer, though at Samarcand a sovereign and a legislator. He
gave up Anatolia to the sons of Bajazet; but the unity of their
power was broken; and the Ottoman kingdom, like those which
had preceded, experienced the evils of partition and mutual animosity. For about twenty years an opportunity was given to
the Greeks of recovering part of their losses; but they were incapable of making the best use of this advantage, and, though
they regained possession of part of Roumania, did not extirpate
a strong Turkish colony that held the city of Gallipoli in the
Chersonesus. When Amurath II, therefore, reunited under his
vigorous sceptre the Ottoman monarchy, Constantinople was
exposed to another siege and to fresh losses. Her walls, however, repelled the enemy, and during the reign of Amurath she
had leisure to repeat those signals of distress which the princes
of Christendom refused to observe. The situation of Europe

was, indeed, sufficiently inauspicious: France, the original country of the crusades and of chivalry, was involved in foreign and domestic war; while a schism, apparently interminable, rent the bosom of the Latin Church and impaired the efficiency of the only power that could unite and animate its disciples in a religious war. Even when the Roman pontiffs were best disposed to rescue Constantinople from destruction, it was rather as masters than as allies that they would interfere; their ungenerous bigotry, or rather pride, dictated the submission of her Church and the renunciation of her favourite article of distinctive faith. The Greeks yielded with reluctance and insincerity in the Council of Florence, but soon rescinded their treaty of union. Ugenius IV procured a short diversion on the side of Hungary; but after the unfortunate battle of Warna the Hungarians were abundantly employed in self-defence.

The two monarchies which have successively held their seat in the city of Constantine may be contrasted in the circumstances of their decline. In the present day we anticipate, with an assurance that none can deem extravagant, the approaching subversion of the Ottoman power; but the signs of internal weakness have not yet been confirmed by the dismemberment of provinces; and the arch of dominion, that long since has seemed nodding to its fall and totters at every blast of the north, still rests upon the landmarks of ancient conquest, and spans the ample regions from Bagdad to Belgrade. Far different were the events that preceded the dissolution of the Greek Empire. Every province was in turn subdued—every city opened her gates to the conqueror: the limbs were lopped off one by one; but the pulse still beat at the heart, and the majesty of the Roman name was ultimately confined to the walls of Constantinople. Before Mohammed II planted his cannon against them, he had completed every smaller conquest and deprived the expiring empire of every hope of succour or delay. It was necessary that Constantinople should fall; but the magnanimous resignation of her emperor bestows an honour upon her fall which her prosperity seldom earned. The long-deferred but inevitable moment arrived; and the last of the Cæsars (I will not say of the Palæologi) folded round him the imperial mantle, and remembered the name which he represented in the dignity of heroic death. It is thus that the intellectual principle, when enfeebled by disease or age, is found to rally its energies in the presence of death, and pour the radiance of unclouded reason around the last struggles of dissolution.

Though the fate of Constantinople had been protracted beyond all reasonable expectation, the actual intelligence operated like that of sudden calamity. A sentiment of consternation, perhaps of self-reproach, thrilled to the heart of Christendom. There seemed no longer anything to divert the Ottoman armies from Hungary; and if Hungary should be subdued, it was evident that both Italy and the German Empire were exposed to invasion.[22] A general union of Christian powers was required to withstand this common enemy. But the popes, who had so often armed them against each other, wasted their spiritual and political counsels in attempting to restore unanimity. War was proclaimed against the Turks at the Diet of Frankfort, in 1454; but no efforts were made to carry the menace into execution. No prince could have sat on the imperial throne more unfitted for the emergency than Frederick III; his mean spirit and narrow capacity exposed him to the contempt of mankind—his avarice and duplicity insured the hatred of Austria and Hungary. During the papacy of Pius II, whose heart was thoroughly engaged in this legitimate crusade, a more specious attempt was made by convening a European congress at Mantua. Almost all the sovereigns attended by their envoys; it was concluded that fifty thousand men at arms should be raised, and a tax levied for three years of one tenth from the revenues of the clergy, one thirtieth from those of the laity, and one twentieth from the capital of the Jews.[23] Pius engaged to head this armament in person; but when he appeared next year at Ancona, the appointed place of embarkation, the princes had failed in all their promises of men and money, and he found only a headlong crowd of adventurers, destitute of every necessary, and expecting to be fed and paid at the Pope's expense. It was not by such a body that Mohammed could be expelled from Constantinople. If the Christian sovereigns had given a steady and sincere co-operation, the contest would still have been arduous and uncertain. In the early crusades the superiority of arms, of skill, and even of discipline, had been uniformly on the side of Europe. But the present circumstances were far from similar. An institution, begun by the first and perfected by the second Amurath, had given to the Turkish armies what their enemies still wanted—military subordination and veteran experience. Aware, as it seems, of the real superiority of Europeans in war, these sultans

---

[22] Sive vincitur Hungaria, sive coacta jungitur Turcis, neque Italia neque Germania tuta erit, neque satis Rhenus Gallos securos reddet. (Æn. Sylv., p. 678.) This is part of a discourse pronounced by Æneas Sylvius before the Diet of Frankfort; which, though too declamatory, like most of his writings, is an interesting illustration of the state of Europe and of the impression produced by that calamity. Spondanus, ad ann. 1454, has given large extracts from this oration.

[23] Spondanus. Neither Charles VII nor even Philip of Burgundy, who had made the loudest professions, and pledged himself in a fantastic pageant at his court, soon after the capture of Constantinople, to undertake this crusade, were sincere in their promises. The former pretended apprehensions of invasion from England, as an excuse for sending no troops; which, considering the situation of England in 1459, was a bold attempt upon the credulity of mankind.

selected the stoutest youths from their Bulgarian, Servian, or Albanian captives, who were educated in habits of martial discipline, and formed into a regular force, with the name of Janizaries. After conquest had put an end to personal captivity, a tax of every fifth male child was raised upon the Christian population for the same purpose. The arm of Europe was thus turned upon herself; and the Western nations must have contended with troops of hereditary robustness and intrepidity, whose emulous enthusiasm for the country that had adopted them was controlled by habitual obedience to their commanders.[24]

Yet forty years after the fall of Constantinople, at the epoch of Charles VIII's expedition into Italy, the just apprehensions of European statesmen might have gradually subsided. Except the Morea, Negropont, and a few other unimportant conquests, no real progress had been made by the Ottomans. Mohammed II had been kept at bay by the Hungarians; he had been repulsed with some ignominy by the Knights of St. John from the island of Rhodes. A petty chieftain defied this mighty conqueror for twenty years in the mountains of Epirus; and the persevering courage of his desultory warfare with such trifling resources, and so little prospect of ultimate success, may justify the exaggerated admiration with which his contemporaries honoured the name of Scanderbeg. Once only the crescent was displayed on the Calabrian coast; but the city of Otranto remained but a year in the possession of Mohammed. On his death a disputed succession involved his children in civil war. Bajazet, the eldest, obtained the victory; but his rival brother Zizim fled to Rhodes, from whence he was removed to France, and afterward to Rome. Apprehensions of this exiled prince seem to have dictated a pacific policy to the reigning Sultan, whose character did not possess the usual energy of Ottoman sovereigns.

[24] In the long declamation of Æneas Sylvius before the Diet of Frankfort in 1454, he has the following contrast between the European and Turkish militia; a good specimen of the artifice with which an ingenious orator can disguise the truth, while he seems to be stating it most precisely : Conferamus nunc Turcos et vos invicem; et quid sperandum sit si cum illis pugnetis, examinemus. Vos nati ad arma, illi tracti. Vos armati, illi inermes; vos gladios versatis, illi cultris utuntur; vos balistas tenditis, illi arcus trahunt; vos loricæ thoracesque protegunt, illos culcitra tegit; vos equos regitis, illi ab equis reguntur; vos nobiles in bellum ducitis, illi servos aut artifices cogunt, etc., p. 685. This, however, had little effect upon the hearers, who were better judges of military affairs than the secretary of Frederick III. Pius II, or Æneas Sylvius, was a lively writer and a skilful intriguer. Long experience had given him a considerable insight into European politics; and his views are usually clear and sensible. Though not so learned as some popes, he knew much better what was going forward in his own time. But the vanity of displaying his eloquence betrayed him into a strange folly when he addressed a very long letter to Mohammed II, explaining the Catholic faith, and urging him to be baptized; in which case, so far from preaching a crusade against the Turks, he would gladly make use of their power to recover the rights of the Church. Some of his inducements are curious, and must, if made public, have been highly gratifying to his friend Frederick III. Quippe ut arbitramur, si Christianus fuisses, mortuo Ladislao Ungariæ et Bohemiæ rege, nemo præter te sua regna fuisset adeptus. Sperassent Ungari post diuturna bellorum mala sub tuo regimine pacem, et illos Bohemi secuti fuissent; sed cum esses nostræ religionis hostis, elegerunt Ungari, etc. (Epist., 396.)

CHAPTER VII

ECCLESIASTICAL POWER DURING THE MIDDLE AGES

Wealth of the clergy—Its sources—Encroachments on ecclesiastical property—Their jurisdiction arbitrative, coercive—Their political power—Supremacy of the crown —Charlemagne—Change after his death, and encroachments of the Church in the ninth century—Primacy of the See of Rome—Its early stage—Gregory I—Council of Frankfort—" False Decretals "—Progress of papal authority—Effects of excommunication—Lothaire—State of the Church in the tenth century—Marriage of priests—Simony—Episcopal elections—Imperial authority over the popes—Disputes concerning investitures—Gregory VII and Henry IV—Concordat of Calixtus—Election by chapters—General system of Gregory VII—Progress of papal usurpations in the twelfth century—Innocent III—His character and schemes—Continual progress of the papacy—Canon law—Mendicant orders—Dispensing power—Taxation of the clergy by the popes—Encroachments on rights of patronage—Mandates, reserves, etc.—General disaffection toward the See of Rome in the thirteenth century—Progress of ecclesiastical jurisdiction—Immunity of the clergy in criminal cases—Restraints imposed upon their jurisdiction—Upon their acquisition of property—Boniface VIII—His quarrel with Philip the Fair—Its termination—Gradual decline of papal authority—Louis of Bavaria—Secession to Avignon and return to Rome—Conduct of Avignon popes—Contested election of Urban and Clement produces the great schism—Council of Pisa—Constance—Basle—Methods adopted to restrain the papal usurpations in England, Germany, and France—Liberties of the Gallican Church—Decline of the papal influence in Italy.

A
T the irruption of the northern invaders into the Roman Empire they found the clergy already endowed with extensive possessions. Besides the spontaneous oblations upon which the ministers of the Christian Church had originally subsisted, they had obtained, even under the pagan emperors, by concealment or connivance—for the Roman law did not permit a tenure of lands in mortmain—certain immovable estates, the revenues of which were applicable to their own maintenance and that of the poor.[1] These, indeed, were precarious and liable to confiscation in times of persecution. But it was among the first effects of the conversion of Constantine to give not only a security, but a legal sanction, to the territorial acquisitions of the Church. The edict of Milan, in 313, recognises the actual estates of ecclesiastical corporations.[2] Another, published in 321, grants to all the subjects of the empire the

---

[1] Giannone, " Istoria di Napoli," l. ii, c. 8; Gibbon, chaps. 15 and 20; F. Paul's " Treatise on Benefices," c. 4. The last writer does not wholly confirm this posi-tion, but a comparison of the three seems to justify my text.
[2] Giannone; Gibbon, ubi supra; F. Paul, c. 5.

power of bequeathing their property to the Church.[3] His own
liberality and that of his successors set an example which did
not want imitators. Passing rapidly from a condition of distress
and persecution to the summit of prosperity, the Church degenerated as rapidly from her ancient purity, and forfeited the respect
of future ages in the same proportion as she acquired the blind
veneration of her own. Covetousness especially became almost
a characteristic vice. Valentinian I, in 370, prohibited the clergy
from receiving the bequests of women—a modification more dis-
creditable than any general law could have been. And several
of the fathers severely reprobate the prevailing avidity of their
contemporaries.[4]

The devotion of the conquering nations, as it was still less
enlightened than that of the subjects of the empire, so was it
still more munificent. They left, indeed, the worship of Hesus
and Taranis in their forests; but they retained the elementary
principles of that and of all barbarous idolatry, a superstitious
reverence for the priesthood, a credulity that seemed to invite
imposture, and a confidence in the efficacy of gifts to expiate
offences. Of this temper it is undeniable that the ministers of
religion, influenced probably not so much by personal covetousness as by zeal for the interests of their order, took advantage.
Many of the peculiar and prominent characteristics in the faith
and discipline of those ages appear to have been either introduced or sedulously promoted for the purposes of sordid fraud.
To those purposes conspired the veneration for relics, the worship of images, the idolatry of saints and martyrs, the religious
inviolability of sanctuaries, the consecration of cemeteries, but,
above all, the doctrine of purgatory and masses for the relief
of the dead. A creed thus contrived, operating upon the minds
of barbarians, lavish though rapacious, and devout though dissolute, naturally caused a torrent of opulence to pour in upon
the Church. Donations of land were continually made to the
bishops, and, in still more ample proportion, to the monastic
foundations. These had not been very numerous in the West
till the beginning of the sixth century, when Benedict established his celebrated rule.[5] A more remarkable show of piety,
a more absolute seclusion from the world, forms more im-
pressive and edifying, prayers and masses more constantly repeated, gave to the professed in these institutions an advantage
in public esteem over the secular clergy.

The ecclesiastical hierarchy never received any territorial en-
dowment by law, either under the Roman Empire or the king-

---

[3] F. Paul.
[4] Giannone, ubi supra; F. Paul, c. 6.
[5] Giannone, l. iii, c. 6; l. iv, c. 12;

"Treatise on Benefices," c. 8; Fleury,
"Huitième Discours sur l'Hist. Ecclésiastique"; Muratori, Dissert. 65.

doms erected upon its ruins. But the voluntary munificence of princes, as well as their subjects, amply supplied the place of a more universal provision. Large private estates, or, as they were termed, patrimonies, not only within their own dioceses, but sometimes in distant countries, sustained the dignity of the principal sees, and especially that of Rome.[6] The French monarchs of the first dynasty, the Carlovingian family and their great chief, the Saxon line of emperors, the Kings of England and Leon, set hardly any bounds to their liberality, as numerous charters still extant in diplomatic collections attest. Many churches possessed seven or eight thousand mansi; one with but two thousand passed for only indifferently rich.[7] But it must be remarked that many of these donations are of lands uncultivated and unappropriated.[8] The monasteries acquired legitimate riches by the culture of these deserted tracts and by the prudent management of their revenues, which were less exposed to the ordinary means of dissipation than those of the laity. Their wealth, continually accumulated, enabled them to become the regular purchasers of landed estates, especially in the time of the crusades, when the fiefs of the nobility were constantly in the market for sale or mortgage.[9]

If the possessions of ecclesiastical communities had all been as fairly earned, we could find nothing in them to reprehend. But other sources of wealth were less pure, and they derived their wealth from many sources. Those who entered into a monastery threw frequently their whole estates into the common stock, and even the children of rich parents were expected to make a donation of land on assuming the cowl. Some gave their property to the Church before entering on military expeditions; gifts were made by some to take effect after their lives, and bequests by many in the terrors of dissolution. Even those legacies to charitable purposes, which the clergy could with more decency and speciousness recommend, and of which the administration was generally confined to them, were frequently applied to their own benefit.[10] They failed not, above all, to inculcate upon the wealthy sinner that no atonement could be so acceptable to Heaven as liberal presents to its earthly delegates.[11] To die

[6] St. Marc, tome i, p. 281; Giannone, l. iv, c. 12.

[7] Schmidt, tome ii, p. 205.

[8] Muratori, Dissert. 65; Du Cange, voc. Eremus.

[9] Heeren, "Essai sur les Croisades," p. 166; Schmidt, tome ii, p. 293.

[10] Primò sacris pastoribus data est facultas, ut hæreditatis portio in pauperes et egenos dispergeretur; sed sensim ecclesiæ quoque in pauperum censum venerunt, atque intestatæ gentis mens credita est proclivior in eas futura fuisse: quâ ex re pinguius illarum patrimonium evasit. Immò episcopi ipsi in rem suam ejusmodi consuetudinem interdum convertebant: ac tributum evasit, quod antea pii moris fuit. (Muratori, "Antiquitates Italiæ," tome v, Dissert. 67.)

[11] Muratori, Dissert. 67 ("Antiquit. Italiæ," tome v, p. 1055), has preserved a curious charter of an Italian count, who declares that, struck with reflections upon his sinful state, he had taken counsel with a certain religious how he should atone for his offences. Accepto consilio ab iis, excepto si renunciare sæculo possem, nullum esse melius inter

without allotting a portion of worldly wealth to pious uses was accounted almost like suicide or a refusal of the last sacraments; and hence intestacy passed for a sort of fraud upon the Church, which she punished by taking the administration of the deceased's effects into her own hands. This, however, was peculiar to England, and seems to have been the case there only from the reign of Henry III to that of Edward III, when the bishop took a portion of the intestate's personal estate for the advantage of the Church and poor, instead of distributing it among his next of kin.[12] The canonical penances imposed upon repentant offenders, extravagantly severe in themselves, were commuted for money or for immovable possessions—a fertile though scandalous source of monastic wealth, which the popes afterward diverted into their own coffers by the usage of dispensations and indulgences.[13] The Church lands enjoyed an immunity from taxes, though not in general from military service, when of a feudal tenure.[14] But their tenure was frequently in what was called frankalmoign, without any obligation of service. Hence it became a customary fraud of lay proprietors to grant estates to the Church, which they received again by way of fief or lease, exempted from public burdens. And, as if all these means of accumulating what they could not legitimately enjoy were insufficient, the monks prostituted their knowledge of writing to the purpose of forging charters in their own favour, which might easily impose upon an ignorant age, since it has required a peculiar science to detect them in modern times. Such rapacity might seem incredible in men cut off from the pursuits of life and the hope of posterity if we did not behold every day the unreasonableness of avarice and the fervour of professional attachments.[15]

As an additional source of revenue, and in imitation of the Jewish law, the payment of tithes was recommended or enjoined. These, however, were not applicable at first to the main-

---

eleemosinarum virtutes, quàm si de propriis meis substantiis in monasterium concederem. Hoc consilium ab iis libenter, et ardentissimo animo ego accepi.

[12] Selden, vol. iii, p. 1676; Prynne's "Constitutions," vol. iii, p. 18; Blackstone, vol. ii, c. 32. In France the lord of the fief seems to have taken the whole spoil. (Du Cange, voc. Intestatus.)

[13] Muratori, Dissert. 68.

[14] Palgrave has shown that the Anglo-Saxon clergy were not exempt, originally at least, from the trinoda necessitas imposed on all allodial proprietors. They were better treated on the Continent; and Boniface exclaims that in no part of the world was such servitude imposed on the Church as among the English. ("English Commonwealth," i, 158.) But

when we look at the charters collected in Kemble's "Codex Diplomaticus" (most or nearly all of them in favour of the Church), we shall hardly think they were ill off, though they might be forced sometimes to repair a bridge or send their tenants against the Danes.

[15] Muratori's sixty-fifth, sixty-seventh, and sixty-eighth dissertations on the "Antiquities of Italy" have furnished the principal materials of my text, with Father Paul's "Treatise on Benefices," especially chaps. 19 and 29. Giannone, loc. cit. and l. iv, c. 12; l. v, c. 6; l. x, c. 12. Schmidt, "Hist. des Allemands," tome i, p. 370; tome ii, pp. 203, 462; tome iv, p. 202. Fleury, III. "Discours sur l'Hist. Ecclés." Du Cange, voc. Precaria.

tenance of a resident clergy. Parochial divisions, as they now exist, did not take place, at least in some countries, till several centuries after the establishment of Christianity.[16] The rural churches, erected successively as the necessities of a congregation required or the piety of a landlord suggested, were in fact a sort of chapels dependent on the cathedral, and served by itinerant ministers at the bishop's discretion.[17] The bishop himself received the tithes, and apportioned them as he thought fit. A capitulary of Charlemagne, however, regulates their division into three parts: one for the bishop and his clergy, a second for the poor, and a third for the support of the fabric of the Church.[18] Some of the rural churches obtained by episcopal concessions the privileges of baptism and burial, which were accompanied with a fixed share of tithes, and seem to imply the residence of a minister. The same privileges were gradually extended to the rest, and thus a complete parochial division was finally established. But this was hardly the case in England till near the time of the conquest.[19]

The slow and gradual manner in which parochial churches became independent appears to be of itself a sufficient answer to those who ascribe a great antiquity to the universal payment of tithes. There are, however, more direct proofs that this species of ecclesiastical property was acquired not only by degrees but with considerable opposition. We find the payment of tithes first enjoined by the canons of a provincial council in France near the end of the sixth century. From the ninth to the end of the twelfth, or even later, it is continually enforced by similar authority.[20] Father Paul remarks that most of the sermons

[16] Muratori, Dissert. 74, and Fleury, "Institutions au Droit Ecclésiastique," tome i, p. 162, refer the origin of parishes to the fourth century; but this must be limited to the most populous part of the empire.

[17] These were not always itinerant; commonly, perhaps, they were dependents of the lord, appointed by the bishop on his nomination. Lehuerou, "Institut. Carolingiennes," p. 526, who quotes a capitulary of the Emperor Lothaire in 825: "De clericis vero laicorum, unde nonnulli eorum conqueri videantur, eo quod quidam episcopi ad eorum preces nolint in ecclesiis suis eos, cum utiles sint, ordinare, visum nobis fuit, ut . . . et cum caritate et ratione utiles et idonei eligantur; et si laicus idoneum utilemque clericum obtulerit nulla qualibet occasione ab episcopo sine ratione certa repellatur; et si rejiciendus est, propter scandalum vitandum evidenti ratione manifestetur." Another capitulary of Charles the Bald, in 864, forbids the establishment of priests in the churches of patrons, or their ejection without the bishop's consent : "De his qui sine consensu episcopi presbyteros in ecclesiis suis constituunt, vel de ecclesiis dejiciunt." Thus the churches are recognised as the property of the lord; and the parish may be considered as an established division, at least very commonly, so early as the Carlovingian empire. I do not by any means deny that it was partially known in France before that time.

Guizot reckons the patronage of churches by the laity among the circumstances which diminished or retarded ecclesiastical power. (Leçon 13.) It may have been so; but without this patronage there would have been very few parish churches. It separated, in some degree, the interests of the secular clergy from those of the bishops and the regulars.

[18] Schmidt, tome ii, p. 206. This seems to have been founded on an ancient canon. (F. Paul, c. 7.)

[19] Collier's "Ecclesiastical History," p. 229.

[20] Selden's "History of Tithes," vol. iii, p. 1108, edit. Wilkins. Tithes are said by Giannone to have been enforced by some papal decrees in the sixth century (l. iii, c. 6).

preached about the eighth century inculcate this as a duty, and even seem to place the summit of Christian perfection in its performance.[21] This reluctant submission of the people to a general and permanent tribute is perfectly consistent with the eagerness displayed by them in accumulating voluntary donations upon the Church. Charlemagne was the first who gave the confirmation of a civil statute to these ecclesiastical injunctions; no one at least has, so far as I know, adduced any earlier law for the payment of tithes than one of his capitularies.[22] But it would be precipitate to infer either that the practice had not already gained ground to a considerable extent, through the influence of ecclesiastical authority, or, on the other hand, that it became universal in consequence of the commands of Charlemagne.[23] In the subsequent ages it was very common to appropriate tithes, which had originally been payable to the bishop, either toward the support of particular churches or, according to the prevalent superstition, to monastic foundations.[24] These arbitrary consecrations, though the subject of complaint, lasted, by a sort of prescriptive right of the landholder, till about the year 1200. It was nearly at the same time that the obligation of paying tithes, which had been originally confined to those called predial, or the fruits of the earth, was extended, at least in theory, to every species of profit, and to the wages of every kind of labour.[25]

Yet there were many hindrances that thwarted the clergy in their acquisition of opulence, and a sort of reflux that set sometimes very strongly against them. In times of barbarous violence nothing can thoroughly compensate for the inferiority of physical strength and prowess. The ecclesiastical history of the middle ages presents one long contention of fraud against robbery; of acquisitions made by the Church through such means as I have described, and torn from her by lawless power. Those very men who in the hour of sickness and impending death showered the gifts of expiatory devotion upon her altars, had passed the sunshine of their lives in sacrilegious plunder. Notwithstanding the frequent instances of extreme reverence for religious institutions among the nobility, we should be deceived in supposing this to be their general character. Rapacity,

---

[21] "Treatise on Benefices," c. 11.

[22] Mably (" Observations sur l'Hist. de France," tome i, pp. 238 et 438) has, with remarkable rashness, attacked the current opinion that Charlemagne established the legal obligation of tithes, and denied that any of his capitularies bear such an interpretation. Those which he quotes have indeed a different meaning; but he has overlooked an express enactment in 789 (" Baluzii Capitularia," tome i, p. 253), which admits of no question, and I believe that there are others in confirmation.

[23] The grant of Ethelwolf in 855 has appeared to some antiquaries the most probable origin of the general right to tithes in England. [Note I.] It is said by Marina that tithes were not legally established in Castile till the reign of Alfonso X. (" Ensayo sobre les Siete Partidas," c. 359.)

[24] Selden, p. 1114 et seq.; Coke, 2 Inst., p. 641.

[25] Selden's " History of Tithes "; " Treatise on Benefices," c. 28; Giannone, l. x, c. 12.

not less insatiable than that of the abbots, was commonly united with a daring fierceness that the abbots could not resist.[26] In every country we find continual lamentation over the plunder of ecclesiastical possessions. Charles Martel is reproached with having given the first notorious example of such spoliation. It was not, however, commonly practised by sovereigns. But the evil was not the less universally felt. The parochial tithes especially, as the hand of robbery falls heaviest upon the weak, were exposed to unlawful seizure. In the tenth and eleventh centuries nothing was more common than to see the revenues of benefices in the hands of lay impropriators, who employed curates at the cheapest rate—an abuse that has never ceased in the Church.[27] Several attempts were made to restore these tithes; but even Gregory VII did not venture to proceed in it;[28] and, indeed, it is highly probable that they might be held in some instances by a lawful title.[29] Sometimes the property of monasteries was dilapidated by corrupt abbots, whose acts, however clandestine and unlawful, it was not easy to revoke. And both the bishops and convents were obliged to invest powerful lay protectors, under the name of advocates, with considerable fiefs, as the price of their assistance against depredators. But these advocates became too often themselves the spoilers, and oppressed the helpless ecclesiastics for whose defence they had been engaged.[30]

If it had not been for these drawbacks, the clergy must, one would imagine, have almost acquired the exclusive property of the soil. They did enjoy, according to some authorities, nearly one half of England, and, I believe, a greater proportion in some countries of Europe.[31] They had reached, perhaps, their

[26] The Church was often compelled to grant leases of her lands, under the name of precariæ, to laymen, who probably rendered little or no service in return, though a rent or census was expressed in the instrument. These precariæ seem to have been for life, but were frequently renewed. They are not to be confounded with terræ censuales, or lands let to a tenant at rack-rent, which, of course, formed a considerable branch of revenue. The grant was called precaria from being obtained at the prayer of a grantee; and the uncertainty of its renewal seems to have given rise to the adjective precarious.

In the ninth century, though the pretensions of the bishops were never higher, the Church itself was more pillaged under pretext of these precariæ, and in other ways, than at any former time. (See Du Cange for a long article on Precariæ.)

[27] Du Cange, voc. Abbas.

[28] Schmidt, tome iv, p. 204. At an assembly held at St. Denis in 997 the bishops proposed to restore the tithes to the secular clergy; but such a tumult

was excited by this attempt that the meeting was broken up. ("Recueil des Historiens," tome xi, præfat., p. 212.)

[29] Selden's "Hist. of Tithes," p. 1136. The third Council of Lateran restrains laymen from transferring their impropriated tithes to other laymen. (Velly, "Hist. de France," tome iii, p. 235.) This seems tacitly to admit that their possession was lawful, at least by prescription.

[30] For the injuries sustained by ecclesiastical proprietors, see Muratori, Dissert. 72. Du Cange, voc. Advocatus. Schmidt, tome ii, pp. 220, 470; tome iii, p. 290; tome iv, pp. 188, 202. "Recueil des Historiens," tome xi, præfat., p. 184, Martenne, "Thesaurus Anecdotorum," tome i, p. 595. Vaissette, "Hist. de Languedoc," tome ii, p. 109, and appendix, passim.

[31] Turner's "Hist. of England," vol. ii, p. 413, from Avesbury. According to a calculation founded on a passage in Knyghton, the revenue of the English Church in 1337 amounted to 730,000 marks per annum. Macpherson's "Annals of Commerce," vol. i, p. 519; "His-

zenith in respect of territorial property about the conclusion of the twelfth century.[32] After that time the disposition to enrich the clergy by pious donations grew more languid, and was put under certain legal restraints, to which I shall hereafter advert; but they became rather more secure from forcible usurpations.

The acquisitions of wealth by the Church were hardly so remarkable, and scarcely contributed so much to her greatness, as those innovations upon the ordinary course of justice which fall under the head of ecclesiastical jurisdiction and immunity. It is hardly, perhaps, necessary to caution the reader that rights of territorial justice, possessed by ecclesiastics in virtue of their fiefs, are by no means included in this description. Episcopal jurisdiction, properly so called, may be considered as depending upon the choice of litigant parties, upon their condition, and upon the subject-matter of their differences.

1. The arbitrative authority of ecclesiastical pastors, if not coeval with Christianity, grew up very early in the Church, and was natural, or even necessary, to an insulated and persecuted society.[33] Accustomed to feel a strong aversion to the imperial tribunals, and even to consider a recurrence to them as hardly consistent with their profession, the early Christians retained somewhat of a similar prejudice even after the establishment of their religion. The arbitration of their bishops still seemed a less objectionable mode of settling differences. And this arbitrative jurisdiction was powerfully supported by a law of Constantine, which directed the civil magistrate to enforce the execution of episcopal awards. Another edict, ascribed to the same emperor, and annexed to the Theodosian code, extended the jurisdiction of the bishops to all causes which either party chose to refer to it, even where they had already commenced in a secular court, and declared the bishop's sentence not subject to appeal. This edict has clearly been proved to be a forgery. It is evident, by a novel of Valentinian III, about 450, that the Church had still no jurisdiction in questions of a temporal nature, except by means of the joint reference of contending parties. Some expressions, indeed, used by the emperor seem intended to repress the spirit of encroachment upon the civil magistrates, which

---

toire du Droit public Ecclés. François," tome i, p. 214.) Anthony Harmer (Henry Wharton) says that the monasteries did not possess one fifth of the land; and I incline to think that he is nearer the truth than Mr. Turner, who puts the wealth of the Church at above 28,000 knights' fees out of 53,215. The bishops' lands could not by any means account for the difference, so that Mr. Turner was probably deceived by his authority.

[32] The great age of monasteries in England was the reigns of Henry I,

Stephen, and Henry II. (Littleton's "Henry II," vol. ii, p. 329.) David I of Scotland, contemporary with Henry II, was also a noted founder of monasteries. (Dalrymple's "Annals.")

[33] 1 Corinth., v, 4. The word ἐξουθενημένους, rendered in our version "of no reputation," has been interpreted by some to mean persons destitute of coercive authority, referees. The passage at least tends to discourage suits before a secular judge.

had probably begun to manifest itself. Charlemagne, indeed, in one of his capitularies, is said by some modern writers to have repeated all the absurd and enormous provisions of the spurious constitution in the Theodosian code.[34] But this capitulary is erroneously ascribed to Charlemagne. It is only found in one of the three books subjoined by Benedict Levita to the four books of capitularies collected by Ansegisus; these latter relating only to Charlemagne and Louis, but the others comprehending many of later emperors and kings. And, what is of more importance, it seems exceedingly doubtful whether this is any genuine capitulary at all. It is not referred to any prince by name, nor is it found in any other collection. Certain it is that we do not find the Church, in her most arrogant temper, asserting the full privileges contained in this capitulary.[35]

2. If it was considered almost as a general obligation upon the primitive Christians to decide their civil disputes by internal arbitration, much more would this be incumbent upon the clergy. The canons of several councils, in the fourth and fifth centuries, sentence a bishop or priest to deposition who should bring any suit, civil or even criminal, before a secular magistrate. This must, it should appear, be confined to causes where the defendant was a clerk, since the ecclesiastical court had hitherto no coercive jurisdiction over the laity. It was not so easy to induce laymen, in their suits against clerks, to prefer the episcopal tribunal. The emperors were not at all disposed to favour this species of encroachment till the reign of Justinian, who ordered civil suits against ecclesiastics to be carried only before the bishops. Yet this was accompanied by a provision that a party dissatisfied with the sentence might apply to the secular magistrate, not as an appellant, but a co-ordinate jurisdiction; for if different judgments were given in the two courts, the process was ultimately referred to the emperor.[36] But the early Merovingian kings adopted the exclusive jurisdiction of the bishop over causes wherein clerks were interested, without any of the checks which Justinian had provided. Many laws enacted during their reigns and under Charlemagne strictly prohibit the temporal magistrates from entertaining complaints against the children of the Church.

This jurisdiction over the civil causes of clerks was not immediately attended with an equally exclusive cognizance of criminal offences imputed to them, wherein the state is so deeply

[34] " Baluzii Capitularia," tome i, p. 9018.
[35] Gibbon, c. xx. Giannone, l. ii, c. 8; l. iii, c. 6; l. vi, c. 7. Schmidt, tome ii, p. 208. Fleury, "7me Discours," and "Institutions au Droit Ecclésiastique," tome ii, p. 1. " Mémoires de l'Académie des Inscriptions," tome xxxix, p. 566.

[36] This was also established about the same time by Athalaric, King of the Ostrogoths, and of course affected the popes who were his subjects. (St. Marc, tome i, p. 60; Fleury, " Hist. Ecclés.," tome vii, p. 292.)

interested, and the Church could inflict so inadequate a punishment. Justinian appears to have reserved such offences for trial before the imperial magistrate, though with a material provision that the sentence against a clerk should not be executed without the consent of the bishop or the final decision of the emperor. The bishop is not expressly invested with this controlling power by the laws of the Merovingians; but they enact that he must be present at the trial of one of his clerks, which probably was intended to declare the necessity of his concurrence in the judgment. The episcopal order was indeed absolutely exempted from secular jurisdiction by Justinian—a privilege which it had vainly endeavoured to establish under the earlier emperors. France permitted the same immunity; Chilperic, one of the most arbitrary of her kings, did not venture to charge some of his bishops with treason, except before a council of their brethren. Finally, Charlemagne seems to have extended to the whole body of the clergy an absolute exemption from the judicial authority of the magistrate.[37]

3. The character of a cause, as well as of the parties engaged, might bring it within the limits of ecclesiastical jurisdiction. In all questions simply religious the Church had an original right of decision; in those of a temporal nature the civil magistrate had, by the imperial constitution, as exclusive an authority.[38] Later ages witnessed strange innovations in this respect, when the spiritual courts usurped, under sophistical pretences, almost the whole administration of justice. But these encroachments were not, I apprehend, very striking till the twelfth century; and as about the same time measures, more or less vigorous and successful, began to be adopted in order to restrain them, I shall defer this part of the subject for the present.

In this sketch of the riches and jurisdiction of the hierarchy I may seem to have implied their political influence, which is naturally connected with the two former. They possessed, however, more direct means of acquiring temporal power. Even under the Roman emperors they had found their road into palaces; they were sometimes ministers, more often secret counsellors, always necessary but formidable allies, whose support was to be conciliated and interference to be respected. But they

---

[37] " Mémoires de l'Académie," ubi supra; Giannone, l. iii, c. 6; Schmidt, tome ii, p. 236; Fleury, ubi supra.
Some of these writers do not state the law of Charlemagne so strongly. Nevertheless, the words of a capitulary in 789, Ut clerici ecclesiastici ordinis si culpam incurrerint apud ecclesiasticos judicentur, non apud sæculares, are sufficiently general (" Baluz. Capitul.," tome i, p. 227); and the same is expressed still more forcibly in the collection published by Ansegisus under Louis the Debonair. (Id., pp. 904 and 1115. See other proofs in Fleury, " Hist. Eccles.," tome ix, p. 607.)
[38] Quoties de religione agitur, episcopos oportet judicare; alteras vero causas quæ ad ordinarios cognitores vel ad usum publici juris pertinent, legibus oportet audiri. (" Lex Arcadii et Honorii," apud " Mém. de l'Académie," tome xxxix, p. 571.)

assumed a far more decided influence over the new kingdoms of the West. They were entitled, in the first place, by the nature of those free governments, to a privilege unknown under the imperial despotism, that of assisting in the deliberative assemblies of the nation. Councils of bishops, such as had been convoked by Constantine and his successors, were limited in their functions to decisions of faith or canons of ecclesiastical discipline. But the northern nations did not so well preserve the distinction between secular and spiritual legislation. The laity seldom, perhaps, gave their suffrage to the canons of the Church; but the Church was not so scrupulous as to trespassing upon the province of the laity. Many provisions are found in the canons of national and even provincial councils which relate to the temporal constitution of the state. Thus one held at Calcluith (an unknown place in England), in 787, enacted that none but legitimate princes should be raised to the throne, and not such as were engendered in adultery or incest. But it is to be observed that, although this synod was strictly ecclesiastical, being summoned by the Pope's legate, yet the Kings of Mercia and Northumberland, with many of their nobles, confirmed the canons by their signature. As for the councils held under the Visigoth Kings of Spain during the seventh century, it is not easy to determine whether they are to be considered as ecclesiastical or temporal assemblies.[39] No kingdom was so thoroughly under the bondage of the hierarchy as Spain.[40] The first dynasty of France seem to have kept their national convention, called the Field of March, more distinct from merely ecclesiastical councils.

The bishops acquired and retained a great part of their ascendency by a very respectable instrument of power—intellectual superiority. As they alone were acquainted with the art of writing, they were naturally intrusted with political correspondence, and with the framing of the laws. As they alone knew the elements of a few sciences, the education of royal families devolved upon them as a necessary duty. In the fall of Rome their influence upon the barbarians wore down the asperities of conquest, and saved the provincials half the shock of that tremendous revolution. As captive Greece is said to have subdued her Roman conqueror, so Rome, in her own turn of servitude, cast the fetters of a moral captivity upon the fierce invaders of the north. Chiefly through the exertions of the bishops, whose ambition may be forgiven for its effects, her religion, her language, in part even her laws, were transplanted into the courts of Paris and Toledo, which became a degree less barbarous by imitation.[41]

[39] Marina, "Teoria de las Cortes," tome i, p. 9.
[40] See instances of the temporal power of the Spanish bishops in Fleury, "Hist. Ecclés.," tome viii, pp. 368, 397; tome ix, p. 68, etc.
[41] Schmidt, tome i, p. 365.

27

Notwithstanding, however, the great authority and privileges of the Church, it was decidedly subject to the supremacy of the crown, both during the continuance of the Western Empire and after its subversion. The emperors convoked, regulated, and dissolved universal councils; the Kings of France and Spain exercised the same right over the synods of their national churches.[42] The Ostrogoth Kings of Italy fixed by their edicts the limits within which matrimony was prohibited on account of consanguinity, and granted dispensations from them.[43] Though the Roman emperors left episcopal elections to the clergy and people of the diocese, in which they were followed by the Ostrogoths and Lombards, yet they often interfered so far as to confirm a decision or to determine a contest. The Kings of France went further, and seem to have invariably either nominated the bishops, or, what was nearly tantamount, recommended their own candidate to the electors.

But the sovereign who maintained with the greatest vigour his ecclesiastical supremacy was Charlemagne. Most of the capitularies of his reign relate to the discipline of the Church; principally, indeed, taken from the ancient canons, but not the less receiving an additional sanction from his authority.[44] Some of his regulations, which appear to have been original, are such as men of high-church principles would, even in modern times, deem infringements of spiritual independence: that no legend of doubtful authority should be read in the churches, but only the canonical books, and that no saint should be honoured whom the whole Church did not acknowledge. These were not passed in a synod of bishops, but enjoined by the sole authority of the emperor, who seems to have arrogated a legislative power over the Church which he did not possess in temporal affairs. Many of his other laws relating to the ecclesiastical constitution are enacted in a general council of the lay nobility as well as of prelates, and are so blended with those of a secular nature that the two orders may appear to have equally consented to the whole. His father Pepin, indeed, left a remarkable precedent in a council held in 744, where the Nicene faith is declared to be established, and even a particular heresy condemned, with the consent of the bishops and nobles. But whatever share we may imagine the laity in general to have had in such matters, Charlemagne himself did not consider even theological decisions as beyond his

[42] Encyclopédie, art. Concile. Schmidt, tome i, p. 384. De Marca, " De Concordantiâ Sacerdotii et Imperii," 1. ii, chaps. 9, 11; et 1. iv, passim.
The last of these sometimes endeavours to extenuate the royal supremacy, but his own work furnishes abundant evidence of it, especially l. vi, c. 19, etc. For the ecclesiastical independence of Spain, down to the eleventh century, see Marina, " Ensayo sobre las Siete Partidas," c. 322, etc, and De Marca, l. vi, c. 23.
[43] Giannone, l. iii, c. 6.
[44] " Baluzii Capitularia," passim ; Schmidt, tome ii, p. 239; Gaillard, " Vie de Charlemagne," tome iii.

province; and, in more than one instance, manifested a determination not to surrender his own judgment, even in questions of that nature, to any ecclesiastical authority.[45]

This part of Charlemagne's conduct is duly to be taken into the account before we censure his vast extension of ecclesiastical privileges. Nothing was more remote from his character than the bigotry of those weak princes who have suffered the clergy to reign under their names. He acted upon a systematic plan of government, conceived by his own comprehensive genius, but requiring too continual an application of similar talents for durable execution. It was the error of a superior mind, zealous for religion and learning to believe that men dedicated to the functions of the one, and possessing what remained of the other, might, through strict rules of discipline, enforced by the constant vigilance of the sovereign, become fit instruments to reform and civilize a barbarous empire. It was the error of a magnanimous spirit to judge too favourably of human nature, and to presume that great trusts would be fulfilled and great benefits remembered.

It is highly probable, indeed, that an ambitious hierarchy did not endure without reluctance this imperial supremacy of Charlemagne, though it was not expedient for them to resist a prince so formidable, and from whom they had so much to expect. But their dissatisfaction at a scheme of government incompatible with their own objects of perfect independence produced a violent recoil under Louis the Debonair, who attempted to act the censor of ecclesiastical abuses with as much earnestness as his father, though with very inferior qualifications for so delicate an undertaking. The bishops, accordingly, were among the chief instigators of those numerous revolts of his children which harassed this emperor. They set, upon one occasion, the first example of a usurpation which was to become very dangerous to society—the deposition of sovereigns by ecclesiastical authority. Louis, a prisoner in the hands of his enemies, had

[45] Charlemagne had apparently devised an ecclesiastical theory, which would now be called Erastian, and perhaps not very short of that of Henry VIII. He directs the clergy what to preach in his own name, and uses the first person in ecclesiastical canons. Yet, if we may judge by the events, the bishops lost no part of their permanent ascendency in the state through this interference, though compelled to acknowledge the supremacy of a great mind. By a vigorous repression of those secular propensities which were displaying themselves among the superior clergy, he endeavoured to render their moral influence more effective. This, however, could not be achieved in the ninth century; nor could it have been brought about by any external power. Nor was it easily consistent with the continual presence of the bishops in national assemblies, which had become essential to the polity of his age, and with which he would not, for several reasons, have wholly dispensed. Yet it appears, by a remarkable capitulary of 811, that he had perceived the inconvenience of allowing the secular and spiritual powers to clash with each other: Discutiendum est atque interveniendum in quantum se episcopus aut abbas rebus secularibus debeat inserere, vel in quantum comes, vel alter laicus, in ecclesiastica negotia. But as the laity, himself excepted, had probably interfered very little in church affairs, this capitulary seems to be restrictive of the prelates.

been intimidated enough to undergo a public penance; and the
bishops pretended that, according to a canon of the Church, he
was incapable of returning afterward to a secular life or preserving the character of sovereignty.[46] Circumstances enabled him
to retain the empire in defiance of this sentence; but the Church
had tasted the pleasure of trampling upon crowned heads, and
was eager to repeat the experiment. Under the disjointed and
feeble administration of his posterity in their several kingdoms,
the bishops availed themselves of more than one opportunity
to exalt their temporal power. Those weak Carlovingian princes,
in their mutual animosities, encouraged the pretensions of a common enemy. Thus Charles the Bald and Louis of Bavaria, having driven their brother Lothaire from his dominions, held an
assembly of some bishops, who adjudged him unworthy to reign,
and, after exacting a promise from the two allied brothers to
govern better than he had done, permitted and commanded them
to divide his territories.[47] After concurring in this unprecedented
encroachment, Charles the Bald had little right to complain when,
some years afterward, an assembly of bishops declared himself
to have forfeited his crown, released his subjects from their allegiance, and transferred his kingdom to Louis of Bavaria. But,
in truth, he did not pretend to deny the principle which he had
contributed to maintain. Even in his own behalf he did not
appeal to the rights of sovereigns, and of the nation whom they
represent. " No one," says this degenerate grandson of Charlemagne, " ought to have degraded me from the throne to which
I was consecrated, until at least I had been heard and judged
by the bishops, through whose ministry I was consecrated, who

[46] Habitu sæculi se exuens habitum
pœnitentis per impositionem manuum
episcoporum suscepit; ut post tantam
talemque pœnitentiam nemo ultra ad
militiam sæcularem redeat. Acta ex-
auctorationis Ludovici, apud Schmidt,
tome ii, p. 68. There was a sort of precedent, though not, I think, very apposite,
for this doctrine of implied abdication,
in the case of Wamba, King of the Visigoths in Spain, who, having been clothed
with a monastic dress, according to a
common superstition, during a dangerous
illness, was afterward adjudged by a
council incapable of resuming his crown,
to which he voluntarily submitted. The
story, as told by an original writer,
quoted in Baronius ad A. D. 681, is too
obscure to warrant any positive inference; though I think we may justly
suspect a fraudulent contrivance between
the bishops and Ervigius, the successor
of Wamba. The latter, besides his monastic attire, had received the last sacraments; after which he might be deemed
civilly dead. Fleury, " 3me Discours sur
l'Hist. Ecclésiast.," puts this case too
strongly when he tells us that the bishops

deposed Wamba; it may have been a
voluntary abdication, influenced by superstition, or, perhaps, by disease. A
late writer has taken a different view of
this event, the deposition of Louis at
Compiègne. It was not, he thinks, une
hardiesse sacerdotale, une témérité ecclésiastique, mais bien une lâcheté politique.
Ce n'était point une tentative pour
élever l'autorité religieuse au-dessus de
l'autorité royale dans les affaires tempo-
relles; c'était, au contraire, un abaisse-
ment servile de la première devant le
monde. (Fauriel, " Hist. de la Gaule Méridionale," iv, 150.) In other words, the
bishops lent themselves to the aristocratic
faction which was in rebellion against
Louis. Ranke, as has been seen in an
early note, thinks that they acted out of
revenge for his deviation from the law of
817, which established the unity of the
empire. The bishops, in fact, had so
many secular and personal interests and
sympathies that we can not always judge
of their behaviour upon general principles.
[47] Schmidt, tome ii, p. 77. Velly, tome
ii, p. 61; see, too, p. 74.

are called the thrones of God, in which God sitteth, and by whom he dispenses his judgments; to whose paternal chastisement I was willing to submit, and do still submit myself." [48]

These passages are very remarkable, and afford a decisive proof that the power obtained by national churches, through the superstitious prejudices then received, and a train of favourable circumstances, was as dangerous to civil government as the subsequent usurpations of the Roman pontiff, against which Protestant writers are apt too exclusively to direct their animadversions. Voltaire, I think, has remarked that the ninth century was the age of the bishops, as the eleventh and twelfth were of the popes. It seemed as if Europe was about to pass under as absolute a domination of the hierarchy as had been exercised by the priesthood of ancient Egypt or the Druids of Gaul. There is extant a remarkable instrument recording the election of Boson, King of Arles, by which the bishops alone appear to have elevated him to the throne, without any concurrence of the nobility.[49] But it is inconceivable that such could have really been the case; and if the instrument is genuine, we must suppose it to have been framed in order to countenance future pretensions. For the clergy, by their exclusive knowledge of Latin, had it in their power to mould the language of public documents for their own purposes; a circumstance which should be cautiously kept in mind when we peruse instruments drawn up during the dark ages.

It was with an equal defiance of notorious truth that the Bishop of Winchester, presiding as papal legate at an assembly of the clergy in 1141, during the civil war of Stephen and Matilda, asserted the right of electing a King of England to appertain principally to that order, and, by virtue of this unprecedented claim, raised Matilda to the throne.[50] England, indeed, has been obsequious, beyond most other countries, to the arrogance of her hierarchy; especially during the Anglo-Saxon period, when the nation was sunk in ignorance and effeminate superstition. Every one knows the story of King Edwy in some form or other, though I believe it impossible to ascertain the real circumstances of that controverted anecdote.[51] But, upon the supposition least favourable to the king, the behaviour of Archbishop Odo and Dunstan was an intolerable outrage of spiritual tyranny.

But while the prelates of these nations, each within his respective sphere, were prosecuting their system of encroachment

[48] Schmidt, tome ii, p. 217.
[49] "Recueil des Historiens," tome ix, p. 304.
[50] Ventilata est causa, says the legate, coram majori parte cleri Angliæ, ad cujus jus potissimùm spectat principem eligere, simulque ordinare. Invocatâ ita-que primò in auxlium Divinitate, filiam pacifici regis, etc., in Anglia Normanniæque dominam eligimus, et ei fidem et manutenementum promittimus. (Gul. Malmsb., p. 188.)
[51] [Note II.]

upon the laity, a new scheme was secretly forming within the bosom of the Church, to enthral both that and the temporal governments of the world under an ecclesiastical monarch. Long before the earliest epoch that can be fixed for modern history, and, indeed, to speak fairly, almost as far back as ecclesiastical testimonies can carry us, the Bishops of Rome had been venerated as first in rank among the rulers of the Church. The nature of this primacy is doubtless a very controverted subject. It is, however, reduced by some moderate Catholics to little more than a precedency attached to the See of Rome in consequence of its foundation by the chief of the apostles, as well as the dignity of the imperial city.[52] A sort of general superintendence was admitted as an attribute of this primacy, so that the Bishops of Rome were entitled, and indeed bound, to remonstrate when any error or irregularity came to their knowledge, especially in the Western churches, a greater part of which had been planted by them, and were connected, as it were by filiation, with the common capital of the Roman Empire and of Christendom.[53] Various causes had a tendency to prevent the Bishops of Rome from augmenting their authority in the East, and even to diminish that which they had occasionally exercised—the institution of patriarchs at Antioch, Alexandria, and afterward at Constantinople, with extensive rights of jurisdiction; the difference of rituals and discipline; but, above all, the many disgusts taken by the Greeks, which ultimately produced an irreparable schism between the two churches in the ninth century. But within the pale of the Latin Church every succeeding age enhanced the power and dignity of the Roman See. By the constitution of the Church, such at least as it became in the fourth century, its divisions being arranged in conformity to those of the empire, every province ought to have its metropolitan, and every vicariate its ecclesiastical exarch or primate. The Bishop of Rome presided, in the latter capacity, over the Roman vicariate, comprehending southern Italy and the three chief Mediterranean

[52] These foundations of the Roman primacy are indicated by Valentinian III, a great favourer of that see, in a novel of the year 455: Cum igitur sedis apostolicæ primatum B. Petri meritum, qui est princeps sacerdotalis coronæ et Romanæ dignitas civitatis, sacræ etiam synodi firmavit auctoritas. The last words allude to the sixth canon of the Nicene Council, which establishes or recognises the patriarchal supremacy, in their respective districts, of the Churches of Rome, Antioch, and Alexandria. (De Marca, " De Concordantiâ Sacerdotii et Imperii," l. i, c. 8.) At a much earlier period, Irenæus rather vaguely, and Cyprian more positively, admit, or rather assert, the primacy of the Church of Rome, which the latter seems even to

have considered as a kind of centre of Catholic unity, though he resisted every attempt of that church to arrogate a controlling power.—See his treatise, " De Unitate Ecclesiæ," 1818. [Note III.]

[53] Dupin, " De antiquâ Ecclesiæ Disciplinâ," p. 306 et seq.; " Histoire du Droit Public Ecclésiastique François," p. 149. The opinion of the Roman See's supremacy, though apparently rather a vague and general notion, as it still continues in those Catholics who deny its infallibility, seems to have prevailed very much in the fourth century. Fleury brings remarkable proofs of this from the writings of Socrates, Sozomen, Ammianus Marcellinus, and Optatus. (" Hist. Ecclés.," tome iii, pp. 282, 320, 449; tome iv, p. 227.)

islands. But, as it happened, none of the ten provinces forming this division had any metropolitan; so that the popes exercised all metropolitical functions within them, such as the consecration of bishops, the convocation of synods, the ultimate decision of appeals, and many other sorts of authority. These provinces are sometimes called the Roman patriarchate; the Bishops of Rome having always been reckoned one, generally indeed the first, of the patriarchs; each of whom was at the head of all the metropolitans within his limits, but without exercising those privileges which by the ecclesiastical constitution appertained to the latter. Though the Roman patriarchate, properly so called, was comparatively very small in extent, it gave its chief, for the reason mentioned, advantages in point of authority which the others did not possess.[54]

I may perhaps appear to have noticed circumstances interesting only to ecclesiastical scholars. But it is important to apprehend this distinction of the patriarchate from the primacy of Rome, because it was by extending the boundaries of the former, and by applying the maxims of her administration in the south of Italy to all the Western churches, that she accomplished the first object of her scheme of usurpation, in subverting the provincial system of government under the metropolitans. Their first encroachment of this kind was in the province of Illyricum, which they annexed in a manner to their own patriarchate, by not permitting any bishops to be consecrated without their consent.[55] This was before the end of the fourth century. Their subsequent advances were, however, very gradual. About the middle of the sixth century we find them confirming the elections of Archbishops of Milan.[56] They came by degrees to exercise, though not always successfully, and seldom without opposition, an appellant jurisdiction over the causes of bishops deposed or censured in provincial synods. This, indeed, had been granted, if we believe the fact, by the canons of a very early council, that of Sardica, in 347, so far as to permit the Pope to order a revision of the process, but not to annul the sentence.[57] Valentinian III, influenced by Leo the Great, one of the most

[54] Dupin, " De Antiquâ Eccles. Disciplinâ," p. 39, etc.; Giannone, "Ist. di Napoli," l. ii, c. 8; l. iii, c. 6; De Marca, l. i, c. 7 et alibi. There is some disagreement among these writers as to the extent of the Roman patriarchate, which some suppose to have even at first comprehended all the Western churches, though they admit that, in a more particular sense, it was confined to the vicariate of Rome.

[55] Dupin, p. 66; Fleury, " Hist. Ecclés.," tome v, p. 373. The ecclesiastical province of Illyricum included Macedonia. Siricius, the author of this encroachment, seems to have been one of the first usurpers. In a letter to the Spanish bishops (A. D. 375), he exalts his own authority very high. (De Marca, l. i, c. 8.)

[56] St. Marc, tome i, pp. 139, 153.

[57] Dupin, p. 109; De Marca, l. vi, c. 14. These canons have been questioned, and Dupin does not seem to lay much stress on their authority, though I do not perceive that either he or Fleury (" Hist. Ecclés.," tome iii, p. 372) doubts their genuineness. Sardica was a city of Illyricum, which the translator of Mosheim has confounded with Sardes.

ambitious of pontiffs, had gone a great deal further, and established almost an absolute judicial supremacy in the Holy See.[58] But the metropolitans were not inclined to surrender their prerogatives; and, upon the whole, the papal authority had made no decisive progress in France, or perhaps anywhere beyond Italy, till the pontificate of Gregory I.

This celebrated person was not distinguished by learning, which he affected to depreciate, nor by his literary performances, which the best critics consider as below mediocrity, but by qualities more necessary for his purpose—intrepid ambition and unceasing activity. He maintained a perpetual correspondence with the emperors and their ministers, with the sovereigns of the Western kingdoms, with all the hierarchy of the Catholic Church, employing, as occasion dictated, the language of devotion, arrogance, or adulation.[59] Claims hitherto disputed, or half preferred, assumed under his hands a more definite form, and nations too ignorant to compare precedents or discriminate principles yielded to assertions confidently made by the authority which they most respected. Gregory dwelt more than his predecessors upon the power of the keys, exclusively, or at least principally, committed to St. Peter, which had been supposed in earlier times, as it is now by the Gallican Catholics, to be inherent in the general body of bishops, joint sharers of one indivisible episcopacy. And thus the patriarchal rights, being manifestly of mere ecclesiastical institution, were artfully confounded or, as it were, merged in the more paramount supremacy of the papal chair. From the time of Gregory the popes appear in a great measure to have thrown away that scaffolding, and relied in preference on the pious veneration of the people, and on the opportunities which might

Consultations or references to the Bishop of Rome, in difficult cases of faith or discipline, had been common in early ages, and were even made by provincial and national councils. But these were also made to other bishops eminent for personal merit or the dignity of their sees. The popes endeavoured to claim this as a matter of right. Innocent I asserts (A. D. 402) that he was to be consulted, quoties fidei ratio ventilatur; and Gelasius (A. D. 492), quantum ad religionem pertinet, non nisi apostolicæ sedi, juxtà canones, debetur summa judicii totius. As the oak is in the acorn, so did these maxims contain the system of Bellarmin. (De Marca, l. i, c. 10, and l. vii, c. 12; Dupin.)

[58] Some bishops belonging to the province of Hilary, metropolitan of Arles, appealed from his sentence to Leo, who not only entertained their appeal, but presumed to depose Hilary. This assumption of power would have had little effect if it had not been seconded by the emperor in very unguarded language; hoc perenni sanctione decernimus, ne

quid tam episcopis Gallicanis, quam aliarum provinciarum, contra consuetudinem veterem liceat sine auctoritate viri venerabilis papæ urbis æternæ tentare; sed illis omnibusque pro lege sit, quidquid sanxit vel sanxerit apostolicæ sedis auctoritas. (De Marca, "De Concordantiâ Sacerdotii et Imperii," l. i, c. 8.) The same emperor enacted that any bishop who refused to attend the tribunal of the Pope when summoned should be compelled by the governor of his province; ut quisquis episcoporum ad judicium Romani episcopi evocatus venire neglexerit, per moderatorem ejusdem provinciæ adesse cogatur. (Id., l. vii, c. 13; Dupin, "De Ant. Discipl.," pp. 29 et 171.)

[59] The flattering style in which this pontiff addressed Brunehaut and Phocas, the most flagitious monsters of his time, is mentioned in all civil and ecclesiastical history. Fleury quotes a remarkable letter to the Patriarchs of Antioch and Alexandria wherein he says that St. Peter has one see, divided into three, Rome, Antioch, and Alexandria; stoop-

occur for enforcing their dominion with the pretence of divine authority.[60]

It can not, I think, be said that any material acquisitions of ecclesiastical power were obtained by the successors of Gregory for nearly one hundred and fifty years.[61] As none of them pos-

ing to this absurdity, and inconsistence with his real system, in order to conciliate their alliance against his more immediate rival, the Patriarch of Constantinople. (" Hist. Ecclés.," tome viii, p. 124.)

[60] Gregory seems to have established the appellant jurisdiction of the See of Rome, which had been long in suspense. Stephen, a Spanish bishop, having been deposed, appealed to Rome. Gregory sent a legate to Spain, with full powers to confirm or rescind the sentence. He says in his letter on this occasion, à sede apostolicâ, quæ omnium ecclesiarum caput est, causa hæc audienda ac didimenda fuerat. (De Marca, l. vii, c. 18.) In writing to the Bishops of France, he enjoins them to obey Virgilius, Bishop of Arles, whom he has appointed his legate in France, secundùm antiquam consuetudinem; so that, if any contention should arise in the Church, he may appease it by his authority, as vicegerent of the apostolic see; auctoritatis suæ vigore, vicibus nempe apostolicæ sedis functus, discretâ moderatione compescat. (" Gregorii Opera," tome ii, p. 783, edit. Benedict.; Dupin, p. 34; Pasquier, " Recherches de la France," l. iii, c. 9.)

[61] I observe that some modern publications annex considerable importance to a supposed concession of the title of universal bishop, made by the Emperor Phocas in 606 to Boniface III, and even appear to date the papal supremacy from this epoch. Those who have imbibed this notion may probably have been misled by a loose expression in Mosheim's " Ecclesiastical History," vol. ii, p. 169, though the general tenor of that passage by no means gives countenance to their opinion. But there are several strong objections to our considering this as a leading fact, much less as marking an era in the history of the papacy. 1. Its truth, more than commonly stated, appears more than questionable. The Roman pontiffs, Gregory I and Boniface III, had been vehemently opposing the assumption of this title by the Patriarch of Constantinople, not as due to themselves, but as one to which no bishop could legitimately pretend. There would be something almost ridiculous in the emperor's immediately conferring an appellation on themselves which they had just disclaimed ; and though this objection would not stand against evidence, yet when we find no better authority quoted for the fact than Baronius, who is no authority at all, it retains considerable weight. And, indeed, the want of early testimony is so decisive an objection to any alleged historical fact that, but for the strange prepossessions of some

men, one might rest the case here. Fleury takes no notice of this part of the story, though he tells us that Phocas compelled the Patriarch of Constantinople to resign his title. 2. But if the strongest proof could be advanced for the authenticity of this circumstance, we might well deny its importance. The concession of Phocas could have been of no validity in Lombardy, France, and other western countries, where nevertheless the papal supremacy was incomparably more established than in the East. 3. Even within the empire it could have had no efficacy after the violent death of that usurper, which followed soon afterward. 4. The title of universal bishop is not very intelligible ; but, whatever it meant, the Patriarchs of Constantinople had borne it before, and continued to bear it ever afterward. (Dupin, " De Antiquâ Disciplinâ," p. 329.) 5. The preceding popes, Pelagius II and Gregory I had constantly disclaimed the appellation, though it had been adopted by some toward Leo the Great in the Council of Chalcedon (Fleury, tome viii, p. 95); nor does it appear to have been retained by the successors of Boniface. It is even laid down in the decretum of Gratian that the Pope is not styled universal: nec etiam Romanus pontifex universalis appellatur (p. 303, edit. 1591), though some refer its assumption to the ninth century. (" Nouveau Traité de Diplomatique," tome v, p. 93.) In fact, it has never been a usual title. 6. The popes had unquestionably exercised a species of supremacy for more than two centuries before this time, which had lately reached a high point of authority under Gregory I. The rescript of Valentinian III in 455, quoted in a former note, would certainly be more to the purpose than the letter of Phocas. 7. Lastly, there are no sensible marks of this supremacy making a more rapid progress for a century and a half after the pretended grant of that emperor. [1818.] The earliest mention of this transaction that I have found, and one which puts an end to the pretended concession of such a title as universal bishop, is in a brief general chronology, by Bede, entitled " De Temporum Ratione." He only says of Phocas: Hic, rogante papa Bonifacio, statuit sedem Romanæ et apostolicæ ecclesiæ caput esse omnium ecclesiarum, quia ecclesia Constantinopolitana primam se omnium ecclesiarum scribebat. (" Bedæ Opera," curâ Giles, vol. vi, p. 323.) This was probably the exact truth; and the subsequent additions were made by some zealous partisans of Rome, to be seized hold of in a later age, and turned against her by some of her

sessed vigour and reputation equal to his own, it might even appear that the papal influence was retrograde. But in effect the principles which supported it were taking deeper root, and acquiring strength by occasional though not very frequent exercise. Appeals to the Pope were sometimes made by prelates dissatisfied with a local sentence; but his judgment of reversal was not always executed, as we perceive by the instance of Bishop Wilfrid.[62] National councils were still convoked by princes, and canons enacted under their authority by the bishops who attended. Though the Church of Lombardy was under great subjection during this period, yet those of France, and even of England, planted as the latter had been by Gregory, continued to preserve a tolerable measure of independence.[63] The first striking infringement of this was made through the influence of an Englishmen, Winfrid, better known as St. Boniface, the apostle of Germany. Having undertaken the conversion of Thuringia, and other still heathen countries, he applied to the Pope for a commission, and was consecrated bishop without any determinate see. Upon this occasion he took an oath of obedience, and became ever afterward a zealous upholder of the apostolical chair. His success in the conversion of Germany was great, his reputation eminent, which enabled him to effect a material revolution in ecclesiastical government. Pelagius II had, about 580, sent a pallium, or vest peculiar to metropolitans, to the Bishop of Arles, perpetual vicar of the Roman See in Gaul.[64] Gregory I had made a similar present to other metropolitans. But it

equally zealous enemies. The distinction generally made is, that the Pope is "universalis ecclesiæ episcopus," but not "episcopus universalis"; that is, he has no immediate jurisdiction in the dioceses of other bishops, though he can correct them for the undue exercise of their own. The Ultramontanes, of course, go further.

[62] I refer to the English historians for the history of Wilfrid, which neither altogether supports, nor much impeaches, the independency of our Anglo-Saxon Church in 700; a matter hardly worth so much contention as Usher and Stillingfleet seem to have thought. The consecration of Theodore by Pope Vitalian in 668 is a stronger fact, and can not be got over by those injudicious Protestants who take the bull by the horns. The history of Wilfrid has been lately put in a light as favourable as possible to himself and to the authority of Rome by Dr. Lingard. We have for this to rely on Eddius (published in Gale's "Scriptores"), a panegyrist in the usual style of legendary biography—a style which has, on me at least, the effect of producing utter distrust. Mendacity is the badge of all the tribe. Bede is more respectable; but in this case we do not learn

much from him. It seems impossible to deny that, if Eddius is a trustworthy historian, Dr. Lingard has made out his case; and that we must own appeals to Rome to have been recognised in the Anglo-Saxon Church. Nor do I perceive any improbability in this, considering that the Church had been founded by Augustin, and restored by Theodore, both under the authority of the Roman See. This intrinsic presumption is worth more than the testimony of Eddius. But we see by the rest of Wilfrid's history that it was not easy to put the sentence of Rome in execution. The plain facts are that, having gone to Rome claiming the See of York, and having had his claim recognised by the Pope, he ended his days as Bishop of Hexham.

[63] Schmidt, tome i, pp. 386, 394.

[64] Ut ad instar suum, in Galliarum partibus primi sacerdotis locum obtineat, et quidquid ad gubernationem vel dispensationem ecclesiastici status gerendum est, servatis patrum regulis, et sedis apostolicæ constitutis, faciat. Præterea, pallium illi concedit, etc. (Dupin, p. 34.) Gregory I confirmed this vicariate to Virgilius, Bishop of Arles, and gave him the power of convoking synods. (De Marca, l. vi, c. 7.)

was never supposed that they were obliged to wait for this favour before they received consecration, until a synod of the French and German bishops, held at Frankfort in 742, by Boniface, as legate of Pope Zachary. It was here enacted that, as a token of their willing subjection to the See of Rome, all metropolitans should request the pallium at the hands of the Pope, and obey his lawful commands.[65] This was construed by the popes to mean a promise of obedience before receiving the pall, which was changed in after times by Gregory VII into an oath of fealty.[66]

This Council of Frankfort claims a leading place as an epoch in the history of the papacy. Several events ensued, chiefly of a political nature, which rapidly elevated that usurpation almost to its greatest height. Subjects of the throne of Constantinople, the popes had not as yet interfered, unless by mere admonition, with the temporal magistrate. The first instance wherein the civil duties of a nation and the rights of a crown appear to have been submitted to his decision was in that famous reference as to the deposition of Childeric. It is impossible to consider this in any other light than as a point of casuistry laid before the first religious judge in the Church. Certainly, the Franks who raised the king of their choice upon their shields never dreamed that a foreign priest had conferred upon him the right of governing. Yet it was easy for succeeding advocates of Rome to construe this transaction very favourably for its usurpation over the thrones of the earth.[67]

I shall but just glance at the subsequent political revolutions of that period—the invasion of Italy by Pepin, his donation of the exarchate to the Holy See, the conquest of Lombardy by Charlemagne, the patriarchate of Rome conferred upon both these princes, and the revival of the Western Empire in the person of the latter. These events had a natural tendency to exalt

[65] Decrevimus, says Boniface, in nostro synodali conventu, et confessi sumus fidem catholicam, et unitatem et subjectionem Romanæ ecclesiæ fine tenus servare, S. Petro et vicario ejus velle subjici, metropolitanos pallia ab illâ sede quærere, et, per omnia, præcepta S. Petri canonicè sequi. (De Marca, l. vi, c. 7; Schmidt, tome i, pp. 424, 438, 446.) This writer justly remarks the obligation which Rome had to St. Boniface, who anticipated the system of Isidore. We have a letter from him to the English clergy, with a copy of canons passed in one of his synods, for the exaltation of the apostolic see, but the Church of England was not then inclined to acknowledge so great a supremacy in Rome. (Collier's " Eccles. History," p. 128.)
In the eighth general council, that of

Constantinople in 872, this prerogative of sending the pallium to metropolitans was not only confirmed to the Pope, but extended to the other patriarchs, who had every disposition to become as great usurpers as their more fortunate elder brother.
[66] De Marca, ubi supra; Schmidt, tome ii, p. 262. According to the latter, this oath of fidelity was exacted in the ninth century; which is very probable, since Gregory VII himself did but fill up the sketch which Nicholas I and John VIII had delineated. I have since found this confirmed by Gratia (p. 305).
[67] Eginhard says that Pepin was made king per auctoritatem Romani pontificis; an ambiguous word, which may rise to command, or sink to advice, according to the disposition of the interpreter.

the papal supremacy, which it is needless to indicate. But a circumstance of a very different nature contributed to this in a still greater degree. About the conclusion of the eighth century there appeared, under the name of one Isidore, an unknown person, a collection of ecclesiastical canons, now commonly denominated the "False Decretals." [68] These purported to be rescripts or decrees of the early Bishops of Rome; and their effect was to diminish the authority of metropolitans over their suffragans, by establishing an appellant jurisdiction of the Roman See in all causes, and by forbidding national councils to be holden without its consent. Every bishop, according to the decretals of Isidore, was amenable only to the immediate tribunal of the Pope, by which one of the most ancient rights of the provincial synod was abrogated. Every accused person might not only appeal from an inferior sentence, but remove an unfinished process, before the supreme pontiff. And the latter, instead of directing a revision of the proceedings by the original judges, might annul them by his own authority; a strain of jurisdiction beyond the canons of Sardica, but certainly warranted by the more recent practice of Rome. New sees were not to be erected, nor bishops translated from one see to another, nor their resignations accepted, without the sanction of the Pope. They were still, indeed, to be consecrated by the metropolitan, but in the Pope's name. It has been plausibly suspected that these decretals were forged by some bishop, in jealousy or resentment; and their general reception may at least be partly ascribed to such sentiments. The archbishops were exceedingly powerful, and might often abuse their superiority over inferior prelates; but the whole episcopal aristocracy had abundant reason to lament their acquiescence in a system of which the metropolitans were but the earliest victims. Upon these spurious decretals was built the great fabric of papal supremacy over the different national churches—a fabric which has stood after its foundation crumbled beneath it; for no one has pretended to deny, for the last two centuries, that the imposture is too palpable for any but the most ignorant ages to credit. [69]

<hr>

[68] The era of the False Decretals has not been precisely fixed; they have seldom been supposed, however, to have appeared much before 800. But there is a genuine collection of canons published by Adrian I in 785, which contain nearly the same principles, and many of which are copied by Isidore, as well as Charlemagne in his capitularies. (De Marca, l. vii, c. 20: Giannone, l. v, c. 6; Dupin, "De Antiquâ Disciplinâ," p. 133.) Fleury ("Hist. Eccles.," tome ix, p. 500) seems to consider the decretals as older than this collection of Adrian; but I have not observed the same opinion in any

other writer. The right of appeal from a sentence of the metropolitan deposing a bishop to the Holy See is positively recognised in the capitularies of Louis the Debonair (Baluze, p. 1000); the last three books of which, according to the collection of Ansegisus, are said to be apostolicâ auctoritate roborata, quia his cudendis maximè apostolica interfuit legatio (p. 1132).

[69] I have not seen any account of the decretals so clear and judicious as in Schmidt's "History of Germany," tome ii, p. 249. Indeed, all the ecclesiastical part of that work is executed in a very

The Gallican Church made for some time a spirited though unavailing struggle against this rising despotism. Gregory IV, having come into France to abet the children of Louis the Debonair in their rebellion, and threatened to excommunicate the bishops who adhered to the emperor, was repelled with indignation by those prelates. " If he comes here to excommunicate," said they, " he shall depart hence excommunicated." [70] In the subsequent reign of Charles the Bald a bold defender of ecclesiastical independence was found in Hincmar, Archbishop of Rheims, the most distinguished statesman of his age. Appeals to the Pope even by ordinary clerks had become common, and the provincial councils, hitherto the supreme spiritual tribunal, as well as legislature, were falling rapidly into decay. The frame of church government, which had lasted from the third or fourth century, was nearly dissolved; a refractory bishop was sure to invoke the supreme court of appeal, and generally met there with a more favourable judicature. Hincmar, a man equal in ambition, and almost in public estimation, to any pontiff, sometimes came off successfully in his contentions with Rome.[71] But time is fatal to the unanimity of coalitions; the French bishops were accessible to superstitious prejudice, to corrupt influence, to mutual jealousy. Above all, they were conscious that a persuasion of the Pope's omnipotence had taken hold of the laity. Though they complained loudly, and invoked, like patriots of a dying state, names and principles of a freedom that was no more, they submitted almost in every instance to the continual usurpations of the Holy See. One of those which most annoyed their aristocracy was the concession to monasteries of exemption from episcopal authority. These had been very uncommon till about the eighth century, after which they were studiously multiplied.[72] It was naturally a favourite object with the abbots;

superior manner. (See also De Marca, l. iii, c. 5; l. vii, c. 20.) The latter writer, from whom I have derived much information, is by no means a strenuous adversary of ultramontane pretensions. In fact, it was his object to please both in France and at Rome, to become both an archbishop and a cardinal. He failed nevertheless of the latter hope; it being impossible at that time (1650) to satisfy the papal court without sacrificing altogether the Gallican Church and the crown.

[70] De Marca, l. iv, c. 11; Velly, etc.

[71] De Marca, l. iv, c. 68, etc.; l. vi, c. 14, 28; l. vii, c. 21. Dupin, p. 133. etc. " Hist. du Droit Ecclés. François," pp. 188, 224. Velly, etc. Hincmar, however, was not consistent; for, having obtained the See of Rheims in an equivocal manner, he had applied for confirmation at Rome, and in other respects impaired the Gallican rights. (Pasquier, " Recherches de la France," l. iii, c. 12.)

[72] The earliest instance of a papal exemption is in 455, which, indeed, is a respectable antiquity. Others scarcely occur till the pontificate of Zachary in the middle of the eighth century, who granted an exemption to Monte Casino, ita ut nullius juri subjaceat, nisi solius Romani pontificis. (See this discussed in Giannone, l. v, c. 6.) Precedents for the exemption of monasteries from episcopal jurisdiction occur in Marculfus's forms compiled toward the end of the seventh century, but these were by royal authority. The Kings of France were supreme heads of their national church. (Schmidt, tome i, p. 382; De Marca, l. iii, c. 16; Fleury, " Institutions au Droit," tome i, p. 228.) Muratori, Dissert. 70 (tome iii, p. 104, Italian), is of opinion that exemptions of monasteries from episcopal visitation did not become frequent in Italy till the eleventh century, and that many charters of this kind are forgeries. It is held also by some English

and sovereigns, in those ages of blind veneration for monastic establishments, were pleased to see their own foundations rendered, as it would seem, more respectable by privileges of independence. The popes had a closer interest in granting exemptions, which attached to them the regular clergy, and lowered the dignity of the bishops. In the eleventh and twelfth centuries whole orders of monks were declared exempt at a single stroke; and the abuse began to awaken loud complaints, though it did not fail to be aggravated afterward.

The principles of ecclesiastical supremacy were readily applied by the popes to support still more insolent usurpations. Chiefs by divine commission of the whole Church, every earthly sovereign must be subject to their interference. The bishops, indeed, had, with the common weapons of their order, kept their own sovereigns in check, and it could not seem any extraordinary stretch in their supreme head to assert an equal prerogative. Gregory IV, as I have mentioned, became a party in the revolt against Louis I, but he never carried his threats of excommunication into effect. The first instance where the Roman pontiffs actually tried the force of their arms against a sovereign was the excommunication of Lothaire, King of Lorraine, and grandson of Louis the Debonair. This prince had repudiated his wife, upon unjust pretexts, but with the approbation of a national council, and had subsequently married his concubine. Nicolas I, the actual Pope, despatched two legates to investigate this business, and decide according to the canons. They hold a council at Metz, and confirm the divorce and marriage. Enraged at this conduct of his ambassadors, the Pope summons a council at Rome, annuls the sentence, deposes the Archbishops of Treves and Cologne, and directs the king to discard his mistress. After some shuffling on the part of Lothaire, he is excommunicated;

antiquaries that no Anglo-Saxon monastery was exempt, and that the first instance is that of Battle Abbey under the Conqueror, the charters of an earlier date having been forged. (Hody on "Convocations," pp. 20 and 170.) It is remarkable that this grant is made by William, and confirmed by Lanfranc. (Collier, p. 256.) Exemptions became very usual in England afterward. (Henry, vol. v, p. 337.) It is nevertheless to be admitted that the bishops had exercised an arbitrary and sometimes a tyrannical power over the secular clergy; and after the monks became part of the Church, which was before the close of the sixth century, they also fell under a control not always fairly exerted. Both complained greatly, as the acts of councils bear witness: Un fait important et trop peu remarque se révèle çà et là dans le cours de cette époque; c'est la lutte des prêtres de paroisse contre les évêques. (Guizot, " Hist. de la Civilis. en France, leçon 13.) In this contention the weaker must have given way: but the regulars, sustained by public respect, and having the countenance of the See of Rome, which began to encroach upon episcopal authority, came out successful in securing themselves by exemptions from the jurisdiction of the bishops. The latter furnished a good pretext by their own relaxation of manners. The monasteries in the eighth and ninth centuries seem not to have given occasion to much reproach, at least in comparison with the prelacy. Au commencement du huitième siècle, l'église était elle tombée dans un désordre presque égal à celui de la société civile. Sans supérieurs et sans inférieurs à redouter, dégagés de la surveillance des métropolitains comme des conciles et de l'influence des prêtres, une foule d'évêques se livraient aux plus scandaleux excès.

and, in a short time, we find both the king and his prelates, who
had begun with expressions of passionate contempt toward the
Pope, suing humbly for absolution at the feet of Adrian II, successor of Nicolas, which was not granted without difficulty. In
all its most impudent pretensions the Holy See has attended to
the circumstances of the time. Lothaire had powerful neighbours, the Kings of France and Germany, eager to invade his
dominions on the first intimation from Rome, while the real
scandalousness of his behaviour must have intimidated his conscience and disgusted his subjects.

Excommunication, whatever opinions may be entertained as
to its religious efficacy, was originally nothing more in appearance than the exercise of a right which every society claims—
the expulsion of refractory members from its body. No direct
temporal disadvantages attended this penalty for several ages;
but as it was the most severe of spiritual censures, and tended
to exclude the object of it not only from a participation in religious rites, but in a considerable degree from the intercourse of
Christian society, it was used sparingly and upon the gravest
occasions. Gradually, as the Church became more powerful and
more imperious, excommunications were issued upon every
provocation, rather as a weapon of ecclesiastical warfare than
with any regard to its original intention. There was certainly
some pretext for many of these censures, as the only means of
defence within the reach of the clergy when their possessions
were lawlessly violated.[73] Others were founded upon the necessity of enforcing their contentious jurisdiction, which, while it
was rapidly extending itself over almost all persons and causes,
had not acquired any proper coercive process. The spiritual
courts in England, whose jurisdiction is so multifarious, and,
in general, so little of a religious nature, had till lately no means
even of compelling an appearance, much less of enforcing a sentence, but by excommunication.[74] Princes who felt the inadequacy of their own laws to secure obedience called in the assistance of more formidable sanctions. Several capitularies of
Charlemagne denounce the penalty of excommunication against
incendiaries or deserters from the army. Charles the Bald procured similar censures against his revolted vassals. Thus the
boundary between temporal and spiritual offences grew every
day less distinct; and the clergy were encouraged to fresh encroachments as they discovered the secret of rendering them successful.[75]

The civil magistrate ought undoubtedly to protect the just

[73] Schmidt, tome iv, p. 217; Fleury,
" Institutions au Droit," tome ii, p. 192.
[74] By a recent statute, 53 G., iii, c. 127,
the writ De excommunicato capiendo, as
a process in contempt, was abolished in
England, but retained in Ireland.
[75] " Mém. de l'Acad. des Inscript.,"
tome xxxix, p. 596, etc.

rights and lawful jurisdiction of the Church. It is not so evident that he should attach temporal penalties to her censures. Excommunication has never carried such a presumption of moral turpitude as to disable a man, upon any solid principles, from the usual privileges of society. Superstition and tyranny, however, decided otherwise. The support due to Church censures by temporal judges is vaguely declared in the capitularies of Pepin and Charlemagne. It became in later ages a more established principle in France and England, and, I presume, in other countries. By our common law an excommunicated person is incapable of being a witness or of bringing an action, and he may be detained in prison until he obtains absolution. By the "Establishments" of St. Louis, his estate or person might be attached by the magistrate.[76] These actual penalties were attended by marks of abhorrence and ignominy still more calculated to make an impression on ordinary minds. They were to be shunned, like men infected with leprosy, by their servants, their friends, and their families. Two attendants only, if we may trust a current history, remained with Robert, King of France, who, on account of an irregular marriage, was put to this ban by Gregory V, and these threw all the meats which had passed his table into the fire.[77] Indeed, the mere intercourse with a proscribed person incurred what was called the lesser excommunication, or privation of the sacraments, and required penitence and absolution. In some places a bier was set before the door of an excommunicated individual, and stones thrown at his windows: a singular method of compelling his submission.[78] Everywhere the excommunicated were debarred of a regular sepulture, which, though obviously a matter of police, has, through the superstition of consecrating burial grounds, been treated as belonging to ecclesiastical control. Their carcasses were supposed to be incapable of corruption, which seems to have been thought a privilege unfit for those who had died in so irregular a manner.[79]

But as excommunication, which attacked only one and perhaps a hardened sinner, was not always efficacious, the Church had recourse to a more comprehensive punishment. For the offence of a nobleman she put a county, for that of a prince his entire kingdom, under an interdict or suspension of religious

[76] "Ordonnances des Rois," tome i, p. 121. But an excommunicated person might sue in the lay though not in the spiritual court. No law seems to have been so severe in this respect as that of England, though it is not strictly accurate to say with Dr. Cosens (Gibson's "Codex," p. 1102) that the writ De excommun. capiendo is a privilege peculiar to the English Church.

[77] Velly, tome ii.
[78] Vaissette, "Hist. de Languedoc," tome iii, appendix, p. 350; Du Cange, voc. Excommunicatio.
[79] Du Cange, voc. Imblocatus: where several authors are referred to, for the constant opinion among the members of the Greek Church that the bodies of excommunicated persons remain in statu quo.

offices. No stretch of her tyranny was perhaps so outrageous as this. During an interdict the churches were closed, the bells silent, the dead unburied, no rite but those of baptism and extreme unction performed. The penalty fell upon those who had neither partaken nor could have prevented the offence; and the offence was often but a private dispute, in which the pride of a pope or bishop had been wounded. Interdicts were so rare before the time of Gregory VII that some have referred them to him as their author; instances may, however, be found of an earlier date, and especially that which accompanied the above-mentioned excommunication of Robert, King of France. They were afterward issued not infrequently against kingdoms, but in particular districts they continually occurred.[80]

This was the mainspring of the machinery that the clergy set in motion, the lever by which they moved the world. From the moment that these interdicts and excommunications had been tried the powers of the earth might be said to have existed only by sufferance. Nor was the validity of such denunciations supposed to depend upon their justice. The imposer, indeed, of an unjust excommunication was guilty of a sin, but the party subjected to it had no remedy but submission. He who disregards such a sentence, says Beaumanoir, renders his good cause bad.[81] And indeed, without annexing so much importance to the direct consequences of an ungrounded censure, it is evident that the received theory of religion concerning the indispensable obligation and mysterious efficacy of the rights of communion and confession must have induced scrupulous minds to make any temporal sacrifice rather than incur their privation. One is rather surprised at the instances of failure than of success in the employment of these spiritual weapons against sovereigns or the laity in general. It was perhaps a fortunate circumstance for Europe that they were not introduced, upon a large scale, during the darkest ages of superstition. In the eighth or ninth centuries they would probably have met with a more implicit obedience. But after Gregory VII, as the spirit of ecclesiastical usurpation became more violent, there grew up by slow degrees an opposite feeling in the laity, which ripened into an alienation of sentiment from the Church, and a conviction of that sacred truth which superstition and sophistry have endeavoured to eradicate from the heart of man, that no tyrannical government can be founded on a divine commission.

Excommunications had very seldom, if ever, been levelled at the head of a sovereign before the instance of Lothaire. His

---

[80] Giannone, l. vii, c. 1; Schmidt, tome iv, p. 220; Dupin, " De Antiquâ Eccl. Disciplinâ," p. 288; St. Marc, tome ii, p. 535; Fleury, " Institutions," tome ii, p. 200.
[81] P. 261.

ignominious submission and the general feebleness of the Carlovingian line produced a repetition of the menace at least, and in
cases more evidently beyond the cognizance of a spiritual authority.   Upon the death of this Lothaire, his uncle, Charles the
Bald, having possessed himself of Lorraine, to which the Emperor Louis II had juster pretensions, the Pope Adrian II warned
him to desist, declaring that any attempt upon that country
would bring down the penalty of excommunication.   Sustained
by the intrepidity of Hincmar, the king did not exhibit his usual
pusillanimity, and the Pope in this instance failed of success.[82]
But John VIII, the next occupier of the chair of St. Peter, carried his pretensions to a height which none of his predecessors
had reached.   The Carlovingian princes had formed an alliance
against Boson, the usurper of the kingdom of Arles.   The Pope
writes to Charles the Fat: " I have adopted the illustrious Prince
Boson as my son; be content, therefore, with your own kingdom, for I shall instantly excommunicate all who attempt to injure my son." [83]   In another letter to the same king, who had
taken some property from a convent, he enjoins him to restore
it within sixty days, and to certify by an envoy that he had obeyed
the command, else an excommunication would immediately
ensue, to be followed by still severer castigation, if the king
should not repent upon the first punishment.[84]   These expressions seem to intimate a sentence of deposition from his throne,
and thus anticipate by two hundred years the famous era of
Gregory VII, at which we shall soon arrive.   In some respects
John VIII even advanced pretensions beyond those of Gregory.
He asserts very plainly a right of choosing the emperor, and may
seem indirectly to have exercised it in the election of Charles
the Bald, who had not primogeniture in his favour.[85]   This
prince, whose restless ambition was united with meanness as well
as insincerity, consented to sign a capitulation, on his coronation at Rome, in favour of the Pope and Church—a precedent
which was improved upon in subsequent ages.[86]   Rome was now
prepared to rivet her fetters upon sovereigns, and at no period
have the condition of society and the circumstances of civil
government been so favourable for her ambition.   But the consummation was still suspended, and even her progress arrested,
for more than a hundred and fifty years.   This dreary interval
is filled up, in the annals of the papacy, by a series of revolutions
and crimes.   Six popes were deposed, two murdered, one mutilated.   Frequently two or even three competitors, among whom
it is not always possible by any genuine criticism to distinguish

[82] De Marca, l. iv, c. 11.
[83] Schmidt, tome ii, p. 260.
[84] Durioribus deinceps sciens te ver-
beribus erudiendum. (Schmidt, p. 261.)

[85] " Baluz. Capitularia," tome ii, p.
251; Schmidt, tome ii, p. 197.
[86] Schmidt, tome ii, p. 199.

the true shepherd, drove each other alternately from the city.
A few respectable names appear thinly scattered through this
darkness; and sometimes, perhaps, a pope who had acquired
estimation by his private virtues may be distinguished by some
encroachment on the rights of princes or the privileges of national churches. But in general the pontiffs of that age had
neither leisure nor capacity to perfect the great system of
temporal supremacy, and looked rather to a vile profit from
the sale of episcopal confirmations or of exemptions to monasteries.[87]

The corruption of the head extended naturally to all other
members of the Church. All writers concur in stigmatizing the
dissoluteness and neglect of decency that prevailed among the
clergy. Though several codes of ecclesiastical discipline had
been compiled by particular prelates, yet neither these nor the
ancient canons were much regarded. The bishops, indeed, who
were to enforce them had most occasion to dread their severity.
They were obtruded upon their sees, as the supreme pontiffs
were upon that of Rome, by force or corruption. A child of
five years old was made Archbishop of Rheims. The See of
Narbonne was purchased for another at the age of ten.[88] By
this relaxation of morals the priesthood began to lose its hold
upon the prejudices of mankind. These are nourished chiefly,
indeed, by shining examples of piety and virtue, but also, in a
superstitious age, by ascetic observances, by the fasting and
watching of monks and hermits, who have obviously so bad a
lot in this life that men are induced to conclude that they must
have secured a better reversion in futurity. The regular clergy
accordingly, or monastic orders, who practised, at least apparently, the specious impostures of self-mortification, retained at all
times a far greater portion of respect than ordinary priests, though
degenerated themselves, as was admitted, from their primitive
strictness.

Two crimes, of at least violations of ecclesiastical law, had
become almost universal in the eleventh century, and excited
general indignation—the marriage or concubinage of priests and
the sale of benefices. By an effect of those prejudices in favour
of austerity to which I have just alluded, celibacy had been, from
very early times, enjoined as an obligation upon the clergy. It
was perhaps permitted that those already married for the first
time, and to a virgin, might receive ordination; and this, after
prevailing for a length of time in the Greek Church, was sanc-

[87] Schmidt, tome ii, p. 414; Mosheim; St. Marc; Muratori, "Ann. d' Italia," passim.
[88] Vaissette, "Hist. de Languedoc," tome ii, p. 252. It was almost general in the Church to have bishops under twenty years old. (Id., p. 149.) Even the Pope Benedict IX is said to have been only twelve, but this has been doubted.

tioned by the Council of Trullo in 691,[89] and has ever since continued one of the distinguishing features of its discipline. The Latin Church, however, did not receive these canons, and has uniformly persevered in excluding the three orders of priests, deacons, and subdeacons, not only from contracting matrimony, but from cohabiting with wives espoused before their ordination. The prohibition, however, during some ages existed only in the letter of her canons. In every country the secular or parochial clergy kept women in their houses, upon more or less acknowledged terms of intercourse, by a connivance of their ecclesiastical superiors, which almost amounted to a positive toleration. The sons of priests were capable of inheriting by the law of France and also of Castile.[90] Some vigorous efforts had been made in England by Dunstan, with the assistance of King Edgar, to dispossess the married canons, if not the parochial clergy, of their benefices; but the abuse, if such it is to be considered, made incessant progress, till the middle of the eleventh century. There was certainly much reason for the rulers of the Church to restore this part of their discipline, since it is by cutting off her members from the charities of domestic life that she secures their entire affection to her cause, and renders them, like veteran soldiers, independent of every feeling but that of fidelity to their commander and regard to the interests of their body. Leo IX,

[89] This council was held at Constantinople in the dome of the palace, called Trullus by the Latins. The nominative Trullo, though solœcistical, is used, I believe, by ecclesiastical writers in English. (St. Marc, tome i, p. 294; "Art de vérifier les Dates," tome i, p. 157; Fleury, "Hist. Ecclés.," tome x, p. 110.) Bishops are not within this permission, and can not retain their wives by the discipline of the Greek Church. Lingard says of the Anglo-Saxon Church: "During more than two hundred years from the death of Augustin the laws respecting clerical celibacy, so galling to the natural propensities of man, but so calculated to enforce an elevated idea of the sanctity which becomes the priesthood, were enforced with the utmost rigour: but during part of the ninth century and most of the tenth, when the repeated and sanguinary devastations of the Danes threatened the destruction of the hierarchy no less than of the government, the ancient canons opposed but a feeble barrier to the impulse of the passions." ("Ang.-Sax. Church," p. 176.) Whatever may have been the case in England, those who look at the abstract of the canons of French and Spanish councils, in Dupin's "Ecclesiastical History," from the sixth to the eleventh century, will find hardly one wherein there is not some enactment against bishops or priests retaining wives in their houses. Such provisions were not repeated certainly without reason; so that the remark of Fleury (tome xi, p. 594) that he has found no instance of clerical marriage before 893 can not weigh for a great deal. It is probable that bishops did not often marry after their consecration; but this can not be presumed of priests. Southey, in his "Vindiciæ Ecclesiæ Anglicanæ," p. 290, while he produces some instances of clerical matrimony, endeavours to mislead the reader into the supposition that it was even conformable to ecclesiastical canons.*

[90] "Recueil des Historiens," tome xi,

* A late writer, who has glossed over every fact in ecclesiastical history which could make against his own particular tenets, asserts, "In the earliest ages of the Church no restriction whatever had been placed on the clergy in this respect." (Palmer's "Compendious Ecclesiastical History," p. 115.) This may be, and I believe it is, very true of the apostolical period; but the "earliest ages" are generally understood to go further: and certainly the prohibition of marriage to priests was an established custom of some antiquity at the time of the Nicene Council. The question agitated there was, not whether priests should marry, contrary as it was admitted by their advocate to ἀρχαία ἐκκλησίας παράδοσις, but whether married men should be ordained. I do not see any difference in principle, but the Church had made one.

accordingly, one of the first pontiffs who retrieved the honour of the apostolic chair, after its long period of ignominy, began in good earnest the difficult work of enforcing celibacy among the clergy.[91] His successors never lost sight of this essential point of discipline. It was a struggle against the natural rights and strongest affections of mankind, which lasted for several ages, and succeeded only by the toleration of greater evils than those it was intended to remove. The laity, in general, took part against the married priests, who were reduced to infamy and want, or obliged to renounce their dearest connections. In many parts of Germany no ministers were left to perform divine services.[92] But perhaps there was no country where the rules of celibacy met with so little attention as in England. It was acknowledged in the reign of Henry I that the greater and better part of the clergy were married, and that prince is said to have permitted them to retain their wives.[93] But the hierarchy never

preface; Marina, " Ensayo sobre las Siete Partidas," chaps. *221, 223.* This was by virtue of the general indulgence shown by the customs of that country to concubinage, or baragania; the children of such a union always inheriting in default of those born in solemn wedlock. (Ibid.)

[91] St. Marc, tome iii, pp. *152, 164, 219, 602,* etc.

[92] Schmidt, tome iii, p. *279*; Martenne, " Thesaurus Anecdotorum," tome i, p. *230.* A Danish writer draws a still darker picture of the tyranny exercised toward the married clergy, which, if he does not exaggerate, was severe indeed: alii membris truncabantur, alii occidebantur, alii de patriâ expellebantur, pauci sua retinuere. (Langebek, " Script. Rerum Danicarum," tome i, p. *380.*) The prohibition was repeated by Waldemar II in *1222,* so that there seems to have been much difficulty then. (Id., pp. *287* and *272.*)

[93] Wilkins, "Concilia," p. *387*; "Chronicon Saxon"; Collier, pp. *248, 286, 294*; Littleton, vol. iii, p. *328.* The third Lateran Council fifty years afterward speaks of the detestable custom of keeping concubines long used by the English clergy. Cum in Angliâ pravâ et detestabili consuetudine et longo tempore fuerit obtentum, ut clerici in domibus suis fornicarias habeant. (Labbé, " Concilia," tome x, p. *1633.*) Eugenius IV sent a legate to impose celibacy on the Irish clergy. (Littleton's " Henry II," vol. ii, p. *42.*)

The English clergy long set at naught the fulminations of the Pope against their domestic happiness; and the common law, or at least irresistible custom, seems to have been their shield. There

is some reason to believe that their children were legitimate for the purposes of inheritance, which, however, I do not assert. The sons of priests are mentioned in several instruments of the twelfth and thirteenth centuries; but we can not be sure that they were not born before their fathers' ordination, or that they were reckoned legitimate.*

An instance, however, occurs in the " Rot. Cur. Regis," A. D. *1194,* where the assize find that there has been no presentation to the Church of Dunstan, but the parsons have held it from father to son. Sir Francis Palgrave, in his introduction to these records (p. *29*), gives other proofs of this hereditary succession in benefices. Giraldus Cambrensis, about the end of Henry II's reign (apud Wright's " Political Songs of England," p. *353*), mentions the marriage of the parochial clergy as almost universal. More sacerdotum parochialium Angliæ fere cunctorum damnabili quidem et detestabili, publicam secum habebat comitem individuam, et in foco focariam, et in cubiculo concubinam. They were called focariæ, as living at the same hearth; and this might be tolerated, perhaps, on pretence of service; but the fellowship, we perceive, was not confined to the fireside. It was about this time that a poem, " De Concubinis Sacerdotum," commonly attributed to Walter Mapes, but alluding by name to Pope Innocent III, humorously defends the uncanonical usage. It begins thus:

" Prisciani regula penitus cassatur,
Sacerdos per hic et hæc olim declinabatur,
Sed per hic solummodo nunc articulatur,

* Among the witnesses to some instruments in the reign of Edward I, printed by Mr. Hudson Gurney from the court rolls of the manor of Keswick in Norfolk, we have more than once Walter filius presbyteri. But the rest are described by the father's surname, except one, who is called filius Beatricis; and as he may be suspected of being illegitimate, we can not infer the contrary as to the priest's son.

relaxed in their efforts; and all the councils, general or provincial, of the twelfth century utter denunciations against concubinary priests.[94] After that age we do not find them so frequently mentioned; and the abuse by degrees, though not suppressed, was reduced within limits at which the Church might connive.

Simony, or the corrupt purchase of spiritual benefices, was the second characteristic reproach of the clergy in the eleventh century. The measures taken to repress it deserve particular consideration, as they produced effects of the highest importance in the history of the middle ages. According to the primitive custom of the Church, an episcopal vacancy was filled up by election of the clergy and people belonging to the city or diocese. The subject of their choice was, after the establishment of the federate or provincial system, to be approved or rejected by the metropolitan and his suffragans, and, if approved, he was consecrated by them.[95] It is probable that, in almost every case, the clergy took a leading part in the selection of their bishops; but the consent of the laity was absolutely necessary to render it valid.[96]. They were, however, by degrees excluded from any real participation, first in the Greek and finally in the Western Church. But this was not effected till pretty late times; the

Cum per nostrum præsulem hæc amoveatur."
The last lines are better known, having been often quoted:
" Ecce jam pro clericis multum allegavi,
Necnon pro presbyteris multa comprobavi;
Pater-noster nunc pro me, quoniam peccavi,
Dicat quisque presbyter cum suâ suavi."
(" Poems ascribed to Mapes," p. 171, Camden Society, 1841.)
Several other poems in this very curious volume allude to the same subject. In a dialogue between a priest and a scholar, the latter having taxed him with keeping a presbytera in his house, the parson defends himself by recrimination:
" Malo cum presbytera pulcra fornicari,
Servituros domino filios lucrari,
Quam vagas satellites per antra sectari;
Est inhonestissimum sic dehonestari."
(p. 256.)
John, on occasion of the interdict pronounced against him in 1208, seized the concubines of the priests and compelled them to redeem themselves by. a fine. Presbyterorum et clericorum focariæ per totam Angliam a ministris regis captæ sunt, et ad se redimendum graviter compulsæ. (Matt. Paris, p. 190.) This is omitted by Lingard.
It is said by Raumer (" Gesch. der Hohenstauffen," vi, 235) that there was a married Bishop of Prague during the

pontificate of Innocent III, and that the custom of clerical marriages lasted in Hungary and Sweden to the end of the thirteenth century.
The marriages of English clergy are noticed and condemned in some provincial constitutions of 1237. (Matt. Paris, p. 381.) And there is, even so late as 1404, a mandate by the Bishop of Exeter against married priests. (Wilkins, " Concilia," tome iii, p. 277.)
[94] Quidam sacerdotes Latini, says Innocent III, in domibus suis habent concubinas, et nonnulli aliquas sibi non metuunt desponsare. (" Opera Innocent III," p. 558; see also pp. 300 and 407.) The latter can not be supposed a very common case, after so many prohibitions; the more usual practice was to keep a female in their houses, under some pretence of relationship or servitude, as is still said to be usual in Catholic countries. (Du Cange, voc. Focaria.) A writer of respectable authority asserts that the clergy frequently obtained a bishop's license to cohabit with a mate. (Harmer's [Wharton's] " Observations on Burnet," p. 11.) I find a passage in Nicholas de Clemangis about 1400, quoted in Lewis's " Life of Pecock," p. 30: Plerisque in diocesibus, rectores parochiarum ex certo et conducto cum his prælatis pretio, passim et publicè concubinas tenent. This, however, does not amount to a direct license.
[95] Marca, " De Concordantiâ," etc., l. vi, c. 2.
[96] Father Paul on " Benefices," c. 7.

people fully preserved their elective rights at Milan in the eleventh century, and traces of their concurrence may be found both in France and Germany in the next age.[97]

It does not appear that the early Christian emperors interposed with the freedom of choice any further than to make their own confirmation necessary in the great patriarchal sees, such as Rome and Constantinople, which were frequently the objects of violent competition, and to decide in controverted elections.[98] The Gothic and Lombard Kings of Italy followed the same line of conduct.[99] But in the French monarchy a more extensive authority was assumed by the sovereign. Though the practice was subject to some variation, it may be said generally that the Merovingian kings, the line of Charlemagne, and the German emperors of the house of Saxony, conferred bishoprics either by direct nomination or, as was more regular, by recommendatory letters to the electors.[100] In England also, before the conquest, bishops were appointed in the witenagemot; and even in the reign of William it is said that Lanfranc was raised to the see of Canterbury by consent of Parliament.[101] But, independently of this prerogative, which length of time and the tacit sanction of the people have rendered unquestionably legitimate, the sovereign had other means of controlling the election of a bishop. Those estates and honours which compose the temporalities of the see, and without which the naked spiritual privileges would not have tempted an avaricious generation, had chiefly been granted by former kings, and were assimilated to lands held on a beneficiary tenure. As they seemed to partake of the nature of fiefs, they required similar formalities—investiture by the lord and an oath of fealty by the tenant. Charlemagne is said to have introduced this practice; and, by way of visible symbol, as usual in feudal institutions, to have put the ring and crozier into the

[97] De Marca, ubi supra; Schmidt, tome iv, p. 173. The form of election of a Bishop of Puy, in 1053, runs thus: Clerus, populus, et militia elegimus. (Vaissette, "Hist. de Languedoc," tome ii, appendix, p. 220.) Even Gratian seems to admit in one place that the laity had a sort of share, though no decisive voice, in filling up an episcopal vacancy. Electio clericorum est, petitio plebis. (Decret., l. i, distinctio 62.) And other subsequent passages confirm this.

[98] Gibbon, c. 20; St. Marc, "Abrégé Chronologique," tome i, p. 7.

[99] Fra Paolo on "Benefices," c. 9; Giannone, l. iii, c. 6; l. iv, c. 12; St. Marc, tome i, p. 37.

[100] Schmidt, tome i, p. 386; tome ii, pp. 245, 487. This interference of the kings was perhaps not quite conformable to their own laws, which only reserved to them the confirmation. Episcopo decedente, says a constitution of Clotaire II

in 615, in loco ipsius, qui a metropolitano ordinari debet, a provincialibus, a clero et populo eligatur: et si persona condigna fuerit, per ordinationem principis ordinetur. ("Baluz. Capitul.," tome i, p. 21.) Charlemagne is said to have adhered to this limitation, leaving elections free, and only approving the person, and conferring investiture on him. (Father Paul on "Benefices," c. 15.) But a more direct influence was restored afterward. Ivon, Bishop of Chartres, about the year 1100, thus concisely expresses the several parties concurring in the creation of a bishop: Eligente clero, suffragante populo, dono regis, per manum metropolitani, approbante Romano pontifice. (Du Chesne, "Script. Rerum Gallicarum," tome iv, p. 174.)

[101] Littleton's "Hist. of Henry II," vol. iv, p. 144. But the passage which he quotes from the "Saxon Chronicle" is not found in the best edition.

hands of the newly consecrated bishop. And this continued for more than two centuries afterward without exciting any scandal or resistance.[102]

The Church has undoubtedly surrendered part of her independence in return for ample endowments and temporal power, nor could any claim be more reasonable than that of feudal superiors to grant the investiture of dependent fiefs. But the fairest right may be sullied by abuse; and the sovereigns, the lay patrons, the prelates of the tenth and eleventh centuries, made their powers of nomination and investiture subservient to the grossest rapacity.[103] According to the ancient canons, a benefice was avoided by any simoniacal payment or stipulation. If these were to be enforced, the Church must almost be cleared of its ministers. Either through bribery in places where elections still prevailed, or through corrupt agreements with princes, or at least customary presents to their wives and ministers, a large proportion of the bishops had no valid tenure in their sees. The case was perhaps worse with inferior clerks; in the Church of Milan, which was notorious for this corruption, not a single ecclesiastic could stand the test, the archbishop exacting a price for the collation of every benefice.[104]

The Bishops of Rome, like those of inferior sees, were regularly elected by the citizens, laymen as well as ecclesiastics. But their consecration was deferred until the popular choice had received the sovereign's sanction. The Romans regularly despatched letters to Constantinople or to the exarchs of Ravenna, praying that their election of a pope might be confirmed. Exceptions, if any, are infrequent while Rome was subject to the Eastern Empire.[105] This, among other imperial prerogatives, Charlemagne might consider as his own. He possessed the city, especially after his coronation as emperor, in full sovereignty; and even before that event had investigated, as supreme chief, some accusations preferred against the Pope Leo III. No vacancy of the papacy took place after Charlemagne became emperor; and it must be confessed that, in the first which happened under Louis the Debonair, Stephen IV was consecrated in haste without that prince's approbation.[106] But Gregory IV, his successor, waited till his election had been confirmed; and, upon

---

[102] De Marca, p. 416; Giannone, l. vi, c. 7.

[103] Boniface, Marquis of Tuscany, father of the Countess Matilda, and by far the greatest prince in Italy, was flogged before the altar by an abbot for selling benefices. (Muratori, ad ann. 1046.) The offence was much more common than the punishment, but the two combined furnish a good specimen of the eleventh century.

[104] St. Marc, tome iii, pp. 65, 188, 219,

230, 206, 568; Muratori, A. D. 958, 1057, etc.; Fleury, " Hist. Ecclés.," tome xiii, p. 73. The sum, however, appears to have been very small: rather like a fee than a bribe.

[105] Le Blanc, " Dissertation sur l'Autorité des Empereurs." This is subjoined to his " Traité des Monnoyes "; but not in all copies, which makes those that want it less valuable. (St. Marc and Muratori, passim.)

[106] Muratori, A. D. 817; St. Marc.

the whole, the Carlovingian emperors, though less uniformly than their predecessors, retained that mark of sovereignty.[107] But during the disorderly state of Italy which followed the last reigns of Charlemagne's posterity, while the sovereignty and even the name of an emperor were in abeyance, the supreme dignity of Christendom was conferred only by the factious rabble of its capital. Otho the Great, in receiving the imperial crown, took upon him the prerogatives of Charlemagne. There is even extant a decree of Leo VIII, which grants to him and his successors the right of naming future popes. But the authenticity of this instrument is denied by the Italians.[108] It does not appear that the Saxon emperors went to such a length as nomination, except in one instance (that of Gregory V, in 996); but they sometimes, not uniformly, confirmed the election of a pope, according to ancient custom. An explicit right of nomination was, however, conceded to the Emperor Henry III in 1047, as the only means of rescuing the Roman Church from the disgrace and depravity into which it had fallen. Henry appointed two or three very good popes, acting in this against the warnings of a selfish policy, as fatal experience soon proved to his family.[109]

This high prerogative was perhaps not designed to extend beyond Henry himself. But even if it had been transmissible to his successors, the infancy of his son, Henry IV, and the factions of that minority, precluded the possibility of its exercise. Nicolas II, in 1059, published a decree which restored the right of election to the Romans, but with a remarkable variation from the original form. The cardinal bishops (seven in number, holding sees in the neighbourhood of Rome, and consequently suffragans of the Pope as patriarch or metropolitan) were to choose the supreme pontiff, with the concurrence first of the cardinal priests and deacons (or ministers of the parish churches of Rome), and afterward of the laity. Thus elected, the new Pope was to be presented for confirmation to Henry, " now king, and hereafter to become emperor," and to such of his successors as should personally obtain that privilege.[110] This decree is the foundation of that celebrated mode of election in a conclave of cardinals which has ever since determined the headship of the Church. It was intended not only to exclude the citizens, who had, in-

[107] Le Blanc; Schmidt, tome ii, p. 186; St. Marc, tome i, pp. 387, 303, etc.
[108] St. Marc has defended the authenticity of this instrument in a separate dissertation (tome iv, p. 1167), though admitting some interpolations. Pagi, in " Baronium," tome iv, p. 8, seemed to me to have urged some weighty objections; and Muratori, " Annali d' Italia," A. D. 962, speaks of it as a gross imposture, in which he probably goes too far.

It obtained credit rather early, and is admitted into the Decretum of Gratian, notwithstanding its obvious tendency (p. 211, edit. 1591).
[109] St. Marc; Muratori; Schmidt: Struvius.
[110] St. Marc, tome iii, p. 276. The first canon of the third Lateran Council makes the consent of two thirds of the college necessary for a pope's election. (Labbé, " Concilia," tome x, p. 1508.)

deed, justly forfeited their primitive right, but as far as possible to prepare the way for an absolute emancipation of the papacy from the imperial control, reserving only a precarious and personal concession to the emperors instead of their ancient legal prerogative of confirmation.

The real author of this decree, and of all other vigorous measures adopted by the popes of that age, whether for the assertion of their independence or the restoration of discipline, was Hildebrand, Archdeacon of the Church of Rome, by far the most conspicuous person of the eleventh century. Acquiring by his extraordinary qualities an unbounded ascendency over the Italian clergy, they regarded him as their chosen leader and the hope of their common cause. He had been empowered singly to nominate a pope on the part of the Romans after the death of Leo IX, and compelled Henry III to acquiesce in his choice of Victor II.[111] No man could proceed more fearlessly toward his object than Hildebrand, nor with less attention to conscientious impediments. Though the decree of Nicolas II, his own work, had expressly reserved the right of confirmation of the young King of Germany, yet on the death of that pope, Hildebrand procured the election and consecration of Alexander II without waiting for any authority.[112] During this pontificate he was considered as something greater than the Pope, who acted entirely by his counsels. On Alexander's decease, Hildebrand, long since the real head of the Church, was raised with enthusiasm to its chief dignity, and assumed the name of Gregory VII.

Notwithstanding the late precedent at the election of Alexander II, it appears that Gregory did not yet consider his plans sufficiently mature to throw off the yoke altogether, but declined to receive consecration until he had obtained the consent of the King of Germany.[113] This moderation was not of long continuance. The situation of Germany speedily afforded him an opportunity of displaying his ambitious views. Henry IV, through a very bad education, was arbitrary and dissolute; the Saxons were engaged in a desperate rebellion; and secret disaffection had spread among the princes to an extent of which the Pope was much better aware than the king.[114] He began by excommunicating some of Henry's ministers on pretence of simony, and made it a ground of remonstrance that they were not instantly dismissed. His next step was to publish a decree, or rather to renew one of Alexander II, against lay investitures.[115]

---

[111] St. Marc, p. 97.
[112] Id., p. 306.
[113] St. Marc, p. 552. He acted, however, as pope, corresponding in that character with bishops of all countries, from the day of his election (p. 554).

[114] Schmidt; Saint Marc. These two are my principal authorities for the contest between the Church and the empire.
[115] St. Marc, tome iii, p. 670.

The abolition of these was a favourite object of Gregory, and formed an essential part of his general scheme for emancipating the spiritual and subjugating the temporal power. The ring and crosier, it was asserted by the papal advocates, were the emblems of that power which no monarch could bestow; but even if a less offensive symbol were adopted in investitures, the dignity of the Church was lowered, and her purity contaminated, when her highest ministers were compelled to solicit the patronage or the approbation of laymen. Though the estates of bishops might strictly be of temporal right, yet, as they had been inseparably annexed to their spiritual office, it became just that what was first in dignity and importance should carry with it those accessory parts. And this was more necessary than in former times on account of the notorious traffic which sovereigns made of their usurped nomination to benefices, so that scarcely any prelate sat by their favour whose possession was not invalidated by simony.

The contest about investitures, though begun by Gregory VII, did not occupy a very prominent place during his pontificate, its interest being suspended by other more extraordinary and important dissensions between the Church and empire. The Pope, after tampering some time with the disaffected party in Germany, summoned Henry to appear at Rome and vindicate himself from the charges alleged by his subjects. Such an outrage naturally exasperated a young and passionate monarch. Assembling a number of bishops and other vassals at Worms, he procured a sentence that Gregory should no longer be obeyed as lawful Pope. But the time was past for those arbitrary encroachments, or at least high prerogatives, of former emperors. The relations of dependency between Church and state were now about to be reversed. Gregory had no sooner received accounts of the proceedings at Worms than he summoned a council in the Lateran palace, and by a solemn sentence not only excommunicated Henry, but deprived him of the kingdoms of Germany and Italy, releasing his subjects from their allegiance, and forbidding them to obey him as sovereign. Thus Gregory VII obtained the glory of leaving all his predecessors behind, and astonishing mankind by an act of audacity and ambition which the most emulous of his successors could hardly surpass.[116]

[116] The sentence of Gregory VII against the Emperor Henry was directed, we should always remember, to persons already well disposed to reject his authority. Men are glad to be told that it is their duty to resist a sovereign against whom they are in rebellion, and will not be very scrupulous in examining conclusions which fall in with their inclinations and interests. Allegiance was in those turbulent ages easily thrown off, and the right of resistance was in continual exercise. To the Germans of the eleventh century a prince unfit for Christian communion would easily appear unfit to reign over them; and though Henry had not given much real provocation to the Pope, his vices and tyranny might seem to challenge any spiritual censure or temporal chastisement. A nearly con-

The first impulses of Henry's mind on hearing this denunciation were indignation and resentment. But, like other inexperienced and misguided sovereigns, he had formed an erroneous calculation of his own resources. A conspiracy, long prepared, of which the Dukes of Swabia and Carinthia were the chiefs, began to manifest itself. Some were alienated by his vices, and others jealous of his family. The rebellious Saxons took courage; the bishops, intimidated by excommunications, withdrew from his side, and he suddenly found himself almost insulated in the midst of his dominions. In this desertion he had recourse, through panic, to a miserable expedient. He crossed the Alps with the avowed determination of submitting, and seeking absolution from the Pope. Gregory was at Canossa, a fortress near Reggio, belonging to his faithful adherent, the Countess Matilda. It was in a winter of unusual severity. The emperor was admitted, without his guards, into an outer court of the castle, and three successive days remained from morning till evening in a woollen shirt and with naked feet; while Gregory, shut up with the countess, refused to admit him to his presence. On the fourth day he obtained absolution; but only upon condition of appearing on a certain day to learn the Pope's decision whether or no he should be restored to his kingdom, until which time he promised not to assume the ensigns of royalty.

This base humiliation, instead of conciliating Henry's adversaries, forfeited the attachment of his friends. In his contest with the Pope he had found a zealous support in the principal Lombard cities, among whom the married and simoniacal clergy had great influence.[117] Indignant at his submission to Gregory, whom they affected to consider as a usurper of the papal chair, they now closed their gates against the emperor, and spoke openly of deposing him. In this singular position between oppo-

temporary writer combines the two justifications of the rebellious party. Nemo Romanorum pontificem reges a regno deponere posse denegabit, quicunque decreta sanctissimi papæ Gregorii non proscribenda judicabit. Ipse enim vir apostolicus. . . . Præterea, liberi homines Henricum eo pacto sibi præposuerunt in regem, ut electores suos justè judicare et regali providentiâ gubernare satageret, quod pactum ille postea prævaricari et contemnere non cessavit, etc. Ergo, et absque sedis apostolicæ judicio principes eum pro rege meritò refutare possent, cum pactum adimplere contempserit, quod iis pro electione su promiserat; quo non adimpleto, nec rex esse poterat. ("Vita Greg. VII," in Muratori, "Script. Rer. Ital.," tome iii, p. 342.)

Upon the other hand, the friends and supporters of Henry, though ecclesiastics, protested against this novel stretch of prerogative in the Roman see. Sev-

eral proofs of this are adduced by Schmidt, tome iii, p. 315.

[117] There had been a kind of civil war at Milan for about twenty years before this time, excited by the intemperate zeal of some partisans who endeavoured to execute the papal decrees against irregular clerks by force. The history of these feuds has been written by two contemporaries, Arnulf and Landulf, published in the fourth volume of Muratori's "Scriptores Rerum Italicarum"; sufficient extracts from which will be found in St. Marc, tome iii, p. 230, etc., and in Muratori's "Annals." The Milanese clergy set up a pretence to retain wives, under the authority of their great archbishop, St. Ambrose, who, it seems, has spoken with more indulgence of this practice than most of the fathers. Both Arnulf and Landulf favour the married clerks, and were perhaps themselves of that description. (Muratori.)

site dangers, Henry retrod his late steps, and broke off his treaty with the Pope; preferring, if he must fall, to fall as the defender rather than the betrayer of his imperial rights. The rebellious princes of Germany chose another king, Rodolph, Duke of Swabia, on whom Gregory, after some delay, bestowed the crown, with a Latin verse importing that it was given by virtue of the original commission of St. Peter.[118] But the success of this pontiff in his immediate designs was not answerable to his intrepidity. Henry both subdued the German rebellion and carried on the war with so much vigour, or rather so little resistance, in Italy that he was crowned in Rome by the antipope Guibert, whom he had raised in a council of his partisans to the government of the Church instead of Gregory. The latter found an asylum under the protection of Roger Guiscard, at Salerno, where he died an exile. His mantle, however, descended upon his successors, especially Urban II and Paschal II, who strenuously persevered in the great contest for ecclesiastical independence; the former with a spirit and policy of Gregory VII, the latter with steady but disinterested prejudice.[119] They raised up enemies against Henry IV out of the bosom of his family, instigating the ambition of two of his sons successively, Conrad and Henry, to mingle in the revolts of Germany. But Rome, under whose auspices the latter had not scrupled to engage in an almost parricidal rebellion, was soon disappointed by his unexpected tenaciousness of that obnoxious prerogative which had occasioned so much of his father's misery. He steadily refused to part with the right of investiture, and the empire was still committed in open hostility with the Church for fifteen years of his reign. But Henry V being stronger in the support of his German vassals than his father had been, none of the popes with whom he was engaged had the boldness to repeat the measures of Gregory VII. At length, each party grown weary of this ruinous contention, a treaty was agreed upon between the emperor and Calixtus II, which put an end by compromise to the question of ecclesiastical investitures. By this compact the emperor resigned forever all pretence to invest bishops by the ring and crosier, and recognised the liberty of elections. But in return it was agreed that elections should be

---

[118] Petra dedit Petro, Petrus diadema Rodolpho.

[119] Paschal II was so conscientious in his abhorrence of investitures that he actually signed an agreement with Henry V in 1110, whereby the prelates were to resign all the lands and other possessions which they held in fief of the emperor, on condition of the latter renouncing the right of investiture, which indeed, in such circumstances, would fall of itself. This extraordinary concession, as may be imagined, was not very satisfactory to the cardinals and bishops about Paschal's court, more worldly minded than himself, nor to those of the emperor's party, whose joint clamour soon put a stop to the treaty. (St. Marc, tome iv, p. 976.) A letter of Paschal to Anselm (Schmidt, tome iii, p. 304) seems to imply that he thought it better for the Church to be without riches than to enjoy them on condition of doing homage to laymen.

made in his presence or that of his officers, and that the new bishop should receive his temporalities from the emperor by the sceptre.[120]

Both parties in the concordat at Worms receded from so much of their pretensions that we might almost hesitate to determine which is to be considered as victorious. On the one hand, in restoring the freedom of episcopal elections the emperors lost a prerogative of very long standing, and almost necessary to the maintenance of authority over not the least turbulent part of their subjects. And though the form of investiture by the ring and crosier seemed in itself of no importance, yet it had been in effect a collateral security against the election of obnoxious persons. For the emperors, detaining this necessary part of the pontificals until they should confer investiture, prevented a hasty consecration of the new bishop, after which, the vacancy being legally filled, it would not be decent for them to withhold the temporalities. But then, on the other hand, they preserved by the concordat their feudal sovereignty over the estates of the Church, in defiance of the language which had recently been held by its rulers. Gregory VII had positively declared, in the Lateran Council of 1080, that a bishop or abbot receiving investiture from a layman should not be reckoned as a prelate.[121] The same doctrine had been maintained by all his successors, without any limitation of their censures to the formality of the ring and crosier. But Calixtus II himself had gone much further, and absolutely prohibited the compelling ecclesiastics to render any service to laymen on account of their benefices.[122] It is evident that such a general immunity from feudal obligations for an order who possessed nearly half the lands in Europe struck at the root of those institutions by which the fabric of society was principally held together. This complete independency had been the aim of Gregory's disciples; and by yielding to the continuance of lay investitures in any shape Calixtus may, in this point of view, appear to have relinquished the principal object of contention.[123]

[120] St. Marc, tome iv, p. 1093; Schmidt, tome iii, p. 178. The latter quotes the Latin words.
[121] St. Marc, tome iv, p. 774. A bishop of Placentia asserts that prelates dishonoured their order by putting their hands, which held the body and blood of Christ, between those of impure laymen (p. 956). The same expressions are used by others, and are levelled at the form of feudal homage, which, according to the principles of that age, ought to have been as obnoxious as investiture.
[122] Id., pp. 1061, 1067.
[123] Ranke observes that, according to the concordat of Worms, predominant influence was yielded to the emperor in Germany and to the Pope in Italy; an agreement, however, which was not expressed with precision, and which contained the germ of fresh disputes. ("Hist. of Reform.," i, 34.) But even if this victory should be assigned to Rome in respect of Germany, it does not seem equally clear as to England. Lingard says of the agreement between Henry I and Paschal II: "Upon the whole, the Church gained little by this compromise. It might check, but did not abolish, the principal abuse. If Henry surrendered an unnecessary ceremony, he still retained the substance. The right which he assumed of nominating bishops and abbots was left un-

The emperors were not the only sovereigns whose practice of investiture excited the hostility of Rome, although they sustained the principal brunt of the war. A similar contest broke out under the pontificate of Paschal II with Henry I of England; for the circumstances of which, as they contain nothing peculiar, I refer to our own historians. It is remarkable that it ended in a compromise not unlike that adjusted at Worms, the king renouncing all sorts of investitures, while the Pope consented that the bishop should do homage for his temporalities. This was exactly the custom of France, where an investiture by the ring and crosier is said not to have prevailed; [124] and it answered the main end of sovereigns by keeping up the feudal dependency of ecclesiastical estates. But the Kings of Castile were more fortunate than the rest; discreetly yielding to the pride of Rome, they obtained what was essential to their own authority, and have always possessed, by the concession of Urban II, an absolute privilege of nomination to bishoprics in their dominions [125]—an early evidence of that indifference of the popes toward the real independence of national churches to which subsequent ages were to lend abundant confirmation.

When the emperors had surrendered their pretensions to interfere in episcopal elections, the primitive mode of collecting the suffrages of clergy and laity in conjunction, or at least of the clergy with the laity's assent and ratification, ought naturally to have revived. But in the twelfth century neither the people, nor even the general body of the diocesan clergy, were considered as worthy to exercise this function. It soon devolved altogether upon the chapters of cathedral churches.[126] The original

impaired." (" Hist. of Engl.," ii, 169.) But if this nomination by the crown was so great an abuse, why did the popes concede it to Spain and France? The real truth is, that no mode of choosing bishops is altogether unexceptionable. But, upon the whole, nomination by the crown is likely to work better than any other, even for the religious good of the Church. As a means of preserving the connection of the clergy with the state, it is almost indispensable.

Schmidt observes, as to Germany, that the dispute about investitures was not wholly to the advantage of the Church; though she seemed to come out successfully, yet it produced a hatred on the part of the laity, and, above all, a determination in the princes and nobility, to grant no more lands over which their suzerainty was to be disputed (iii, 269). The emperors retained a good deal—the regale, or possession of the temporalities during a vacancy; the prerogative, on a disputed election, of investing whichever candidate they pleased; above all, perhaps, the recognition of a great principle, that the Church was, as to its temporal estate, the subject of the civil magistrate.

The feudal element of society was so opposite to the ecclesiastical that whatever was gained by the former was so much subtracted from the efficacy of the latter. This left an importance to the imperial investiture after the Calixtin concordat, which was not intended probably by the Pope. For the words, as quoted by Schmidt (iii, 301), Habeat imperatoria dignitas electum liber, consecratum canonicè, regaliter per sceptrum sine pretio tamen investire soleniter, imply nothing more than a formality. The emperor is, as it were, commanded to invest the bishop after consecration. But in practice the emperors always conferred the investiture before consecration. (Schmidt, iv, 153.)

[124] " Histoire du Droit Public Ecclésiastique François," p. 261. I do not fully rely on this authority.

[125] F. Paul on " Benefices," c. 24; Zurita, " Annales de Aragon," tome iv, p. 305. Fleury says that the Kings of Spain nominate to bishoprics by virtue of a particular indulgence, renewed by the Pope for the life of each prince. (" Institutions au Droit," tome i, p. 106.)

[126] Fra Paolo (" Treatise on Bene-

of these may be traced very high. In the earliest ages we find a college of presbytery consisting of the priests and deacons, assistants as a council of advice, or even a kind of Parliament, to their bishops. Parochial divisions, and fixed ministers attached to them, were not established till a later period. But the canons, or cathedral clergy, acquired afterward a more distinct character. They were subjected by degrees to certain strict observances, little differing, in fact, from those imposed on monastic orders. They lived at a common table, they slept in a common dormitory, their dress and diet were regulated by peculiar laws. But they were distinguished from monks by the right of possessing individual property, which was afterward extended to the enjoyment of separate prebends or benefices. These strict regulations, chiefly imposed by Louis the Debonair, went into disuse through the relaxation of discipline; nor were they ever effectually restored. Meantime the chapters became extremely rich; and as they monopolized the privilege of electing bishops, it became an object of ambition with noble families to obtain canonries for their younger children as the surest road to ecclesiastical honours and opulence. Contrary, therefore, to the general policy of the Church, persons of inferior birth have been rigidly excluded from these foundations.[127]

The object of Gregory VII, in attempting to redress those more flagrant abuses which for two centuries had deformed the face of the Latin Church, is not incapable, perhaps, of vindication, though no sufficient apology can be offered for the means he employed. But the disinterested love of reformation, to which candour might ascribe the contention against investitures, is belied by the general tenor of his conduct, exhibiting an arrogance without parallel, and an ambition that grasped at universal and unlimited monarchy. He may be called the common enemy of all sovereigns whose dignity as well as independence mortified his infatuated pride. Thus we find him menacing Philip I of France, who had connived at the pillage of some Italian merchants and pilgrims, not only with an interdict, but a sentence of deposition.[128] Thus, too, he asserts, as a known historical fact, that the kingdom of Spain had formerly belonged, by spe-

fices," c. 24) says that between 1122 and 1145 it became a rule almost everywhere established that bishops should be chosen by the chapter. Schmidt, however, brings a few instances where the consent of the nobility and other laics is expressed, though perhaps little else than a matter of form. Innocent II seems to have been the first who declared that whoever had the majority of the chapter in his favour should be deemed duly elected; and this was confirmed by Otho IV in the capitulation upon his acces-

sion. (" Hist. des Allemands," tome iv, p. 175.) Fleury thinks that chapters had not an exclusive election till the end of the twelfth century. The second Lateran Council in 1139 represses their attempts to engross it. (" Institutions au Droit Ecclés.," tome i, p. 100.)

[127] Schmidt, tome ii, pp. 224, 473; tome iii, p. 281; Encyclopédie, art. Chanoine; F. Paul on "Benefices," c. 16; Fleury, "8me Discours sur l'Hist. Ecclés."

[128] St. Marc, tome iii, p. 628; Fleury, "Hist. Ecclés.," tome xiii, pp. 281, 284.

cial right, to St. Peter; and by virtue of this imprescriptible claim he grants to a certain Count de Rouci all territories which he should reconquer from the Moors, to be held in fief from the Holy See by a stipulated rent.[129] A similar pretension he makes to the kingdom of Hungary, and bitterly reproaches its sovereign, Solomon, who had done homage to the emperor, in derogation of St. Peter, his legitimate lord.[130] It was convenient to treat this apostle as a great feudal suzerain, and the legal principles of that age were dexterously applied to rivet more forcibly the fetters of superstition.[131]

While temporal sovereigns were opposing so inadequate a resistance to a system of usurpation contrary to all precedent and to the common principles of society, it was not to be expected that national churches should persevere in opposing pretensions for which several ages had paved the way. Gregory VII completed the destruction of their liberties. The principles contained in the decretals of Isidore, hostile as they were to ecclesiastical independence, were set aside as insufficient to establish the absolute monarchy of Rome. By a constitution of Alexander II, during whose pontificate Hildebrand himself was deemed the effectual Pope, no bishop in the Catholic Church was permitted to exercise his functions until he had received the confirmation of the Holy See:[132] a provision of vast importance, through which, beyond perhaps any other means, Rome has sustained, and still sustains, her temporal influence, as well as her ecclesiastical supremacy. The national churches, long abridged of their liberties by gradual encroachments, now found themselves subject to an undisguised and irresistible despotism. Instead of affording protection to bishops against their metropolitans, under an insidious pretence of which the popes of the ninth century had subverted the authority of the latter, it became the favourite policy of their successors to harass all prelates with citations to Rome.[133] Gregory obliged the metropolitans to attend in person for the pallium.[134] Bishops were summoned

[129] The language he employs is worth quoting as a specimen of his style: Non latere vos credimus, regnum Hispaniæ ab antiquo juris sancti Petri fuisse, et adhuc licet diu a paganis sit occupatum, lege tamen justitiæ non evacuatâ, nulli mortalium, sed soli apostolicæ sedi ex æquo pertinere. Quod enim auctore Deo semel in proprietates ecclesiarum justè pervenerit, manente Eo, ab usu quidem, sed ab earum jure, occasione transeuntis temporis, sine legitimâ concessione divelli non poterit. Itaque comes Evalus de Roceio, cujus famam apud vos haud obscuram esse putamus, terram illam ad honorem Sti. Petri ingredi, et a paganorum manibus eripere cupiens, hanc concessionem ab apostolicâ sede obtinuit, ut partem illam, unde paganos suo studio et adjuncto sibi aliorum auxilio expellere possit, sub conditione inter nos factæ pactionis ex parte Sti. Petri possideret. (Labbé, " Concilia," tome x, p. 10.) Three instances occur in the Corps Diplomatique of Dumont, where a Duke of Dalmatia (tome i, p. 53), a Count of Provence (p. 58), and a Count of Barcelona (ibid.) put themselves under the feudal superiority and protection of Gregory VII. The motive was sufficiently obvious.

[130] St. Marc, tome iii, pp. 624, 674; Schmidt, p. 73.

[131] The character and policy of Gregory VII are well discussed by Schmidt, tome iii, p. 307.

[132] St. Marc, p. 460.

[133] Schmidt, tome iii, pp. 80, 322.

[134] Id., tome iv, p. 170.

even from England and the northern kingdoms to receive the commands of the spiritual monarch. William the Conqueror having made a difficulty about permitting his prelates to obey these citations, Gregory, though in general on good terms with that prince, and treating him with a deference which marks the effect of a firm character in repressing the ebullitions of overbearing pride,[135] complains of this as a persecution unheard of among pagans.[136] The great quarrel between Archbishop Anselm and his two sovereigns, William Rufus and Henry I, was originally founded upon a similar refusal to permit his departure for Rome.

This perpetual control exercised by the popes over ecclesiastical and in some degree over temporal affairs was maintained by means of their legates, at once the ambassadors and the lieutenants of the Holy See. Previously to the latter part of the tenth age these had been sent not frequently and upon special occasions. The legatine or vicarial commission had generally been intrusted to some eminent metropolitan of the nation within which it was to be exercised, as the Archbishop of Canterbury was perpetual legate in England. But the special commissioners, or legates a latere, suspending the Pope's ordinary vicars, took upon themselves an unbounded authority over the national churches, holding councils, promulgating canons, deposing bishops, and issuing interdicts at their discretion. They lived in splendour at the expense of the bishops of the province. This was the more galling to the hierarchy, because simple deacons were often invested with this dignity, which set them above primates. As the sovereigns of France and England acquired more courage, they considerably abridged this prerogative of the Holy See, and resisted the entrance of any legates into their dominions without their consent.[137]

From the time of Gregory VII no pontiff thought of awaiting the confirmation of the emperor, as in earlier ages, before he was installed in the throne of St. Peter. On the contrary, it was pretended that the emperor was himself to be confirmed by the Pope. This had, indeed, been broached by John VIII two hundred years before Gregory.[138] It was still a doctrine not calculated for general reception; but the popes availed them-

---

[135] St. Marc, pp. 628, 788; Schmidt, tome iii, p. 82.

[136] St. Marc, tome iv, p. 761; Collier, p. 252.

[137] De Marca, l. vi, chaps. 28, 30, 31; Schmidt, tome ii, p. 498; tome iii, pp. 312, 320; "Hist. du Droit Public Eccl. François," p. 250; Fleury, "4me Discours sur l'Hist. Ecclés.," c. 10.

[138] Vide supra. It appears manifest that the scheme of temporal sovereignty was only suspended by the disorders of the Roman See in the tenth century.

Peter Damian, a celebrated writer of the age of Hildebrand, and his friend, puts these words into the mouth of Jesus Christ, as addressed to Pope Victor II: Ego claves totius universalis ecclesiæ meæ tuis manibus tradidi, et super eam te mihi vicarium posui, quam proprii sanguinis effusione redemi. Et si pauca sunt ista, etiam monarchias addidi: immo sublato rege de medio totius Romani imperii vacantis tibi jura permisi. (Schmidt, tome iii, p. 78.)

FREDERICK BARBAROSSA AT THE FEET
OF THE POPE.

Photogravure from a painting by Albert Maignan.

Goupilgravure

selves of every opportunity which the temporizing policy, the negligence or bigotry of sovereigns threw into their hands. Lothaire coming to receive the imperial crown at Rome, this circumstance was commemorated by a picture in the Lateran palace, in which, and in two Latin verses subscribed, he was represented as doing homage to the Pope.[139]   When Frederick Barbarossa came upon the same occasion, he omitted to hold the stirrup of Adrian IV, who, in his turn, refused to give him the usual kiss of peace; nor was the contest ended but by the emperor's acquiescence, who was content to follow the precedents of his predecessors.   The same Adrian, expostulating with Frederick upon some slight grievance, reminded him of the imperial crown which he had conferred, and declared his willingness to bestow, if possible, still greater benefits.   But the phrase employed (majora beneficia) suggested the idea of a fief; and the general insolence which pervaded Adrian's letter confirming this interpretation, a ferment arose among the German princes in a congress of whom this letter was delivered.   "From whom, then," one of the legates was rash enough to say, "does the emperor hold his crown, except from the Pope?" which so irritated a prince of Wittelsbach, that he was with difficulty prevented from cleaving the priest's head with his sabre.[140]   Adrian IV was the only Englishman that ever sat in the papal chair. It might, perhaps, pass for a favour bestowed on his natural sovereign, when he granted to Henry II the kingdom of Ireland; yet the language of this donation, wherein he asserts all islands to be the exclusive property of St. Peter, should not have had a very pleasing sound to an insular monarch.

I shall not wait to comment on the support given to Becket by Alexander III, which must be familiar to the English reader, nor on his speedy canonization; a reward which the Church has always held out to its most active friends, and which may be compared to titles of nobility granted by a temporal sovereign.[141]   But the epoch when the spirit of papal usurpation was most strikingly displayed was the pontificate of Innocent III. In each of the three leading objects which Rome has pursued—independent sovereignty, supremacy over the Christian Church, control over the princes of the earth—it was the fortune of this pontiff to conquer.   He realized, as we have seen in another

---

[139] " Rex venit ante fores, jurans prius urbis honores:
  Post homo fit papæ, sumit quo dante coronam."
    (Muratori, " Annali," A. D 1157.)
  There was a pretext for this artful line.   Lothaire had received the estate of Matilda in fief from the Pope, with a reversion to Henry the Proud, his son-in-law. (Schmidt, p. 349.)

[140] Muratori, ubi supra; Schmidt, tome iii, p. 393.
[141] The first instance of a solemn papal canonization is that of St. Udalric by John XVI, in 993. However, the metropolitans continued to meddle with this sort of apotheosis till the pontificate of Alexander III, who reserved it, as a choice prerogative, to the Holy See. (" Art. de vérifier les Dates," tome i, pp. 247 and 290.)

place, that fond hope of so many of his predecessors, a dominion over Rome and the central parts of Italy. During his pontificate Constantinople was taken by the Latins; and, however he might seem to regret a diversion of the crusaders, which impeded the recovery of the Holy Land, he exulted in the obedience of the new patriarch and the reunion of the Greek Church. Never, perhaps, either before or since, was the great Eastern schism in so fair a way of being healed; even the Kings of Bulgaria and of Armenia acknowledged the supremacy of Innocent, and permitted his interference with their ecclesiastical institutions.

The maxims of Gregory VII were now matured by more than a hundred years, and the right of trampling upon the necks of kings had been received, at least among churchmen, as an inherent attribute of the papacy. "As the sun and the moon are placed in the firmament" (such is the language of Innocent), "the greater as the light of the day, and the lesser of the night, thus are there two powers in the Church—the pontifical, which, as having the charge of souls, is the greater; and the royal, which is the less, and to which the bodies of men only are intrusted." [142] Intoxicated with these conceptions (if we may apply such a word to successful ambition), he thought no quarrel of princes beyond the sphere of his jurisdiction. "Though I can not judge of the right to a fief," said Innocent to the Kings of France and England, "yet it is my province to judge where sin is committed, and my duty to prevent all public scandals." Philip Augustus, who had at that time the worse in his war with Richard, acquiesced in this sophism; the latter was more refractory till the papal legate began to menace him with the rigour of the Church.[143] But the King of England, as well as his adversary, condescended to obtain temporary ends by an impolitic submission to Rome. We have a letter from Innocent to the King of Navarre, directing him, on pain of spiritual censures, to restore some castles which he detained from Richard.[144] And the latter appears to have entertained hopes of recovering his ransom paid to the emperor and Duke of Austria through the Pope's interference.[145] By such blind sacrifices of the greater to the less,

[142] " Vita Innocentii Tertii," in Muratori, " Scriptores Rerum Ital.," tome iii, pars i, p. 448. This life is written by a contemporary. (St. Marc, tome v, p. 325; Schmidt, tome iv, p. 227.)

[143] Philippus rex Franciæ in manu ejus datâ fide promisit se ad mandatum ipsius pacem vel treugas cum rege Angliæ initurum. Richardus autem rex Angliæ se difficilem ostendebat. Sed cum idem legatus ei cepit rigorem ecclesiasticum intentare, saniori ductus consilio acquievit. (" Vita Innocentii Tertii," tome iii, pars i, p. 503.)

[144] "Innocentii Opera" (Coloniæ, 1574), p. 124.

[145] Id., p. 134. Innocent actually wrote some letters for this purpose, but without any effect, nor was he probably at all solicitous about it (pp. 139 and 141). Nor had he interfered to procure Richard's release from prison : though Eleanor wrote him a letter, in which she asks, " Has not God given you the power to govern nations and kings? " (Velly, " Hist. de France," tome iii, p. 382.)

of the future to the present, the sovereigns of Europe played continually into the hands of their subtle enemy.

Though I am not aware that any pope before Innocent III had thus announced himself as the general arbiter of differences and conservator of the peace throughout Christendom, yet the scheme had been already formed, and the public mind was in some degree prepared to admit it. Gerohus, a writer who lived early in the twelfth century, published a theory of perpetual pacification, as feasible certainly as some that have been planned in later times. All disputes among princes were to be referred to the Pope. If either party refused to obey the sentence of Rome, he was to be excommunicated and deposed. Every Christian sovereign was to attack the refractory delinquent under pain of a similar forfeiture.[146] A project of this nature had not only a magnificence flattering to the ambition of the Church, but was calculated to impose upon benevolent minds, sickened by the cupidity and oppression of princes. No control but that of religion appeared sufficient to restrain the abuses of society; while its salutary influence had already been displayed both in the Truce of God, which put the first check on the custom of private war, and more recently in the protection afforded to crusaders against all aggression during the continuance of their engagement. But reasonings from the excesses of liberty in favour of arbitrary government, or from the calamities of national wars in favour of universal monarchy, involve the tacit fallacy that perfect, or at least superior, wisdom and virtue will be found in the restraining power. The experience of Europe was not such as to authorize so candid an expectation in behalf of the Roman See.

There were certainly some instances where the temporal supremacy of Innocent III, however usurped, may appear to have been exerted beneficially. He directs one of his legates to compel the observance of peace between the Kings of Castile and Portugal, if necessary, by excommunication and interdict.[147] He enjoins the King of Aragon to restore his coin, which he had lately debased, and of which great complaint had arisen in his kingdom.[148] Nor do I question his sincerity in these or in any other cases of interference with civil government. A great mind, such as Innocent III undoubtedly possessed, though prone to sacrifice every other object to ambition, can never be indifferent to the beauty of social order and the happiness of mankind. But, if we may judge by the correspondence of this remarkable person, his foremost gratification was the display of unbounded power. His letters, especially to ecclesiastics, are full of unprovoked rudeness. As impetuous as Gregory VII, he is unwilling to owe anything to favour; he seems to anticipate denial; heats

[146] Schmidt, tome iv, p. 232.   [147] " Innocent. Opera," p. 146.   [148] P. 378.

himself into anger as he proceeds, and, where he commences with solicitation, seldom concludes without a menace.[149] An extensive learning in ecclesiastical law, a close observation of whatever was passing in the world, an unwearied diligence, sustained his fearless ambition.[150] With such a temper, and with such advantages, he was formidable beyond all his predecessors, and perhaps beyond all his successors. On every side the thunder of Rome broke over the heads of princes. A certain Swero is excommunicated for usurping the crown of Norway. A legate, in passing through Hungary, is detained by the king: Innocent writes in tolerably mild terms to this potentate, but fails not to intimate that he might be compelled to prevent his son's succession to the throne. The King of Leon had married his cousin, a princess of Castile. Innocent subjects the kingdom to an interdict. When the clergy of Leon petition him to remove it, because, when they ceased to perform their functions, the laity paid no tithes, and listened to heretical teachers when orthodox mouths were mute, he consented that divine service with closed doors, but not the rites of burial, might be performed.[151] The king at length gave way, and sent back his wife. But a more illustrious victory of the same kind was obtained over Philip Augustus, who, having repudiated Isemburga of Denmark, had contracted another marriage. The conduct of the king, though not without the usual excuse of those times, nearness of blood, was justly condemned; and Innocent did not hesitate to visit his sins upon the people by a general interdict. This, after a short demur from some bishops, was enforced throughout France; the dead lay unburied, and the living were cut off from the offices of religion, till Philip, thus subdued, took back his divorced wife. The submission of such a prince, not feebly superstitious, like his predecessor, Robert, nor vexed with seditions, like the Emperor Henry IV, but brave, firm, and victorious, is perhaps the proudest trophy in the scutcheon of Rome. Compared with this, the subsequent triumph of Innocent over our pusillanimous John seems cheaply gained, though the surrender of a powerful kingdom into the vassalage of the Pope may strike us as a proof of

[149] Pp. 31, 73, 76, etc.
[150] The following instance may illustrate the character of this pope, and his spirit of governing the whole world, as much as those of a more public nature. He writes to the chapter of Pisa that one Rubens, a citizen of that place, had complained to him that, having mortgaged a house and garden for two hundred and fifty-two pounds, on condition that he might redeem it before a fixed day, within which time he had been unavoidably prevented from raising the money, the creditor had now refused to accept it; and directs them to inquire into the facts, and, if they prove truly stated, to compel the creditor by spiritual censures to restore the premises, reckoning their rent during the time of his mortgage as part of the debt, and to receive the remainder. (Id., tome ii, p. 17.) It must be admitted that Innocent III discouraged in general those vexatious and dilatory appeals from inferior ecclesiastical tribunals to the court of Rome, which had gained ground before his time, and especially in the pontificate of Alexander III.
[151] " Innocent. Opera," tome ii, p. 411; " Vita Innocent III."

stupendous baseness on one side, and audacity on the other.[152] Yet, under this very pontificate, it was not unparalleled. Peter II, King of Aragon, received at Rome the belt of knighthood and the royal crown from the hands of Innocent III; he took an oath of perpetual fealty and obedience to him and his successors; he surrendered his kingdom, and accepted it again to be held by an annual tribute, in return for the protection of the Apostolic See.[153] This strange conversion of kingdoms into spiritual fiefs was intended as the price of security from ambitious neighbours, and may be deemed analogous to the change of allodial into feudal, or, more strictly, to that of lay into ecclesiastical tenure, which was frequent during the turbulence of the darker ages.

I have mentioned already that among the new pretensions advanced by the Roman See was that of confirming the election of an emperor. It had, however, been asserted rather incidentally than in a peremptory manner. But the doubtful elections of Philip and Otho after the death of Henry VI gave Innocent III an opportunity of maintaining more positively this pretended right. In a decretal epistle addressed to the Duke of Zahringen, the object of which is to direct him to transfer his allegiance from Philip to the other competitor, Innocent, after stating the mode in which a regular election ought to be made, declares the Pope's immediate authority to examine, confirm, anoint, crown, and consecrate the elect emperor, provided he shall be worthy; or to reject him if rendered unfit by great crimes, such as sacrilege, heresy, perjury, or persecution of the Church; in default of election, to supply the vacancy; or, in the event of equal suffrages, to bestow the empire upon any person at his discretion.[154] The princes of Germany were not much influenced by this hardy assumption, which manifests the temper of Innocent III and of his court, rather than their power. But Otho IV at his coronation by the Pope signed a capitulation, which cut off several privileges enjoyed by the emperors, even since the

---

[152] The stipulated annual payment of one thousand marks was seldom made by the Kings of England: but one is almost ashamed that it should ever have been so. Henry III paid it occasionally when he had any object to attain, and even Edward I for some years; the latest payment on record is in the seventeenth of his reign. After a long discontinuance, it was demanded in the fortieth of Edward III (1366), but the Parliament unanimously declared that John had no right to subject the kingdom to a superior without their consent, which put an end forever to the applications. (Prynne's " Constitutions," vol. iii.)
[153] Zurita, " Annales de Aragon," tome i, fol. 91. This was not forgotten toward the latter part of the same century, when Peter III was engaged in the Sicilian war, and served as a pretence for the Pope's sentence of deprivation.

[154] " Decretal," l. i, tit. 6, c. 34, commonly cited Venerabilem. The rubric or synopsis of this epistle asserts the Pope's right electum imperatorem examinare, approbare et inungere, consecrare et coronare, si est dignus; vel rejicere si est indignus, ut quia sacrilegus, excommunicatus, tyrannus, fatuus et hæreticus, paganus, perjurus, vel ecclesiæ persecutor. Et electoribus nolentibus eligere, papa supplet. Et data paritate, vocum eligentium, nec accedente majore concordiâ, papa potest gratificari cui vult. The epistle itself is, if possible, more strongly expressed.

Concordat of Calixtus, in respect of episcopal elections and investitures.[155]

The noonday of papal dominion extends from the pontificate of Innocent III inclusively to that of Boniface VIII; or, in other words, through the thirteenth century. Rome inspired during this age all the terror of her ancient name. She was once more the mistress of the world, and kings were her vassals. I have already anticipated the two most conspicuous instances when her temporal ambition displayed itself, both of which are inseparable from the civil history of Italy.[156] In the first of these, her long contention with the house of Swabia, she finally triumphed. After his deposition by the Council of Lyons the affairs of Frederick II went rapidly into decay. With every allowance for the enmity of the Lombards and the jealousies of Germany, it must be confessed that his proscription by Innocent IV and Alexander IV was the main cause of the ruin of his family. There is, however, no other instance, to the best of my judgment, where the pretended right of deposing kings has been successfully exercised. Martin IV absolved the subjects of Peter of Aragon from their allegiance, and transferred his crown to a prince of France, but they did not cease to obey their lawful sovereign. This is the second instance which the thirteenth century presents of interference on the part of the popes in a great temporal quarrel. As feudal lords of Naples and Sicily, they had indeed some pretext for engaging in the hostilities between the houses of Anjou and Aragon, as well as for their contest with Frederick II. But the pontiffs of that age, improving upon the system of Innocent III, and sanguine with past success, aspired to render every European kingdom formally dependent upon the See of Rome. Thus Boniface VIII, at the instigation of some emissaries from Scotland, claimed that monarchy as paramount lord, and interposed, though vainly, the sacred panoply of ecclesiastical rights to rescue it from the arms of Edward I.[157]

This general supremacy effected by the Roman Church over mankind in the twelfth and thirteenth centuries derived material support from the promulgation of the canon law. The foundation of this jurisprudence is laid in the decrees of councils, and in the rescripts or decretal epistles of popes to questions propounded upon emergent doubts relative to matters of discipline and ecclesiastical economy. As the jurisdiction of the spiritual tribunals increased, and extended to a variety of persons and causes, it became almost necessary to establish a uniform system for the regulation of their decisions. After several minor compilations had appeared, Gratian, an Italian monk, published

---

[155] Schmidt, tome iv, pp. 149, 175.
[156] See chapter iii.

[157] Dalrymple's "Annals of Scotland," vol. i, p. 267.

about the year 1140 his "Decretum," or general collection of canons, papal epistles, and sentences of fathers, arranged and digested into titles and chapters, in imitation of the "Pandects," which very little before had begun to be studied again with great diligence.[158] This work of Gratian, though it seems rather an extraordinary performance for the age when it appeared, has been censured for notorious incorrectness as well as inconsistency, and especially for the authority given in it to the false decretals of Isidore, and consequently to the papal supremacy. It fell, however, short of what was required in the progress of that usurpation. Gregory IX caused the five books of "Decretals" to be published by Raimond de Pennafort in 1234. These consist almost entirely of rescripts issued by the later popes, especially Alexander III, Innocent III, Honorius III, and Gregory himself. They form the most essential part of the canon law, the "Decretum" of Gratian being comparatively obsolete. In these books we find a regular and copious system of jurisprudence, derived in a great measure from the civil law, but with considerable deviation, and possibly improvement. Boniface VIII added a sixth part, thence called the Sext, itself divided into five books, in the nature of a supplement to the other five, of which it follows the arrangement, and composed of decisions promulgated since the pontificate of Gregory IX. New constitutions were subjoined by Clement V and John XXII, under the name of Clementines and Extravagantes Johannis; and a few more of later pontiffs are included in the body of canon law, arranged as a second supplement after the manner of the Sext, and called Extravagantes Communes.

The study of this code became, of course, obligatory upon ecclesiastical judges. It produced a new class of legal practitioners, or canonists; of whom a great number added, like their brethren, the civilians, their illustrations and commentaries, for which the obscurity and discordance of many passages, more especially in the "Decretum," gave ample scope. From the general analogy of the canon law to that of Justinian, the two systems became, in a remarkable manner, collateral and mutually intertwined, the tribunals governed by either of them borrowing their rules of decision from the other in cases where their peculiar jurisprudence is silent or of dubious interpretation.[159] But the canon law was almost entirely founded upon the legislative authority of the Pope; the "Decretals" are, in fact, but a new arrangement of the bold epistles of the most usurping pontiffs, and especially of Innocent III, with titles or rubrics compre-

---

[158] Tiraboschi has fixed on 1140 as the date of its appearance (iii, 343), but others bring it down some years later.

[159] Duck, "De Usu Juris Civilis," l. i, c. 8.

hending the substance of each in the compiler's language. The
superiority of ecclesiastical to temporal power, or at least the
absolute independence of the former, may be considered as a
sort of key-note which regulates every passage in the canon
law.[160] It is expressly declared that subjects owe no allegiance
to an excommunicated lord, if after admonition he is not reconciled to the Church.[161] And the rubric prefixed to the declaration of Frederick II's deposition in the Council of Lyons asserts
that the Pope may dethrone the emperor for lawful causes.[162]
These rubrics to the " Decretals " are not perhaps of direct authority as part of the law, but they express its sense, so as to be
fairly cited instead of it.[163] By means of her new jurisprudence,
Rome acquired in every country a powerful body of advocates,
who, though many of them were laymen, would, with the usual
bigotry of lawyers, defend every pretension or abuse to which
their received standard of authority gave sanction.[164]

Next to the canon law, I should reckon the institution of
the mendicant orders among those circumstances which principally contributed to the aggrandizement of Rome. By the
acquisition, and in some respects the enjoyment, or at least
ostentation, of immense riches, the ancient monastic orders had
forfeited much of the public esteem.[165] Austere principles as
to the obligation of evangelical poverty were inculcated by the
numerous sectaries of that age, and eagerly received by the people, already much alienated from an established hierarchy. No
means appeared so efficacious to counteract this effect as the
institution of religious societies strictly debarred from the insidious temptations of wealth. Upon this principle were founded

[160] Constitutiones principum ecclesiasticis constitutionibus non præeminent,
sed obsequuntur. (" Decretum," distinct. 10.) Statutum generale laicorum
ad ecclesias vel ad ecclesiasticas personas, vel eorum bona, in earum præ-
judicium non extenditur. (" Decretal,"
l. i, tit. 2, c. 10.) Quæcunque a principibus in ordinibus vel in ecclesiasticis rebus decreta inveniuntur, nullius auctoritatis esse monstrantur. (" Decretum,"
distinct. 96.)
[161] Domino excommunicato manente,
subditi fidelitatem non debent; et si
longo tempore in e perstiterit, et moni-
tus non pareat ecclesiæ, ab ejus debito
absolvuntur. (" Decretal," l. v, tit. 37,
c. 18). I must acknowledge that the
decretal epistle of Honorius III scarcely warrants this general proposition of
the rubric, though it seems to lead
to it.
[162] Papa imperatorem deponere potest
ex causis legitimis (l. ii, tit. 13, c. 2).
[163] If I understand a bull of Gregory
XIII, prefixed to his recension of the
canon law, he confirms the rubrics or
glosses along with the text: but I can

not speak with certainty as to his
meaning.
[164] For the canon law I have consulted, besides the " Corpus Juris Canonici,"
Tiraboschi, " Storia della Litteratura,"
tomes iv and v; Giannone, l. xiv, c. 3;
l. xix, c. 3; l. xxii. c. 8; Fleury, " Institutions au Droit Ecclésiastique," tome
i, p. 10, and " 5me Discours sur l'Histoire Ecclés.; Duck, " De Usu Juris
Civilis," l. i, c. 8; Schmidt, tome iv, p.
39; F. Paul, " Treatise of Benefices," c.
31. I fear that my few citations from
the canon law are not made scientifically;
the proper mode of reference is to the
first word, but the book and title are
rather more convenient, and there are
not many readers in England who will
detect this impropriety.
[165] It would be easy to bring evidence
from the writings of every successive
century to the general viciousness of the
regular clergy, whose memory it is sometimes the fashion to treat with respect.
(See particularly Muratori, Dissert. 65;
and Fleury, " 8me Discours.") The latter observes that their great wealth was
the cause of this relaxation in discipline.

the orders of Mendicant Friars, incapable, by the rules of their foundation, of possessing estates, and maintained only by alms and pious remunerations. Of these, the two most celebrated were formed by St. Dominic and St. Francis of Assisi, and established by the authority of Honorius III in 1216 and 1223. These great reformers, who have produced so extraordinary an effect upon mankind, were of very different characters: the one, active and ferocious, had taken a prominent part in the crusade against the unfortunate Albigeois, and was among the first who bore the terrible name of inquisitor; while the other, a harmless enthusiast, pious and sincere, but hardly of sane mind, was much rather accessory to the intellectual than to the moral degradation of his species. Various other mendicant orders were instituted in the thirteenth century; but most of them were soon suppressed, and, besides the two principal, none remain but the Augustin and the Carmelites.[166]

These new preachers were received with astonishing approbation by the laity, whose religious zeal usually depends a good deal upon their opinion of sincerity and disinterestedness in their pastors. And the progress of the Dominican and Franciscan friars in the thirteenth century bears a remarkable analogy to that of our English Methodists. Not deviating from the faith of the Church, but professing rather to teach it in greater purity, and to observe her ordinances with greater regularity, while they imputed supineness and corruption to the secular clergy, they drew round their sermons a multitude of such listeners as in all ages are attracted by similar means. They practised all the stratagems of itinerancy, preaching in public streets, and administering the communion on a portable altar. Thirty years after their institution a historian complains that the parish churches were deserted, that none confessed except to these friars—in short, that the regular discipline was subverted.[167] This uncontrolled privilege of performing sacerdotal functions, which their modern antitypes assume for themselves, was conceded to the mendicant orders by the favour of Rome. Aware of the powerful support they might receive in turn, the pontiffs of the thirteenth century accumulated benefits upon the disciples of Francis and Dominic. They were exempted from episcopal authority; they were permitted to preach or hear confessions without leave of the ordinary,[168] to accept of legacies, and to inter in their churches. Such privileges could not be granted without resistance from the other

[166] Mosheim's " Ecclesiastical History "; Fleury, " 8me Discours": Crevier, " Histoire de l'Université de Paris," tome i, p. 318.
[167] Matt. Paris, p. 607.
[168] Another reason for preferring the friars is given by Archbishop Peckham:

quoniam casus episcopales reservati episcopis ab homine, vel a jure, communiter a Deum timentibus episcopis ipsis fratribus committuntur, et non presbyteris, quorum simplicitas non sufficit aliis dirigendis. (Wilkins, " Concilia," tome ii, p. 169.)

clergy; the bishops remonstrated, the University of Paris maintained a strenuous opposition; but their reluctance served only to protract the final decision. Boniface VIII appears to have peremptorily established the privileges and immunities of the mendicant orders in 1295.[169]

It was naturally to be expected that the objects of such extensive favours would repay their benefactors by a more than usual obsequiousness and alacrity in their service. Accordingly, the Dominicans and Franciscans vied with each other in magnifying the papal supremacy. Many of these monks became eminent in canon law and scholastic theology. The great lawgiver of the schools, Thomas Aquinas, whose opinions the Dominicans especially treat as almost infallible, went into the exaggerated principles of his age in favour of the See of Rome.[170] And as the professors of those sciences took nearly all the learning and logic of the times to their own share, it was hardly possible to repel their arguments by any direct reasoning. But this partiality of the new monastic orders to the popes must chiefly be understood to apply to the thirteenth century, circumstances occurring in the next which gave in some degree a different complexion to their dispositions in respect of the Holy See.

We should not overlook, among the causes that contributed to the dominion of the popes, their prerogative of dispensing with ecclesiastical ordinances. The most remarkable exercise of this was as to the canonical impediments of matrimony. Such strictness as is prescribed by the Christian religion with respect to divorce was very unpalatable to the barbarous nations. They, in fact, paid it little regard; under the Merovingian dynasty, even private men put away their wives at pleasure.[171] In many capitularies of Charlemagne we find evidence of the prevailing license of repudiation and even polygamy.[172] The principles which the Church inculcated were in appearance the very reverse of this laxity, yet they led indirectly to the same effect. Mar-

[169] Crevier, "Hist. de l'Université de Paris," tome i et tome ii, passim; Fleury, ubi supra; "Hist. du Droit Ecclésiastique François," tome i, pp. 394, 396, 446; Collier's "Ecclesiastical History," vol. i, pp. 437, 448, 452; Wood's "Antiquities of Oxford," vol. i, pp. 376, 480 (Gutch's edition).

[170] It was maintained by the enemies of the mendicants, especially William St. Amour, that the Pope could not give them a privilege to preach or perform the other duties of the parish priests. Thomas Aquinas answered that a bishop might perform any spiritual functions within his diocese, or commit the charge to another instead, and that the Pope, being to the whole Church what a bishop is to his diocese, might do the same everywhere. (Crevier, tome i, p. 474.)

[171] "Marculfi Formulæ," l. ii, c. 30.

[172] Although a man might not marry again when his wife had taken the veil, he was permitted to do so if she was infected with the leprosy. (Compare "Capitularia Pippini," A. D. 752 and 755.) If a woman conspired to murder her husband, he might remarry. (Id., A. D. 753.) A large proportion of Pepin's laws relate to incestuous connections and divorces. One of Charlemagne seems to imply that polygamy was not unknown even among priests. Si sacerdotes plures uxores habuerint, sacerdotio priventur; quia sæcularibus deteriores sunt. (Capitul., A. D. 769.) This seems to imply that their marriage with one was allowable, which nevertheless is contradicted by other passages in the capitularies.

riages were forbidden, not merely within the limits which Nature, or those inveterate associations which we call Nature, have rendered sacred, but as far as the seventh degree of collateral consanguinity, computed from a common ancestor.[173] Not only was affinity, or relationship by marriage, put upon the same footing as that by blood, but a fantastical connection, called spiritual affinity, was invented in order to prohibit marriage between a sponsor and godchild. A union, however innocently contracted, between parties thus circumstanced, might at any time be dissolved, and their subsequent cohabitation forbidden; though their children, I believe, in cases where there had been no knowledge of the impediment, were not illegitimate. One readily apprehends the facilities of abuse to which all this led; and history is full of dissolutions of marriage, obtained by fickle passion or cold-hearted ambition, to which the Church has not scrupled to pander on some suggestion of relationship. It is so difficult to conceive, I do not say any reasoning, but any honest superstition, which could have produced those monstrous regulations that I was at first inclined to suppose them designed to give, by a side wind, that facility of divorce which a licentious people demanded, but the Church could not avowedly grant. This refinement would, however, be unsupported by facts. The prohibition is very ancient, and was really derived from the ascetic temper which introduced so many other absurdities.[174] It was not until the twelfth century that either this or any other established rules of discipline were supposed liable to arbitrary dispensation; at least the stricter churchmen had always denied that the Pope could infringe canons, nor had he asserted any right to do so.[175] But Innocent III laid down as a maxim that out of the plenitude of his power he might lawfully dispense with the law; and accordingly granted, among other instances of this prerogative, dispensations from impediments of marriage to the Emperor Otho IV.[176] Similar indulgences were given by his successors, though they did not become usual for some ages.

[173] See the canonical computation explained in St. Marc, tome iii, p. 376. Also in Blackstone's law tracts, "Treatise on Consanguinity." In the eleventh century an opinion began to gain ground in Italy that third cousins might marry, being in the seventh degree according to the civil law. Peter Damian, a passionate abettor of Hildebrand and his maxims, treats this with horror, and calls it a heresy. (Fleury, tome xiii, p. 152; St. Marc, ubi supra.) This opinion was supported by a reference to the "Institutes of Justinian"; a proof, among several others, how much earlier that book was known than is vulgarly supposed.

[174] Gregory I pronounces matrimony to be unlawful as far as the seventh degree; and even, if I understand his meaning, as long as any relationship could be traced; which seems to have been the maxim of strict theologians, though not absolutely enforced. (Du Cange, voc. Generatio; Fleury, "Hist. Ecclés.," tome ix, p. 211.)

[175] De Marca, l. iii, chaps. 7, 8, 14; Schmidt, tome iv, p. 235. Dispensations were originally granted only as to canonical penances, but not prospectively to authorize a breach of discipline. Gratian asserts that the Pope is not bound by the canons, in which, Fleury observes, he goes beyond the False Decretals. ("Septième Discours," p. 291.)

[176] Secundum plenitudinem potestatis de jure possumus supra jus dispensare. (Schmidt, tome iv, p. 235.)

The fourth Lateran Council in 1215 removed a great part of the restraint by permitting marriages beyond the fourth degree, or what we call third cousins; [177] and dispensations have been made more easy when it was discovered that they might be converted into a source of profit. They served a more important purpose by rendering it necessary for the princes of Europe, who seldom could marry into one another's houses without transgressing the canonical limits, to keep on good terms with the court of Rome, which, in several instances that have been mentioned, fulminated its censures against sovereigns who lived without permission in what was considered an incestuous union.

The dispensing power of the popes was exerted in several cases of a temporal nature, particularly in the legitimation of children, for purposes even of succession. This Innocent III claimed as an indirect consequence of his right to remove the canonical impediment which bastardy offered to ordination; since it would be monstrous, he says, that one who is legitimate for spiritual functions should continue otherwise in any civil matter.[178] But the most important and mischievous species of dispensations was from the observance of promissory oaths. Two principles are laid down in the " Decretals "—that an oath disadvantageous to the Church is not binding; and that one extorted by force was of slight obligation, and might be annulled by ecclesiastical authority.[179] As the first of these maxims gave the most unlimited privilege to the popes of breaking all faith of treaties which thwarted their interest or passion, a privilege which they continually exercised,[180] so the second was equally convenient to princes weary of observing engagements toward their sub-

---

[177] Fleury, " Institutions au Droit Ecclésiastique," tome i, p. 296.

[178] " Decretal," l. iv, tit. 17, c. 13.

[179] Juramentum contra utilitatem ecclesiasticam præstium non tenet. (" Decretal," l. ii, tit. 24, c. 27, et Sext., l. i, tit. 11, c. 1.) A juramento per metum extorto ecclesia solet absolvere, et ejus transgressores ut peccantes mortaliter non punientur. (Eodem lib. et tit., c. 15.) The whole of this title in the decretals upon oaths seems to have given the first opening to the lax casuistry of succeeding times.

[180] Take one instance out of many. Piccinino, the famous condottiere of the fifteenth century, had promised not to attack Francis Sforza, at that time engaged against the Pope. Eugenius IV (the same excellent person who had annulled the compatacta with the Hussites, releasing those who had sworn to them, and who afterward made the King of Hungary break his treaty with Amurath II) absolves him from this promise, on the express ground that a treaty disadvantageous to the Church ought not to be kept. (Sismondi, tome ix, p. 196.) The Church in that age was synonymous with the papal territories in Italy.

It was in conformity to this sweeping principle of ecclesiastical utility that Urban VI made the following solemn and general declaration against keeping faith with heretics: Attendentes quod hujusmodi confœderationes, colligationes, et ligæ seu conventiones factæ cum hujusmodi hæreticis seu schismaticis postquam tales effecti erant, sunt temerariæ, illicitæ, et ipso jure nullæ (etsi forte ante ipsorum lapsum in schisma, seu hæresin initæ seu factæ fuissent), etiam si forent juramento vel fide datâ firmatæ, aut confirmatione apostolicâ vel quâcunque firmitate aliâ roboratæ, postquam tales, ut præmittitur, sunt effecti. (Rymer, tome vii, p. 352.)

It was of little consequence that all divines and sound interpreters of canon law maintain that the Pope can not dispense with the divine or moral law, as De Marca tells us (l. iii, c. 15), though he admits that others of less sound judgment assert the contrary, as was common enough, I believe, among the Jesuits at the beginning of the seventeenth century. His power of interpreting the law was of itself a privilege of dispensing with it.

jects or their neighbours. They protested with a bad grace against the absolution of their people from allegiance by an authority to which they did not scruple to repair in order to bolster up their own perjuries. Thus Edward I, the strenuous asserter of his temporal rights, and one of the first who opposed a barrier to the encroachments of the clergy, sought at the hands of Clement V a dispensation from his oath to observe the great statute against arbitrary taxation.

In all the earlier stages of papal dominion the supreme head of the Church had been her guardian and protector; and this beneficent character appeared to receive its consummation in the result of that arduous struggle which restored the ancient practice of free election to ecclesiastical dignities. Not long, however, after this triumph had been obtained, the popes began by little and little to interfere with the regular constitution. Their first step was conformable, indeed, to the prevailing system of spiritual independence. By the concordat of Calixtus it appears that the decision of contested elections was reserved to the emperor, assisted by the metropolitan and suffragans. In a few cases during the twelfth century this imperial prerogative was exercised, though not altogether undisputed.[181] But it was consonant to the prejudices of that age to deem the supreme pontiff a more natural judge, as in other cases of appeal. The point was early settled in England, where a doubtful election to the archbishopric of York, under Stephen, was referred to Rome, and there kept five years in litigation.[182] Otho IV surrendered this among other rights of the empire to Innocent III by his capitulation,[183] and from that pontificate the papal jurisdiction over such controversies became thoroughly recognised. But the real aim of Innocent, and perhaps of some of his predecessors, was to dispose of bishoprics, under pretext of determining contests, as a matter of patronage. So many rules were established, so many formalities required by their constitutions, incorporated afterward into the canon law, that the court of Rome might easily find means of annulling what had been done by the chapter, and bestowing the see on a favourite candidate.[184] The popes soon assumed not only a right of decision, but of devolution—that is, of supplying the want of election, or the unfitness of the elected,

---

[181] Schmidt, tome iii, p. 299; tome iv, p. 149. According to the concordat, elections ought to be made in the presence of the emperor or his officers; but the chapters contrived to exclude them by degrees, though not perhaps till the thirteenth century. (Compare Schmidt, tome iii, p. 296; tome iv, p. 146.)
[182] Henry's "Hist. of England," vol. v, p. 324; Littleton's "Henry II," vol. i, p. 356.
[183] Schmidt, tome iv, p. 149. One of

these was the spolium, or movable estate of a bishop, which the emperor was used to seize upon his decease (p. 154). It was certainly a very leonine prerogative; but the popes did not fail, at a subsequent time, to claim it for themselves. (Fleury, "Institutions au Droit," tome i, p. 425; Lenfant, "Concile de Constance," tome ii, p. 130.)
[184] F. Paul, c. 30; Schmidt, tome iv, pp. 177, 247.

by a nomination of their own.[185] Thus Archbishop Langton, if not absolutely nominated, was at least chosen in an invalid and compulsory manner by the order of Innocent III, as we may read in our English historians. And several succeeding Archbishops of Canterbury equally owed their promotion to the papal prerogative. Some instances of the same kind occurred in Germany, and it became the constant practice in Naples.[186]

While the popes were thus artfully depriving the chapters of their right of election to bishoprics, they interfered in a more arbitrary manner with the collation of inferior benefices. This began, though in so insensible a manner as to deserve no notice but for its consequences, with Adrian IV, who requested some bishops to confer the next benefice that should become vacant on a particular clerk.[187] Alexander III used to solicit similar favours.[188] These recommendatory letters were called mandates. But though such requests grew more frequent than was acceptable to patrons, they were preferred in moderate language, and could not decently be refused to the apostolic chair. Even Innocent III seems in general to be aware that he is not asserting a right; though in one instance I have observed his violent temper break out against the chapter of Poitiers, who had made some demur to the appointment of his clerk, and whom he threatens with excommunication and interdict.[189] But, as we find in the history of all usurping governments, time changes anomaly into system, and injury into right; examples beget custom, and custom ripens into law; and the doubtful precedent of one generation becomes the fundamental maxim of another. Honorius III requested that two prebends in every church might be preserved for the Holy See; but neither the bishops of France nor England, to whom he preferred this petition, were induced to comply with it.[190] Gregory IX pretended to act generously in limiting himself to a single expectative, or letter directing a particular clerk to be provided with a benefice in every church.[191] But his practice went much further. No country was so intolerably treated by this Pope and his successors as England throughout the ignominious reign of Henry III. Her Church seemed to have been so richly endowed only as the free pasture of Italian priests, who were placed, by the mandatory letters of Gregory IX and Innocent IV, in all the best benefices. If

[185] Thus we find it expressed, as captiously as words could be devised, in the "Decretals," l. i, tit. 6, c. 22: Electus a majori et saniori parte capituli, si est, et erat idoneus tempore electionis, confirmabitur; si autem erit indignus in ordinibus scientiâ vel ætate, et fuit scienter electus, electus a minori parte, si est dignus, confirmabitur.
A person canonically disqualified when presented to the Pope for confirmation was said to be postulatus, not electus.

[186] Giannone, l. xiv, c. 6; l. xix, c. 5.
[187] St. Marc, tome v, p. 41; "Art de vérifier les Dates," tome i, p. 288; Encyclopédie, art. Mandats.
[188] Schmidt, tome iv, p. 239.
[189] "Innocent III Opera," p. 502.
[190] M. Paris, p. 267; De Marca, l. iv, c. 9.
[191] F. Paul on "Benefices," c. 30.

we may trust a solemn remonstrance in the name of the whole nation, they drew from England, in the middle of the thirteenth century, sixty or seventy thousand marks every year—a sum far exceeding the royal revenue.[192] This was asserted by the English envoys at the Council of Lyons. But the remedy was not to be sought in remonstrances to the court of Rome, which exulted in the success of its encroachments. There was no defect of spirit in the nation to oppose a more adequate resistance; but the weak-minded individual upon the throne sacrificed the public interest sometimes through habitual timidity, sometimes through silly ambition. If England, however, suffered more remarkably, yet other countries were far from being untouched. A German writer about the beginning of the fourteenth century mentions a cathedral where, out of about thirty-five vacancies of prebends that had occurred within twenty years, the regular patron had filled only two.[193] The case was not very different in France, where the continual usurpations of the popes produced the celebrated Pragmatic Sanction of St. Louis. This edict, the authority of which, though probably without cause, has been sometimes disputed, contains three important provisions; namely, that all prelates and other patrons shall enjoy their full rights as to the collation of benefices, according to the canons; that churches shall possess freely their rights of election; and that no tax or pecuniary exaction shall be levied by the Pope without consent of the king and of the national Church.[194] We do not find, however, that the French govern-

---

[192] M. Paris, pp. 579, 740.

[193] Schmidt, tome vi, p. 104.

[194] "Ordonnances des Rois de France," tome i, p. 97. Objections have been made to the authenticity of this edict, and in particular that we do not find the king to have had any previous differences with the See of Rome; on the contrary, he was just indebted to Clement IV for bestowing the crown of Naples on his brother, the Count of Provence. Velly has defended it, "Hist. de France," tome vi, p. 57; and in the opinion of the learned Benedictine editors of "L'Art de vérifier les Dates," tome i, p. 585, cleared up all difficulties as to its genuineness. In fact, however, the "Pragmatic Sanction" of St. Louis stands by itself, and can only be considered as a protestation against abuses which it was still impossible to suppress.

Of this law, which was published in 1268, Sismondi says: En lisant la pragmatique sanction, on se demande avec étonnement ce qui a pu causer sa prodigieuse célébrité. Elle n'introduit aucun droit nouveau; elle ne change rien à l'organisation ecclésiastique; elle déclare seulement que tous les droits existans seront conservés, que toute la législation canonique soit exécutée. A l'exception de l'article v, sur la levées d'argent de la cour de Rome, elle ne contient rien que cette cour n'eut pu publier elle-même; et quant à cet article, qui paroit seul dirigé contre la chambre apostolique, il n'est pas plus précis que ceux que bien d'autres rois de France, d'Angleterre, et d'Allemagne, avaient déjà promulgués à plusieurs réprises, et toujours sans effet. (" Hist. des Franc.," v. 106.) But Sismondi overlooks the fourth article, which enacts that all collations of benefices shall be made according to the maxims of councils and fathers of the Church. This was designed to repress the dispensations of the Pope; and if the French lawyers had been powerful enough, it would have been successful in that object. He goes on, indeed, himself to say: Ce qui changea la pragmatique sanction en une barrière puissante contre les usurpations de la cour de Rome, c'est que les légistes s'en emparèrent; ils prirent soin de l'expliquer, de la commenter; plus elle était vague, et plus, entre leurs mains habiles, elle pouvoit recevoir d'extension. Elle suffisait seule pour garantir toutes les libertés du royaume; une fois que les parlemens étoient résolus de ne jamais permettre qu'elle fût violée, tout empiétement de la cour de Rome ou des tribunaux ecclésiastiques, toute levée de deniers or-

ment acted up to the spirit of this ordinance; and the Holy See continued to invade the rights of collation with less ceremony than they had hitherto used. Clement IV published a bull in 1266, which, after asserting an absolute prerogative of the supreme pontiff to dispose of all preferments, whether vacant or in reversion, confines itself in the enacting words to the reservation of such benefices as belong to persons dying at Rome (vacantes in curiâ).[195] These had for some time been reckoned as a part of the Pope's special patronage; and their number, when all causes of importance were drawn to his tribunal, when metropolitans were compelled to seek their pallium in person, and even by a recent constitution exempt abbots were to repair to Rome for confirmation,[196] not to mention the multitude who flocked thither as mere courtiers and hunters after promotion, must have been very considerable. Boniface VIII repeated this law of Clement IV in a still more positive tone;[197] and Clement V laid down as a maxim that the Pope might freely bestow, as universal patron, all ecclesiastical benefices.[198] In order to render these tenable by their Italian courtiers, the canons against pluralities and non-residence were dispensed with, so that individuals were said to have accumulated fifty or sixty preferments.[199] It was a consequence from this extravagant principle that the Pope might prevent the ordinary collator upon a vacancy; and as this could seldom be done with sufficient expedition in places remote from his court, that he might make reversionary grants during the life of an incumbent, or reserve certain benefices specifically for his own nomination.

The persons as well as estates of ecclesiastics were secure from arbitrary taxation in all the kingdoms founded upon the ruins of the empire, both by the common liberties of freemen, and more particularly by their own immunities and the horror of sacrilege.[200] Such at least was their legal security, whatever violence might occasionally be practised by tyrannical princes. But this exemption was compensated by annual donatives, probably to a large amount, which the bishops and monasteries were accustomed, and as it were compelled, to make to their sovereigns.[201] They were subject also, generally speaking, to the

donnée par elle, toute élection irrégulière, toute excommunication, tout interdit, qui touchoient l'autorité royale ou les droits du sujet, furent dénoncés par les légistes en parlement, comme contraires aux franchises des églises de France, et à la pragmatique sanction. Ainsi s'introduisait l'appel comme d'abus qui réussit seul à contenir la jurisdiction ecclésiastique dans de justes bornes.
[195] " Sext. Decretal," l. iii, tome iv, c. 2; F. Paul on " Benefices," c. 35. This writer thinks the privilege of nominating benefices vacant in curiâ to have been

among the first claimed by the popes, even before the usage of mandates (c. 30).
[196] Matt. Paris, p. 817.
[197] " Sext. Decret.," l. iii, tome iv, c. 3. He extended the vacancy in curiâ to all places within two days' journey of the papal court.
[198] F. Paul, c. 35.
[199] Id., chaps. 33–35; Schmidt, tome iv, p. 104.
[200] Muratori, Dissert. 70 ; Schmidt, tome iii, p. 211.
[201] Schmidt, tome iii, p. 211; Du Cange, voc. Dona.

feudal services and prestations. Henry I is said to have extorted a sum of money from the English Church.[202] But the first eminent instance of a general tax required from the clergy was the famous Saladine tithe: a tenth of all movable estate, imposed by the Kings of France and England upon all their subjects, with the consent of their great councils of prelates and barons, to defray the expense of their intended crusade. Yet even this contribution, though called for by the imminent peril of the Holy Land after the capture of Jerusalem, was not paid without reluctance, the clergy doubtless anticipating the future extension of such a precedent.[203] Many years had not elapsed when a new demand was made upon them, but from a different quarter. Innocent III (the name continually recurs when we trace the commencement of a usurpation) imposed in 1199 upon the whole Church a tribute of one fortieth of movable estate, to be paid to his own collectors, but strictly pledging himself that the money should only be applied to the purposes of a crusade.[204] This crusade ended, as is well known, in the capture of Constantinople. But the word had lost much of its original meaning, or rather that meaning had been extended by ambition and bigotry. Gregory IX preached a crusade against the Emperor Frederick, in a quarrel which only concerned his temporal principality, and the Church of England was taxed by his authority to carry on this holy war.[205] After some opposition, the bishops submitted, and from that time no bounds were set to the rapacity of papal exactions. The usurers of Cahors and Lombardy, residing in London, took up the trade of agency for the Pope; and in a few years he is said, partly by levies of money, partly by the revenues of benefices, to have plundered the kingdom of nine hundred and fifty thousand marks; a sum equivalent, perhaps, to not less than fifteen millions sterling at present. Innocent IV, during whose pontificate the tyranny of Rome, if we consider her temporal and spiritual usurpations together, seems to have reached its zenith, hit upon the device of ordering the English prelates to furnish a certain number of men at arms to defend the Church at their expense. This would soon have been

[202] Eadmer, p. 83.
[203] Schmidt, tome iv, p. 212; Littleton's "Henry II," vol. iii, p. 472; Velly, tome iii, p. 316.
[204] Innocent, "Opera," p. 266.
[205] M. Paris, p. 470. It was hardly possible for the clergy to make any effective resistance to the Pope without unravelling a tissue which they had been assiduously weaving. One English prelate distinguished himself in this reign by his strenuous protestation against all abuses of the Church. This was Robert Grosstete, Bishop of Lincoln, who died in 1253, the most learned Englishman of his time, and the first who had any tincture of Greek literature. Matthew Paris gives him a high character, which he deserved for his learning and integrity; one of his commendations is for keeping a good table. But Grosstete appears to have been imbued in a great degree with the spirit of his age as to ecclesiastical power, though unwilling to yield it up to the Pope: and it is a strange thing to reckon him among the precursors of the Reformation. (M. Paris, p. 754; Berington's "Literary History of the Middle Ages," p. 378.)

commuted into a standing escuage instead of military service.[206]
But the demand was perhaps not complied with, and we do not
find it repeated. Henry III's pusillanimity would not permit any
effectual measures to be adopted; and, indeed, he sometimes
shared in the booty, and was indulged with the produce of taxes
imposed upon his own clergy to defray the cost of his projected
war against Sicily.[207] A nobler example was set by the kingdom
of Scotland: Clement IV having, in 1267, granted the tithes of
its ecclesiastical revenues for one of his mock crusades, King
Alexander III, with the concurrence of the Church, stood up
against this encroachment, and refused the legate permission to
enter his dominions.[208] Taxation of the clergy was not so outrageous in other countries; but the popes granted a tithe of benefices to St. Louis for each of his own crusades, and also for the
expedition of Charles of Anjou against Manfred.[209] In the Council of Lyons, held by Gregory X in 1274, a general tax in the
same proportion was imposed on all the Latin Church for the
pretended purpose of carrying on a holy war.[210]

These gross invasions of ecclesiastical property, however sub-
missively endured, produced a very general disaffection toward
the court of Rome. The reproach of venality and avarice was
not indeed cast for the first time upon the sovereign pontiffs;
but it had been confined, in earlier ages, to particular instances,
not affecting the bulk of the Catholic Church. But, pillaged
upon every slight pretence, without law and without redress, the
clergy came to regard their once paternal monarch as an arbitrary oppressor. All writers of the thirteenth and following centuries complain in terms of unmeasured indignation, and seem
almost ready to reform the general abuses of the Church. They
distinguished, however, clearly enough between the abuses which
oppressed them and those which it was their interest to preserve,
nor had the least intention of waiving their own immunities
and authority. But the laity came to more universal conclusions. A spirit of inveterate hatred grew up among them, not
only toward the papal tyranny, but the whole system of ecclesiastical independence. The rich envied and longed to plunder
the estates of the superior clergy; the poor learned from the
Waldenses and other sectaries to deem such opulence incompatible with the character of evangelical ministers. The itiner-

[206] M. Paris, p. 613. It would be endless to multiply proofs from Matthew
Paris, which, indeed, occur in almost
every page. His laudable zeal against
papal tyranny, on which some Protestant
writers have been so pleased to dwell,
was a little stimulated by personal feelings for the abbey of St. Alban's; and
the same remark is probably applicable
to his love of civil liberty.
[207] Rymer, tome i, p. 599, etc. The

substance of English ecclesiastical history during the reign of Henry III may
be collected from Henry, and still better
from Collier.
[208] Dalrymple's " Annals of Scotland,"
vol. i, p. 179.
[209] Velly, tome iv, p. 343; tome v, p.
343; tome vi, p. 47.
[210] Idem, tome vi, p. 308; St. Marc,
tome vi, p. 347.

ant minstrels invented tales to satirize vicious priests, which
a predisposed multitude eagerly swallowed. If the thirteenth
century was an age of more extravagant ecclesiastical pretensions than any which had preceded, it was certainly one in which
the disposition to resist them acquired greater consistence.

To resist had, indeed, become strictly necessary, if the temporal governments of Christendom would occupy any better
station than that of officers to the hierarchy. I have traced already the first stage of that ecclesiastical jurisdiction, which,
through the partial indulgence of sovereigns, especially Justinian
and Charlemagne, had become nearly independent of the civil
magistrate. Several ages of confusion and anarchy ensued, during which the supreme regal authority was literally suspended
in France, and not much respected in some other countries.
It is natural to suppose that ecclesiastical jurisdiction, so far
as even that was regarded in such barbarous times, would be
esteemed the only substitute for coercive law, and the best security against wrong. But I am not aware that it extended itself
beyond its former limits till about the beginning of the twelfth
century. From that time it rapidly encroached upon the secular
tribunals, and seemed to threaten the usurpation of an exclusive
supremacy over all persons and causes. The bishops gave the
tonsure indiscriminately, in order to swell the list of their subjects. This sign of a clerical state, though below the lowest of
their seven degrees of ordination, implying no spiritual office, conferred the privileges and immunities of the profession on all who
wore an ecclesiastical habit and had only once been married.[211]
Orphans and widows, the stranger and the poor, the pilgrim and
the leper, under the appellation of persons in distress (miserabiles
personæ), came within the peculiar cognizance and protection
of the Church; nor could they be sued before any lay tribunal.
And the whole body of crusaders, or such as merely took the vow
of engaging in a crusade, enjoyed the same clerical privileges.

But where the character of the litigant parties could not,
even with this large construction, be brought within their pale,
the bishops found a pretext for their jurisdiction in the nature
of the dispute. Spiritual causes alone, it was agreed, could appertain to the spiritual tribunal. But the word was indefinite; and,
according to the interpreters of the twelfth century, the Church
was always bound to prevent and chastise the commission of

[211] Clerici qui cum unicis et virginibus contraxerunt, si tonsuram et vestes deferant clericales, privilegium retineant —— præsenti declaramus edicto, hujusmodi clericos conjugatos pro commissis ab iis excessibus vel delictis, trahi non posse criminaliter aut civiliter ad judicium sæculare. (Bonifacius Octavus, in "Sext. Decretal," l. iii, tit. 2, c. I.)

Philip the Bold, however, had subjected these married clerks to taxes, and later ordinances of the French kings rendered them amenable to temporal jurisdiction; from which, in Naples, by various provisions of the Angevin line, they always continued free. (Giannone, l. xix, c. 5.)

sin. By this sweeping maxim, which we have seen Innocent III apply to vindicate his control over national quarrels, the common differences of individuals, which generally involve some charge of wilful injury, fell into the hands of a religious judge. One is almost surprised to find that it did not extend more universally, and might praise the moderation of the Church. Real actions, or suits relating to the property of land, were always the exclusive province of the lay court, even where a clerk was the defendant.[212] But the ecclesiastical tribunals took cognizance of breaches of contract, at least where an oath had been pledged, and of personal trusts.[213] They had not only an exclusive jurisdiction over questions immediately matrimonial, but a concurrent one with the civil magistrate in France, though never in England, over matters incident to the nuptial contract, as claims of marriage portion and of dower.[214] They took the execution of testaments into their hands, on account of the legacies to pious uses which testators were advised to bequeath.[215] In process of time, and under favourable circumstances, they made still greater strides. They pretended a right to supply the defects, the doubts, or the negligence of temporal judges; and invented a class of mixed causes, whereof the lay or ecclesiastical jurisdiction took possession according to priority. Besides this extensive authority in civil disputes, they judged of some offences which naturally belong to the criminal law, as well as of some others which participate of a civil and criminal nature. Such were perjury, sacrilege, usury, incest, and adultery;[216] from the punishment of all which the secular magistrate refrained, at least in England, after they had become the province of a separate jurisdiction. Excommunication still continued the only chastisement which the Church could directly inflict. But the bishops acquired a right of having their own prisons for lay offenders,[217] and the monasteries were the appropriate prisons of clerks. Their sentences of excommunication were enforced by the temporal magistrate by imprisonment or sequestration of effects; in some cases by confiscation or death.[218]

[212] " Decretal," l. ii, tome ii; " Ordonnances des Rois," tome i, p. 40 (A. D. 1189). In the Council of Lambeth in 1261 the bishops claim a right to judge inter clericos suos, vel inter laicos conquerentes et clericos defendentes, in personalibus actionibus super contractibus, aut delictis aut quasi—i. e., quasi dilictis. (Wilkins, " Concilia," tome i, p. 747.)
[213] " Ordonnances des Rois," p. 319 (A. D. 1290).
[214] Id., pp. 40, 121, 220, 319.
[215] Id., p. 319; Glanvil, l. vii, c. 7. Sancho IV gave the same jurisdiction to the clergy of Castile, " Teoria de las Cortes," tome iii, p. 20; and in other respects followed the example of his father, Alfonso X, in favouring their encroachments. The Church of Scotland seems to have had nearly the same jurisdiction as that of England. (Pinkerton's " History of Scotland," vol. i, p. 173.)
[216] It was a maxim of the canon, as well as the common law, that no person should be punished twice for the same offence; therefore, if a clerk had been degraded, or a penance imposed on a layman, it was supposed unjust to proceed against him in a temporal court.
[217] Charlemagne is said by Giannone to have permitted the bishops to have prisons of their own (l. vi, c. 7).
[218] Giannone, l. xix, c. 5, tome iii; Schmidt, tome iv, p. 195; tome vi, p. 125;

The clergy did not forget to secure along with this jurisdiction their own absolute exemption from the criminal justice of the state. This, as I have above mentioned, had been conceded to them by Charlemagne; and this privilege was not enjoyed by clerks in England before the conquest, nor do we find it proved by any records long afterward; though it seems, by what we read about the constitutions of Clarendon, to have grown into use before the reign of Henry II. As to France and Germany, I can not pretend to say that the law of Charlemagne granting an exemption from ordinary criminal process was ever abrogated. The " False Decretals " contain some passages in favour of ecclesiastical immunity, which Gratian repeats in his collection.[219] About the middle of the twelfth century the principle obtained general reception, and Innocent III decided it to be an inalienable right of the clergy, whereof they could not be divested even by their own consent.[220] Much less were any constitutions of princes, or national usages, deemed of force to abrogate such an important privilege.[221] These, by the canon law, were invalid when they affected the rights and liberties of holy Church.[222] But the spiritual courts were charged with scandalously neglecting to visit the most atrocious offences of clerks with such punishment as they could inflict. The Church could always absolve from her own censures; and confinement in a monastery, the usual sentence upon criminals, was frequently slight and temporary. Several instances are mentioned of heinous outrages that remained nearly unpunished through the shield of ecclesiastical privilege.[223] And as the temporal courts refused their assistance to a rival jurisdiction, the clergy had no redress for their own injuries, and even the murder of a priest at one time, as we are told, was only punishable by excommunication.[224]

Such an incoherent medley of laws and magistrates, upon the symmetrical arrangement of which all social economy mainly depends, could not fail to produce a violent collision. Every

Fleury, " 7me Discours," " Mém. de l'Acad. des Inscript.," tome xxxix, p. 603. Ecclesiastical jurisdiction not having been uniform in different ages and countries, it is difficult without much attention to distinguish its general and permanent attributes from those less completely established. Its description, as given in the " Decretals," lib. ii, tit. 2, De foro competenti, does not support the pretensions made by the canonists, nor come up to the sweeping definition of ecclesiastical jurisdiction by Boniface VIII in the " Sext.," l. iii, tit. 23, c. 40, sive ambæ partes hoc voluerint, sive una super causis ecclesiasticis, sive quæ ad forum ecclesiasticum ratione personarum, negotiorum, vel rerum de jure vel de antiquâ consuetudine pertinere noscuntur.

[219] Fleury, " 7me Discours."
[220] Id.; " Institutions au Droit Ecclés.," tome ii, p. 8.
[221] In criminalibus causis in nullo casu possunt clerici ab aliquo quàm ab ecclesiastico judice condemnari, etiamsi consuetudo regia habeat ut fures a judicibus sæcularibus judicentur. (" Decretal," l. i, tit. 1, c. 8.)
[222] " Decret.," distinct. 96.
[223] Collier, vol. i, p. 351. It is laid down in the canon laws that a layman can not be a witness in a criminal case against a clerk. (" Decretal," l. ii, tit. 20, c. 14.)
[224] Littleton's " Henry II," vol. iii, p. 332. This must be restricted to that period of open hostility between the Church and state.

sovereign was interested in vindicating the authority of the constitutions which had been formed by his ancestors or by the
people whom he governed. But the first who undertook this
arduous work, the first who appeared openly against ecclesiastical
tyranny, was our Henry II. The Anglo-Saxon Church, not so
much connected as some others with Rome, and enjoying a sort
of barbarian immunity from the thraldom of canonical discipline, though rich, and highly respected by a devout nation,
had never, perhaps, desired the thorough independence upon
secular jurisdiction at which the continental hierarchy aimed.
William the Conqueror first separated the ecclesiastical from the
civil tribunal, and forbade the bishops to judge of spiritual causes
in the hundred court.[225] His language is, however, too indefinite
to warrant any decisive proposition as to the nature of such
causes; probably they had not yet been carried much beyond
their legitimate extent. Of clerical exemption from the secular
arm we find no earlier notice than in the coronation oath of
Stephen; which, though vaguely expressed, may be construed
to include it.[226] But I am not certain that the law of England
had unequivocally recognised that claim at the time of the constitutions of Clarendon. It was at least an innovation, which
the legislature might without scruple or transgression of justice
abolish. Henry II, in that famous statute, attempted in three
respects to limit the jurisdiction assumed by the Church; asserting for his own judges the cognizance of contracts, however confirmed by oath, and of rights of advowson, and also that of
offences committed by clerks, whom, as it is gently expressed,
after conviction or confession the Church ought not to protect.[227]
These constitutions were the leading subject of difference between the king and Thomas à Becket. Most of them were annulled by the Pope, as derogatory to ecclesiastical liberty. It
is not improbable, however, that, if Louis VII had played a
more dignified part, the See of Rome, which an existing schism
rendered dependent upon the favour of those two monarchs,
might have receded in some measure from her pretensions. But
France implicitly giving way to the encroachments of ecclesias-

---

[225] Ut nullus episcopus vel archidiaco-
nus de legibus episcopalibus amplius in
Hundret placita teneant, nec causam
quæ ad regimen animarum pertinet, ad
judicium sæcularium hominum adducant.
(Wilkins, " Leges Anglo-Saxon," 230.)
　Before the conquest the bishop and
earl sat together in the court of the
county or hundred, and, as we may infer from the tenor of this charter, ecclesiastical matters were decided loosely,
and rather by the common law than according to the canons. This practice
had been already forbidden by some
canons enacted under Edgar (id., p. 83),
but apparently with little effect. The

separation of the civil and ecclesiastical
tribunals was not made in Denmark till
the reign of Nicholas, who ascended the
throne in 1105. (Langebek, " Script. Rer.
Danic.," tome iv, p. 380.) Others refer
the law to St. Canut, about 1080 (tome ii,
p. 209).
　[226] Ecclesiasticarum personarum et omnium clericorum, et rerum eorum justitiam et potestatem, et distributionem
honorum ecclesiasticorum, in manu episcoporum esse perhibeo, et confirmo.
(Wilkins, " Leges Anglo-Saxon," p. 310.)
　[227] Wilkins, " Leges Anglo-Saxon," p.
323; Littleton's " Henry II "; Collier,
etc.

tical power, it became impossible for Henry completely to withstand them.

The constitutions of Clarendon, however, produced some effect, and in the reign of Henry III more unremitted and successful efforts began to be made to maintain the independence of temporal government. The judges of the king's court had until that time been themselves principally ecclesiastics, and consequently tender of spiritual privileges.[228] But now, abstaining from the exercise of temporal jurisdiction, in obedience to the strict injunctions of their canons,[229] the clergy gave place to common lawyers, professors of a system very discordant from their own. These soon began to assert the supremacy of their jurisdiction by issuing writs of prohibition whenever the ecclesiastical tribunals passed the boundaries which approved use had established.[230] Little accustomed to such control, the proud hierarchy chafed under the bit; several provincial synods protest against the pretensions of laymen to judge the anointed ministers whom they were bound to obey;[231] the cognizance of rights of patronage and breaches of contract is boldly asserted;[232] but firm and cautious, favoured by the nobility, though not much by the king, the judges receded not a step, and ultimately fixed a barrier which the Church was forced to respect.[233] In the ensuing reign of Edward I an archbishop acknowledges the abstract right of the king's bench to issue prohibitions;[234] and the statute entitled Circumspectè agatis, in the thirteenth year of that prince, while by its mode of expression it seems designed to guarantee the actual privileges of spiritual jurisdiction, had a tendency, especially with the disposition of the judges, to preclude the assertion of some which are not therein mentioned. Neither the right of advowson nor any temporal contract is specified in this act as pertaining to the Church; and, accordingly, the temporal courts have ever since maintained an undisputed jurisdiction over them.[235] They succeeded also partially in prevent-

[228] Dugdale's "Origines Juridicales," c. 8.

[229] "Decretal," l. i, tit. 37, c. 1; Wilkins, "Concilia," tome ii, p. 4.

[230] Prynne has produced several extracts from the pipe rolls of Henry II, where a person has been fined quia placitavit de laico feodo in curiâ christianitatis. And a Bishop of Durham is fined five hundred marks quia tenuit placitum de advocatione cujusdam ecclesiæ in curiâ christianitatis. (Epistle dedicatory to Prynne's "Records," vol. iii.) Glanvil gives the form of a writ of prohibition to the spiritual court for inquiring de feodo laico; for it had jurisdiction over lands in frankalmoign. This is conformable to the constitutions of Clarendon, and shows that they were still in force. (See also Littleton's "Henry II," vol. iii, p. 97.)

[231] Cum judicandi Christos domini nulla sit laicis attributa potestas, apud quos manet necessitas obsequendi. (Wilkins, "Concilia," tome i, p. 747.)

[232] Id., ibid.; et tome ii, p. 90.

[233] Vide Wilkins, "Concilia," tome ii, passim.

[234] Licet prohibitiones hujusmodi a curiâ christianissimi regis nostri justè proculdubio, ut diximus, concedantur. (Id., tome ii, pp. 100 and 115.)

[235] The statute Circumspectè agatis—for it is acknowledged as a statute, though not drawn up in the form of one—is founded upon an answer of Edward I to the prelates who had petitioned for some modification of prohibitions. Collier, always prone to exaggerate church authority, insinuates that the jurisdiction of the spiritual court over breaches of

ing the impunity of crimes perpetrated by clerks. It was enacted by the statute of Westminster, in 1275, or rather a construction was put upon that act, which is obscurely worded, that clerks indicted for felony should not be delivered to their ordinary until an inquest had been taken of the matter of accusation, and, if they were found guilty, that their real and personal estate should be forfeited to the crown. In later times the clerical privilege was not allowed till the party had pleaded to the indictment, and being duly convict, as is the practice at present.[236]

The civil magistrates of France did not by any means exert themselves so vigorously for their emancipation. The same or rather worse usurpations existed, and the same complaints were made, under Philip Augustus, St. Louis, and Philip the Bold; but the laws of those sovereigns tend much more to confirm than to restrain ecclesiastical encroachments.[237] Some limitations were attempted by the secular courts; and a historian gives us the terms of a confederacy among the French nobles in 1246, binding themselves by oath not to permit the spiritual judges to take cognizance of any matter, except heresy, marriage, and usury.[238] Unfortunately, Louis IX was almost as little disposed as Henry III to shake off the yoke of ecclesiastical dominion. But other sovereigns in the same period, from various motives, were equally submissive. Frederick II explicitly adopts the exemption of clerks from criminal as well as civil jurisdiction of seculars.[239] And Alfonso X introduced the same system in Castile—a kingdom where neither the papal authority nor the independence of the Church had obtained any legal recognition until the promulgation of his code, which teems with all the prin-

contract, even without oath, is preserved by this statute; but the express words of the king show that none whatever was intended, and the archbishop complains bitterly of it afterward. (Wilkins, " Concilia," tome ii, p. 118; Collier's " Ecclesiast. History," vol. i, p. 487.) So far from having any cognizance of civil contracts not confirmed by oath, to which I am not certain that the Church ever pretended in any country, the spiritual court had no jurisdiction at all, even where an oath had intervened, unless there was a deficiency of proof by writing or witnesses. (Glanvil, l. x, c. 12; Constitut. Clarendon, art. 15.)

[236] 2 Inst., p. 163. This is not likely to mislead a well-informed reader, but it ought, perhaps, to be mentioned that by the " clerical privilege " we are only to understand what is called benefit of clergy, which, in fact, is, or rather was till recent alterations of the law since the first edition of this work, no more than the remission of capital punishment for the first conviction of felony, and that not for the clergy alone, but for all culprits alike. They were not called upon at any time, I believe, to prove their claim as clergy, except by reading the neck-verse after trial and conviction in the king's court. They were then in strictness to be committed to the ordinary or ecclesiastical superior, which probably was not often done.

[237] It seems deducible from a law of Philip Augustus, " Ordonnances des Rois," tome i, p. 39, that a clerk convicted of some heinous offences might be capitally punished after degradation; yet a subsequent ordinance (p. 43) renders this doubtful, and the theory of clerical immunity became afterward more fully established.

[238] Matt. Paris, p. 629.

[239] Statuimus, ut nullus ecclesiasticam personam, in criminali quæstione vel civili, trahere ad judicium sæculare præsumat. " Ordonnances des Rois de France," tome i, p. 611, where this edict is recited and approved by Louis Hutin. Philip the Bold had obtained leave from the Pope to arrest clerks accused of heinous crimes, on condition of remitting them to the bishop's court for trial. (" Hist. du Droit Eccl. Franç.," tome i, p. 426.) A council at Bourges, held in 1276, had so absolutely condemned all

ciples of the canon law.[240] It is almost needless to mention that all ecclesiastical powers and privileges were incorporated with the jurisprudence of the kingdom of Naples, which, especially after the accession of the Angevin line, stood in a peculiar relation of dependence upon the Holy See.[241]

The vast acquisitions of landed wealth made for many ages by bishops, chapters, and monasteries, began at length to excite the jealousy of sovereigns. They perceived that, although the prelates might send their stipulated proportion of vassals into the field, yet there could not be that active co-operation which the spirit of feudal tenures required, and that the national arm was palsied by the diminution of military nobles. Again the reliefs upon succession, and similar dues upon alienation, incidental to fiefs, were entirely lost when they came into the hands of these undying corporations, to the serious injury of the feudal superior. Nor could it escape reflecting men, during the contest about investitures, that, if the Church peremptorily denied the supremacy of the state over her temporal wealth, it was but a just measure of retaliation, or rather self-defence, that the state should restrain her further acquisitions. Prohibitions of gifts in mortmain, though unknown to the lavish devotion of the new kingdoms, had been established by some of the Roman emperors to check the overgrown wealth of the hierarchy.[242] The first attempt at a limitation of this description in modern times was made by Frederick Barbarossa, who, in 1158, enacted that no fief should be transferred, either to the Church or otherwise, without the permission of the superior lord. Louis IX inserted a provision of the same kind in his " Establishments." [243] Castile had also laws of a similar tendency.[244] A license from the crown is said to have been necessary in England before the conquest for alienations in mortmain; but, however that may be, there seems no reason to imagine that any restraint was put upon them by the common law before Magna Charta, a clause of which statute was construed to prohibit all gifts to religious houses without the consent of the lord of the fee. And by the 7th Edward I alienations in mortmain are absolutely taken away, though the king might always exercise his prerogative of granting a

interference of the secular power with clerks that the king was obliged to solicit this moderate favour (p. 421).

[240] Marina, " Ensayo Historico-Critico sobre las Siete Partidas," c. 320, etc.; " Hist. du Droit Ecclés. Franç.," tome i, p. 442.

[241] Giannone, l. xix, c. v; l. xx, c. 8. One provision of Robert, King of Naples, is remarkable: it extends the immunity of clerks to their concubines. (Ibid.) Villani strongly censures a law made at Florence in 1345, taking away the personal immunity of clerks in criminal cases. Though the state could make such a law, it had no right to do so against the liberties of holy Church (l. xii, c. 43).

[242] Giannone, l. iii.

[243] " Ordonnances des Rois," p. 213. See, too, p. 303 and alibi. Du Cange, voc. Manus morta. Amortissiment, in Denisart and other French law-books. Fleury, " Instit. au Droit," tome i, p. 350.

[244] Marina, " Ensayo sobre las Siete Partidas," c. 235.

license, which was not supposed to be affected by the statute.[245]

It must appear, I think, to every careful inquirer that the papal authority, though manifesting outwardly more show of strength every year, had been secretly undermined, and lost a great deal of its hold upon public opinion, before the accession of Boniface VIII, in 1294, to the pontifical throne. The clergy were rendered sullen by demands of money, invasions of the legal right of patronage, and unreasonable partiality to the mendicant orders; a part of the mendicants themselves had begun to declaim against the corruptions of the papal court; while the laity, subjects alike and sovereigns, looked upon both the head and the members of the hierarchy with jealousy and dislike. Boniface, full of inordinate arrogance and ambition, and not sufficiently sensible of this gradual change in human opinion, endeavoured to strain to a higher pitch the despotic pretensions of former pontiffs. As Gregory VII appears the most usurping of mankind till we read the history of Innocent III, so Innocent III is thrown into shade by the superior audacity of Boniface VIII. But independently of the less favourable dispositions of the public, he wanted the most essential quality for an ambitious pope—reputation for integrity. He was suspected of having procured through fraud the resignation of his predecessor, Celestine V, and his harsh treatment of that worthy man afterward seems to justify the reproach. His actions, however, display the intoxication of extreme self-confidence. If we may credit some historians, he appeared at the Jubilee in 1300, a festival successfully instituted by himself to throw lustre around his court and fill his treasury,[246] dressed in imperial habits, with the two swords borne before him, emblems of his temporal as well as spiritual dominion over the earth.[247]

It was not long after his elevation to the pontificate before Boniface displayed his temper. The two most powerful sovereigns of Europe, Philip the Fair and Edward I, began at the same moment to attack in a very arbitrary manner the revenues of the Church. The English clergy had, by their own voluntary grants, or at least those of the prelates in their name, paid frequent sub-

[245] 2 Inst., p. 74; Blackstone, vol. ii, c. 18.

[246] The Jubilee was a centenary commemoration in honour of St. Peter and St. Paul, established by Boniface VIII on the faith of an imaginary precedent a century before. The period was soon reduced to fifty years, and from thence to twenty-five, as it still continues. The court of Rome at the next jubilee will, however, read with a sigh the description given of that in 1300: Papa innumerabilem pecuniam ab iisdem recepit, quia die et nocte duo clerici stabant ad altare

sancti Pauli, tenentes in eorum manibus rastellos, rastellantes pecuniam infinitam. (Auctor apud Muratori, " Annali d' Italia.") Plenary indulgences were granted by Boniface to all who should keep their jubilee at Rome, and I suppose are still to be had on the same terms. Matteo Villani gives a curious account of the throng at Rome in 1350.

[247] Giannone, l. xxi, c. 3; Velly, tome vii, p. 149. I have not observed any good authority referred to for this fact, which is, however, in the character of Boniface.

sidies to the crown from the beginning of the reign of Henry III. They had nearly in effect waived the ancient exemption, and retained only the common privilege of English freemen to tax themselves in a constitutional manner. But Edward I came upon them with demands so frequent and exorbitant that they were compelled to take advantage of a bull issued by Boniface, forbidding them to pay any contribution to the state. The king disregarded every pretext, and, seizing their goods into his hands, with other tyrannical proceedings, ultimately forced them to acquiesce in his extortion. It is remarkable that the Pope appears to have been passive throughout this contest of Edward I with his clergy. But it was far otherwise in France. Philip the Fair had imposed a tax on the ecclesiastical order without their consent, a measure perhaps unprecedented, yet not more odious than the similar exactions of the King of England. Irritated by some previous differences, the Pope issued his bull known by the initial words Clericis laicos, absolutely forbidding the clergy of every kingdom to pay, under whatever pretext of voluntary grant, gift, or loan, any sort of tribute to their government without his special permission. Though France was not particularly named, the king understood himself to be intended, and took his revenge by a prohibition to export money from the kingdom. This produced angry remonstrances on the part of Boniface; but the Gallican Church adhered so faithfully to the crown, and showed, indeed, so much willingness to be spoiled of their money, that he could not insist upon the most unreasonable propositions of his bull, and ultimately allowed that the French clergy might assist their sovereign by voluntary contributions, though not by way of tax.

For a very few years after these circumstances the Pope and King of France appeared reconciled to each other; and the latter even referred his disputes with Edward I to the arbitration of Boniface, " as a private person, Benedict of Gaeta (his proper name), and not as pontiff "; an almost nugatory precaution against his encroachment upon temporal authority.[248] But a terrible storm broke out in the first year of the fourteenth century. A bishop of Pamiers, who had been sent as legate from Boniface with some complaint, displayed so much insolence and

---

[248] Walt. Hemingford, p. 150. The award of Boniface, which he expresses himself to make both as Pope and Benedict of Gaeta, is published in Rymer, tome ii, p. 819, and is very equitable. Nevertheless, the French historians agreed to charge him with partiality toward Edward, and mention several proofs of it, which do not appear in the bull itself. Previous to its publication it was allowable enough to follow common fame; but Velly has repeated mere false-hoods from Mezeray and Baillet, while he refers to the instrument itself in Rymer, which disproves them. (" Hist. de France," tome vii, p. 139.) M. Gaillard, one of the most candid critics in history that France ever produced, pointed out the error of her common historians in the " Mém. de l'Académie des Inscriptions," tome xxxix, p. 642; and the editors of " L'Art de vérifier les Dates " have also rectified it.

such disrespect toward the king that Philip, considering him as his own subject, was provoked to put him under arrest, with a view to institute a criminal process. Boniface, incensed beyond measure at this violation of ecclesiastical and legatine privileges, published several bulls addressed to the king and clergy of France, charging the former with a variety of offences, some of them not at all concerning the Church, and commanding the latter to attend a council which he had summoned to meet at Rome. In one of these instruments, the genuineness of which does not seem liable to much exception, he declares in concise and clear terms that the king was subject to him in temporal as well as spiritual matters. This proposition had not hitherto been explicitly advanced, and it was now too late to advance it. Philip replied by a short letter in the rudest language, and ordered his bulls to be publicly burned at Paris. Determined, however, to show the real strength of his opposition, he summoned representatives from the three orders of his kingdom. This is commonly reckoned the first assembly of the States-General. The nobility and commons disclaimed with firmness the temporal authority of the Pope, and conveyed their sentiments to Rome through letters addressed to the college of cardinals. The clergy endeavoured to steer a middle course, and were reluctant to enter into an engagement not to obey the Pope's summons; yet they did not hesitate unequivocally to deny his temporal jurisdiction.

The council, however, opened at Rome; and notwithstanding the king's absolute prohibition, many French prelates held themselves bound to be present. In this assembly Boniface promulgated his famous constitution, denominated Unam sanctam. The Church is one body, he therein declares, and has one head. Under its commands are two swords, the one spiritual, and the other temporal; that to be used by the supreme pontiff himself; this by kings and knights, by his license and at his will. But the lesser sword must be subject to the greater, and the temporal to the spiritual authority. He concludes by declaring the subjection of every human being to the See of Rome to be an article of necessary faith.[249] Another bull pronounces all persons of whatever rank obliged to appear when personally cited before the audience or apostolical tribunal at Rome; "since such is our pleasure, who, by divine permission, rule the world." Finally, as the rupture with Philip grew more evidently irreconcilable,

---

[249] Uterque est in potestate ecclesiæ, spiritalis scilicet gladius et materialis. Sed is quidem pro ecclesiâ, ille vero ab ecclesiâ exercendus: ille sacerdotis, is manu regum ac militum, sed ad nutum et patientiam sacerdotis. Oportet autem gladium esse sub gladio, et temporalem auctoritatem spiritali subjici potestati. Porro subesse Romano pontifici omni humanæ creaturæ declaramus, dicimus, definimus et pronunciamus omnino esse de necessitate fidei. ("Extravagant.," l. i, tit. 8, c. 1.)

and the measures pursued by that monarch more hostile, he not only excommunicated him, but offered the crown of France to the Emperor Albert I. This arbitrary transference of kingdoms was, like many other pretensions of that age, an improvement upon the right of deposing excommunicated sovereigns. Gregory VII would not have denied that a nation, released by his authority from its allegiance, must re-enter upon its original right of electing a new sovereign. But Martin IV had assigned the crown of Aragon to Charles of Valois; the first instance, I think, of such a usurpation of power, but which was defended by the homage of Peter II, who had rendered his kingdom feudally dependent, like Naples, upon the Holy See.[250] Albert felt no eagerness to realize the liberal promises of Boniface; who was on the point of issuing a bull absolving the subjects of Philip from their allegiance, and declaring his forfeiture, when a very unexpected circumstance interrupted all his projects.

It is not surprising, when we consider how unaccustomed men were in those ages to disentangle the artful sophisms, and detect the falsehoods in point of fact, whereon the papal supremacy had been established, that the King of France should not have altogether pursued the course most becoming his dignity and the goodness of his cause. He gave too much the air of a personal quarrel with Boniface to what should have been a resolute opposition to the despotism of Rome. Accordingly, in an assembly of his states at Paris, he preferred virulent charges against the Pope, denying him to have been legitimately elected, imputing to him various heresies, and ultimately appealing to a general council and a lawful head of the Church. These measures were not very happily planned; and experience had always shown that Europe would not submit to change the common chief of her religion for the purposes of a single sovereign. But Philip succeeded in an attempt apparently more bold and singular. Nogaret, a minister who had taken an active share in all the proceedings against Boniface, was secretly despatched into Italy, and, joining with some of the Colonna family, proscribed as Ghibelins, and rancorously persecuted by the Pope, arrested him at Anagnia, a town in the neighbourhood of Rome, to which he had gone without guards. This violent action was not, one

---

[250] Innocent IV had, however, in 1245, appointed one Bolon, brother to Sancho II, King of Portugal, to be a sort of co-adjutor in the government of that kingdom, enjoining the barons to honour him as their sovereign, at the same time declaring that he did not intend to deprive the king or his lawful issue, if he should have any, of the kingdom. But this was founded on the request of the Portuguese nobility themselves, who were dissatisfied with Sancho's administration. ("Sext. Decretal," 1. i, tit. 8, c. 2; "Art de vérifier les Dates," tome i, p. 778.)

Boniface invested James II of Aragon with the crown of Sardinia, over which, however, the See of Rome had always pretended to a superiority by virtue of the concession (probably spurious) of Louis the Debonair. He promised Frederick, King of Sicily, the empire of Constantinople, which, I suppose, was not a fief of the Holy See. (Giannone, 1. xxi, c. 3.)

HALLAM'S MIDDLE AGES

would imagine, calculated to place the king in an advantageous light, yet it led accidentally to a favourable termination of his dispute. Boniface was soon rescued by the inhabitants of Anagnia; but rage brought on a fever which ended in his death; and the first act of his successor, Benedict XI, was to reconcile the King of France to the Holy See.[251]

The sensible decline of the papacy is to be dated from the pontificate of Boniface VIII, who had strained its authority to a higher pitch than any of his predecessors. There is a spell wrought by uninterrupted good fortune, which captivates men's understanding, and persuades them, against reasoning and analogy, that violent power is immortal and irresistible. The spell is broken by the first change of success. We have seen the working and the dissipation of this charm with a rapidity to which the events of former times bear as remote a relation as the gradual processes of Nature to her deluges and her volcanoes. In tracing the papal empire over mankind we have no such marked and definite crisis of revolution. But slowly, like the retreat of waters, or the stealthy pace of old age, that extraordinary power over human opinion has been subsiding for five centuries. I have already observed that the symptoms of internal decay may be traced further back. But as the retrocession of the Roman terminus under Adrian gave the first overt proof of decline in the ambitious energies of that empire, so the tacit submission of the successors of Boniface VIII to the King of France might have been hailed by Europe as a token that their influence was beginning to abate. Imprisoned, insulted, deprived eventually of life by the violence of Philip, a prince excommunicated, and who had gone all lengths in defying and despising the papal jurisdiction, Boniface had every claim to be avenged by the inheritors of the same spiritual dominion. When Benedict XI rescinded the bulls of his predecessor and admitted Philip the Fair to communion, without insisting on any concessions, he acted perhaps prudently, but gave a fatal blow to the temporal authority of Rome.

Benedict XI lived but a few months, and his successor, Clement V, at the instigation, as is commonly supposed, of the King of France, by whose influence he had been elected, took the extraordinary step of removing the papal chair to Avignon. In this city it remained for more than seventy years, a period which Petrarch and other writers of Italy compare to that of the Babylonish captivity. The majority of the cardinals was always French, and the popes were uniformly of the same nation. Timidly dependent upon the court of France, they neglected the interests and lost the affections of Italy. Rome, forsaken by her

---

[251] Velly, " Hist. de France," tome vii, pp. 109–258; Crevier, " Hist. de l'Université de Paris," tome ii, p. 170, etc.

sovereign, nearly forgot her allegiance; what remained of papal authority in the ecclesiastical territories was exercised by cardinal legates, little to the honour or advantage of the Holy See. Yet the series of Avignon pontiffs were far from insensible to Italian politics. These occupied, on the contrary, the greater part of their attention. But engaging in them from motives too manifestly selfish, and being regarded as a sort of foreigners from birth and residence, they aggravated that unpopularity and bad reputation which from various other causes attached itself to their court.

Though none of the supreme pontiffs after Boniface VIII ventured upon such explicit assumptions of a general jurisdiction over sovereigns by divine right as he had made in his controversy with Philip, they maintained one memorable struggle for temporal power against the Emperor Louis of Bavaria. Maxims long boldly repeated without contradiction, and ingrafted upon the canon law, passed almost for articles of faith among the clergy and those who trusted in them; and in despite of all ancient authorities, Clement V laid it down that the popes, having transferred the Roman Empire from the Greeks to the Germans, and delegated the right of nominating an emperor to certain electors, still reserved the prerogative of approving the choice, and of receiving from its subject upon his coronation an oath of fealty and obedience.[252] This had a regard to Henry VII, who denied that his oath bore any such interpretation, and whose measures, much to the alarm of the court of Avignon, were directed toward the restoration of his imperial rights in Italy. Among other things he conferred the rank of vicar of the empire upon Matteo Visconti, Lord of Milan. The popes had for some time pretended to possess that vicariate, during a vacancy of the empire; and after Henry's death insisted upon Visconti's surrender of the title. Several circumstances, for which I refer to the political historians of Italy, produced a war between the Pope's legate and the Visconti family. The Emperor Louis sent assistance to the latter, as heads of the Ghibelin or imperial party. This interference cost him above twenty years of trouble. John XXII, a man as passionate and ambitious as Boniface himself, immediately published a bull in which he asserted the right of administering the empire during its vacancy (even in Germany, as it seems from the generality of his expression), as well as of deciding in a doubtful choice of the electors, to appertain to the Holy See; and commanded

[252] Romani principes, etc. . . . Romano pontifici, a quo approbationem personæ ad imperialis celsitudinis apicem assumendæ, necnon unctionem, consecrationem et imperii coronam accipiunt, sua submittere capita non reputârunt indignum, seque illi et eidem ecclesiæ, quæ a Græcis imperium transtulit in Germanos, et a quâ ad certos eorum principes jus et potestas eligendi regem, in imperatorem postmodum promovendum, pertinet, adstringere vinculo juramenti, etc. (Clement, l. ii, tome ix.) The terms of the oath, as recited in this constitution, do not warrant the Pope's interpretation, but imply only that the emperor shall be the advocate or defender of the Church.

31

Louis to lay down his pretended authority until the supreme jurisdiction should determine upon his election. Louis's election had indeed been questionable; but that controversy was already settled in the field of Mühldorf, where he had obtained a victory over his competitor, the Duke of Austria; nor had the Pope ever interfered to appease a civil war during several years that Germany had been internally distracted by the dispute. The emperor, not yielding to this peremptory order, was excommunicated; his vassals were absolved from their oath of fealty, and all treaties of alliance between him and foreign princes annulled. Germany, however, remained firm; and if Louis himself had manifested more decision of mind and uniformity in his conduct, the court of Avignon must have signally failed in a contest from which it did not in fact come out very successful. But while at one time he went intemperate lengths against John XXII, publishing scandalous accusations in an assembly of the citizens of Rome, and causing a Franciscan friar to be chosen in his room, after an irregular sentence of deposition, he was always anxious to negotiate terms of accommodation, to give up his own active partisans, and to make concessions the most derogatory to his independence and dignity. From John indeed he had nothing to expect; but Benedict XII would gladly have been reconciled, if he had not feared the Kings of France and Naples, political adversaries of the emperor, who kept the Avignon popes in a sort of servitude. His successor, Clement VI, inherited the implacable animosity of John XXII toward Louis, who died without obtaining the absolution he had long abjectly solicited.[253]

Though the want of firmness in this emperor's character gave sometimes a momentary triumph to the popes, it is evident that their authority lost ground during the continuance of this struggle. Their right of confirming imperial elections was expressly denied by a Diet held at Frankfort in 1338, which established as a fundamental principle that the imperial dignity depended upon God alone, and that whoever should be chosen by a majority of the electors became immediately both king and emperor, with all prerogatives of that station, and did not require the approbation of the Pope.[254] This law, confirmed as it was by subsequent usage, emancipated the German Empire, which was immediately

[253] Schmidt, " Hist. des Allemands," tome iv, pp. 446–536, seems the best modern authority for this contest between the empire and papacy. See also Struvius, " Corp. Hist. German.," p. 591.

[254] Ouòd imperialis dignitas et potestas immediatè ex solo Deo, et quòd de jure et imperii consuetudine antiquitùs approbatâ postquam aliquis eligitur in imperatorem sive regem ab electoribus imperii concorditer, vel majori parte eorundem, statim ex solâ electione est rex verus et imperator Romanorum censendus et nominandus, et eidem debet ab omnibus imperie subjectis obediri, et administrandi jura imperii, et cætera faciendi, quæ ad imperatorem verum pertinent, plenariam habet potestatem, nec papæ sive sedis apostolicæ aut alicujus alterius approbatione, confirmatione, auctoritate indiget vel censusu. (Schmidt, p. 513.)

concerned in opposing the papal claims. But some who were
actively engaged in these transactions took more extensive views,
and assailed the whole edifice of temporal power which the Roman
See had been constructing for more than two centuries. Several
men of learning, among whom Dante, Ockham, and Marsilius
of Padua are the most conspicuous, investigated the foundations
of this superstructure, and exposed their insufficiency.[255] Literature, too long the passive handmaid of spiritual despotism, began
to assert her nobler birthright of ministering to liberty and truth.
Though the writings of these opponents of Rome are not always
reasoned upon very solid principles, they at least taught mankind
to scrutinize what had been received with implicit respect, and
prepared the way for more philosophical discussions. About this
time a new class of enemies had unexpectedly risen up against the
rulers of the Church. These were a part of the Franciscan order,
who had seceded from the main body on account of alleged de-
viations from the rigour of their primitive rule. Their schism was
chiefly founded upon a quibble about the right of property in
things consumable, which they maintained to be incompatible
with the absolute poverty prescribed to them. This frivolous
sophistry was united with the wildest fanaticism; and as John
XXII attempted to repress their follies by a cruel persecution,
they proclaimed aloud the corruption of the Church, fixed the
name of Antichrist upon the papacy, and warmly supported the
Emperor Louis throughout all his contention with the Holy
See.[256]

Meanwhile the popes who sat at Avignon continued to invade
with surprising rapaciousness the patronage and revenues of the
Church. The mandates or letters directing a particular clerk to be
preferred seem to have given place in a great degree to the more
effectual method of appropriating benefices by reservation or
provision, which was carried to an enormous extent in the fourteenth century. John XXII, the most insatiate of pontiffs, reserved to himself all the bishoprics in Christendom.[257] Benedict XII assumed the privilege for his own life of disposing of all
benefices vacant by cession, deprivation, or translation. Clement
VI naturally thought that his title was equally good with his

---

[255] Giannone, l. xxii, c. 8; Schmidt,
tome vi, p. 152. Dante was dead before
these events, but his principles were the
same. Ockham had already exerted his
talents in the same cause by writing, in
behalf of Philip IV, against Boniface, a
dialogue between a knight and a clerk on
the temporal supremacy of the Church.
This is published among other tracts of
the same class in Goldastus, " Monarchia
Imperii," p. 13. This dialogue is translated entire in the " Songe du Vergier,"
a more celebrated performance, ascribed
to Raoul de Presles under Charles V.

[256] The schism of the rigid Franciscans
or Fratricelli is one of the most singular
parts of ecclesiastical history, and had a
material tendency both to depress the
temporal authority of the papacy and to
pave the way for the Reformation. It is
fully treated by Mosheim, cent. 13 and
14, and by Crevier, " Hist. de l'Université
de Paris," tome ii, pp. 233-264, etc.

[257] Fleury, " Institutions," etc., tome i,
p. 368; F. Paul on " Benefices," c. 37.

predecessor's, and continued the same right for his own time; which soon became a permanent rule of the Roman chancery.[258] Hence the appointment of a prelate to a rich bishopric was generally but the first link in a chain of translation which the Pope could regulate according to his interest. Another capital innovation was made by John XXII in the establishment of the famous tax called annates, or first fruits of ecclesiastical benefices, which he imposed for his own benefit. These were one year's value, estimated according to a fixed rate in the books of the Roman chancery, and payable to the papal collectors throughout Europe.[259] Various other devices were invented to obtain money, which these degenerate popes, abandoning the magnificent schemes of their predecessors, were content to seek as their principal object. John XXII is said to have accumulated an almost incredible treasure, exaggerated perhaps by the ill-will of his contemporaries; [260] but it may be doubted whether even his avarice reflected greater dishonour on the Church than the licentious profuseness of Clement VI.[261]

These exactions were too much encouraged by the Kings of France, who participated in the plunder, or at least required the mutual assistance of the popes for their own imposts on the clergy. John XXII obtained leave of Charles the Fair to levy a tenth of ecclesiastical revenues; [262] and Clement VI, in return, granted two tenths to Philip of Valois for the expenses of his war. A similar tax was raised by the same authority toward the ransom of John.[263] These were contributions for national purposes unconnected with religion, which the popes had never before pretended to impose, and which the king might properly have levied with the consent of his clergy, according to the practice of England. But that consent might not always be obtained with ease, and it seemed a more expeditious method to call in the authority of the Pope. A manlier spirit was displayed by our ancestors. It

[258] F. Paul, c. 38. Translations of bishops had been made by the authority of the metropolitan till Innocent III reserved this prerogative to the Holy See. (De Marca, l. vi, c. 8.)

[259] F. Paul, c. 38; Fleury, p. 424; De Marca, l. vi, c. 10; Pasquier, l. lii, c. 28. The popes had long been in the habit of receiving a pecuniary gratuity when they granted the pallium to an archbishop, though this was reprehended by strict men, and even condemned by themselves. (De Marca, ibid.) It is noticed as a remarkable thing of Innocent IV that he gave the pall to a German archbishop without accepting anything. (Schmidt, tome iv, p. 172.) The original and nature of annates is copiously treated in Lenfant, " Concile de Constance," tome ii, p. 133.

[260] G. Villani puts this at 25,000,000

florins, which it is hardly possible to believe. The Italians were credulous enough to listen to any report against the Popes of Avignon. (L. xi, c. 20; Giannone, l. xxii, c. 8.)

[261] For the corruption of morals at Avignon during the secession, see De Sade, " Vie de Pétrarque," tome i, p. 70, and several other passages.

[262] Continuator Gul. de Nangis, in " Spicilegio d'Achery," tome iii, p. 86 (folio edition). Ita miseram ecclesiam, says this monk, unus tondet, alter excoriat.

[263] Fleury, " Institut. au Droit Ecclesiastique," tome ii, p. 245; Villaret, tome ix, p. 431. It became a regular practice for the king to obtain the Pope's consent to lay a tax on his clergy, though he sometimes applied first to themselves. (Garnier, tome xx, p. 141.)

was the boast of England to have placed the first legal barrier to the usurpations of Rome, if we except the insulated Pragmatic Sanction of St. Louis, from which the practice of succeeding ages in France entirely deviated. The English barons had, in a letter addressed to Boniface VIII, absolutely disclaimed his temporal supremacy over their crown, which he had attempted to set up by intermeddling in the quarrel of Scotland.[264] This letter, it is remarkable, is nearly coincident in point of time with that of the French nobility; and the two combined may be considered as a joint protestation of both kingdoms, and a testimony to the general sentiment among the superior ranks of the laity. A very few years afterward, the Parliament of Carlisle wrote a strong remonstrance to Clement V against the system of provisions and other extortions, including that of first fruits, which it was rumoured, they say, he was meditating to demand.[265] But the court of Avignon was not to be moved by remonstrances; and the feeble administration of Edward II gave way to ecclesiastical usurpations at home as well as abroad.[266] His magnanimous son took a bolder line. After complaining ineffectually to Clement VI of the enormous abuse which reserved almost all English benefices to the Pope, and generally for the benefit of aliens,[267] he passed in 1350 the famous statute of provisors. This act, reciting one supposed to have been made at the Parliament of Carlisle, which, however, does not appear,[268] and complaining in strong language of the mischief sustained through continual reservations of benefices, enacts that all elections and collations shall be free, according to law, and that, in case any provision or reservation should be made by the court of Rome, the king should for that turn have the collation of such a benefice, if it be of ecclesiastical election or patronage.[269] This devolution to the crown, which seems a little arbitrary, was the only remedy that could be effectual against the connivance and timidity of chapters and spiritual patrons. We can not assert that a statute so nobly planned was executed with equal steadiness. Sometimes

[264] Rymer, tome ii, p. 373; Collier, vol. i, p. 725.

[265] "Rotuli Parliamenti," vol. i, p. 204. This passage, hastily read, has led Collier and other English writers, such as Henry and Blackstone, into the supposition that annates were imposed by Clement V. But the concurrent testimony of foreign authors refers this tax to John XXII, as the canon law also shows. ("Extravagant. Communes," l. iii, tit. 2, c. 11.)

[266] The statute called Articuli cleri, in 1316, was directed rather toward confirming than limiting the clerical immunit in criminal cases.

[267] Collier, p. 546.

[268] It is singular that Sir E. Coke should assert that this act recites and is founded upon the statute 35 E. I, De asportatis religiosorum (2 Inst., 580): whereas there is not the least resemblance in the words, and very little, if any, in the substance. Blackstone, in consequence, mistakes the nature of that act of Edward I, and supposes it to have been made against papal provisions, to which I do not perceive even an allusion. Whether any such statute was really made in the Carlisle Parliament of 35 E. I, as is asserted both in 25 E. III and in the roll of another Parliament, 17 E. III ("Rot. Parl.," tome ii, p. 144), is hard to decide; and perhaps those who examine this point will have to choose between wilful suppression and wilful interpolation.

[269] 25 E. III, stat. 6.

by royal dispensation, sometimes by neglect or evasion, the papal
bulls of provision were still obeyed, though fresh laws were enacted to the same effect as the former. It was found on examination in 1367 that some clerks enjoyed more than twenty benefices by the Pope's dispensation.[270] And the Parliaments both of
this and of Richard II's reign invariably complain of the disre-
gard shown to the statutes of provisors. This led to other measures, which I shall presently mention.

The residence of the popes at Avignon gave very general offence to Europe, and they could not themselves avoid perceiving
the disadvantage of absence from their proper diocese, the city of
St. Peter, the source of all their claims to sovereign authority.
But Rome, so long abandoned, offered but an inhospitable reception: Urban V returned to Avignon, after a short experiment
of the capital; and it was not till 1376 that the promise, often
repeated and long delayed, of restoring the papal chair to the
metropolis of Christendom, was ultimately fulfilled by Gregory
XI. His death, which happened soon afterward, prevented, it is
said, a second flight that he was preparing. This was followed
by the great schism, one of the most remarkable events in ecclesiastical history. It is a difficult and by no means an interesting
question to determine the validity of that contested election
which distracted the Latin Church for so many years. All contemporary testimonies are subject to the suspicion of partiality
in a cause where no one was permitted to be neutral. In one fact,
however, there is a common agreement, that the cardinals, of
whom the majority were French, having assembled in conclave,
for the election of a successor to Gregory XI, were disturbed by
a tumultuous populace, who demanded with menaces a Roman,
or at least an Italian, pope. This tumult appears to have been
sufficiently violent to excuse, and in fact did produce, a considerable degree of intimidation. After some time the cardinals made
choice of the Archbishop of Bari, a Neapolitan, who assumed
the name of Urban VI. His election satisfied the populace, and
tranquility was restored. The cardinals announced their choice
to the absent members of their college, and behaved toward
Urban as their pope for several weeks. But his uncommon
harshness of temper giving them offence, they withdrew to a
neighbouring town, and, protesting that his election had been
compelled by the violence of the Roman populace, annulled the
whole proceeding, and chose one of their own number, who took
the pontifical name of Clement VII. Such are the leading circumstances which produced the famous schism. Constraint is
so destructive of the essence of election, that suffrages given
through actual intimidation ought, I think, to be held invalid,

[270] Collier, p. 568.

even without minutely inquiring whether the degree of illegal force was such as might reasonably overcome the constancy of a firm mind. It is improbable that the free votes of the cardinals would have been bestowed on the Archbishop of Bari; and I should not feel much hesitation in pronouncing his election to have been void. But the sacred college unquestionably did not use the earliest opportunity of protesting against the violence they had suffered; and we may infer almost with certainty that, if Urban's conduct had been more acceptable to that body, the world would have heard little of the transient riot at his election. This, however, opens a delicate question in jurisprudence, namely, under what circumstances acts, not only irregular, but substantially invalid, are capable of receiving a retroactive confirmation by the acquiescence and acknowledgment of parties concerned to oppose them. And upon this, I conceive, the great problem of legitimacy between Urban and Clement will be found to depend.[271]

Whatever posterity may have judged about the pretensions of these competitors, they at that time shared the obedience of Europe in nearly equal proportions. Urban remained at Rome; Clement resumed the station at Avignon. To the former adhered Italy, the Empire, England, and the nations of the north; the latter retained in his allegiance France, Spain, Scotland, and Sicily. Fortunately for the Church, no question of religious faith intermixed itself with this schism; nor did any other impediment to reunion exist than the obstinacy and selfishness of the contending parties. As it was impossible to come to any agreement on the original merits, there seemed to be no means of healing the wound but by the abdication of both popes and a fresh undisputed election. This was the general wish of Europe, but urged with particular zeal by the court of France, and, above all, by the University of Paris, which esteems this period the most honourable in her annals. The cardinals, however, of neither obedience would recede so far from their party as to suspend the election of a successor upon a vacancy of the pontificate, which would have at least removed one half of the obstacle. The Roman conclave accordingly placed three pontiffs successively, Boniface IX, Innocent VI, and Gregory XII, in the seat of Urban VI; and the cardinals at Avignon, upon the death of Clement in 1394 elected Benedict XIII (Peter de Luna), famous for his inflexible obstinacy in prolonging the schism. He repeatedly promised to sacrifice his dignity for the sake of union. But there

---

[271] Lenfant has collected all the original testimonies on both sides in the first book of his "Concile de Pise." No positive decision has ever been made on the subject, but the Roman popes are numbered in the commonly received list, and those of Avignon are not. The modern Italian writers express no doubt about the legitimacy of Urban; the French at most intimate that Clement's pretensions were not to be wholly rejected.

was no subterfuge to which this crafty pontiff had not recourse in order to avoid compliance with his word, though importuned, threatened, and even besieged in his palace at Avignon. Fatigued by his evasions, France withdrew her obedience, and the Gallican Church continued for a few years without acknowledging any supreme head. But this step, which was rather the measure of the University of Paris than of the nation, it seemed advisable to retract; and Benedict was again obeyed, though France continued to urge his resignation. A second subtraction of obedience, or at least declaration of neutrality, was resolved upon, as preparatory to the convocation of a general council. On the other hand, those who sat at Rome displayed not less insincerity. Gregory XII bound himself by oath on his accession to abdicate when it should appear necessary. But while these rivals were loading each other with the mutual reproach of schism, they drew on themselves the suspicion of at least a virtual collusion in order to retain their respective stations. At length the cardinals of both parties, wearied with so much dissimulation, deserted their masters, and summoned a general council to meet at Pisa.[272]

The council assembled at Pisa deposed both Gregory and Benedict, without deciding in any respect as to their pretensions, and elected Alexander V by its own supreme authority. This authority, however, was not universally recognised; the schism, instead of being healed, became more desperate; for, as Spain adhered firmly to Benedict, and Gregory was not without supporters, there were now three contending pontiffs in the Church. A general council was still, however, the favourite and indeed the sole remedy; and John XXIII, successor of Alexander V, was reluctantly prevailed upon, or perhaps trepanned, into convoking one to meet at Constance. In this celebrated assembly he was himself deposed; a sentence which he incurred by that tenacious clinging to his dignity, after repeated promises to abdicate, which had already proved fatal to his competitors. The deposition of John, confessedly a legitimate pope, may strike us as an extraordinary measure. But, besides the opportunity it might afford of restoring union, the council found a pretext for this sentence in his enormous vices, which indeed they seem to have taken upon common fame without any judicial process. The true motive, however, of their proceedings against him was a desire to make a signal display of a new system which had rapidly gained ground, and which I may venture to call the whig principles of the Catholic Church. A great question was at issue, whether the polity of that establishment should be an absolute or an exceedingly limited monarchy. The papal tyranny, long endured and still

[272] Villaret; Lenfant, " Concile de Pise "; Crevier, " Hist. de l'Université de Paris," tome iii.

increasing, had excited an active spirit of reformation which the most distinguished ecclesiastics of France and other countries encouraged. They recurred, as far as their knowledge allowed, to a more primitive discipline than the canon law, and elevated the supremacy of general councils. But in the formation of these they did not scruple to introduce material innovations. The bishops have usually been considered the sole members of ecclesiastical assemblies. At Constance, however, sat and voted not only the chiefs of monasteries, but the ambassadors of all Christian princes, the deputies of universities, with a multitude of inferior theologians, and even doctors of law.[273] These were naturally accessible to the pride of sudden elevation, which enabled them to control the strong and humiliate the lofty. In addition to this the adversaries of the court of Rome carried another not less important innovation. The Italian bishops, almost universally in the papal interests, were so numerous that, if suffrages had been taken by the head, their preponderance would have impeded any measures of transalpine nations toward reformation. It was determined, therefore, that the council should divide itself into four nations, the Italian, the German, the French, and the English, each with equal rights; and that, every proposition having been separately discussed, the majority of the four should prevail.[274] This revolutionary spirit was very unacceptable to the cardinals, who submitted reluctantly, and with a determination, that did not prove altogether unavailing, to save their papal monarchy by a dexterous policy. They could not, however, prevent the famous resolutions of the fourth and fifth sessions, which declare that the council has received, by divine right, an authority to which every rank, even the papal, is obliged to submit, in matters of faith, in the extirpation of the present schism, and in the reformation of the Church both in its head and its members; and that every person, even a pope, who shall obstinately refuse to obey that council, or any other lawfully assembled, is liable to such punishment as shall be necessary.[275] These decrees are great pillars of that moderate theory with respect

[273] Lenfant, "Concile de Constance," tome i, p. 107 (edit. 1727); Crevier, tome iii, p. 405. It was agreed that the ambassadors could not vote upon articles of faith, but only on questions relating to the settlement of the Church. But the second order of ecclesiastics were allowed to vote generally.

[274] This separation of England, as a coequal limb of the council, gave great umbrage to the French, who maintained that, like Denmark and Sweden, it ought to have been reckoned along with Germany. The English deputies came down with a profusion of authorities to prove the antiquity of their monarchy, for which they did not fail to put in requisition the immeasurable pedigrees of Ireland. Joseph of Arimathea, who planted Christianity and his stick at Glastonbury, did his best to help the cause. The recent victory of Agincourt, I am inclined to think, had more weight with the council. (Lenfant, tome ii, p. 46.)

At a time when a very different spirit prevailed, the English bishops under Henry II and Henry III had claimed as a right that no more than four of their number should be summoned to a general council. (Hoveden, p. 320; Carte, vol. ii, p. 84.) This was like boroughs praying to be released from sending members to Parliament.

[275] Id., p. 164; Crevier, tome iii, p. 417.

to the papal authority which distinguished the Gallican Church, and is embraced, I presume, by almost all laymen and the major part of ecclesiastics on this side of the Alps.[276] They embarrass the more popish churchmen, as the Revolution does our English Tories; some boldly impugn the authority of the Council of Constance, while others chicane upon the interpretation of its decrees. Their practical importance is not, indeed, direct; universal councils exist only in possibility; but the acknowledgment of a possible authority paramount to the See of Rome has contributed, among other means, to check its usurpations.

The purpose for which these general councils had been required, next to that of healing the schism, was the reformation of abuses. All the rapacious exactions, all the scandalous venality of which Europe had complained, while unquestioned pontiffs ruled at Avignon, appeared light in comparison of the practices of both rivals during the schism. Tenths repeatedly levied upon the clergy, annates rigorously exacted and enhanced by new valuations, fees annexed to the complicated formalities of the papal chancery, were the means by which each half of the Church was compelled to reimburse its chief for the subtraction of the other's obedience. Boniface IX, one of the Roman line, whose fame is a little worse than that of his antagonists, made a gross traffic of his patronage; selling the privileges of exemption from ordinary jurisdiction, of holding benefices in commendam, and other dispensations invented for the benefit of the Holy See.[277] Nothing had been attempted at Pisa toward reformation. At Constance the majority were ardent and sincere; the representatives of the French, German, and English churches met with a determined and, as we have seen, not always unsuccessful resolution to assert their ecclesiastical liberties. They appointed a committee of reformation, whose recommendations, if carried into effect, would have annihilated almost entirely that artfully constructed machinery by which Rome had absorbed so much of the revenues and patronage of the Church. But men, interested in perpetuating these abuses, especially the cardinals, improved the advantages which a skilful government always enjoys in playing against a popular assembly. They availed themselves of the jealousies arising out of the division of the council into nations, which exterior political circumstances had enhanced. France, then at war with England, whose pretensions to be counted as a fourth nation she had warmly disputed, and not well disposed toward the Emperor Sigismund, joined with the Italians

[276] This was written in 1816. The present state of opinion among those who belong to the Gallican Church has become exceedingly different from what it was in the last two centuries. [1847.]

[277] Lenfant, " Hist. du Concile de Pise," passim; Crevier; Villaret; Schmidt; Collier.

against the English and German members of the council in a matter of the utmost importance, the immediate election of a pope before the articles of reformation should be finally concluded. These two nations, in return, united with the Italians to choose the Cardinal Colonna, against the advice of the French divines, who objected to any member of the sacred college. The court of Rome were gainers in both questions. Martin V, the new Pope, soon evinced his determination to elude any substantial reform. After publishing a few constitutions tending to redress some of the abuses that had arisen during the schism, he contrived to make separate conventions with the several nations, and as soon as possible dissolved the council.[278]

By one of the decrees passed at Constance, another general council was to be assembled in five years, a second at the end of seven more, and from that time a similar representation of the Church was to meet every ten years. Martin V accordingly convoked a council at Pavia, which, on account of the plague, was transferred to Siena; but nothing of importance was transacted by this assembly.[279] That which he summoned seven years afterward to the city of Basle had very different results. The Pope, dying before the meeting of this council, was succeeded by Eugenius IV, who, anticipating the spirit of its discussions, attempted to crush its independence in the outset by transferring the place of session to an Italian city. No point was reckoned so material in the contest between the popes and reformers as whether a council should sit in Italy or beyond the Alps. The Council of Basle began, as it proceeded, in open enmity to the court of Rome. Eugenius, after several years had elapsed in more or less hostile discussions, exerted his prerogative of removing the assembly to Ferrara, and from thence to Florence. For this he had a specious pretext in the negotiation, then apparently tending to a prosperous issue, for the reunion of the Greek Church; a triumph, however transitory, of which his council at Florence obtained the glory. On the other hand, the assembly of Basle, though much weakened by the defection of those who adhered to Eugenius, entered into compacts with the Bohemian insurgents, more essential to the interests of the Church than any union with the Greeks, and completed the work begun at Constance by abolishing the annates, the reservations of benefices, and other abuses of papal authority. In this it received the approbation of most princes; but when, provoked by the endeavours of the Pope to frustrate its decrees, it proceeded so

[278] Lenfant, " Concile de Constance." The copiousness as well as impartiality of this work justly renders it an almost exclusive authority. Crevier (" Hist. de l'Université de Paris," tome iii) has given a good sketch of the council, and Schmidt (" Hist. des Allemandes," tome v) is worthy of attention.

[279] Lenfant, " Guerre des Hussites," tome i, p. 223.

far as to suspend and even to depose him, neither France nor Germany concurred in the sentence. Even the Council of Constance had not absolutely asserted a right of deposing a lawful pope except in case of heresy, though their conduct toward John could not otherwise be justified.[280] This question indeed of ecclesiastical public law seems to be still undecided. The fathers of Basle acted, however, with greater intrepidity than discretion, and, not perhaps sensible of the change that was taking place in public opinion, raised Amadeus, a retired Duke of Savoy, to the pontifical dignity by the name of Felix V. They thus renewed the schism, and divided the obedience of the Catholic Church for a few years. The empire, however, as well as France, observed a singular and not very consistent neutrality; respecting Eugenius as a lawful pope, and the assembly at Basle as a general council. England warmly supported Eugenius, and even adhered to his council at Florence; Aragon and some countries of smaller note acknowledged Felix. But the partisans of Basle became every year weaker; and Nicholas V, the successor of Eugenius, found no great difficulty in obtaining the cession of Felix, and terminating this schism. This victory of the court of Rome over the Council of Basle nearly counterbalanced the disadvantageous events at Constance, and put an end to the project of fixing permanent limitations upon the head of the Church by means of general councils. Though the decree that prescribed the convocation of a council every ten years was still unrepealed, no absolute monarchs have ever more dreaded to meet the representatives of their people than the Roman pontiffs have abhorred the name of those ecclesiastical synods: once alone, and that with the utmost reluctance, has the Catholic Church been convoked since the Council of Basle; but the famous assembly to which I allude does not fall within the scope of my present undertaking.[281]

It is a natural subject of speculation, what would have been the effects of these universal councils, which were so popular in the fifteenth century, if the decree passed at Constance for their periodical assembly had been regularly observed. Many Catholic writers, of the moderate or cisalpine school, have lamented their disuse, and ascribed to it that irreparable breach which the

[280] The Council of Basle endeavoured to evade this difficulty by declaring Eugenius a relapsed heretic. (Lenfant, " Guerre des Hussites," tome ii, p. 98.) But as the Church could discover no heresy in his disagreement with that assembly, the sentence of deposition gained little strength by this previous decision. The bishops were unwilling to take this violent step against Eugenius; but the minor theologians, the democracy of the Catholic Church, whose right of suffrage seems rather an anomalous infringement of episcopal authority, pressed it with much heat and rashness. See a curious passage on this subject in a speech of the Cardinal of Arles. (Lenfant, tome ii, p. 225.)

[281] There is not, I believe, any sufficient history of the Council of Basle. Lenfant designed to write it from the original acts, but, finding his health decline, intermixed some rather imperfect notices of its transactions with his history of the Hussite war, which is commonly quoted under the title of " History of the Council of Basle." Schmidt, Crevier, and Villaret are still my other authorities.

Reformation has made in the fabric of their Church. But there is almost an absurdity in conceiving their permanent existence. What chemistry could have kept united such heterogeneous masses, furnished with every principle of mutual repulsion? Even in early times, when councils, though nominally general, were composed of the subjects of the Roman Empire, they had been marked by violence and contradiction: what then could have been expected from the delegates of independent kingdoms, whose ecclesiastical polity, whatever may be said of the spiritual unity of the Church, had long been far too intimately blended with that of the state to admit of any general control without its assent? Nor, beyond the zeal, unquestionably sincere, which animated their members, especially at Basle, for the abolition of papal abuses, is there anything to praise in their conduct, or to regret in their cessation. The statesman who dreaded the encroachments of priests upon the civil government, the Christian who panted to see his rights and faith purified from the corruption of ages, found no hope of improvement in these councils. They took upon themselves the pretensions of the popes whom they attempted to supersede. By a decree of the fathers at Constance, all persons, including princes, who should oppose any obstacle to a journey undertaken by the Emperor Sigismund, in order to obtain the cession of Benedict, are declared excommunicated, and deprived of their dignities, whether secular or ecclesiastical.[282] Their condemnation of Huss and Jerome of Prague, and the scandalous breach of faith which they induced Sigismund to commit on that occasion, are notorious. But perhaps it is not equally so that this celebrated assembly recognised by a solemn decree the flagitious principle which it had practised, declaring that Huss was unworthy, through his obstinate adherence to heresy, of any privilege; nor ought any faith or promise to be kept with him, by natural, divine, or human law, to the prejudice of the Catholic religion.[283] It will be easy to estimate the claims

---

[282] Lenfant, tome i, p. 439.

[283] Nec aliqua sibi fides aut promissio, de jure naturali, divino, et humano, fuerit in prejudicium Catholicæ fidei observanda. (Lenfant, tome i, p. 491.)

This proposition is the great disgrace of the council in the affair of Huss. But the violation of his safe-conduct being a famous event in ecclesiastical history, and which has been very much disputed with some degree of erroneous statement on both sides, it may be proper to give briefly an impartial summary. 1. Huss came to Constance with a safe-conduct of the emperor very loosely worded, and not directed to any individuals. (Lenfant, tome i, p. 59.) 2. This pass, however, was binding upon the emperor himself, and was so considered by him when he remonstrated against the arrest of Huss.

(Id., pp. 73, 83.) 3. It was not binding on the council, who possessed no temporal power, but had a right to decide upon the question of heresy. 4. It is not manifest by what civil authority Huss was arrested, nor can I determine how far the imperial safe-conduct was a legal protection within the city of Constance. 5. Sigismund was persuaded to acquiesce in the capital punishment of Huss, and even to make it his own act (Lenfant, p. 409); by which he manifestly broke his engagement. 6. It is evident that in this he acted by the advice and sanction of the council, who thus became accessory to the guilt of his treachery.

The great moral to be drawn from the story of John Huss's condemnation is, that no breach of faith can be excused by our opinion of ill desert in the party, or

of this congress of theologians to our veneration, and to weigh
the retrenchment of a few abuses against the formal sanction of
an atrocious maxim.

It was not, however, necessary for any government of tolerable energy to seek the reform of those abuses which affected the
independence of national churches, and the integrity of their
regular discipline, at the hands of a general council. Whatever
difficulty there might be in overturning the principles founded
on the decretals of Isidore, and sanctioned by the prescription of
many centuries, the more flagrant encroachments of papal tyranny were fresh innovations, some within the actual generation,
others easily to be traced up, and continually disputed. The
principal European nations determined, with different degrees
indeed of energy, to make a stand against the despotism of Rome.
In this resistance England was not only the first engaged, but the
most consistent; her free Parliament preventing, as far as the
times permitted, that wavering policy to which a court is liable.
We have already seen that a foundation was laid in the statute
of provisors under Edward III. In the next reign many other
measures tending to repress the interference of Rome were
adopted, especially the great statute of præmunire, which subjects all persons bringing papal bulls for translation of bishops
and other enumerated purposes into the kingdom to the penalties of forfeiture and perpetual imprisonment.[284] This act received, and probably was designed to receive, a larger interpretation than its language appears to warrant. Combined with the
statute of provisors, it put a stop to the Pope's usurpation of patronage, which had impoverished the Church and kingdom of
England for nearly two centuries. Several attempts were made
to overthrow these enactments; the first Parliament of Henry IV
gave a very large power to the king over the statute of provisors,
enabling him even to annul it at his pleasure.[285] This, however,
does not appear in the statute-book. Henry indeed, like his predecessors, exercised rather largely his prerogative of dispensing
with the law against papal provisions; a prerogative which, as to
this point, was itself taken away by an act of his own, and another
of his son Henry V.[286] But the statute always stood unrepealed;
and it is a satisfactory proof of the ecclesiastical supremacy of

by a narrow interpretation of our own
engagements. Every capitulation ought
to be construed favourably for the
weaker side. In such cases it is emphatically true that, if the letter killeth, the
spirit should give life.

Gerson, the most eminent theologian
of his age, and the coryphæus of the
party that opposed the transalpine principles, was deeply concerned in this atrocious business. (Crevier, p. 432.)

[284] 16 Ric. II, c. 5.

[285] " Rot. Parl.," vol. iii, p. 428.

[286] 7 H. IV, c. 8; 3 H. V, c. 4. Martin
V published an angry bull against the
" execrable statute " of præmunire; enjoining Archbishop Chicheley to procure
its repeal. (Collier, p. 653.) Chicheley
did all in his power; but the commons
were always inexorable on this head (p.
636), and the archbishop even incurred
Martin's resentment by it. (Wilkins,
" Concilia," tome iii, p. 483.)

the legislature that in the concordat made by Martin V at the Council of Constance with the English nation we find no mention of reservation of benefices, of annates, and the other principal grievances of that age,[287] our ancestors disdaining to accept by compromise with the Pope any modification or even confirmation of their statute law. They had already restrained another flagrant abuse, the increase of first fruits by Boniface IX; an act of Henry IV forbidding any greater sum to be paid on that account than had been formerly accustomed.[288]

It will appear evident to every person acquainted with the contemporary historians and the proceedings of Parliament that, besides partaking in the general resentment of Europe against the papal court, England was under the influence of a peculiar hostility to the clergy, arising from the dissemination of the principles of Wicliff.[289] All ecclesiastical possessions were marked for spoliation by the system of this reformer; and the House of Commons more than once endeavoured to carry it into effect, pressing Henry IV to seize the temporalities of the Church for public exigencies.[290] This recommendation, besides its injustice, was not likely to move Henry, whose policy had been to sustain the prelacy against their new adversaries. Ecclesiastical jurisdiction was kept in better control than formerly by the judges of common law, who, through rather a strained construction of the statute of præmunire, extended its penalties to the spiritual courts when they transgressed their limits.[291] The privilege of clergy in criminal cases still remained, but it was acknowledged not to comprehend high treason.[292]

Germany, as well as England, was disappointed of her hopes

[287] Lenfant, tome ii, p. 444.

[288] 6 H. IV, c. 1.

[289] See, among many other passages, the articles exhibited by the Lollards to Parliament against the clergy in 1394. Collier gives the substance of them, and they are noticed by Henry, but they are at full length in Wilkins, tome iii, p. 221.

[290] Walsingham, pp. 371, 379; "Rot. Parl.," 11 H. IV, vol. iii, p. 645. The remarkable circumstances detailed by Walsingham in the former passage are not corroborated by anything in the records. But as it is unlikely that so particular a narrative should have no foundation, Hume has plausibly conjectured that the roll has been wilfully mutilated. As this suspicion occurs in other instances, it would be desirable to ascertain, by examination of the original rolls, whether they bear any external marks of injury. The mutilators, however, if such there were, have left a great deal. The rolls of Henry IV and V's Parliaments are quite full of petitions against the clergy.

[291] "3 Inst.," p. 121; Collier, vol. i, p. 668.

[292] "2 Inst.," p. 634, where several instances of priests executed for coining and other treasons are adduced. And this may also be inferred from 25 E. III, stat. 3, c. 4; and from 4 H. IV, c. 3. Indeed, the benefit of clergy has never been taken away by statute from high treason. This renders it improbable that Chief-Justice Gascoyne should, as Carte tells us (vol. ii, p. 664), have refused to try Archbishop Scrope for treason, on the ground that no one could lawfully sit in judgment on a bishop for his life. Whether he might have declined to try him as a peer is another question. The Pope excommunicated all who were concerned in Scrope's death, and it cost Henry a large sum to obtain absolution. But Boniface IX was no arbiter of the English law. Edward IV granted a strange charter to the clergy, not only dispensing with the statutes of præmunire, but absolutely exempting them from temporal jurisdiction in cases of treason as well as felony. (Wilkins, "Concilia," tome iii, p. 583; Collier, p. 678.) This, however, being an illegal grant, took no effect, at least after his death.

of general reformation by the Italian party of Constance; but she did not supply the want of the council's decrees with sufficient decision. A concordat with Martin V left the Pope in possession of too great a part of his recent usurpations.[293] This, however, was repugnant to the spirit of Germany, which called for a more thorough reform with all the national roughness and honesty. The Diet of Mentz, during the continuance of the Council of Basle, adopted all those regulations hostile to the papal interests which occasioned the deadly quarrel between that assembly and the court of Rome.[294] But the German Empire was betrayed by Frederick III, and deceived by an accomplished but profligate statesman, his secretary, Æneas Sylvius. Fresh concordats, settled at Aschaffenburg in 1448, nearly upon a footing of those concluded with Martin V, surrendered great part of the independence for which Germany had contended. The Pope retained his annates, or at least a sort of tax in their place; and instead of reserving benefices arbitrarily, he obtained the positive right of collation during six alternate months of every year. Episcopal elections were freely restored to the chapters, except in case of translation, when the Pope still continued to nominate; as he did also if any person, canonically unfit, were presented to him for confirmation.[295] Such is the concordat of Aschaffenburg, by which the Catholic principalities of the empire have always been governed, though reluctantly acquiescing in its disadvantageous provisions. Rome, for the remainder of the fifteenth century, not satisfied with the terms she had imposed, is said to have continually encroached upon the right of election.[296] But she purchased too dearly her triumph over the weakness of Frederick III, and the Hundred Grievances of Germany, presented to Adrian VI by the Diet of Nuremberg in 1522, manifested the working of a long-treasured resentment, that had made straight the path before the Saxon reformer.

I have already taken notice that the Castilian Church was in the first ages of that monarchy nearly independent of Rome. But after many gradual encroachments the code of laws promulgated by Alfonso X had incorporated a great part of the decretals, and thus given the papal jurisprudence an authority which it nowhere else possessed in national tribunals.[297] That

---

[293] Lenfant, tome ii, p. 428; Schmidt, tome v, p. 131.

[294] Schmidt, tome v, p. 221; Lenfant.

[295] Schmidt, tome v, p. 250; tome vi, p. 94, etc. He observes that there is three times as much money at present as in the fifteenth century: if, therefore, the annates are now felt as a burden, what must they have been? (p. 113). To this Rome would answer, If the annates were but sufficient for the Pope's maintenance at that time, what must they be now?

[296] Schmidt, p. 98; Æneas Sylvius, Epist. 369 and 371; and "De Moribus Germanorum," pp. 1041, 1061. Several little disputes with the Pope indicate the spirit that was fermenting in Germany throughout the fifteenth century. But this is the proper subject of a more detailed ecclesiastical history, and should form an introduction to that of the Reformation.

[297] Marina, "Ensayo Historico-Critico," c. 320, etc.

richly endowed hierarchy was a tempting spoil. The popes filled up its benefices by means of expectatives and reserves with their own Italian dependents. We find the Cortes of Palencia in 1388 complaining that strangers are beneficed in Castile, through which the churches are ill supplied, and native scholars can not be provided, and requesting the king to take such measures in relation to this as the Kings of France, Aragon, and Navarre, who do not permit any but natives to hold benefices in their kingdoms. The king answered to this petition that he would use his endeavours to that end.[298] And this is expressed with greater warmth by a Cortes of 1473, who declare it to be the custom of all Christian nations that foreigners should not be promoted to benefices, urging the discouragement of native learning, the decay of charity, the bad performance of religious rites, and other evils arising from the non-residence of beneficed priests, and request the king to notify to the court of Rome that no expectative or provision in favour of foreigners can be received in future.[299] This petition seems to have passed into a law; but I am ignorant of the consequences. Spain certainly took an active part in restraining the abuses of pontifical authority at the Councils of Constance and Basle; to which I might add the name of Trent, if that assembly were not beyond my province.

France, dissatisfied with the abortive termination of her exertions during the schism, rejected the concordat offered by Martin V, which held out but a promise of imperfect reformation.[300] She suffered in consequence the papal exactions for some years, till the decrees of the Council of Basle prompted her to more vigorous efforts for independence, and Charles VII enacted the famous Pragmatic Sanction of Bourges.[301] This has been deemed a sort of Magna Charta of the Gallican Church; for though the law was speedily abrogated, its principle has remained fixed as the basis of ecclesiastical liberties. By the Pragmatic Sanction a general council was declared superior to the Pope; elections of bishops were made free from all control; mandates or grants in expectancy, and reservations of benefices, were taken away; first fruits were abolished. This defalcation of wealth, which had now become dearer than power, could not be patiently borne at Rome. Pius II, the same Æneas Sylvius who had sold himself to oppose the Council of Basle, in whose service he had been originally distinguished, used every endeavour to procure the repeal of this ordinance. With Charles VII he had no success; but Louis XI, partly out of blind hatred to

[298] Id.; " Teoria de las Cortes," tome iii, p. 126.
[299] " Teoria de las Cortes," tome ii, p. 364; Mariana, " Hist. Hispan.," l. xix, c. 1.
[300] Villaret, tome xv, p. 126.

[301] Idem, p. 263; "Hist. du Droit Public Ecclés. François," tome ii, p. 234; Fleury, "Institutions au Droit"; Crevier, tome iv, p. 100; Pasquier, " Recherches de la France," l. iii, c. 27.

his father's memory, partly from a delusive expectation that the Pope would support the Angevin faction in Naples, repealed the Pragmatic Sanction.[302] This may be added to other proofs that Louis XI, even according to the measures of worldly wisdom, was not a wise politician. His people judged from better feelings; the Parliament of Paris constantly refused to enregister the revocation of that favourite law, and it continued in many respects to be acted upon until the reign of Francis I.[303] At the States-General of Tours, in 1484, the inferior clergy, seconded by the two other orders, earnestly requested that the Pragmatic Sanction might be confirmed; but the prelates were timid or corrupt, and the regent Anne was unwilling to risk a quarrel with the Holy See.[304] This unsettled state continued, the Pragmatic Sanction neither quite enforced nor quite repealed, till Francis I, having accommodated the differences of his predecessor with Rome, agreed upon a final concordat with Leo X, the treaty that subsisted for almost three centuries between the papacy and the kingdom of France.[305] Instead of capitular election or papal provision, a new method was devised for filling the vacancies of episcopal sees. The king was to nominate a fit person, whom the Pope was to collate. The one obtained an essential patronage, the other preserved his theoretical supremacy. Annates were restored to the Pope; a concession of great importance. He gave up his indefinite prerogative of reserving benefices, and received only a small stipulated patronage. This convention met with strenuous opposition in France; the Parliament of Paris yielded only to force; the university hardly stopped short of sedition; the zealous Gallicans have ever since deplored it, as a fatal wound to their liberties. There is much exaggeration in this, as far as the relation of the Gallican Church to Rome is concerned; but the royal nomination to bishoprics impaired, of course, the independence of the hierarchy. Whether this prerogative of the crown were upon the whole beneficial to France, is a problem that I can not affect to solve; in this country there seems little doubt that capitular elections, which the statute of Henry VIII has reduced to a name, would long since have degenerated into the corruption of close boroughs; but the circumstances of the Gallican establishment may not have been entirely similar, and the question opens a variety of considerations that do not belong to my present subject.

From the principles established during the schism, and in the Pragmatic Sanction of Bourges, arose the far-famed liberties

[302] Villaret, and Garnier, tome xvi; Crevier, tome iv, pp. 256, 274.
[303] Garnier, tome xvi, p. 432; tome xvii, p. 222, et alibi; Crevier, tome iv, p. 318, et alibi.
[304] Garnier, tome xix, pp. 216 and 321.
[305] Garnier, tome xxiii, p. 151; "Hist. du Droit Public Ecclés. Fr.," tome ii, p. 243; Fleury, "Institutions au Droit," tome i, p. 107.

of the Gallican Church, which honourably distinguished her from other members of the Roman communion. These have been referred by French writers to a much earlier era; but except so far as that country participated in the ancient ecclesiastical independence of all Europe, before the papal encroachments had subverted it, I do not see that they can be properly traced above the fifteenth century. Nor had they acquired even at the expiration of that age the precision and consistency which was given in later times by the constant spirit of the Parliaments and universities, as well as by the best ecclesiastical authors, with little assistance from the crown, which, except in a few periods of disagreement with Rome, has rather been disposed to restrain the more zealous Gallicans. These liberties, therefore, do not strictly fall within my limits; and it will be sufficient to observe that they depended upon two maxims: one, that the Pope does not possess any direct or indirect temporal authority; the other, that his spiritual jurisdiction can only be exercised in conformity with such parts of the canon law as are received by the kingdom of France. Hence the Gallican Church rejected a great part of the Sext and Clementines, and paid little regard to modern papal bulls, which, in fact, obtained validity only by the king's approbation.[306]

The pontifical usurpations which were thus restrained, affected, at least in their direct operation, rather the Church than the state; and temporal governments would only have been half emancipated, if their national hierarchies had preserved their enormous jurisdiction.[307] England, in this also, began the work, and had made a considerable progress, while the mistaken piety or policy of Louis IX and his successors had laid France open to vast encroachments. The first method adopted in order to check them was rude enough—by seizing the bishop's effects when he exceeded his jurisdiction.[308] This jurisdiction, according to the construction of churchmen, became perpetually larger:

[306] Fleury, "Institutions au Droit," tome ii, p. 226, etc., and "Discours sur les Libertés de l'Église Gallicane." The last editors of this dissertation go far beyond Fleury, and perhaps reach the utmost point in limiting the papal authority which a sincere member of that communion can attain. (See notes, pp. 417 and 445.)

[307] It ought always to be remembered that ecclesiastical, and not merely papal, encroachments are what civil governments and the laity in general have had to resist; a point which some very zealous opposers of Rome have been willing to keep out of sight. The latter arose out of the former, and perhaps were in some respects less objectionable. But the true enemy is what are called high-church principles; be they main-

tained by a pope, a bishop, or a presbyter. Thus Archbishop Stratford writes to Edward III: Duo sunt, quibus principaliter regitur mundus, sacra pontificalis auctoritas, et regalis ordinata potestas: in quibus est pondus tanto gravius et sublimius sacerdotum, quanto et de regibus illi in divino reddituri sunt examine rationem; et ideo scire debet regia celsitudo ex illorum vos dependere judicio, non illos ad vestram dirigi posse voluntatem. (Wilkins, "Concila," tome ii, p. 663.) This amazing impudence toward such a prince as Edward did not succeed; but it is interesting to follow the track of the star which was now rather receding, though still fierce.

[308] De Marca, "De Concordantiâ," l. iv, c. 18.

even the reforming Council of Constance give an enumeration of ecclesiastical causes far beyond the limits acknowledged in England, or perhaps in France.[309] But the Parliament of Paris, instituted in 1304, gradually established a paramount authority over ecclesiastical as well as civil tribunals. Their progress was indeed very slow. At a famous assembly in 1329, before Philip of Valois, his advocate general, Peter de Cugnières, pronounced a long harangue against the excesses of spiritual jurisdiction. This is a curious illustration of that branch of legal and ecclesiastical history. It was answered at large by some bishops, and the king did not venture to take any active measures at that time.[310] Several regulations were, however, made in the fourteenth century, which took away the ecclesiastical cognizance of adultery, of the execution of testaments, and other causes which had been claimed by the clergy.[311] Their immunity in criminal matters was straitened by the introduction of privileged cases, to which it did not extend; such as treason, murder, robbery, and other heinous offences.[312] The Parliament began to exercise a judicial control over episcopal courts. It was not, however, till the beginning of the sixteenth century, according to the best writers, that it devised its famous form of procedure, the "appeal because of abuse."[313] This, in the course of time, and through the decline of ecclesiastical power, not only proved an effectual barrier against encroachments of spiritual jurisdiction, but drew back again to the lay court the greater part of those causes which by prescription, and indeed by law, had appertained to a different cognizance. Thus testamentary, and even, in a great degree, matrimonial causes were decided by the Parliament; and in many other matters that body, being the judge of its own competence, narrowed, by means of the appeal because of abuse, the boundaries of the opposite jurisdiction.[314] This remedial process appears to have been more extensively applied than our English writ of prohibition. The latter merely restrains the interference of the ecclesiastical courts in matters which the law has not com-

[309] De Marca, " De Concordantiâ," l. iv, c. 15; Lenfant, " Conc. de Constance," tome ii, p. 331. De Marca (l. iv, c. 15) gives us passages from one Durandus about 1309, complaining that the lay judges invaded ecclesiastical jurisdiction, and reckoning the cases subject to the latter, under which he includes feudal and criminal causes in some circumstances, and also those in which the temporal judges are in doubt; si quid ambiguum inter judices sæculares oriatur.

[310] Velly, tome viii, p. 234; Fleury, " Institutions," tome ii, p. 12; " Hist. du Droit Ecclés. Franç.," tome ii, p. 86.

[311] Villaret, tome xi, p. 182.

[312] Fleury, " Institutions au Droit," tome ii, p. 138. In the famous case of

Balue, a bishop and cardinal, whom Louis XI detected in a treasonable intrigue, it was contended by the king that he had a right to punish him capitally. (Du Clos, " Vie de Louis XI," tome i, p. 422; Garnier, " Hist. de France," tome xvii, p. 330.) Balue was confined for many years in a small iron cage, which till lately was shown in the castle of Loches.

[313] Pasquier, l. iii, c. 33; " Hist. du Droit Ecclés. François," tome ii, p. 119; Fleury, " Institutions au Droit Ecclés. François," tome ii, p. 221; De Marca, " De Concordantiâ Sacerdotii et Imperii," l. iv, c. 19. The last author seems to carry it rather higher.

[314] Fleury, " Institutions," tome ii, p. 42, etc.

mitted to them. But the Parliament of Paris considered itself, I apprehend, as conservator of the liberties and discipline of the Gallican Church; and interposed the appeal because of abuse whenever the spiritual court, even in its proper province, transgressed the canonical rules by which it ought to be governed.[315]

While the Bishops of Rome were losing their general influence over Europe, they did not gain more estimation in Italy. It is, indeed, a problem of some difficulty whether they derived any substantial advantage from their temporal principality. For the last three centuries it has certainly been conducive to the maintenance of their spiritual supremacy, which, in the complicated relations of policy, might have been endangered by their becoming the subjects of any particular sovereign. But I doubt whether their real authority over Christendom in the middle ages was not better preserved by a state of nominal dependence upon the empire, without much effective control on one side, or many temptations to worldly ambition on the other. That covetousness of temporal sway which, having long prompted their measures of usurpation and forgery, seemed, from the time of Innocent III and Nicholas III, to reap its gratification, impaired the more essential parts of the papal authority. In the fourteenth and fifteenth centuries the popes degraded their character by too much anxiety about the politics of Italy. The veil woven by religious awe was rent asunder, and the features of ordinary ambition appeared without disguise. For it was no longer that magnificent and original system of spiritual power which made Gregory VII, even in exile, a rival of the emperor, which held forth redress where the law could not protect, and punishment where it could not chastise, which fell in sometimes with superstitious feeling, and sometimes with political interest. Many might believe that the Pope could depose a schismatic prince, who were disgusted at his attacking an unoffending neighbour. As the cupidity of the clergy in regard to worldly estate had lowered their character everywhere, so the similar conduct of their head undermined the respect felt for him in Italy. The censures of the Church, those excommunications and interdicts which had made Europe tremble, became gradually despicable as well as odious when they were lavished in every squabble for territory which the Pope was pleased to make his own.[316]

---

[315] De Marca, " De Concordantiâ," l. iv, c. 9; Fleury, tome ii, p. 224. In Spain, even now, says De Marca, bishops or clerks not obeying royal mandates that inhibit the excesses of ecclesiastical courts are expelled from the kingdom and deprived of the rights of denizenship.

[316] In 1290 Pisa was put under an interdict for having conferred the signiory on the Count of Montefeltro; and he was ordered, on pain of excommunication, to lay down the government within a month. (Muratori ad ann.) A curious style for the Pope to adopt toward a free city! Six years before the Venetians had been interdicted because they would not allow their galleys to be hired by the King of Naples. But it would be almost endless to quote every instance.

Even the crusades, which had already been tried against the heretics of Languedoc, were now preached against all who espoused a different party from the Roman See in the quarrels of Italy. Such were those directed at Frederick II, at Manfred, and at Matteo Visconti, accompanied by the usual bribery, indulgences, and remission of sins. The papal interdicts of the fourteenth century wore a different complexion from those of former times. Though tremendous to the imagination, they had hitherto been confined to spiritual effects, or to such as were connected with religion, as the prohibition of marriage and sepulture. But Clement V, on account of an attack made by the Venetians upon Ferrara in 1309, proclaimed the whole people infamous, and incapable for three generations of any office, their goods, in every part of the world, subject to confiscation, and every Venetian, wherever he might be found, liable to be reduced into slavery.[317] A bull in the same terms was published by Gregory XI in 1376 against the Florentines.

From the termination of the schism, as the popes found their ambition thwarted beyond the Alps, it was diverted more and more toward schemes of temporal sovereignty. In these we do not perceive that consistent policy which remarkably actuated their conduct as supreme heads of the Church. Men generally advanced in years, and born of noble Italian families, made the papacy subservient to the elevation of their kindred, or to the interest of a local faction. For such ends they mingled in the dark conspiracies of that bad age, distinguished only by the more scandalous turpitude of their vices from the petty tyrants and intriguers with whom they were engaged. In the latter part of the fifteenth century, when all favourable prejudices were worn away, those who occupied the most conspicuous station in Europe disgraced their name by more notorious profligacy than could be paralleled in the darkest age that had preceded; and at the moment beyond which this work is not carried, the invasion of Italy by Charles VIII, I must leave the pontifical throne in the possession of Alexander VI.

It has been my object in the present chapter to bring within the compass of a few hours' perusal the substance of a great and interesting branch of history; not certainly with such extensive reach of learning as the subject might require, but from sources of unquestioned credibility. Unconscious of any partialities that could give an oblique bias to my mind, I have not been very solicitous to avoid offence where offence is so easily taken. Yet there is one misinterpretation of my meaning which I would gladly obviate. I have not designed, in exhibiting without disguise the usurpations of Rome during the middle ages, to furnish

[317] Muratori.

materials for unjust prejudice or unfounded distrust. It is an advantageous circumstance for the philosophical inquirer into the history of ecclesiastical dominion that, as it spreads itself over the vast extent of fifteen centuries, the dependence of events upon general causes, rather than on transitory combinations or the character of individuals, is made more evident, and the future more probably foretold from a consideration of the past, than we are apt to find in political history. Five centuries have now elapsed, during every one of which the authority of the Roman See has successively declined. Slowly and silently receding from their claims to temporal power, the pontiffs hardly protect their dilapidated citadel from the revolutionary concussions of modern times, the rapacity of governments, and the growing averseness to ecclesiastical influence. But if, thus bearded by unmannerly and threatening innovation, they should occasionally forget that cautious policy which necessity has prescribed, if they should attempt (an unavailing expedient!) to revive institutions which can be no longer operative, or principles that have died away, their defensive efforts will not be unnatural, nor ought to excite either indignation or alarm. A calm, comprehensive study of ecclesiastical history, not in such scraps and fragments as the ordinary partisans of our ephemeral literature obtrude upon us, is perhaps the best antidote to extravagant apprehensions. Those who know what Rome has once been are best able to appreciate what she is; those who have seen the thunderbolt in the hands of the Gregories and the Innocents will hardly be intimidated at the sallies of decrepitude, the impotent dart of Priam amid the crackling ruins of Troy.[318]

[318] It is again to be remembered that this paragraph was written in 1816.